Usability in Government Systems

User Experience Design for Citizens and Public Servants

Usability in Government Systems

User Experience Design for Citizens and Public Servants

Elizabeth Buie

Dianne Murray

AMSTERDAM • BOSTON • HEIDELBERG • LONDON
NEW YORK • OXFORD • PARIS • SAN DIEGO
SAN FRANCISCO • SINGAPORE • SYDNEY • TOKYO
Morgan Kaufmann is an imprint of Elsevier

Acquiring Editor: Todd Green
Development Editor: Robyn Day
Project Manager: André Cuello
Designer: Joanne Blank

Morgan Kaufmann is an imprint of Elsevier
225 Wyman Street, Waltham, MA 02451, USA

Notices
Knowledge and best practice in this field are constantly changing. As new research and experience broaden our understanding, changes in research methods or professional practices may become necessary. Practitioners and researchers must always rely on their own experience and knowledge in evaluating and using any information or methods described herein. In using such information or methods, they should be mindful of their own safety and the safety of others, including parties for whom they have a professional responsibility.

To the fullest extent of the law, neither the Publisher nor the authors, contributors, or editors assume any liability for any injury and/or damage to persons or property as a matter of products liability, negligence or otherwise, or from any use or operation of any methods, products, instructions, or ideas contained in the material herein.

Library of Congress Cataloging-in-Publication Data
Application submitted

British Library Cataloguing-in-Publication Data
A catalogue record for this book is available from the British Library.

ISBN: 978-0-12-391063-9

For information on all MK publications visit our website at www.mkp.com

*To my late husband, **Antonio Vallone,** who inspired and challenged me to explore with him the role of human-computer interaction in the engineering of complex government systems and who learned alongside me as we did so.* (Elizabeth Buie)

*To my sons, **Mark Rennie** and **Gavin David**, who will live in the world we are now creating. (*Dianne Murray*)*

Men standing in opposite hemispheres will converse and deride each other and embrace each other, and understand each other's language.

Leonardo da Vinci

Contents

SECTION III: UX ISSUES COMMON TO PUBLIC AND INTERNAL SYSTEMS

Foreword

Arguably, government systems have the largest user base of any technology—that is, everyone. The range of activities that government systems support is enormous, including everything from providing information to citizens about the location of drivers' license offices to supporting real-time intelligence and collaboration among emergency first responders in an urban crisis. In many ways, governments were early adopters of human-centered design and usability analysis because the military realized decades ago that many of their systems were "human-in-the-loop" systems for which it was critical to design for minimizing error and maximizing accuracy. The realization that the field of human–computer interaction (HCI) was relevant to more mundane, civilian applications was slower to develop, but as citizens have become more enmeshed in a global sociotechnical information and communication web, it has become more obvious that HCI will be critical to the development, deployment, and understanding of digital government systems for citizens, policymakers, legislators, and other stakeholders.

Hence this book comes at a perfect time and fills an important void. e-Government systems have always been a small domain area within the field of HCI, and HCI has always been an interesting technical highlight within the field of government information technology systems. Perhaps this book can help place the study of user experience issues in e-gov in a more central position, or even move us toward defining a field.

Sometimes people think that usability is about the size of type, the color of backgrounds, and the labels on buttons. The fact is that those kinds of problems are well understood. What challenges us now in the area of user-centered technology are the same issues that challenge society at large as we struggle with the growth and globalization of information collection, dissemination, decision, communication, and collaboration systems. What is privacy anymore? How can we assure the security of sensitive information? What are the implications and causes of inequities in information access and how can they be overcome? How can we trust information systems that handle such sensitive matters as voting or health data? What does it mean when citizens and politicians mix in an unmediated digital social sphere? What are the ethical issues of government monitoring of online social movements? Who is responsible in situations involving remote control warfare? These are some central questions of a field of human-centered digital government.

The contributors to this volume are a mix of practitioners and academics. The editors, also a practitioner and an academic, have clearly asked each chapter's author(s) to offer design guidelines and implications. Hence, the book is rich with case studies that provide valuable insights into what has and has not worked in the past. Case studies, well described and followed by insights and recommendations, are the designer's best friend. With good guidance, it is easy to understand a story and apply valuable lessons learned from prior experience to current problems. Digital government experiments have been taking place in several countries, across various forms of government, and throughout different levels of government since the early days of "digital cities" (see Ishida & Isbister, 2000). By now there have been plenty of successes and failures. In this book we can read about both, and we can view cross-cultural approaches to the same problems in order to inform design.

The advent of social media and the use of multiple personal platforms may be game changers for e-participation. As this book appears, we are entering a period of widespread social unrest and political activism in which new forms of social media are playing an important role. At the same time, governments are trying to add social aspects to policy functions, for example, public comment on proposed legislation, and politicians are embracing social media for their campaigning and governing activities. Governments are also keen to mine social media activities for a variety of purposes, some good and some bad. This book includes contributions discussing multiple instances of social media use from which design guidelines are explicitly derived.

This book includes some straightforward contributions on the realities of the information technology business in the context of government that will be useful to practitioners, including how to incorporate usability in contract proposals, the need for organizational commitment to usability, and the interplay between policy and design. We often talk about how "politics" intrudes on the progress of what might otherwise be a smooth . In e-Government, however, "politics" is not a euphemism. It is incumbent upon HCI researchers and practitioners to advocate for usability in e-Gov and make sure that HCI is integrated with all phases of e-Gov technology planning, development, deployment, and follow-up.

On his way to a more famous quote, Winston Churchill said that "[m]any forms of Government have been tried, and will be tried in this world of sin and woe." Although he didn't know it, he was describing in the context of government the iterative development process that has become enshrined in the information technology industry. Enlightened and successful technology companies have integrated HCI into the iterative development process. In doing so, it was necessary to develop a cyclic and agile process with many break points, ways of communicating easily between HCI researchers from the human sciences and engineers from the STEM disciplines, and design principles and patterns that derived from an understanding of human affect, cognition, perception, and behavior. It is a maxim in HCI that when we develop new systems for human use, even if we are careful to fully understand how the activities they support are carried out, we also change the nature of those activities. Thus, as we venture into new digital technologies for e-Gov, we will be changing the way government works. We will be modifying the relationships and understandings among citizens and between citizens and their governments. This book is an argument for doing so with our eyes open to the human implications.

Scott Robertson
Information and Computer Sciences Department
University of Hawaii at Manoa, USA.

Reference

Ishida, T., & Isbister, K. (2000). *Digital cities: Experiences, technologies, and future perspectives. Lecture notes in computer science* Vol. 1765. Berlin: Springer-Verlag.

Preface

Both of us have worked in human-computer interaction for more than three decades — since the early days of the field, when it had only just stopped being called "Man-Machine Integration." Before beginning this collaboration, we had each attended numerous ACM/SIGCHI conferences over the years, had known of each other's work, and had even corresponded — via snail mail! — about the 1985 conference. It was only a few short years ago, however, that our paths crossed physically — we finally met in person at the CHI 2008 conference in Florence, Italy. We had a wonderful lunch together at a "Slow Food" hole-in-the-wall *trattoria* full of locals, and a camaraderie was born. It was based on a shared love of good food, good wine, and — last but certainly not least — HCI.

At CHI 2009, in Boston, Dianne suggested writing a book. We went to the Morgan Kaufmann booth to identify a gap that we might fill, and after less than a minute of looking over the titles Elizabeth exclaimed, "Government systems!" Elizabeth has spent most of her career working on government systems as a practitioner on the contractor side, and Dianne started her career as a scientific civil servant in a government national research laboratory — so it seemed a natural fit. Elizabeth lives in the Washington, DC area and knows many user experience experts who work in the US government domain (both in the United States and around the world). Dianne, as the long-standing editor of *Interacting with Computers*, knows almost everyone else.

Our author list fell into place quite easily, as almost everyone we approached about writing a chapter was excited about contributing to what they saw as a very important book. Those of us in HCI and user experience (UX) tend to be passionate about designing technology to improve people's lives — and on a day-to-day basis, what affects people's lives more immediately than the state and the government under which they live?

Both of us saw this book as an opportunity to begin to collect (for the first time, we believe) the knowledge and wisdom of expert consultants, researchers, and practitioners in designing usable computer systems specifically for "the government" in all its myriad aspects. Our commitment to usability and user experience means that we focus on improving the ability of government systems to streamline and facilitate the activities of the human beings who use them. It is hoped that our skills, knowledge, and sheer weight of experience will allow this commitment to bear fruit in future government computing systems.

Whether your expertise is in government systems or in usability and user experience, we hope that you will learn something here that will help you increase, not just the cost-effectiveness and operational efficiency of your government, but citizen engagement with it via greater satisfaction with its online and interactive services.

We have chosen our quotations from medieval and Renaissance Italy, in honor of the city where we met.

Dianne Murray and Elizabeth Buie
Teddington and Silver Spring, November 17, 2011

Editors' Biographies

ELIZABETH BUIE

Elizabeth Buie has 35 years of experience in information systems, of which over 30 have involved user interfaces, usability, and the user experience. Approximately 90% of her work has involved government systems of one sort or another, both internal and public facing. She has performed research, analysis, specification, design, development, and evaluation of human-computer interaction (HCI) for web sites, web applications, desktop and mainframe applications, and complex systems such as spacecraft control centers and air-traffic control applications. Her experience has also included several years in system engineering, which includes the specification and analysis of system and software requirements and the integration of the HCI process into the system lifecycle. She has Master's degrees in Mathematics and in Human Development, extensive technical and nontechnical writing experience, and proficiency in the Italian language. She serves on the editorial board of the UPA's online *Journal of Usability Studies* and served for several years on the editorial board of ACM's *interactions* magazine. She plans to begin a PhD program in October of 2012.

In the mid-1990s, Elizabeth initiated the effort to promote awareness of HCI in government systems. She co-chaired a workshop at CHI'95 and a SIG at CHI'96 and was one of the organizers of three symposia at the National Institute of Standards and Technology (NIST) on HCI in government.

DIANNE MURRAY

Dianne Murray has a joint honors degree in Computer Science and Psychology and has been in the HCI field since 1979. Her first career was as a research scientist in one of the first HCI groups in the UK, at the National Physical Laboratory. Her second career was as an HCI and Software Engineering academic, at City University London, Kings College London, and for the University of London International Degree Program. Her third career brought her a Senior Research Fellowship in the Social and Computer Sciences (SCS) Research Group at University of Surrey. Her fourth career as a Usability / HCI consultant with her partner, Neil Sandford, at Putting People Before Computers and her fifth as Editor-in-Chief of the international journal *Interacting with Computers: The Interdisciplinary Journal of Human-Computer Interaction* (an official publication of the British Computer Society) have taken place in parallel since 1984, when she was a founder member of *interaction* (originally the British HCI Group).

After working on the design and development of a CBT authoring system she published some of the first research in the now-burgeoning area of adaptivity, user modeling and intelligent interfaces. She been involved with many national and international groups and activities, was International Chair and on the executive committee of ACM SIGCHI for almost ten years, and has frequently acted as an expert Evaluator and Technical Rapporteur for EU research programmes. She has previously edited 2 books of HCI readings and published in both the HCI and CSCW field.

Contributors' Biographies

RAHEL ANNE BAILIE

Rahel Anne Bailie is a content strategist with a skill set encompassing content management, business analysis, information architecture, and communications. She operates IntentionalDesign.ca, helping clients analyze their business requirements and spectrum of content to get the right fit for their content development and management needs, and facilitates transitions to new business processes, content models, and technology implementations. Her experience gives her an intimate understanding of end-to-end processes, from requirements gathering to implementation.

NIGEL BEVAN

Nigel Bevan is an independent usability consultant with wide industrial and research experience. He has been the editor of several international standards, including ISO9241-11 and ISO/IEC 25010, and contributed to many others, including ISO 9241-210 and ISO 18529. Nigel leads the UPA Usability Body of Knowledge project. He was a member of the National Academy of Science Committee on Human-System Design Support for Changing Technology. He has authored over 80 publications and has a chapter providing a framework for cost benefits in *Cost-Justifying Usability* (Bias and Mayhew, 2005). Nigel has first degrees in Physics and in Psychology and a Ph.D. in MMI.

GEORGE BUCHANAN

George Buchanan is an Associate Professor in the Centre for Human–Computer Interaction Design at City University London, UK. George ran a software publishing house for nearly a decade before obtaining his Ph.D. in HCI. His main research interests are the usability issues surrounding search engines and mobile devices.

RAVEN CHAI

Raven Chai is the principal consultant and founder of UX Consulting, a user experience research and design company based in Singapore. He is currently on the leadership team of the Usability Professionals' Association Asia and was one of the founders of UXSG, a local UX community for UX practitioners in Singapore. He has been engaged by SingTel as the lead usability consultant since 2008 and has been instrumental in creating a user-centric design culture, translating SingTel's business vision into actionable roadmaps and building an internal UX team. Raven is a former technologist at Arthur Andersen with over 12 years of experience in the IT industry and has managed many user-centered projects that synthesized marketing, technology, and user goals from concept to launch.

TORKIL CLEMMENSEN

Torkil Clemmensen is an Associate Professor in the Department of IT Management, Copenhagen Business School, Denmark. He has more than 20 years of academic and industrial experience with human-centered methods and techniques for analysis, design, and evaluation of information and communication technology and digital media and how these are designed and used in organizational, human, social, and cultural contexts.

ANGUS DOULTON

Angus Doulton was appointed director of the UK's National Interactive Video Centre (NIVC) in 1984. NIVC was the only entirely independent center for advice on all aspects of interactive technologies in Great Britain and, possibly, the world. He rapidly became convinced that what aspiring users needed most was not advice on technology but on implementation. In particular, he began to define "interface" as the complete action from the moment the user first came through "the door" to the end of interaction. More projects failed because computers were put in inappropriate places than because they didn't actually work. Following NIVC, founded CDW & Associates Ltd. in 1991 and has spent 20 years assisting local and central governments with transformation projects where technology implementation was a key success factor.

LAURA L. DOWNEY

Laura Downey is a senior information technology professional who thrives on making technology work for people. She has B.A. and M.S. degrees in Computer Science and 20 years' experience in usability and information architecture across government, industry, and academia. Laura currently heads the Applied Architecture Branch in the Enterprise Architecture Division of the Transportation Security Administration.

CATHY DUDEK

Cathy Dudek is a research associate who has been involved with HCI for over 10 years through her affiliation with the Human Oriented Technology Lab (HOTLab) at Carleton University, Canada. Her research interests include user satisfaction, aesthetics, usability, trust, and relationships among them as they contribute to the holistic Web user experience. She also consults on projects involving emergency response systems and emergency preparedness planning applications. Cathy holds a Ph.D. in Psychology from Carleton University in Ottawa, Canada.

JONATHAN EARTHY

Jonathan Earthy is a Principal Specialist for Lloyd's Register, where he has worked for 19 years in consulting, strategic, audit, and research roles across a range of industries, including defense and the public sector. His technical specialty is assurance of the quality of human factors work. Jonathan has participated in standards development since the mid-1980s. He is convener of ISO TC159/SC4/WG6 Human-Centered Design for Interactive Systems and UK Head of Delegation and Ergonomics Liaison to ISO/IECJTC1 SC7 Systems and Software Engineering.

KATHY E. GILL

Kathy Gill is a consultant, writer, and digital media educator at the University of Washington (Seattle), USA, whose interests center on the intersection of communication technology and institutions of power such as government and the media. She has been analyzing and writing about the usability of government web sites since the late 1990s. Kathy has helped political campaigns and government agencies develop web sites that don't treat visitors rudely. She is writing a book about how early adopter organizations use social networking sites such as Twitter and Google+.

JAN GULLIKSEN

Jan Gulliksen is Professor of HCI and Dean of the School of Computer Science and Communication at KTH — the Royal Institute of Technology in Stockholm, Sweden. He holds an M.Sc. in Engineering Physics and a Ph.D. in Systems Analysis and was previously a professor at Uppsala University, Sweden. He has conducted a number of EU Action Research projects with Swedish public authorities with the purpose of introducing more user-centered design methodologies and was a founder of the NordiCHI conference series. He has been involved in writing ISO standards on usability, accessibility, and human-centered design and is the current chair of IFIP TC 13, Human Computer Interaction. Jan has authored more than 100 publications and has been active as a consultant in industry.

CAROLINE JARRETT

Caroline Jarrett is a user experience consultant. After 13 years as a project manager, she founded Effortmark Ltd. in 1994. She has a long-held fascination with making forms easy to fill in, particularly focusing on government, official, and other complex forms and transactions. Caroline is coauthor of *User Interface Design and Evaluation* and *Forms That Work: Designing Web Forms for Usability*. Her next book, *Surveys that Work*, will be published in 2012.

CHRIS JOHNSON

Chris Johnson is Professor of Computing Science at the University of Glasgow, Scotland. His research develops new techniques for incident and accident investigation. He has worked with EUROCONTROL to develop guidelines for mishap reporting in air traffic management and has recently helped develop similar guidance for training accident investigators on behalf of the European Railway Agency. He has held fellowships from NASA and the USAF, most recently working with the safety teams for the International Space Station, and is a member of the IAASS suborbital safety team. He is cochair for the EU's scientific advisory board to the three-billion euro SESAR program on the modernization of air traffic management. His recent work has focused on the impact that cyberthreats have for the safety of space-based infrastructures.

TIMO JOKELA

Timo Jokela is an independent usability consultant and Adjunct Professor at both the University of Helsinki and the University of Oulu in Finland. He holds a Ph.D. in Information Processing Science. He was previously a full professor at the University of Oulu and a usability pioneer at Nokia. Timo has worked with and developed approaches for a wide spectrum of usability issues: most recently for the procurement and development of government systems, and previously for strategic usability, from usability maturity models to usability requirements definition and measures. He has published more than 100 articles on usability and is a member of ISO working groups on usability standards.

DINESH KATRE

Dinesh Katre is presently Associate Director and Head of Development (HOD) of the Human-Centered Design & Computing Group at C-DAC, India. He has been exploring HCI and usability through sponsored R&D projects in diverse areas such as museum archives, educational game design, public information systems, and mobile applications. He is also the principal designer of many software, multimedia, and educational products.

SUSAN KLEIMANN

Susan Kleimann is the president of Kleimann Communication Group, a consultancy near Washington, DC. She has worked with many US government agencies on research, design, and testing projects to transform critical documents into a form that consumers can understand and use. For example, with her key team, she developed and tested a privacy disclosure, now used voluntarily by nearly all major US financial institutions; major mortgage documents; and an electronic privacy policy for personal health records, also now used voluntarily by major institutions. Susan holds a Ph.D. in English from the University of Maryland, USA.

JONATHAN LAZAR

Jonathan Lazar is a full Professor of Computer and Information Sciences, Director of the undergraduate program in information systems, and Director of the Universal Usability Laboratory, all at Towson University, USA. Jonathan is involved in teaching and research, — specifically in Web usability, Web accessibility, user-centered design methods, assistive technology, and public policy in the HCI area. He is the author of five books related to accessibility, usability, and HCI. He holds a Ph.D. in Information Systems from the University of Maryland Baltimore County, in Maryland, USA.

GITTE LINDGAARD

Gitte Lindgaard was Director of the Human Oriented Technology Lab (HOTLab), full professor in the Department of Psychology, Carleton University, Ottawa, Canada, and holder of the prestigious Canadian Natural Science & Engineering Senior Industry Research Chair in User-Centered Design for the past 11 years. She is now a Distinguished Research Professor at Carleton and Professor in Neuro-Affective Psychology at Swinburne University of Technology in Melbourne, Australia. She is a Fellow of the HF&ESA, a Deputy Editor of the journal *Interacting with Computers*, and an associate editor of several international HCI journals. Her research interests include multimedia/multimodal and mobile technologies, aesthetics and emotion in computing, and human decision making, especially in diagnostic medicine. She has published over 200 refereed papers, books, and book chapters.

MARK T. MAYBURY

Mark Maybury is Chief Scientist of the US Air Force. He serves as chief scientific and technical advisor to the Chief of Staff and the Secretary of the Air Force. Mark is currently on a leave of absence as an executive director at the MITRE Corporation. Fellow of the IEEE, he has served on the ACM Intelligent User Interfaces Steering Council and as an AAAI counselor. He has edited or coauthored 10 books, published over 60 refereed articles, and was awarded three US patents. Mark holds degrees from College of the Holy Cross, Rensselaer Polytechnic Institute, USA. (MBA), and Cambridge University, England (M.Phil, Ph.D.).

JESS MCMULLIN

Jess McMullin is the founder of the Centre for Citizen Experience in Canada — a startup "do tank" dedicated to advancing design innovation in the public sector. Jess works with public sector clients to design services, systems, and policies that make a difference in the daily lives of citizens. He also pursues design advocacy opportunities to improve design competency, change organizational culture, and promote design as a key for reinventing service delivery and public policy.

PATRICK J. NOONAN

Patrick Noonan is a Research Assistant in the Human-Oriented Technology Lab (HOTLab) in Ottawa, Ontario, Canada. After receiving his Master's degree in 2010, Patrick has been consulting for Ottawa-based software companies while publishing in both scholarly journals and magazines. His research interests include mobile usability, music psychology, aesthetics, and user experience with robots.

PHILIPPE PALANQUE

Philippe Palanque is Professor in Computer Science at the University Toulouse 3–Paul Sabatier and is head of the Interactive Critical Systems group at the Institut de Recherche en Informatique de Toulouse (IRIT) in France. He has worked on research projects to improve interactive ground segment systems at the Centre National d'Etudes Spatiales (CNES) for more than 10 years and is also involved in the development of software architectures and user interface modeling for interactive cockpits in large civil aircraft (funded by Airbus). The main driver of his research over the last 20 years has been to place the human at the center of the development processes. His current research deals with formal description techniques to support the design and construction of resilient interactive systems, taking into equal account usability, safety, and dependability.

MONICA PALMIRANI

Monica Palmirani is Associate Professor of Computer Science and Law at CIRSFID, University of Bologna University School of Law, Italy. She teaches several courses in legal informatics, e-government, legal drafting techniques, and legal XML. Her principal field of research is legislative and legal informatics, legal drafting techniques, and software tools for supporting legislative processes in public administration bodies in Italy, Europe, and Uruguay. She serves on several technical committees for the standardization of legal documents.

WHITNEY QUESENBERY

Whitney Quesenbery is a user experience researcher and usability expert with a passion for clear communication. Her projects include work for the US National Cancer Institute, the UK's Open University, and IEEE. Pursuing her interest in the usability of civic life, she has served on two US government advisory committees: updating Section 508 accessibility regulations and creating usability and accessibility guidelines for US elections. Whitney is the author, with Daniel Szuc, of *Global UX* and, with Kevin Brooks, of *Storytelling for User Experience*.

JANICE (GINNY) REDISH

For more than 30 years, Ginny Redish has brought her background in linguistics (Ph.D., Harvard, USA) and her passion for UX and plain language to her research and practice. She helps clients and colleagues create products in which people can find what they need, understand what they find, and use that to meet their needs. Ginny's extensive publication list includes the award-winning book, *Letting Go of the Words — Writing Web Content That Works*.

KAREN RENAUD

Karen Renaud is a computing scientist at the University of Glasgow in Scotland. Her primary focus is in improving the accessibility of security software. She has more than 20 years of industrial and academic experience as a software engineer and usability and usable security researcher.

SYLVIA ROSALES

Sylvia Rosales is a technology consultant based in Washington, DC. Her career interests include mobile usability, social networking, user-centered design, and information architecture. Sylvia graduated from the University of Virginia, USA in 2009 with a B.S. in Systems Engineering.

NEIL SANDFORD

Neil Sandford began his career in an area of computing once described — still partially true 40 years later — as "the bit that isn't quite working yet." He ran one of the pioneering multimedia companies in the 1980s, gaining the UK's Design Council recognition as an HCI/ergonomics consultant in 1989, and now consults under the strap-line "Putting People before Computers." He was once told by the Institute of Defense Analyses: "Either you guys address the problem or we'll have to, and you know what that would mean."

BRIAN SHERWOOD JONES

Brian Sherwood Jones has over 35 years of experience in human factors aspects of complex systems. His interest has been in providing usability assurance, that is, assurance of safe and effective operation from the early stages of a system through to operational use. Prior to setting up Process Contracting Ltd., Brian worked at YARD Ltd. in Glasgow, Scotland and at Westland Helicopters Ltd. in Somerset, UK.

BRIAN STANTON

Brian Stanton is a Cognitive Scientist in the Visualization and Usability Group at the US National Institute of Standards and Technology (NIST) where he works on the Common Industry Format project, developing usability standards, and investigates biometric usability issues ranging from interface design and analysis to anthropometric concerns. He has worked on biometric projects for the Department of Homeland Security, for the Federal Bureau of Investigation's Hostage Rescue Team, and with latent fingerprint examiners. Previously he worked in private industry designing user interfaces for air traffic control systems and B2B Web applications.

MILICA STOJMENOVIC

Milica Stojmenovic is a Master's student at the Human Oriented Technology Lab (HOTLab) at Carleton University, Canada. Her research interests include crisis management, design and testing of emergency response systems, teamwork, communication, social networks, usability, and aesthetics. She has seven publications, including book chapters, refereed papers, and technical reports. She was awarded several scholarships and awards, including the Senate Medal for Outstanding Academic Achievement at Carleton University Canada for her undergraduate degree.

LIVIA SUMEGI

Livia Sumegi works in the area of user experience design and is currently a usability specialist with OpenText Corporation, a Canadian enterprise software company. She holds an M.A. degree in Psychology from Carleton University, Canada, and specialized in HCI. In this field, she has a number of publications relating to usability and assistive technology. Her research interests include accessibility, Web aesthetics, and interaction design.

ALISTAIR SUTCLIFFE

Alistair Sutcliffe retired from the University of Manchester, UK in October 2011; however, he continues his research as a Visiting Professor at University College London and the University of Lancaster. He has been principal investigator on numerous EPSRC and EU projects. His research interests in HCI are in the theory and models of user experience, interaction design, social media, and design of complex sociotechnical systems. In software engineering he specializes in requirements engineering methods and tools, scenario-based design, and theories of domain knowledge. He serves on several journal editorial boards and as editor of ISO standard 14915, on "Multimedia User Interface Design." He has over 250 publications, including five books, and was awarded the IFIP "Silver Core" in 2000.

DANIEL SZUC

Daniel Szuc is a principal consultant at Apogee, based in Hong Kong China. He worked previously on a usability team for Telstra Australia and was VP of UPA International. He lectures about UX globally and recently wrote a book on *Global UX* with Whitney Quesenbery and cowrote a "Usability Kit" with Gerry Gaffney. Daniel holds a B.S. in Information Management from Melbourne University, Australia.

MARY FRANCES THEOFANOS

Mary Frances Theofanos is a Computer Scientist at the National Institute for Standards and Technology (NIST), where she is the program manager of the Industry Usability Reporting Project developing standards for usability. She is a member of ISO/IEC JTC1 SC7 and the Convener of the SC7 TC 159/SC4 Joint Working Group. She is the principal architect of the Biometrics Usability Program evaluating the human factors and usability of biometric systems. She spent 15 years as a program manager for software technology at the Oak Ridge National Laboratory complex of the US Department of Energy. Mary Frances received the NIST Bronze Medal in 2005.

BRUCE TSUJI

Bruce Tsuji is a Professor of Psychology at CEGEP Heritage College in Gatineau, Quebec, and also teaches at Carleton University, both in Canada. His research interests include expertise technologies to assist those with visual impairment, and how people understand data. He has held product management, marketing, and business development roles at a number of technology companies and currently provides user experience consulting for several startups. Bruce is a coinventor on numerous patents and holds a Ph.D. in Psychology from Carleton University, Canada.

FABIO VITALI

Fabio Vitali is an Associate Professor in Computer Science at the University of Bologna, Italy. His main areas of research interest are in Web technologies and user-centered software design. He has been working in the field of languages and tools for the legislative process since his Ph.D. years and has contributed to shaping the Italian standard NormeInRete, the European standard CEN Metalex, and the international standard Akoma Ntoso for expression in XML of legislative and parliamentary documents.

KATE WALSER

Kate Walser is a user experience consultant with 14 years of experience in planning and designing software, Web, and mobile apps that people can use and enjoy. She specializes in collaboration and rich application design. She has provided user experience strategy, information architecture, design, usability testing, and accessibility services for large government and commercial organizations, including the US Departments of Health and Human Services, Defense, and Veterans Affairs. She served on the US government advisory committee tasked with updating Section 508 accessibility standards and is a Center for Plain Language executive board member.

BRIAN WENTZ

Brian Wentz is an Assistant Professor in the Department of Computer Science and Information Technologies at Frostburg State University. His research interests include HCI, accessibility, user-centered design, social computing, policy implications of accessibility and usability, and making business practices more accessible. He holds a M.S. in information systems from Penn State University and a D.Sc. in Information Technology from Towson University in Maryland, both in the USA.

MARCO WINCKLER

Marco Winckler is Assistant Professor in Computer Science at the University Toulouse 3–Paul Sabatier, France. His research is focused on the development of tools, methods, and notations for engineering interactive systems. He has been involved in several French national projects related to the design, development, and evaluation of e-government applications. His current research interests include topics on engineering interactive systems, HCI, and Web engineering.

JOSEPHINE WONG

Josephine Wong is the cofounder of Apogee and has been in usability consulting and project management for more than 10 years. She is a senior member of the team with insights across every Apogee project since its foundation. Josephine speaks fluent Cantonese, English, and Mandarin; is the lead Chinese consultant; and has practiced usability and promoted customer-centered design in both Hong Kong and China. She holds a B.S. in Information Management from Melbourne University, Australia.

Acknowledgments

Both editors greatly acknowledge the support, help, and encouragement of family, friends, and colleagues on the long road toward bringing this book into being.

Elizabeth's acknowledgments especially go to

- **Thomas Vander Wal**, for idea bouncing and sanity checking
- **Douglas Lang**, for reassuring me that I understood government procurement fairly well and filling in where I didn't
- **Jane Baluss**, for checking in with me and helping keep me sane during the last intense weeks of manuscript preparation
- **Computer Sciences Corporation**, for giving me more than 30 years of government contracting experience

Dianne's acknowledgments especially go to

- **Neil Sandford**, for being there, always, when needed
- **Lauren, Katharine, Mark,** and **Gavin Sandford**, for support and understanding
- **Gitte Lindgaard** and **Karmen Guevara,** for friendship and encouragement

We also thank all of our contributing authors for taking part in this endeavor and to the staff at Elsevier/Morgan Kaufmann. For their hard work, patience and forbearance, without which etcetera . . .

- **Heather Scherer, Steve Elliot, Andre Cuello, Rachel Roumeliotis,** and **David Bevans**

Dianne Murray and Elizabeth Buie

London and Washington, 17th November 2011

Introduction

"Reader, if thou to credit what is here
Art slow, 'tis no surprise, since I can scarce
Believe, who saw it all as clear as clear."
— Dante Alighieri, *L'Inferno*, Canto XXV, lines 46-48

WHY WE WROTE THIS BOOK

Bookstores abound with offerings on "usability" and "user experience" (2352 and 293 search results, respectively, on Amazon.com as of this writing). The number doubles for "government contracting" (4275 results) and jumps by almost 50 times for "government systems" (106,957 — again, as of this writing). This book, however, is unique. Although a search on "usability and government" finds 89 titles, not one of them is like this book. Books on e-government mention usability as a success factor (e.g., Roebuck, 2011). Government publications offer usability information related to a single domain, such as Web design (US Government, 2011a) or aviation cockpit displays (e.g., US Government, 2011b). Conference proceedings include academic research papers (e.g., Sørum, 2011) on usability in e-Gov But none of these titles covers the topic broadly or focuses on it exclusively, as this book does.

Yet countless citizens worldwide use government web sites and other systems to obtain information from their government and to do business with it. Tremendous numbers of government employees conduct their nation's business via desktop computer and intranet sites. It is impossible to say exactly how many people will use a government system themselves during their lifetimes, but it is a safe bet that these systems will touch everyone's life in some way.

But how usable are these systems? How consistent and predictable are the web sites for those who have to navigate the maze of government information and online services? How well do internal applications support the productivity of government employees? Functionality apart, how well do government systems actually serve the citizenry?

The US government is the largest consumer of information technology in the world (Colvin, 2011). In the summer of 2011 the White House reported that the government had a shocking number — more than 24,000 — of different web sites (White House, 2011). US President Obama announced the Campaign to Cut Waste, whose charter includes finding ways of presenting the public with Web-based information and services that are better connected and presented more consistently.

Other governments have had similar concerns. In March of 2004 the United Kingdom launched DirectGov (BBC, 2004) to consolidate access to much of its national government information for citizens, and in January 2007 it announced a decision to eliminate almost 60% of the 951 sites it had at the time (BBC, 2007). A 2011 study by the China Software Testing Center, as reported in the China Daily (Uking, 2011), found that 79% of national government websites in China, although they provide more information than ever, have various functional and usability problems; and the problem is even worse in provincial and local governments. As of this writing, the United Nations has issued two reports on e-gov (United Nations, 2010; United Nations, 2011), and the Association for Computing Machinery has held several annual conference on e-gov, in which both of us participated in 2011 (Robertson, Buie, & Murray, 2011).

Almost every national government in the world has at least one public web site United Nations, 2011, and we would be surprised to learn of a government that didn't have computers, at least in its national offices.

And yet no book exists that addresses usability in government systems. Until now.

This is the first book that concentrates on the role of usability in government systems. It covers designing government systems to provide effectiveness, efficiency, and a pleasant and satisfying experience to the people who use them, whether they are interacting with their government from the outside or working for the government on the inside.

This book opens with the history of usability and user experience in government systems. **Laura Downey** (US) and **Sylvia Rosales** (US) provide a survey of the history of government involvement in various aspects of UX, which began almost a century ago. The armed forces have always been a leader in human factors and ergonomics, Downey and Rosales tell us, beginning in the United Kingdom during World War I and expanding into the United States and Canada during World War II and into China in the 1950s. Governments have, they report, funded research, consumed technologies, provided information, and implemented policy and legislation, not to mention provided training in UX topics and employment to UX professionals. The authors caution, however, that although much UX progress has been made in the public sector, involvement of government institutions in UX varies widely — as reflected in the different levels of usability present — or to the complete lack of attention paid to user experience, in government systems around the globe. "Increased coverage of UX in government systems is an important goal," Downey and Rosales state, "and one in which multiple groups share responsibility and, ultimately, the benefits. We hope chroniclers, in future histories, are able to report that UX in government systems continued the positive trend and became a best practice."

The rest of the book is divided into five sections. The first three address usability issues related to who will use the system. Some issues are particular to systems used by members of the public (Section I); some concern systems whose users work inside government (Section II); and still others relate to both types of systems (Section III). Section IV covers the incorporation of usability and user-centered design into the government procurement process, and Section V takes a step back and addresses some wider concerns beyond the immediate user experience of interactive technology. We will let those sections introduce themselves to you when you reach them.

THE AUDIENCE

We have planned and prepared the content of this book with three audiences in mind.

Our first audience is government and contractor professionals responsible for government system projects. We write for project/product managers, business analysts, system architects and engineers, writers of requests for proposals, business development managers, and quality assurance and testing specialists — people who recognize that it is important to make government information technology better meet the needs of the users, but who may not know where and how to start improving usability or how to integrate the activities into their projects. We hope to help them start understanding how to do that.

Our second audience is professionals in usability and user experience looking to expand their careers into government systems or who aspire to use their knowledge and skills to help improve their government's ability to meet its citizens' needs. We aim to give them some understanding of the constraints and requirements under which government projects operate and some insights into how their skills might fit into this environment.

Our third audience is policymakers and legislators. These people are in a position to influence the very policies and laws that affect the inclusion of usability in government systems. We hope that this book will show them the potential need for new policies or legislation, or for changes to those already in existence, to improve the environment for usability as a component of government procurements, in the same way that laws around the world have worked to improve accessibility for people with disabilities, as described in Chapter 12. We anticipate that these readers will lead the effort to make those changes.

References

BBC. (2004). *Doubts cloud e-government sites.* Retrieved 21 November 2011 from http://news.bbc.co.uk/2/hi/technology/3747021.stm

BBC. (2007). *Government to close 551 websites.* Retrieved 21 November 2011 from http://news.bbc.co.uk/2/hi/uk_news/politics/6247703.stm

Colvin, G. (2011). *Uncle Sam's first CIO.* CNN Money. Retrieved 21 November 2011 from http://money.cnn.com/2011/07/13/news/companies/vivek_kundra_leadership.fortune/index.htm

Robertson, S. P., Buie, E. A., & Murray, D. M. (2011). Interaction design for citizen engagement and digital government. In: *Proceedings of the 12th annual international digital government research conference: Digital government innovation in challenging times (dg.o '11)*, New York: ACM.

Roebuck, K. (2011). *e-Government: High-impact strategies — what you need to know: Definitions, adoptions, impact, benefits, maturity, vendors.* Tebbo.

Sørum, H. (2011). An empirical investigation of user involvement, website quality and perceived user satisfaction in eGovernment environments. In K. N. Anderson, E. Francesconi, A. Grönlund & T. M. van Engers (Eds.), *Proceedings of EGOVIS 2011* (pp. 122–134). Toulouse, France: Springer.

United Nations Department of Economic and Social Affairs. (2010). *E-government survey 2010: Leveraging e-government at a time of financial and economic crisis.* ST/ESA/PAD/SER.E/131 New York: United Nations.

United Nations Department of Economic and Social Affairs. (2012). E-Government Survey 2012: E-Government for the People (UN, New York, N.Y.) www.upan.org/e-government.

Uking. (2011). *80% of gov't websites nonfunctional.* Retrieved 4 December 2011 from http://www.chinadaily.com.cn/china/2011-12/03/content_14208579.htm

US Government. (2011a). *Research-based web design & usability guidelines.* Washington DC: Books LLC.

US Government. (2011b). Usability and effectiveness of advanced general aviation cockpit displays for instrument flight procedures. Washington DC: Books LLC.

White House. (2011). *TooManyWebsites.gov.* The White House Blog. Retrieved 21 November 2011 from http://www.whitehouse.gov/blog/2011/06/13/toomanywebsitesgov

CHAPTER

A Brief History of User Experience in Government Systems

1

Laura L. Downey[1],*, Sylvia Rosales†
Fairfax, VA, USA Vienna, VA, USA†*

"I was taught that the way of progress is neither swift nor easy."
— Marie Curie

INTRODUCTION

In the early days of user experience (UX), government participation occurred as a result of a specific government need, or with government organizations providing funding for research and innovation. In later years, government and those that did business with the government also realized the tangible benefits of UX in government systems. Benefits were often related to safety, accuracy, and productivity. From cockpit design and battle systems to sophisticated interactive training and information systems — military personnel, government workers, and citizens benefit from UX in government systems.

ORIGINS OF UX

Before examining the history of UX in government systems, we will briefly review its origins. UX is concerned with the encounters a human has while interacting with products and services (Roto, Law, Vermeeren, & Hoonhout, 2011). UX is also an umbrella field that encompasses several disciplines and areas of study. Over the past 80 years, multiple disciplines have emerged and evolved, each offering significant contributions to the UX of technology and products. Three major contributors are human factors and ergonomics (HF&E), human-computer interaction (HCI), and usability. Related design processes and disciplines also arose alongside these foundational disciplines. User-centered design (UCD) (also known as human-centered design, or HCD), interaction design (IxD), and information architecture (IA) are notable contributors. Additionally, the umbrella discipline of UX involves many areas of study, including psychology, industrial design, systems engineering, computer science, anthropology, cognitive science, information systems, and library science. A brief look back provides the context in which UX developed and in which governments influenced and utilized it.

[1]The information, comments, and views presented here are solely those of the authors and editors, and do not represent the views of the Transportation Security Administration, the Department of Homeland Security, or the United States.

During World War I, scientists in the United Kingdom investigated human issues in ordnance (military weapons and equipment) factories (Shackel, 2009). In the 1930s, Henry Dreyfuss, an American pioneer in industrial design, established his design practice based on a holistic view of the user. He also contributed to the field of ergonomics. Much of the early work in HF&E stemmed from military application across multiple countries:

- HF&E in the United States and Canada substantially began during World War II, with the design of human operated systems (DRDC, 2010; HFES, 2010). The aircraft cockpit is an example of a user interface that was targeted for review. The US military called in engineering psychologists to study the configuration of controls and arrangement of instrument displays to aid human performance and reduce crashes (Shaver & Braun, 2009).
- Those in the United Kingdom focused on ergonomics in World War II by matching military equipment to human capacity (Shackel, 2009).
- China established an aviation psychology lab in the 1950s (Liu, Zhang, Zhang, & Chen, 2011).
- In 1972, the Israeli Air Force began using human factors research in the development of its technology (Eliav & Sharon, 2011).
- In 1978, the "Ergocenter" opened as part of the Soviet Academy of Sciences and primarily served the Russian military (Belyshkin, 2011).

The 1980s ushered in the rise of personal computers and prompted a greater focus on successful interaction between humans and computers (Carroll, 2011). The complexity of software versus single-use devices presented a distinct design challenge. As a result, the study of HCI began in various places around the world in the 1980s — e.g., the United States, United Kingdom, Brazil, Australia, Japan, and New Zealand (Carroll, 2011; Douglas & Liu, 2011; Human Factors and Ergonomics Society of Australia (HFESA), 2011). Over the next decade, research and practice expanded and matured, and the 1990s saw the rise of HCI in other countries such as Mexico, Poland, Russia, and China (Douglas & Liu, 2011). Organizations devoted to HCI sprang up around the globe. The Association for Computing Machinery's (ACM's) Special Interest Group on Computer and Human Interaction (SIGCHI) held its first HCI conference at the US National Institute of Standards and Technology (NIST) in 1982 (Pew, 2003). The *interaction* group (previously the UK HCI Group) of the British Computer Society (BCS) was established in 1984 and is the oldest national HCI group in Europe (BCS, 2011). BCS collaborates with government and industry on work practices, standards, codes of conduct, and skills definition. The French-speaking HCI community organized its first conference IHM (Interaction Human-Machine) in 1989 (HCIRN, 2011). INTERACT, an international HCI conference sponsored by the International Federation for Information Processing (IFIP), started in 1984 (HCIRN, 2011). In the 1990s, other groups across the globe formed and held conferences dedicated to HCI. The first Australian HCI conference, OZCHI, was held in 1991, and the East-West Conferences on HCI were held annually from 1992 to 1996 in Russia (Belyshkin, 2011; HCIRN, 2011).

Closely following the early years of HCI practice, the usability profession appeared on the scene somewhere between 1988 and 1993 (Dumas, 2007). Usability and usability engineering research and work started in the 1980s. John Whiteside introduced the phrase "usability engineering" (Whiteside, Bennett, & Holzblatt, 1988). Usability promoted an engineering approach and the use of applied methods for the design and testing of technology, instead of the more traditional research methods of HF&E and early HCI. The Usability Professionals Association (UPA) was launched in 1991 and included individuals from government and industrial organizations, who helped design and evaluate government systems. Today UPA has chapters around the world.

Two user-focused approaches that appeared in the 1980s were UCD and IxD. UCD promoted involvement of the user in the design of systems and products. IxD "defines the structure and behavior of interactive systems" (Interaction Design Association [IxDA], n.d.). Although IxD began in the 1980s, mainstream use of the term "interaction design" occurred in the mid-1990s (Cooper, 2007). IxDA, an international organization devoted to IxD formed in 2003, includes practitioners who work on government and corporate systems.

With the advent of the World Wide Web ("the Web") in the 1990s, and the subsequent explosion of available information at the fingertips of millions of users, IA and search became a prominent part of UX. IA is the "the art and science of organizing information so that it is findable, manageable and useful" (Bailey, 2002). The US Library of Congress regularly applies IA techniques to its digital libraries and library catalogs. The Smithsonian Institution has applied IA practices to its systems that deal with digital collections of artifacts.

The Web also offered a medium for a rich visual experience, and thus visual designers played an important role in creating a good UX. Many government web sites around the world, both intranets and public-facing sites, include the work of graphic and visual designers, information architects, and interaction designers.

Don Norman coined the phrase "user experience" in the mid-1990s, but its use to describe an industry did not occur until the late 1990s and early 2000s (Brazen, 2009). Books and conferences began appearing with "UX" in the title. Adaptive Path held one of the first UX conferences, called "UX Week," in 2003. In 2012, UX has matured into a field with a diverse set of contributors working toward a common goal — designing products and services that enable users to be productive while also enjoying the experience.

UX IN GOVERNMENT SYSTEMS

The history of UX in government systems presented here spans the 1950s to the present. We explore the early years, the transition years, the growth years, and the partnership years. Figure 1.1 illustrates the timeline of UX in government systems including these groupings along with major activities. Many people and governments of the world have contributed to this history, and if we have not mentioned them in particular or included examples of their work, it does not indicate that they have not participated or that we do not value their contributions. The examples, activities, and stories in this chapter come from our personal knowledge and from information readily available via a variety of sources.

1950-1970s: the early years

HF&E played a significant role from the 1950s through the 1970s (Pew, 2003). The military needed successful battlefield and defense technology — including systems operated on the ground, in the air, and in the sea (HFES, 2010). HF&E was a critical contributor to this success. Command-and-control systems were the primary types of systems where HF&E was applied. IBM was the first computer company to set up a human factors group, and the group's original focus was on military systems during WWII (Pew, 2003). In the 1950s, the US Air Force commissioned Project SAGE (Strategic Air-Ground Environment) — an air defense system — which included a human factors group led by J.C.R. Licklider (Dalakov, 2011). Work on this system

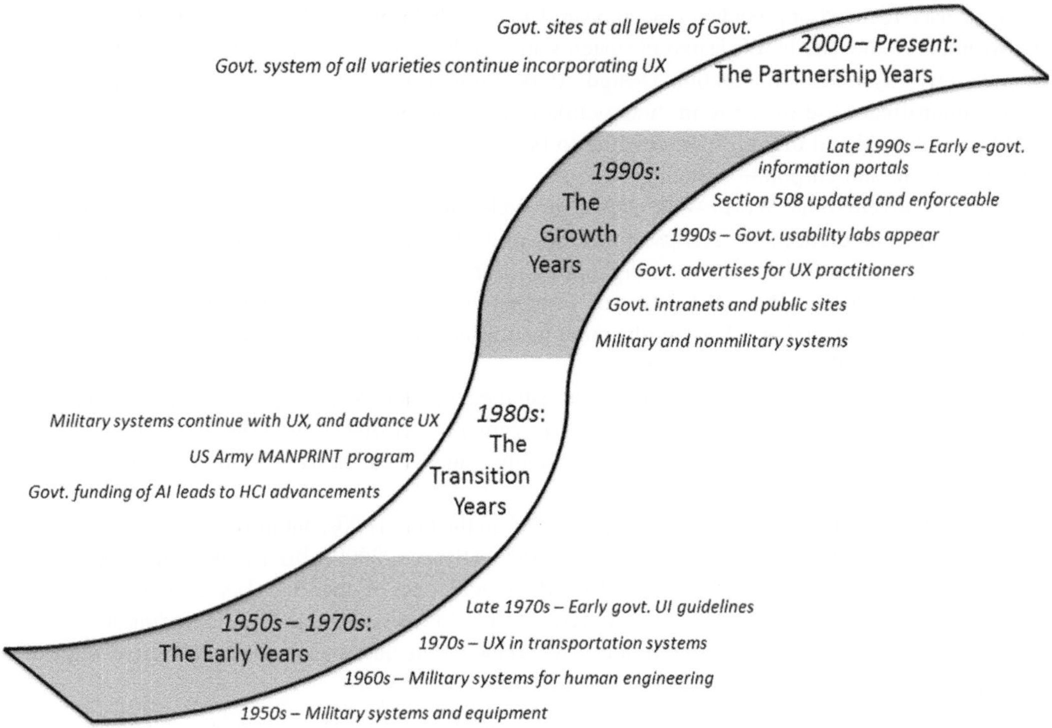

FIGURE 1.1 UX in government systems: timeline

contributed to Licklider's 1960 seminal notion of human-machine symbiosis, which laid a foundation for interactive systems (Dalakov, 2011).

Military standards were first developed during this period, and they became an important factor in government systems across the globe. They were often specified in the procurement process and even when they were not specified, the government still developed and implemented many systems using military standards. One of the most prominent standards related to UX was MIL-STD-1472. The US Department of Defense (DOD) developed the standard in 1968 based on test and evaluation results of the US Army Human Engineering Laboratory (Poston, 2003). (In 1994, the reform of military standards converted many of the human factors standards to handbooks or design criteria standards [Poston, 2003].)

In addition to military systems, transportation systems began to consider human factors concerns in their designs — e.g., air-traffic control systems of several governments around the world. Airline accidents were a primary driver of UX-related considerations in the 1970s and 1980s. According to SKYbrary (2011), HF in aviation focused on reducing workload in the 1970s and situational awareness in the 1980s. HF aviation professionals concentrated on nontechnical skills and crew resource management training in the early 1980s (SKYbrary, 2011).

Government funding played a critical role in initiating and advancing HCI technologies, resulting in increased application of HCI in government systems. According to Card (1996), government funding built intellectual capital and trained the research teams in HCI. Douglas Engelbart designed one of the "pioneer systems" of HCI. Engelbart's NLS (oN-Line-System) introduced a number of interaction features like the mouse, hypertext, and groupware concepts. The US Air Force, the US National Aeronautics and Space Administration (NASA), and the US Defense Advanced Research Projects Agency (previously known as ARPA) funded this work. The US DOD and NASA have a long history of involvement in funding innovative projects and the use of UX in their systems. For example, display designs in weapons, cockpits, rockets, and the space shuttle have gone through a series of redesigns, each iteration containing improvement goals for UX. NASA developed the first space shuttle user interfaces in the 1970s (NASA, 2000).

Screen design was fairly simple in the 1970s, with a finite set of screens and a sequential structure built anew for each application (Pew, 2003). However, it was during this time that some of the early UX style guides were produced. Pew and Rollins (Pew, 2003) developed a set of guidelines for a planned system at the US Department of Agriculture. Government managers wanted to make sure that agricultural field agents with no computer experience could use the system and enter data while conducting interviews. The guidelines were developed for programmers, to help them deal with screen design, information presentation, task analysis, terminology, and user interaction. Although the system was never deployed, this activity demonstrated government interest in UX in its office systems.

In the late 1970s, Sidney L. Smith of the Mitre Corporation began work on a set of guidelines for the USAF (Smith & Mosier, 1986), which became widely referenced in government systems, not only in the United States but internationally. Smith and Mosier produced the final set of guidelines in 1986; the comprehensive guidelines are the largest collection of publicly available user interface guidelines in the world (Travis, 2007).

One of the earliest series of government usability activities occurred at the US Social Security Administration (SSA) in 1978 (Pew, 2003). Contractors at SSA performed design activities that allowed SSA field users to evaluate alternative designs for a planned interactive system that would be deployed to the field. Although the system was not implemented, SSA did embrace many usability activities, then and in later years.

1980s: the transition years

Government funding continued in the early 1980s. Japanese, UK, and European governmental organizations all provided significant funding that supported development of HCI capabilities (Shackel, 2009). The Japanese Fifth Generation Project, the UK Alvey Programme, and the European initiative ESPRIT (European Strategic Programme for Research in Information Technology) were primarily focused on Artificial Intelligence (AI). These programs led to advancements in HCI (Grudin, 2009). DARPA's (Defense Advanced Research Projects Agency) funding of AI computing led to human factors issues being considered in military systems — e.g., the Autonomous Land Vehicle, a Pilot's Associate, and a Battle Management system (Grudin, 2011). Technologies employed in these systems — e.g., speech recognition, language technologies, and head-up displays — all highlighted UX challenges.

The military were still some of the main governmental organizations building UX into their system designs in the 1980s. The US Army established the Manpower and Personnel Integration (MANPRINT) program in 1981 (US Army, 2007) and used it to incorporate human considerations throughout the system lifecycle. The program defined the human as part of the system — whether hardware, software, or a weapon. The success of MANPRINT led to the concept of Human Systems Integration (HSI), which was adopted by the US DOD and many other government agencies (US Army, 2007). The US Navy also established the Navy Center for Applied Research in AI (NCARAI) in 1981 (US Naval Research Laboratory, n.d.). NCARAI has been involved in AI, human factors, and human-centered computing since its founding. The center focuses on issues in adaptive systems, intelligent systems, interaction systems, and immersive simulations. In 1987, the Israeli Air Force undertook the Lavi project — the design of a fighter jet. Even though the project was eventually canceled, HCI researchers were included, which contributed to the development and use of HCI and usability methods in Israel (Eliav & Sharon, 2011).

The invention of the graphical user interface (GUI) and associated concepts of multiple windows, menus, widgets, icons, and the mouse paved the way for more sophisticated systems. While the GUI introduced more options and control for the user, it also increased use and design complexities, requiring a stronger focus on HCI. As a result, governments were building prototypes and systems with an emphasis on HCI. The Atmospheric Environment Service of the Canadian government built a prototype to allow weather forecasters to digitally render sketches of weather depiction charts used in forecasting (Trafford, 1987). The primary goals of the system included ease, speed, and accuracy to compete with manual chart production.

In 1988, the US Air Force Logistics Command commissioned the Reliability and Maintainability Information System (REMIS), with human engineering, including HCI design, as a broad requirement for the procurement (Lorenzetti, Williamson, Hoffman, Beck, & Maguire, 1988). The Air Force intended this large-scale information system to enable logistics managers to maintain combat systems during peacetime and to sustain the systems during war. The variety of information planned for REMIS included inventory, status, maintenance, and configuration for multiple equipment types such as aircraft, communications, and test equipment. This example represents UX applied in a government information system. The success of the HSI program in military systems provided a foundation for applying these same principles to related information systems.

In 1986, the United States passed its accessibility law, known as Section 508, which deals with accessibility of electronic and information technology. Section 508 would have far-reaching effects for US government systems, but not until after 1998, when the US Congress amended the law and made it more enforceable. The most recent update to Section 508 occurred in 2000. Chapter 12, Ensuring Accessibility for People with Disabilities, covers more information on accessibility.

1990s: the growth years

A series of occurrences led to the growth of UX in government systems in the 1990s. Usability and HCI spread from research to industry in the late 1980s. UX in the commercial world rapidly advanced in the 1990s. Government traditionally tends to defer wide adoption of techniques and technologies until after they have matured (Scholtz, 2003). A certain level of maturity had been reached and it continued during the growth years. Companies, consultants, and government practitioners began focusing on the value that UX could bring to government information systems. With this convergence of events, the 1990s ushered in the decade in which UX became much more widely applied in the government arena. UX was actively promoted and encouraged. The Web was born. Usability had coalesced as a profession, and eager practitioners conducted design activities and usability evaluations on many government applications — internal systems, intranets, and public web sites. Incorporating UX into the development cycle and usability evaluation constituted key themes in this era.

Practitioners applied UX techniques across a variety of systems and organizations developed policies that emphasized UX. In the early 1990s, SSA worked with NIST to produce a prototype information-retrieval system aimed at modernizing a wage-verification process. Willman and Downey (1994) incorporated new indexing and search techniques and also introduced a GUI as part of the prototype. Development involved process analysis, interviews, observations, task analysis, user profiling, and usability testing. The prototype won two federal awards: one for excellence in applications and the other for contributing to reengineering government. In 1993, the FAA issued an official policy that specified responsibility for managing and incorporating human factors in its systems and activities (FAA, 1993). HF regulations in aviation re-emphasized organizational safety and auditing (SKYbrary, 2011). The US Army continued to make sure users were involved in systems development. Mastaglio and Williamsonn (1995) reported on the UCD of the Close Combat Tactical Trainer, a large-scale networked virtual environment used for training. The system used simulators, workstations, and a virtual environment to mimic real-world terrain. In 1998, members of a groupware project for the German government applied user advocacy in participatory design (Mambrey, Mark, & Pankoke-Babatz, 1998).

Government researchers, practitioners, and contractors actively encouraged and pursued incorporating UX into government systems. Winkler and Buie (1995) held a workshop at the CHI'95 conference to address HCI Challenges in Government Systems. From 1996 to 1998, NIST conducted a series of usability engineering symposia aimed at fostering collaboration between industry and government to increase the usability of government and corporate systems. At the 1996 symposium, participants shared government success stories (Downey & Laskowski, 1997). Usability specialists reported on applying usability methods at the Federal Intelligent Document Understanding Laboratory and creating a usability methodology called TIGERS (Tactical Information GUI Engineering & Requirements Specification). TIGERS was developed for combat systems and utilized in the development of the NATO Sea Sparrow Surface Missile System (a US Navy system). SSA shared a success story about setting up a usability team aimed at evaluating and improving in-house systems. The team also trained over 120 people at SSA in the basic understanding of usability (Stoos, 1996). Today, SSA has a division devoted to usability, accessibility, and project support which helps ensure usability in its systems.

The 1997 NIST symposium welcomed more government success stories. UCD and evaluation were key themes. One story described usability processes and evaluation applied to tax forms and tax returns of the United Kingdom's Inland Revenue (Bevan, 1997). This work led to the Inland Revenue adopting usability methods and receiving an innovation award from the UK Central Government (Bevan, 2005). Federal staff and contractors presented work on usability testing of the different internal and external web sites of the US Bureau of Labor Statistics (Levi, 1997), as well as work on the development and use of a set of user interface guidelines for systems at NASA's Goddard Space Flight Center (Uehling, 1997).

The final NIST symposium in 1998 occurred in conjunction with the annual UPA conference and focused on practical techniques for government systems. The major themes were making the case for usability to government management, usability measurement, and specifying usability in the government procurement process (Buie & Kreitzberg, 1998; Downey & Scholtz, 1998; Rohn & Coyne, 1998).

The positive trend continued. Presentations focused on government systems became more prominent at popular UX conferences. Reengineering of legacy systems, UX promotion and implementation, evaluation of existing products, and design and evaluation of sophisticated device control software are examples of topics from the 1996 and 1998 UPA conferences:

- At the UPA 1998 Conference, Kreitzberg (1998) reported on the reengineering of a legacy system and associated usability issues of a system from Maryland's Department of Juvenile Justice. The case study described moving from a character-based legacy system with 3270 terminals that lacked important features, to a desktop system with a GUI designed as an integrated performance support system.
- At the UPA Conference in 1998, Ng and Pittass (1998) reported on efforts to encourage UX in government systems in Singapore. They provided consulting services on more than 10 government projects.
- Comparative usability testing that evaluated commercial off-the-shelf financial management software as part of a NASA procurement (Horst & Autry, 1998) was presented at the UPA Annual Conference in 1998. This was an example of usability being specified as a major criterion for evaluation in government procurement.
- Donkers (1998) shared information about UX issues in the design and evaluation of NASA's Hubble Space Telescope Control Center software at the UPA Conference in 1998.

It was an exciting time to be involved in UX in government. In the past, US government jobs for UX practitioners were primarily for human factors engineers and psychologists, but government job postings began appearing for usability specialists, visual designers, and eventually for information architects. The broad field of UX had arrived. With the coming of the Web, government intranets and web applications also benefited from UX techniques. Novak and Thomas (1999) described the evolution from 1994 to 1999 of a large, distributed intranet with over 3500 users at Pacific Northwest National Laboratory, US Department of Energy. The process included requirements analysis, prototyping, and usability testing. Usability was a key differentiator for user acceptance.

Government policy and standards played an expected role in government systems. The International Organization for Standardization (ISO), which includes both public- and private-sector members, established a variety of UX standards. Two of the more well known are ISO 9241-11 on usability and ISO 13407 on HCD in context (superseded by 9241-210). Both were formalized in the late 1990s and are partially based on Brian Shackel's definition of context of use and the concepts of efficiency, effectiveness, and satisfaction. Just as the previously mentioned military standards become contractual obligations when inserted in government contracts, so too did national and international standards when specified in government procurements. Chapter 17, Standards in the UCD Process, covers more information on UX standards.

Some government agencies also set up their own internal usability labs to test their systems and web sites. Examples in the United States include SSA, the Bureau of Labor Statistics (BLS), the US Census Bureau, and the National Cancer Institute (NCI), a part of the US Department of Health and Human Services (HHS). HHS offers its labs for use free of charge to other federal agencies. HHS also sponsors Usability.gov — a web site developed by HHS that is dedicated to usability in the government (http://www.usability.gov). The research-based web design guidelines offered on Usability.gov help many government web designers create usable sites.

During the 1990s, several countries passed laws that covered accessibility of information technology and affected their government systems and web sites: Australia passed the Disability Discrimination Act in 1992; the United Kingdom passed its Disability Discrimination Act in 1995 and the Equality Act in, 2010. Accessibility would become even more prominent in the coming e-government (e-gov) age. In the latter part of the decade, governments began forming e-gov strategies and government information portals began appearing (Spremić, Šimurina, Jaković, & Ivanov, 2009). In 1999, China launched the Government Online Project, aimed at helping create national and municipal government web sites (Zhou, 2005). The activities and efforts of multiple governments set the stage for the explosion of e-gov in the next decade.

2000 to present: the partnership years

The new century saw the full-fledged arrival of UX. Government employees and contractors further broadened UX benefits across government systems, intranets, and public web sites. Partnership and collaboration received increased focus and attention. UX was seen as a key enabler. The knowledge economy emphasized information sharing — within an agency, between government agencies, between governments, and between governments and their citizens. Information and services spanned a wide field and included areas such as intelligence, health care, benefits, drivers' licenses, political processes, safety recalls, and much more. UX specialists emphasized IA, search, forms, usable semantic technology, and analytics displays in information-rich government systems and web sites.

Universal usability, the digital divide, and privacy emerged as critical themes in government-to-citizen systems. Universal usability is the design of information and technology such that it accounts for user differences while allowing successful use of technology including access to information (Shneiderman, 2000). Universal usability aims to provide the benefits of technology to every citizen, as governments are concerned with equal opportunity regarding access to information and services. In this way, universal usability is a natural extension of accessibility in that it focuses on designing for a variety of differences. Governments also developed policy efforts designed to bridge the "digital divide" between the technology haves and have-nots. In the 1990s, the definition of the digital divide focused on issues of technology access across various socioeconomic groups (Jesse, 2004). In the 2000s, researchers and practitioners raised issues on the differences in skills, information, and knowledge among technology users (Bertot, 2003; Dewan & Riggins, 2005; Hargittai, 2003).

Many governments take the responsibility of protecting the privacy rights of their citizens very seriously. The presentation and communication of privacy laws and usage became a key UX concern. With so many citizens using technology and providing personal information, governments evolved their rules and regulations to address privacy. Many government web sites include privacy provisions, and commercial web sites are often required to address privacy issues depending on a specific nation's laws. Lastly, governments also have to balance privacy and national security concerns. Many internal government systems include mechanisms for addressing and protecting the privacy of citizens and user information. Design for universal usability, equal information access, and privacy issues have all influenced UX in government systems. Chapter 5, Privacy and the Citizen, covers this area.

In the 2000s, government transportation, military, and security systems with their life-critical components and mission focus continued their long UX association. The US Department of Homeland Security formed an HSI community of practice whose members are government practitioners that share successes and strategies on UX in government systems. In 2000, the Shuttle Atlantis flew with a new cockpit design, the Multifunction Electronic Display System, a "glass cockpit" (digital LCDs) similar to that in many commercial airliners and private planes (NASA, 2000). Many of NASA's systems have incorporated UX features and systems such as robots, hand-held equipment, instruction cards, and computer systems. The FAA continued incorporating human factors and usability into their various systems, including air-traffic control, facilities and maintenance systems, and web-based applications. Singapore developed an Advanced Combatman System, which included a variety of UX factors to deal with such features as helmet-mounted displays, mobile computing interactions, situation awareness, and data fusion (Lim, 2011).

In this decade, governments also looked more closely at the information they supplied, such as voting systems, statistics, and forms. In 2004, Ferguson (2004) shared international perspectives on voting systems at the UPA Conference. The report included variations across countries, paper versus electronic media, and whether governments addressed usability in voting systems. The survey included the United Kingdom, Ireland, France, Belgium, Switzerland, India, Brazil, and Australia. The United States passed the Help America Vote Act in 2002 (H.R. 3295, 2001). One of the provisions specifically called for a report on UX in voting systems (Laskowski, 2004).

Information presentation gained a revived focus with respect to universal usability. Usability specialists described work done to improve user interfaces for understanding US federal statistics (Marchionini, Hert, Liddy, & Shneiderman, 2000). Forms were redesigned for usability to help citizens. Jarrett and Quesenbery (2006) shared a case study at the UPA Conference in Denver, Colorado, United States, regarding form redesign on a local government web site in Oxfordshire, United Kingdom. Barnett (2009) reported on the redesign of a set of government forms from the Australian Department of Human Services that dealt with social security, veterans, and other similar payments and benefits. Chapter 4, UX of Transactions, covers more information on the UX of government forms.

With access to technology rapidly increasing, shrinking budgets, and government concern over equal access to information and services, governments launched many e-gov initiatives in the 2000s. E-gov is a mechanism for disseminating information and services to the population more quickly and more economically. The US General Services Administration (GSA) launched the official portal of the US government in 2000. GSA also participates in the Federal Web Manager's Council — set up in 2004 *per* government mandate — and jointly sponsors the Web Manager University — a training program provided by the government and aimed specifically at government web managers (federal, state, local, and tribal) that provides affordable training in web usability. The United States passed the E-Government Act of 2002, which includes language stating that sites and services will be citizen-centric and measurable (H.R. 2458, 2001). The UK government published a strategic e-gov framework in 2000, which encouraged innovation in the public sector, mandated development of e-business strategies within all major departments, and also outlined the need for required infrastructure and leadership to make e-gov a reality (Cabinet Office, 2000). Two major UK e-gov sites for citizens are Directgov (http://www.direct.gov.uk) and the Government Gateway (http://www.gateway.gov.uk/). Directgov provides a listing of public services all in one place, as well as news and government information. The Government Gateway is for UK citizens to conduct a variety of secure online transactions and communicate with the government. There is also an e-gov site dedicated to business called Business Link (http://www/businesslink.gov.uk). In 2012 GOV.UK (https://www.gov.uk/), an experimental trial ('beta') replacement for Directgov and the first step towards a single government web site was launched.

Many countries have created e-gov programs with a usability focus. Beginning in 2001, Japan formed the e-Japan strategy, which initiated e-gov services (Kurosu, 2011). After discovering low usage of the services, the Japanese government ordered a usability overhaul of the central government web sites in 2008. In 2004, the Australian government developed a set of best practices on IA to guide government agencies in the design of their intranets and public-facing web sites (Commonwealth of Australia, 2008). In Brazil, digital inclusion — which includes usability — is a primary concern and goal. As one example, the state of São Paulo set up an HCI lab specifically for testing its e-gov services (Filgueiras, Aquino, Tokairim, Torres, & Barbarian, 2004). One of the grand challenges identified in a 2006 Brazilian Computer Society report was, "participative and universal access to knowledge for the Brazilian Citizen" (Prates & Filgueiras, 2011). These are just a few examples of national and state governments applying UX to provide better access to government information and services.

City and local governments have also taken notice of UX. Since 2002, Rutgers University and Sungkyunkwan University (SKKU) have conducted surveys of municipal e-gov web sites. One of the five measures is usability (Rutgers University, 2010). The top 10 city e-gov web sites for 2009, according to the Rutgers/SKKU study, were Seoul, Prague, Hong Kong, New York, Singapore, Shanghai, Madrid, Vienna, Auckland, and Toronto. Seoul, South Korea, claimed the top spot in 2003, 2005, 2007, and 2009. Seoul's continuous top rankings may be attributed to South Korea's commitment to usable government web sites. South Korea's National Information Society Agency conducts an annual assessment of all its public web sites of government institutions (Lee & Lee, 2011). The assessment includes a variety of usability and accessibility criteria. Chapter 3, Government 2.0, presents more in-depth information on the treatment of UX in e-gov.

The first decade of the new century saw global application of UX in government systems, especially in e-gov. Governments worldwide took major policy steps to specify and require usability. The advancement of technology, the explosion of available information, and the recognized benefit of collaboration between various stakeholders fueled the partnership years.

SUMMARY

The history of UX in government illustrates the progression of human considerations in system design for the benefit of public servants and citizens. Governments have been involved in various aspects of UX for over 80 years. Major roles include funder of research, consumer of techniques and technology, provider of information, and implementer of policy and legislation (Scholtz, 2003). Government agencies and organizations have also hired UX specialists, both as employees and contractors, to design internal systems and to help produce usable public-facing technology. Government organizations have promoted and offered UX training for both government employees and private sector employees, further supporting UX in government systems.

Although much UX progress has been made in the public sector, involvement of government institutions in UX varies widely. This is reflected in the different levels of usability present, or complete lack of attention to UX, in government systems around the globe. We have presented many success stories in this chapter, but challenges remain. In those situations, practitioners in the government arena may employ unobtrusive techniques to enable UX, "flying under the radar," so to speak (Buie, 2011). UX professionals are creative, flexible, and adaptable in their quest to improve UX in government systems. Even though challenges exist, many members of the public sector — including decision makers, employees, and contractors — embrace UX activities with the goal of improving UX for both internal systems and public-facing technology. Increased coverage of UX in government systems is an important goal — one in which multiple groups share the responsibility and, ultimately, the benefits. We hope that chroniclers, in future histories, will be able to report that UX in government systems continued the positive trend and became a best practice.

References

Bailey, S. (2002, February 7). *Do you need a taxonomy strategy?* Inside knowledge, 5. Retrieved 21 September 2011 from http://www.ikmagazine.com/xq/asp/sid.0/articleid.E4F31EEC-FB65-413A-A24B-13AA6ACDD12D/eTitle. Do_you_need_a_taxonomy_strategy_A_primer_on_information_architecture_and_taxonomy_development/qx/display.html

Barnett, R. (2009). Redesigning Centrelink forms: A case study of government forms. *User Experience Magazine*, *8*(2), 12–16.

Belyshkin, A. (2011). Usability in Russia. In I. Douglas & Z. Liu (Eds.), *Global usability* (pp. 273–284). London, UK: Springer-Verlag London Limited. doi:10.1007/978-0-85729-304-6_17.

Bertot, J. C. (2003, April). The multiple dimensions of the digital divide: More than the technology "haves" and "have nots." *Government Information Quarterly*, *20*, 185–191.

Bevan, N. (1997, March). Achieving usability through user-centered design. In *Proceedings of the usability engineering 2: Measurement and methods (UE2) symposium, Gaithersburg, MD, USA.*

Bevan, N. (2005). Cost-benefit framework and case studies. In G. B. Randolph & J. M. Deborah (Eds.), *Cost-justifying usability* (pp. 575–600). (2nd ed.). doi:10.1016/B978-012095811-5/50020-1.

Brazen, T. (Producer). (2009, March 10). The history and evolution of user experience design [Audio podcast]. Retrieved 6 November 2011 from http://www.teawithteresa.com/podcasts/the-history-evolution-of-user-experience-design

British Computer Society. About interaction. (2011). Retrieved 31 October 2011 from http://www.bcs.org/category/14297

Buie, E. (2011, May). *UX under the Radar: An approach to user experience work in the government systems world. In Presented at the CHI 2011 conference, Vancouver, British Columbia, Canada.* Presentation retrieved 6 November 2011 from www.slideshare.net/ebuie/ux-under-the-radar-7940005

Buie, E., & Kreitzberg, C. (1998). Using the RFP to get the usability you need. In *Proceedings of usability engineering 3: Practical techniques for government systems, Washington, DC, USA.*

Cabinet Office. (2000). *E-government: A strategic framework for public services in the information age.* London, UK: Crown Copyright.

Card, S. (1996). Pioneers and settlers: methods used in successful user interface design. In M. Rudisill, C. Lewis, P. Polson & T. McKay (Eds.), *Human-computer interface design: Success stories, emerging methods, and real-world context* (pp. , ?122–169). San Francisco, CA, USA: Morgan Kaufmann, 122–169.

Carroll, J. (2011). *Human computer interaction (HCI).* In M. Soegaard & R. Dam (Eds.), *Encyclopedia of human-computer interaction.* Retrieved 21 September 2011 from http://www.interaction-design.org/encyclopedia/human_computer_interaction_hci.html

Commonwealth of Australia. Better practice checklist-15. Information architecture for websites. (2008). Retrieved 21 September 2011 from http://www.finance.gov.au/e-government/better-practice-and-collaboration/better-practice-checklists/information-architecture.html

Cooper, A. (2007). *About Face 3.0: The essentials of interaction design.* New York, NY, USA: John Wiley & Sons, Inc.

Dalakov, G. (2011). *History of computers: Hardware, software, internet.* Retrieved 21 September 2011 from http://history-computer.com/index.html

Defence Research and Development Canada (DRDC). About Defence Research and Development Canada (DRDC)—Toronto. (2010). Retrieved 6 November 2011 from http://www.toronto.drdc-rddc.gc.ca/about-apropos/history-histoire-eng.asp

Dewan, S., & Riggins, E. (2005). The digital divide: Current and future research directions. *Journal of the Association for Information Systems, 6*(12), 298–337.

Disability Discrimination Act 1992 (as amended up to Act No. 124 of 2009) [Australia], Act No. 135 of 1992 as amended, 1992, November 5. Retrieved 6 November 2011 from http://www.unhcr.org/refworld/docid/4b4716162.html

Disability Discrimination Act 1995. (1995). London: HMSO.

Donkers, A. (1998, June). User interface issues and methodological approaches to re-designing the Hubble space telescope control software for web-based operations. In *Proceedings of the usability professionals' association annual conference, Washington, DC, USA*, (pp. 7–11).

Douglas, I., & Liu, Z. (Eds.), (2011). *Global usability*. London, UK: Springer-Verlag London Limited. doi:10.1007/978-0-85729-304-6.

Downey, L., & Laskowski, S. (Eds.), (1997). In *Usability engineering: Industry-government collaboration for system effectiveness and efficiency, symposium transcription* (NIST Special Publication 500-237). Washington, DC, USA: US Government Printing Office.

Downey, L., & Scholtz, J. (1998). What to measure: Making choices about usability metrics. In *Proceedings of usability engineering 3: Practical techniques for government systems, Washington, DC, USA*.

Dumas, J. (2007). The great leap forward: The birth of the usability profession (1988-1993). *Journal of Usability Studies, 2*(2), 54–60.

Eliav, O., & Sharon, T. (2011). Usability in Israel. In I. Douglas & Z. Liu (Eds.), *Global usability* (pp. 169–194). London, UK: Springer-Verlag London Limited.

Equality Act 2010. (2010). London: HMSO.

Federal Aviation Administration (FAA). Human factors policy (DOT Order No. 9550.8). (1993). Retrieved 6 November 2011 from https://www.hf.faa.gov/docs/508/docs/FAA%20Order%209550.8_1993.pdf

Ferguson, L. (2004, June). *Voting: International perspectives. In Presented at the usability professionals' association conference, Minneapolis, MN, USA.* Retrieved 6 November 2011 from http://www.usabilityprofessionals.org/civiclife/voting/documents/international_ferguson.pdf

Filgueiras, L., Aquino, P., Tokairim, V., Torres, C., & Barbarian, I. (2004). Usability evaluation as quality assurance of E-government services. In W. Lamersdorf, V. Tschammer & S. Amarger (Eds.), *Building the E-service society* (pp. 77–87). Norwell, MA, USA: Kluwer Academic Publishers. doi:10.1007/1-4020-8155-3_5.

Grudin, J. (2009). Brian Shackel's contribution to the written history of human-computer interaction. *Interacting with Computers, 21*(5-6), 370–374.

Grudin, J. (2012). A moving target: The evolution of HCI. In J. Jacko (Ed.), *Human-computer interaction handbook* (pp. 1–39). (3rd ed.). Boca Raton, FL: CRC Press.

H.R. 2458—107th Congress: E-Government Act of 2002. (2001). In GovTrack.us (database of federal legislation). Retrieved 16 October 2011 from http://www.govtrack.us/congress/bill.xpd?bill=h107-2458

H.R. 3295—107th Congress: Help America Vote Act of 2002. (2001). In GovTrack.us (database of federal legislation). Retrieved 16 October 2011 from http://www.govtrack.us/congress/bill.xpd?bill=h107-3295

Hargittai, E. (2003). The digital divide and what to do about it. In D. C. Jones (Ed.), *New economy handbook* (pp. 822–841). San Diego, CA, USA: Academic Press.

Horst, R., & Autry, M. (1998, June). Lessons learned in the comparative usability testing of commercial off-the-shelf financial management software for a government procurement. In *Proceedings of the usability professionals' association annual conference, Washington, DC, USA*, (pp. 31–35).

Human Factors and Ergonomics Society (HFES). About HFES: HFES history. (2010). Retrieved 21 September 2011 from http://www.hfes.org/web/AboutHFES/history.html

Human Factors & Ergonomics Society of Australia (HFESA). Special Interest Groups: CHISIG. (2011). Retrieved 31 October 2011 from http://www.ergonomics.org.au/

Human-Computer Interaction Resource Network (HCIRN). HCIRN: Events. (2011). Retrieved 6 November 2011 from http://www.hcirn.com/res/event/index.php

Interaction Design Association (IxDA) (n.d.). Definition of IxD. Retrieved 21 September 2011 from http://www.ixda.org/about/ixda-mission

Jarrett, C., & Quesenbery, W. (2006, June). *How to look at a form . . . in a hurry. In Presented at the usability professionals' association conference, Denver, CO, USA.* Retrieved 6 November 2011 from http://www.formsthatwork.com/files/Articles/how-to-look-at-a-form.pdf

Jesse, J. (2004). The digital divide: Policy myth or political reality. In W. Aspray (Ed.), *Chasing Moore's law: Information technology policy in the United States* (pp. 247–272). Raleigh, NC, USA: SciTech Publishing, Inc.

Kreitzberg, C. B. (1998). Usability issues in the re-engineering of legacy systems. In *Proceedings of the usability professionals' association fifth annual conference, Copper Mountain, CO, USA.*

Kurosu, M. (2011). Usability in Japan. In I. Douglas & Z. Liu (Eds.), *Global usability* (pp. 195–209). London, UK: Springer-Verlag London Limited. doi:10.1007/978-0-85729-304-6_11.

Laskowski, S. (2004, June). *Voting systems in the US: Standards and testing for usability and accessibility. In Presented at the usability professionals' association conference, Minneapolis, MN, USA.* Retrieved 6 November 2011 from http://www.usabilityprofessionals.org/civiclife/voting/documents/voting_in_us_laskowski.pdf

Lee, K., & Lee, J. (2011). Usability in Korea—From GUI to user experience design. In I. Douglas & Z. Liu (Eds.), *Global usability* (pp. 309–331). London, UK: Springer-Verlag London Limited. doi:10.1007/978-0-85729-304-6_19.

Levi, M. (1997, March). Usability testing web sites at the Bureau of Labor Statistics (BLS). In *Proceedings of the usability engineering 2: Measurement and methods (UE2) symposium, Gaithersburg, MD, USA.*

Lim, K. (2011). Usability in Singapore. In I. Douglas & Z. Liu (Eds.), *Global usability* (pp. 285–307). London: Springer-Verlag London Limited. doi:10.1007/978-0-85729-304-6_18.

Liu, Z., Zhang, J., Zhang, H., & Chen, J. (2011). Usability in China. In I. Douglas & Z. Liu (Eds.), *Global usability* (pp. 111–135). London, UK: Springer-Verlag London Limited. doi:10.1007/978-0-85729-304-6_7.

Lorenzetti, R., Williamson, J., Hoffman, L., Beck, T., & Maguire, F. (1988). A case study in large scale computer human interaction design. In *Proceedings of the human factors society 32nd annual meeting, Santa Monica, CA, USA*, (pp. 1041–1045).

Mambrey, P., Mark, G., & Pankoke-Babatz, U. (1998). User advocacy in participatory design: Designers' experiences with a new communication channel. *Computer Supported Cooperative Work (CSCW), 7*(3), 291–313. doi:10.1023/A:1008687122083.

Marchionini, G., Hert, C., Liddy, L., & Shneiderman, B. (2000). Extending understanding of federal statistics in tables. In *Proceedings of the 2000 annual national conference on digital government research*, (pp. 1–7).

Mastaglio, T., & Williamson, J. (1995). Design briefings: Managing complex data. In *Proceedings of ACM CHI'95 conference on human factors in computing systems, Denver, CO, USA*, (pp. 546–552).

National Aeronautics and Space Administration (NASA). The glass cockpit. (2000). Retrieved 21 September 2011 from http://www.nasa.gov/centers/langley/news/factsheets/Glasscockpit.html

Ng, J., & Pittas, M. (1998). Encouraging HCI technology in the government agencies' system development. In *Proceedings of the usability professionals' association annual conference, Washington, DC, USA*, (pp. 13–16).

Novak, P., & Thomas, S. (1999). Building a better intranet. In *Proceedings of the usability professionals' association ninth annual conference, Scottsdale, AZ, USA*, (pp. 31–39).

Pew, R. (2003). The evolution of human-computer interaction: From memex to bluetooth and beyond. In J. A. Jacko & A. Sears (Eds.), *The human-computer interaction handbook* (pp. 1–17). Hillsdale, NJ, USA: L. Erlbaum Associates Inc.

Poston, A. (2003). The current state of human factors standardization. Human systems information analysis center (HSIAC) gateway newsletters, XIV(2), 1-5. Retrieved 6 November 2011 from http://www.dtic.mil/dticasd/docs-gw/gw_xiv_2.pdf

Prates, R., & Filgueiras, L. (2011). Usability in Brazil. In I. Douglas & Z. Liu (Eds.), *Global usability* (pp. 91–109). London, UK: Springer-Verlag London Limited. doi:10.1007/978-0-85729-304-6_6.

Rohn, J., & Coyne, K. (1998). Making the case for usability engineering to management: Total cost of ownership & cost/benefit analysis. In *Proceedings of usability engineering 3: Practical techniques for government systems, Washington, DC, USA.*

Roto, V., Law, E., Vermeeren, A., & Hoonhout, J. (2011). User experience white paper: Bringing clarity to the concept of user experience. In *Result from Dagstuhl seminar on demarcating user experience, September 15, 2010, Wardern, Germany.*

Rutgers University. Seoul and Prague achieve top rankings in E-government web portal excellence [News Release]. (2010, July 13). Retrieved 21 September 2011 from http://news.rutgers.edu/medrel/news-releases/2010/07/seoul-and-prague-ach-20100713

Scholtz, J. (2003). Government roles in human-computer interaction. In J. Jacko & A. Sears (Eds.), *The human-computer interaction handbook: Fundamentals, evolving technologies and emerging applications* (pp. 790–807). Hillsdale, NJ, USA: L. Erlbaum Associates, Inc.

Shackel, B. (2009). Designing for people in the age of information. *Interacting with Computers*, *21*(5-6), 325–330.

Shaver, E., & Braun, C. (2009, January 5). Human factors and ergonomics initiatives make good business sense. *Idaho Business Review*, pp. 4A.

Shneiderman, B. (2000). Universal usability: Pushing human-computer interaction research to empower every citizen. *Communications of the ACM*, *43*(5), 85–91.

SKYbrary. Human factors strategy. SKYbrary. (2011). Retrieved 6 November 2011 from http://www.skybrary.aero/index.php/Human_Factors_Strategy_(OGHFA_BN)

Smith, S., & Mosier, J. (1986). *Guidelines for designing user interface software (Research Report MTR-10090).* Bedford, MA, USA: The MITRE Corporation.

Spremić, M., Šimurina, J., Jaković, B., & Ivanov, M. (2009). E-government in transition economies. *World Academy of Science, Engineering and Technology*, *53*(84), 518–526.

Stoos, P. (1996, February). A usability success story at the social security administration. In *Proceedings of the usability engineering: Industry-government collaboration for system effectiveness and efficiency symposium, Gaithersburg, MD, USA.*

Trafford, R. (1987). Graphical entry of weather forecasts. *ACM SIGCHI Bulletin*, *19*(2), 56–57. doi:10.1145/36111.1045601.

Travis, D. (2007, April 16). *Usability expert reviews: Beyond heuristic evaluation.* Retrieved 6 November 2011 from http://www.userfocus.co.uk/articles/expertreviews.html

Uehling, D. (1997, March). Development and use of guidelines at NASA's GSFC. In *Proceedings of the usability engineering 2: Measurement and methods (UE2) symposium, Gaithersburg, MD, USA.*

US Army. MANPRINT history. (2007). Retrieved 21 September 2011 from http://www.manprint.army.mil/manprint/history.html

US Naval Research Laboratory. (n.d.). Navy center for applied research in artificial intelligence. Retrieved 21 September 2011 from http://www.nrl.navy.mil/aic/

Whiteside, J., Bennett, J., & Holzblatt, K. (1988). Usability engineering: Our experience and evolution. In M. Helander, T. Landauer & P. Prabhu (Eds.), *Handbook of human-computer interaction* (pp. 791–817). Amsterdam: Elsevier.

Willman, N., & Downey, L. (1994). *The design and development of an information retrieval system for the EAMATE data* (Vol. I). (NIST Internal Report 5394). Washington, DC, USA: US Government Printing Office.

Winkler, I., & Buie, E. (1995). HCI challenges in government contracting: A CHI '95 workshop. *SIGCHI Bulletin*, *27*(4), 35–37.

Zhou, Q. (2005). National & municipal government websites: A comparison between the United States and China. In *Proceedings of the 2005 national conference on digital government research, Atlanta, GA, USA*, (pp. 317–318).

SECTION

Public-Facing Systems I

"All of our knowledge has its origins in our perceptions."
— Leonardo da Vinci

This section illustrates many of the important issues that affect the usability of public-facing systems and Web sites. The section has four chapters:

- *Chapter 2,* Usability of Public web sites
- *Chapter 3,* Usability and Government 2.0
- *Chapter 4,* UX of Transactions
- *Chapter 5,* Privacy and the Citizen

The chapters in this section detail various usability issues that governments face when governments provide information to, conduct transactions with, and collect data from their citizens. These chapters describe the two roles that government web sites fulfill, the three factors that distinguish government transactions from business transactions, and the ways in which citizen interaction is like a relationship and requires showing respect, building trust, and speaking a common language.

- In Chapter 2, **Kathy Gill** (USA) gives an overview of the usability problems with government web sites and the foundations of best-practice recommendations for user-centered design.

She explains why incorporating usability is an important business decision for government web sites and introduces us to the two roles of government web sites: providing information and conducting transactions. Gill uses two scenarios — adding a motorcycle endorsement to a driver's license and paying a ticket for going through a red light — to explore examples of successful and not-so-successful government web sites with respect to both of these roles. The designers of the sites she reviews have taken pains, she says, to make the experience feel familiar, but their payment systems have a distinctly different look and feel from the main sites. She finds less consistency across sites in using language that reflects how citizens think and what they are trying to accomplish. Gill closes with five recommendations for government Web designers related to usefulness, aesthetics, accessibility, social networking, and mobile access. "We do not have the luxury of a slow rate of change when we are creating web sites," she observes. "To best serve our citizens, we must acknowledge that our web sites are becoming the place our citizens go to first when they have questions about or want to interact with government. Our designs need to match their growing need for both information and service."

- In Chapter 3, **Kate Walser** (USA) explores the ways in which a combination of government data and tools - known as Gov 2.0 - can allow citizens to see more clearly into government operations and offer solutions to major challenges, partnering with government to achieve transparency and participatory democracy. As the use of social media and open standards frameworks has spread, observes Walser, so has the use of Government 2.0. She draws on examples from Gov 2.0 efforts around the world to illustrate the importance of user experience for both citizens and public servants — including diversity and access, awareness and trust, and context and tools — in the success of these efforts. She lists the activities that contribute to making a relationship successful and explains how they map to Gov 2.0 activities. "Agencies that treat Gov 2.0 as a relationship and address these facets of the user experience," says Walser, "will be more successful in collaborating with citizens."

- In Chapter 4, **Caroline Jarrett** (UK) discusses the many ways in which governments conduct transactions with the public and the ways in which government forms are used to collect data from them. Transactions with the public are essential to governance, she observes, and notes that from the user's perspective government transactions are typically compulsory, lengthy, and lacking in competition. Moving transactions to the Web, Jarrett says, offers obvious cost savings for government, and should offer improvements in convenience for businesses and citizens, although governments need to support multiple channels because not all citizens have Internet access. Jarrett illustrates the principles of government form design with examples of good and not-so-good forms, using a scenario of paying a parking ticket, and she offers guidance for designing usable forms. She comments that transactions are like conversations and reinforces Walser's point that government needs to pay attention to its relationship with its citizens: "But if you do not pay enough attention to relationship and conversation," Jarrett says, "then your users really will be in difficulty. You will have to deal with their phone calls, letters, and emails, leading to higher costs to you and burden for them. They may even give up altogether, failing to obtain benefits to which they are entitled, or failing to comply with the law."

- In Chapter 5, **Dianne Murray** (UK) and **Karen Renaud** (UK) discuss current and pertinent concerns about citizens' trust of government sites and applications, and issues in personal privacy, given the growth of e-democracy and a strong emphasis on digital inclusion. They explore the implications of governments' collection of vast amounts of data about their citizens, which is usually promoted as being in the public interest or for the citizens' own benefit, and they point out that it is easier for people to "opt out" of data collection by businesses than by governments. Murray and Renaud explain the ways in which governments can, and do, invade the privacy of their citizens, and they urge governments to be accountable to their citizens and to treat them with respect. They present examples from different world regions to illustrate how UX designers can realistically build in suitable controls to address such concerns.

These chapters start with general aspects of usability in e-government and proceed to more specific issues.

CHAPTER

2 Usability of Public Web Sites

Kathy Gill
Lynnwood, WA, USA

"The role of the designer is that of a very good, thoughtful host anticipating the needs of his guests."
— Charles Eames

INTRODUCTION

This chapter explains and illustrates why incorporating usability is an important business decision for government web sites. It shows how government web sites serve two very different roles, one informational and one transactional, and it analyzes examples of successful and less-than-successful government web sites from the perspectives of these two roles. Finally, it describes the origin of web site design best practice recommendations that focus on usability.

Importance of usability to external audiences

Think about the last time you read a book, the paper kind. Did you have trouble finding the table of contents? How easy was it to find a specific page or chapter? What about figuring out who wrote the book — was that a challenge?

Books, in a word, are usable. They conform to an accepted structural framework.

Publishers have had centuries to perfect the interface that is the book and yet it remains, in many respects, almost unchanged from the days of Gutenberg (Ayiter, n.d.). The web, on the other hand, is only two decades old. Is it any wonder that our web site visitors too often tap their mice in frustration?

For the purposes of this chapter, a usable web site is one where a site visitor can easily find what she is looking for and successfully do what she came to the web site to do without resorting to "search" in frustration or finding herself pressing the back button with the urgency of Pavlov's dog seeking a treat.

A usable web site is one that "doesn't make me think," according to Krug (2005):

> *When I'm looking at a page that doesn't make me think, all the thought balloons over my head say things like "OK, there's the ____. And that's a _____. And there's the thing that I want." (p. 12)*

Many government web sites do not meet this definition, whether the function is to allow a citizen to complete a transaction or to serve up needed information. These are two different roles, but both need to be easy to accomplish.

Current state of government web site use

Recent data from the Pew Internet & American Life Project (Smith, 2010) suggest that 8 in 10 Americans who are online (78% of American adults) visit government web sites. Americans are not alone in wanting access to online government information. In Australia, the numbers are similar: in 2010, 8 in 10 Australians reported having broadband access at home (Thomler, 2011). In a 2008 survey, for most participants, the Internet was the most recent channel used to contact government (Australian Government Information Management Office, 2009).

However, Internet adoption is not quite as robust in the European Union. In 2010, Europa reported that only 6 in 10 adults had Internet access. In 2006, the percentage of EU citizens who contacted government officials ranged widely, from 3% in Romania to 61% in Iceland.

In the minds and actions of most of our citizens, web sites are, or are becoming, mainstream. The Internet is the modern-day equivalent of yesterday's small town courthouse. In the United States, about half of our web site visitors are checking out agency services; they are trying to get something done. Services range from renewing automobile license plates to finding out how to apply for unemployment benefits. These are the kinds of services that, before the Web, would have necessitated a visit to a local government office.

Another one in two online American adults seek public policy information online (Smith, 2010). This information was once doled out by local newspapers or shared by public officials in periodic newsletters. The Internet makes it easier for citizens to be informed — a cornerstone of democracy — but only if citizens can find the information that they are looking for.

Providing online information can be easier than building an application that substitutes for a visit to government offices, but only about half of the Americans interviewed told Pew researchers that they succeeded with "everything" they were trying to do on government web sites. Another one in three accomplished "most" of what they were trying to do. But 20% said that they had an unsuccessful experience (Smith, 2010).

What Pew researchers failed to ask was how difficult it was to accomplish "everything." In other words, how much did citizens have to "think" in order to succeed in their tasks? In early 2011, ForeSee Results (2011a, 2011b) asked 330,000 Americans how satisfied they were with their experience at 110 government web sites; a question about satisfaction gets us closer to understanding frustration. The ForeSee numbers mirror the Pew results: the satisfaction rate was 75%.

This means, however, that as many as one in four Americans visit government web sites and leave either feeling unsatisfied or without having had a successful experience. We can, and should, do better.

ForeSee researchers asked Americans what government agencies needed to do to improve their web sites. Tied for first place were improvements to functionality and transparency. Functionality — the usefulness, convenience, and variety of online features available on the web site — relates to replacing that trip downtown with a trip to the browser. Transparency — how thoroughly, quickly, and accessibly the web site discloses information — relates to information availability. Therefore these represent the two roles, transaction and information.

Making web sites more usable saves money because usability reduces service costs (Bias & Mayhew, 2005; Donahue, Weinschenk, & Nowicki, 1999; Marcus, 2004; Nielsen Norman Group, n.d.). It is less expensive for all concerned — citizen and agency — if I can pay my property taxes online. In addition, enhanced customer satisfaction improves the brand that is government service. Moreover, "highly satisfied" citizens are more likely than others to participate with that government agency in the future and rate the agency higher on a scale measuring trust, according to the ForeSee Results research.

Although interaction designers and usability professionals have studied what works (and what does not) on the Web, too often this information is misunderstood or not accessible to those who make budget decisions. These following case studies are designed to illustrate concepts related to web site usability.

CASE STUDIES

When *Wired* was launched in the 1990s, it challenged conventional publishing standards and audience expectations of what a "magazine" was supposed to look like. *Wired*'s designers experimented with a color palette reminiscent of 1960s psychedelic art. Carr (2003) described it as "neon-suffused, anarchic design." The magazine stood in stark contrast to conventional, pedestrian publications with their black ink on white paper.

However, in other interface matters, the magazine conformed to norms. The table of contents was in the front; the magazine read from front to back. Today, *Wired*'s print designers experiment in other ways; feature stories are, in the main, classic dark-on-light but the magazine covers can still be delightfully colorful and avant-garde.

This story provides four key usability lessons:

- *Make the experience feel familiar.* Readers and web site visitors want their experience to be comfortable; for this to happen, designers must honor expected patterns. For *Wired*, placing the table of contents at the front of a book or magazine gave a nod to an established norm. What about page numbers? Placing page numbers along the inside of the page may look attractive to a designer but they are not functional for the reader, who may search for them in vain. The better design: placing page numbers on the outside corners, where readers can find them.

  Even though it is *possible* to execute an edgy design, it might not be the *right* thing to do if it causes the reader to feel so unsettled that she cannot accomplish what she set out to do.
- *Understand your audience.* What is it that your customer wants to do with your product? This user-centered question differs dramatically from the orientation of many communication efforts that start with, "what we want our customers to do." If your design makes it harder for a reader to feel successful, she will not be in your audience very long.

  Part of understanding your audience means thinking about the mental models of your customers. A mental model is a person's internal expectation for how something is supposed to work, based on prior experience with similar things. Robert Hoekman, Jr. writes in *Designing the Obvious* (Hoekman, 2006) that mental models shape "how we assimilate new things into our existing knowledge" (p. ?). Designs that violate a person's mental model result in unease and disorientation. *Wired* was hard to read, and the designers adapted.
- *Practice appropriate consistency.* We can manipulate design to call attention to text or images, and we can also use design to provide cohesion, to make disparate elements feel like a whole. There are conventions that relate to the genre — publishing in the case of *Wired*, Web publishing in the case of government web sites. But we should also establish conventions within our own project, such as the design grid, the color pattern, the typefaces used.

Our goal with this design should be to make the web site experience feel frictionless, without the cognitive overload that leads to frustration and failure. Consistency can also nurture a feeling of familiarity.

- *Test and evaluate your designs.* We use research to inform both the initial design and any redesign. For example, there is a reason most magazine feature stories are printed with dark ink on light-colored paper: it is easier to read (Scharff & Ahumada, 2005). We need the contrast that was missing from *Wired*'s experiment with neon green on hot pink.

When we think about usable web sites, however, we have another factor to consider: interactivity. Novels are linear and are usually read front to back. Magazines and newspapers cluster thematic nuggets; usually it does not matter in what order we read them. Web site content is more like a magazine or newspaper than a novel; it is a series of discrete units connected by theme, not by narrative. However, web applications, such as paying property taxes, look and feel more like a traditional software application.

In addition, as site owners, we do not control how our citizens "enter" our sites. Citizens are as likely to arrive through a side door (a search result or a shared link) as through the front door (home page). Thus we also must incorporate wayfinding signals into our design that help people understand where they are, where they can go, and where they have been. Both the information and the functional sides of our sites have to accommodate citizen interaction.

With this background in mind, we will explore three examples. The first, obtaining a motorcycle endorsement, is primarily an information task. The second, paying the fine associated with a parking ticket, is primarily a functional one. The third, contacting an agency using social networking sites (SNSs), is primarily informational.

Obtaining a motorcycle endorsement

To drive an automobile or motorcycle, a citizen must have a license; a motorcycle endorsement is an addendum to a driver's license. In this scenario, Betsy has a valid Pennsylvania driver's license with a motorcycle endorsement. We will chart the experience Betsy might have if she were to move to Illinois, Utah (within the United States), or New South Wales (in Australia). She is trying to determine the licensing requirements in her new home state and would like to schedule an appointment at the Department of Motor Vehicles. Although the licensing agency may think of these as distinct tasks, for Betsy there is only one goal: get a new driver's license with a motorcycle endorsement.

This scenario epitomizes most citizen interaction with government web sites: it is task-focused and not something Betsy will do over and over. She will always be a novice at this task, so the system must be very clear; designers cannot rely on her learning system idiosyncrasies. Understanding how citizens approach this task is important; according to the 2010 Pew report, 33% of Americans who are online had renewed a driver's license or auto registration.

There are two ways Betsy might begin this project. She could go straight to the state government home page. Conversely, she might enter through a side door, either by employing a search engine or by asking friends if they know where this information can be found.

Traditional government web site home pages have been organized as portals, an entry that displays a diversity and breadth of information in a systematic way. For example, Europa.eu is the official portal for the European Union; USA.gov is the portal for the US federal government; and Australia.gov.au is "your connection with government" if you are Australian. Emerging government web site design acknowledges the far-ranging scope of information and minimizes visual clutter by focusing on search as the tool for access. If Betsy chooses to start at the state government home page, her experience will be shaped by these two distinct styles of information organization.

State of Illinois

The state of Illinois (United States, population 13 million) uses a standard portal design. Betsy scans the home page, looking for "driver's license." The home page (Figure 2.1) reflects a portal design; less than a quarter of the visible portion of the page is devoted to actions that might have triggered a citizen visit.

Betsy might see the "How Do I?" link in the lower right. Or she might "mouseover" the primary navigation nouns; if she does, she will discover hidden information: links to additional services. What she will not find is the phrase "driver's license" or even "DMV" (an abbreviation for the Department of Motor Vehicles, the licensing agency in her home state of Pennsylvania). Because the web site is structured primarily like an organization chart, Betsy is being forced to think.

Johnson (2010), writing in *Designing with the Mind in Mind*, explains that when we are focused on a task we tend to notice only the things that match our goals. This is sometimes described as following the

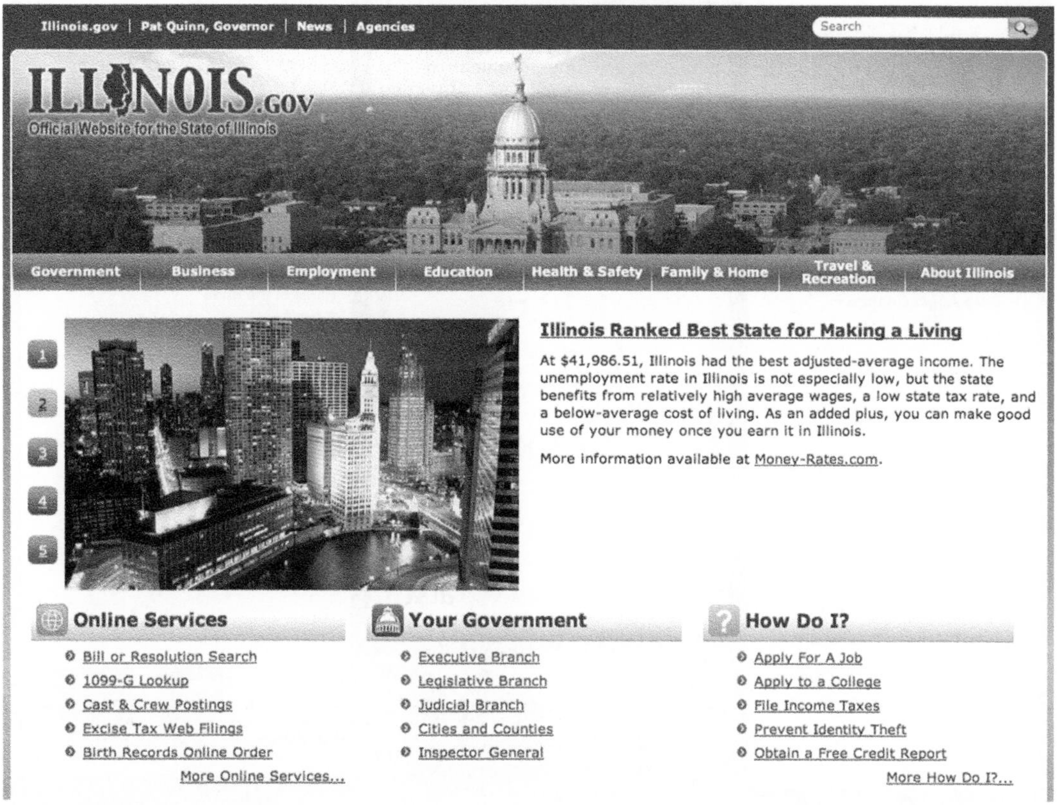

FIGURE 2.1 The Illinois.gov home page

(For color version of this figure, see the web version of this chapter)

"scent" of information. Web site visitors are framed as foragers who use cues, such as phrases or images, to make a judgment about whether or not the page at the end of the link will meet their needs (Chi, Pirolli, Chen, & Pitkow, 2001). To create a web site that helps citizens accomplish their goals, designers need to understand thoroughly both the goal and the requisite steps. They also need to understand the language used by citizens rather than relying on the language used by government insiders.

According to Spool, Perfetti, and Brittan (2004), web site visitors turn to search when they do not see their trigger words, so it is probable that Betsy would resort to search. After she types "driver's license" into the search box, she sees a link for CyberDriveIllinois.com.

On the CyberDriveIllinois web site, Betsy is greeted with a barrage of 35 unordered links, phrases that are not grouped by function nor are they in alphabetical order. In addition, as Figure 2.2 shows,

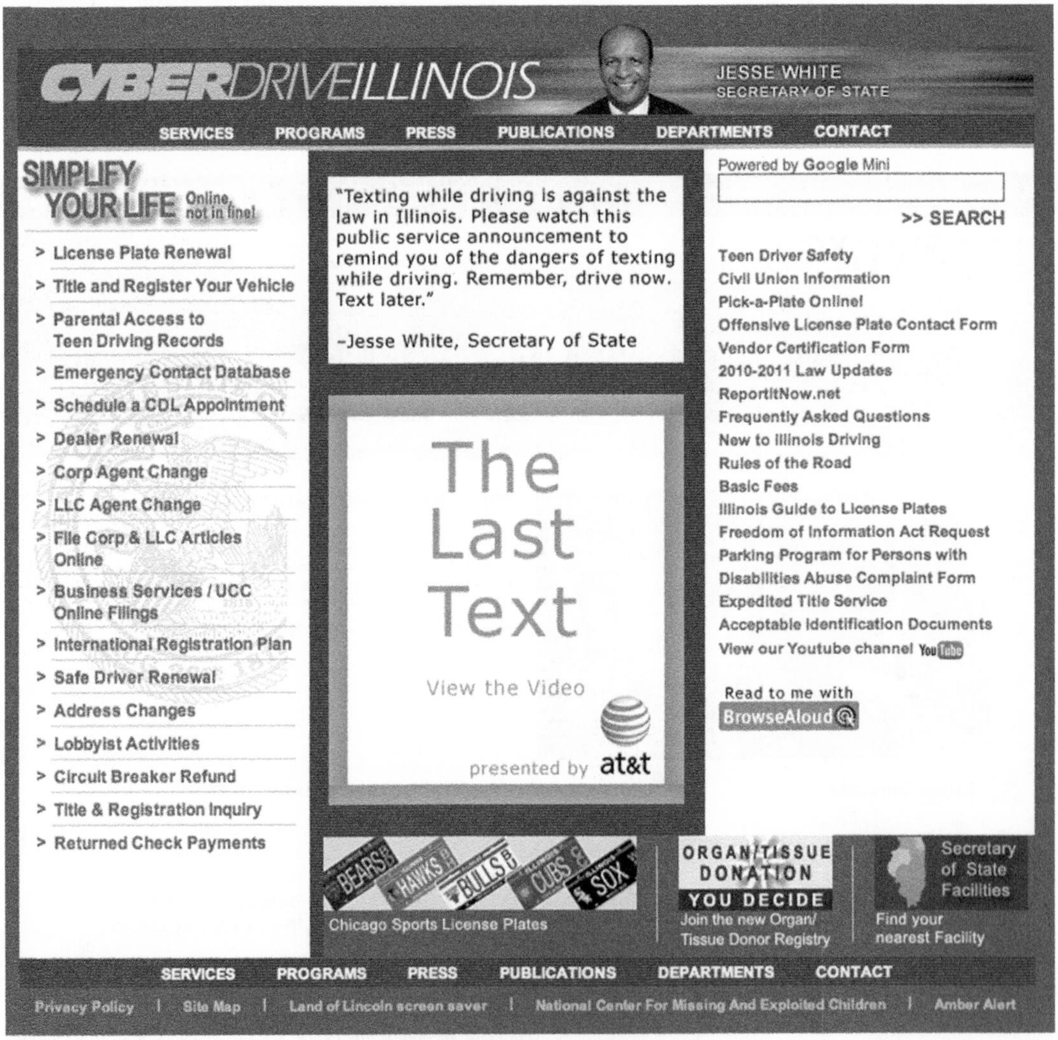

FIGURE 2.2 The Illinois Secretary of State manages driver's licenses

(For color version of this figure, see the web version of this chapter)

fully one-third of the page is devoted to a government message: don't text and drive. Imagine how difficult it would be to find an article in a magazine if there were no hierarchy to the table of contents, and it was also full of advertisements. That is what this page is like for Betsy.

Because this site is operated by the Secretary of State, content ranges from getting a title for a vehicle to filing lobbyist reports. To help Betsy quickly process such varied information, designers should chunk these links into logical groups, such as auto-related links. Within each group, the links should appear in alphabetical order.

Such visual structure reduces cognitive load. Johnson (2010) argues that information should be terse and structured. Krug (2005) explains that without visual hierarchy (structure), "everything looks equally important" (p. 33). On the Illinois site, the unstructured design causes Betsy to slow down as she to tries to impose order on the information.

She is still looking for the words "driver's license" but the phrase is not on this new home page, either. She clicks Services on the primary navigation bar (there are no mouseover menus on this site, a lack of consistency with the home site) and spots the link "services for motorists." There is light at the end of the tunnel!

Two more clicks before Betsy finds the "Driver's License" page. However, there is no link for people who have just moved into the state. Moreover, the motorcycle page contains information only for graduates of the Illinois Motorcycle Rider Course. The page that answers all of her questions is the Frequently Asked Questions (FAQ), which she finds after exhausting the more obvious choices.

Remember that it is important to provide navigation cues for people who enter a site via a side door, such as from a search engine. To accommodate those visitors, Illinois web designers implemented what is known as a breadcrumb trail in the navigation, as shown in Figure 2.3. A well-designed set of location breadcrumbs is one way to provide way-finding information because the links can clearly answer the question "Where am I?" Keith Instone (2004) described location breadcrumbs as being static; in other words, they reflect the site hierarchy, not the path that a visitor used to arrive at the page.

If the hypertext changes color to reflect different states (pages I have visited and pages I have not visited), then the links also clearly answer the question "Where have I been?" Breadcrumb trails are less helpful in providing clues as to "Where can I go from here?"

As you can see from examining the breadcrumb trail in Figure 2.3, the Illinois site has a linear structure that mirrors that of the government agency. This is not task-focused or user-centered design. Moreover, the visited page breadcrumb links are represented in white text on a light blue background; this is hard to read because of insufficient contrast (Cronin, 2009; Hall & Hanna, 2003; World Wide Web Consortium, 2010). The result is a site that is not as easy to use as it could be.

FIGURE 2.3 The CyberDriveIllinois site

(For color version of this figure, see the web version of this chapter)

Moreover, Betsy will not be able to make an appointment at her local Secretary of State facility in Champaign, IL. But she can find the address, phone number, and hours of operation. It has taken quite a long time to find what she needs to know, but she thinks it was better than spending time on her phone with interactive voice response system prompts.

State of Utah

The Interactive Media Council (2011) awarded the state of Utah (United States, population 3 million) a "best in class" award for its search- and task-centric web site. This design reflects a dramatically different approach to helping citizens find information, compared with the Illinois site. The striking design of the home page, Figure 2.4, is reminiscent of the design of the Microsoft Bing home page.

On the home page, Betsy places her mouse over "Residents" and immediately sees "Newcomers Guide." The very first link? "Getting a Driver License." The Utah home page makes good use of mouseover menus and functional navigation nouns.

Betsy may have been taken aback at the dramatic change in visual appearance after she clicked the "Getting a Driver License" link, however. The Utah Department of Public Safety web site looks nothing like Utah.gov. But the "Utah.Gov Services" bar along the top of the page, shown in Figure 2.5, provides the needed visual cue that the site is part of the state information system. The bar provides consistency and familiarity.

After clicking "Licensing" in the left-hand navigation, Betsy sees examples of Utah driver's licenses. It may not be clear that she is supposed to click on an image. If there is any doubt that an image is clickable, be sure to have a prominent text link.

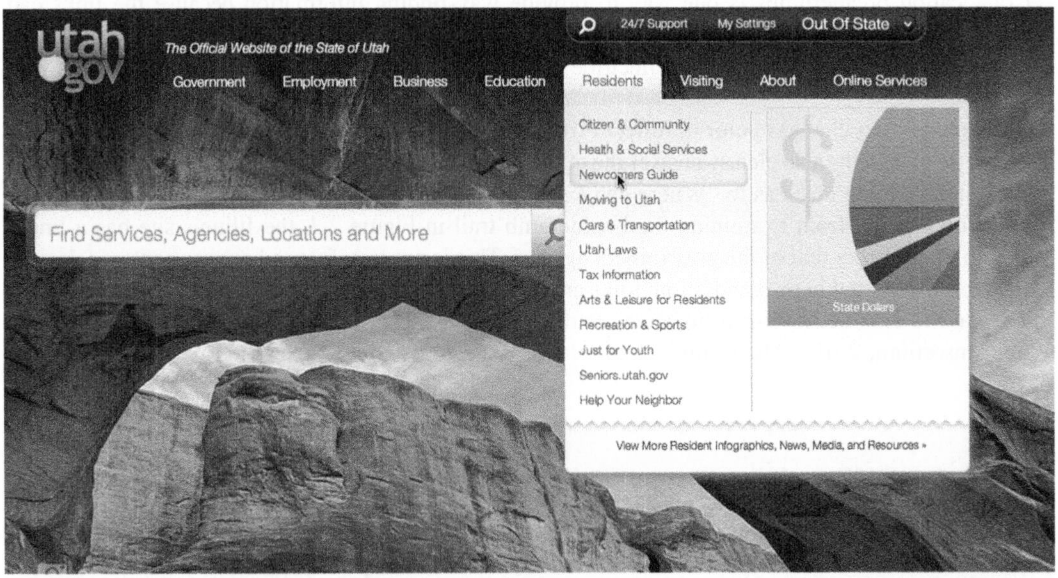

FIGURE 2.4 Utah.gov home page

(For color version of this figure, see the web version of this chapter)

FIGURE 2.5 The Utah.Gov Services bar on the Public Safety web site

(For color version of this figure, see the web version of this chapter)

Betsy finds the "Motorcycle" link in the "Quick Links" panel. She is rewarded with detailed information that explains how to get a license with or without having taken a Utah-sponsored motorcycle safety course.

As in the Illinois scenario, Betsy will not be able to use the web site to make an appointment at her local Department of Public Safety office in Logan, UT. But she can find the address, phone number, and hours of operation. More importantly, she learns that the Logan office requires that citizens telephone the agency to make an appointment for road tests.

State of New South Wales

The government of New South Wales (Australia, population 7 million) web site is a portal, and the information is structured around citizen information, not the government's organizational chart, as shown in Figure 2.6. Betsy's employer has transferred her to Australia. When she goes to the home page, which is structured exclusively around citizen tasks in citizen phrasing, she immediately spots her task phrase: "Get a driver license." Having this task-oriented link on the home page reflects current usability research: "the addition of a single link can enhance performance if the link is germane to the task at hand" (Scharff & Kortum, 2009, p. 18).

With one click, Betsy is rewarded with information about both auto and motorcycle license requirements, including links to fees, tests, office locations (no scheduling here, either), and handbooks for test prep. Moreover, there is a link specifically for new residents of NSW. This is without question the most usable and user-centered design of the three sites, as Figure 2.7 attests.

Here is a scorecard for how well these three web sites solve a basic information task, using a matrix similar to that developed for Chapter 4, UX of Transactions: overall it worked well ✓, it worked okay O, or it posed problems ✗.

Jurisdiction	Steps to Find Driver's License Link	Overall Impression
Illinois	10	✗
New South Wales	1	✓
Utah	4	O

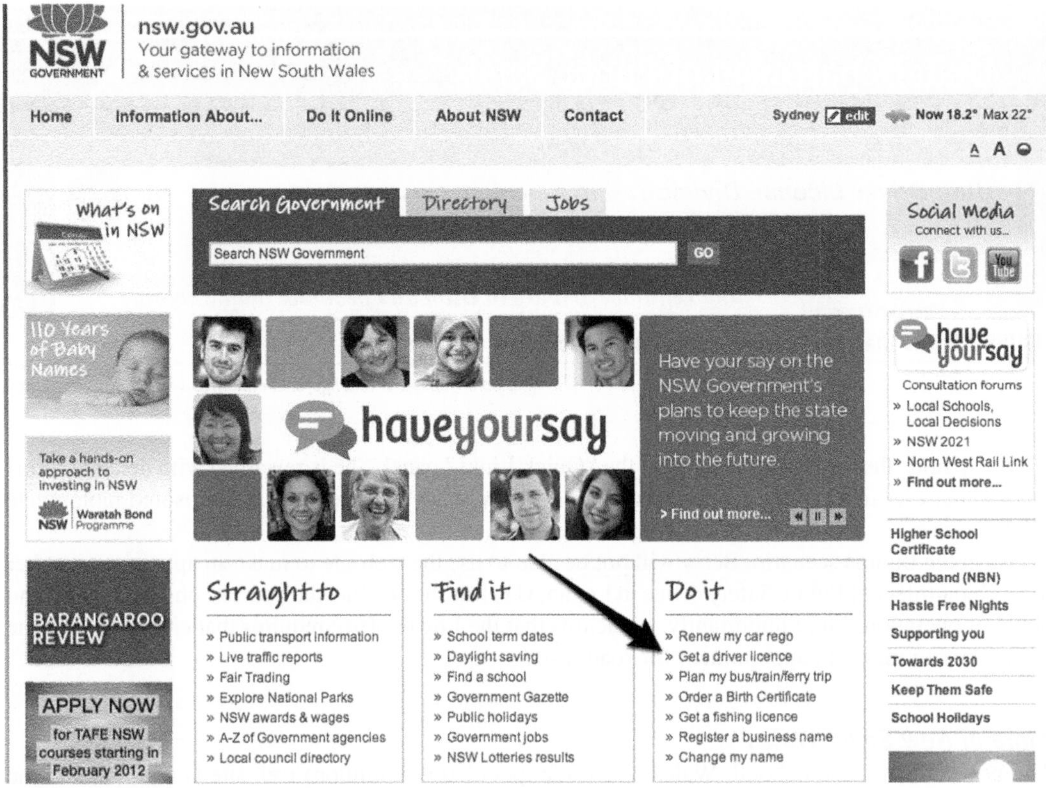

FIGURE 2.6 The New South wales web site

(For color version of this figure, see the web version of this chapter)

Pay for a parking or red-light ticket

According to Wylie (2011), "unpaid parking citation fines represent a hidden — and potentially large — source of untapped revenue owed to governments" (p. 24) if only the money could be recovered. The city of Seattle, WA (United States, population 563,000) raised $10 million from parking meters in 2002; at that time, about 25% of all tickets were sent to collections, potentially another $3+ million. Thus there is a clear financial incentive for making it easy for citizens to pay tickets online.

In Chapter 4, UX of Transactions, Caroline Jarrett assesses the performance of seven government web sites regarding paying for parking tickets online. She discovered that four UK sites did not have this capability but three North American sites did: Vancouver, Canada; Montgomery County, Maryland; and San Francisco, California.

Parking tickets are not the only automobile-related ticket we might want to pay online. Cash-strapped local governments in the United States have begun implementing automated enforcement technology, such as cameras that capture automobiles running a red light. In 2004, Washington, DC, added almost $5 million to its budget with red-light tickets (Wilber & Willis, 2005). According to

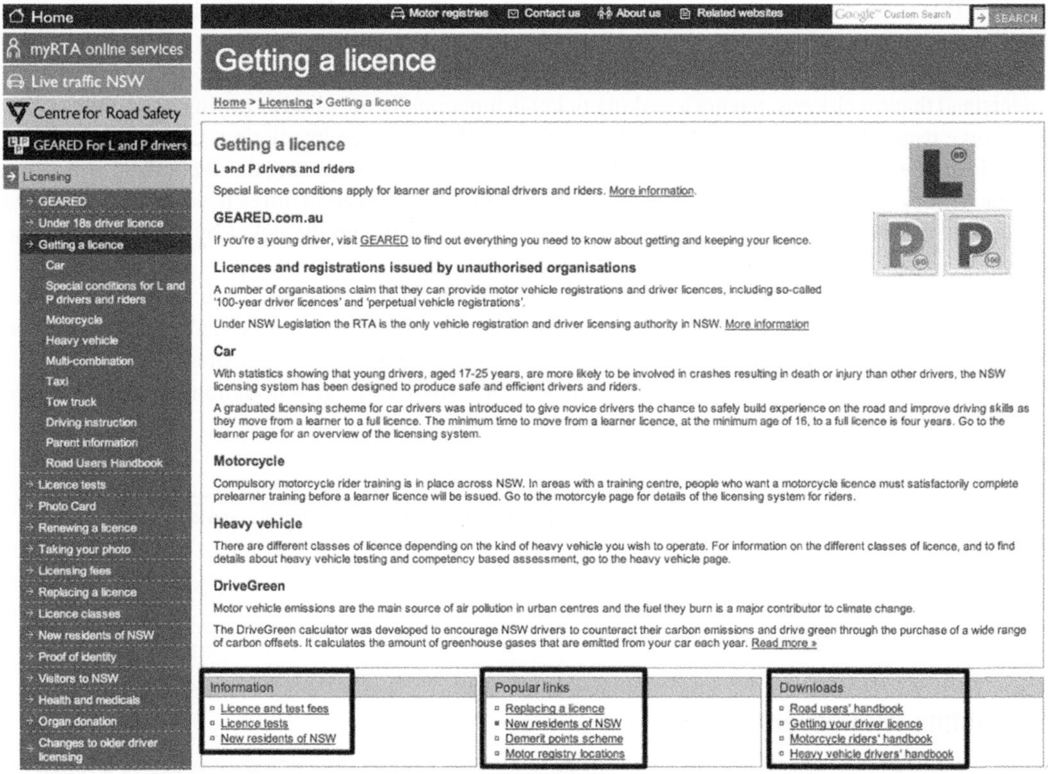

FIGURE 2.7 The New South Wales comprehensive license page

(For color version of this figure, see the web version of this chapter)

the Insurance Institute for Highway Safety (2011), approximately 555 communities have implemented red-light cameras, and 104 have added speed cameras.

My home, Lynnwood, WA (United States, population 35,836), has a one-stop permit center for businesses on the home page of the web site but nothing obvious for citizens to pay red-light camera tickets. I found the section of the web site that addresses traffic cameras by using Google search. Once I arrived on that page, however, I could not find a "pay your ticket" link. Instead, the site is written in government-speak: Violation Review, Payment, or Schedule a Hearing. Click that mouthful and off you go to ViolationInfo.com, the "pay your ticket site" hosted by American Traffic Solutions. Do not lose the ticket you got in the mail because there is no lookup-by-license-plate option.

Like the state of Utah, the city of Seattle, WA (United States, population 563,374) has been honored with awards; its web site was named the top city site in the 2011 contest sponsored by the Center for Digital Government and *Government Technology* magazine (Heaton, 2011). But that does not mean I could easily find out how to pay a red-light camera ticket. I resorted to web site search, which worked perfectly; the first search result was the right page that contained a prominent link: Pay Your Ticket

Online. This is the same service — and page — for paying Seattle parking tickets; it is just not easy to find on the web site.

Designers of the Baltimore, MD (United States, population 636,919) web site, on the other hand, understand that for citizens, paying a parking ticket is functionally the same as paying a red-light ticket. The home page, shown in Figure 2.8, is designed to facilitate citizen interaction. Clever use of white space leads the eye to the "I want to" box. For citizens with experience using the Web, the down arrow communicates, "put your mouse here, and I'll tell you more." No need to move beyond the home page to find the right link. And if you misplace the mail, you can look up the ticket by your license plate number.

In summary, Seattle and Lynnwood were plagued by hard-to-navigate web sites. Usability at Lynnwood's site was further complicated by the use of insider language instead of the colloquial language of citizens. Both cities should study the success of Baltimore's web site.

Here is a scorecard for how well these three web sites solved a basic transaction: overall it worked well ✓, it worked okay O, or it posed problems ✗.

Jurisdiction	Steps to Find Payment Link	Overall Impression
Baltimore, MD	1	✓
Lynnwood, WA	3	✗
Seattle, WA	3	O

Interacting with government

Effective citizen interaction with government officials — elected or appointed — is key to a functioning democracy. Equally important are the communication technologies used to mediate these interactions. Because of the 2001 anthrax scare, many US Senators and Representatives discourage citizens from sending mail to the nation's capitol. For example, Congressman Linda Sanchez (D-CA) asks constituents (2011) to use alternative methods of contact:

> *Because Congress has had delayed mail delivery since the Anthrax threat in 2001, e-mails, phone calls, faxes, and in-person visits are the most effective ways to communicate with my office. You may also mail directly to my Cerritos office for a quicker response.*

Today, many citizens also expect to be able to interact with government officials at SNSs such as Facebook or Twitter. In a 2010 report, Pew Internet & American Life Project noted that 31% of adults who are online have connected with government using tools such as SNS, online video, blogs, email, and text alerts.

After analyzing the 15 US government executive department web sites, recommended that agencies develop one set of links to SNS and place them on each page of the web site. In addition, the links should be identified with clarifying text such as "Stay Connected" or "Connect With Us." Finally, agencies that have multiple accounts should create a social media page to showcase accounts on each platform. How well are government web site designers implementing these best practices?

FIGURE 2.8 The city of Baltimore home page

(For color version of this figure, see the web version of this chapter)

The US military has embraced digital networking sites like Facebook, Twitter, YouTube, and Flickr, although adoption got off to a rocky start. In 2007, the US Department of Defense (DoD) began banning access to SNS such as MySpace and YouTube. Then in February 2010, the DoD opened its unclassified computer network to the SNS universe (Gohring, 2010).

This move is strategically astute. The majority of those in the Army are 18-24 years of age. According to the Pew Internet & American Life Project (Zickurh, 2010), 83% of adults younger than 34 frequent sites like Facebook.

The US Navy has been at the forefront in its use of these digital spaces. As of this writing, the US Navy Facebook page is liked by about 396,000 people; it has almost 31,000 followers on Twitter and 1.2 million upload views on its YouTube channel. Therefore it is not surprising that the Navy makes it very easy to connect using alternative digital channels. Not only are these primary SNS linked directly

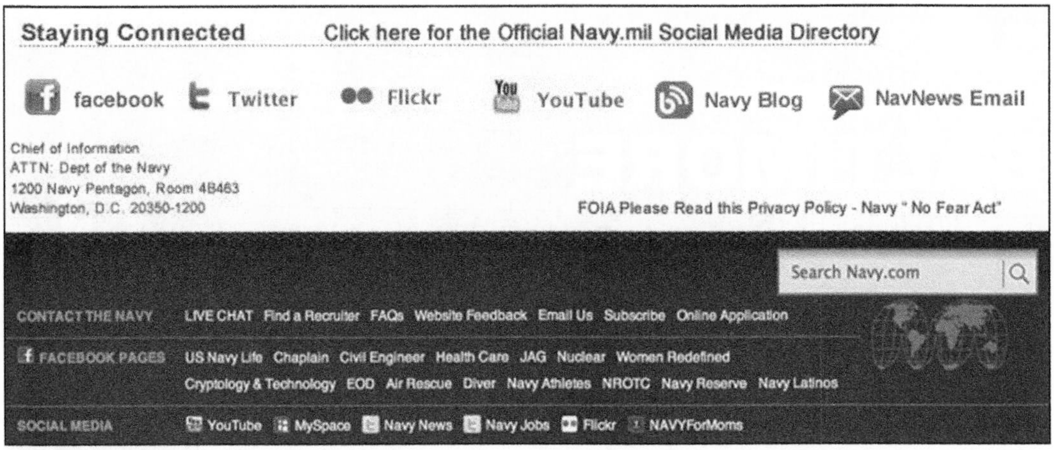

FIGURE 2.9 The footer of the US Navy home page (top) and the US Navy careers site (bottom)

(For color version of this figure, see the web version of this chapter)

from the web site home page, but the Navy also maintains a directory of auxiliary accounts. However, the SNS links can be found only on the home page.

However, if you go to "Careers," you will not only find yourself on navy.com, but you will see a new set of SNS links, as shown in Figure 2.9. On navy.com, the footer information is repeated throughout the site. Thus the primary external-facing site, the site designed for recruits, best conforms with ForeSee recommendations.

The office of the British Prime Minister (PM) is a pioneer in the use of Twitter to share information with citizens. As of this writing, the account, which was launched in March of 2008, has almost two million followers. Like the US Navy, the PM web site includes links to its Twitter, Facebook (almost 150,000 "likes"), and Flickr accounts on the home page. It also promotes an iPhone application, which delivers content such as speeches, press releases, and podcasts to citizen phones. However, the block of SNS links can be overlooked because it is not at the top or at the bottom of the page, the two places we normally look for such information. Moreover, these links are not repeated on the formal "Contact Us" web page; the Navy site misses this opportunity, also. These alternative forms of contact should also be present on the "Contact Us" page.

Conversely, Illinois has no SNS links on its home page and no SNS directory. Various Illinois government agencies have Twitter and Facebook accounts, but there is no easy way to find any of the Illinois SNS accounts.

Utah has no SNS links on its home page, but second level pages have a standard footer with links for Twitter and Facebook accounts. Each of these pages links to a "mobile and social" portal. However, once you leave the main Utah.gov site for a specific agency, you may or may not see SNS links.

FIGURE 2.10 The New South Wales Social Media directory

(For color version of this figure, see the web version of this chapter)

New South Wales includes Twitter and Facebook links on the home page as well as a link to a social directory, as shown in Figure 2.10. These links are replicated throughout the second level but tend to be missing from actual content pages. Both Seattle and Baltimore have some SNS links on the home page, but only Baltimore has a directory.

This analysis suggests that thinking about alternative means of contacting government officials is a new task for web site designers and government communicators. Designers should look to New South Wales and Baltimore for examples of effective integration of SNS sites.

Here is a scorecard for how well these web sites implemented three SNS best practices: having links on the home page, having an SNS directory, and using call to action language such as "Connect With Us" as a headline for the links; the legend is implemented ✓ or not implemented ✗.

Jurisdiction	Home Page Links	Directory	"Connect" Text
Baltimore, MD	✓	✓	✗
Illinois	✗	✗	✗
Lynnwood	✗	✗	✗
New South Wales	✓	✓	✓
Seattle	✓	✗	✗
UK PM	✓	✗	✗
US Navy	✓	✓	✗
Utah	✗	✓	✗

SUCCESS FACTORS

As more citizens turn to the Internet to find answers and solve problems, government web site designers need to make web site usability a design priority. Although a usable web site is one that does not "make us think," there are other factors that are critical to a web site's success.

Be Useful. The most usable web sites are useful. Visual appeal is important (more on that in a moment), but the sites must first be useful. To be useful, the design must embody a clear understanding of tasks and motivations and be structured to support the visitor's mental model, not that of the designer or that of the organization. In these case studies, the New South Wales web site stands out as a model to emulate.

Be Accessible. The Web Accessibility Initiative (2011) of the World Wide Web Consortium (W3C) emphasizes the universal nature of the Web. In the United States, government web sites must conform to Section 508 of the US code; information on the Web must be accessible to people with disabilities. But accessibility is more than thinking about the blind or hearing impaired; it also means making sure your site works in multiple browsers and across computing platforms. Chapter 12, Ensuring Accessibility for People with Disabilities, provides more depth.

Be Attractive. We have all heard the aphorism "you only have one chance to make a good first impression." Research suggests that for web sites, not only is there only one chance but we make up our minds in a blink, in as little as 50 ms (Lindgaard, Fernandes, Dudek, & Brown, 2006). In addition, visual appeal (or lack thereof) is directly related to perceptions of usability; a positive first impression may lead to the "potentially negative aspects" (p. 115) of a web site being overlooked.

Be Social. Government exists to serve citizens; in order to extend that service, many have established a presence on digital networks such as Twitter, Facebook, Flickr, and YouTube. Make it easy for your constituents to find you in the social sphere. Check out the Baltimore and New South Wales web sites, which offer two different approaches to designing a social media directory. In each case, the directory is featured prominently on the home page.

Think "Mobile." By 2014, analysts believe, there will be more people accessing the Web via mobile devices than via personal computers (Ingram, 2010). This means that governments need to decide which services are logical candidates for mobile access. Top of the list: services that have a direct relationship to being on the go, such as knowing what rush-hour traffic looks like, when the next bus or train arrives, or how to find an office. Lower on the priority list: paying your property taxes or filing for a business license.

SUMMARY

We began this discussion of web site usability by looking at an older form of communication, printed books and magazines, but even those stalwarts are under pressure to evolve as our information space becomes increasingly digitized.

Creating usable and useful web sites remains a balancing act: first, understand the environment that is the Web so that you can leverage design norms that make sites easier to use; second, figure out what your citizens are trying to do online and make it easy for them to tackle that task; and third, figure out how to allocate resources so that you can take advantage of emerging trends.

In each of the driver's license scenarios as well as the red-light camera ticket scenarios, the web site designers have taken pains to *make the experience feel familiar*. Sites conform to evolving Web design norms. One potentially jarring experience is the choice by Illinois and the US Navy to use .com web sites instead of a .gov domain. Also, ticket-payment systems have a distinctly different look and feel from the referring web pages.

There was less consistency across web site designs in demonstrating that designers *understood the audience*. It is important that the language used on the web site reflects how our citizens think as well as the tasks they are trying to accomplish. Web sites should be organized around audience needs rather than be structured like an organizational chart. We need to ask ourselves: "what are our citizens trying to do?" Make the home page a place where citizens find it easy to spot key phrases on an initial scan, so that they can begin the most common tasks with a single click. The sites in this review that do this best: New South Wales, Baltimore, and Utah.

Because the state of Utah elected to have its home page serve more like a search engine than a traditional portal, designers had to devise a way to *practice appropriate consistency*, so that citizens felt they were in an integrated place when they left home base. This is why we see a thin services bar atop all Utah government sites. This solution is less resource intensive (a money saving feature) than forcing all sites to undergo a redesign in order to conform to a standard template. Consider this technique for incorporating SNS links into a consistent footer.

The scenario analysis in this chapter is an example of *testing and evaluating your designs*. In a heuristic analysis, usability experts assess how well a design conforms to a specific (small) set of heuristics or rules. In an expert analysis, usability experts examine a web site to tease out possible problems. These forms of evaluation are generally less expensive than usability testing with representative citizens; however, expert and heuristic analyses are important but should not be a substitute for testing. To learn more about testing, see Chapter 20, Evaluation in Government Environments.

If you were to be tasked with printing a 32-page, four-color magazine today, you would approach it differently from how you did it 30 years ago, but your approach has probably changed little in the past decade. We do not have the luxury of a slow rate of change when we are creating web sites. To best serve our citizens, we must acknowledge that our web sites are becoming the place our citizens go to first when they have questions about or want to interact with government. Our designs need to match their growing need for both information and service.

References

Australian Government Information Management Office. Australians' use and satisfaction with e-government services. (2009) Retrieved 27 September 2011 from http://www.finance.gov.au/publications/interacting-with-government-2009/

Ayiter, E. (n.d.). from The history of visual communication: the printing press. Sabanci University. Retrieved 27 September 2011 from http://citrinitas.com/history_of_viscom/press.html

Bias, R., & Mayhew, D. (Eds.), (2005). *Cost-justifying usability: An update for the Internet age.* (2nd ed.). Boston, MA: Morgan Kaufmann.

Carr, D. (2003, July 27). *The coolest magazine on the planet.* In *The New York Times.* Retrieved 27 September 2011 from http://www.nytimes.com/2003/07/27/books/the-coolest-magazine-on-the-planet.html?pagewanted=all

Chi, E. H., Pirolli, P., Chen, K., & Pitkow, J. (2001). Using information scent to model user information needs and actions on the web. Presented at CHI 2001, March 31 to April 4, Seattle, WA, USA. Retrieved 27 September 2011 from the ACM Digital Library, DOI 10.1145/365024.365325.

Cronin, M. (2009, March 18). *10 Principles for readable web typography.* In *Smashing Magazine.* Retrieved 14 November 2011 from http://www.smashingmagazine.com/2009/03/18/10-principles-for-readable-web-typography/

Donahue, G. M., Weinschenk, S., & Nowicki, J. (1999, July 27). *Usability is good business.* In *Compuware.* Retrieved 5 November 2011 from http://www.theomandel.com/docs/Usability_Is_Good_Business.pdf

Europa. Household survey reveals more Europeans on-line but concerned about costs and security. (2010, October 13). In *Press Release.* Retrieved 27 September 2011 from http://europa.eu/rapid/pressReleasesAction.do?reference=IP/10/1328

Europa. Individuals using the Internet for interaction with public authorities. (2011, August 12). In *Chart.* Retrieved 27 September 2011 from http://epp.eurostat.ec.europa.eu/tgm/table.do?tab=table&init=1&language=en&pcode=tin00105&plugin=1

ForeSee Results. Making the case for e-gov. (2011a, April 26). Retrieved 27 September 2011 from http://www.foreseeresults.com/research-white-papers/acsi-e-gov-index-q1-2011-foresee.shtml

ForeSee Results. Federal social media usage and citizen satisfaction update. (2011b, October 25). Retrieved 5 November 2011 from http://www.ForeSee.com/research-white-papers/acsi-e-gov-satisfaction-index-q3-form-2011-foresee.shtml

Gohring, N. (2010, March 1). *US Defense Department OKs social networking.* In *PC World.* Retrieved 5 November 2011 from http://www.pcworld.com/article/190457/us_defense_department_oks_social_networking.html

Hall, R. H., & Hanna, P. (2003). *The effect of web page text-background color combinations on retention and perceived readability, aesthetics, and behavioral intention.* In *Proceedings of the Americas conference on information systems (AMCIS),* 2149–2156 Retrieved 14 November 2011 from http://ctel.mst.edu/documents/amcis_03.pdf

Heaton, B. (2011, September 1). *2011 Best of web award winners announced.* In *Government Technology.* Retrieved 27 September 2011 from http://www.govtech.com/e-government/2011-Best-of-the-Web-Award-Winners-Announced.html

Hoekman, R., Jr., (2006). *Designing the obvious* (Kindle edition). A division of Pearson Education, Peachpit Press, Berkeley, CA, USA: New Riders Press.

Ingram, M. (2010, April 12). *Mary Meeker: Mobile Internet will soon overtake fixed Internet.* In *GigaOm.* Retrieved 27 September 2011 from http://gigaom.com/2010/04/12/mary-meeker-mobile-internet-will-soon-overtake-fixed-internet/

Instone, K. (2004, January 1). Location, Path & Attribute Breadcrumbs. Retrieved 5 November 2011 from http://instone.org/breadcrumbs

Insurance Institute for Highway Safety. Communities using red light and/or speed cameras. (November 2011). Retrieved 9 November 2011 from http://www.iihs.org/laws/cameramap.aspx

Interactive Media Council. Best in class, government winner page. (2011, July 21). Retrieved 27 September 2011 from http://www.interactivemediaawards.com/winners/certificate.asp?param=86484&cat=1

Johnson, J. (2010). *Designing with the mind in mind* (Kindle edition). Burlington, MA: Morgan Kaufmann.

Krug, S. (2005). *Don't make me think, a common sense approach to web usability* (2nd ed., Kindle edition). A division of Pearson Education, Peachpit Press, Berkeley, CA, USA: New Riders Press.

Lindgaard, G., Fernandes, G., Dudek, C., & Brown, J. (March-April 2006). Attention web designers. You have 50 milliseconds to make a good first impression!. *Behaviour & Information Technology*, *25*(2) Retrieved 27 September 2011 from http://www.ext.colostate.edu/conferences/ace-netc/lindgaard.pdf

Marcus, A. (2004, April 1). *Return on investment for usable user-interface design: examples and statistics.* In *Experience intelligent design*. Retrieved 5 November 2011 from http://www.amanda.com/joomla_uploads/whitepapers/AM+A_ROIWhitePaper_20Apr0%201.pdf

Nielsen Norman Group. (n.d.). Usability return on investment. Retrieved 5 November 2011 from http://www.nngroup.com/reports/roi/

Sanchez, L. (2011). *Contact Linda. U.S. House of Representatives.* Retrieved 9 November 2011 from https://forms.house.gov/lindasanchez/webforms/issue_subscribe.htm

Scharff, L. V., & Ahumada, A. J. (2005, September 23). Why is light text harder to read than dark text? *Journal of Vision*, *5*(8). doi:10.1167/5.8.812.

Scharff, L. V., & Kortum, P. (November 2009). When links change: How additions and deletions of single navigation links affect user performance. *Journal of Usability Studies*, *5*(1), 8–20. Retrieved 27 September 2011 from http://www.upassoc.org/upa_publications/jus/2009november/scharff1.html

Smith, A. (2010, April 27). *How Americans use government websites.* In *Pew Internet & American Life Project.* Retrieved 27 September 2011 from http://www.pewinternet.org/Reports/2010/Government-Online/Part-One/How-Americans-use-government-websites.aspx

Spool, J., Perfetti, C., & Brittan, D. (2004). *Designing for the scent of information.* In *User Interface Engineering*. Retrieved 8 November 2011 from http://uwf.edu/ddawson/d3net/documents/web_usability/Designing%20for%20Scent.pdf

Thomler, C. (2011, May 1). *Australian Internet users more social, connected and politically aware than non-users.* In *Government in the lab*. Retrieved 27 September 2011 from http://govinthelab.com/australian-internet-users-more-social-connected-and-politically-aware-than-non-users/

Wilber, D. Q., & Willis, D. (2005, October 4). *D.C. red-light cameras fail to reduce accidents.* In *The Washington Post*. Retrieved 9 November 2011 from http://www.washingtonpost.com/wp-dyn/content/article/2005/10/03/AR2005100301844.html

World Wide Web Consortium. Contrast (minimum). (2010). In *Understanding WCAG 2.0.* Retrieved 14 November 2011 from http://www.w3.org/TR/UNDERSTANDING-WCAG20/visual-audio-contrast-contrast.html

World Wide Web Consortium. Web accessibility initiative. (2011, March 11). Retrieved 14 November 2011 from http://www.w3.org/WAI/

Wylie, S. (2011). *Transforming delinquent parking tickets into revenue.* In *The Parking Professional.* Retrieved 27 September 2011 from http://www.publicans.com/documents/Presto%20Change-O%20article%20by%20S%20Wylie.pdf

Zickurh, K. (2010, December 16). *Generations 2010.* In *Pew Internet & American Life Project.* Retrieved 5 November 2011 from http://www.pewinternet.org/Reports/2010/Generations-2010.aspx

Further reading

Books

Brown, D. M. (2006). *Communicating design: Developing website documentation for design and planning.* New Riders Press.

Goto, K., & Cotler, E. (2001). *Web redesign: Workflow that works* (1st ed.). New Riders Press.

Lynch, P. J., & Horton, S. (2009). *Web style guide* (3rd ed.). Yale University Press.

Norman, D. A. (1990). *The design of everyday things.* Doubleday Business.

Articles

Government Use of Social Media — "In Addition To" Not "In Lieu Of," http://steveradick.com/2010/04/27/government-use-of-social-media-in-addition-to-not-in-lieu-of/

Human-to-Human Design, http://www.alistapart.com/articles/humantohuman/

Strategies for determining your top tasks, http://www.usa.gov/webcontent/usability/toptasks.shtml

Usability: how to make a good design brilliant, http://www.coolhomepages.com/cda/usability/

Visual Decision Making, http://www.alistapart.com/articles/visual-decision-making/

Web quality: Readability, http://www.w3schools.com/quality/quality_readability.asp

Web Sites

http://ec.europa.eu/ipg/standards/accessibility/

http://ec.europa.eu/ipg/

http://plainlanguage.gov

http://section508.gov

http://usableweb.com/

http://usability.gov

CHAPTER

Usability and Government 2.0

3

Kate Walser

CX Insights, Centreville, VA, USA

"Change will not come if we wait for some other person, or if we wait for some other time. We are the ones we've been waiting for. We are the change that we seek."

— Then-Senator Barack Obama (D-Ill.), February 6, 2008 (Super-Tuesday — primary elections)

INTRODUCTION

As the use of social media and open standards frameworks spreads, the idea of Government 2.0, or Gov 2.0, has taken off. A combination of government data and tools holds the promise of making government more transparent, by publishing data and insights into government operations, and participatory, by inviting citizens to offer solutions to major challenges.

In several countries — including the United States, Brazil, the United Kingdom, Canada, Australia, New Zealand, and Iceland — the average citizen has increasing opportunity to partner with agencies and actively contribute solutions. Technology and data enablers coupled with agency policies are spurring a larger movement in which citizens — business people, stay-at-home individuals, students, voters, developers, journalists, and others — are shaping the future and priorities of government agencies. Gov 2.0 is alive and growing, offering an improved way of doing business in government by collaborating directly with citizens. Examples abound.

In December 2009, the Obama administration directed US agencies to publish, on a new OpenGov web site (e.g., ed.gov/open, energy.gov/open), Open Government Plans and at least three "high-value data sets" not available before, and to invite the public, for the first time, to offer ideas for the future of those agencies (Orszag, 2009). In the United Kingdom, citizens can see how the government is spending their tax money, and can check data such as agency performance. In July 2011, Iceland's Constitutional Council delivered its crowd-sourced constitution with citizen ideas and feedback collected at http://stjornlagarad.is. Egypt followed in July 2011, inviting citizens to comment on a proposed constitution at Wathiqah.com. The United States' SeeClickFix (seeclickfix.com) and Australia's "It's Buggered Mate" (mashupaustralia.org/mashups/its-buggered-mate) combine map data with feedback, to let citizens report potholes, signage, and public service issues.

Gov 2.0 has accelerated as technology innovations make it easier for agencies to publish data and collect ideas. Information that previously required citizens to file formal requests under freedom of information laws is now available on agency web sites as downloadable data sets.

Gov 2.0 can give citizens expanded and improved government services, quicker access to providing ideas, and the chance to provide agencies with ideas and actual solutions, if agencies consider the user experience. Too often, in the rush to implement technology as a solution, initiatives fail because users and their goals are not considered. Gov 2.0 will fall short if agencies fail to design a usable and compelling experience for both citizens and public servants.

KEY CONSIDERATIONS

Successful initiatives start most often by focusing on objectives and the end goal. Although many describe Gov 2.0 in terms of the technology enablers — technology that enables citizens to participate in government — others define it in terms of objectives related to the citizens and public servants involved: open government, transparency, and crowd-sourced innovation. Agencies with the most successful initiatives view Gov 2.0 as a partnership between public servants and citizens to achieve one or both of the following goals:

- Public outreach and participation to transform government
- Outsourcing of innovation, as agencies ask citizens for help solving challenging issues.

For Gov 2.0 to succeed in either of these respects, government leaders must consider several critical aspects that affect this partnership. Four factors — diversity and access; awareness and trust; context, tools, and instructions; and public servant consideration — will affect every interaction that agencies wish to have with citizens.

Diversity and access

Consider several countries with Gov 2.0 initiatives: the United States (whitehouse.gov/open), the United Kingdom (direct.gov.uk), Brazil (www.portaltransparencia.gov.br), and New Zealand (data.govt.nz). Citizens differ widely in several key attributes that affect how they interact with agencies and technology. Age, background, education, primary language, and understanding of government all influence how citizens interact with agencies and technology, and what they need if they are going to feel comfortable and to participate. Younger citizens who grew up with the Internet may feel more at ease interacting with agencies and participating in initiatives that involve technology and social media, while older citizens require more introduction and understanding to participate. Literacy rates differ among citizens and across countries: is the ability to read and write an acceptable prerequisite for participatory government, or are there ways to include citizens who may be in most need of having a voice in government? Understanding and addressing diversity will affect how we design successful interactions.

Demographics also affect the form factors — mobile phone, personal computer, tablet device — that citizens will use to participate in government. While mobile device adoption and use is rising globally, adoption among older adults lags adoption and use by younger audiences. A Pew Research Center survey in the spring of 2011 (Smith, 2011) found that 35% of American adults own a smartphone, with 18-46-year-olds heavily skewing the number. Agencies that use mobile apps as the main channel for Gov 2.0 initiatives will miss user audiences who have yet to adopt fuller-featured smartphones that make mobile apps more realistic. See Chapter 13, Mobile Access.

Gov 2.0 has the potential either to narrow or to widen the digital divide. Gov 2.0 initiatives rely heavily on technology enablers, including Internet access, web sites, social media, and smartphones.

Physical abilities, access to technology and tools, geography, education, and economic means can affect how much citizens can access those technology enablers and, therefore, how much they can participate in Gov 2.0. Accessibility for people with different physical abilities, which Lazar and Wentz discuss in detail in Chapter 12, Ensuring Accessibility for People with Disabilities, is probably better understood among government agencies than accessibility related to the availability of technology, location, and economic means. In the second quarter of 2011, 17.5% of UK adults lacked Internet access (UK Office for National Statistics, 2011). The United States still lags behind several nations in Internet access: as of October 2010, according to the US National Telecommunications and Information Administration (NTIA), 28.9% of Americans lacked Internet connectivity at home and 28.3% lacked connectivity anywhere (NTIA, 2011). Statistics such as these suggest that when countries host Gov 2.0 initiatives that require Internet access, 15-30% of their citizens could be left out of the discussion.

For those who do have Internet access, timing and location can affect participation. Virtual town hall meetings hosted on Twitter, such as those recently launched in the United States, require that citizens who wish to participate know what Twitter is, have an account, know how to use it, and are in a place where they can use it when the town hall meeting occurs. Major Gov 2.0 announcements that are communicated solely through Twitter, Facebook, or YouTube channels during business hours also overlook citizens who cannot use these social network sites at work.

Web sites such as the United States' Data.gov and Data.Medicare.gov allow citizens to create and view different filtered views of the data sets, but first prompt them to create a (free) account. The agency may have an important reason for wanting users to create accounts, but this practice presents a barrier to those who find the data and just wish to explore it.

Addressing diversity and access challenges seems more doable when teams sit down to identify and describe the Gov 2.0 audience and what capabilities they bring to the initiative.

Use personas and top tasks to anticipate hurdles to Gov 2.0's success

Ideally, teams can create personas after conducting user research and identifying their key audiences. The personas would help reveal any assumptions, especially related to when, where, and how citizens can access government initiatives and offerings. In the rush to launch the most recent Gov 2.0 initiatives, time may be a scarce resource, and having top tasks and simple questions can help.

Identifying the top tasks — the most frequently requested information or transactions — will give the agency insights into citizen needs. Reviewing the site's web analytics and search engine referrals can provide clues to what information and transactions citizens wanted to find. These insights will help agencies prioritize improved services, new apps, and data sets that may be published. It will also give agencies ideas about what sites, search engines, and language citizens use; information that will prove useful in deciding where to host Gov 2.0 initiatives and how to describe and publicize them to the public. Talking with agency call centers and public outreach teams is also a valuable resource for understanding citizens and what they need.

At a minimum, government leaders can answer a basic set of questions to identify any assumptions that will impact the success of their initiatives. For example, launching a mobile initiative but using Adobe Flash-based components and tools will alienate users who cannot access Flash because of organizational policies or mobile device limitations (e.g., the iPhone and iPad do not support Flash), and

Table 3.1 Sample Questions to Ask When Considering User Diversity

Sample Questions	Examples	Considerations
What technology will citizens have to access the Gov 2.0 initiative?	Personal computer	What type of connection will users have? Will they have the tools and Internet access to connect from home or work?
	Mobile device, including smartphone	Do we need/plan to use any rich features or code that would not work on these devices? (e.g., Flash on Apple's mobile devices)
	Cell phone	Can users access the information and functionality? If not, what can we change or provide?
Where would the target audience be most likely to participate?	Agency's web site (.gov, governo.it, .gov.uk, etc.)	Should we promote the initiative beyond our agency? Should we involve the media? Can we ask citizens to spread the word?
	Initiative-centric site (e.g., Challenge.gov)	What information will citizens want about who is sponsoring the initiative? Who will serve as points of contacts in case users have questions? How will we promote the URL? Is it easy to remember? Do we have clear links from the sponsor agencies to the agency site to help build trust?
	Third-party hosted .com site (e.g., Apps for Democracy)	Are there clear links from our agency web sites, to verify the relationship? Can we brand the hosted site to reflect the agency or initiative? Can we customize the look and feel? Is it accessible?
	Third-party social network site (SNS) (e.g., Facebook, YouTube, GitHub [site where developers find open source code])	Will users have accounts on this site? Does the benefit of attracting a key audience by taking the initiative to them offset the barrier created by requiring SNS accounts? Are there clear links from our agency web sites, to verify the relationship?

will disenfranchise those without access to mobile devices. Table 3.1 lists some basic questions that can help an agency plan for its user audience's needs.

When possible, include citizens in the planning stages

The biggest challenges to technology projects are the assumptions and questions that go unanswered. Agencies have an opportunity to include citizens informally, asking those they have interactions with on social networks or call centers for feedback on ideas. They also may create longer-term citizen advisory committees, similar to the customer advisory committees that companies create to gather insights about their user audience and collect feedback on concepts and vision. Even quick conversations with the target audience can reveal key information at little to no cost. Take the following example:

Agency:	"We launch the campaign and ask citizens to suggest ideas."
Citizen:	"How would I find out about it?"
Agency:	"Through our web site."
Citizen:	"I visit your web site only when I need to find something. Last year I went there once, via a search engine."
Agency:	"How would you find out about something like this?"
Citizen:	"TV, radio, friends on Facebook or Twitter."
Agency:	"We need to publicize this via TV, newspaper, radio, and post messages to Facebook, Twitter, and email lists."

If you cannot talk directly to users, talk with people who know them

Time and budget do not always enable agencies to talk directly with citizens. Think about who knows your target audience. Chances are that subject matter experts (SMEs) within your agency — in special program groups, public relations, and communications groups, or citizen advisory committees — do know your target audience and can share insights about citizens. Conferences — either with the target audience or with SMEs who know them — also provide a venue for learning about your target audience. Ask people in your own neighborhood. Asking the wrong demographic for their views can be misleading, but in the case of Gov 2.0, your neighbors and others in your social networks outside government represent a part of the target audience.

If agencies include citizens in the planning stage, the citizens may be so excited about the initiative that they serve as powerful advocates, helping to publicize it.

Use all available channels to engage citizens, not just Web-centric channels

Gov 2.0 is thought of as a web-based movement largely because technology enablers are web-based tools. The Web or access to a computer will be essential in some cases — such as visualization of tax money use or map mashups showing crime data in your neighborhood. But plenty of Gov 2.0 situations will work with access via other channels. For example, citizens who do not have smartphones with quick-response code readers could check bus schedules by calling a phone number and punching in a corresponding code. Citizens can contribute ideas by sending a short message service (SMS) message or tweeting their ideas via mobile phone. Some tools, such as SeeClickFix.com, factor in alternate channels — citizens can report issues in their neighborhood through a web site, mobile app, widget, email, or a toll-free phone number.

If you cannot use alternate channels for an initiative, consider ways to include those who otherwise cannot participate. Provide a longer time period for ideas, questions, and comments, and advertise the opportunity well in advance at all levels of government (federal, state, local).

Awareness and trust

As Gill describes in Chapter 2, Usability of Public web sites, and Jarrett in Chapter 4, UX of Transactions, citizens' interactions with government agencies often amount to required transactions (e.g., renewing a license, paying taxes) or finding information (e.g., establishing a business). The typical citizen does not frequent government web sites. A Pew Research Center study in late 2009 (Smith, 2010) found that of 2258 American adults surveyed, including both English and Spanish speakers, 61% of the respondents had visited a government web site in the prior 12 months to find specific information or complete a transaction. The respondents used external search engines to find what they needed (Smith, 2010), and were likely to miss the agency home page or sections publicizing Gov 2.0.

Trends in other countries likely reflect similar dynamics: citizens interact with agencies primarily when they need to learn or do something. Citizens will be unlikely to learn about Gov 2.0 initiatives solely through the web site of the government agencies involved. Awareness is key for citizen participation and will require publicizing beyond the agency web site.

In the past, many agencies did not invite citizen ideas, and access to data required formal requests. As agencies make their data available and invite citizens to contribute, it seems natural for citizens to be skeptical and wonder, "Why now?", They may also wonder, "Is this all the data they have?" or "Is this a biased subset?" and "What will they do with my comments?".

Gov 2.0 spans many types of web sites — nonprofit organizations seeking transparency, technology firms supporting Gov 2.0 initiatives, and the agencies' own web sites. Agencies that partner with industry to provide tools or collect ideas may host their Gov 2.0 initiatives on third-party sites with non-government branding. Factors that affect trust — including clearly communicating identity, purpose, and branding — must factor into any Gov 2.0 planning.

Make it easy to remember and find

The OpenGov web sites that US federal agencies established in 2010 (complete list available at www.whitehouse.gov/open/around) are a good example of a way to brand an initiative and build trust. The Obama administration instructed agencies to create an "open" domain to collaborate with the public on agency priorities and plans (Orszag, 2009). The "open" address had three key benefits: government leaders could mention it easily in announcements (e.g., "visit www.hhs.gov/open to share your ideas"), citizens had an easy-to-remember address, and the domain reinforced the tone of the initiative ("open for business, open for ideas . . ."). Citizens knew where to look and what to expect at each site. The consistency and expectation setting made it easier and more likely that they would contribute.

Today, citizens can return to those sites (www.hhs.gov/open, www.epa.gov/open, etc.) to find the history and activities related to the agency's initiatives. Agencies published the plans that resulted from all of the ideas citizens contributed at those "/open" web sites. By including the plans there as well, the OpenGov initiative closed the loop with citizens, affirming that the public servants had listened to their ideas and incorporated them into their strategic plan. This affirmation helps build trust. In a similar manner, Brazil publishes its government expenditures on the Portal da Transparência (Transpency Portal) at portaltransparencia.gov.br. The United Kingdom publishes its data and collects citizen ideas on Data.gov.uk and Data.gov.uk/ideas.

Identify your agency and any other organizations involved

Trust is a critical element for Gov 2.0 success. Citizens in many countries trust that a web site, app, or campaign sponsored by a government agency is legitimate and follows certain rules, including privacy, security, and, often, accessibility guidelines. They associate "gov," "governo," "gobierno," or similar government indicators in web addresses with government agencies. If the initiative exists on an external domain, especially one that is not a recognized government domain (e.g., .gov in the United States, governo.it in Italy, gov.au in Australia), the agency should publicize it via their web site, Facebook page, Twitter feeds, and any other channels it uses (e.g., magazine advertisements or radio spots) and should link to that campaign from its own site.

Gov 2.0 web sites and data sets should have a clear link back to the agency's site where citizens can learn about the initiative and verify that the agency really is sponsoring the program. Agencies should describe any partner organizations — vendors who host the tools or provide user accounts to participate — in an "About" or "FAQ" area. Knowing who is who establishes trust.

Set expectations

In a good conversation, both sides pay attention and acknowledge what the other has said. Gov 2.0 is no different. For action-requested initiatives (e.g., crowd-sourcing the constitution in Iceland, gathering ideas for US agencies), users will want to know two key things: who is listening, and what will happen with the ideas. An agency that describes how ideas will be collected and reviewed will seem more open than one that seems like a black box.

Share outcomes

Telling people how you used their ideas and which ones were chosen also helps foster trust. It lets contributors know their ideas were heard, and — in the case of innovation contests and crowd-sourcing — that they were considered and judged fairly. Something as basic as acknowledging each contribution and publishing outcomes helps.

Tools, context, and instructions

For citizens to truly experience transparency in government, open data are a small, though valuable, part of the equation. With no context or supporting tools, County and Regional Analyses data (UK Government Finances, n.d.) shown in Figure 3.1 almost make government seem less transparent. The average citizen will not recognize the "COFOG" acronym to mean "Classification of the Functions

Dept Code	Dept Name	COFOG Level 1	HMT Functional Classification
Dept020	Office of Gas and Electricity Markets	4. Economic affairs	4. Economic affairs - of which: enterprise and econom
Dept020	Office of Gas and Electricity Markets	4. Economic affairs	4. Economic affairs - of which: enterprise and econom
Dept020	Office of Gas and Electricity Markets	4. Economic affairs	4. Economic affairs - of which: enterprise and econom
Dept020	Office of Gas and Electricity Markets	4. Economic affairs	4. Economic affairs - of which: enterprise and econom
Dept020	Office of Gas and Electricity Markets	4. Economic affairs	4. Economic affairs - of which: enterprise and econom
Dept020	Office of Gas and Electricity Markets	4. Economic affairs	4. Economic affairs - of which: enterprise and econom
Dept020	Office of Gas and Electricity Markets	4. Economic affairs	4. Economic affairs - of which: enterprise and econom
Dept020	Office of Gas and Electricity Markets	4. Economic affairs	4. Economic affairs - of which: enterprise and econom
Dept020	Office of Gas and Electricity Markets	4. Economic affairs	4. Economic affairs - of which: enterprise and econom
Dept020	Office of Gas and Electricity Markets	4. Economic affairs	4. Economic affairs - of which: enterprise and econom
Dept020	Office of Gas and Electricity Markets	4. Economic affairs	4. Economic affairs - of which: enterprise and econom
Dept020	Office of Gas and Electricity Markets	4. Economic affairs	4. Economic affairs - of which: enterprise and econom
Dept020	Office of Gas and Electricity Markets	4. Economic affairs	4. Economic affairs - of which: enterprise and econom
Dept020	Office of Gas and Electricity Markets	4. Economic affairs	4. Economic affairs - of which: enterprise and econom
Dept020	Office of Gas and Electricity Markets	4. Economic affairs	4. Economic affairs - of which: enterprise and econom
Dept020	Office of Gas and Electricity Markets	4. Economic affairs	4. Economic affairs - of which: enterprise and econom
Dept020	Office of Gas and Electricity Markets	4. Economic affairs	4. Economic affairs - of which: enterprise and econom
Dept020	Office of Gas and Electricity Markets	4. Economic affairs	4. Economic affairs - of which: enterprise and econom
Dept020	Office of Gas and Electricity Markets	4. Economic affairs	4. Economic affairs - of which: enterprise and econom
Dept020	Office of Gas and Electricity Markets	4. Economic affairs	4. Economic affairs - of which: enterprise and econom
Dept020	Office of Gas and Electricity Markets	4. Economic affairs	4. Economic affairs - of which: enterprise and econom
Dept020	Office of Gas and Electricity Markets	4. Economic affairs	4. Economic affairs - of which: enterprise and econom
Dept020	Office of Gas and Electricity Markets	4. Economic affairs	4. Economic affairs - of which: enterprise and econom

FIGURE 3.1 County and regional analyses — raw data (subset)

of Government," or know what to do with that information. Unitless numbers, such as 0.05 and 13.52, further cloud the issue.

Present the data as a visualization, as shown in Figure 3.2 (Open Knowledge Foundation, 2011), and even citizens with lower literacy can see how the United Kingdom is spending their tax money.

Transparency and citizen participation are possible if citizens have the context and tools to make sense of data that agencies publish and if they have some basic background to understand challenges that agencies face. Visualization tools, guiding instructions, and legends that explain any acronyms and units for numbers will promote understanding and opportunity to participate. Sample visualizations, from which citizens can learn how to use the data and tools, also help.

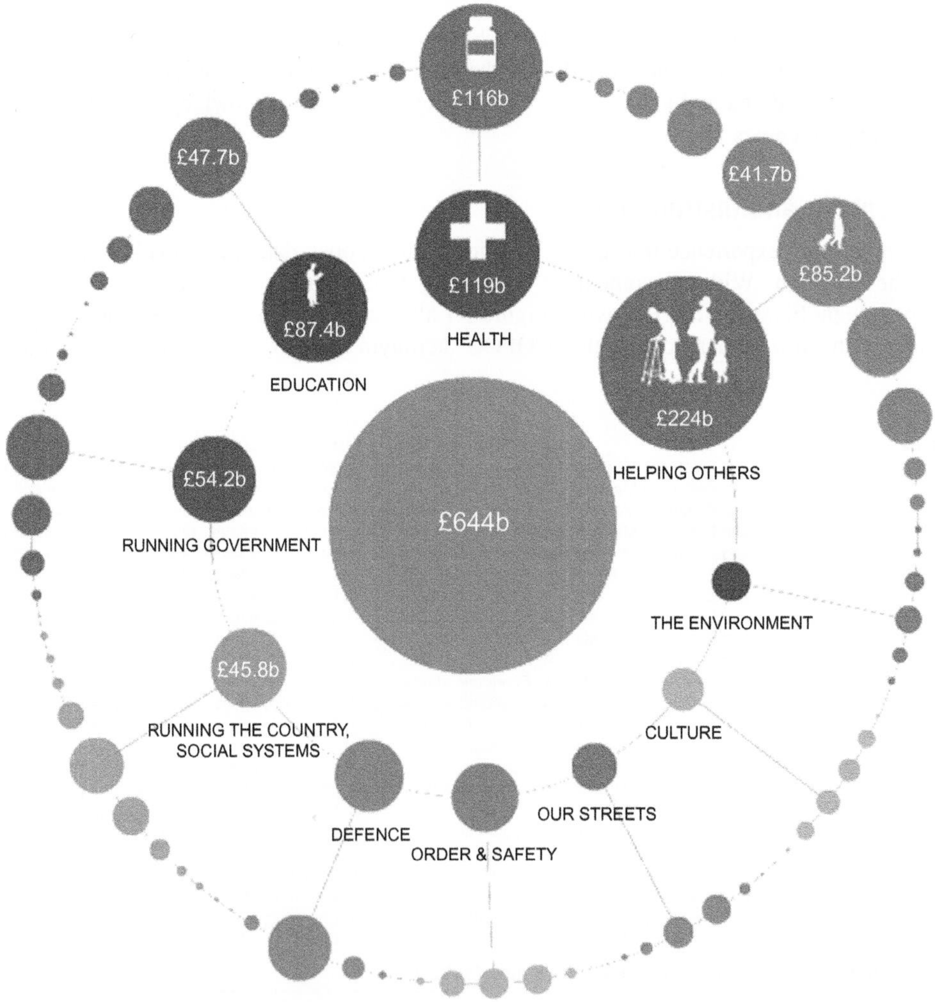

FIGURE 3.2 County and regional analyses — visualization

(For color version of this figure, see the web version of this chapter)

Include a clear call to action

Whether you use the Web, a mobile app, sidewalk signs, or other means, the call to action for any Gov 2.0 initiative needs to be clear, obvious, and one that grabs visitors' attention. Think of how differently users will respond to different phrases — "get more involved in government" usually means voting or writing to a congressperson. "Suggest ideas" and "Solve problems" are clearer and more intriguing than phrases like "Act Now" or "Participate."

Provide context and clarify purpose

Just as it is when outsourcing an initiative to another party, it is helpful to set the stage and list any requirements or limiting factors. In some cases, as with Apps for Democracy, there may be no boundaries aside from available data sets and technologies. In others, such as Challenge.gov, agencies may have specific problems for which they want solutions. As Figure 3.3 shows, each Challenge.gov entry

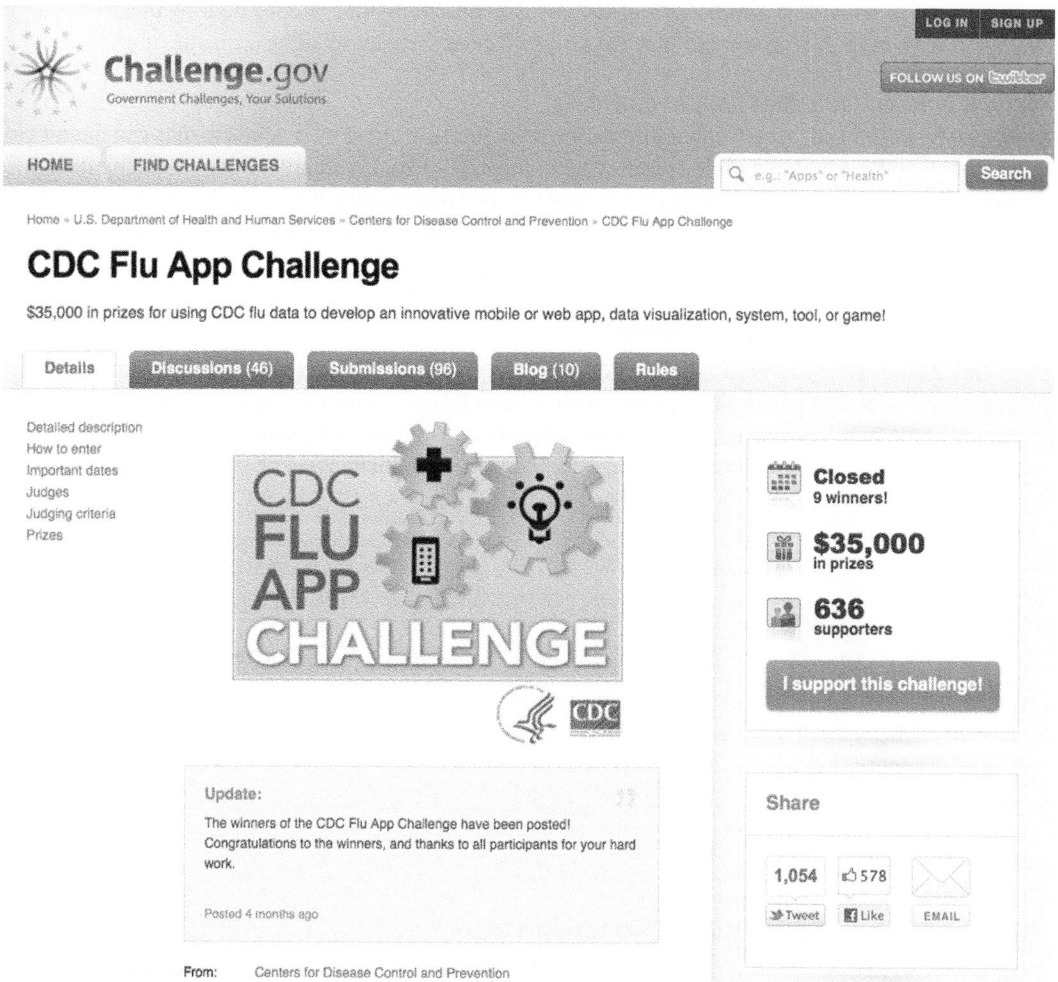

FIGURE 3.3 Challenge.gov entry

(For color version of this figure, see the web version of this chapter)

includes a description of the problem, supporting information, a link to the sponsor agency's web site, and incentives.

For a web-based call for ideas, context would include relevant history, information about the agency's overall mission, and objectives and timelines. Other Gov 2.0 initiatives, especially those involving open data and visualizations, should provide context such as time periods, acronyms, and other relevant details that bound the data to avoid misinterpretation.

Ask specialists to create reasonable instructions that users with some basic knowledge of a tool can use

If an agency publishes a large data set, a small set of users may know how to use and interact with the data. The data set will, however, have plenty of other users who, with some basic instructions, could find different ways to explore the data and may provide new perspectives. To help the latter group, work with tool specialists and plain language experts (see Chapter 11, Plain Language in Government) to provide a simple and clear set of instructions that people new to the technology can use if they have the basic tools (database, spreadsheets, access to some web site, etc.).

Include links to tools that people may need

The Open New Zealand initiative includes online communities where interested citizens can interact to build tools — GPS-enabled mobile apps, tax mapping apps, social community apps — using data that the government publishes (NZ Open Government Online Groups, July 2011). Visitors can learn how to participate (How Tos, Showcase, and Help) and explore helpful examples and links posted by others, as Figure 3.4 shows.

Considerations for public servants

Each Gov 2.0 initiative has at least two major user groups — citizens, and the public servants who will manage or contribute to the initiative. In the rush to launch Gov 2.0 initiatives, agencies often overlook the needs of the public servants. These public servants may publish data sets, collect and share information from their agencies, moderate discussion boards, post challenges, or set up entire initiatives.

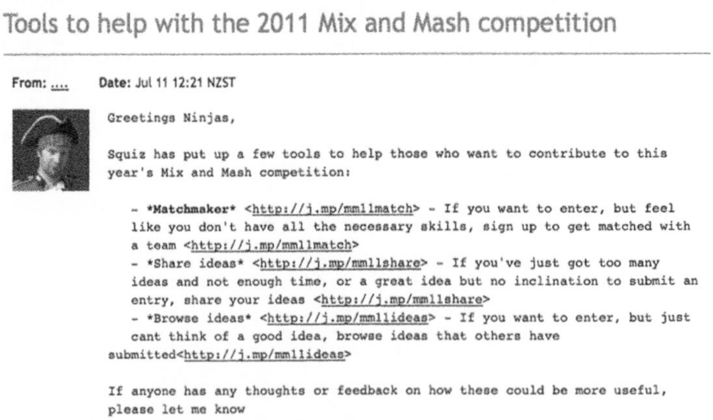
Tools to help with the 2011 Mix and Mash competition

From: .... Date: Jul 11 12:21 NZST

Greetings Ninjas,

Squiz has put up a few tools to help those who want to contribute to this year's Mix and Mash competition:

- *Matchmaker* <http://j.mp/mml1match> - If you want to enter, but feel like you don't have all the necessary skills, sign up to get matched with a team <http://j.mp/mml1match>
- *Share ideas* <http://j.mp/mml1share> - If you've just got too many ideas and not enough time, or a great idea but no inclination to submit an entry, share your ideas <http://j.mp/mml1share>
- *Browse ideas* <http://j.mp/mml1ideas> - If you want to enter, but just cant think of a good idea, browse ideas that others have submitted<http://j.mp/mml1ideas>

If anyone has any thoughts or feedback on how these could be more useful, please let me know

FIGURE 3.4 Open New Zealand post, with links to helpful tools

(For color version of this figure, see the web version of this chapter)

They are a critical piece of Gov 2.0: any tools involved in the initiative must be easy, efficient, and engaging, to enable them to participate effectively.

Out-of-the-box or off-the-shelf products may have all possible functionality and features enabled by default. Usually, these features can be adjusted and configured in a way that makes sense to the user audience. Features can be hidden or moved, labels can be changed, and in some cases workflow and activities can be modified. Agencies will recognize the need for these changes only if they think of public servants as a user audience.

Discussions of transparency and open government around the world often include mantras such as "release the data," "listen to citizens," and other well-intentioned battle cries. An assumption seems to exist among some in the Gov 2.0 community that agencies do not want to publish their data or do not want to use the tools. In the same way that agencies may forget to consider citizens' technology, resource, and access needs, agencies and vendors may fail to envision how public servants will use the required tools or to design them in a way that makes sense.

Before the US General Services Administration launched Challenge.gov, the team worked with the tool vendor to design the screens that public servants would see when they posted challenges and, later, moderated the challenges and awarded prizes. They recognized that these public servants would not be logged in to the Challenge.gov site waiting for submissions. Instead, the tool sends an email alerting them that submissions exist and gives them simple screens for reviewing and judging the submissions. The effect of this planning shows: Challenge.gov published its 100th challenge about 10 months after the site's launch.

Storyboard the entire interaction

Telling the story of how a great interaction would look and feel is invaluable. Describing what each party does and how the interaction should make them feel can uncover assumptions, and required tools and information. This is especially important for the public servants' view of Gov 2.0: an initiative that makes it harder for public servants to do their job will decrease their motivation to participate and use the tools, regardless of how strongly they feel about Gov 2.0.

Interview or shadow public servants to understand their workflow

Seeing how people moderate or manage content, data, and transactions makes it easier to design tools that they can use. It may seem tempting and easy to implement a tool "as is", in an out-of-box configuration. Realistically, however, the out-of-the-box experience does not always satisfy users, as it usually includes all possible options and a workflow that does not align with how they operate. If the tool is adjusted and designed to make it easy for public servants to use and complete their work, they not only will be more likely to use it, but will be more enthusiastic about it as well. That enthusiasm will flow through to citizens with whom they interact.

GOV 2.0 AS A RELATIONSHIP

If Gov 2.0 is meant to be a partnership between citizens and public servants, then viewing it with that lens makes it easier to plan, design, and achieve success. In its simplest form, a successful Gov 2.0 relationship means introducing yourself, finding a place to meet that works well for both sides, speaking a common language, engaging the other party, and building trust. Table 3.2 translates these relationship facets into the guidelines described earlier and summarized below.

Table 3.2 Gov 2.0 as a Relationship

Relationship Practice	Gov 2.0 Usability Principle	Guideline
1. Introduce yourself	– Clear branding – List of players involved – Links to learn more	– Identify your agency and any other organizations involved – Set expectations
2. Find a place to meet that works well for both sides	Consider factors that will affect participation: – Consider time – Choose place – Select technologies – Offer alternatives for those with access issues	– Use personas and top tasks to anticipate Gov 2.0 hurdles – If you can't talk directly to citizens, talk with people who know them – Use all available channels to engage citizens, not just Web-centric channels – Make it easy to remember and find
3. Speak a common language	– Clear labels – Clear call to action – Simple, clear wording – Images to support discussion	– Use plain language (see Chapter 11, Plain Language in Government) – When possible, include citizens in the planning stages
4. Engage the other party	– Clear language – Acknowledgments of what the citizens contribute – Removal of explanations that users do not read	– Include a clear call to action – Share outcomes – Make it interactive and interesting – Offer rewards or compelling reasons to participate
5. Build trust	– Related and supporting information – Context, supporting tools – Examples or sample data sets – Accessible options	– Storyboard the entire interaction – Provide context and clarify purpose – Ask specialists to create clear instructions that users with basic knowledge of a tool can use – Interview public servants to understand their workflow

SUCCESS FACTORS

Gov 2.0 holds tremendous promise for enabling citizens to innovate and tackle government challenges. Inviting citizens to contribute is a small piece. Agencies can follow these steps to design an experience that makes citizens and public servants want to collaborate:

- *Use personas and top tasks to anticipate hurdles to Gov 2.0 success.* Describing citizens and public servants and how they will participate will uncover assumptions or special needs such as outreach or technology access.
- *When possible, include citizens in the planning stages.* Citizens will spot holes in a Gov 2.0 strategy quickly and provide insights in how to address them.
- *If you cannot talk directly to users, talk with people who know them.* If you lack time and budget, talk with SMEs and outreach and program teams who know citizens.
- *Use all available channels to engage citizens, not just Web-centric channels.* Mobile phones, apps, email, and phone provide other avenues for collecting citizen feedback.
- *Make it easy to remember and find.* Sites such as ed.gov/open and hhs.gov/open work because they are easy for citizens to remember where to go to participate.

- *Identify your agency and any other organizations involved.* Trust is key to widespread participation in Gov 2.0. The first step is identifying all parties involved.
- *Set expectations.* Describe the process and steps involved. Citizens want to know what will happen with their ideas to decide whether participating is worth their time.
- *Share outcomes.* Follow up and share the final results and contest winners so citizens know they were heard and ideas were reviewed openly and fairly.
- *Include a clear call to action.* "Get involved" is not as obvious as "Suggest an idea." Clear calls to action tell citizens how to participate.
- *Provide context and clarify purpose.* Citizens need to understand the problem before they can tackle it. Define acronyms and provide context to help citizens understand the problem.
- *Ask specialists to create reasonable instructions that users with some basic knowledge of a tool can use.* Even a novice can offer new insights if he has a chance to explore data sets. Use plain language to teach citizens about the data and tools.
- *Include links to tools that people may need.* Without visualization tools, massive data sets are still just a bunch of numbers. Provide access to tools that let citizens explore.
- *Storyboard the entire interaction.* Tell the story of how citizens and public servants will interact in the initiative to see if any support or tools are needed for either side.
- *Interview or shadow public servants to understand their workflow.* Any technology used should make it easy, not a burden, for public servants to support.

SUMMARY

Gov 2.0 requires collaboration between citizens and public servants to achieve participation and innovation by citizens. Merely throwing new technologies at the challenge will not produce success. Agencies must consider what will affect collaboration — and plan, design, and implement with citizens and public servants in mind.

This means addressing several challenging factors that affect participation: diversity and access, awareness and trust, context and tools, and the involvement of public servants. Viewing Gov 2.0 as a relationship offers a way for agencies to address each of these facets. Agencies are more likely to succeed with Gov 2.0 initiatives if they make the initial introduction, find times and places to include the most citizens, speak in plain language, engage citizens in clear and intriguing ways, and establish trust.

The guidelines described above map directly to these components of a strong relationship. Agencies that treat Gov 2.0 as a relationship and address these facets of the user experience will be more successful in collaborating with citizens.

References

National Telecommunications and Information Administration, US Department of Commerce. Digital nation: Expanding Internet usage. (US Department of Commerce, 2011, February). Retrieved 3 November 2011 from http://www.ntia.doc.gov/reports/2011/NTIA_Internet_Use_Report_February_2011.pdf

NZ Open Government Online Groups. Tools to help with the 2011 Mix and Mash competition. (2011, July 11). Retrieved 3 November 2011 from http://groups.open.org.nz/groups/ninja-talk/messages/topic/6F23l8qQJiQaMCnMlIE8vW

Open Knowledge Foundation. Where does my money go. (2011). Retrieved 3 November 2011 from http://wheredoesmymoneygo.org/about

Orszag, P. *Executive Office of the President, US Office of Management and Budget. Open Government Directive, Memorandum M-10-06.* (US Office of Management and Budget, 2009, December 8). Washington, DC: US Government Printing Office. Retrieved 3 November 2011 from *http://www.whitehouse.gov/sites/default/files/omb/assets/memoranda_2010/m10-06.pdf*

Smith, A. (2010, April 27). *The Internet gives citizens new paths to government services and information. In Pew Research Center's Internet & American Life Project.* Retrieved 3 November 2011 from http://www.pewinternet.org/Reports/2010/Government-Online/Summary-of-Findings.aspx

Smith, A. (2011, August 15). *Americans and their cell phones. In Pew Research Center's Internet & American Life Project.* Retrieved 3 November 2011 from http://pewinternet.org/Reports/2011/Cell-Phones.aspx

United Kingdom Office for National Statistics. Internet access quarterly update 2011 Q2. (2011, August 31). Retrieved 3 November 2011 from http://www.ons.gov.uk/ons/rel/rdit2/internet-access-quarterly-update/2011-q2/art-internet-access-q2.html#tab-Summary

UK Government Finances. (n.d.). Country and regional analyses 2010. Retrieved 3 November 2011 from http://thedatahub.org/dataset/ukgov-finances-cra

Further reading

Intellitics, Inc. (n.d.). ParticipateDBβ. Retrieved 3 November 2011 from http://participatedb.com/

Lathrop, D., & Ruma, L. (2010). *Open government: Collaboration, transparency, and participation in practice.* Sebastopol, CA: O'Reilly Media, Inc.

Open Government Partnership. Country commitments. (2011, December). Retrieved 3 November 2011 from http://www.opengovpartnership.org/country-commitments

UBM TechWeb & O'Reilly Conferences. (2010). Gov 2.0 Expo. Retrieved 3 November 2011 from http://www.gov2expo.com/gov2expo2010

World Wide Web Consortium. eGovernment at W3C: Better government through better use of the web. (2011). Retrieved 3 November 2011 from http://www.w3.org/egov/

Tambouris, E., Macintosh, A., & de Bruijn, H. (2011). *Electronic participation: Third IFIP WG 8.5 international conference, ePart 2011, Delft, The Netherlands, August 29 - September 1, 2011. Proceedings.* New York, NY: Springer.

CHAPTER

UX of Transactions

4

Caroline Jarrett

Effortmark Ltd., Leighton Buzzard, UK

"This form, this form in particular I am absolutely fine with and it is not a concern. Often I'll actually give this form to a colleague and they will complete it. Not a problem. Other [government] forms, ohh, when they [are] on the desk you are just thinking oh my goodness, nightmare."

— Employer, interviewed (Dowling, 2006)

INTRODUCTION

If citizen and government never came into contact with each other, we would have no need to consider the user experience of transactions. But governments feel the urge to count, to make records, and to tax — and have done so for several thousand years.

Even when transactions were necessarily face to face, administrators found that it was worth recording them. One explanation of the origin of writing is that it was invented to make it easier to deal with administrative transactions; certainly, vast numbers of Mesopotamian clay tablets that still exist are administrative records. As Gus O'Donnell, Cabinet Secretary and Head of the British Civil Service, commented on a clay tablet from around 3000 BCE (BBC, 2010)

> *You've got a civil service here, starting to come into place in order to record what is going on. Here is very clearly the state paying some workers for some work that's been done. They need to keep a track of the public finances, they need to know how much they have paid the workers and it needs to be fair.*

After the introduction of writing, the next crucial technological development in government transactions was the form. Instead of a free-format method of obtaining and recording information, the form offered a series of prescribed questions with specific requirements for the answers that helped to structure transactions into predictable sequences, with corresponding opportunities for increased efficiency. The exact origins of this approach are unclear, but a well-known example is the Domesday Book, compiled from a survey taken in 1086 (National Archives, 2010).

The invention of printing with moveable type offered the next technological step for transactions. Some of the earliest printed documents were forms: Schwesinger (2012) cites a papal indulgence printed by Gutenberg in 1445, and also includes a tax form printed in France in 1790. But the real period of growth for forms as part of government transactions was the nineteenth century, and by the early 1900s forms had become the everyday artifacts with which we are familiar today — even if the format has changed somewhat (Figure 4.1).

TO BE FILLED IN BY COLLECTOR.

List. No. ....

.... *District of* ....

Date received ....

Form 1040.

INCOME TAX.

THE PENALTY
FOR FAILURE TO HAVE THIS RETURN IN THE HANDS OF THE COLLECTOR OF INTERNAL REVENUE ON OR BEFORE MARCH 1 IS $20 TO $1,000.
(SEE INSTRUCTIONS ON PAGE 4.)

TO BE FILLED IN BY INTERNAL REVENUE BUREAU.

File No. ....

Assessment List ....

Page .... *Line* ....

UNITED STATES INTERNAL REVENUE.

RETURN OF ANNUAL NET INCOME OF INDIVIDUALS.

(As provided by Act of Congress, approved October 3, 1913.)

RETURN OF NET INCOME RECEIVED OR ACCRUED DURING THE YEAR ENDED DECEMBER 31, 191 ....
(FOR THE YEAR 1913, FROM MARCH 1, TO DECEMBER 31.)

Filed by (or for) .... *of* ....
(Full name of individual.) (Street and No.)

in the City, Town, or Post Office of .... *State of* ....
(Fill in pages 2 and 3 before making entries below.)

1. Gross Income (see page 2, line 12)		$
2. General Deductions (see page 3, line 7)		$
3. Net Income		$
Deductions and exemptions allowed in computing income subject to the normal tax of 1 per cent.		
4. Dividends and net earnings received or accrued, of corporations, etc., subject to like tax. (See page 2, line 11)	$	
5. Amount of income on which the normal tax has been deducted and withheld at the source. (See page 2, line 9, column A)		
6. Specific exemption of $3,000 or $4,000, as the case may be. (See Instructions 3 and 19)		
Total deductions and exemptions. (Items 4, 5, and 6)		$
7. Taxable Income on which the normal tax of 1 per cent is to be calculated. (See Instruction 3)		$

8. When the net income shown above on line 3 exceeds $20,000, the additional tax thereon must be calculated as per schedule below:

		INCOME.	TAX.
1	per cent on amount over $20,000 and not exceeding $50,000	$	$
2	" " 50,000 " " 75,000		
3	" " 75,000 " " 100,000		
4	" " 100,000 " " 250,000		
5	" " 250,000 " " 500,000		
6	" " 500,000		
	Total additional or super tax		$
	Total normal tax (1 per cent of amount entered on line 7)		$
	Total tax liability		$

FIGURE 4.1 Form 1040 (the United States Federal Tax Return) from 1913

In the twenty-first century, a face-to-face transaction is expensive. For example, a study found that the cost to a government agency of a face-to-face transaction was more than twice that of the same transaction conducted by phone, which was in turn more than nine times the cost of the same transaction on the Web (Socitm Insight, 2011). The cheapest transaction of all is transferring data computer-to-computer, without involving people at all.

KEY CONSIDERATIONS

Much of the conventional advice about web sites in general, and forms in particular, assumes that the transaction is

- *Discretionary*: the user can choose whether to do it or not
- *Transitory*: the length of engagement will be short
- *Competitive*: the user can choose whether to do it on this web site or some other web site

In contrast, a typical government transaction is

- *Compulsory*: the law requires the user to engage with it
- *Lengthy*: it may be complex in its own right; the transaction itself may be simple but be repeated over long periods, even lifetimes; or it may even be both of these
- *Lacking in competition*: as a citizen or business person, you can choose to deal with it yourself, to pay someone else to deal with it for you, or to ignore the whole issue and risk retribution — but you cannot easily go to a different government

There is the old saying, "Nothing is certain but death and taxes" — and in many jurisdictions, even dying will not let you wriggle out of a tax bill.

Who is the user in a business?

User experience is all about focusing on the person who is at the heart of the experience: the user. When considering businesses, it is easy to be misled into thinking that you are dealing with "the business." You are not: you are dealing with a person in that business who has to take responsibility for the transaction.

In her investigation of compulsory transactions that collect official statistics in the United States and United Kingdom, Dowling (2006) noted:

> *This notion of a "forms person" is something that arose within other companies, particularly in the larger ones. When a new person starts (or is promoted/transferred) and they are directed to take over completion of a particular questionnaire, it often transpires that they end up completing all the others that come into their department. Perhaps unsurprisingly, it is a task from which people are keen to be relieved and thus is transferred to newer, often more junior, members of staff. However, this is not always the case as a few of the participants are senior managers in some of the larger companies.*

Bearing in mind that more than 90% of businesses are micro-businesses — i.e., have nine employees or fewer (U.S. Census Bureau, 2007) — the "forms person" nearly always has to do that work as an extra:

> *And it is not my job is it? You [the government] are sending the forms and they have to be done, it is just on top of your job. And the boss certainly doesn't see it as part of the job . . . forms to be filled I guess but other things are a priority in his book.*
>
> **— Person working in a small business (Dowling, 2006)**

When I was part of a team that investigated the ways in which people in micro-businesses deal with their tax responsibilities as employers, we too found that the "forms person" was struggling to fit these transactions, and mastering the regulations and instructions that go with them, into working life. I particularly remember the woman who could keep up with the flood of materials only by reading them in bed at night. At least in a micro-business, the person dealing with the forms usually has immediate access to the answers.

In large businesses, the problems are different but even more complex. Dealing with transactions is now a specific job function, but one on which whole departments work — or even share responsibility, across (for example) finance, human resources, and production. These also bring in the challenge of determining where one business ends and another begins: if this large enterprise is a group, is the transaction about the group as a whole, a specific business within the group, the activities of that business that fall within this jurisdiction (particularly for international businesses), or some combination?

Medium-sized businesses may be connected in various ways with each other, or may be in business to provide services to other businesses (such as accountancy).

And that brings us back to the micro-businesses, where a number of businesses may be separate legally but in fact are operated by a common cast of individuals — as illustrated by one of the families in "The Archers," a long-running radio soap opera in the United Kingdom, where Tony and Pat run an organic farm with the assistance of their daughter, who sells their dairy products and vegetables in her shop, and their son, who has his own sausage business. Although their various responsibilities for the specific businesses are theoretically clear, in times of crisis they can get mixed and overlap.

What does this mean for e-government transactions?

- Do not assume that there is a single user.
- Allow for sharing one transaction between multiple users.
- Allow for protecting parts of a transaction from some users.
- Provide save-and-resume features that allow information to be collected and entered into a form sporadically and in any order; do not assume that all the answers are easily available.

Who is the user as a citizen?

When the transaction is with an individual citizen, is the picture any clearer? Possibly, but possibly not. Where private enterprise can choose to market to specific segments of the general public, government has no such choice. If the legislation requires a citizen to undertake a transaction, then some way of dealing with that citizen — or, rather, allowing that citizen to deal with government — must be found. We, or at least our parents, have to start our official lives at birth when they register that event — or possibly even before, should they be planning a home birth (Figure 4.2).

An individual may be unable or unwilling to act for all sorts of reasons. Too young, too old, too disabled, too disorganized, too frightened of officialdom — or too busy.

How do I begin the registration process?	Contact the local health department in the jurisdiction (county or Baltimore City) where the birth occurred. Some jurisdictions have procedures in place to allow parents to "preregister" in anticipation of a home birth. Preregistration simplifies the registration process that will take place after the baby is born.
What information is needed to register my baby's birth?	You will be required to provide information that verifies the following facts of birth: 1. Identity of parent(s); 2. Fact of pregnancy; 3. Fact of live birth; and 4. Place of delivery. You will also be required to: 1. Complete the Mother's Worksheet, which will be provided by the local health department; and 2. Provide information required by the Department of Health and Mental Hygiene for public health purposes.

FIGURE 4.2 The transaction for registering a home birth may start before birth, http://vsa.maryland.gov/html/home-birth.cfm

Conversely, government should not assume that an individual does prefer to have someone else act. In the United Kingdom, the Mental Capacity Act makes it very clear that simply making a foolish decision does not indicate lack of capacity.

The principles

(1) The following principles apply for the purposes of this Act.
(2) A person must be assumed to have capacity unless it is established that he lacks capacity.
(3) A person is not to be treated as unable to make a decision unless all practicable steps to help him to do so have been taken without success.
(4) A person is not to be treated as unable to make a decision merely because he makes an unwise decision.
(5) An act done, or decision made, under this Act for or on behalf of a person who lacks capacity must be done, or made, in his best interests.
(6) Before the act is done, or the decision is made, regard must be had to whether the purpose for which it is needed can be as effectively achieved in a way that is less restrictive of the person's rights and freedom of action.

(Mental Capacity Act, 2005)

What does this mean for e-gov transactions?

Respect the right of the citizen to act without assistance.

- Equally, respect the right of the citizen to
  - ask another person to act for all or part of the transaction
  - have that person be informed about all of a transaction or about only specific parts of it.
- Allow for protecting parts of a transaction from some users.

- Provide mechanisms to allow information to be collected and entered into a form sporadically; do not assume that all the answers are easily available, or that the person undertaking the transaction knows the answers personally.

GENERAL CONSIDERATIONS FOR ALL TRANSACTIONS

These are four key drivers for transactions:

- *Relationship*: the combination of the government agency's reasons for the transaction and the user's
- *Conversation*: the question-and-answer sequence that makes up the meat of a form, plus the route to finding the form and the information exchange that follows its completion
- *Appearance*: the visual layout of the elements of the conversation
- *Implementation*: organizing the different technological and human elements in the transaction so that they all work together, and on time

The structure of the transaction: relationship

Every form issued by government is issued for some purpose. Similarly, citizens rarely engage with government without having some goal in mind, whether it is getting their trash collected or complying with legislation that requires them to complete a statistical survey on behalf of their business. In this section, I will discuss these key points about the structure of the transaction:

- Have you allocated the tasks appropriately?
- Are you supporting multiple channels?
- What level of online form is appropriate for this transaction?
- Are you expecting too much from your online forms project?

Have You Allocated the Tasks Appropriately?

When the UK Inland Revenue was preparing for a major change to the personal tax system, I did a lot of observation of work in tax offices. One of the most depressing sights was watching tax officials typing tax returns into a computer — from printouts that had been printed by another computer. At that time (the early 1990s), there was no provision for online filing of tax returns. Fast-forward: by 2011, 78% of UK personal tax returns were filed online: computer to computer.

Can you organize the transaction so that people do not have to be involved?

If people do have to be involved, they need to take six steps:

1. Find the appropriate form(s).
2. Work out which one(s) they have to use, and when.
3. Fill out the form.
4. Wait for a reply, acknowledgment, or other receipt — possibly including notification of errors.
5. Deal with the errors, queries, or follow-up questions.
6. Deal with any follow-up activity, such as paying tax due.

Notice that the form itself is only one step within the transaction, but a complex one, itself consisting of six steps:

1. Understand the questions.
2. Find the appropriate answers, including liaising with others.
3. Perform any necessary calculations, for example, to aggregate answers.
4. Put the answers into the correct spaces on the form.
5. If it is an electronic form, deal with any errors.
6. Send the form on paper or transmit it electronically.

If people do have to be involved, have you done these four things?

1. Made it easy to understand the requirements of the transaction
2. Made it easy to find the relevant form(s) and identify the correct one
3. If calculations are involved, provided a way for a computer to do the calculation
4. Provided reassurance at the end of the transaction that it is all finished

Are You Supporting Multiple Channels?

Although access to the Internet is growing rapidly everywhere, it is still by no means universal. Even in South Korea, a country with wonderfully fast, almost universal broadband provision, 19% of its citizens did not have access to the Internet in 2009 (World Bank, 2011). In the United States, the "digital generation" (18-to-29-year-olds) has grown up alongside the Internet, yet 5% of them do not have access (PewInternet.org, 2011).

This lack of provision is unequally distributed: if you are poor, or unemployed, or disabled, or old, then you are far more likely to lack Internet access (Helsper, 2008). But it is exactly those groups that have a disproportionately high level of interaction with government.

So if you cannot assume that everyone has Internet access, you must assume that you will have to support multiple channels or find some other way of dealing with the inevitable exceptions. For example, Irish Tax and Customs (2011) mandates that all corporations and employers file returns and pay tax electronically, but also says this:

> *[We] may exclude a person from the obligation to pay and file electronically, if [we] are satisfied that the person does not have the capacity to do so. In this context "capacity" is defined to mean access to the requisite technology, both hardware and software.*

Despite these caveats, if an online transaction can be offered to the majority then considerable cost savings for the agency, and possibly time savings for the user, can be achieved.

Are You Allowing for Rare Exceptions?

One of the fascinations of government is the "Law of large numbers."

This was explained to me by a project manager at a government agency. He was installing a complex system and had been assured by the vendor that the chance of a particular failure was "only one in a million." As the project manager explained: "Of course, we had 8 million users so it happened the first day."

Let us look at this from the point of view of transactions. Let us take, for example, a compliance system: a government agency — let us call it the Department of Oversight (DoO) — requires organizations to inform them about every instance of an activity. DoO officials will investigate some activities — those that it considers to be unusual — and will prosecute if they are revealed to be illegal. Most organizations comply with the law; unusual activity is rare, and the proportion of unusual activity that proves to be illegal is tiny. The challenge for the officials is to identify the unusual.

Organizations can choose to send in their returns of activity electronically, and most of them do: in fact, out of the annual 100 million returns, 99.9% are indeed sent electronically; leaving only 0.1% (1 in 1000) that must be sent on paper. This means that DoO receives 99,900,000 electronic submissions, and 100,000 paper submissions.

What do we know about these submissions? They are lots of electronic ones, and very few on paper. We might almost say: "there might be something unusual about those paper submissions." And indeed, when the officials start to investigate, while they only find one unusual submission in about ten thousand electronic submissions, they find that about one in ten of paper ones is about an unusual activity (Table 4.1).

Table 4.1 Unusual Activities by Type of Submission

Type of Submission	Number	Rate of Unusual Activity	Number of Unusual Activities Reported
Electronic	99,900,000	1 in 10,000	9900
Paper	100,000	1 in 10	10,000

Clearly, if the officials invest at least as much time on the rare paper returns as on the vast number of electronic returns, they will reap large benefits.

What happens if DoO then decides to require organizations to send all returns electronically? Yes, it will achieve a small saving in processing time. But it now becomes much harder to identify the unusual cases.

This example illustrates a case where aiming for totally online transactions may be a step too far. Because of the Law of large numbers, it is far from atypical. Rare exceptions will always occur, whether for technological or practical reasons. The cost of pursuing them, and of programming systems to allow for them, may be disproportionate.

What Level of Online Form is Appropriate For This Transaction?

Online transactions can offer considerable benefits in terms of cost savings for the government agency, and increased convenience for the user. But what level of online form is appropriate for this transaction?

Killam (2009) describes five levels of online forms:

1. *Print-on-Demand (POD). Essentially, paper forms that are made available electronically. The most familiar technology is Adobe's PDF. Users print the form for filling in manually. The main user benefit is that the form is available immediately. The main organizational benefit is that the form does not have to be printed, stored, or sent out to the user. There is no obsolescence cost if it gets updated, and only the current version is available to the user. So POD forms save organizations a lot of money, but the user still has to print and send in the form. POD forms also have the disadvantage that the organization is likely to receive a lot of hand-written forms, which*

are harder to process. Despite their problems, POD forms can still be a good solution for getting forms to people who do not have their own computer but can get someone else to print out a form for them for completion later.

2. *Fill-and-print (F/P). These are an improvement on POD forms. The user fills the form online, then prints and sends in. There is usually a tab order, some field restrictions, some masking, and special fields such as check boxes and simple drop-down selections. These forms provide the same advantages as POD, and are easier to fill out, more legible, and contain fewer errors. These forms are often a good solution where the organization requires a real signature, or the user has to attach another document that may not be electronic.*
3. *Intelligent electronic forms (IEF). These have more intelligence such as calculations, conditional fields, logic choices, logon access, hidden fields, and help messages. They are truly online from the user's perspective, but data collected is not integrated with enterprise applications. Many ordinary web forms fall into this category by accident: the organization has thought about how to collect the data, but not paid enough attention to what to do with it when it arrives within the organization. IEFs do work well, however, as a further improvement on F/P forms for forms with complex internal routing.*
4. *Enterprise-enabled (EE). These employ email connections, database connections, secure access, intranet/Internet access, usage tracking, edition control, ecommerce connections, electronic signatures, and other enterprise features. They can eliminate or reduce paper from the process, improve productivity, improve customer service, and eliminate or reduce filing.*
5. *Complete business applications (CBA). A full CBA typically employs multiple forms and subforms in an integrated business solution. It may have a mixture of IEF and EE forms, pulled together into a system that routes forms from the user to the different parts of the business as needed. CBAs require custom programming to build business rules and logic into the forms set. A CBA has the potential to save costs across a business, eliminating paper and duplicate keystrokes, and making sure that the data gets to the people who need it.*

Killam does not mention the drawbacks of EE and CBA forms such as the high costs of implementation, and less resilience in the face of the inevitable cycles of change:

- Annual
- As legislation changes
- As agencies reorganize for internal or political reasons

Choosing the appropriate level of electronic form can be tricky. For example, the major benefits from CBA arise when work needs to flow around the agency, efficiently directing it in turn to each person who needs to deal with it. But one major UK government department canceled a workflow project when we investigated and found that the work did not flow: the department was organized so efficiently that each worker dealt with his or her caseload in its entirety, apart from a tiny proportion of cases referred for technical investigation. No flow, no merit in CBA.

The details of the transaction: conversation

I would say 70% of the form I can just fill out off the top of my head. Probably 20% I probably have to just work out some numbers and look things up and 10% I have to refer to other people.

— Person working in a small business (Dowling, 2006)

Let us make the assumption that you have followed the advice on plain language in Chapter 11, Plain Language in Government, and made sure that your questions are clear and written so that the users understand them in the same way that you do.

A government transaction is not a quiz, where users can reasonably expect to know every single one of the answers off the top of their heads — and if not, to give up on the transaction. Each question must be answered using one of these four strategies, presented in increasing order of burden:

1. *Slot-in answers*: these are the "top of the head" information that most people will know without looking it up, such as their own name and address.
2. *Gathered answers*: ones that have to be looked up and copied, or looked up and then manipulated, such as calculating total income from savings by looking up details on two or three bank accounts and adding them together.
3. *Third-party answers*: ones that have to be referred to other people, such as obtaining a certified copy of a document to support an application.
4. *Created answers*: ones where original thought is necessary, such as filling in a government job application that requires a statement of competency, or writing a justification for a planning application.

Burden is not necessarily a problem if the administrative benefit has been proven, but it must be understood.

Two specific areas can cause problems:

- The actual strategy that a user takes to find the answer does not match the official concept of the strategy. For example, the official form asks for a child's name to be entered exactly as shown on a passport, but the mother writes down the child's name according to the way she usually thinks of it. (Official strategy: gathered answer; actual strategy: slot-in answer.)
- The strategies match, and the user gathers the answer or asks a third party, but does not have access to the source of the answer. For example, the official form expects the user to copy the answer from another document but the user has lost it, or has never had it in the first place.

What does this mean for e-gov transactions?

- Think about how the user will obtain the answer. Which strategy do you expect the person to use? Is there any risk that the strategy that you expect might differ from the one that will actually be used?
- Consider whether the burden of finding the answers is truly justified by the administrative benefit of having that answer. For third-party answers: could you ask the third party directly? For gathered answers: could you collect the data from the other document(s) directly and simply get the user to confirm the answers?

Making it look good: appearance

In the early days of the Web, users quickly learned that good design is expensive, and came to regard well-designed sites as more trustworthy (Karvonen, 2000).

> *"If a web site strikes me as beautiful, I will gladly give away my credit card number—is that how it goes?"*
>
> *With our Swedish users, that is exactly what we experienced: users admitted to making intuitive, and rather emotional, on-the-spot decisions to trust a service provider when shopping online.*
>
> *A user comment included: "if it looks pleasant, I just trust it."*

FIGURE 4.3 The complexity of language on official forms

(courtesy Effortmark Ltd).

Since then, this research has been replicated (e.g., Lindgaard, Dudek, Sen, Sumegi, & Noonan, 2011). If your site looks attractive and orderly, it will be perceived as easier to use — and therefore, users will approach it with a more positive attitude.

Exactly the same considerations apply to forms. An orderly form that looks airy and uncluttered will encourage your users. Crush it all together, add long paragraphs of complex notes, throw in plenty of convoluted language, and it will seem highly intimidating (Figure 4.3).

Making it happen: implementation

Implementing a typical, rather simple, government transaction will involve dozens of stakeholders:

- The Web team
- The content people, often across different policy areas
- The staff who deal with paper forms
- The staff who deal with phone calls and face-to-face transactions
- Payment technologies and other specific services, often bought in or outsourced to a third-party service provider
- Marketing and publicity
- And, maybe, many more

These different groups all have their own different points of view, responsibilities, and reporting lines. A successful transaction needs them all to work together to create a seamless and coordinated user experience.

If the groups do not coordinate, disaster can result. For example, I recall a UK tax transaction, where the policy people responsible for forms decreed that incoming forms should be processed within 90 days; the policy people responsible for letters decreed that incoming letters should be processed within 30 days; the publicity people were running a major national campaign inviting the public to send in forms; and the staffing people had not yet got the planned level of staff in place. The few staff available were spending all their time answering letters from irate members of the public asking why their forms had not been dealt with — the letters had a shorter target than the actual forms.

CASE STUDY: FIND THE FORM TO PAY A PARKING TICKET

Although all of the different considerations are likely to apply to any particular transaction, I have chosen a case study to illustrate some selected aspects of the issues.

- *Area:* Aspect of the consideration illustrated in this case study.
- *Relationship:* Make it easy to find the appropriate form.
- *Conversation:* Use the terminology that is familiar to your users, and use it consistently.
- *Appearance:* Use consistent branding across all the elements of the transaction.
- *Implementation:* When purchasing a forms solution from a third-party vendor, make sure you include usability in your requirements.

A small but frequent transaction: paying a parking ticket

Some people live in areas where parking tickets are irrelevant; others treat them as an everyday hazard, blithely park where they wish, and get their staff to deal with the consequences. Most of us are somewhere in the middle: we occasionally forget the time, misunderstand the rules of an unfamiliar area, or suffer some other misfortune that leads to the dreaded notice attached to our vehicle — and usually that means an encounter with an agency of local government.

For many local government agencies, parking tickets are an important source of revenue but also a contentious one as they try to balance the competing interests of residents, visitors, and businesses.

I chose to visit the web sites of four UK local authorities, drawing on Jarrett (2011), and also found the web sites relevant to parking tickets issued in Vancouver, Canada; Bethesda, Maryland, USA and San Francisco, California, USA — chosen because I have visited those cities recently.

Each site offered some good and bad experiences

A quick search reveals that the appropriate authority for Bethesda is Montgomery County (Figure 4.4). Then it gets hard. The home page offers two routes to paying a parking fine: "I want to" and "Online Services." Neither mentions parking; both are obvious if you work in government, but obscure if you do not. Maybe people in Montgomery County are meticulous about their parking; maybe Montgomery County's parking policies mean that they rarely hand out tickets. But it still seems unlikely that "County Executive" is a more popular choice than paying a parking ticket.

Reading Borough Council in the United Kingdom does a better job here, featuring eight tasks prominently on its home page, including "Pay a Parking Ticket" (Figure 4.5)

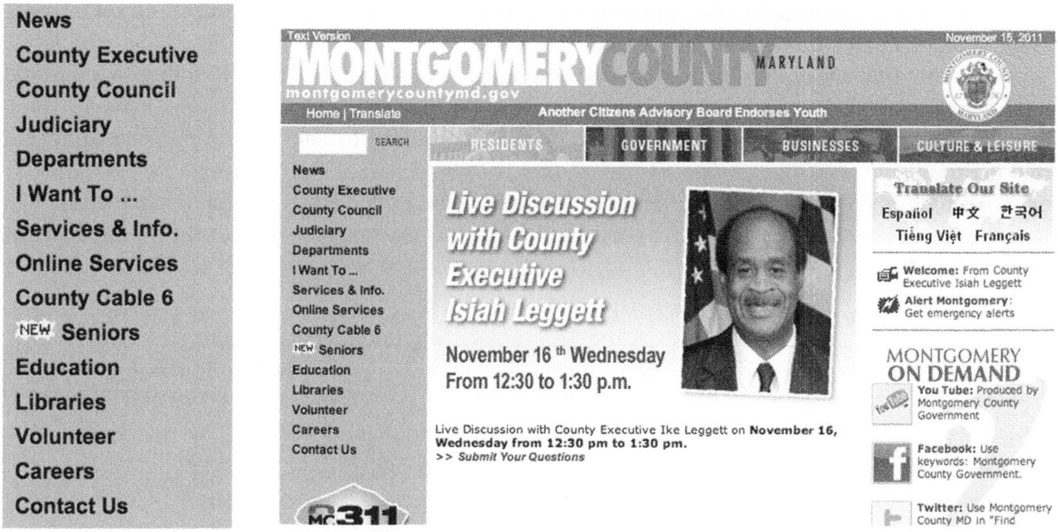

FIGURE 4.4 Menu and upper part of home page of Montgomery County, Maryland web site

(For color version of this figure, see the web version of this chapter.)

It is tempting to say that steps in a forms process are good, bad, or indifferent — but it is a bit more complicated than that. A page might be a good page in that it is well written, has appropriate links, and an attractive design, but it might still fail because the user arrives at it with the expectation of a different page, or because the choices it offers are irrelevant to that task. A question on a form might be clearly written but still difficult to answer because the information required is not at hand, or because the choices on offer are not suitable.

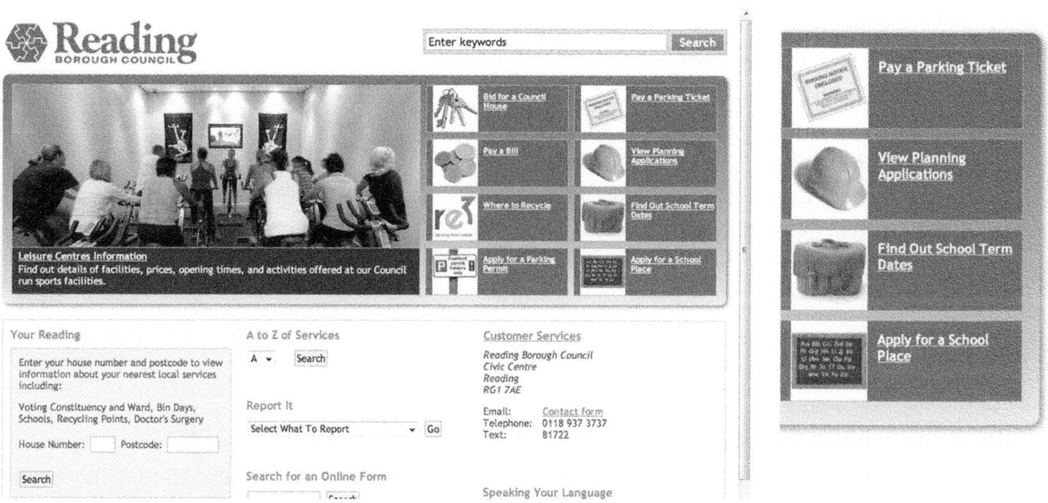

FIGURE 4.5 Home page and featured tasks on Reading Borough Council web site

(For color version of this figure, see the web version of this chapter.)

As I worked through each of the seven web sites, I noted whether the page worked well for me (✓), posed a problem (✗), or made no difference (○).

I could not find a way to pay a lost parking ticket online in any of the four UK authorities. I would have had to telephone to ask what to do.

All three North American authorities offered me the opportunity to enter my license plate number to find the ticket.

This might suggest that the user experience was poor in the United Kingdom, and successful outside it. But in fact every experience had its good and bad points, rearranged below to show how many of each I encountered.

Authority	Parking ticket	Number of good, no-difference, and poor steps
Brighton and Hove City Council	Telephoned after 10 steps	✓✓✓✓✓○○○✗✗
City of Edinburgh Council	Telephoned after 6 steps	✓✓○○○✗
Reading Borough Council	Telephoned after 5 steps	✓✓○○✗
London Borough of Richmond on Thames	Telephoned after 11 steps	✓✓✓✓○○○○✗✗✗
Montgomery County Government	Asked to enter license plate number after 5 steps	✓○○✗✗
City of Vancouver, British Columbia	Asked to enter license plate number after 4 steps	✓✓○✗
City and County of San Francisco	Asked to enter license plate number after 6 steps	✓○○○✗✗

One common problem: using unfamiliar terminology

One issue often tripped me up: the differences in terminology between the everyday phrase "parking ticket" and the official phrases. For example, on just the UK sites I found all these variations, sometimes (but not always) used alongside the everyday phrase:

- Charge notice
- Fixed Penalty Notice (New Roads and Street Works Act 1991) (UK)
- Parking and Bus Lane Fines
- Parking or Bus Lane Penalty Charge Notice
- Parking penalty charge notice
- PCN (acronym used without expansion or explanation)
- Penalty charge notice

If you work in government, you will probably accept that they are all equivalent — but what if you are not so familiar with official terminology?

Using a third-party system without specifying usability requirements

All of the UK sites failed to allow for the possibility of a lost parking ticket. I suspect that they are all using third-party payment systems, and that those payment systems all had the same defect.

Clearly, using a purchased module or service to handle your transactions can offer benefits such as lower programming and maintenance costs — but your users will experience that as part of your site, not as a separate matter. It is vital that you identify your usability requirements and ensure that they are specified in the contract (see Chapter 16, Getting UX into the Contract).

SUCCESS FACTORS

To achieve success with a transaction with a public, follow these steps:

- *Make common transactions easy to find on the home page.* Make popular transactions clearly visible, and use terminology that citizens are likely to recognize.
- *Make your forms orderly and attractive.* This may help people find information more easily, and it *will* help produce positive reactions and encourage people to feel better about doing business online with your agency.
- *Match your transactions to users' strategies for finding answers.* Aim to reduce the effort which people need to expend to provide the required information.
- *Support multiple channels.* Ensure that every citizen has a choice of how to do business with your agency. Do not require all transactions to be conducted online.
- *Allow for rare exceptions.* Governments conduct so many transactions that even a one-in-a-million frequency of a particular exception could mean that you will see several of them every day.
- *Specify usability requirements in contracts with third-party vendors.* If you are using commercial transaction services, ensure that you procure ones that can provide your citizens with appropriate usability.

And of course, above all: do plenty of testing with your target audience

SUMMARY

Given so much to think about, what matters most?

It is tempting to a claim, "All of it." But my experience has been that in a typical government project, two considerations receive the most attention from the project team:

- Information technology (IT) aspects of implementation
- Detailed aspects of appearance, such as where to put the labels with respect to the fields on the form and whether or not to have a colon on the end of the label

For the users, the citizens and business people dealing with the transactions, IT considerations are also very important. For example, I did a small survey to investigate why some people continue to file their taxes on paper, and one of the top reasons they gave was a previous bad experience with the technology, such as the transaction crashing part-way through.

In contrast, few users care very much about the detailed aspects of appearance. In nearly 20 years of usability testing paper and online forms, I have yet to meet a user who notices whether the labels have colons, or expresses an opinion about it. Label placement is a little bit more important, but provided that the users can work out which label goes with which field fairly quickly, they will be able to deal with the form without difficulty. Most other detailed aspects of appearance fall into the same area: make some adequate decisions, implement them consistently, and you will be fine.

But if you do not pay enough attention to relationship and conversation, then your users really will be in difficulty. You will have to deal with their phone calls, letters, and emails, leading to higher costs to you and burden for them. They may even give up altogether, failing to obtain benefits to which they are entitled, or failing to comply with the law.

Acknowledgments

I would like to thank Zoë Dowling and Ray Killam for permission to quote from their respective publications, and Ginny Redish for her perceptive comments on an early version of this chapter.

References

BBC, (2010). Early writing tablet. *A History of the World in 100 Objects*, Retrieved 12 September 2011 from http://www.bbc.co.uk/ahistoryoftheworld/objects/TnAQ0B8bQkSJzKZFWo6F-g

Dowling, Z. (2006). *Web data collection for mandatory business surveys: An exploration of new technology and expectations.* Ph.D. Thesis, University of Surrey, Guildford, GU2 7XH.

Helsper, D. E. J. (2008). *Digital inclusion: An analysis of social disadvantage and the information society.* Oxford Internet Institute (OII).

Irish Tax and Customs, (2011). *Mandatory electronic filing and payment of tax—Implementation of phase 3.* Retrieved 24 September 2011 from http://www.revenue.ie/en/practitioner/ebrief/2011/no-042011.html

Jarrett, C. (2011). A review of easy and hard forms. In *Better Connected 2011, a snapshot of all local authority websites.* Socitm Insight.

Karvonen, K. (2000). The beauty of simplicity. In *Paper presented at the proceedings on the 2000 conference on universal usability.*

Killam, R. (2009). Forms management: What forms managers think about. *User Experience, the Magazine of the Usability Professionals' Association, 8*, 3.

Lindgaard, G., Dudek, C., Sen, D., Sumegi, L., & Noonan, P. (2011). An exploration of relations between visual appeal, trustworthiness and perceived usability of homepages. *ACM Transactions on Computer-Human Interaction, 18*(1), 1–30.

Mental Capacity Act, (2005). *Part 1, the Principles, Section 1.* Retrieved 15 November 2011 from http://www.legislation.gov.uk/ukpga/2005/9/section/1

National Archives, (2010). *Domesday book: Research guide.* Retrieved 23 September 2011 from http://www.nationalarchives.gov.uk/records/research-guides/domesday.htm

PewInternet.org, (2011). *Demographics of Internet users.* Retrieved 1 October 2011 from http://pewinternet.org/Trend-Data/Whos-Online.aspx

Schwesinger, B. (2010). *The form book: best practice in creating forms for printed and online use.* London: Thames & Hudson.

Socitm Insight, (2011). *Better connected 2011: a snapshot of all local authority websites.* Society of Information Technology Management.

U.S. Census Bureau, (2007). *Statistics about business size (including small business).* Retrieved 1 October 2011 from http://www.census.gov/econ/smallbus.html

World Bank, (2011). *Internet users (per 100 people).* Retrieved 15 November 2011 from http://data.worldbank.org/indicator/IT.NET.USER.P2

Further reading

Jarrett, C., & Gaffney, G. (2009). *Forms that work: Designing web forms for usability.* Boston, MA: Morgan Kaufmann.

CHAPTER

Privacy and the Citizen

5

Dianne Murray*, Karen Renaud†

Putting People Before Computers, Teddington, UK School of Computing Science, University of Glasgow, Glasgow, UK†*

"Relying on the government to protect your privacy is like asking a Peeping Tom to install your window blinds."
— John Perry Barlow

INTRODUCTION

The first step in addressing this question is to define the concept of privacy. Here we meet our first hurdle because arriving at a widely accepted definition is not a trivial task. The reality is that privacy means different things to different people (Kumaraguru & Cranor, 2005), and different cultures have different needs for privacy (Kaya & Weber, 2003). The Calcutt Committee in the United Kingdom adopted the following definition (Calcutt, 1990):

> *The right of the individual to be protected against intrusion into his personal life or affairs, or those of his family, by direct physical means or by publication of information.*

The right to privacy is an ancient concept, with mentions in the Bible[1] (Moore, 1984) and in classical Greece (Burke, 2000). The Hippocratic oath included the statement "I will not divulge, as reckoning that all such should be kept secret" (Keenan, 2005, p. 5). In 1361, King Edward passed laws that made eavesdropping punishable[2] (Michael, 1994).

What about the right of a twenty-first-century citizen to expect to have these privacy concepts respected by their government? Privacy is still important today, as evidenced by the following quote from Article 8 of the European Convention for the Protection of Human Rights and Fundamental Freedoms 1950 (Council of Europe, 1950), that states:

> *(1) Everyone has the right to respect for his private and family life, his home and his correspondence.*
> *(2) There shall be no interference by a public authority with the exercise of this right except as in accordance with the law and is necessary in a democratic society in the interests of national security, public safety or the economic well-being of the country, for the prevention of disorder or crime, for the protection of health of morals, or for the protection of the rights and freedoms of others.*

[1]But when you pray, go into your room, close the door and pray. (Matthew 6:6)
[2]Justices of the Peace Act, 1361 (Eng.), 34 Edw. 3, c. 1.

Table 5.1 Privacy Concepts as Identified by Privacy International

Information Privacy	*The protection of government records about individuals.*
Bodily Privacy	*Protection of our bodies (e.g., against cavity searches).*
Privacy of Communications	*Privacy of interpersonal communications such as email and telephone conversations.*
Territorial Privacy	*The right to be left in isolation.*

Privacy International (www.privacyinternational.org/article/overview-privacy) explores the concept of privacy in greater depth, and divides "privacy" into the concepts shown in Table 5.1.

In the last few years, the right to privacy has been eroded in a number of ways in many countries of the world. Some governments have a poor track record with respect to confidentiality. The UK government, for example, has an unenviable reputation of not preserving the confidentiality of citizens' information (Mathieson, 2007; Espiner, 2007; Harrison, 2008). Citizens' trust has been betrayed when data has been leaked to unauthorized individuals. This emphasizes citizens' responsibility to be aware of their right to privacy and their responsibility to ensure that they entrust their data only to trustworthy individuals or institutions.

It is important, at this stage, to understand the difference between privacy and confidentiality. Citizens often divulge their *private* and personal details to government agencies. The government has a responsibility to preserve the *confidentiality* of such data. So, governments can potentially violate a citizen's privacy by collecting data, either because citizens are forced to forgo their right to privacy (coercion) or because they collect data without their knowledge or consent (surveillance). Coercion does not have to be violent; in many cases it is manipulative rather than overtly aggressive. A citizen could be forced by necessity to divulge personal information in order to gain access to a service, such as voting or benefits. Surveillance is sometimes overt, but often covert (BBC, 2010; Martin, 2010). If the government agency leaks such data to unauthorized bodies, it is the *confidentiality* of the data that has been violated. In a nutshell, privacy is related to collection, and confidentiality to protection and preservation.

The second privacy concept relates to our bodies. Patients have to give consent before doctors are permitted to carry out any investigations on their bodies that accord with this privacy principle. Sometimes health professionals do not ask for permission. Unruh (2009) reports that newborns' DNA was collected without their parents' permission in Minnesota. The privacy of travelers is notoriously disregarded. Airline travelers are often presented with the choice between a full body scan, which reveals their body beneath their clothes, or a pat down by a security officer (Egan, 2011). Neither of these options respects the person's right to privacy, but such invasions are permitted by the laws of many countries, and accepted without reservation by most travelers.

A worrying trend is the use of biometrics within schools (Little Brother, 2006). This recording is often carried out to support fairly innocuous functions. It might be used to record attendance, or to manage the use of resources such as libraries. It is often sold to parents as a "faster" way of doing things, proving once again that one can sell anything that makes things more convenient (Rush, 2007). Thus the children's privacy is being invaded and their right thereto denied in the name of convenience for staff members. This collection and storage of underage biometrics seems to be happening in an unregulated fashion, with few guarantees about how long the biometric data will be kept, what other purposes it will be used for, or whether children, and their parents, are permitted to opt out.

Probably the most personal and intimate biometric is DNA. Some governments collect the DNA of their citizens, and often the citizens have no choice. The United Kingdom has over 5 million DNA samples, mostly collected when people are suspected of crime (Turvill, 2011). Russia plans to collect and store the DNA of criminals (Lekarev, 2011). There are grave concerns in the United Kingdom about the retention of innocents' and underage children's DNA. In Scotland, the DNA is destroyed if the person is not convicted but a landmark case in 2008 (BBC, 2009) required two innocent English men to appeal to the European Court of Human Rights to have their DNA removed from the database.

The third privacy concept relates to privacy of communication. Although these were previously considered sacrosanct, the events of September 11th in New York and the 7th of July in London have led to some governments wanting more access to personal communications. The United Kingdom and The Netherlands have argued for "the right balance between privacy and the needs of the law enforcement agencies in the light of the battle against terrorism" (van Buuren, 2001). In 2002, the European Union adopted the "Privacy and Electronic Communications Directive", allowing member countries to pass laws that permit them to retain information about all communications in the interests of national security or crime prevention and/or prosecution. The balance now appears to be skewed in favor of governments invading personal communications at will (Figure 5.1).

The final privacy concept relates to a person's right to be left in isolation, to be left alone. This right is impacted by the use of CCTV cameras in public spaces. The United Kingdom is somewhat notorious for having the most CCTV cameras carrying out surveillance on their citizens in public spaces (Johnston, 2006). Clearly UK residents do not have the right not to be photographed as they go about their business. It is ironic that a British writer, George Orwell, wrote about this kind of

FIGURE 5.1 Privacy of communications

(courtesy of Keagan Renaud).

surveillance in his book "1984". Concerns are being expressed by various people. Philip Johnston writes, "The individual citizen is in no position either to accept or reject surveillance. This heightens the sense that we may be developing a 'Big Brother' society" (Johnston, 2007) (Figure 5.2). Ian Pearson, speaking to the City IT and IT Security Forum, predicts a backlash against this widespread surveillance (Collins, 2008). At the other end of the spectrum is Switzerland, whose government actively defends their citizens' rights to privacy. Associated Press reported, in 2009, that the privacy watchdog in Switzerland was to sue Google for taking photos of their cities (Associated Press, 2009). Google also encountered widespread resistance in Germany (Evans, 2010).

FIGURE 5.2 Banksy painting on a wall in London

(courtesy of Gideon). (For color version of this figure, see the web version of this chapter)

Although one can spot a surveillance camera and thereby realize that one is being watched, governments are starting to use more secret ways of tracking citizens. Isikoff (2010) writes that Americans are being tracked by means of their mobile phones. Furthermore, this is carried out on a widespread scale, without the search warrants that would cover more traditional kinds of privacy intrusion.

The discussion thus far has looked at privacy in broad terms. We will now focus on the citizen's experience of privacy in terms of e-government (e-gov) systems. Research suggests that trust in e-gov builds on previously established trust in governments (Avgerou, Ganzaroli, Poulymenakou, & Reinhard, 2007). Trust in the institution of government is essential (Warkentin, Pavlou, & Rose,

2002) — hence, government web sites will not engender or improve trust levels. If governments have this trust, and this encourages citizens to start using e-gov systems they will have to ensure that such trust is maintained. Regrettable incidents such as those reported by Swabey (2008), Fricker (2008), and Gross (2006) make citizens very concerned about entrusting government agencies with their personal data.

Bélanger and Carter (2008) say, "If government agencies expect citizens to provide sensitive information and complete personal transactions online, they must acknowledge and enhance citizens' views concerning the credibility of e-government services." It is therefore imperative for e-gov web sites to respect the privacy of their citizens, and to be seen to do so.

PROTECTING PRIVACY

Privacy International enumerates four models of privacy protection:

- *Comprehensive Laws*: Countries pass a general law about the use and dissemination of personal information. This is usually overseen and enforced by a state-legitimized compliance body. This is the approach followed by countries within the European Union.
- *Sectoral Laws*: These are laws covering specific areas. For example, the United States has specific laws about video rental records.
- *Self-Regulation*: In this case, it is left to individual organizations to implement their own codes of practice and to police themselves. This is the approach applied in Japan and Singapore.
- *Technologies of Privacy*: In this case, the citizens take the protection of privacy into their own hands.

The United Kingdom has comprehensive laws about data protection, which try to cover all areas. Yet they fall short in protecting the public. For example, consider the widespread use of CCTV cameras in the United Kingdom. The Information Commissioner (Information Commissioner's Office, undated) states that organizations should have a retention policy. Its web site says: "They should only keep the images for as long as necessary to meet the purpose of recording them." This rather vague rule opens the way for organizations to argue a continuing need to retain footage much longer than is required for solving crime.

Even if laws do exist, citizens should self-regulate their personal data. The right to privacy can be measured by the extent to which citizens feel they have control over their own data. Do governments give citizens the right to control the personal data they disclose on e-gov web sites? We now consider the privacy policies governments publish on their web sites.

Government systems and privacy policies

Westin (1967) claimed that people naturally fall into three groups with respect to their attitude to privacy: fundamentalist, pragmatic, and unconcerned. Gandy (1995) has argued against these categories, saying that people's privacy concerns are formed primarily by their exposure to narratives about the potential or actual misuses of personal information. Whether people naturally fall into these categories, or whether they become more finely attuned to privacy over time, the fact is that citizens need to be able to explore their privacy options, and to make an informed decision about whether to use an e-gov site or not.

Table 5.2 Stated Governmental Privacy Policy

SCAN Principles	Canada	Australia	Scotland (EU)
Security *Show that an effort is made to protect personal information*	Not mentioned	Not mentioned	Mentions secure storage in database
Choice *Offering citizens a choice about how personal information is managed and used*	Purpose disclosed at time of data collection	Information shared only for stated purpose	Information managed by an outside contractor
Access *Citizens should be able to access and correct their personal information*	Yes	Yes	Yes
Notice *Citizens should be able to obtain information on how sites collect and use information*	Provided	Provided	Provided

What do governments say about how they protect citizens' privacy when using e-gov web sites? It is sadly true that many people do not even bother to read privacy policies (Vila, Greenstadt, & Molnar, 2003). However, those who do should be able to do so. We have chosen three governments to compare and contrast their stated privacy policies with respect to e-gov web sites, as shown in Table 5.2. These three countries were chosen because they fall into three distinct categories as classified by Privacy International based on surveillance levels (Privacy International, 2006). Canada was classified as "consistently upholding human rights standards," Australia as "failing to uphold safeguards," and the United Kingdom as implementing "endemic surveillance." (America also falls into the latter category, perhaps this is why the majority of Americans express privacy concerns [Hart-Teeter, 2001].)

The left-hand column enumerates those aspects that Kuzma (2010) suggests should be provided by all e-gov sites. Canada (www.canada.gc.ca/importantnotices.html), Australia (www.australia.gov.au/about/privacy-statement), and Scotland (www.scotland.gov.uk/Disclaimers) provide a snapshot of what ought to be provided. Other countries do not provide any easily accessible information about their privacy policies; examples are South Africa (www.gov.za), Ghana (www.ghana.gov.gh), and Guyana (www.gina.gov.gy).

Government use of physiological biometrics

A government may require their citizens to carry identity cards, and record their biometrics for storing on the identity card. Biometric data is undeniably personal.

Chapter 15, Biometrics explains the topic while this chapter discusses the use of biometric applications for physical and data access control, employee security management, and personal verification; it is evident that such technology is no longer used solely for law enforcement purposes but is increasingly common in the public domain and used more frequently now by the general public. As the impact that usability can have on the performance and reliability of biometric devices grows, and Smart card, iris recognition, and radiofrequency identification (RFID) technologies improve, we urgently need to address the indisputable privacy, security, and confidentiality dangers such improvements also create.

Would a government allow citizens to opt out? If not, what measures and controls would be implemented to ensure that this coerced suspension of the right to privacy is not betrayed?

We carried out an informal survey on a randomly chosen selection of countries that use biometrics, and the results are shown in Table 5.3. Issues identified range from the loss of voter anonymity with

Table 5.3 Governments' Use of Physiological Biometrics

Country	Biometrics Used	Purpose	Opt Out Allowed?	Documented Problems
Armenia	Fingerprints	Passport ID card	No	Discrimination against people who do not hold legitimate passport.
Brazil	Fingerprints	ID card Voting	No	Voting is compulsory and can be identified and checked through digital ID card.
Bulgaria	Fingerprints Facial measurements	Passport	No	IT systems suffer overload problems.
Canada	Iris scan	Airport border control	Yes	
Italy	Fingerprints	Passport ID card Residence permit	No	Concerns amongst the Roma population as children are fingerprinted (Kington, 2008).
Japan	Fingerprint	Border control	No	Two South Korean women arrested on suspicion of illegally entering Japan, bypassing cutting-edge fingerprint-reading machines by using special tape bearing the fingerprints (Mah, 2009).
Malaysia	Fingerprint	Passport with RFID	No	First country to introduce biometric passports (1998).
The Netherlands	Fingerprints	Passport ID cards	Mandatory	Expensive equipment means that only the home country can issue new passports, discriminating against expatriates.
Philippines	Fingerprints	Passport Voting	No	Since a passport is more expensive, the poorest may be discriminated against.
South Africa	Fingerprints	Passport Smart card (social security; potential monitoring of HIV/AIDs treatment)	No	Data creep/leakage on 5-7 year lifespan of Smart card. Perceived "immaturity" of technology and legislation.

digital ID cards for mandatory voting to the problems encountered with complex technology and the inventive ways that it can be fooled. The opportunity for opt-out is rare and, in some countries, the collection of biometric data is mandatory and a prerequisite to service provision.

TRUST

It is important that citizens be able to trust their government. Carter and Bélanger (2005) report "trustability" as another important indicator of usage of e-gov sites. If such trust is eroded, perhaps because personal data has been leaked by an e-gov site, it could affect more than just usage of that system. Citizens might well vote for another government at the next election. How governments treat and respect citizens' personal data will play a role in how people feel about the government.

Trust in government

Governments do not want people to consider disclosing their data too risky. A study (Cullen, 2011) comparing New Zealand and Japanese citizens' concepts of information privacy and trust in their government indicated that trust levels do differ, with Japanese citizens demonstrating lower levels of trust, but with both knowing little about national privacy legislation, and citizens of both states admitting to concerns about modern privacy practices. Sandman claims that perceived risk depends on the real extent of the hazard being amplified by the measure of outrage perceived by each individual (Sandman, 1987). When data is lost through carelessness one can expect a high level of outrage. When this happens regularly, the hazard will be perceived to be high.

In the foreword to a report on the changing concept of *identity* in an information society (Rannenberg, Royer, & Deuker, 2009), Viviane Reding (Member of the European Commission Responsible for Information Society and Media at the time) opens with a telling depiction of the issue of trust between citizen and government:

> *Given the "... massive amounts of personal data being generated, collected, analyzed and processed, exchanged, recombined, and stored sometimes for a life-time or more. The contours of the digital age have rapidly taken shape and with this, the creation and management of individual identity has emerged as one of the central challenges in digital life. Citizens look for value in the activities they do on the Internet. Therefore, they want to be able to trust the technology and services provided and the actors behind it."*

Chapter 1, A Brief History of User Experience in Government Systems, gives more details of the development of European Union policies aimed at reducing the "digital divide" and fostering Europe's IT capabilities to build an effective and efficient digitally enhanced Information Society. It is, however, only relatively recently that the potentially damaging side effects in terms of loss of personal freedoms, hard-won rights, and control over one's own personal data have been fully recognized.

Against the background of the rapid growth of an Information Society and the quality of a person's future digital life, Reding identified the need for people to have confidence in safeguards that provide suitable protection against malicious behavior and that effectively foster accountability and liability for both personal dignity and legitimate business interests. Such a "rule of law in digital space" would require a strong privacy protecting identity management framework and associated authentication mechanisms to be developed. This was what was proposed in the policy framework precursor to the EU's current *Digital Agenda for Europe* (www.ec.europa.eu/information_society/digital-agenda/index_en.htm), the *i2010 — A European Information Society for growth and employment* (www.ec.europa.eu/information_society/eeurope/i2010/index_en.htm). Notably, it identified security, trust, and privacy as one of the four major challenges to be met in order to attain digital convergence and, equally notably, one of the key drivers identified was that of usability. Reding did, however, raise a cautionary note: "There is no single 'silver bullet' solution to information identity risks."

As indicated in Table 5.1, it seems as if the four tenets described are regularly discounted by governments and corporations, with the citizens of some countries having their rights respected more than others. One country that has managed well the issue of trust and its effective implementation at the heart of government services is Canada (Media Awareness Network, undated); another is Australia with the creation of a new Office of the Australian Information Commissioner (Australian Government, undated); while New Zealand's stated policy was assessed quite early on and its future needs articulated by democracy researchers (Cullen & Houghton, 2000):

> *The Vision Statement, "Electronic Government in New Zealand," issued by the government in October 1996 extends the notion of access and accountability to cover all government services in which the government interacts with an individual in the provision of information, services, feedback, and a wide range of intra-governmental networks. The vision is that "e-government will harness people and technology to revolutionize the delivery of government services to New Zealanders. The new services will be tailored, inexpensive, easy to use, personal and friendly.*

The call was for the introduction of standards for use of the Web across all New Zealand government agencies in order to address the concerns raised by those authors' studies:

> *The independent evaluation of government agency sites has shown some major areas of concern in the performance of the sites overall:*
>
> - *Lack of a clear purpose for government web sites, and a failure to communicate this purpose to users;*
> - *Lack of good meta-data;*
> - *Lack of good contacts for feedback and update of information;*
> - *Statements about, and adequate provision for, confidentiality and privacy of personal data, statements of liability, and copyright;*
> - *Access for disabled users; and*
> - *Availability of publications in both electronic and print formats.*
>
> *These are key points for government web designers to bear in mind and issues that someone within government needs to take responsibility for overall.*

One government that has singularly failed to do so is South Africa (Peekhaus, 2011). Recently published research into the state of play in international e-gov has surveyed the scene *vis-a-vis* public information access (Relly, 2010) and identified the best and worst of situations. The country that is deemed by many indices to be foremost in protecting its citizens' rights and privacy and that takes top position in a table of the "Top 20 countries in e-government development" (UN, 2010) is that of South Korea, but it is a rare beacon. Is it then surprising that people mistrust government intentions and fail to demonstrate much trust in manifestations of e-gov as evinced by web sites, one-stop shop kiosks, Web portals, and information repositories?

Trust and health

In some countries, the health system is government run, and in that case the privacy of health-related data is in the government's remit. In this chapter, we are not exploring health data, but rather the kinds of personal data that all countries store about their citizens. This is the case in the United Kingdom. Unfortunately, there is much evidence that this information is not being treated with the respect it deserves (Big Brother Watch, 2011). Health data has also been lost in the United States (Fogarty, 2011) and Canada (Canadian Press, 2009). The Danish government, on the other hand, gathers and stores extensive data about their citizens including health data, but there are signs that they are concerned enough about privacy to protect this data (Frank, 2000).

Some useful investigations into attitudes toward seeking health advice online, with its necessary levels of self-disclosure (Sillence, Briggs, Harris, & Fishwick, 2007), posited "a staged model of trust in which mistrust or rejection of web sites is based on design factors and trust or selection of web sites is based on content factors such as source credibility and personalization." From this, the researchers derived design implications or proposed guidelines for creating much more trustworthy health web sites. In addition to online interactions that disclose and discuss highly personal health details — which are expected to become more and more common — people can now expect that some of their personal health care will be increasingly provided in the form of assistive technologies (Doukas et al., 2011) where ubiquitous and pervasive sensor devices monitor, collect, and analyze personal health data, usually of older, housebound citizens.

One further aspect of potential privacy problems with government health data management is the whole issue of Electronic Patient Records (EPR). Such EPRs have a vast potential for misuse and for accountability mismanagement — extensively highlighted in many health-related publications — but the level of knowledge and awareness of the general public is poor. The views of younger people, however, are engagingly illustrated in a recent report from the United Kingdom's Royal Academy of Engineering (2010), which sampled their view on privacy and health data sharing:

> *Young people have significant concerns regarding EPRs. These arise due to the perceived inherent weaknesses of an EPR system, including both the robustness (or not) of the technology and the potential errors that will be made by the users. Young people noticed that this could lead to incorrect data within a patient's record, data loss (massive or individual), or the data reaching the "wrong hands". The consequences were deemed to be very serious and include the improper treatment of patients, fundamental breaches in privacy, the misuse and inappropriate exploitation of the data, prejudice, and discrimination.*
>
> *The "wrong hands" were those organisations or individuals that young people felt had "no right" to the data, irrespective of whether they had achieved "official" access (i.e., by the EPR regulators) or by using improper methods such as hacking or bribing the system users. The "wrong hands" included commercial companies, marketing and advertising agencies, insurance companies, employers or potential employers, and the media. Young people frequently mentioned that parents should not automatically have access to their records, while adults also considered the Government to be the "wrong hands".*

Next steps for e-gov

In the last few years, there has been an incredible growth in the number of people who use social networking web sites. Government is often a few steps behind industry, but it generally adopts technologies and techniques that clearly work in industry. Hence we can expect government to start utilizing social networking techniques extensively in the very near future as discussed in Chapter 2, Government 2.0.

Recent publications show that studies and guidance on how to achieve this are well underway in the United Kingdom (House of Lords, 2011; Cabinet Office, 2010; COI, 2009), and in North America (House of Tweets, United States Government Accountability Office). Hassani (2010) lists the top government social networking sites. Howard (2010) argues that government works better when they utilize social networking. In the United Kingdom, significant investment has been made into the uptake of social media methods in order to catch benefit frauds (Jupp, 2009; Storrar, 2011; BBC, 2010). Gomez (2010), on the other hand, expresses grave reservations about the privacy implications of government use of social networking to monitor citizens.

The other technique that government is bound to use, sooner or later, is recommender technology. Iskold (2007) enumerates four kinds of recommender approach used in industry:

- Personalized recommendation — based on your previous purchases
- Social recommendation — based on the purchases of others with similar purchases
- Item recommendation — items linked to the item you are viewing
- A hybrid approach based on the above.

All of these are based on information gathered from previous interactions with the web site. It would be trivial for governments to collect the usage data from all their various e-gov sites, collate such data, and use it not to recommend, but to monitor and police citizens.

If governments betray their citizens' trust in this way, it could have domino effects on their use of other, essential, e-gov sites. It would be best for governments to ensure that if they do go down this route, they guarantee that the privacy of their citizens is respected, and assured.

In the near future

The speed of development and change in immersive artificial realities, in gaming, in online social communications, and in virtual lives means that, for many in the digital generation, the concept of identity has become fluid and multiple. In a number of vignettes (Rannenberg, Royer, & Deuker, 2009), researchers describe the experiences and lives a new "digerati" may have and identify problematic issues that may arise. Many of these are related to privacy, digital rights, transparency, and trust while others focus on legal aspects, forensic implications, and Identity Rights Management (IRM) problems that stem from supporting and emerging technologies such as biometrics and RFID, Ambient Intelligence, and ubicomp. Questions to do with the identity and privacy rights — to say nothing of the democratic rights — of partial identities or "Virtual Persons" such as avatars, robots, and intelligent agents will come to the fore. Hertzum et al. (2002) have investigated ways in which to build user trust in virtual agents such as suggestions that agents be recommended by independent third parties rather than by being trusted simply at face value.

We have, already, in 2011, seen a furor over pseudonyms created by the insensitive handling of identities when Google+ came into being; the so-called "Nymwars" (Carmody, 2011). Google+ did not believe that people should be allowed to use pseudonyms. The reason people are concerned about using their own names is because this creates a tangible and undeniable link between their behaviors and their identity, which could easily come back to haunt them in later years. The use of pseudonyms is a widely accepted and established practice in publishing: Mary Ann Evans published as George Eliot, and Eric Blair wrote as George Orwell. One has to wonder why it is so important for Google to force people to use their real names and why the company was so resistant to a policy change.

Such challenges are likely to be exacerbated by extended use and application of automatic furore techniques and technologies based on data mining and modeling of individual user behaviors. Such techniques are now common in the plethora of sophisticated recommender systems that exist in commercial enterprises. Consider the examples given earlier and think about Amazon's recommendations of what you might like, based on your past purchasing and browsing behavior, applied to the personal data a person must entrust to governmental agencies as part of the shared contract of citizenhood. Then consider how difficult it has been made to opt-out of such pervasive targeted and personalized behavioral advertising (Leon et al., 2011; Loftus, 2011) despite long-standing studies and investigations into the practice (TRUSTe, 2009). What will this mean for a citizen's trust in a governmental data repository that may be shared between many departments or suborned into use as a resource for profiling terrorism suspects, investigating social security or tax fraud, or keeping track of deviant behavior (Birrer, 2005; McCarthy & Yates, 2010)? How can identity, privacy, and an individual's ownership of personal data be not just *managed*, openly *maintained*, and *safeguarded*, but also be made resistant to harvesting, misuse, and manipulation? In other words, how can a citizen's trust in government, with its oversight of individual identity, be fostered (Figure 5.3)?

DESIGNING FOR USER EXPERIENCE

Carter and Bélanger (2005) found that ease of use was one of the primary factors influencing people's intention to use e-gov web sites. Governments are clearly aware of this. The US government has a special site for designers of government web sites (www.howto.gov/web-content) that provides advice about how to design usable web sites. It advises focusing on the citizen's goals, on the agency's goals and how the web site can be used to meet such goals, and on user-centered design. It also talks about the importance of setting key performance measures so that particular usability aspects can be measured. Success should be measured from the customer's perspective, and not merely from the agency's point of view. One of the most frequently requested pages on this web site is related to privacy requirements of web sites, so clearly this issue is important to both developers and citizens. There are now numerous other initiatives — many of which are discussed in other chapters — including the important US Department of Health and Human Services' (HHS's) "Research-Based Web Design and Usability Guidelines" (www.usability.gov/guidelines).

Other governments provide similar guidelines, aggregated together (www.usabilitygeek.com/official-usability-web-site-guidelines-of-governments-from-around-the-world/), or as shown in Table 5.4 where some are listed. A recent book, *Global Usability*, also comprehensively covers many aspects from an international perspective (Douglas & Liu, 2011).

FIGURE 5.3 The right to be left alone

(courtesy of Keagan Renaud).

Table 5.4 A Selection of Individual Government's Usability and Accessibility Guidance Resources

Accessibility features (Canada)	www.servicecanada.gc.ca/eng/common/acc_help.shtml#accfsc
Enabling accountability (South Korea)	Wong & Welch. Does E-Government Promote Accountability? www.wiki.dbast.com/images/4/49/Does_E-Government_Promote_Accountability.pdf
Feedback (Canada)	www.canada.gc.ca/comments-commentaires/think-pensez-eng.html
Good practice (Denmark)	Guidelines for Internet Publishing: www.netsteder.dk/publ/index.html
Good web site design (UK)	Quality Framework for UK Government website Design: What is a good government web site? www.rightdynamic.com/casestudy_4.html
Modernization and improving effectiveness (USA)	TooManywebsites.gov: www.whitehouse.gov/blog/2011/06/13/toomanywebsitesgov
Privacy (Sweden)	Swedish National Guidelines for Public Sector web sites: http://www.eutveckling.se/static/doc/swedish-guidelines-public-sector-websites.pdf

The crucial point is succinctly made by the authors of a handbook commissioned by United Kingdom Cabinet Office (2003), which counsels how to incorporate users' needs into the design process:

> *When considering user-centred design, it is important to remember that there is no single kind of user. Therefore, different levels of Internet experience, interest in the subject matter and individual need for services should be taken into consideration when planning a good government web site.*

It is heartening to see that the Swedish guidelines specifically address privacy concerns, but concerning that the others do not.

SUCCESS FACTORS

The key recommendation to all citizens must be to take steps to enforce their right to privacy. It may be the case that a current government is trustworthy but governments change, and some governments do not have the best interests of their citizens in mind. Even if they do, Governments can easily draw the wrong conclusions about people based on collected data, even if they do indeed have the best intentions.

In order for e-gov to retain the trust of citizens, and to encourage the use of e-gov web sites, the following are the minimum steps to take:

- Display a link to your privacy policy on all pages of all government web sites.
- Explain what data is being collected, the purpose for which it is being collected, and how people can see such data and correct it.
- Allow citizens to change data that is incorrect, and do not erect bureaucratic barriers to impede this.
- Take stringent steps to preserve the confidentiality of any and all personal data that citizens divulge to government agencies and web sites.
- Explain how the data is secured in your privacy policy.
- Ensure that all government staff are well briefed in the requirements of confidentiality, and that deliberate leakages lead to dismissals.
- Scrutinize data-handling processes within the government agencies to ensure that accidental leakage of information is made extremely unlikely.

The warning to e-gov developers must be that trust, once lost, is very hard to regain. By following these guidelines, it might be possible to regain the trust of citizens that is being eroded by ever more privacy invasive governmental practices.

SUMMARY

Benjamin Franklin is thought to have said, "They who can give up essential liberty to gain a little temporary safety deserve neither liberty nor safety."* The governments of the twenty-first century often err on the side of too much control, too much surveillance, and too little respect for the personal privacy of

*This statement first appeared in a letter from the Pennsylvania Assembly, dated November 11, 1755, to the Governor of Pennsylvania.

FIGURE 5.4 The transient nature of privacy

(courtesy of Alan Cleaver). (For color version of this figure, see the web version of this chapter)

their citizens. It ill behooves us to give up that which, once lost, cannot be regained. The citizen needs to stand up for the ancient and crucial right to be his/her own person. As Ronald Reagan famously said, "Government's first duty is to protect the people, not run their lives." In protecting the people in a post-9/11 era, the average citizen should keep reminding the government of the essential balance expressed in these wise words (Figure 5.4).

References

Associated Press. (2009, November 13). Privacy watchdog to sue Google over street view. *Fox News*, Retrieved 11 November 2011 from www.foxnews.com/scitech/2009/11/13/privacy-watchdog-sue-google-street-view/

Australian Government. (undated). *Protecting information rights—advancing information privacy.* Retrieved 15 November 2011 from http://www.oaic.gov.au/privacy-portal/index.html

Avgerou, C., Ganzaroli, A., Poulymenakou, A., & Reinhard, N. (2007). ICT and citizens' trust in government: Lessons from electronic voting in Brazil. In *Proceedings of the 9th International Conference on Social Implications of Computers in Developing Countries, São Paulo, Brazil, May.*

BBC. (2009, February 6). Warning over "surveillance state." *BBC News*, Retrieved 11 November 2011 from news.bbc.co.uk/1/hi/uk_politics/7872425.stm

BBC. (2010, August 10). Benefit fraud. Cameron defends use of credit rate firms. *BBC News*, Retrieved 12 November 2011 from www.bbc.co.uk/news/uk-10922261

Bélanger, F., & Carter, L. (2008). Trust and risk in e-government adoption. *The Journal of Strategic Information Systems*, *17*(2), 165–176.

Big Brother Watch. NHS breaches of data protection law. (2011). Retrieved 15 November 2011 from http://www.bigbrotherwatch.org.uk/files/NHS_Breaches_Data_Protection.pdf

Birrer, F. J. (2005). Data mining to combat terrorism and the roots of privacy concerns. *Ethics and Information Technology*, (7), 211–220.

Burke, S. (2000). Delos: Investigating the notion of privacy within the ancient Greek house. PhD Thesis. Retrieved 21 January 2012 from https://lra.le.ac.uk/handle/2381/8947

Cabinet Office, Behavioural Insights Team. (2010). *Behavioural insights: Annual update 2010–11*. London: HMSO.

Cabinet Office, Office of the e-Envoy. Quality framework for UK government website design: Usability issues for government websites. (2003). Retrieved 15 November 2011 from http://www.umic.pt/images/stories/publicacoes/quality_framework_uk.pdf

Calcutt, D. (1990). *Report of the committee on privacy and related matters*. Chairman David Calcutt QC, 1990, Cmnd. 1102. London: HMSO.

Canadian Press. Ontario's privacy commissioner probing missing health records in Durham region. (2009, December 23). Retrieved 15 November 2011 from http://www.cumberlandnewsnow.com/Technologies/2009-12-23/article-816075/Ontarios-privacy-commissioner-probing-missing-health-records-in-Durham-Region/1

Carmody, T. (2011, July 26). Google+ identity crisis: What's at stake with real names and privacy? *Wired*, Retrieved 13 November 2011 from www.wired.com/epicenter/2011/07/google-plus-user-names/

Carter, L., & Bélanger, F. (2005). The utilization of e-government services: citizen trust, innovation and acceptance factors. *Information Systems Journal*, *15*(1), 5–25.

Central Office of Information. (2009). Communications and behaviour change. Retrieved 21 January 2012 from http://coi.gov.uk/documents/commongood/commongood-behaviourchange.pdf

Collins, T. (2008, November 9). *IT suppliers at risk of backlash as public reject surveillance state*. Retrieved 11 November 2011 from www.computerweekly.com/Articles/2008/11/10/233272/IT-suppliers-at-risk-of-backlash-as-public-reject-surveillance.htm

Council of Europe. Convention for the protection of human rights and fundamental freedoms, (ETS No: 005) open for signature. (1950). November 4, 1950, entry into force September 3, conventions.coe.int/Treaty/EN/cadreprincipal.htm

Cullen, R. (2011). Privacy and personal information held by government: A comparative study, Japan and New Zealand. In S. Assar, I. Boughzala & I. Boydens (Eds.), *Practical studies in e-government: Best practices from around the world*. New York, NY: Springer.

Cullen, R., & Houghton, C. (2000). Democracy online: An assessment of New Zealand government web sites. *Government Information Quarterly*, *17*(3), 243–267.

Douglas, I., & Liu, Z. (Eds.), (2011). *Global usability*. New York, NY: Springer.

Doukas, C., et al. (2011). Digital cities of the future: Extending @home assistive technologies for the elderly and the disabled. *Telematics and Informatics*, (28), 176–190.

Egan, K. (2011, October 5). Column: Full-body search at airport leaves woman in tears. *Ottawa Citizen*, Retrieved 11 November 2011 from www.ottawacitizen.com/health/Column+Full+body+search+airport+leaves+woman+tears/5502469/story.html

Espiner, T. (2007, December 18). *U.K. government loses data on driving-test candidates*. Retrieved 11 November 2011 from www.news.cnet.com/U.K.-government-loses-data-on-driving-test-candidates/2100-1029_3-6223292.html

Evans, S. (2010, September 20). *Wary Germans say no to Google cameras*. Retrieved 15 November 2011 from http://www.bbc.co.uk/news/world-europe-11371557

Fogarty, K. (2011, March 15). *Insurer's data loss deserves a drastic punishment.* Retrieved 15 November 2011 from http://www.itworld.com/legal/140208/health-net-data-breach-far-worse-others-drew-heavy-fines

Frank, L. (2000). When an entire country is a cohort. *Science*, (287), 5462, 2398–2399.

Fricker, M. (2008, October 14). MoD loses data on up to 1.7m people who wanted to join the armed forces. *Mirror*, Retrieved 8 November 2011 from www.mirror.co.uk/news-old/top-stories/2008/10/14/mod-loses-data-on-up-to-1-7m-people-who-wanted-to-join-the-armed-forces-115875-20801745/

Gandy, O. H. (Jr)., (1995). The role of theory in the policy process. A response to professor Westin. In C. Firestone & J. Schement (Eds.), *Toward an information bill of rights and responsibilities* (pp. 99–106). Washington DC: The Aspen Institute Communications and Society Program.

Gomez, D. (2010, October 13). Government uses social networking to infiltrate people's lives. *TG Daily*, Retrieved 8 November 2011 from www.tgdaily.com/opinion-features/52013-government-uses-social-networking-to-infiltrate-peoples-lives

Gross, G. (2006, May 22). US agency loses data containing 26 million Ids. *IT World Canada*, Retrieved 8 November 2011 from www.itworldcanada.com/news/us-agency-loses-data-containing-26-million-ids/01396

Harrison, D. (2008, January 6). Government's record year of data loss. *Daily Telegraph*, Retrieved 8 November 2011 from www.telegraph.co.uk/news/politics/1574687/Governments-record-year-of-data-loss.html

Hart-Teeter survey reported in e-government: The Next American Revolution. The council for excellence in government, February. (2001). Retrieved 8 November 2011 from excelgov.org/usermedia/images/uploads/PDFs/bpnt4c.pdf

Hassani, S. (2010, January 27). The top 6 government social networks. *OhMyGov*, Retrieved 8 November 2011 from ohmygov.com/blogs/general_news/archive/2010/01/27/The-top-6-government-social-networks.aspx

Hertzum, M., et al. (2002). Trust in information sources: seeking information from people, documents, and virtual agents. *Interacting with Computers*, (14), 575–599.

House of Lords, Science and Technology Select Committee. (2011). 2nd Report of session 2010–12. In *Behaviour change*. London: HMSO.

Howard, A. (2010, May 10). 5 Ways government works better with social media. *Mashable Social Media*, Retrieved 8 November 2011 from mashable.com/2010/05/10/social-media-government/

Information Commissioner's Office. (Undated). *CCTV—guide for the public*. Retrieved 15 November 2011 from http://www.ico.gov.uk/for_the_public/topic_specific_guides/cctv.aspx

Isikoff, J. (2010, Feburary 18). The snitch in your pocket. *Newsweek Magazine*, Retrieved 8 November 2011 from www.thedailybeast.com/newsweek/2010/02/18/the-snitch-in-your-pocket.html

Iskold, A. (2007). The art, science and business of recommendation engines. *ReadWriteWeb*, Retrieved 12 November 2011 from www.readwriteweb.com/archives/recommendation_engines.php

Johnston, P. (2006, November 2). Britain: the most spied on nation in the world. *Daily Telegraph*, Retrieved 8 November 2011 from www.telegraph.co.uk/news/uknews/1533054/Britain-the-most-spied-on-nation-in-the-world.html

Johnston, P. (2007, March 27). Big Brother is harming you, warns report. *Daily Telegraph*, Retrieved 8 November 2011 from www.telegraph.co.uk/news/uknews/1546764/Big-Brother-is-harming-you-warns-report.html

Jupp, R. (2009, March 24). Fraud teams use facebook to catch benefit cheats. *ChronicleLive.co.uk*, Retrieved 12 November 2011 from www.chroniclelive.co.uk/north-east-news/evening-chronicle-news/2009/03/24/fraud-teams-use-facebook-to-catch-benefit-cheats-72703-23221169/

Kaya, N., & Weber, M. J. (2003). Cross-cultural differences in the perception of crowding and privacy regulation: American and Turkish students. *Journal of Environmental Psychology*, *23*(3), 301–309.

Keenan, K. M. (2005). *Invasion of Privacy: A Reference Handbook.* Santa Barbara, CF: ABC-CLIO Ltd.

Kington, T. (2008, June 27). Unicef among critics of Italian plan to fingerprint Roma children. *The Guardian*, Retrieved 13 November 2011 from www.guardian.co.uk/world/2008/jun/27/race.italy

Kumaraguru, P., & Cranor, L. F. (2005). *Privacy indexes: A survey of Westin's studies.* Technical Report CMU-ISRI-05-138.pdf. Institute for Software Research International. Pittsburgh: Carnegie Mellon University.

Kuzma, J. (2010). An examination of privacy policies of US Government Senate web sites. *Electronic Government, an International Journal*, *3*(7), 270–280.

Lekarev, P. (2011, October 19). Russia to create severe offenders DNA database. *The Voice of Russia*, Retrieved 12 November 2011 from english.ruvr.ru/radio_broadcast/25950828/58992992.html

Leon, P. G., Ur, B., Balebako, R., Faith Cranor, L., Shay, R., & Yang Wang, Y. (2011). *Why Johnny can't opt out: A usability evaluation of tools to limit online behavioral advertising*. Technical Reports: Cmu-Cylab-11-017. Pittsburgh: Carnegie Mellon University.

Little Brother. (2006). Alarming rise of children's ID databases and biometrics in schools. *IndyMedia UK*, Retrieved 12 November 2011 from www.indymedia.org.uk/en/2006/08/348865.html

Loftus, T. (2011). Study: usability issues plague tools that limit online behavioral advertising. *The Wall Street Journal*, Retrieved 11 November 2011 from blogs.wsj.com/digits/2011/10/31/study-usability-issues-plague-tools-that-limit-online-behavioral-advertising/?mod=WSJBlog&utm_source=twitterfeed&utm_medium=twitter

Mah, P. (2009, December 9). Fierce CIO tech watch. *Woman Foils Security to Enter Japan*, Retrieved 13 November 2011 from www.fiercecio.com/techwatch/story/woman-foils-fingerprint-security-enter-japan/2009-12-08

Martin, A. (2010). ABC news video—Whistleblowers expose massive government violations of privacy. *Examiner.com*, Retrieved 11 November 2011 from www.examiner.com/conservative-in-national/abc-news-video-whistleblowers-expose-massive-government-violations-of-privacy#ixzz1baZiQCv6

Mathieson, S. A. (2007, November 20). UK government loses data on 25 million Britons. *Computer Weekly*, Retrieved 11 November 2011 from www.computerweekly.com/Articles/2007/11/20/228216/UK-government-loses-data-on-25-million-Britons.htm

McCarthy, L., & Yates, D. (2010). The use of cookies in federal agency web sites: Privacy and recordkeeping issues. *Government Information Quarterly*, (27), 231–237.

Media Awareness Network. (undated). Canadian Privacy Legislation. Retrived 15 November 2011 from http://www.media-awareness.ca/english/issues/privacy/canadian_legislation_privacy.cfm

Michael, J. (1994). *Privacy and human rights*. New York, NY: UNESCO.

Moore, B. (1984). *Privacy: Studies in social and cultural history*. Armonk, NY: M. E. Sharpe.

Peekhaus, W. (2011). Biowatch South Africa and the challenges in enforcing its constitutional right to access to information. *Government Information Quarterly*, (28), 542–552.

Privacy International. National privacy ranking 2006—European Union and leading surveillance societies. (2006). Retrieved 15 November 2011 from https://www.privacyinternational.org/survey/phr2005/phrtable.pdf

Rannenberg, K., Royer, D., & Deuker, A. (Eds.), (2009). *The future of identity in the information society: Challenges and opportunities*. Berlin: Springer-Verlag.

Relly, J. E. (2010). A study of e-government and political indicators in developing nations with and without access-to-information laws. In C. E. Reddick (Ed.), *Comparative e-government*.

Royal Academy of Engineering. Privacy and prejudice: Young people's views on the development and use of electronic patient records. (2010). Retrieved 13 November 2011 from www.raeng.org.uk/societygov/public_engagement/current_issues/electronic_patient_records.htm

Rush, A. J. (2007). STAR*D: What have we learned. *The American Journal of Psychiatry*, *2*(164), 201–204.

Sandman, P. M. (1987). Risk communication: Facing public outrage. *Environmental Protection Journal*, November 13, 21–22.

Sillence, E., Briggs, P., Harris, P., & Fishwick, L. (2007). Health Websites that people can trust—The case of hypertension. *Interacting with Computers*, (19), 32–42.

Storrar, K. (2011, February 22). Facebook wedding photos catches out benefit cheats. *Mirror*, Retrieved 12 November 2011 from www.mirror.co.uk/news/top-stories/2011/02/22/facebook-wedding-photos-catches-out-benefits-cheat-115875-22940340/

Swabey, P. (2008, August 22). Government contractor loses data on entire UK prison population. *Information Age*, Retrieved 8 November 2011 from www.information-age.com/channels/security-and-continuity/news/637266/government-contractor-loses-data-on-entire-uk-prison-population.thtml

TRUSTe. (2009). Online behavioral advertising: A checklist of practices that impact consumer trust. *TechRepublic*, Retrieved 8 November 2011 from www.techrepublic.com/whitepapers/online-behavioral-advertising-a-checklist-of-practices-that-impact-consumer-trust/1115625

Turvill, W. (2011, October 25). DNA data—A political party's nightmare. *Huff Post Politics*, Retrieved 12 November 2011 from www.huffingtonpost.co.uk/william-turvill/post_2570_b_1029943.html

United Nations Department of Economic and Social Affairs. (2010). *e-government survey 2010*. New York: United Nations.

Unruh, B. (2009, March 12). Parents sue state over babies' DNA. Minnesota accused of depriving newborns "of lawful privacy rights." *WorldNetDaily*, Retrieved 8 November 2011 from www.wnd.com/?pageId=91520

van Buuren, J. (2001, October 17). Telecommunication council wants new investigation into privacy rules. *Heise Online*, Retrieved 8 November 2011 from www.heise.de/tp/artikel/9/9838/1.html

Vila, T., Greenstadt, R., & Molnar, D. (2003). Why we can't be bothered to read privacy policies: models of privacy economics as a lemons market. In *Proceedings of the 5th international conference on Electronic commerce (ICEC '03)*. New York, NY: ACM.

Warkentin, D. G., Pavlou, P. A., & Rose, G. M. (2002). Encouraging citizen adoption of e-government by building trust. *Electronic Markets, 12*(3), 157–162.

Westin, A. F. (1967). *Privacy and freedom*. New York, NY: Atheneum.

Further reading

Bozdag, E., & Timmermans, J. (2011). Values in the filter bubble: Ethics of personalization algorithms in cloud computing. In *Proceedings of the 13th IFIP TC13 conference on human-computer interaction (interact), workshop on values in design – building bridges between HCI, RE and Ethics, Lisbon, Portugal*.

Dempsey, J. X., Anderson, P., & Schwartz, A. (2011). Privacy and e-government: a report to the United Nations department of economic and social affairs as background for the *world public sector report: E-government. Center for Democracy and Technology*, Retrieved 8 November 2011 from www.internetpolicy.net/privacy/20030523cdt.pdf

Etzioni, A. (1999). *The limits of privacy*. New York, NY: Basic Books.

Garfinkel, S. (2000). *Database nation. The death of privacy in the 21st century*. Sebastopol, CA: O'Reilly.

Kizza, J. M. (2010). *Ethical and social issues in the information age* (4th ed.). Berlin: Springer-Verlag.

Rosen, J. (2000). *The unwanted gaze. The destruction of privacy in America*. New York, NY: Random House.

Slobogin, C. (2007). *Privacy at risk. The new government surveillance and the fourth amendment*. Chicago, IL: The University of Chicago Press.

Solove, D. J. (2005). *A taxonomy of privacy*. George Washington University Public Law Research Paper No. 129. 2005. Retrieved 8 November 2011 from papers.ssrn.com/sol3/papers.cfm?abstract_id=667622

Westin, A. (1967). *Privacy and freedom*. New York, NY: Atheneum.

Wong, W., & Welch, E. (date unknown). Does e-government promote accountability? A comparative analysis of website openness and government accountability. Retrieved 13 November 2011 from www.wiki.dbast.com/images/4/49/Does_E-Government_Promote_Accountability.pdf

3TU. Centre for Ethics and Technology. A EU-sponsored Centre of Excellence in The Netherlands, studying the ethics and philosophy of new technologies. www.ethicsandtechnology.eu/about/

SECTION

Internal Systems

II

"Simplicity is the ultimate sophistication."
— Leonardo da Vinci

This section illustrates some of the usability issues that are unique to government systems whose users are inside the government. The section has four chapters:

- *Chapter 6*, Usability in Defense Systems: Examples from Aviation
- *Chapter 7*, Emergency Response in Simulated Terrorist Attacks: Usability Lessons Learned
- *Chapter 8*, National Critical Infrastructures
- *Chapter 9*, Legislative Drafting Systems

The first three deal with systems for managing unpredictable conditions: military aviation, terrorist attacks, and disruptions to critical infrastructures such as transportation and communications. The fourth deals with systems that support long-established roles and procedures that are very resistant to change, even when that change could improve usability.

- In Chapter 6, **Mark Maybury** (USA) describes the rich, challenging, and critical environment for usability that defense systems provide. As Chapter 1, A Brief History of User Experience in Government Systems, highlighted the military has been a leader in usability since the early days of human factors engineering. Major factors in its involvement are the complexity of the environments and the user tasks as well as the severity and life-critical importance of "getting it right." In this chapter, Maybury describes the broad range of defense missions, people who operate defense systems, and the environments in which they work. He relates these to several important dimensions of usability and illustrates his points with two examples from military aviation: ground control stations for remotely piloted aircraft and air traffic management systems. By describing crowded conditions, information overload, and the need for constant vigilance in an ever-changing situation, he explores how advances in machine autonomy and human control promise to enhance operator situation awareness and control in these and similar cases. Maybury presents five components of successful usability efforts in military systems; implementing them, he says, "promises capability increases, manpower efficiencies, and cost reductions through increased employment of autonomous systems."

- In Chapter 7, **Gitte Lindgaard** and her colleagues (Canada) outline some lessons that her research team has learned over the past decade from their involvement with the design, development, and evaluation of applications to support the management of the response to large-scale chemical, biological, radiological, nuclear, and explosives (CBRNE) events that result in large numbers of casualties. The team's work on a command post for medical and casualty response revealed how important it is to create a *plausible* scenario for use in requirements gathering — so that prospective users will find it easier to act out their roles and provide the input the team needs to design the user interface. Lindgaard and her colleagues then discuss issues that they encountered in two other projects — one providing support for police, hazardous materials technicians, and emergency medical services teams and the other involving a commercial tool for consolidating several extremely diverse sets of information on commercial explosives and articles into a standardized database. Finally, they present what they have learned about designing and evaluating applications for users who must act quickly in the face of uncertain, often unpredictable conditions. "Although these lessons were learned in the specific context of designing UIs for supporting the management of CBRNE events," Lindgaard and her colleagues observe, "we believe that they are generalizable to other types of projects."

- In Chapter 8, **Chris Johnson** (UK) describes and analyzes the myriad challenges confronting governments in their attempts to respond to events that disrupt national critical infrastructures such as telephone, transportation, and Internet. From natural disasters (e.g., Hurricane Katrina) to terrorist attacks (e.g., the 2004 Madrid bombings), such events require strong coordination efforts among different government agencies (e.g., police, fire, rescue, public health, regulatory bodies), different levels of government (from national to local), nongovernmental organizations, and private citizens. Governments are often very slow to respond to civil contingencies, Johnson observes, and often their assistance has little practical benefit — which increases loss of life and property and exacerbates the impact of such events. He describes the obstacles that cause difficulties for information exchange about these events and government's responses to them. Johnson explores the role of usability, ultimately tracing the root causes of difficulties to political concerns over who owns the data and to conflicting views about the role that central government should play in protecting the public from civil emergencies. "Further work is urgently required," Johnson tells us, "not just to assess whether usability concerns can be adequately represented within national e-governance initiatives . . . but also whether those same initiatives can support the information needs of the general public as they work to protect local communities in the aftermath of natural disasters and terrorist attacks."

- In Chapter 9, **Fabio Vitali** (Italy) and **Monica Palmirani** (Italy) analyze, and describe in detail, the issues they have encountered in introducing document editors based on the Extensible Markup Language (XML) into the legislative drafting offices (where the creation of the text of a piece of legislation takes place) of several legislative bodies, both at the national level and below it. These tools can have a critical impact on the general population of a jurisdiction, even if no direct interaction is involved, as their usability can concretely affect the efficiency and transparency of the democratic processes they support. The authors explain the legislative drafting process and describe the role that such tools play in marking up a draft during the legislative process of amending and approving it. Although they are convinced that XML carries great promise for increasing the efficiency of the legislative process, they offer some interesting — and cautionary — conclusions from their experiences in designing and testing three such tools for the back offices of legislative bodies in several countries. Although the authors were able to make a good case for the long-term benefits that XML tools could bring to the organization, end users found them unbearable if they deviated in any way from the traditional divisions of tasks, responsibilities, and roles — "which in most cases long predated not only XML but computers themselves. We remain convinced," Vitali and Palmirani tell us, "that this is not an isolated case, and that similar situations exist in a number of different professional contexts, especially in public administration." They urge us to ensure that any change we make in technology supports the existing competencies and roles of the individuals who will use it. "Details matter," they assure us — "a lot."

All four chapters involve highly complex activities and coordination among individuals, in some cases even among different organizations and levels of government.

CHAPTER

6 Usability in Defense Systems: Examples from Aviation

Mark T. Maybury
United States Air Force, Washington, DC, USA

"If we slide into one of those rare moments of military honesty, we realize that the technical demands of modern warfare are so complex a considerable percentage of our material is bound to malfunction even before it is deployed against a foe. We no longer waste manpower by carrying the flag into battle. Instead we need battalions of electronic engineers to keep the terrible machinery grinding."

— Ernest K. Gann

INTRODUCTION

Operator interfaces to defense systems encompass a broad set of categories of missions, environments, and users. For example, they include relatively simple office automation systems that enable logistics and business operations. But they also include complex analytic environments for multiple security level and multisource exploitation of imagery, signals, and open-source intelligence or high-fidelity cockpit simulations for aviation training. Moreover, they include real-time command-and-control environments to manage life-critical activities in air, ground, sea, space, or cyber operations. Users vary significantly and might include active duty uniformed personnel, reservists, national guard, civilians, contractors, or even foreign coalition partners who have different social and cultural backgrounds and expectations. Given such a broad set of missions, environments, and users, interfaces in defense face a broad range of human factors challenges. Operator interfaces range from the real-time challenges of tactical interfaces for advanced land, air, sea, and spacecraft to interfaces for strategic tasks including situational awareness, campaign planning, and execution management of complex, multidomain, cross-cultural information sources and resources across multiple time and space scales. Discussing human factors in military systems encompasses a broad spectrum of challenges and solutions. Usability takes on added importance in defense systems because of the potentially life-critical consequences of error or failure.

This chapter first provides an overview of some of the primary characteristics of the interfaces required to address the broad range of environments faced by the defense community. To illustrate some of these dimensions, challenges, and solutions concretely, it provides a more detailed deep dive into the rapidly growing area of remotely piloted aircraft (RPA) and the related but distinct mission of air traffic management (ATM). The article concludes by summarizing several lessons learned from applied human factors in defense domains.

DEFENSE MISSIONS, ENVIRONMENTS, AND USABILITY

Defense systems are utilized to train, support, and employ military forces. As the first column in Table 6.1 illustrates, these systems can be used for a variety of strategic, operational, or tactical joint military essential tasks (*Universal Joint Task Manual*, 2011). These tasks cover the range of operations performed by military users to observe, orient, decide, and act in warfare, the so called OODA-loop. As listed in the first column, these include intelligence, command and control of operations (including course of action analysis and execution monitoring and assessment), performance of operations, force protection, and support of combat operations (e.g., education, medical, mobility, and refueling). Accordingly, the environments in which forces and users operate can range significantly as shown in the second column of Table 6.1. Environments range physically (e.g., land, air, sea, and space), temporally (from real time to long term), politically (national vs. international users; degree of domestic and international unity), in terms of freedom of movement (uncontested vs. contested vs. denied), culturally (e.g., language, religion), economically (expense of the system acquisition and use), collaboration-wise (single vs. group), distribution-wise (collocated vs. distributed), and in terms of their realism (live vs. virtual vs. constructed).

As is evident from this discussion, broad sets of missions and environments can drive a variety of dimensions of usability such as physical, perceptual, cognitive, emotional, or collaborative. Accordingly, usability of defense systems needs to take into account measures often beyond traditional assessments of physical, perceptual, and cognitive ergonomics and supporting accessibility. Given the harsh environments, it is important to also take into consideration issues such as system reliability, error recoverability (both for unintentional user errors as well as malicious insiders), reliability and robustness under adverse conditions including adversary attacks, and autonomy in complex environments.

Table 6.1 Defense Missions, Environments, and Usability

Missions	Environment	Usability Requirements
Strategic/tactical intelligence (planning, tasking, processing exploitation, dissemination)	*Physical*: Air, space, ground, sea, and associated conditions (terrain, weather, freedom of movement)	Utility (relevant, useful)
Command and control (mission/operation/campaign)	*Temporal*: Real time vs. long term (e.g., tactical vs. strategic)	Simplicity/accessibility/self-evidency/transparency
Military operations	*Political*: National vs. international; unity vs. polarity	Consistency
Force protection	*Freedom of movement*	Error prevention/recovery affordances
Mobility	*Cultural*: Language, religion	Efficiency
Education and training	*Economics*: Acquire, use	Reliability/robustness
Medical	*Collaboration*: Solitary vs. team	Customizability
	Distribution: Collocated vs. distributed	Autonomy (manual vs. automated)
	Realism: Live vs. virtual vs. constructed	Ergonomics – Physical, perceptual, cognitive, emotional

In order to better understand the relation among missions, environment, and usability, we consider a particular case study, namely the rapid growth of RPA and associated RPA pilots.

CASE STUDY: RPA

To understand some of the challenges and solutions to usability of defense systems, consider one of the newest missions in aerospace. RPAs have grown rapidly in support of humanitarian relief, border security, and surveillance and reconnaissance missions. RPAs encompass a broad range of aircraft, from small, hand-launched aircraft that operate in a range of only a few nautical miles and carry a few pounds of payload for short mission durations (e.g., the RQ-11 Raven) to large aircraft (e.g., MQ-1 Predator, MQ-9 Reaper, and RQ-4 Global Hawk) that can carry up to a thousand pounds of payload and fly 20,000–50,000 feet in the air for over 20 hours over thousands of miles.

Because of strong operational needs, early systems such as the Predator were rapidly developed as advanced concept technology demonstrations (ACTDs). While ACTDs are an excellent mechanism for accelerating development and responding to urgent operational requirements, one limitation is that they can result in solutions that do not fully address the full spectrum of requirements such as reliability, affordability, security, and usability.

Indeed, in their RPA study, the Air Force Scientific Advisory Board (2010) found that "poorly-designed operator control stations (OCSs) fail to provide effective, robust, and safe mission management" (Zacharias & Maybury, 2010, p. 1). Indeed, Tvaryanas and Thompson (2008) found that OCS design deficiencies were a significant contributor to lost Predator aircraft. Figure 6.1 concretely illustrates several key usability problems in the RPA ground control system. The figure shows RPA operators (a pilot, sensor operator, and observers) cramped next to one another, interacting with a multiplicity of traditional controls (e.g., joystick, interaction panels, multiple keyboards, digital displays). Fourteen displays and innumerable switches, buttons, and warning lights are visible to the four depicted individuals resulting in visual overload. Poor physical ergonomics are exacerbated by an excessive need for input, limited task awareness, and lack of graceful degradation. In spite of this visual information overload, operators suffer sensory deprivation. Unlike a normal airborne pilot, by design remote operations mean that users have no direct visual or physical access to the environment outside the distant aircraft. The pilot's environmental sensing cues are solely limited to the visual domain, via onboard cameras with limited resolution and field of view. They literally cannot see icing on wings, feel vibration of fuselage parts, hear the strain of the engine, or experience air turbulence. Further exacerbating situational awareness, the actual launch and recovery element might, in fact, be on a different continent than are the RPA pilot and sensor operator. As a consequence, they cannot do a preflight check and/or walk-around of the aircraft, although the landing/recovery unit, local to the aircraft, could perform such a check. Moreover, the referenced SAB study found that "insufficient and inflexible platform and sensor automation increase operator workload and limit mission effectiveness." Exacerbating this situation, the study noted further that "Concepts of operations (CONOPS) and tactics, techniques, and procedures (TTPs) are developed after system development and deployment, rather than as a concurrent effort in an 'incremental development' program."

Thunberg and Tvaryanas (2008) document a human-centered usability process for the emerging OCS in the Advanced Cockpit program encompassing operator capabilities/competencies, workload,

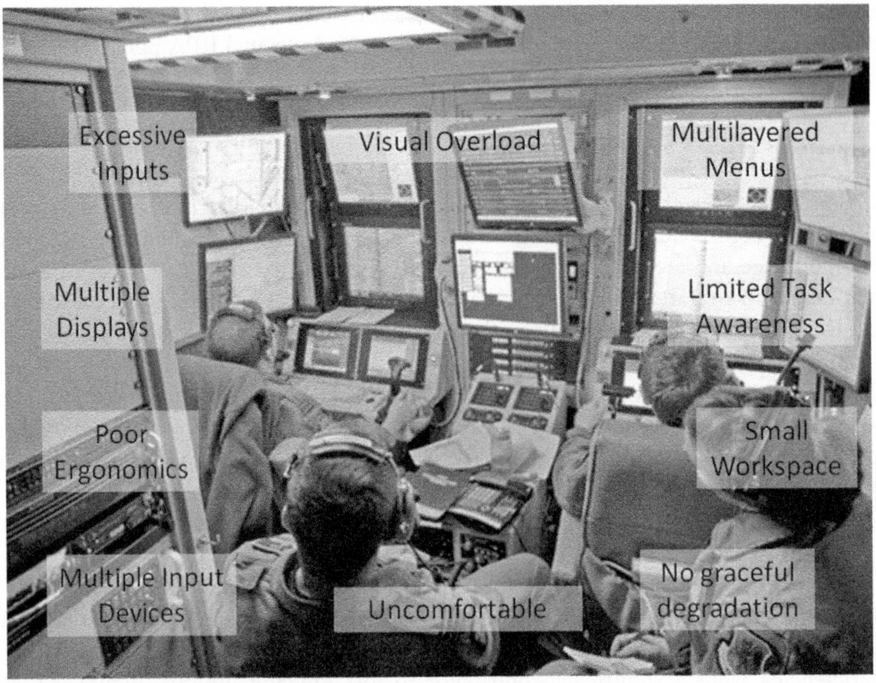

FIGURE 6.1 Usability challenges with RPA ground control stations

(For color version of this figure, see the web version of this chapter.)

and fitness. Draper et al. (2007) describe efforts to enhance RPA operator interfaces. Arguing that ground stations are more heterogeneous than necessary, Nelson (2011) recommends revisions to the current acquisition strategy that manages RPA such as the Predator RQ-1, Reaper MQ-9, and Global Hawk RQ-4 independently to facilitate cross-platform multi-vehicle control, for example, by acquiring interoperable architectures. Well-designed cockpits/ground stations that consider human-systems integration from the start can overcome current usability limitations and not only enhance human effectiveness but also ensure more robust performance in dull, dirty, or dangerous environments such as in congested or contested air space or in adverse weather conditions.

CASE STUDY: ATM

RPAs operate in military, civil, and international air space. Accordingly, RPA pilots must interact with a diverse set of air space managers, another military career field that sheds insight into usability in defense. As illustrated in Figure 6.2, ATM is a mission in which air space managers are often co-located in local towers; however, they collaborate with others via two types of communication — synchronous (e.g., radio, face-to-face communication) and asynchronous (e.g., email, chat). These operators may work across multiple operating environments: national airspace, international airspace,

FIGURE 6.2 Air traffic management

(For color version of this figure, see the web version of this chapter.)

and military airspace, each of which often has its own rules, regulations, procedures, and systems. As in most professions, towers include controllers who have specialized but interdependent roles and tasks, such as ground vehicle vs. air vehicle control. Their work environment must be designed to include visual situational awareness but also access to real-time displays of aircraft positions, weather information, and flight plans. The air traffic control system has evolved to ensure graceful degradation. For example, it allows controllers to deal with system outages by smoothly moving from highly automated processes such as machine-to-machine data exchanges and semi-automated routing all the way down to controllers visually tracking aircraft and keeping records on manual paper strips. Ensuring system robustness across humans and machines is essential to enhance safety (e.g., air and ground collision avoidance). However, achieving system robustness is extremely challenging because of imperfect automation and human error. One mitigation is the concept of mixed initiative in which human and machine collaborate to perform tasks. This transition from total human control to machine automation will be discussed further below. Nowhere is the need for automation and enhancements to human-machine interaction more apparent than in the emerging area of RPAs operating with manned aircraft in national airspace. The same SAB study referenced above found that "manually intensive airspace deconfliction and management is inefficient, will not scale, and hampers manned/unmanned integration."

MACHINE AUTONOMY AND HUMAN CONTROL

Automation of manual tasks and increasing levels of machine autonomy (e.g., automated takeoff and landing, ground collision detection and warning, and dynamic route [re]planning) are important in defense systems to increase efficiency, effectiveness, and safety. For example, machine-to-machine information exchange can simultaneously increase the situational awareness of both RPA operators and air traffic managers. Yet automation can equally decrease situational awareness if operators are not aware of the machine-to-machine communication and resultant autonomous decisions. And even though the "loss of link" between a ground controller and airborne platform is an infrequent event, remotely piloted aircraft will need the ability to make a graceful and successful transition from "remotely-piloted" to "unmanned," to avoid incidents. Under these conditions, they will need to independently sense and avoid (SAA) potential collisions, safely complete their mission, if needed, and navigate home and land autonomously. Analogously, if catastrophic failure occurs during ATM (e.g., natural disaster or terrorist act), the system (human or semi-automated) must be robust and ensure semi-automated airspace deconfliction, air and ground collision avoidance, and terminal area operations.

In addition to increasingly complex environments and systems, as illustrated by the above two cases, robustness to adversary attack is a key additional burden required to be addressed by defense systems which can entail severe usability requirements. Autonomy can provide increased performance and resiliency although it has additional benefits such as (manpower) efficiency (freeing up humans to do higher level tasks), speed (especially important in long latency environments such as undersea or in space), and predictability given well-specified environmental conditions. As expressed in the Air Force's Technology Horizons (Dahm, 2010), "As natural human capacities become increasingly mismatched to data volumes, processing capabilities, and decision speeds, augmenting human performance will become essential for gaining the benefits that other technology advances can offer." The real-time nature of cyber operations can require millisecond sense and response strategies. Whereas the attention and communications requirements to command and control even a modest swarm of RPAs exceed human capacity, the necessary sensing and communication would be trivial for most computers. An alternative solution would be to develop goal-directed supervisory control interfaces where the operator issues high-level goals and constraints and replanning needs to the automation. Automation is a key element in the Office of Secretary of Defense Unmanned Systems Roadmap (2009-2034), which focuses on four mission areas including reconnaissance and surveillance, target identification and designation, counter-mine warfare, and chemical, biological, radiological, nuclear, and explosive tactics. Similarly, the Army's 2009 robotic strategy emphasizes automation in five key areas: logistics, security, engineering, medical, and maintenance (Cruz, 2011).

Automation is valued by society and the defense community not only for speed, cost, and performance but also to assist or completely perform tasks (autonomously) in dull, dangerous, and dirty environments. Increasingly, escalating manpower requirements and associated costs are driving interest in autonomy because of the self-directed and self-sufficient characteristics of autonomy. Figure 6.3 distinguishes and exemplifies differing degrees and levels of autonomy. The "degree" of autonomy—that is, the degree of machine independence from human control—can range from none (manual control) to partial automation (often with the human "in the loop" manually performing some of the tasks), to supervisory control (human "on the loop" overseeing and often guiding tasks or selecting among possible alternative actions), to full autonomy (no human intervention other than to start or cancel an operation). One can also talk about "levels" of autonomy, such as at lower-level tasks (e.g., simple sensors and actuators to support basic flight control and guidance such as maintaining altitude), at a medium-level mission level (e.g., SAA, which requires more robust, cross-modal sensing and response reasoning), and a higher campaign level (e.g., planning or operating multi-ship tasks such as distributed search, tracking, and engagement). As shown in the upper right quadrant in Figure 6.3, given current limitations in machine representation of knowledge of the world, reasoning about courses of action, and learning from experience, autonomous campaigns remain beyond the state of the art.

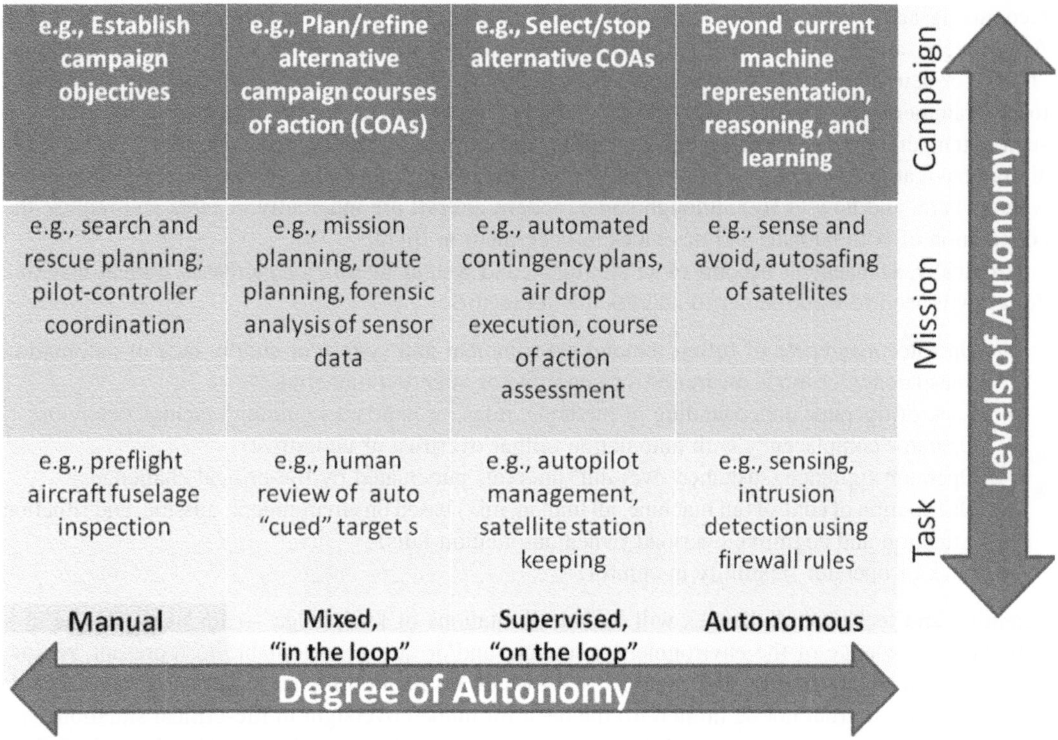

e.g., Establish campaign objectives
e.g., Plan/refine alternative campaign courses of action (COAs)
e.g., Select/stop alternative COAs
Beyond current machine representation, reasoning, and learning
Campaign
e.g., search and rescue planning; pilot-controller coordination
e.g., mission planning, route planning, forensic analysis of sensor data
e.g., automated contingency plans, air drop execution, course of action assessment
e.g., sense and avoid, autosafing of satellites
Mission
e.g., preflight aircraft fuselage inspection
e.g., human review of auto "cued" target s
e.g., autopilot management, satellite station keeping
e.g., sensing, intrusion detection using firewall rules
Task
Levels of Autonomy
Manual
Mixed, "in the loop"
Supervised, "on the loop"
Autonomous
Degree of Autonomy

FIGURE 6.3 Degree and levels of autonomy

(For color version of this figure, see the web version of this chapter.)

There are several published hierarchies of autonomy. For example, Sheridan and Verplank (1978) and Parasuraman, Sheridan and Wickens (2000) proposed 10 levels which vary the degree of human vs. machine control. These typically view autonomy as levels of machine independence from human control. However, an alternative perspective is to view the man-machine relationship in terms of interdependence: either humans can either be supported by machines, or we can in turn support the autonomous machines when they need it. Of course, computers are great at accuracy and processing speed, while humans are better at perception, pattern recognition, and abstract thinking. Combining these strengths as a team can yield new capabilities that we may have not yet thought of, with the human and machine working as a team to apply their unique strengths in mixed initiative systems.

However, autonomy suffers many limitations such as rigidity, brittleness, reliability, and opacity. For example, today there exist aircraft that can take off autonomously, follow a prespecified (by a human) route (though perhaps including branching logic), and return home and self land. However, today's aircraft guidance, navigation, and control systems can neither independently negotiate with air traffic control, nor automatically SAA other aircraft, nor manage novel emergency situations. More generally, there remain a number of gaps in machine intelligence including, but not limited to, limitations in machine visual perception and understanding, auditory sensing and understanding, recognizing and reasoning about real-world objects and events, fine control actuation, and so on. Accordingly, automation is only as good as the coded knowledge (often represented as methods, "rules", or heuristics), as few systems have the ability to learn from experience and thus are limited to programmers' imaginations. Advances in sensing and understanding environmental phenomena, such as temperature, pressure, humidity, altitude, and attitude, are today already used in "fly by wire" aircraft navigation and control systems. Typically, humans are guiding those systems (e.g., telling them when, where, and how to fly) although some modern aircraft are inherently instable and require the cooperation of both humans and machines to keep them in flight.

Ironically, as machines become more intelligent and system automation increases, human-machine design will need to work harder to address human factors:

- Operator awareness of (often remote) environment and system or simply lack of automation transparency or mode awareness or cognitive or attention tunneling
- Lack of operator understanding of methods, rules, or heuristics guiding machine behavior
- Operator complacency with automation (either overtrust or undertrust)
- Operator vigilance (sustained over dull intervals punctuated by life-critical challenges)
- Distribution of control (all machine, all human, mix) based on environment, mission, and situation
- Attention and cognitive overload (when automation fails)
- Lack of operator flexibility in control.

Scientific and technical challenges will include limitations of knowledge — for example, the systems lack knowledge of the environment, situation, and/or task or are unable to represent, reason, and communicate uncertainty and complexity — which results in brittleness. Similarly, ethical challenges will include (but not be limited to) the need for human oversight in life-critical situations and the challenge of assigning accountability to operator vs. machine vs. designer/developer in failure situations.

In addition to system automation, humans may increasingly experience their own onboard automation. Technologies to augment human vigilance, perception, and cognition have long been the subject of study in defense. For example, nearly 50 years ago, Dewan (1967) at the Air Force Cambridge Research Lab demonstrated that users could be taught to control their eye movement voluntarily, to send messages in Morse code using electroencephalogram activity associated with eye movements. Today, researchers have demonstrated not only noninvasive electrophysiological measures (measuring positive potential around 300 ms after an event) but also the use of magnetoencephalography, functional magnetic resonance imaging, and near-infrared systems. While medical implants are used today to improve audition and vision, future augmentation may improve not only visual/aural/tactile/olfactory acuity, but also alertness, memory, and perhaps even cognition.

Automation and autonomy solutions continue to be advanced for the future to enhance system usability and user-machine effectiveness. For example, the Phraselator (www.voxtec.com/phraselator) enables hand-held, real-time natural language translation to enhance human-human communication, and the DARPA Communicator Program yielded a two-way, open-source, spoken-language infrastructure (Seneff et al., 1998). Future systems will extend spoken language to gesture and facial expression recognition as well as sentiment detection and modeling, to enable understanding of operator attention/intention/emotion detection and tracking to enhance user modeling and user-adapted interaction. In the meantime, a number of best practices can be employed to overcome today's technology gaps, several of which are identified in the next section.

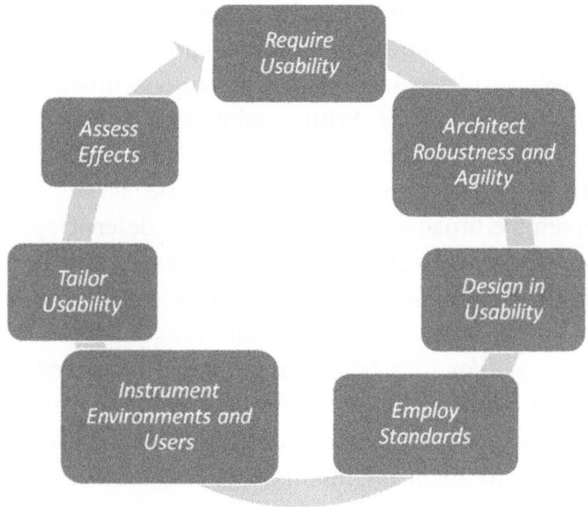

FIGURE 6.4 Usability best practices in defense systems

(For color version of this figure, see the web version of this chapter.)

SUCCESS FACTORS

As one of the largest sectors of the economy, defense systems represent a major area of experience in the advancement and employment of usability knowledge. Some of the lessons learned that can be garnered from this experience (see Figure 6.4) include these suggested practices:

- *Require Usability.* Given that most modern systems include humans either as critical elements of missions and/or in supervisory control roles over systems, it is essential to consider usability as a key performance parameter. Lack of consideration of usability requirements up front often results in defense systems that suffer failures in situational awareness, safety, and/or effectiveness.
- *Architect Robustness and Agility.* Architect processes, operations, and employments that incorporate affordances and fault tolerance to ensure graceful degradation of human-system operations in the face of automation failures, human (physical, perceptual, attention, cognitive) deficiencies, and/or communications and/or environmental (lighting, heating, vibration, acceleration, noise) challenges.
- *Design Usability In.* Engage human factors experts to perform usability analysis at the inception of new systems. Perform cognitive task analyses early on to understand the key tasks and resources required by users to accomplish specific missions. Usability needs to be designed into systems, and not applied as a Band-Aid after a system is created. If, however, systems have already been designed or are in a maintenance or sustainment phase, all is not lost. For example, heuristic analysis by experienced usability experts can be very useful in rapidly and inexpensively identifying and prioritizing areas for usability improvement. These experts can progress through common operational or mission threads and, using checklists, can quickly note various deficiencies in interface and/or interaction (e.g., sequencing, timing, workflow). Similarly, cognitive walkthroughs conducted by experienced users of the system to verbalize what they are thinking while performing tasks in validated use cases can also reveal usability problems.

- *Employ Standards.* Common standards broadly employed can increase system learnability, interoperability, and robustness. Standards range from common policies, operating procedures, physical and logical controls, displays, and even terminology/symbology (MIL-STD-2525C, 2008).
- *Instrument Environments and Users.* While maintaining privacy, it is essential to instrument system and user activity to help identify the relative importance of system elements, system improvements, and user and group challenges and/or needs.
- *Tailor Usability.* Given the broad range of interfaces to defense systems in terms of individual vs. group, real-time vs. non-real-time, tactical vs. strategic, single media (e.g., text or audio only) vs. multimodal, and so on, it is essential to tailor usability to the mission, tasks, environment, and user population. Indeed, modern capabilities such as user modeling and adaptation promise to track usage and/or user behavior to enable increased intelligent support to users if not actual interaction modification tailored to individual user and/or situational needs.
- *Assess Effects.* Leveraging models of expected user expertise, tasks/activity, and behaviors evaluate the effects of the environment and modify services, interactions, or affordances to optimize performance.

REMAINING CHALLENGES

While human physiology, perception, and cognition change slowly, defense systems have seen many revolutions in form and function, with accelerated change expected in the future. Accordingly, new challenges arise in usability of defense systems including but not limited to:

- Increasing complexity of environments, missions, and procedures
- Increased volumes and speed of data caused by high-fidelity, heterogeneous sensors
- Increasing connectivity and interactivity of human-human, machine-machine, and human-machine
- Shrinking timelines for decisions and sometimes increasing criticality of consequences
- The need for quantitative and qualitative models of human-system environments for a range of tasks
- The need for improved calibration, validation, verification, certification, and accreditation of human performance, machine performance, and the combination to increase trust in automation
- Finding the right balance of operator trust in the autonomy algorithms that are part of the control and decision-making software
- The increased need to employ modeling and simulation, testing, and training to facilitate rapid knowledge, understanding, and trust
- Prediction of future performance of machines (and operators) that learn from experience
- Economical, rapidly implementable, and broadly applicable usability solutions

Particular defense missions and systems may have additional challenges. For example, in the RPA domain discussed in detail above, the Human Effectiveness Directorate in the Air Force Research Laboratory is presently pursuing (1) enhancements to operator situational awareness, (2) prioritization of functions to automate, (3) context-determined degree of automation, and (4) manned-unmanned platform interaction. Included are efforts to achieve multi-aircraft control (Eggers and Draper, 2006; Draper, 2010). A significant amount of work remains to create processes, flight rules, and safety systems to enable the joint use of both manned and unmanned assets in a controlled airspace, not to mention the more severe case of defense systems operations in contested airspace.

SUMMARY

Complexity, severity, and life-critical importance place defense systems necessarily on the cutting edge of usability. This chapter has presented an overview of some of the primary characteristics of the interfaces required to address the broad range of environments in which defense systems need to operate. It detailed how these challenges manifest in both RPA and ATM, and it highlighted several lessons learned from applied human factors in military domains.

Next-generation systems will need to enhance usability through enhanced awareness of and response to operators. Successful systems of the future must do the following:

- Enhance situational awareness of both human and machine, along with situational awareness shared between them.
- Advance multi-level and multi-partner automation to enable situation-adaptive, mixed initiative human-machine interaction.
- Understand fundamental capabilities and skill sets required for each defense specialty and exploit current training and simulation technologies to enhance operator depth and breadth of experience (including exposure to contested/denied access environments).
- Develop CONOPS and TTPs for defense systems that enable distributed global operations and coevolve CONOPS/TTPs with system development.
- Appropriately apply ACTDs to develop prototypes and shift successful projects to the acquisition process, incorporating rigorous systems engineering practices including human-systems integration.

Doing so promises capability increases, manpower efficiencies, and cost reductions through increased employment of autonomous systems.

References

Air Force Scientific Advisory Board Study on operating next-generation remotely piloted aircraft (RPA) for irregular warfare (IW). (2010). www.sab.hq.af.mil/TORs/2010/Abstract_UIW.pdf

Cruz, A. Lt Col, USA. (2011). The robot general: Implications of Watson on military operations. *Armed Forces Journal*, 20 (June). Retrieved 12 February 2012 from www.armedforcesjournal.com/2011/06/6187209. On line article is at: http://www.armedforcesjournal.com/2011/06/6187209

Dahm, W. (2010). *United States Air Force Chief Scientist (AF/ST) technology horizons: A vision for Air Force Science & Technology during 2010-2030.* Vol. 1, AF/ST-TR-10-01-PR, 15 May 2010.

Dewan, E. M. (1967). Occipital alpha rhythm eye position and lens accommodation. *Nature*, *214*(5092), 975–977. June 3.

Draper, M. H. (2010). *Supervisory control interface research for next generation UAS.* Human Effectiveness Directorate, Air Force Research Laboratory. Wright Patterson AFB, OH. 11 May.

Draper, M. H., Barry, T., Calhoun, G., Clark, J., Draper, M., Goodrich, M., et al. (2007). *Advanced UMV operator interfaces.* RTO HFM-078/RTG-017 uninhabited military vehicles (UMVs): Human factors issues in augmenting the force. Neuilly-sur-Seine, Cedex: NATO RTO. http://ftp.rta.nato.int/public/PubFullText/RTO/TR/RTO-TR-HFM-078/TR-HFM-078-06.pdf

Eggers, J. W., & Draper, M. H. (2006). *Multi-UAV control for tactical reconnaissance and close air support missions: Operator perspectives and design challenges.* Human Factors and Medicine Panel of the NATO Research and Technology Organization.

MIL-STD-2525C. (2008). *Common warfighting symbology*. Department of Defense Interface Standard. Defense Information Systems Agency (DISA).

Nelson, E. Lt. Col., USAF, (2011). *Exploiting remotely piloted aircraft: Understanding the impact of strategy on the approach to autonomy*. Master's thesis. Air University, Maxwell AFB, AL. June.

Parasuraman, R., Sheridan, T. B., & Wickens, C. D. (2000). A model for types and levels of human interaction with automation. *IEEE Transactions on Systems, Man, and Cybernetics –Part A: Systems and Humans*, *30*(3), 286–297, IEEE May 2000.

Seneff, S., Hurley, E., Lau, R., Pao, C., Schmid, P., & Zue, V. (1998). *Galaxy-II: A reference architecture for conversational system development. In Proc. ICSLP 98, Sydney, Australia*, paper 1153. November 1998. See also communicator.sourceforge.net/index.shtml

Sheridan, T. B., & Verplank, W. (1978). *Human and Computer Control of Undersea Teleoperators*. Cambridge, MA: Man-Machine Systems Laboratory, Department of Mechanical Engineering, MIT.

Thunberg, C., & Tvaryanas, A. (2008). Human-centered ground control station design: The predator/reaper approach. In *AUVSI. Association for Unmanned Vehicle Systems International (AUVSI), June 10-12, 2008*, pp. 395–409.

Tvaryanas, A. P., & Thompson, W. T. (2008). Recurrent error pathways in HFACS data: Analysis of 95 mishaps with remotely piloted aircraft. *Aviation, Space, and Environmental Medicine*, *79*(5), 525–532.

Universal Joint Task Manual. CJCSM 3500.04F. (2011). Washington, DC: Joint Staff. www.dtic.mil/cjcs_directives/cdata/unlimit/m350004.pdf. June.

Zacharias, G., & Maybury, M. (2010). 7 July. *Operating next-generation remotely piloted aircraft for irregular warfare*. Washington, DC: Air Force Scientific Advisory Board. www.sab.hq.af.mil/TORs/2010/Abstract_UIW.pdf

CHAPTER

7 Emergency Response in Simulated Terrorist Attacks: Usability Lessons Learned

Gitte Lindgaard*, Cathy Dudek†, Bruce Tsuji‡, Patrick Noonan§, Livia Sumegi||, Milica Stojmenovic¶

Manotick, Canada Manotick, Canada† Ottawa, Canada‡ Toronto, Canada§ Ottawa, Canada|| Ottawa, Canada¶*

"Each problem that I solved became a rule, which served afterwards to solve other problems."
— Rene Descartes

INTRODUCTION

Television shows such as *CSI Miami* (Crime Scene Investigation) have done much to raise public interest in, and awareness of, the advanced science, technology, detective work, and human know-how that go into solving serious crimes. They have, however, also created some misconceptions concerning the time it takes to conduct these investigations and the level of resources that first-responder agencies have at their disposal. In reality, there is room for improvement in all aspects of support for managing criminal events, including in the range of existing database systems and technologies. This chapter outlines some of the most important lessons we have learned from our involvement in the definition, UI design, and usability evaluation of applications intended to support the management of large-scale chemical, biological, radiological, nuclear, and explosives (CBRNE) events with mass casualties. These projects are funded by Defence Research and Development Canada, an agency within the Federal Department of National Defence, within its CBRNE Research and Technology Initiative (CRTI) preparing Canada's CBRNE response capabilities. Each project involves numerous public and private civilian partners as well as university partners, which is the category to which our team belongs. We are subcontracted by an industry client in charge of developing the software.

When an adverse event escalates into a criminal investigation, it becomes very difficult to control and combine information into a manageable format. Numerous professionals representing different responder agencies, public health authorities, and others are involved, or become involved as the magnitude of an adverse event with mass casualties unfolds. In such events, chaos and uncertainty prevail; things happen very quickly, well before the first responders arrive on the scene, and last until a clearer picture of the nature and scope of the event can be formed, a command post has been set up, and a responsible action plan can be formulated and executed. The combined role of the first-responder teams is to preserve life, property, and equipment, while preventing the damage from spreading, providing triage to casualties on the spot, and identifying potential offending explosive or chemical agents, even before they really know what they are dealing with. There is no way that a team of HCI researchers would be allowed to observe the activities of first responders in a real major CBRNE event, the kind of which has, thankfully, not been experienced in Canada as yet. Instead, simulated events are staged around the country, but as these are extremely time-consuming and expensive to arrange, they occur relatively rarely. In the course of obtaining the necessary data for our HCI tasks, we have had several opportunities to observe, record, and analyze such simulations. Simulated events offer experienced CBRNE teams an opportunity to practice managing these as well as offering additional training for responder teams with limited experience. It is not surprising that few of our standard UCD methods (see e.g., Preece, Rogers, & Sharp, 2011; Shneiderman, Plaisant, Cohen, & Jabobs, 2009) apply comfortably in those environments. Still, our team has been able to contribute to the generation of user requirements and UI design, and the UI evaluation of a suite of such applications over the past 10 years.

The rest of the chapter presents what we have learned in the design, development, and evaluation of three projects in which we have been involved. It ends with a summary of the takeaway messages that we think may be useful to user experience practitioners who face similar uncertain, often unpredictable conditions "in the wild" (Hutchins, 1995).

CBRNE RESPONSE TEAMS' SETUP AND RESPONSIBILITIES

The area in which a CBRNE event has taken place is designated the "hot zone" into which only first responders are allowed. The hot zone is surrounded by the "warm zone" in which, in a large event with mass casualties, a team of operations specialists representing the various responder agencies are located. This is also where first responders and casualties are decontaminated before exiting to the "cold zone" that surrounds the "warm zone." One task of police "generalists" is to seal off all three zones to prevent unauthorized people from entering into the entire controlled area and risk contamination or injury. For safety reasons, the event management team located in the command post is placed well away from the crime scene, often even beyond the designated "cold zone."

In large events, the operations specialists are responsible for directing the actions of the first responders in the hot zone and for relaying relevant information to the management team in the command post. Each member of the command post team is a team leader for their group of responders. The team as a whole is responsible for the strategic management of the event and for the overall action plan and amendments to the same as the event unfolds. In smaller events in which no operations specialists are required, command post team members communicate directly with the first-responder teams in the hot zone.

CBRNE team responsibilities

A CBRNE crime scene involves the presence of numerous civilian agencies such as police, fire, medical, and veterinary responders. Each agency has its own roles and responsibilities, its own procedures, language, reporting formats, and so on, but the management of a large adverse event requires all involved to work together as a team. The command post team typically comprises officers representing Emergency Medical Services (EMS), specialist police officers, and hazardous materials ("hazmat") technicians, who belong to a special branch of the firefighting services, as well as an event manager. Depending on the nature and scope of the event, the event manager may be a police officer, a hazmat technician, or, in the case of a major rapidly spreading infectious disease outbreak such as the Severe Acute Respiratory Syndrome (SARS) in 2003, a public health authority.

The EMS team leader is responsible for the first-responder paramedics, whose role is to perform triage on casualties before they are decontaminated, discharged, or transported to a hospital. In a large-scale event involving mass casualties and possible deaths, a senior public health officer may be called in to direct the flow of patients to different hospitals. That person is also responsible for keeping the media and the Minister of Health informed of the unfolding event. If the event escalates, spreading further and going beyond a certain state/province, federal public health authorities are called in to lead the investigation in collaboration with their state/provincial and local counterparts. If the threat goes beyond a country's border, they are also responsible for reporting it to the World Health Organization (WHO).

The police officers include "generalists" who seal off the area surrounding the cold zone, re-directing traffic around it. A trained bomb technician is responsible for identifying the explosive materials and for preventing further bombs from detonating. He is likely to work closely with the hazmat technician when a "dirty bomb" (Dingle, 2005; Petroff, 2003; Zimmerman & Loeb, 2004) that may involve nuclear materials or other dangerous chemicals as well as explosives is suspected. If, for example, a suspicious package or backpack with unknown contents has been detected in a public area, the bomb technician and hazmat technician may send in a robot to help in the investigation before allowing people into the hot zone. These robots are equipped with remotely controllable equipment, including mobile video cameras and tools with which to take samples of any chemicals to help identify the offending agent without endangering first responders. The Forensic Identification Specialist (called FIS or "Ident") sends his staff into the hot zone once the area has been rendered safe, to collect evidence for a possible subsequent court case. As the interval between the occurrence of an event and the case going to court is often several years, all items found in the hot zone must be given an ID, be photographed, and packaged in several layers of sealed plastic bags for storage. The FIS officer signs each bag as he seals it. If for any reason the item is removed before the court case, it is resealed and the relevant officer again signs each bag. A radiofrequency ID (RFID) tag attached to each exhibit enables the police to retrieve all evidence associated with a given event once the court case goes ahead.

The hazmat team's responsibilities include taking samples of the offending agent in the hot zone and relaying important information to the command post team leader. This may include the color and texture of the agent, any smells or fumes exuding from it, or any other physical or behavioral signs they are able to discern. Together with information about the nature and extent of injuries of people in the hot zone, which the EMS first responders report to their team leader, this information is passed to other members of the hazmat team, located in special fire trucks equipped with a plethora of online and printed resources. Their role is to identify the agent as quickly as possible and communicate their findings to the command post team leader. The team leader decides on the level of Personal Protective Equipment (PPE) that everyone in the hot/warm zones must wear and on the decontamination agent to be used. PPE may involve impervious full body suits, gas masks, heavy boots, and gloves. The team leader also controls the entry into and exit from the hot zone to ensure that only authorized personnel is present. The firefighters decontaminate everyone exiting from the hot zone.

Before entering the hot zone, the EMS team records every first responder's vital signs (pre-vitals) — radial pulse, blood pressure, respiration rate — and notes the precise time of entry. For safety reasons, a first responder is allowed to remain in the hot zone only for a strictly controlled period of time. Once his time is up and after being decontaminated, his post-vitals are recorded to ensure that he has not been unduly affected or even injured while in the hot zone.

Communication between the first responders and their operational team or, in smaller events, with their command post team leaders, is maintained via radio. Each team uses a unique frequency to ensure clear communication between the responders and their team leader. Frequencies are agreed upon at the outset of the response. In addition, some command post team leaders rely on laptops and on cell phones for other communication during the event.

MEDPOST, THE MEDICAL AND CASUALTY COMMAND POST

MedPost presents, in one central place, an aggregate view of the essential information about casualties (number of people affected, who they are, where they are, their condition, etc.). It enables integration of communications between on-scene responders, hospital staff, and the response community involved in managing a CBRNE event. By capturing medical information about casualties and allowing different levels of responders to view it, it maintains, or improves, the situational awareness (Artman & Waern, 1999; Garbis & Altman, 2004; Riley, Endsley, Bolstad, & Cuevas, 2006) of the event among the specialists managing the crisis. Figure 7.1 shows the communication flows and the data sources for people who may be linked to MedPost in the event of a major outbreak.

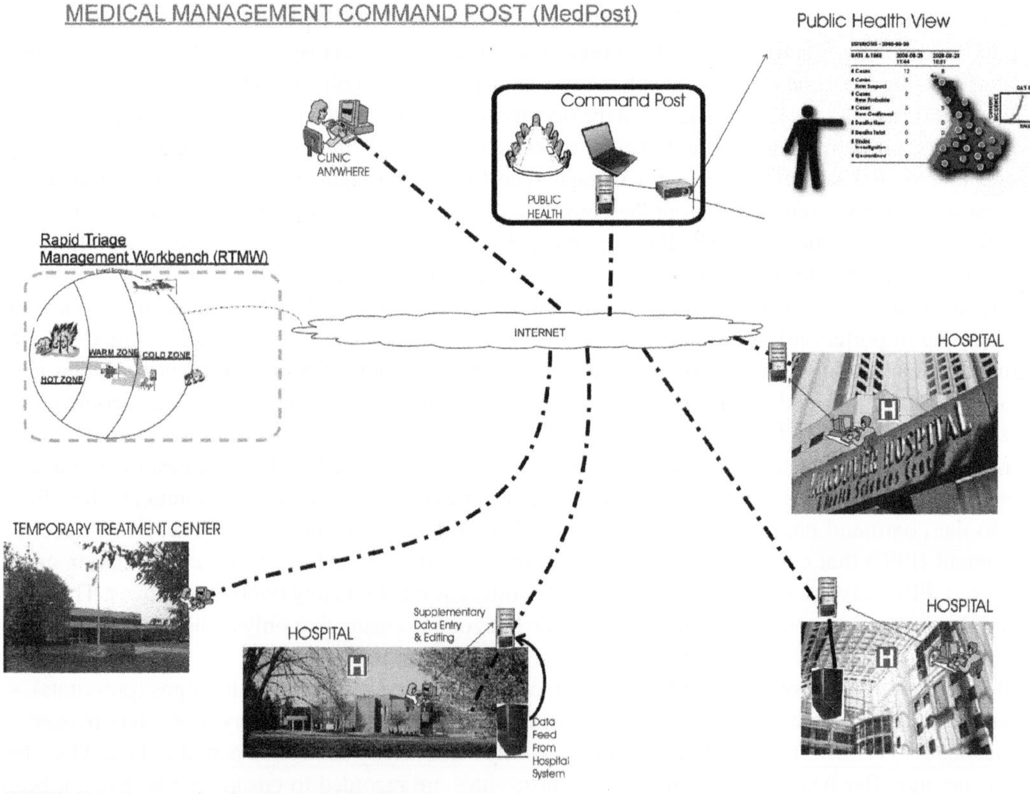

FIGURE 7.1 Communication flows in MedPost

As Figure 7.1 shows, MedPost can communicate with users in several hospitals and temporary treatment centers. The Rapid Triage Management Workbench, a first-responder triage application that shares critical information among people responsible for first response, casualty care, command and control, and public communication, is used to track, manage, and assign casualties to the proper point of care. It facilitates the triaging of casualties from the event scene through to transport at the hospital by capturing initial medical data in the field (Lindgaard et al., 2006). Finally, there is communication with individual clinics, the command post, and with the public health authorities.

To generate user requirements for each target user population, our team had prepared a fictitious but plausible scenario (Rosson & Carroll, 2001) for each type of CBRNE event. The explosion scenario, for example, read as follows:

> *A few minutes ago on the 10AM CBC radio1, you heard news of a terrifying accident in Montréal's Central station. The magnitude of the disaster is not yet known. It is unclear if a highly toxic gas has been accumulating in the city's ageing sewerage system that runs underneath the railway net, or if it is an act of terrorism. Members of the public have apparently been complaining about extremely foul smells in the streets of Old Montréal around that area for over two weeks. However, because garbage handlers have been on strike for the past four weeks, the accumulating garbage in the streets was believed to be the source of the smells. According to the report, a series of at least five deafening explosions occurred in rapid succession around 9:52AM. At least two buses are on fire; the station is apparently in ruins, and it is not known how many passenger trains may also have been hit by the blast. No information is as yet available about the number of casualties.*
>
> *Jeremy Hall, the Mayor of Montréal, is on the line requesting your immediate assistance. Having recently provided funding to install the MedPost system in two of the city-owned hospitals, Mr. Hall is aware of your involvement in its development as well as of your expertise at handling major disasters in Canada and abroad. MedPost has not been fully implemented yet, but Mr. Hall believes it may be possible to use a limited version of it to help monitor the situation. This limited version, which is intended for training medical staff, is capable of tracking up to five types of data selectable from a wider range, but no one in Montréal knows which data types will be most valuable for managing the situation efficiently, perhaps using a mixture of electronic and manual data tracking. They are also unsure as to what can, and what must be, reported to whom, when, and how often. What would you advise?*

While our team prefers to work with the rough hand-drawn paper prototypes (Arnowitz, Arent, & Berger, 2007; Beaudouin-Lafon & Mackay, 2003) that we know encourage lively and informative discussion in participatory design sessions (Schuler & Namioca, 1993), our client was uncomfortable presenting such rough, "unprofessional" looking drawings to future users. Therefore, they had produced quite pretty-looking Hypertext Markup Language (HTML) pages even though none of us knew much about the roles of the different players before the day-long session. Yet, no sooner had the users — in this case, experts who had collaboratively managed the SARS event in 2003 — read the above scenario than they began to act out their respective roles with such an intense urgency and sense of realism that they seemed to have forgotten the artificiality of the situation. No attention whatsoever was paid to the HTML pages displayed on the wall. Perhaps the most important lesson we learned was the kinds of information to which different users must not have access. To keep the Minister of Health and the media informed on progress and prevent accidental information leaks about individual casualties, their present whereabouts, their condition, or any names of people affected, these users must not have access to such detailed information. They see aggregate data only, such as the total number of cases, the number of new cases since the last briefing, the number of suspected and confirmed cases, and the number of deaths believed to be attributable to the event. The coroners' role includes distributing casualties among the surrounding hospitals. The number of patients with severe burns, for example, turned out to be an extremely important item of information for them because there are only eight burns beds in Montréal. Before these are filled, information must therefore be obtained about vacant burns beds in hospitals in other cities. Our very first, very crude mock-up HTML draft of the summary screen, which was subsequently shown to the domain experts for comment, is presented in Figure 7.2. As new information becomes available, the data is automatically updated in MedPost. Two updates are shown, with the most recent report shown next to the relevant field header. Thus the total number of cases (casualties) increased from 17 to 25 in the period 10:20-10:57. Eight new cases had been identified in the intervening period. The user can see when either the minister or the press was last notified, making it easy to focus on the most important data—presented first—namely the total number of cases and the number of new cases since the last report was received. Because the users were able to act out their roles in such detail, the summary screen hardly changed as the design of the application matured. Save for the look and feel of the final application, the content of this crude first prototype for this user population of which the screen in Figure 7.1 is a part remained virtually unchanged.

Teleconferences were subsequently held with the client's epidemiologist and the infection control nurses. Scenarios again informed the discussion identifying their specific requirements. In contrast to the event managers, the epidemiologist needs access to information about suspected and confirmed cases in her geographical region's hospitals, nursing homes, and other institutions. However, unlike

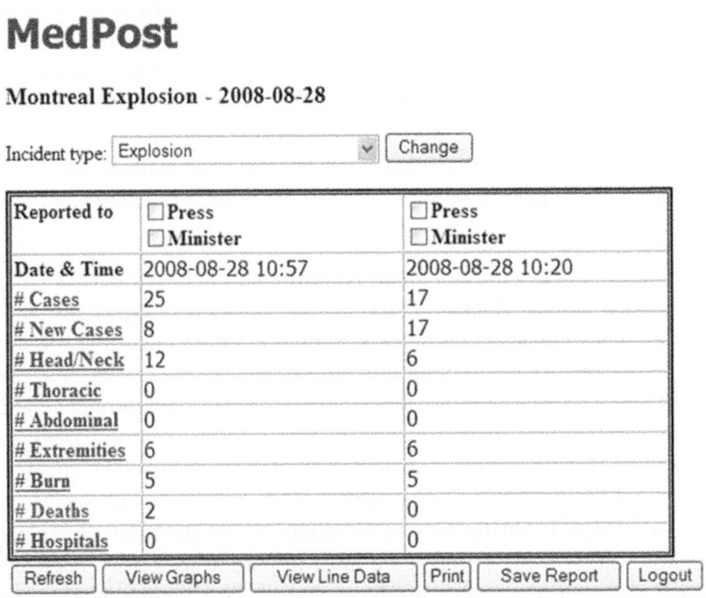

MedPost
Montreal Explosion - 2008-08-28
Incident type: Explosion
Change
Reported to | Press, Minister | Press, Minister
Date & Time | 2008-08-28 10:57 | 2008-08-28 10:20
Cases | 25 | 17
New Cases | 8 | 17
Head/Neck | 12 | 6
Thoracic | 0 | 0
Abdominal | 0 | 0
Extremities | 6 | 6
Burn | 5 | 5
Deaths | 2 | 0
Hospitals | 0 | 0
Refresh
View Graphs
View Line Data
Print
Save Report
Logout

FIGURE 7.2 The very first crude HTML mock-up draft summary screen

(For color version of this figure, see the web version of this chapter.)

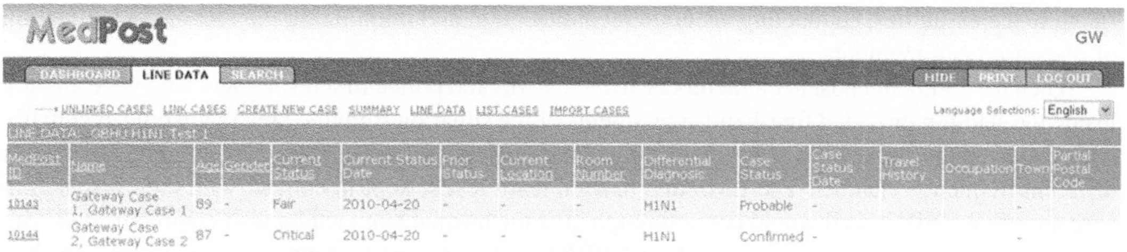

FIGURE 7.3 A partial screen designed for epidemiologists

(For color version of this figure, see the web version of this chapter.)

the infection control nurse, who also needs access to patients' names and home addresses, the epidemiologist cannot see those specific details. Figure 7.3 shows the epidemiologist's view in a more advanced version of the MedPost prototype. Note the blank fields that are filled only for the infection control nurses' view. The conspicuous red button labeled "HIDE" in the upper right corner of the screen was added for security reasons to prevent unauthorized access to the system. Pressing the "HIDE" button logs the user out, requiring him to login again upon his return. MedPost automatically saves the (presumably) half-finished task and takes the user directly back to where he left off rather than forcing him to start from the opening screen. This enables him quickly to continue the task he was working on when he was interrupted.

PROBE: A CRIME SCENE SUPPORT TOOL

The PROBE project combines existing software applications to create an integrated and expandable CBRNE crime scene support tool allowing the various first-responder agencies to communicate and share CBRNE event data and resources in real time. We were able to observe several CBRNE simulations to gather user requirements and in a user-based prototype test. The scenarios given to responders upon arrival at the scene were always prepared by the event organizers, police, or fire chiefs. Researchers thus had no control over the nature, scope, or content of the scenario, and nor was the user test in any way under our control. The first simulation included five command post team leaders: two EMS officers, one bomb technician, one FIS, and one hazmat technician as well as several teams of first responders representing all three agencies, and over 20 stadium employees acting as casualties. Five HCI researchers, each equipped with a digital video camera, a still camera, an audio recorder, and note paper, observed and recorded activities in the command post throughout the event in which we derived user requirements for PROBE.

The simulation took place in a large sports stadium in the center of Toronto with a seating capacity of over 55,000 and in which a baseball game was said to be ongoing at the time. The scenario stated only that an unknown object or objects had been thrown from above into a section of lower-level seats and that an unknown number of people would need medical attention and decontamination as quickly as safety would permit. The command post team's task was to manage the situation by determining how to proceed, allocating resources, distributing manpower in the area while providing rapid medical triage to the casualties, conducting accurate recordkeeping, and minimizing the risk of contamination of response team members.

When the command post team members arrived, EMS and police first responders who were already inside the stadium provided first-hand assessments of the situation from the area that would eventually be declared the hot zone. All team members had their own radios, and each agency communicated on a different frequency channel. The EMS and hazmat team leader kept in contact with their dispatch in case an actual CBRNE call would come through, and the hazmat team leader also communicated with specialist staff in the hazmat vehicle. Three CBRNE calls were made during the simulation, which is highly unusual. This forced the teams to reconfigure because the number of fully trained CBRNE teams is limited.

Three researchers each observed the team leader(s) in the command post (EMS, police, hazmat) throughout the simulation. One captured activities in the command post as a whole, and the fifth researcher recorded first-responder activities in the hot zone. In spite of Williams' (2006) warning that it can be a poor strategy to record everything, all researchers recorded as many activities as possible of the person(s) they were observing. With five channels of simultaneous data collection, it was impossible to keep track of all interactions and thus to identify weaknesses and communication breakdowns on the spot. The event took roughly 3 hours, followed by a 1-hour briefing session in which all responders, team leaders, our client, and our team participated.

For the data analysis, all video and audio recordings were transcribed *ad verbum*, adding any notes taken during the exercise. These were merged into a single file and arranged in a minute-by-minute fashion as recommended in the cognitive ethnographic framework, in an effort to reconstruct the entire event. Table 7.1 shows an extract of the merged data file. The time is shown in the leftmost column, followed by the source of the original data (video, audio, notes), and then the data obtained from each agency. An ID was assigned to each media file, together with its duration in minutes, both shown in bold in the table.

Table 7.1 Extract of the Merged Data File

Time	Source	EMS	Police	Hazmat
10:33	Video	SE's radio: Right now we are looking at 2500 potential victims and that is a very small guesstimate. (SE quickly scribbling down message from radio) SE: Do we know what they are complaining of? SE's radio: Itching, burning — nausea		**File 141203 (8:10)** BH's radio: Exercise, exercise, exercise — HazXXY responding (pause)
10:34	Video	SE to NP: 10:31 MC ... SE's radio: A white powder substance like talcum powder — about 200 people — some are coughing — some are itching and sore eyes ...	**File 141203 (8:10)** NP to radio: So you are gonna have to update me — so what we got, Mate?	BH's radio: The section has been locked down over

This transcript enabled us to reconstruct the entire event, which was useful for identifying communication breakdowns, and from those, infer user requirements that were then given to the developers and expert responders for discussion and verification. For each of the 47 user requirements thus identified, the times and verbatim sources of the underlying rationale were indicated, enabling the experts directly to access the context of our inference from the transcript. Since we are not domain experts in any of the agencies' fields, this was very valuable; several misunderstandings on our part were identified that had led to misinterpretation, and hence to an unjustified user requirement. These were corrected before coding commenced on the advanced prototype. In the end, however, we only needed data obtained in the first half of the event, when responders and team leaders were making sense of the situation. Once they had identified the chemical agent they were dealing with, the number of casualties and types of injuries had been determined, and decontamination was proceeding, the management process settled into a routine that did not require much system support. In subsequent observations, only two researchers were present, but recording equipment was placed next to each command post team leader to capture both his statements and incoming radio information.

THE COMMERCIAL eXplosives IDENTIFICATION TOOL

The commercial eXplosives Identification Tool (XIT) is expected eventually to network with a database of improvised explosive devices yet to be designed, and into Socius, an explosives incident database, which is currently being implemented in 27 languages throughout the European Union. All three form part of the suite of CBRNE-related applications that our client is developing.

By the time our team became involved with the ongoing design of XIT, system and user requirements had already been determined. Our task is therefore to provide prototypes to assist with the UI design and to run usability evaluations. The user requirements stretch over many pages of very detailed items. Two important lessons have been learned so far in this project. First, the concept of a "prototype" varied considerably among members of the project team, and constraints included the need to work with specific development tools that impose a particular UI style or look and feel. Therefore, even our early prototypes were assessed against the very specific requirements, leaving very little room for "thinking outside the UI design box". The second important lesson was that, for this user population, vocabulary, images, and content of the prototypes must precisely match reality and hence the users' rather specific expectations even of an initial low-fidelity prototype. Thus, when turning up to run an extensive, very early prototype pen/paper-based usability test in which we had expected up to 40 participants at a symposium held for first responders from around the country, we were unable to run the test. This was due to concerns with the inaccuracy especially of the images of bomb materials that we had found on the Internet. One screen displaying some of those images is shown in Figure 7.4. This, we were told, would turn the users right off and thus negatively affect eventual user acceptance of the eventual application.

Consistent with UCD methodology, we had focused on testing the navigation model and the advanced search module that allows text and image searches using an approximate approach to the content. Unfortunately, that was unacceptable. Thus, even when attempting to test a low-fidelity, high-level pen/paper prototype presented in Balsamiq (balsamiq.com/products/mockups) the prototype was expected to be a true representation of the eventual system, leaving no room whatsoever for pretending. Evidently, the seriousness of the context in which the application will be used assumed a far

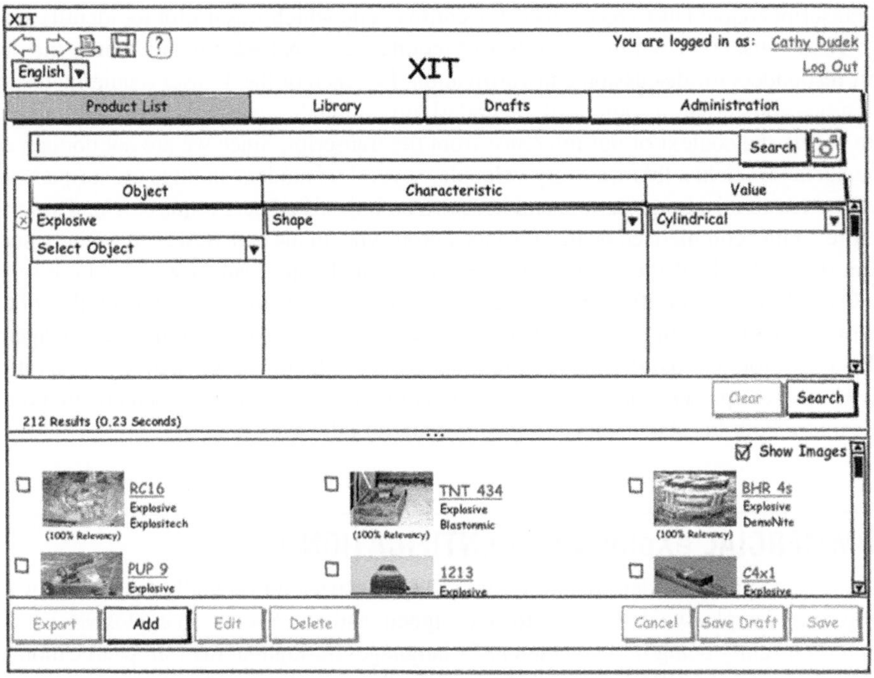

FIGURE 7.4 XIT screen with (inaccurate) images of bomb materials

(For color version of this figure, see the web version of this chapter.)

higher level of importance than we had expected. Instead, we should have presented the "images" at a higher level of abstraction — that is, without pictures — as we did in the next version of the prototype (Figure 7.5).

SUCCESS FACTORS

Space limitations have allowed us to present only some of what we consider the most interesting and compelling lessons we have learned over the past 10 years in the context of assisting with the generation of user requirements for surveillance and threat monitoring, and for its UI design and evaluation.

- *Users may be very sensitive to the authenticity of materials presented in prototypes.* Therefore, be aware of, and respect, your target users' expectations and the level of seriousness they place on even high-level early prototypes.
- *This authenticity concerns text, terminology, and images.* If you cannot obtain authentic high-quality images, use high-level abstractions to represent these instead.
- *People are better at acting out their roles than at talking about them.* Therefore, when writing usage scenarios, make sure you represent your users' reality as closely as possible, enabling them to act out their roles early in the requirements capture stage. Make sure also that you adjust the usage scenarios to each user population.

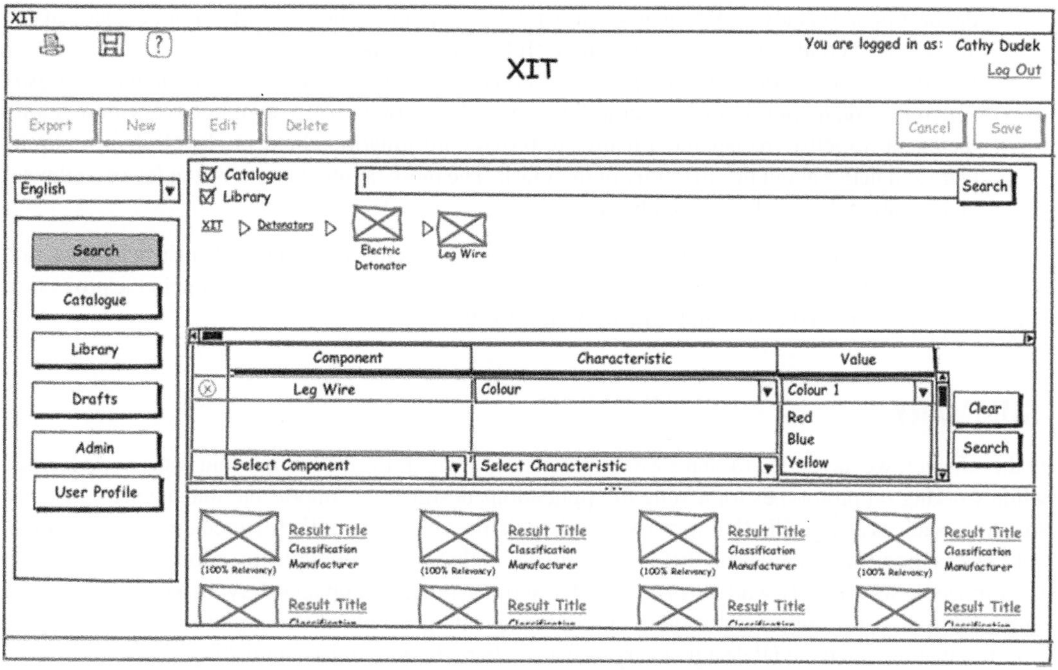

FIGURE 7.5 XIT prototype screen with images preceding the version in Figure 7.4

(For color version of this figure, see the web version of this chapter.)

- *Occasionally, certain users should not be able to access particular items of information.* This is especially important if you are designing a time/safety/mission critical application, as sensitive information could inadvertently be leaked by people who should not know details that are irrelevant to their roles and responsibilities.
- *Record and analyze data only in the first half of a CBRNE or other crisis simulation.* By far, most activity takes place at the beginning of a response to a crisis, when the responders are trying to piece together a coherent picture of the type and magnitude of an unfolding event. Once they know what they are dealing with, they go into a routine response mode in which they can rely on their knowledge and experience.
- *Reconstruct minute-to-minute parts of an adverse event from data transcriptions originating in several files.* By collating all data from different media and possibly from different researchers into one master data file, everyone will have the same picture. When extracting user requirements from that file, keep a reference to the point in time at which the observation was made that led you to articulate the requirement. This greatly facilitates the user requirements reviews with all stakeholders and helps to correct any misunderstandings.
- *Select the episodes in the event that are worthy of detailed analysis.* It is easier to select the best data from smaller sections. Therefore, divide the event data into smaller sections and then perform a quick tally of the relative amount of relevant verbal activity in each section to help select

the best data to analyze. When an event stretches over many hours, it may not be necessary to analyze all verbal episodes to generate useful requirements.

- *Eliminate all unrelated conversations and statements from the data file, but calculate the percentage of such conversations.* An indication of the amount of irrelevant conversation among the event response management team can provide information about the level of stress in the team and hence about the difficulty of their task. The more taxing the task is, the fewer irrelevant conversational episodes are likely to occur.

In our attempts to deliver high-quality products, we work very closely with the client's personnel, and we are constantly trying to help specialists from different disciplines who are involved in the projects to understand the user perspective and how to design for it.

SUMMARY

In this chapter, we have tried to share what we consider some of the most important lessons we learned while working on prototypes for a suite of applications designed to support the management of crisis situations such as a large CBRNE terrorist attack with mass casualties. We selected episodes that stood out to us as requiring a somewhat different approach to that we would typically adopt when designing UIs for people whose daily work does not involve serious threats to human safety. In MedPost, we were surprised to discover the power of the scenario for revealing details of the experts' roles and responsibilities that rendered the UI design a very easy task. In particular, it was interesting to note the importance of knowing which items of information should not be accessible to some users. In PROBE, we had underestimated the value of linking each user requirement to particular points in the minute-by-minute verbalizations captured in the master data file of the event. In the XIT prototype, we were quite taken aback by the importance to users of including authentic images to illustrate how an image-based search might work. Although these lessons were learned in the specific context of designing UIs for supporting the management of CBRNE events, we believe that they are generalizable to other types of projects.

Acknowledgments

We thank all first-responder participants for allowing us to observe their activities, ask questions, and record data in sometimes stressful situations. We also thank our client, AMITA Corporation, and its personnel for their persistent patience, help, feedback, and good humor. This research was sponsored by CRTI Grant #06-0255TA-Medical and Casualty Command Post (MedPost), CRTI Grant # 06-0317TD PROBE — Crime Scene Support Tool for Police, Hazmat, & EMS, and CRTI Grant #08-0131TD Commercial eXplosives Identification Tool (XIT).

References

Arnowitz, J., Arent, M., & Berger, N. (2007). *Effective prototyping for software makers.* Chicago, IL: Morgan Kaufmann.

Artman, H., & Waern, Y. (1999). Distributed cognition in an emergency co-ordination center. *Cognition, Technology and Work, 1*, 237–246.

Beaudouin-Lafon, M., & Mackay, W. E. (2003). Prototyping tools and techniques. In J. Jacko & A. Sears (Eds.), *The human-computer interaction handbook* (pp. 1006–1031). Hillsdale, NJ: Lawrence Erlbaum Associates Inc.

Dingle, J. (2005). Dirty bombs: Real threat? *Security*, *42*(4), 48.

Garbis, C., & Altman, H. (2004). Team situation awareness as communicative practices. In S. Banbury & Y. S. Tremblay (Eds.), *A cognitive approach to situation awareness: Theory and application* (pp. 275–296). Aldershot, Hampshire, UK: Ashgate.

Hutchins, E. (1995). *Cognition in the wild.* Cambridge, MA: MIT Press.

Lindgaard, G., Dillon, R. F., Trbovich, P., White, R., Fernandes, G., Lundahl, S., et al. (2006). User needs analysis and requirements engineering: Theory and practice. *Interacting with Computers*, *18*(1), 47–70.

Petroff, D. M. (2003). Responding to "dirty bombs." *Occupational Health and Safety*, *72*(9), 82–87.

Preece, J., Rogers, Y., & Sharp, H. (2011). *Interaction design: Beyond human-computer interaction.* New York, NY: John Wiley Sons.

Riley, J. M., Endsley, M. R., Bolstad, C. A., & Cuevas, H. M. (2006). Collaborative planning and situation awareness in army command and control. *Ergonomics*, *49*(12-13), 1139–1153.

Rosson, M. B., & Carroll, J. M. (2001). *Usability engineering: Scenario-based development of human computer interaction.* (chap. 1) San Diego, CA: Morgan Kaufmann.

Schuler, D., & Namioca, A. (Eds.), (1993). *Participatory design: Principles and practices.* New York, NY: John Wiley Sons.

Shneiderman, B., Plaisant, C., Cohen, M., & Jabobs, S. (2009). *Designing the user interface: Strategies for effective human-computer interaction* (5th ed.). New York, NY: Addison-Wesley.

Williams, R. F. (2006). Using cognitive ethnography to study instruction. In *Proceedings of the 7th international conference of the learning sciences*, (pp. 838–844) Bloomington, Indiana.

Zimmerman, P. D., & Loeb, C. (2004). Dirty bombs: The threat revisited. *Defense Horizons*, *38*(4), 1–12.

Further reading

Situation awareness

Comfort, L. K., Ko, K., & Zagorecki, A. (2004). Coordination in rapidly evolving disaster response systems. *American Behavioral Scientist*, *48*(3), 295–313.

Cannon-Bowers, J. A., & Salas, E. (1990). Cognitive psychology and team training: Shared mental models in complex systems. In *Proceedings of the 5th annual meeting of the society for industrial and organizational psychology*, (pp. 121–132) Miami, Florida.

Durso, F. T., & Gronlund, S. D. (1999). Situation awareness. In F. T. Durso, R. S. Nickerson, R. W. Schvaneveldt, S. T. Dumais, D. S. Lindsay & M. T. H. Chi (Eds.), *Handbook of applied cognition* (pp. 283–314). New York, NY: John Wiley.

Endsley, M. R. (1995). Towards a theory of situation awareness in dynamic systems. *Human Factors*, *37*, 32–64.

Endsley, M. R. (2000). Theoretical underpinnings of situation awareness: A critical review. In M. R. Endsley & D. J. Garland (Eds.), *Situation awareness analysis and measurement.* Mahwah, NJ: Lawrence Erlbaum Associates Inc.

Endsley, M. R., & Bolstad, C. A. (1994). Individual differences in pilot situation awareness. *International Journal of Aviation Psychology*, *4*(3), 241–264.

Gorman, J. C., Cooke, N. J., & Winner, J. L. (2006). Measuring team situation awareness in decentralized command and control environments. *Ergonomics*, *49*(12-13), (Oct 10-22) 1312–1325.

Guerlain, S., Adams, R., Turrentine, T. S., Guo, H., Collins, S. R., & Calland, F. (2005). Assessing team performance in the operating room: Development and use of a "black box" recorder and other tools for the intraoperative environment. *Journal of American College of Surgery*, *200*(1), 29–37.

Son, J., Aziz, Z., & Pena-Mora, F. (2007). Supporting disaster response and recovery through improved situation awareness. *Structural Survey*, *26*(5), 411–425.

Vollmann, T. E. (1991). Cutting the Gordian Knot of misguided performance measurement. *Industrial Management and Data Systems*, *1*, 24–26.

Wellens, A. R. (1993). Group situation awareness and distributed decision making: From military to civilian applications. In N. J. Castellan (Ed.), *Individual and group decision making: Current issues* (pp. 267–287). Hillsdale, NJ: Lawrence Erlbaum Associates Inc.

Information overload

Hunt, R. E., & Newman, R. G. (1997). Medical knowledge overload: A disturbing trend for physicians. *Health Care Management Review*, *22*, 70–75.

Libowski, Z. (1975). Sensory and information inputs overload: Behavioral effects. *Comprehensive Psychiatry*, *16*, 199–221.

Distributed cognition

Blandford, A., & Furniss, D. (2006). DiCoT: A methodology for applying distributed cognition to the design of team working systems. In S. W. Gilroy & M. D. Harrison (Eds.), *Proceedings of the 12th international workshop on design, specification and verification of interactive systems*, (pp. 26–38). Berlin: Springer-Verlag: LNCS 3941.

Brehmer, B. (1992). Dynamic decision making: Human control of complex systems. *Acta Psychologica*, *81*, 211–241.

Orasanu, J., & Salas, E. (1993). Team decision making in complex environments. In G. A. Klein, J. Orasanu, R. Calderwood & C. E. Zsambok (Eds.), *Decision making in action: Models and methods* (pp. 327–345). Westport, CT: Ablex Publishing.

CHAPTER

National Critical Infrastructures

8

Chris W. Johnson
School of Computing Science, University of Glasgow, Glasgow, UK

"[Effective preparation] requires the commitment of each and every individual to a group effort—that is what makes a team work, a company work, a society work, a civilization work."
— Vince Lombardi

INTRODUCTION

This chapter focuses on government intervention to mitigate the impact of civil contingencies, including natural disasters, terrorist attacks, infrastructure failures, and pandemics. The US National Strategy for the Physical Protection of Critical Infrastructures and Key Assets (National Infrastructure Advisory Council, 2003) focuses on 11 sectors: agriculture and food, water, public health, emergency services, defense industrial base, telecommunications, energy, transportation, banking and finance, chemicals and hazardous materials, and postal and shipping. Similarly, the UK Centre for the Protection of National Critical Infrastructure identifies nine sectors that deliver essential services: energy, food, water, transport, telecommunications, government and public services, emergency services, health, and finance. In contrast, the European Programme for Critical Infrastructure Protection (EPCIP) defines critical infrastructure to be any industry or service whose loss would have a strong negative effect not only on the country in which it is located but also on one or more other member states. The USA PATRIOT Act of 2001 defined critical infrastructure as those physical or virtual systems whose incapacity or destruction would have a debilitating impact on national security, economy, public health, or safety.

CASE STUDIES

This section presents two case studies to illustrate the problems that arise when national governments coordinate the response to contingency events.

Hurricane Katrina, August 2005

The first case study focuses on government response to a major natural disaster. Although Hurricane Katrina had a significant impact on Caribbean states, this chapter focuses on the information and communications technology (ICT) problems created for national and local governments across the United States. It then identifies a broad class of usability issues that reduce the utility of command-and-control systems to support government's response to major contingency events.

There were also considerable, unexpected problems in coordinating the inter-agency response to Hurricane Katrina when so many diverse aspects of the transportation, power, and telecommunications infrastructure were affected by flooding and high winds (Department of Homeland Security, 2006). The storm damaged many 911 emergency call centers. More than three million customers lost telephone service. Almost 50% of radio stations and television stations were affected. High winds and the rising flood waters brought down 50,000 utility poles in Mississippi. The hurricane left an estimated three million people without electricity.

The consequences can be illustrated by the observation that one country coroner was still trying to get a list of missing from the Red Cross in November 2005, more than 2 months after the event. The collapse of communication infrastructure and the loss of both computer-based and paper records hindered this work. The lack of appropriate evacuation plans and the failure of communications networks to summon external help forced many individuals to place their own lives at risk. For example, staff from the East Jefferson General Hospital had to perform ad-hoc evacuations of elderly patients by wading from the emergency department ramp to an elderly care home that was being inundated. Clinicians and support staff at New Orleans' University Hospital had to carry patients down four flights of stairs to take them to an improvised Intensive Care Unit (ICU) when their generators were flooded (US Congress, 2006).

The impact of the hurricane was also felt across the region's computational infrastructure. One month after the hurricane, more than 130 major computer networks remained unreachable across Louisiana, Mississippi, and Alabama. These included networks associated with telecommunications service providers, such as the Network Telephone Company in Pensacola, Florida, as well as the Air2LAN wireless service provider in Mississippi. The routing recovery process was significantly slower than anticipated. The impact around the Gulf states tended to coincide with landfall by the hurricane; those networks that were affected tended to go down and stay down.

BellSouth Corp was the main fixed-line telecommunications provider in the affected region. It estimated that more than 750,000 lines were out of service in the epicenter. It also had some 180 offices running on backup generators. This created a huge demand for fuel deliveries that had to be transported over the damaged and congested road network. In some cases, local authorities would not grant service providers access to the disaster area. Long-distance carriers who exchange traffic with local operators indicated that much of the local routing infrastructure maintained by BellSouth, Alltel Corp., and smaller independent phone companies were out of service after the first landfall.

More than three million people were affected by the secondary effects of communications failures triggered by power failures. The duration of the power failures were, in part, caused by the sheer logistics of the recovery operations. More than 30,000 new poles were needed to support more than 2200 miles of replacement power cabling. At the height of the recovery operations there were more than 22,000 utility crews working in the affected regions.

These failures often had unpredictable consequences for end users. Some Gulf Coast residents who evacuated before the storm hit found they could make calls on cell phones but could not receive them. The problem affected phone numbers with area codes from the affected region, including the New Orleans 504 prefix. The end users did not understand that for most US providers, an account check is made on the home network whenever a call is placed outside the phone's registered area. This check also provides information from the home service provider on how to route the call. After Katrina's initial flood surge, many of the host servers that should have implemented these checks were suffering primary or secondary flood damage. The service providers quickly made alternate arrangements so that other providers could respond to requests to place these calls when evacuees were located in other regions. However, it was technically more difficult to provide routing information for incoming calls when the supporting networks continued to make account checks on the original hosts in the affected areas.

For several years prior to the storm, local agencies had drawn on Federal resources to prepare for potential contingencies. For instance, the Mississippi Emergency Management Agency (MEMA) had used Department of Homeland Security (DHS) emergency management performance grant funds to prepare the technological and management infrastructure needed to increase local resilience. A range of ICT systems had been introduced. Many of these interfaced with federal systems. By 2005, over 1200 first responders had received training in the US National Incident Management System (NIMS). That summer, the senior MEMA staff received NIMS training and drills based on the associated Incident Command System (ICS). This occurred at the same time as the US Federal Emergency Management Agency (FEMA) officials responsible for the national response also participated in extensive drills using the available ICT infrastructure. These focused on the best ways to adapt complex information systems to support large-scale recovery operations. The FEMA officials involved in the emergency response later argued that these exercises and training opportunities enabled them to quickly establish a unified command structure for local and national resources. However, this close integration in Mississippi cannot be said to have characterized the response across all the areas of local government in all the states affected by the disaster.

The coordination of mandatory evacuations provides an illustration of the lack of coordination in command and control both during and immediately after the hurricane. Alabama and Mississippi declared mandatory evacuations prior to landfall. This enabled localities to work with state officials to implement existing plans. The picture was more mixed in Louisiana. Although many areas successfully implemented their emergency plans, New Orleans delayed the declaration of mandatory evacuations. It is no coincidence that this was among the most densely populated areas in the state. Local government officials faced significant logistical challenges to supporting the mass movement of people. The usability and utility of government information systems formed part of a more complex landscape in which many different agencies had to act together to implement a mandatory evacuation. In theory, New Orleans city officials had the authority to commandeer the resources necessary to assist in this mass movement. They could not, however, act in isolation. In particular, arrangements had to be made to support the population in evacuation centers once they had been moved. State officials also had to organize the contraflows and dispatch arrangements that would be necessary to speed the evacuation process. It is estimated that more than 70,000 individuals did not leave before the mandatory evacuation. Many did not have their own means of transportation. This illustrates the limitations of exercises and drills — for instance using evacuation simulators — that fail to capture the scale of the problems that arise during civil contingencies. Partly in consequence, New Orleans officials opened the Superdome rather than coordinating a full evacuation.

State and county officials both criticized the US Army Corps of Engineers' data that was used to plan for evacuations in the areas of Alabama affected by the hurricane. Much of this information was based on coastal studies that were more than 5 years old. In some areas, these surveys did not include detailed information about the potential wind patterns that is needed to anticipate evacuation times. Other limitations included the lack of information about new areas of settlement or about the impact of tourism that significantly increased the population in coastal areas prior to this natural disaster. Local government officials estimated that 28 h would be required for an evacuation; however, this was based on guesswork given the lack of detailed and up-to-date information.

Even when the users of government and local information systems have access to accurate data, political and organizational issues can intervene to undermine command-and-control mechanisms. As the storm approached, the director of the National Hurricane Center provided the Governor of Louisiana with a detailed brief on the potential impact of Katrina. On the Sunday before landfall, the Slidell Office of the National Weather Service argued that Katrina would lead to significant food and water shortages and to widespread damage to other critical infrastructure. However, senior city officials in New Orleans seemed more concerned to determine whether the city would be liable for loss of business during an evacuation. Initial steps to commandeer buses did not begin until almost 3 days after these earlier warnings (US Congress, 2006).

Katrina illustrates the way in which the usability of government information systems plays only a small part in the wider political and organizational context of emergency planning. The problem of persuading stakeholders to make difficult decisions before a contingency is dwarfed by the challenges that arise in marshaling ICT resources to support the response to natural disasters. In particular, the evacuation of the Superdome after Katrina was immensely more complex than previous drills or exercises had envisaged. Many elements of the information infrastructure were damaged by the flood waters and high winds. Servers were off-line, generators flooded, and communications cables severed. In many cases, ICT applications that were supposed to have resilient and distributed backups failed in ways that could not have been anticipated before they were needed. Many of the state and FEMA officials had to rely on manual processes to plan the number of buses needed, to identify accessible routes to the Superdome, etc. This planning occurred in a highly degraded environment that included limited communications that prevented a full understanding of the scope of the needs and even the visibility of deployed resources.

The Madrid bombings, March 2004

The previous section has argued that usability concerns form one component of the complex challenges that natural disasters create for government command-and-control systems at both local and national levels. These problems are even more acute for command-and-control structures that have to be established following terrorist attacks.

One hundred ninety-one people were killed, with 1800 wounded in the Madrid attacks. Improvised explosives were hidden inside backpacks and detonated on the Cercanías commuter train system. Four devices exploded on the same line between Alcalá de Henares and Atocha station in Madrid between 07:37 and 07:40. Bomb-disposal teams detonated two further devices. The final bomb was not discovered until later in the evening among luggage that had been taken from a damaged train.

The emergency response began around 08:00, when relief agencies began arriving at the four sites. Initial reports confirmed that there had been numerous victims, with around 50 wounded and several dead. By 08:30, the emergency ambulance services had established a field hospital in a local sports facility. By 08:43, firefighters reported 15 dead at El Pozo. By 09:00, the police had confirmed the deaths of at least 30 people, and the number of casualties continued to rise during the morning.

Many similarities exist between the problems that faced the public and government response to Hurricane Katrina and those that emerged in the aftermath of the attacks in Spain. In particular, one can see strong parallels in the problems of communicating and in coordinating the rescue efforts. Madrid, Spain, has several Emergency Medical Services (EMSs) with different working procedures, dispatch centers, and staff. The relationships among these various agencies complicated command

and control in the aftermath of the attacks. Usability problems associated with the telecommunications infrastructure were often strongly determined by the complex organizational structures in place at the time of the bombing. These can be summarized as follows: Madrid-112 (M-112) is a call reception center that receives and distributes all emergency telephone calls in the area. It then notifies or transfers them to the appropriate emergency service. It does not maintain radio contact with the responding units. The Servicio de Urgencias Médicas de Madrid (SUMMA) is managed by the regional government, and operates throughout the province of Madrid, including the city of Madrid. The Servicio de Emergencias de la Comunidad de Madrid (SERCAM) is managed by the regional government, and operates in the province of Madrid. However, it does not normally operate within the city. Its ambulances are mainly based at fire stations, whereas those of SUMMA are based in hospitals and health centers. At the time of the attacks, it was in the process of merging with SUMMA.

In addition to the resources controlled by local government, the Servicio de Asistencia Municipal de Urgencia y Rescate-Protección Civil (SAMUR-PC) was managed by Madrid City Council. It operated out of its own stations and had a volunteer section. Similarly, the Cruz Roja Española (CRE) was also staffed by volunteers. Unlike some of the other agencies, it operated more widely across Madrid and the rest of Spain. However, it used the same Madrid-112/SUMMA command and coordination systems. The final elements in this mosaic were provided by civil protection organizations. Again these were staffed by volunteers from the local community. Some of these local organizations were integrated into Madrid-112/SUMMA. Others operated ambulance services that were under direct municipal control without reference to the wider regional control structures.

The usability issues that further complicated these organizational structures can be illustrated by the observation that each agency operated their own communications centers and radio frequencies. After the attacks, it was argued that they lacked common crisis management plans. The frequencies used by each of these agencies listed above were incompatible. There was no shared tactical channel. One consequence of this was that on March 11, the emergency staff were forced to communicate either face to face in the field or using their personal mobile telephones. Although mobile telephones provide a flexible solution to infrastructure problems, they cannot adequately replace the specialist radio communications facilities provided by emergency services. As with Katrina, it can be argued that many of the usability concerns in command-and-control systems stemmed from deeper problems in the organizational structures between national and local governments. In consequence, emergency personnel struggled to piece together information from their remaining communications systems to understand the nature of the threat to public safety. In such a situation, it is almost impossible for local and national governments to maintain adequate situation awareness across all of the first responders. Significant concerns remain that these various agencies might themselves have become the targets for secondary devices in the aftermath of the initial blasts.

There were further usability concerns. One of the Madrid emergency medical radio systems has 10 independent communication channels. During the first 2 hours after the attack, all of the explosion sites used the same channel. The system quickly became overloaded, so that it was hard for some units to coordinate their work with their headquarters staff. As might be expected, staff responded by using their mobile telephones even though these networks were overloaded by members of the public trying to contact friends and relatives. These communications problems had further consequences on emergency response. For instance, the sites of the Atocha and Téllez blasts were relatively close together. Initially, the dispatch centers believed that Atocha and Téllez were different names for the same site. A police officer had diverted some ambulances on the way to Atocha so that they could deal with the

Téllez explosion. Many of these ambulances were aware of the explosions at Atocha only through their vehicle radios and so thought that they had arrived at Atocha. During the critical time immediately after the attacks, many reinforcements were sent only to Atocha. Calls for backup from personnel at Téllez were mistaken as calls from Atocha.

The lack of effective communications and a reliance on the overloaded mobile telephone network created hazards both for the public and for emergency personnel. At two of the sites, many responders did not know about unexploded devices in the wreckage of the trains. Further concerns stemmed from the difficulty of getting calls through to signallers and the train-operating companies. At one of the explosion sites, responders had to get off the tracks when a train continued through the station at high speed. This arguably again illustrates the problems that local and national governments face in integrating command-and-control infrastructure across different industry organizations.

IDENTIFYING SPECIFIC BARRIERS TO THE USABILITY OF CRITICAL INFRASTRUCTURE

Previous sections have argued that usability issues exacerbate wider communications problems as multiple stakeholders coordinate their efforts in uncertain and evolving situations. The remaining sections of this chapter identify higher level barriers that undermine the utility of command-and-control systems across both local and national governments.

Barriers between local and national governments

It is notoriously difficult for national governments to obtain detailed, reliable, and timely information from local governments. Political differences undermine cooperation between the administrations and agencies that operate at different tiers of government. Further problems stem from technical barriers to the exchange of information between the legacy systems procured for local and national governments (Johnson, 2008). Usability concerns are also apparent — even in situations where it is technologically feasible for the central government to obtain information from local IT systems, lack of training and experience often frustrate the exchange of critical data (Johnson, 2007).

Further examples can be provided by the United Kingdom response to the 2007 floods. Central government faced considerable problems in answering even the most basic question: how many people were affected? Initial reports from the Environment Agency suggested that between 3000 and 4000 properties were affected (Pitt, 2007). Several days later, local authorities reported that 30,000 houses were flooded. The discrepancy arose because the Environment Agency counted only properties affected by river flooding; it excluded surface water flooding of urban properties, which was the most significant source of damage during June 2007. Such differences show that usability problems cannot be addressed unless they are accompanied by a root-and-branch reform of the information management systems across national and local governments.

Further examples are provided by the range of different Geographic Information Systems (GISs) used by different branches of government during the UK floods. These had been designed in a piecemeal fashion, with different data formats and interface design standards. In consequence, it was very difficult to correlate data about flood levels and the location of "at-risk" members of the public or the location of Fire and Rescue Personnel and the state of local critical infrastructure (Johnson, 2009). In the aftermath of the floods, it was proposed that the common access methods should be developed to present integrated information on Mobile Data Terminals (Knight, 2008). However, such proposals tend to ignore the organizational differences between local and national tiers of government that help to explain why such different systems were developed and owned by multiple agencies.

Barriers from market deregulation and public-private partnerships

Public agencies must coordinate the work of private and commercial organizations involved in the operation of critical infrastructure. Most western governments no longer have direct control of their critical infrastructure following market deregulation. For instance, in North America energy generation and distribution have been opened to market competition. The Public Utility Regulatory Policy Act (PURPA) was intended to lower costs by encouraging investment in newer, more efficient technologies for energy generation. New entrants can sell energy to utilities without any responsibility for the operation of the transmission infrastructure. This contrasts with traditional market structures where the same companies owned and operated generation, transmission, and distribution. Federal Energy Regulatory Commission (FERC) Order 888 extended access to energy marketers. These private companies gained access to the distribution grid under the same conditions as the utilities. This creates problems when local and national governments must work together with many different stakeholders to increase the resilience of infrastructure prior to events such as Hurricane Katrina.

During an adverse event, it can become increasingly difficult for command-and-control systems to develop an overview of the infrastructure when many different operating companies have access to the networks. During the North American blackouts of 2003, the users of the network monitoring systems had to constantly enter manual values for parameters across the electricity distribution system because some companies had not yet provided automatic information feeds for their components of the grid. This provides a further example of how the usability of information systems is directly influenced by underlying market and governance structures.

The same processes of deregulation that complicate government contingency coordination in the energy industries are also apparent in telecommunications. In the past, national monopolies, such as British Telecom, France Telecom, and Deutsche Telekom, dominated domestic markets. However, by 1998 the European Commission had issued a series of directives that encouraged competition across both voice and data communications networks. These requirements were extended by the 1990 Open Network Provision (ONP) Framework Directive, which established the principles of "fair pricing" for resellers. The 1996 US Telecommunications Act was intended to enable competition between dominated domestic markets sectors of the media, including the provision of digital infrastructure. The provisions of this legislation were supported by technological developments and market changes; for instance, enabling competition between fixed and mobile telecommunications providers. These trends were not restricted to the United States and Europe. The Davidson Enquiry encouraged private sector involvement in the delivery of telecommunications services by recommending an end to the Telecom Australia monopoly.

Deregulation was, typically, intended to reduce costs to industry and domestic consumers by increasing competition. The impact of these different initiatives has subsequently been mitigated by pressures for market consolidation and amalgamation during different stages of the economic cycle. However, increasing levels of competition have created particular problems in ensuring the reliability of critical communications. The events of 9/11, of 7/7 in the United Kingdom, and the Madrid bombings in Spain have forced governments to consider ways in which to ensure that industry partners consider the resilience of their systems. For instance, following the US PATRIOT Act, any company that works in a critical infrastructure must take four steps:

- Assess its vulnerabilities to both physical and cyber-attacks.
- Plan to eliminate significant vulnerabilities.
- Develop systems to identify and prevent attempted attacks.
- Alert, contain, and rebuff attacks; and then, with FEMA, rebuild essential capabilities in the aftermath.

There is, however, no requirement that private commercial information systems integrate with the command-and-control networks maintained by federal agencies in the same way that the Obama healthcare reforms would have clinicians connect to national electronic patient records. This implies that there will not be any common user interfaces to provide a coordinated view across multiple industries and infrastructure in the minutes and hours following future contingencies. Instead, teams must work together using their individual information systems to collate the information required by local and national governments.

Both Hurricane Katrina and the Madrid bombings have illustrated the importance of training and rehearsal in response to terrorist attacks and natural disasters, especially given the lack of integration across the multiple information systems mentioned above. DHS has provided grants to local government and private entities for infrastructure protection, including emergency management, water security training, rail, transit and port security, metropolitan medical response, and terrorism prevention programs. In consequence, some infrastructure providers, including food distribution companies, have developed detailed business continuity plans to maintain the resilience of their organization. In other cases, government agencies have had to take a more proactive approach — for example, by establishing public-private partnerships to plan for a range of potential adverse events. In either case, it can be difficult for local and national governments to make up for the lack of common command-and-control infrastructure across the multiple agencies that support critical infrastructure.

Barriers from complexity

Complexity provides further barriers to the command-and-control mechanisms that help to mitigate civil contingencies. Complexity stems from dynamism and uncertainty. These combine to have a significant impact both on the utility and usability of government information systems. Critical infrastructures change rapidly in response to local needs so that it can be very hard for higher levels of government to keep pace with changes; for instance, in energy infrastructure, in demographic changes or even the deployment of emergency resources. Uncertainty is a problem because it is often difficult to provide government agencies with accurate predictions about the impact of contingencies, including natural disasters and terrorist attacks, upon local or national infrastructure.

Complexity undermines the usability of government command-and-control systems. At first sight, this is related to the mass of data that must be considered — for instance, when planning a coordinated response to a flood or hurricane. Planners must account for the impact on health care, on power distribution, on water, and food supplies, etc. However, the barriers created by the volume of relevant data have gradually been eroded through the development of information systems with sophisticated visualization facilities. Drills and exercises then provide opportunities for decision makers to develop the skills that extract key information from this mass of data.

The quality of information provided to command-and-control functions by these information systems is often undermined by the dynamism of critical infrastructure. For instance, the UK Department of Communities and Local Government (CLG) has developed an innovative GIS application that enables planners to identify the risks associated with almost every building across the country. Census data is integrated with information about business occupations. Records of previous fires can be combined with information about the responses to these incidents. End users can then create different scenarios to determine the costs and benefits from different allocations of resources to the fire and rescue services based on the risk profile of the local community. However, the insights that this information system provides have to be balanced against the difficulty of keeping the data up to date. Significant delays occur between changes taking place in a district and the associated updates in the information system. For example, construction could take several years before new housing appeared in the GIS. These delays are created by the intervals between major data collation exercises— for instance, in the United Kingdom, the national census takes place only once in a decade. Although other information sources are updated more regularly, further barriers complicate the task of updating the CLG toolset. Security concerns about the sensitive nature of this information prevent the distribution of new data over the Internet. Instead, existing tools run on standalone machines. This implies significant overheads for users who must install and configure each new version of the software. The dynamism of local communities and the stasis of many information tools complicate command and control during contingencies; maps, census data, and integrated information systems are unlikely to accurately reflect the situation faced by personnel "on the ground."

Complexity also arises from uncertainty. This is created by the barriers to information transfer both within and between different levels of government. However, there is also an inherent difficulty in predicting the consequence of contingencies on command and control structures during natural disasters, terrorist attacks, or technical failures. Many governments have tried to address this problem through the development of simulation software. The US Sandia National Laboratory has been particularly successful in refining these systems to a point where they can be used by a range of stakeholders, including FEMA. However, the simulations are stochastic: they will often produce very different results for different runs even of the same scenarios. The UK government has pioneered the use of modeling tools to help prepare for terrorist attacks on major transportation centers. These simulations use 3D models of key locations. They also exploit software agents to mimic the potential behavior of crowds exposed to fragmentation and blast from improvised explosive devices. The impact of each attack will vary depending on the reaction of crowds and the emergency services. The precise location of a blast can also affect the results; for example, on non-permanent structures within a building. For the end user, it is very difficult to use these tools to direct command-and-control activities because they provide very different insights into the worst plausible consequences of a civil contingency.

Barriers from the integration of infrastructure

Previous sections have focused on the many different organizational, structural, and technological barriers that have combined to undermine the usability and utility of government command-and-control systems for contingency response. One reason for this is that major IT acquisitions have followed traditional organizational boundaries, which often complicates information integration. Even where attempts have been made to bring systems together, the record has been less than impressive. Previous work (Johnson, 2011) described many of the problems that have undermined attempts to integrate electronic patient records in Europe and North America. A further example is provided by work to centralize the UK's 46 regional command-and-control systems for the fire and rescue services into nine centers. The UK government recently canceled £200 million of FireControl contracts after a series of delays. The minister responsible for this decision subsequently announced that the future command-and-control policy would be based on principles of "localism" (Johnson and Raue, 2010).

Previous piecemeal procurements have arguably been based around traditional organizational boundaries that have undermined coordinated approaches to contingency management. It is important to recognize, however, that governments have taken significant steps to address these problems. Governments across Europe and North America have recently reviewed their provision of electronic information (Johnson, 2011; Johnson and Raue, 2010). These initiatives have considered the use of service-oriented architectures to integrate command-and-control systems, especially at the interfaces between public and private organizations. The UK government's Enterprise Information Architecture (xGEA) provides a specific example. This was intended to provide a reference model to broaden and deepen "professionalism" in the provision of information services. A key objective was to help public organizations share information across organizational boundaries to improve services and save resources.

These themes of sharing and reuse are critical because they create the opportunities for emergency response to be better informed by the integration of data from across government departments. At the same time, these innovations create new concerns about the integrity and application of government information, when it may not originally have been intended for such uses. One of the key concepts in xGEA is a repository that will collect case studies of successful exchanges of data between government agencies. As might be expected, however, the initial focus is on the higher levels of government. Little attention seems to have been paid to the interfaces with local government agencies that played a key role in the response to contingencies such as Hurricane Katrina. These case studies can also provide examples of the exchange of "leading practices" or business processes. UK Cabinet Office documentation identifies four initial types of exemplar. These include a managed service built using existing staff and technical resources. They also include solution exemplars. These require additional investments but are based on proven techniques. A third form of "exemplar" provides patterns that can be followed again. Finally, lessons learned provide more focused recommendations on particular topics (Knight, 2008). These distinctions should be extended to recognize the importance of human-computer interaction.

The UK government has also identified a process by which xGEA supports the exchange of information across government. The identification of business needs leads to a sustained search across the repository of previous exemplars to provide a template for exchange. This is then placed within the broader context of the xGEA — for instance, by mapping elements of the case study to the technical approaches used in previous systems. The final stage is to deliver the service provision within the end user organization. Although it is too early to determine whether or not this approach has yielded the intended benefits, it is clear that the success or failure of these innovations will rest on the degree to which they can provide usable services across the boundaries that exist between local and national governments as well as between private and public organizations well before any contingency takes place.

SUMMARY

A number of civil contingencies, ranging from natural disasters to terrorist attacks, have revealed the limits of government intervention in national critical infrastructure. Very often, central agencies have been slow to respond. When they have been able to assist, the aid has often been of little practical benefit. This chapter has explored some of the reasons for this. In particular, it has identified a range of barriers that hinder the exchange of information between local and national governments, within fire and rescue services, as well as between public and private organizations have been identified. Many of these problems relate to the usability of government information systems. The root causes can be traced back to political concerns over the ownership of data and contradictory views about the role of central government in protecting the population from civil contingencies.

This chapter has focused on the problems of information exchange that have undermined the usability of command-and-control systems as local and national governments work to protect critical infrastructure. These same problems not only affect government agencies, but also have a direct impact on the general public. During the 2007 UK floods, one family saw water pour through the door of their home. They asked the local government agency for sandbags, which arrived 1 week later. This was after their property had sustained significant water damage. When the father called the local fire and rescue service, he was put through to a different county. They were unable to provide any help as he tried to evacuate his family from the rising flood waters. He, therefore, again telephoned the local council and was told to go to a nearby leisure center. He drove his family at some risk through the flood waters only to find that he had been given wrong information. The leisure center was not being used as an evacuation point (Knight, 2008). Individuals were forced to search through dozens of web sites to find information about insurance claims, about whether or not they could drink the water in their main's supply, about the disconnection or restoration of electricity, and about the risk of further flooding. These sites were usually overloaded with inquiries, and response times were very poor. Further work is urgently required not just to assess whether usability concerns can be adequately represented within national e-governance initiatives, such as the xGEA program mentioned above, but also whether those same initiatives can support the information needs of the general public as they work to protect local communities in the aftermath of natural disasters and terrorist attacks.

References

Johnson, C. W. (2007). Establishing public policy as a primary cause of technological failure: Did market deregulation cause the North American blackout, August 14th, 2003? In T. Cant (Ed.), *12th Australian workshop on safety-related programmable systems (SCS'07), volume XXXI, conferences in research and practice in information technology*, Australian Computer Society.

Johnson, C. W. (2008). Understanding failures in international infrastructures: A comparison of major blackouts in North America and Europe. In J. Simmons, D. J. Mohan & M. Mullane (Eds.), *Proceedings of the 26th international conference on systems safety, Vancouver, Canada*, Unionville, VA, USA: International Systems Safety Society 0-9721385-8-7.

Johnson, C. W. (2009). Information management for mobile communications in the European floods of 2007. In J. Loeffler & M. Klann (Eds.), *Mobile response. Lecture Notes in Computing Science, 5424* (pp. 1–11). Springer Verlag ISBN 0302-9743.

Johnson, C. W. (2011). Identifying common problems in the acquisition and deployment of large-scale software projects in the US and UK healthcare systems. *Safety Science*, *5*(49), 735–745 ISSN: 0925-7535.

Johnson, C. W., & Raue, S. (2010). On the safety implications for e-governance: Assessing the hazards of enterprise information architectures in safety-critical applications. In E. Schoitsch (Ed.), *Proceedings of SAFECOMP 2010, 29th international conference on computer safety, reliability and security*, Springer Verlag LNCS 6351, 2010.

Knight, K. (2008, March). *Facing the challenge: The chief fire and rescue adviser's review of the operational response by the fire and rescue service to the widespread flooding in England during 2007*. London, UK: Department for Communities and Local Government.

National Infrastructure Advisory Council. U.S. Department of Homeland Security, US national strategy for the physical protection of critical infrastructures and key assets, Washington DC, February. (2003). Available on http://www.whitehouse.gov/pcipb/physical.html. Accessed March 2008.

Pitt. (2007, December). *Pitt review learning lessons from the 2007 floods (interim report)*. London, UK: UK Cabinet Office.

United States Congress. A failure of initiative: Final report of the select bipartisan committee to investigate the preparation for and response to Hurricane Katrina. (2006). Washington, DC: Government Printing Office. Available on http://www.gpoaccess.gov/katrinareport/mainreport.pdf. Accessed November 2011.

United States Department of Homeland Security. The Federal response to Hurricane Katrina, lessons learned, Washington DC, February. (2006). Available on http://georgewbush-whitehouse.archives.gov/reports/katrina-lessons-learned/. Accessed November 2011.

CHAPTER

Legislative Drafting Systems

9

Monica Palmirani*, Fabio Vitali†

CIRSFID—University of Bologna, Bologna, Italy Dept of Computer Science, University of Bologna, Bologna, Italy†*

"The number of the section must be in italic, and the heading of the section must also be in italic, but the dash separating them must NOT be in italic. That's obvious!"

— An anonymous officer of the legal drafting office of some Parliament

INTRODUCTION

Legislative information systems are computer tools that help, streamline, and manage the activities of legislative offices, mostly the back-office activities of a national parliament or of any assembly entrusted with legislative power. Although the largest part of these tools are not in direct contact with the general population, they have an indirect, yet very important effect on it, and their systematic and correct use can concretely improve the efficiency and transparency of the democratic processes they support. Legislative drafting — i.e., the support of the actual wording of the content of a piece of legislation — is a major activity that such systems need to support and specific tools exist for this very purpose.

Legislative information systems are composed of a number of tools to control the workflow of a legislative assembly. These are aimed at collecting contributions from the political structure of the assembly, organizing the discussions in the official sessions, compiling documents out of these activities (e.g., creating transcripts and structuring bills), and distributing such documents in the subsequent workflow steps, including final publication to the general public in print or on the Web. Some of these activities are straightforwardly similar to other document-centered processes (albeit strongly leaning toward very formalized and structured workflows), but there are a few activities peculiar to legislation (such as consolidation or long-term preservation) that require very specific tools for successful completion (Bing, 2003; Greenleaf, 2004).

The adoption of formats based on Extensible Markup Language (XML) for these documents is an ongoing discussion among experts and practitioners, and the unwarranted optimism of technologists has often conflicted with the equally unwarranted skepticism of traditionalists: rarely has criticism regarded the usefulness and the undisputed advantages of the innovation; more often, it has aimed at the usability of the existing tools, and most frequently at the disruption they would create. Such skepticism was based on the fears that they would be acting directly on existing, tested, and well-understood tasks, processes, and job descriptions, which in many cases have been in place for decades if not for centuries (Marchetti, Megale, Seta, & Vitali, 2002).

Yet technology advancements loom; new functions are first dreamed, then wished, and then outright demanded by interested parties. At the same time, the global economic crisis has posed some serious questions for many items of the classically huge expenditures that Parliaments make for the paper-based management of bills, transcripts, and approved acts.

A case in point is *consolidation* (Seppius, 2008) — the generation of the current form of an act after a modification act that contains only editing instructions such as "delete this structure," "add these words" etc.; in many countries, consolidation is done manually, often by third-party providers with little or no control, authority, or officiality in the generation of the result. Such providers would usually produce the consolidation of codes and acts as printed volumes and/or CD-ROMs and would regularly (e.g., every 3 or 6 months) release them for a fee to professionals such as judges, lawyers, and public administrators, and rather infrequently would sell them to the general public. Giving open and free access to up-to-date legislation is becoming a frequent and pressing request, and this is widely considered a clear democratic advancement. Even more, requests now regard not only up-to-date *current* legislation, but *point-in-time* legislation (Arnold-Moore, 1995; Palmirani, 2005), whereby one can access the full legislative context in force now and at any precise moment of the past. Quite often, past personal, political, administrative, or even judiciary events need to be examined and analyzed under the light of the law as it was in force at the time in which such events occurred, rather than what is in force now. For instance, in many countries, civil cases are evaluated according to the law that was in force at the moment when the cause for litigation arose, rather than what is in force during the case itself (EU Publication Office, 2009).

Introducing XML-based tools into a world that accepted word processors only recently — and uneasily, at that — and where it is not unheard of for cut-and-paste to be done with scissors and glue, and markup with felt pens, is proving rather difficult. (Figure 9.1 shows an example of bill drafting using manual techniques at the Irish Parliament in 2005.)

The real elephant in the room, however, is not the resistance of the workforce, but rather the impact and role of *tradition*. The characteristics of every workflow step, the exact boundaries of every job description, the minute details of every typographical rendering of documents — all these have histories that run decades into the past and cannot be put into discussion; and yet their importance and strictness are downplayed when they are discussed with any of the affected individuals, regardless of whether it is an interview leading to formal requirements or an informal chat at the water fountain. The hard-learned experience, in many cases, is that the real objective of the tools is to mimic as closely as possible the workings and the results of the traditional process, regardless of the complication in the workflow or the very usability of the tools themselves.

Within the SEAL European Project (http://www.leibnizcenter.org/previous-projects/seal), in June 2008 a number of XML-based tools for Parliaments were tested for functionality and usability with real users from the Dutch House of Representatives and from the Italian Senate. The purpose was formative rather than summative: it was requested that functionality and usability weaknesses in the then-current batch of legislative tools be assessed and fixed in a subsequent implementation phase. We were involved in the organization and execution of the Italian tests, where important feedback was gained that allowed the tested tools to be significantly improved and extended.

Due to the very nature of the SEAL Project, no distinction was made between *functionality weaknesses* (the user expects the tool to help him/her in performing a task, when in fact it does not) and *usability weaknesses* (the tool does provide the necessary function, but the user could not use it, or could hardly use it, or found it unhelpful or less than satisfactory) and the resulting report

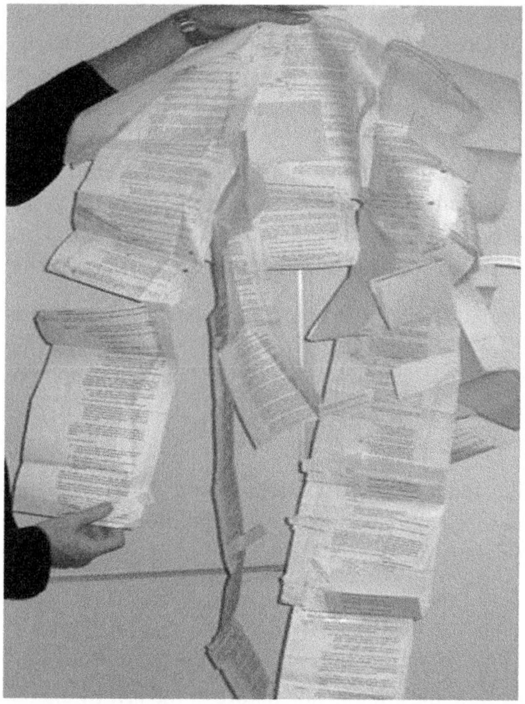

FIGURE 9.1 Example of manual bill drafting in the Irish Parliament before the introduction of automated tools

(Courtesy of Patricia Doran, Clerk to the Joint Committee on Health and Children, Houses of the Oireachtas). (For color version of this figure, see the web version of this chapter.)

(van den Brink & de Maat, 2008) describes both types of weaknesses without distinction. The following sections briefly describe the results of the Italian tests and give pointers to similar tests performed in The Netherlands with different tools.

XML FOR LEGISLATIVE DOCUMENTS: ADVANTAGES AND ISSUES

The new challenge of the Internet era is to put into use all the potentialities of the Web, including the newer Web 2.0 technologies, to improve the interchange between different legislative bodies and to provide for the long-term preservation of digital document collections (see Palmirani, 2011, and Chapter 3, Usability and Government 2.0 of this book). For the legislative resources these issues are dramatically real, and they represent critical points of the digitization process toward a paperless era. This approach, viewed in a long-term perspective, supports the development of projects about e-gov, e-democracy, and e-participation and possibly creates essential prerequirements for a competing and growing economy.

The United States' OpenGov initiative, launched by President Obama in January 2009 (see the Memorandum on Transparency and Open Government, 2009), aims at creating "an unprecedented level of openness in government" for ensuring "the public trust and establish[ing] a system of transparency, public participation, and collaboration. Openness will strengthen our democracy and promote efficiency and effectiveness in government." Similarly, in July 2009 the Australian government declared its endorsement of OpenGov initiatives (Australian Government, 2010), to promote greater participation of the citizens in Australian democracy. It committed itself "to open government based on a culture of engagement, built on better access to and use of government-held information, and sustained by the innovative use of technology."

National Official Gazettes organizations in Europe and outside of Europe alike[1] can play a key role in achieving these ends by adopting a legal XML standard that preserves the legality, authenticity, and authority over time of some of the most fundamental document collections of a country, such as the law corpora. All Official Gazettes are required to safeguard four pillars:

- Grant to all citizens equal access, guaranteeing transparency and independency from proprietary applications,
- Support open access to the legal resources as a fundamental legal value in a modern democracy,
- Foster the usage of public information by the private sector, and
- Henceforth support interoperability across independent implementation and computer systems.

An abstract analysis of the fundamental functions of the Official Gazettes of the European (see Hietanen, 2007) and non-European bodies underlines their three main roles, all independent of the legal tradition or the form of government

- *Provide legal validity* of the normative acts through an official publication instrument (mostly empowered at the constitutional level as cognitive source of law).
- *Ensure the publicity, authenticity, and knowledgeability* of the law.
- *Preserve for the long term* the content and nature of the law by enacting a controlled and authoritative legal deposit of the documents on which it relies.

Recently, those institutional roles, fully endorsed by all democratic establishments, were enriched with new functions:

- *Offer free and authoritative access* to the original sources of the law on the Web.
- *Provide consolidated and updated collections of laws* with annotations.
- *Supply a legally binding form of online publication* of the original texts (e.g., digital authentic publication).
- *Provide new value-adding services to users* (e.g., commentaries, access to relevant jurisprudence, drafting of legal notes, etc.)

Figure 9.2 (elaborated from Publications Office of the European Union, 2009, p. 230) shows some statistics regarding services provided by the Official Gazette offices of all European countries (27 member states plus the European Union institutions themselves).

The new technologies and services that have recently become ubiquitous do provide new opportunities for services, and new expectations from users. The Web 2.0 platform (see Chapter 3, Usability and Government 2.0) has been proposed as a mechanism through which to fight the overproduction of legal information (Noveck, 2009), the crisis of legislation (Sartor, Palmirani, Francesconi, & Biasiotti, 2011), and the disorientation of end users. Among the advantages envisioned, mobile tools such as smartphones, tablets, etc. (see Chapter 13, Mobile Access), can be used to provide

[1]see, e.g., Lupo et al., 2007, for the European Union, http://www.usgovxml.com/ and https://www.niem.gov/Pages/default.aspx for the United States, http://projeto.lexml.gov.br/ for Brazil, Cifuentes-Silva, Sifaqui, & Labra-Gayo, 2011, for Chile

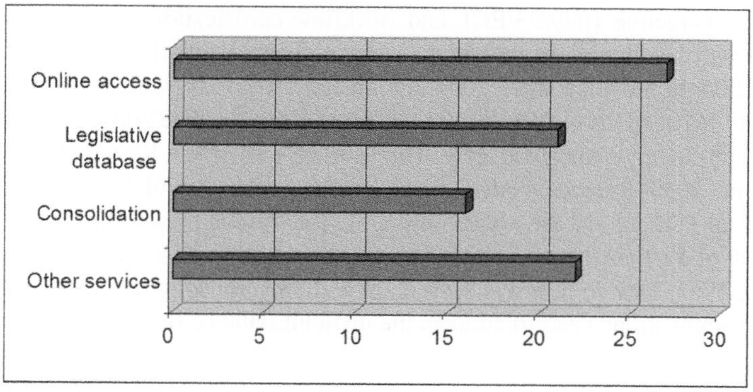

FIGURE 9.2 Advanced ICT services provided by national Official Gazettes in the European Union

(For color version of this figure, see the web version of this chapter.)

navigation of legal content in any context; RSS can be considered for real-time updates of the parliamentary activities; expert tagging can improve the search of legal information by providing sophisticated qualification and interconnection of the legal content; folksonomic tagging (Vander Wal, 2007) may provide a shared outlet of hard-earned field experience from professionals and practitioners on the legal documents, possibly even fostered by semantic Web tools; and social networks can be used to foster jurisprudence and commentary.

These new applications have the increasing potential to remove the barriers of the "digital divide"—still rather high in this domain—and strongly to affect the desirable development of digital democracies. As the Global Information Technology Report 2009-2010 (Dutta & Mia, 2010) states, "Despite the best efforts of governments and the private sector, the broadband digital divide persists as a significant challenge to inclusive and sustainable development, especially in emerging economies" (p. 97). To open the door to these benefits, the use of XML-based formats for legal documents is an undeniable improvement over competing approaches.

There has been a skeptical attitude toward the adoption of XML for legal and legislative documentation (Global Centre for ICT in Parliament, 2010). In part, we believe, this is due to errors made by enthusiastic early adopters, and in many ways it is true that some competing formats, (e.g., PDF or PDF/A) are far easier to generate when managing legislative resources. Nevertheless, many new opportunities to implement Web 2.0 functionalities would be lost without a proper and true markup of the document content and structures via appropriate XML-based formats. Even when the PDF is enriched with metadata (as e.g., in the Global Legal Information Network project, http://www.glin.gov/), an insurmountable fracture remains between the textual content as it is originally delivered and endorsed by the authority and the metadata, which is not and cannot remain aligned to the text. By following this path, we are unable to provide open documents to citizens; nor can we apply reasoning tools to the text or use semantic technologies to manage the legal content.

Yet, in spite of the skepticism toward XML in the legal domain, many parliaments have started the process of electronic publication from an XML document; and only later is the XML transformed into some unmodifiable form (e.g., PDF/A) so as to present the outcome to the end user in human-readable form. In several European countries the increasing use of XML for legislative documents has made it easier to publish the Official Gazette online, keeping its legal validity through different security systems that guarantee authenticity, validity, and integrity (chain of confidence, digital/electronic signatures [see EU Directive 1999/93/EC], and workflow certification). For instance, the paper and electronic versions of legislative documents have been deemed equally valid in Estonia since 2001, in France since 2004, in Slovenia since 2007, and in Italy since 2009. The electronic version of legislative documents has been the only authentic format in Norway since 2001, in Austria since 2004, in Denmark since 2008, and in Spain since 2009. The World e-Parliament Report 2010 (Global Centre for ICT in Parliament, 2010) provides interesting figures on the use of the XML for legislation in Parliaments: 34% of Parliaments are now using XML for various reasons and for different purposes. For instance, 90% of Parliaments use XML for interoperability, 71% for presentation of legislative documents on the Web, 48% to improve searching, and 38% for long-term preservation.

Most of these applications need to address the difficult balance of three main aspects (Barabucci et al., 2010):

1. Preserving, as much as possible, the separation between the document content as delivered by the original author and the metadata added in the post-delivery workflow
2. Preserving the semantic descriptiveness of the document content, structure, and context (hopefully in XML)
3. Maintaining the legal validity of the document manifestation (as expressed in the particular typographical layout that was actually signed by the issuing authority)

Consequently, although the digitization of other types of documents does not pose serious problems, the processes of creation, management, and distribution of legal documents impose more specific issues: authenticity, integrity, validity, and persistence.

At the same time, we aim to guarantee interoperability, interchange, and machine readability during the lawmaking process.

THE ARCHITECTURE OF LEGISLATIVE INFORMATION SYSTEMS

For a correct analysis of the HCI issues necessary in the legislative system, we propose, in Figure 9.3, an abstract architecture for managing the complexities of all legislative parliamentary processes. It is composed of several independent modules accessible using standard World Wide Web protocols such as HyperText Transfer Protocol and Secure HyperText Transfer Protocol (HTTP and HTTPS) via the main Web-based application.

Particularly important in the context of legislative documents is the editor, a module that supports the legal-drafting activities in both the *ex-ante* and *ex-post* phases[2] and is used by the legal experts for their tasks. The legal document needs different types of manipulations during its lifecycle: drafting, modifications, consolidation, refinement, metadata annotation, editorial, and graphical work. A specialized editor has to manage all these functions. In addition, the editor has to manage the specification of the markup, the import and export in XML from external sources (Microsoft Word, HTML, plain text, etc.) and the validation of the resulting document using XML Schemas or Document Type Definitions (DTDs) corresponding to a selected legislative XML standard.

[2] *Ex-ante* phases are all the phases before the official endorsement by the Parliament or by the powered authority. *Ex-post* phases are all the editorial phases done after the official deliberation (e.g. publication in the Official Gazette).

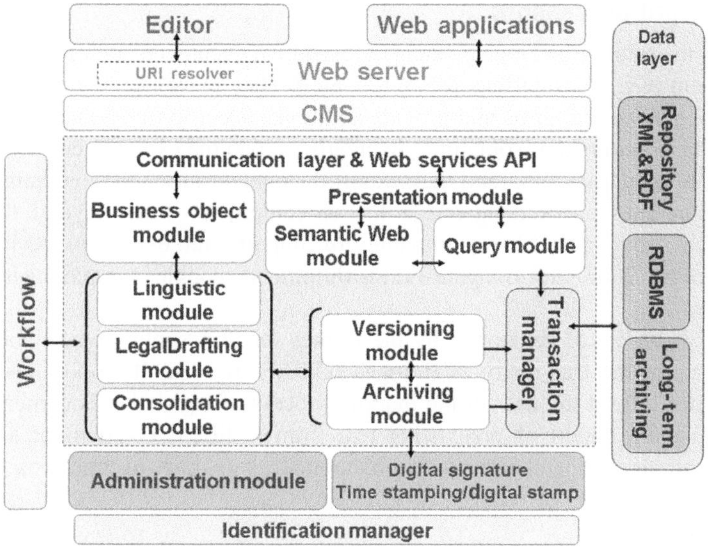

FIGURE 9.3 Abstract architecture of parliamentary information systems

(For color version of this figure, see the web version of this chapter.)

The editors specifically addressing markup in XML of legislative documents have to guarantee a number of specific functions, among which are the following:

- Stand between the user and the XML syntax; allow the markup even if the user is not an XML expert
- Help the user in generating correct markup of the document according to the rules and the best practices of the local legal drafting offices; perform semantic checks on any errors that cannot be captured by the XML schema during the validation process (e.g., an empty heading)
- Provide some automation in the markup, possibly through parsers of the structure, of the normative links, of the annexes, of the images, of the metadata; provide context- and position-dependent suggestions to the user (e.g., as to which could be the correct elements and metadata in any given circumstance)
- Generate or convert the document into XML at any moment during its elaboration; validate even individual fragments of the document (e.g., validate only the header, or only the metadata section, etc.)
- Generate the document in other different formats — PDF, HTML, etc.
- Have a design that is based on the existing workflow and not on the needs of the markup, the XML schema being used, or the editing platform

The existing editors for legislative XML markup can be organized into three main categories: extensions to word processors, customization of native XML editors, and Web-based tools.

Extensions to word processors

These tools allow the creation and management of legislative documents within a standard office automation environment (e.g., Open Office, MS Word, etc.). They make use of existing competencies in using well-known general platforms and provide additional specific functionalities as add-ons to the main interface. These editors use (sometimes in creative ways) the expressiveness of the internal format (styles, custom properties, etc.) and they export the content into XML on demand. The XML is validated and sometimes checked against a list of compliancy rules beyond those included in the XML schema. They also have a module for import and export in XML. Norma-Editor (Palmirani & Benigni, 2007) and Bungeni-Editor (http://code.google.com/p/bungeni-editor/) belong to this category.

Norma-Editor is an editor developed by the Center for Philosophy and Sociology of Law and Computer and Law of the University of Bologna (CIRSFID) 2002. It works in VisualBasic .NET on top of MS Word to lead the user in the markup process of legislative documents in XML, with a focus on helping the import of preexisting text from a different system or authority. Norma-Editor has the peculiarity that it manages in a semiautomatic way point-in-time consolidation, and thus

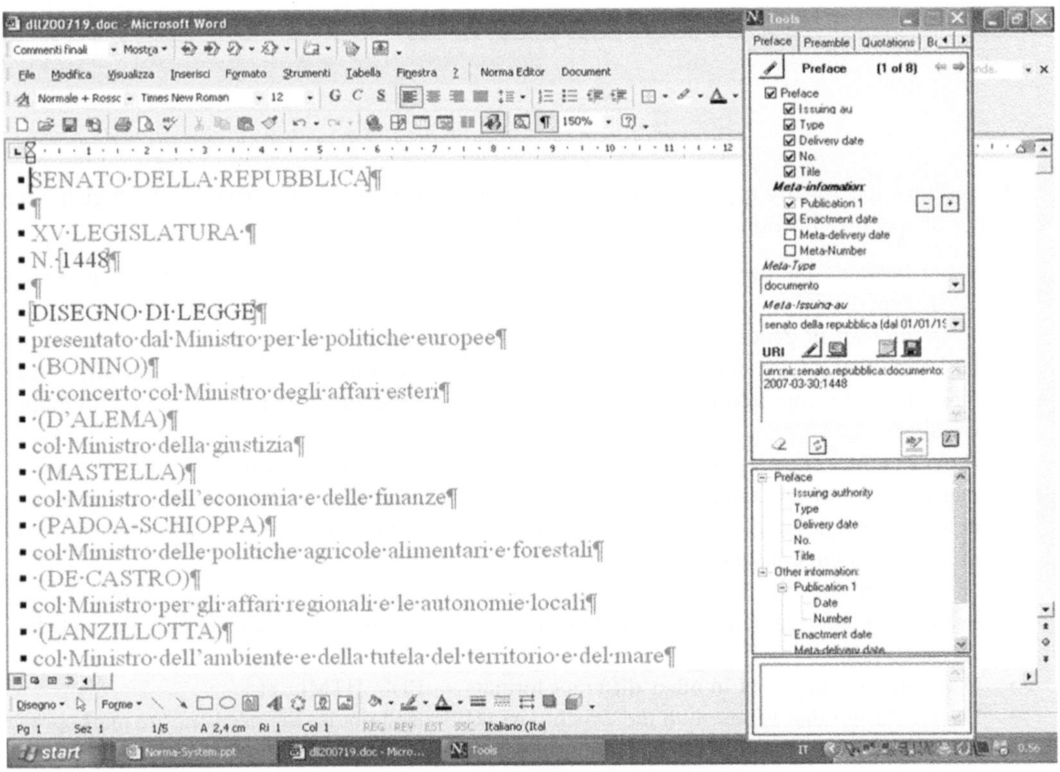

FIGURE 9.4 Example of a bill of the Italian Senate marked up with Norma-Editor

(For color version of this figure, see the web version of this chapter.)

it helps keep the law collections up to date. Norma-Editor has had different releases over time, version, languages, and purposes, the most successful of which is being used daily by the Italian Supreme Court (*Corte di Cassazione*) to mark up in XML (using the *NormeInRete* standard) and consolidate more than 50,000 acts (Figure 9.4).

The Bungeni-Editor[3] has been under development since 2007 by the United Nations Department of Economic and Social Affairs (UNDESA) under the project, "Africa i-Parliaments Action Plan." It is an editor based on OpenOffice 3.1 and developed using Java 6. This means that it is a cross-platform tool (it works in Linux, MacOS, and Windows). The Bungeni-Editor extends the common functionalities of OpenOffice to provide functionalities specific to the parliamentary activities, as well as support for XML import and export according to the Akoma Ntoso schema (Vitali & Zeni, 2007; Vitali, 2011). Starting in 2010, both the Akoma Ntoso schema and the Bungeni-Editor have aimed at a more international audience, with users and adopters both in Europe and in Latin America.

Currently Bungeni supports the markup of acts, bills, and debate records. It does not implement a parser to recognize the document structure but uses a database of suggestions for the user to carry out the markup. For instance, it contains a list of the names of all parliament members, their role, their institutional positions, and the full panoply of steps of the legislative procedure. This helps the markup

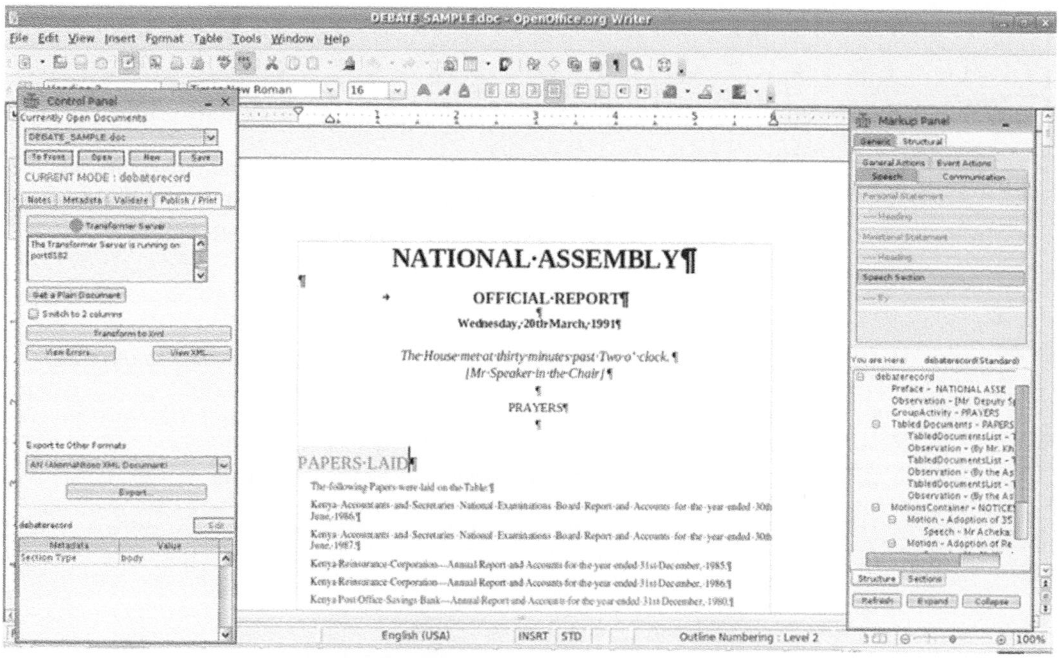

FIGURE 9.5 Example of a Kenyan debate in Bungeni

(For color version of this figure, see the web version of this chapter.)

[3]*Bungeni* is a Kiswahili word meaning *within the Parliament.*

of debate records, which, according to the Akoma Ntoso rules, requires the unambiguous identification of every individual taking a turn in the debate, as well as the position they occupy (e.g., minister, ministerial delegate chair of the main assembly, chair of a commission relevant to the debate, etc.) (Figure 9.5).

Customization of native XML editors

These editors are managed through (and are strictly dependent on) the specific XML schema they support, and at each step they revalidate the document according to the XML schema itself. This feature allows the immediate identification of structural errors, yet it rapidly limits the overall flexibility of the tool: some operations are blocked from even starting, and it is the XML schema, rather than the needs of the user, that determines the sequence of allowed actions. The initial steps of the drafting process require looser control and allow content authors to express themselves freely — only at the end is it important to execute rigorous structural and semantic validations — so most of these automatic checks at every step are redundant and oppressive. Some examples of these editors are

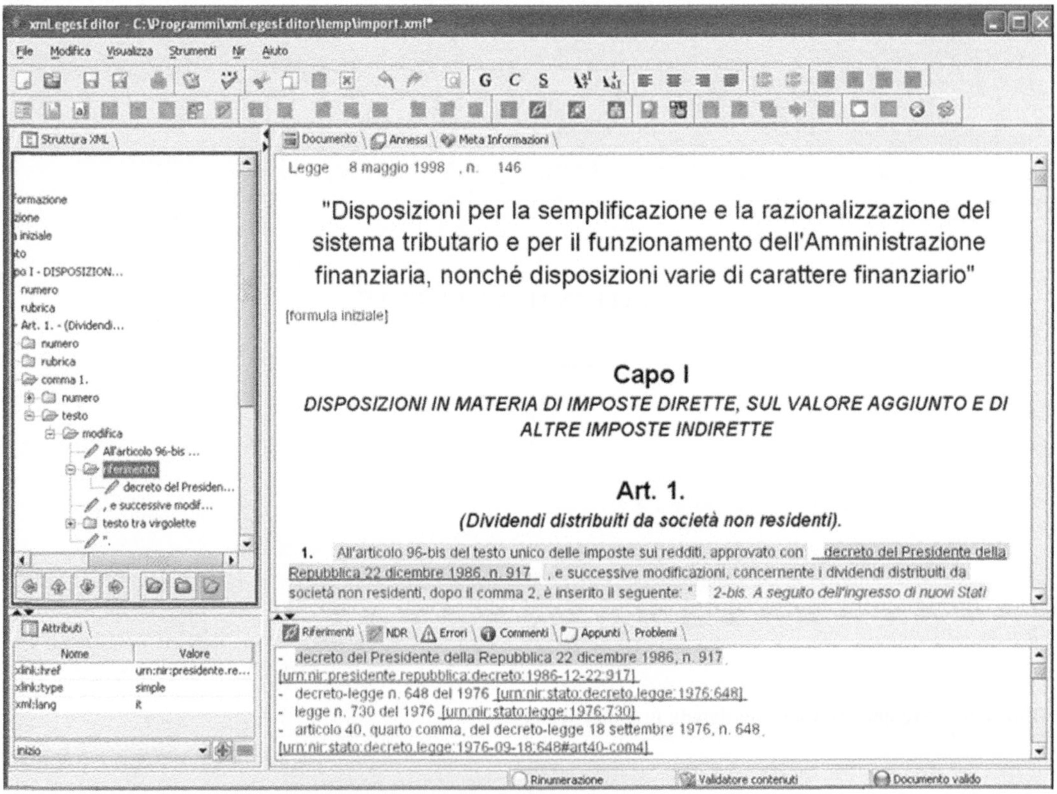

FIGURE 9.6 Example of an Italian law marked up with xmLeges editor

(For color version of this figure, see the web version of this chapter.)

xmLeges, developed by the Institute of Legal Information Theory and Techniques of the Italian National Research Centre in Florence (http://www.xmleges.org; Agnoloni, Francesconi, & Spinosa, 2007), *MetaVox*, developed by Leibniz Center for Law, University of Amsterdam (van de Ven, Hoekstra, Winkels, de Maat, & Kollár, 2008), and *XCential LegisPro*, the editor for the Assembly of the State of California (http://xcential.com/navigate.php?p=legisproxmetal; Vergottini, 2011).

The xmLeges editor has been in continuous development since 2003. This software is designed to lead the user through the phases of the actual drafting of legislative documents rather than checking the markup of already existing legislative documents. xmLeges is a native XML editor that uses a set of grids to aid the user in drafting documents. It was expressly designed for the Italian *NormeInRete* standard (Marchetti et al., 2002), and it represents a powerful instrument for managing documents marked up in that vocabulary. For this reason, its interface does not support languages other than Italian (Figure 9.6).

Xcential LegisPro is a highly customized version of the XmetaL editor, and has been deployed in the assembly of the State of California since 2006. Xcential LegisPro is a native XML editor that provides a quasi-WYSIWYG editing environment suitable for attorneys and other nontechnical staff to draft and amend legislation. In particular, it provides context-sensitive commands and a drag-and-drop

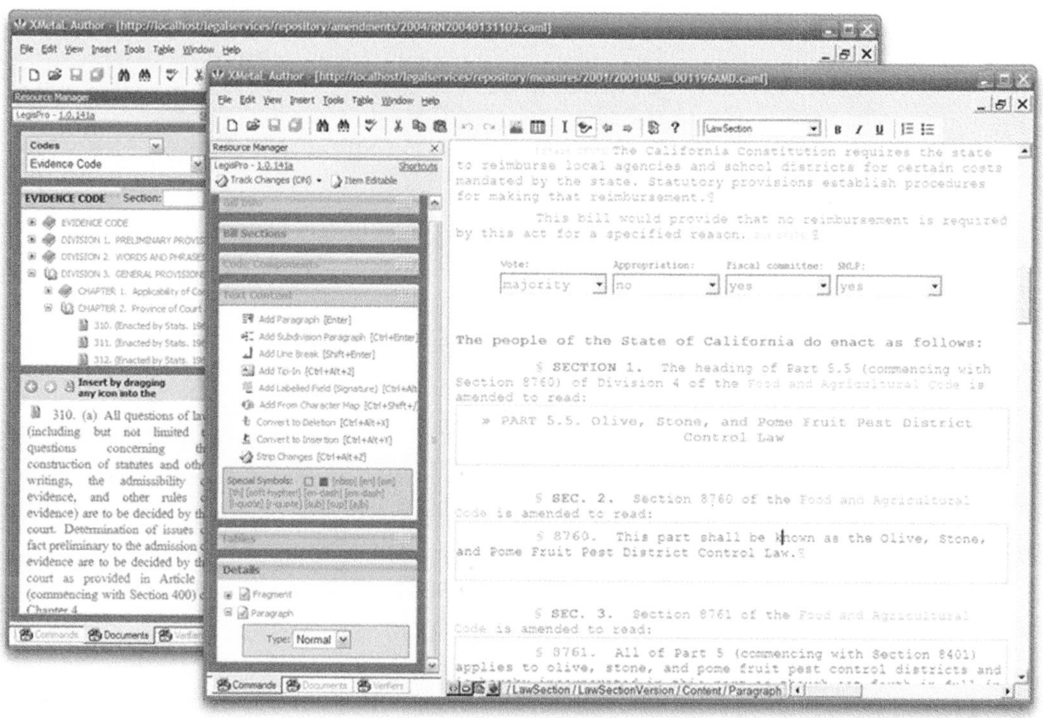

FIGURE 9.7 Example of a bill of the State of California in LegisPro

(For color version of this figure, see the web version of this chapter.)

environment for treating components of legislation as building blocks in drafting new legislation. Underlying LegisPro is a custom legislative XML schema, but the editor can be adapted to various legislative schemas such as Akoma Ntoso by way of configuration — supplying the schema, basic templates, and a set of XML-based configuration files to define appropriate behavior in various contexts. The editor connects with XML repositories, relational databases, or even a simple file system for access editable documents (Figure 9.7).

Web-based editors

These editors are Web-based applications, mostly using technologies based in Asynchronous JavaScript and XML (AJAX) — which, like GoogleDocs, are capable of managing word-processing tasks within a browser window. This type of editor is promising, especially considering the advances in cloud computing, but we must also consider problems such as privacy, security, autonomy, and traceability. A popular application that uses this approach is *the Authoring Tool for Amendments (AT4AM)*,

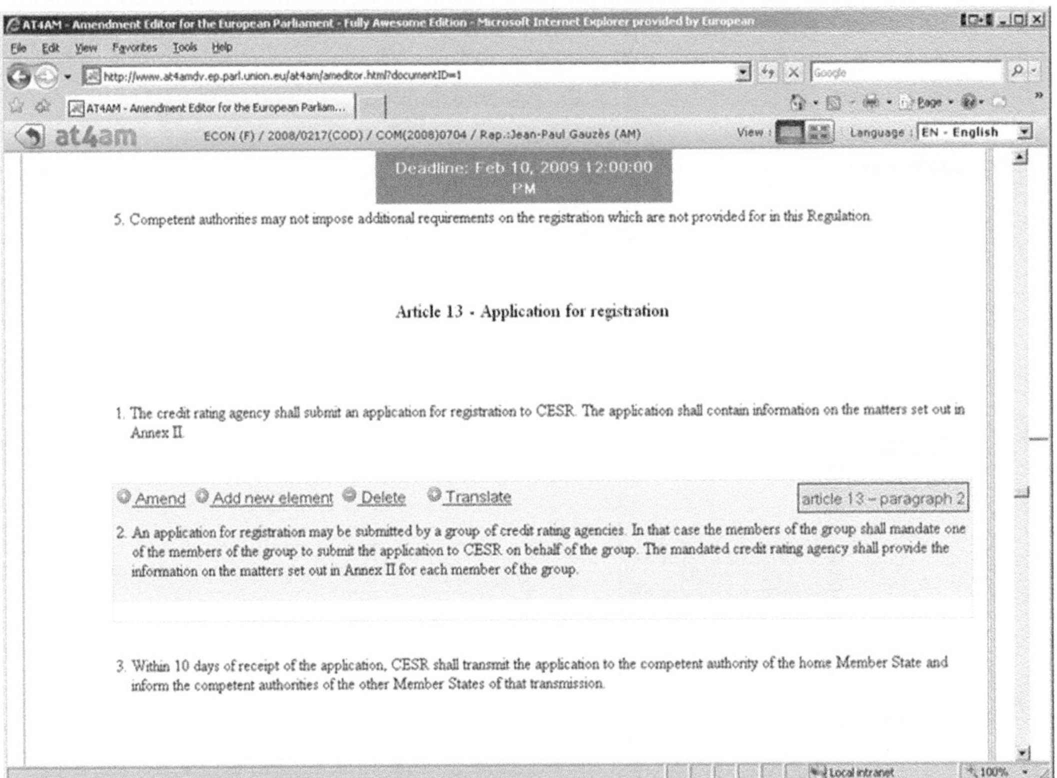

FIGURE 9.8 Example of amendment proposed by AT4AM

(For color version of this figure, see the web version of this chapter.)

developed in 2010 by the European Parliament. AT4AM (Fabiani, 2011) allows Members of the European Parliament (MEPs) to write and send amendments to any European Commission proposal through the Web using any browser. Since amendments are usually short and limited texts, regulated by rigorous procedures and following a set of fixed linguistic constraints, the Web editor proved to be an appropriate solution, much better than the previous one, which was based on hand-filled templates in MS Word, printed out and delivered on paper to the drafting offices.

AM4EP uses the Akoma Ntoso schema and enables all MEPs to see and edit Commission proposals directly onto the original text. The user thus sees the wording of the proposal as it should read if the amendment was accepted, and the tool automatically generates the amendment as a set of editing instructions as expected by the offices. Currently 70% of the amendments of the European Parliament are submitted using this tool and the editor was awarded European Parliament Best Tool for 2010 (Figure 9.8).

CASE STUDY: TESTING LEGISLATIVE SYSTEM TOOLS

In the tests carried out at the Italian Senate, we encountered four different types of end users, each with different needs:

- *Legal Drafting Office of the Assembly*: In 80% of cases, this office converts and fixes existing documents that come from parties, deputies, senators, ministries, government, and other institutional bodies. Therefore its main goal is to have a light tool for checking and fixing existing documents and for marking them up in XML.
- *Committee Secretary's Office*: The initial work of this office is to prepare, order, and assemble amendments for the voting sessions. After a voting session, its main task is to apply the amendments to the document under discussion. The amendments are not the modifications: they are only textual changes and no temporal element affects their application.
- *Office of General Affairs of the Assembly*: This office is tasked with exchanging documents between the different legislative houses, other institutions, and other relevant actors. Its main task is to output the XML file of the internal lifecycle and to import into XML the corresponding input from any of the external bodies. A secondary task is to make a rapid comparison between the two texts (the *synopsis table*).
- *ICT Department*: This department eliminates redundancy in the data, improves the quality of the documents, ensures that each step of the workflow is consistent with the rest, and provides effective tools for the end users to save time, paper, costs, and errors.

This shows that there is no single tool that captures all the required functionality but four main tools differentiated by the type of task:

- Checking, fixing, and creating documents — legal drafting offices
- Managing amendment reports and the consolidation of amendments — committee secretaries' offices
- Comparing different texts coming from different actors, steps, etc. — general office
- Parsing existing documents and translating them into XML — ICT department supporting all the other offices

DISEGNO DI LEGGE D'INIZIATIVA DEL GOVERNO —	DISEGNO DI LEGGE TESTO PROPOSTO DALLA COMMISSIONE —
Art. 1.	Art. 1.
1. Per le attività connesse all'esercizio delle funzioni inerenti al proprio mandato, i parlamentari possono avvalersi di personale esterno alle amministrazioni della Camera dei deputati e del Senato della Repubblica, in qualità di collaboratori .	1. Per le attività connesse all'esercizio delle funzioni inerenti al proprio mandato, i parlamentari possono avvalersi **, oltre che di prestazioni fornite in base a contratti di servizi,** di personale esterno alle amministrazioni della Camera dei deputati e del Senato della Repubblica, in qualità di collaboratori **parlamentari** .
2. Il rapporto di lavoro dei collaboratori parlamentari ha natura fiduciaria e ad esso si applica, sulla base degli accordi tra le parti , la disciplina privatistica in materia di contratti di lavoro subordinato, di collaborazione coordinata e continuativa, ai sensi degli articoli 61 e seguenti del decreto legislativo 10 settembre 2003, n. 276, e successive modificazioni, ovvero di lavoro autonomo.	2. Il rapporto di lavoro dei collaboratori parlamentari ha natura fiduciaria e ad esso si applica, sulla base degli accordi tra le parti **e nel rispetto delle leggi e dei contratti collettivi applicabili,** , la disciplina privatistica in materia di contratti di lavoro subordinato, di collaborazione coordinata e continuativa, ai sensi degli articoli 61 e seguenti del decreto legislativo 10 settembre 2003, n. 276, e successive modificazioni, ovvero di lavoro autonomo.
	2-bis. I contratti di cui al comma 2 dovranno essere certificati presso le sedi competenti, secondo le disposizioni di cui agli articoli 75 e seguenti del decreto legislativo 10 settembre 2003, n. 276.
3. Salvo diverso accordo tra le parti, i contratti di cui al comma 2 hanno durata commisurata a quella della legislatura nel corso della quale sono instaurati e possono essere rinnovati. I contratti medesimi si risolvono di diritto in caso di cessazione anticipata del mandato parlamentare rispetto alla conclusione della legislatura.	3. *Identico*

FIGURE 9.9 A comparative view of an Italian bill returned to the original house after modifications

The Italian legislative process is perfectly bicameral, with two houses that have identical powers and the requirement that both houses pass exactly the same text before a bill can become law. Either house may be the starting point in the discussion of a bill. Within the Italian legislative process, we can thus find two main macro-processes:

1. *Internal processes*: Each house has several internal activities, not all of which allow for the support of computer tools. Thus the workflow must be hybrid: some steps are done with the aid of tools and computers, and some steps must be performed by hand on paper. The workflow should support a hybrid organization of processes with frequent passages of the relevant documents from paper to digital form, and vice versa.
2. *External processes*: these revolve mostly around the exchange of documents between institutions. At the end of each internal process the house finalizes the version of the bill and sends it to the other house. This moment is formal and it is recorded in each house's Official Journal as a sort of check-in, check-out process. Whenever the second house to discuss a bill introduces new modifications, this requires another passage in the first house for the approval of the new form of the bill. The document is presented to the members of the house in a comparative format based on two columns. The first column shows the document as is was when it went out, i.e., as originally approved by the first house, while the second column shows the incoming document from the second house, with all differences duly underlined. The process may be repeated a number of times until both houses approve exactly the same text (Figure 9.9).

Each macro-process is divided into four macro-steps:

1. *Activities before the discussion*: In this phase, the legal drafting office works heavily to readjust and repair the text to improve its formal quality. If this is a returning bill from the other house requiring new approval, the legal drafting office must also identify and mark up the

modifications done in the other house. The same is done for the proposal of modifications coming from the committees.
2. *Discussion and voting*: All activities performed inside of the assembly deputed to approve the text. In this phase, new amendments can arise from the government, from the president of the house, from the presidents of the involved committees, and also from deputies or senators. They are examined, discussed, and voted on for inclusion in the draft of the bill.
3. *Activities after the vote*: After each voting session the legal drafting office applies the new modifications to those approved in previous sessions, producing a new version for the next steps or discussion sessions.
4. *Publishing of the final version*: Once the discussion and voting are finished, the outcome of the process, called *message* ("*messaggio*"), is formally published in the House Official Journal. This document is the authoritative version that becomes the input for the next discussion cycle in the other house. If this is the final vote marking the complete agreement of the two houses, the document is sent to the President of the Republic for signature and promulgation.

This description of the processes naturally creates three main scenarios:

- The markup of an existing document in XML that is going to be sent from the Senate to the Chamber of Deputies after its final approval (*external process*);
- The markup of a problematic document (partially cut/pasted using a number of tools including word processors) delivered from a political actor to the legal drafting office for a strong formal revision (*internal process*);
- The creation of a new document with the list of amendments and their application on the text of the bill as approved by a committee before submitting it to the full assembly or after the assembly debate (*regular process*).

We tested two Italian tools — Norma-Editor and the xmLeges Editor — producing our findings in two reports. Each report includes some issues about the respective editor.

After a verification of the logistics and technical aspects of the pilot locations, the test phase consisted of three different steps:

- *Interviews*: During and after the test, the participants were interviewed about the working environment and their experiences with it. The participants were also asked for recommendations for further functionality and about problems in the working environment.
- *Solving test tasks*: During the different test periods, there were tests consisting of tasks that are part of the daily work of the participants.
- *Debriefing*: After the test, the participants were asked to fill in a questionnaire about their experiences. This questionnaire was based on the initial questionnaire that was used to measure the existing situation and defining requirements for development.

The test phase underwent an iterative process of continuous development of the tools. This process involved several pilot sessions over 7 days. Based on the findings of each session, we immediately revised the tools and the working environments to fix problems and improve user acceptance.

A few issues were too complicated to deal with immediately; these were left pending and were addressed in subsequent weeks. These issues did not undergo final testing and no acceptability information appears in the report, although the implementation took very seriously the suggestions and concerns raised during the tests. A similar test with similar results was performed at the Dutch House of Representatives using the Dutch tool MetaVex.

All in all, 44 findings were found for Norma-Editor, and 34 for xmLeges Editor. Respectively 34 and 28 of these findings were immediately addressed during the test phase and were successfully verified as solved by the test participants, while 10 and 6, respectively, were left open at the end of the test phase and were subsequently solved and closed without a concrete verification by the test participants (although they still had the chance to discuss and approve a textual description of their future solution).

At the end of each test session, a report was produced with a description of the findings. The programmers would then write a solution proposal for each of them, and submit them to the test subjects. Upon approval of each solution, this would be implemented and the new system would be then used for the subsequent tests.

At the end, a report organizing the findings and their status was realized and delivered to the project reviewers, who approved the method and the results. This divides the findings into four categories:

- Repairing and creating XML documents
- Amendment and consolidation
- Synopsis and layout
- Server-side services *(only Norma-Editor)*

The report included a final list of considerations dealing with the use of predefined document templates, the correct parsing of documents coming from external formats such as MS Word, the management of the workflow, the version management, and the general usability of the tools.

SUCCESS FACTORS

More and more countries are looking into ways to improve and speed up the legislation processes using information technologies. XML provides a key technology in this regard, but there are issues that need to be taken good care of. Although it is an incomplete list, we propose the following:

- *Adopt an international standard.* Too often the ease of creating a custom XML vocabulary has tempted clients and tool designers simply to create their own. This is wrong on many different levels: first of all, because it delivers the content of the legislative documents into the hands of the private companies who design the format; second, because this never manages to create a sufficiently large customer base for the tools themselves; and finally, because the large number of incredibly convoluted issues that have been discovered with pain and errors in years of interactions with parliaments by the authors of international standards would need to be discovered, with renewed pain and errors, by the tool designers themselves.
- *Carefully separate presentation from structure and content, and also authorial from editorial content.* The conceptual structure of a legislative document changes with less frequency than its typographical and presentational choices. Carefully preserving only the typographical layout of the original form of the printed document prevents its being reused in newer presentation contexts, promotes subtle semantic differences and trivial clerical errors in presentation to the same conceptual level, prevents sophisticated technical analysis on its structure, etc. Providing a careful legal analysis of the structure and content of a legislative document, on the other hand, allows

the exact original presentation layout to be delivered while at the same time enabling sophisticated functionality to be implemented alongside presentation.

- *Respect competencies, roles, and jobs of your perspective users.* Legislative drafting offices and legislative typographies have been well established in all countries since the very beginning of those countries' very institution as countries. This means that traditions, competencies, and relationships, but also fine points of technical aspects (such as typography and wording), date from decades and centuries in the past. The average reaction to innovation, in these contexts, is suspicion and dread. Only by calmly respecting and supporting the individual competencies and roles of the individuals affected (or, as they would put it, *hit*) by the new tools can one hope to foster their acceptance and give them increased job satisfaction.

Yet we suppose that the real lesson learned in these years is to ignore small-talk reassurances that details do not matter. Details matter a lot, each one of them. You cannot imagine.

SUMMARY

The acceptability of a tool is, possibly, the most important measure of its usability. Yet, if there is one lesson to be drawn from our direct experience with the end users of our legislative XML tools, it is that sometimes acceptability is not determined by the number of successful completions of individual tasks, the low rate of errors, the subjective appreciation of the organization of the commands, the esthetic value of the interface, or the wide reach of its functions. A key factor in a tool's acceptability lies in its capacity to provide a nonconfrontational, nonaggressive, nonchallenging integration with the habits, expectations, and competencies of its designed users- even if it reenacts in a different context the same suboptimal, fragmented, redundant, error-prone, convoluted tasks they had without the tool.

In the case of XML tools, although we were able to mount a good case for the long-term benefits to the organization in adopting such technologies, the impact on their users remained unbearable as long as we did not fully adhere to the existing, traditional divisions of tasks and responsibilities and roles—which in most cases long predated not only XML but computers themselves. We remain convinced that this is not an isolated case, and that similar situations exist in a number of different professional contexts, especially in public administration.

References

Administration of Barack H. Obama. Memorandum on transparency and open government. (January, 2009). Retrieved 14 November 2011 from http://www.gpoaccess.gov/presdocs/2009/DCPD200900010.pdf

Agnoloni, T., Francesconi, E., & Spinosa, P. (2007). xmLegesEditor: An opensource visual XML editor for supporting legal national standards. In C. Biagioli, E. Francesconi & G. Sartor (Eds.), *Proceedings of the V legislative XML workshop*, (pp. 239–251) Florence, Italy: European Press Academic Publishing, ISBN 9788883980466.

Arnold-Moore, T. (1995). Automatically processing amendments to legislation. In *Proceedings of the fifth international conference on artificial intelligence and law, ICAIL '95, May 21-24, 1995, College Park, Maryland, USA*, (pp. 297–306) New York: ACM Press, ISBN 0-89791-758-8.

Australian Government. Declaration of open government. (June, 2010). Retrieved 14 November 2011 from http://www.finance.gov.au/e-government/strategy-and-governance/gov2/declaration-of-open-government.html

Barabucci, G., Cervone, L., Di Iorio, A., Palmirani, M., Peroni, S., & Vitali, F. (2010). Managing semantics in XML vocabularies: an experience in the legal and legislative domain. In *Proceedings of balisage: The markup conference 2010, Montréal, Canada, August 3-6*. ISBN-13 978-1-935958-01-7.

Bing, J. (2003). The policies of legal information services: A perspective of three decades. In L. A. Bygrave (Ed.), *Yulex 2003* (pp. 35–57). Oslo, Norway: Institutt for Rettsinformatikk, ISBN 82-7226-077-8.

Cifuentes-Silva, F., Sifaqui, C., & Labra-Gayo, J. E. (2011). Towards an architecture and adoption process for linked data technologies in open government contexts: a case study for the Library of Congress of Chile. In *I-semantics '11, proceedings of the 7th international conference on semantic systems, Graz (AU), September 07-09*. New York: ACM, ISBN 978-1-4503-0621-8.

Directive 1999/93/EC of the European Parliament and of the Council of 13 December 1999 on a community framework for electronic signatures. Retrieved 14 November 2011 from http://eur-lex.europa.eu/smartapi/cgi/sga_doc?smartapi!celexapi!prod!CELEXnumdoc&numdoc=31999L0093&model=guichett

Dutta, S., & Mia, I. (Eds.), (2010). *Global information technology report 2009–2010*. Retrieved 14 November 2011 from http://www3.weforum.org/docs/WEF_GITR_Report_2010.pdf. ICT for Sustainability, World Economic Forum, 2010.

Fabiani, C. (2011). *Introducing XML at the European Parliament. In Presentation at Cape Town (ZA), January 24*. Retrieved 14 November 2011 from http://www.akomantoso.org/presentations/introducing-xml-at-the-european-parliament/at_download/file

Global Centre for ICT in Parliament. (2010). *World e-parliament report 2010*. UNDESA and IPU. Retrieved 14 November 2011 from http://www.ictparliament.org/wepr2010

Greenleaf, G. (2004). Jon bing and the history of computerised legal research—Some missing links. In O. Torvund & L. Bygrave (Eds.), *Et tilbakeblikk på fremtiden (Looking back at the future)* (pp. 61–75). Oslo, Norway: Institutt for Rettsinformatikk.

Hietanen, A. (2007). *Final report on electronic publishing of legislation—Towards authenticity. In 4th European forum of official gazettes, Helsinki (SF)-Tallinn (EE), 14th-15th June*. Retrieved 14 November 2011 from http://circa.europa.eu/irc/opoce/ojf/info/data/prod/data/pdf/Helsinki2007-authenticity-final.pdf

Lupo, C., Vitali, F., Francesconi, E., Palmirani, M., Winkels, R., de Maat, E., Boer, A., & Mascellani, P. (2007). *General XML formats for legal sources*. Estrella European Project IST-2004-027655. Deliverable 3.1, University of Amsterdam. Retrieved 14 November 2011 from http://www.estrellaproject.org/?page_id=4

Marchetti, A., Megale, F., Seta, E., & Vitali, F. (2002). *Using XML as a means to access legislative documents. ACM SIGAPP Applied Computing Review 10*. (1), Spring 2002. New York: ACM Press.

Noveck, S. B. (2009). *Wiki government*. Washington, DC: Brookings Institution Press.

Palmirani, M. (2005). Time Model in Normative Information Systems. In *Proceedings of the workshop "The Role of Knowledge in e-Government" at ICAIL 2005. Tilburg, NL, 6 June 2005*. (pp. 15–25). Wolf Legal Publishers.

Palmirani, M. (2011). Long-term preservation and legal validity of e-law. In *IRIS 2011 conference, Salzburg (AU), February 23-26*. Wien, Austria: Österreichische Computer Gesellschaft.

Palmirani, M., & Benigni, F. (2007). Norma-system: A legal information system for managing time. In C. Biagioli, E. Francesconi & G. Sartor (Eds.), *Proceedings of the V legislative XML workshop*, (pp. 205–224) Florence, Italy: European Press Academic Publishing, ISBN 9788883980466.

Publications Office of the European Union. *Access to legislation in Europe*. (2009). ISBN 978-92-78-40510-6. Luxembourg (LU). Retrieved 14 November 2011 from http://circa.europa.eu/irc/opoce/ojf/info/data/prod/data/pdf/AccessToLegislationInEuropeGUIDE2009.pdf

Sartor, G., Palmirani, M., Francesconi, E., & Biasiotti, M. A. (2011). Legislative XML for semantic web. Berlin: Springer, ISBN 978-94-007-1886-9.

Seppius, M. (2008). Consolidation, interim report of the working group. In *European forum of official gazettes, 5th meeting in Madrid, September 25-26*. Retrieved 14 November 2011 from http://circa.europa.eu/irc/opoce/ojf/info/data/prod/data/pdf/Madrid2008-consolidation-interimReport.pdf van de Ven, S., Hoekstra, R., Winkels, R., de Maat, E., & Kollár, A. (2008). MetaVex: Regulation drafting meets the semantic web. In G. Sartor & P. Casanovas (Eds.), *Computable models of the law. Languages, dialogues, games, ontologies* (pp. 42–55). *Lecture Notes in Artificial Intelligence,* Vol. 4884 (pp. 42–55). Berlin (D): Springer Verlag.

van den Brink, G., & de Maat, E. (2008). *D4.5 final report.* Seal European Project. Retrieved 14 November 2011 from http://www.leibnizcenter.org/docs/demaat/D4_5_FinalReport.pdf

Vander Wal, T. (2007). *Folksonomy coinage and definition.* Retrieved 14 November 2011 from http://vanderwal.net/folksonomy.html

Vergottini, G. (2011). Legislative time machine—Explore compiled law in the past, present, and future. In *IRIS 2011 conference, Salzburg (AU), February 23-26.* Wien, Austria: Österreichische Computer Gesellschaft.

Vitali, F. (2011). *Akoma Ntoso release notes.* Retrieved 14 November 2011 from http://www.akomantoso.org

Vitali, F., & Zeni, F. (2007). Towards a country-independent data format: The Akoma Ntoso experience. In C. Biagioli, E. Francesconi & G. Sartor (Eds.), *Proceedings of the V legislative XML workshop,* (pp. 67–86) Florence, Italy: European Press Academic Publishing, ISBN 9788883980466.

SECTION

III

UX Issues Common to Public and Internal Systems

"The noblest pleasure is the joy of understanding."
— Leonardo da Vinci

This section addresses a variety of important user experience issues that public-facing and internal systems have in common. The section has six chapters:

- *Chapter 10*, Content Strategy
- *Chapter 11*, Plain Language in Government
- *Chapter 12*, Ensuring Accessibility for People with Disabilities
- *Chapter 13*, Mobile Access
- *Chapter 14*, User Issues in Security
- *Chapter 15*, Usability of Biometric Systems

The chapters in this section discuss issues ranging from content and how it is presented and expressed, to issues surrounding the technologies that people use directly, to issues involving both front-end and back-end components.

- In Chapter 10, **Rahel Bailie** (Canada) describes content strategy, a comprehensive plan that builds a framework to create, manage, deliver, share, and archive or renew content in reliable ways. Content is not static, she observes, but has a complex and iterative life-cycle that requires a level of planning that did not exist before the Web. Content *strategy* says Bailie, considers the technical and business requirements, plus the editorial, social, and process aspects of publishing, in a holistic way. It constitutes a comprehensive plan that builds a framework to create, manage, deliver, share, and archive or renew content in reliable ways. Bailie provides a brief case study to demonstrate how these aspects came together on a successful project for a public-facing municipal web site, and she offers success factors gleaned from interviews with content strategists from three continents. "For content to be the effective agent to facilitate the provision of information, completion of transactions, and engagement of citizens," she states, "content needs to be managed reliably and effectively, throughout its entire lifecycle. Paying attention to the content lifecycle ensures that the increasing complexity of delivering content to multiple audiences is handled in ways that keep content at the center of an organization's digital strategy."

- In Chapter 11, **Ginny Redish** (USA) and **Susan Kleimann** (USA) discuss the importance of using plain language in government systems. Plain language is now required by law for government communications in the United States, and a number of other countries also have programs that require or encourage government writers to communicate clearly with citizens, immigrants, and visitors. Plain language, the authors show, concentrates on three key measures — *find, understand, use* — and requires us to focus on our readers and remember that plain language "is more than words and sentences." Plain language, they explain, involves selecting the right content, organizing it logically, breaking it up into manageable pieces, using familiar language, writing in short sentences with illustrations and lists as appropriate, and designing the appearance to help readers. Redish and Kleimann describe two case studies that showed the value of plain language. "The Swedish Agency for Higher Education Services," they report, "saved 25% of the cost of its contact center through plain language," and "a consortium of eight US federal agencies developed a model plain language notice that most major US financial institutions have adopted." They conclude by providing a set of detailed guidelines for government writers and content developers to use in learning how to write in plain language.

- In Chapter 12, **Jonathan Lazar** (USA) and **Brian Wentz** (USA) describe the legal requirements for building systems that can be used by people with disabilities and present some techniques for achieving accessibility. Government system accessibility, they observe, is a compound responsibility involving laws and policies for implementing accessible technology in government systems, and the monitoring and enforcement of accessible technology. The authors survey accessibility laws, standards, and enforcement approaches around the world — "from very specific and measurable to vague and nonexistent." They offer some ideas on how measures such as training, increased transparency, and the harmonization of international standards could aid in accessibility enforcement and monitoring, thus strengthening moves toward government accessibility. "If government leads the way in IT accessibility," Lazar and Wentz assert, "universal access will ultimately reach beyond government to all areas of life."

- In Chapter 13, **George Buchanan** (UK) describes the ways in which context affects people's use of technology and how this relates particularly to the use of mobile devices for accessing government services. Creating usable mobile services for government is difficult, he says: local, national, and cultural contexts all play a part in shaping the expectations and skills of users. Mobile services provide an opportunity to leap the "digital divide" even where PC ownership is commonplace, many services fit more naturally into a mobile context. However, the novelty of mobile technology and its rapidly changing nature mean that development and implementation costs can be high. "Government bodies," stresses Buchanan, "need to ensure that they scope down the complexity of their mobile services so that they can be affordably sustained in the longer term, and also are genuinely usable for the communities that they serve."

- In Chapter 14, **Karen Renaud** (UK) discusses the issues involved in maintaining the security of access to citizens' personal information which is stored in government databases. In order to achieve and preserve the necessary level of trust from citizens in an age of online transactions she presents the case for designing security with the user in mind, showing how and why usability is as important as back-end security. Most user encounters with e-government security, she observes, involve the need to authenticate themselves to the system, so the discussion centers on the selection and implementation of authentication mechanisms. She points out that the measure of a citizen's perception of security will also depend on how well back-end systems are secured, but since these measures do not inconvenience users, they are unlikely to form the basis of anyone's user experience unless they fail. Renaud concludes by offering some guidance for implementing usable authentication mechanisms. "All that is required," she notes, "is for some rigor to be interjected into the process, so that the burden being imposed on the user is considered, and reduced as much as is possible, while security is maintained."

- In Chapter 15, **Mary Frances Theofanos** (USA) and **Brian Stanton** (USA) discuss the use of biometrics — automated methods of recognizing an individual based on anatomical, physiological, or behavioral characteristics — in government interactions with the public and with its employees and contractors. They describe how their research has shown the importance of usability and human factors in the design of biometric devices. Biometric systems appear in diverse contexts, from customs and immigration to the issuing of identification badges to government employees and contractors. In this chapter, the authors describe how the biometrics group at the US National Institute of Standards and Technology applied usability testing to improve the performance of government biometric systems, using case studies that illustrate the scientific rigor of the research methods and the impact of human factors on deployed biometric systems. They present some factors

> that their studies have found to aid in achieving success in designing biometric systems and integrating biometric devices into exisiting systems. These usability studies have already had an impact on the industry. "We have shown," Theofanos and Stanton emphasize, "that the findings of the NIST experiments and usability tests do translate directly into the field. This is a paradigm shift for the biometric industry, as previous attempts at improving accuracy and performance focused mainly on developing better biometric technologies."

The first three chapters in this section focus on design for everyone, and the last three address specific topics or technologies that can be used in both public-facing and internal systems.

CHAPTER

Content Strategy

10

Rahel Bailie
Intentional Design Inc., Richmond, BC, Canada

"From the beginning, we understood this project would be more like an organ transplant than a facelift."
— Project Director

INTRODUCTION

Understanding the role of a content strategy means understanding several aspects of the strategy and its implementation. The first aspects are the framework and the cornerstones that become the foundation for a content strategy. The next aspect is a platform for content-driven sites. The final aspect discussed in this chapter is how to look for success factors, and the related guidelines and implications.

This chapter also provides a brief case study to demonstrate how these aspects of content strategy come together on a successful project for a public-facing municipal web site.

A FRAMEWORK FOR CONTENT STRATEGY

Content — the text, images, audio, and video that we use to communicate — is an organizational asset, too valuable to be treated like a throw-away commodity. Content is costly to produce, and complicated to manage. Content does not have to be resource intensive to maintain, but if the foundation is not properly laid, then content will not only be complicated to maintain, but expensive as well.

The information age, which started in the late 1970s and gained momentum in the 1990s, brought with it digital literacy. The Web experience evolved faster than most organizations could keep up with. While organizations claimed to have entered the information age, their web sites said otherwise, and the public noticed. Site visitors, also known as content consumers, bring high expectations from their overall Web experience to your web site, and they are easily disappointed and frustrated if the content they are looking for is missing. Financial consumers would lose confidence in their bank if they thought the financial asset management strategy consisted of stuffing money into a mattress. Likewise, content consumers lose confidence in organizations managing content assets by stuffing content into their web site and calling it a strategy.

We may think we are doing a fine job of providing what our consumers need, but it does not really matter what we think. It is what our consumers think that ultimately matters; if they are frustrated because they cannot find information, cannot complete a transaction, or cannot engage civically, there is a disconnect. That is where a good content strategy comes in.

One popular definition of content strategy is "a repeatable process for managing content throughout the content lifecycle" (Bailie, 2010). But what does that mean exactly, and what does it have to do with user experience in a government setting?

The emergence of content strategy

Content may be defined from a technical perspective as contextualized data. Consider this: the number "12" is a piece of data. It has limited usefulness until it is placed into a humanized context: for example, the unit size in which to purchase eggs (12 in a dozen), December (the 12th month), a financial amount ($12), festive days (12 days of Christmas), and so on. But that is only the beginning. There is an important distinction that underpins the entire discussion of content strategy, and that is the difference between content and copy. Copy is the editorial shaping of a message, the writing process. While good content may start with good copy, content actually includes an entire host of processing considerations that give content the ability to be delivered accurately and reliably so that the content consumers at the end of the line can actually use it.

Delivering content, whether it is to your web site or to a print document, or delivered to both the web site *and* print from a single source, has become complicated. The planning of the editorial stream — the copywriting and wordsmithing of content — is perhaps the most straightforward, with a handful of writing guidelines. A publication or web site with multiple writers needs writing guidelines that govern tone, voice, style, vocabulary, and other quality and consistency standards. The writers are also responsible for ensuring that the information presented meets standards for accessibility — which requires an understanding of how to use style sheets properly within the word processing software, and how to ensure that elements such as images and tables meet minimum requirements, such as images that can be viewed by those with color blindness.

Beyond that, however, comes the planning for the other stages of the content lifecycle. There are the standards aspects: from the content will be constructed the "architecture" of each type of content within the publishing system and the international standards to which the content must conform, to be published eventually according to the needs of the organization. For example, is event information manually entered into a web page, which then requires a staff person to cut and paste the event into multiple web sites to advertise the event? Or will that information conform to the international standards that allow other systems to receive that event information immediately after it gets published? When event content conforms to a specific format, readers can subscribe to the event listings through an RSS (Real Simple Syndication). The RSS feed can "grab" and import the published content into a reader because the content is in a common schema that both systems can understand.

The content lifecycle also covers technical management aspects, such as planning for how the content will be handled between the time the author submits the content and the time it is published. This includes workflow and approval systems, which is an automated, controlled sign-off mechanism for reviewing and approving content before it gets published. The system chosen to manage the organization's web sites may also have some limitations, which will dictate how well content interacts with other systems and whether the content can be syndicated, or have data integrated into it, or be converged with other content. For example, for many organizations the publishing of catalogs is a time-consuming and onerous task. The descriptions are written in a word processor, and then schedules and prices are pasted in from a spreadsheet to prepare the copy for publishing; this manual process is repeated for the online version of the catalog, which may also be hooked up to a payment system. Knowing how to automate the integration of scheduling and pricing into the content and the payment system, and then how to make each of those content blocks converge on a web page can have a great impact on productivity, accuracy, time to market, and organizational credibility — if the right technology is in place *and* if there is an understanding, at the content level, of how the content needs to be managed.

To demonstrate, all the content highlighted in red in Figure 10.1 is drawn from a complex database, while the content highlighted in yellow is culled from other sources. The database contains all the information about all of the parks and their amenities. When a viewer asks to see information about either Riverfront Park, or parks in the Killarney area with particular amenities — picnic sites, for example — the "page" is dynamically assembled by the database. The content converges into a single display to the information in a context that makes sense to the reader.

Similarly, Figure 10.2 shows a page with a listing of programs, dates, and costs. (Different types of content are highlighted by rectangles and by rounded-corner rectangles.) This information is maintained in a completely separate database, and drawn into the page. Keeping the pricing data in an event and payment tracking system makes the entry and maintenance far more cost-efficient,

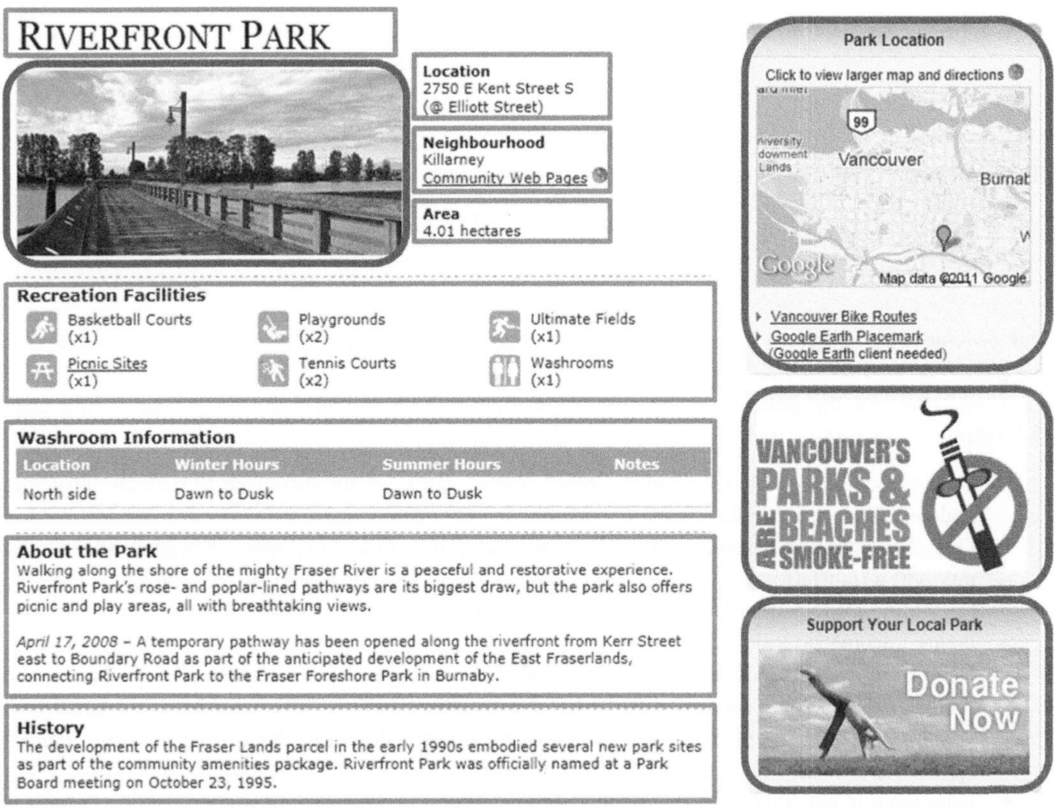

FIGURE 10.1 Convergence of content from multiple sources on a Web page

(For interpretation of the references to color in this figure legend, see the Web version of this chapter.)

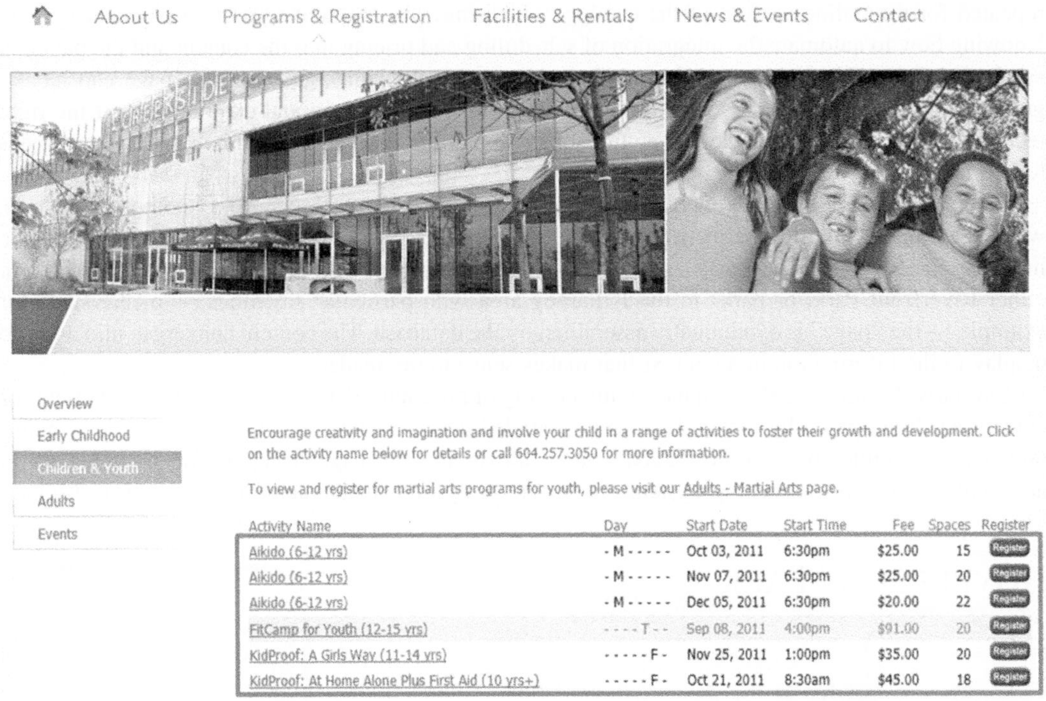

FIGURE 10.2 Web page of integrated content from a database feed

(For color version of this figure, see the Web version of this chapter.)

and provides the ability to pre-sort the current class offerings before integrating that content into the page.

Then there are the publishing aspects of the plan, which includes anything that occurs after publishing:

- Does the content get syndicated? In other words, can a visitor subscribe to receive automatic updates about a particular piece of content?
- Does the content get localized? Localization is adapting content to a specific market, and usually involves a translation component. For example, providing content in North America may mean translating into Spanish for an American market and French for Quebec, plus changing measurements into metric units for the entire Canadian market.
- Does content get archived or destroyed, and if so, according to a retention policy? The public sector often has legal requirements to keep particular types of content for a certain number of years. If the retirement of content involves permanent deletion, the formal schedule can be applied to content in some automated way.
- Does content get edited and republished as a new version; and if so, how are the editing changes tracked?

These decisions are often connected to content governance, which involves the decisions around the daily management of an organization's body of content; most often, content governance determines who has authority to make content decisions at various times and levels of operational importance. However, these decisions are also connected to the publishing process. When an organization subjects any part of the publishing process through a content management system, which automates many of the steps involved in publishing content, the governance decisions need to be programmed into the content management system for it to work properly.

All this is encompassed in content strategy, which is a comprehensive plan that builds a framework to create, manage, deliver, share, and archive or renew content in reliable ways. Content strategy is to writing what house construction is to interior decorating: when a writer creates a piece of copy, its purpose is to inform or engage the audience; when a content strategist plans for the copy to be used as content, their work ensures that the content can be served up and delivered to the right people, at the right time, in the right format, and in the right medium.

CORNERSTONES OF CONTENT STRATEGY

A content strategy has three key aspects:

- Ensure that the content being produced supports not only the organizational goals but also the goals of the organization's constituents and other stakeholders — in other words, the content consumers.
- Ensure that the content infrastructure is robust enough to manage content throughout the entire content lifecycle.
- Put in place a governance model that supports goals and infrastructure, and allows for the resources and processes to carry out the strategy.

The following sections discuss these aspects.

Supporting business and consumer goals

In government, each agency, each department, and sometimes each business unit within a department, has unique goals. Yet overall, there are three universal goals:

- *Location of information.* This is the most basic goal, and is likely to be the hardest to accomplish. Government web sites are notorious for being structured to reflect the organizational structure rather than the user's mental model (Rutter, 2008) — the expectations that people bring with them when interacting with your organization, based on their accumulation of experience with other sites. A general example is that customers renting cars know where the controls are in other cars they have driven, so they can apply this knowledge and drive off with confidence. When dealing with a municipality, a promoter may need several licenses from different city departments to produce an event. The promoter's mental model is to look for information by event type: to go to a page or section of the city's site where all event promotion requirements are outlined, and in which order to apply for the permits — such as a permit to hold the event, a permit to erect a stage, a permit for food, a liquor permit, and a traffic control or security permit. However, a city probably publishes each licensing requirement in an information silo by department: the food permit is described on the health department site; the traffic control permit is described on the police department site;

and so on. The promoter is left to uncover each of these by chance, and possibly proceed without the required permits, or risks getting frustrated and sharing that frustration with other promoters through social media sites such as Twitter or public forums, which other promoters can search to determine which venues are friendly — or frustrating. Understanding the mental model of your most frequent site users is critical, to provide information in a way that is useful to them.

- *Completion of transactions*. Transactions, such as submitting an application for a license or paying property taxes online, make up fewer content pages on a web site, but that content generally supports a high number of transactions. The goal is to explain the context and instructions of the transaction clearly enough that every person who needs to complete the transaction can do so online. The larger the numbers that can complete their transactions online, the fewer resources need to be diverted to assist those stymied by unusable instructions or applications. The success of transactions often depends on two factors: the quality of the applications and the quality of the instructions. To ensure quality of the software applications, the development process should follow the appropriate ISO standards — such as ISO 90003:2004, which governs all aspects of software design and development. To ensure the quality of the instructions, the terminology embedded within the application (called transactional content) should be coordinated with the content throughout the rest of the site. Using consistent terminology across the site *and* in applications makes it easier to understand and complete transactions. (See Chapter 4, UX of Transactions, for more information.)
- *Civic engagement*. Organizations can be assured that, whatever level of transparency they feel they have achieved, the public generally thinks of opportunities for engagement as an impenetrable mystery. When organizations fail to publish and share content in ways that allow the public to — involved with ease, something will fill the vacuum, and with the dramatic rise in the use of social media, often in ways that quickly put a new spin on whatever messaging strategy was in place. Building the opportunity for civic engagement into a web site cannot be done at a tactical level; it is a strategy-level activity that needs to integrate content from across the site and present it to the content consumer at the right time and place. For example, soliciting public feedback through — consultations is more likely to elicit responses when the agency delivers the information, not just to a closed mailing list of community advocates, but also by displaying it in areas of the web site most likely to be noticed by interested community members. These web site areas need to be well thought out, and the content should always appear in consistent ways and in consistent places.

Implementing a content infrastructure

The production and publishing of content have become much more technically challenging than simply writing copy within the type of communications strategy typically used by Communications or Public Relations departments. Content is not part of some supply chain, where you create, publish, and archive. Content has a lifecycle that is complex and often iterative. Web publishing, in particular, has unique needs: publishing now requires a level of planning that addresses the technical and business requirements and the editorial, social, and process aspects of publishing in an integrated, comprehensive way.

Four areas require strategic decisions to be made before any content strategy is implemented. Figure 10.3 provides an overview of the content lifecycle and shows where the decisions are implemented.

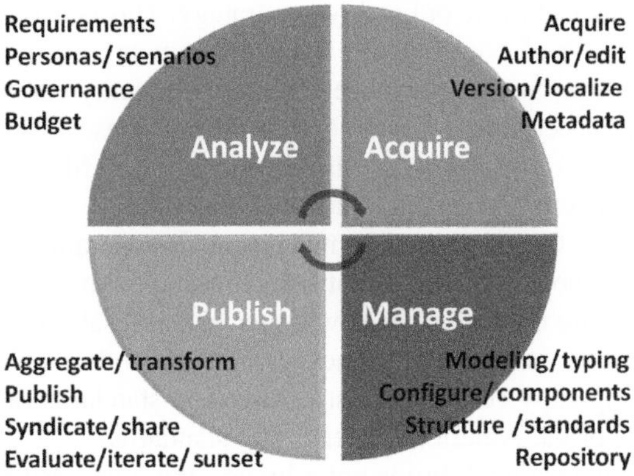

FIGURE 10.3 The content lifecycle

The exact complement of strategic issues to be covered is highly situational, yet several core issues will determine whether content enables people to find and use it as intended:

- *Editorial standards*. The style guide is a tried-and-true tool to ensure that editorial copy—certain standards. The better ones cover not only uniformity in visual style considerations (e.g., colors and page formats) but also guidelines for content structures, grammar, vocabulary, punctuation, tone and voice, and related editorial aspects of copywriting. On a web site, the challenge of maintaining consistency increases with every new author and content type. A universal complaint about copy on government sites is that the required reading levels to understand the content are quite high, which puts the content out of reach of low-literacy and English as a Second Language (ESL) readers, and tests the patience of the rest of their readers (Campbell, 2008).
- *Content types*. In print publications, some content types are visible to readers, and help with comprehension. For example, a procedure is quite apparent to a reader and the numbered steps help a reader understand what to do and in which order. In a Web situation, content types have more complexity, which is not always visible but important to systems that need to process content. Content on a "page" is often not constructed as a page, but as modules of content that converge on a page according to a set of business logic programmed into the web site code. For example, a web page could consist of a block of editorial content that belongs only to that page, plus a photograph that is drawn from an image library; in addition, there may be an area for a news feed that lists the headlines of news items entered elsewhere on the site. There may also be a content block that has been programmed to automatically show on the page after publishing—a disclaimer would be a common example of that. Determining the content types, and building a model for how content flows within a web site, and between systems, must be diagrammed. These content models are given to the software developers, who customize the code so that the content on a web site appears the way it was intended.
- *Technical standards*. Content can conform to varying international technical standards. These standards allow content to be processed by other systems, and even different parts of the same system. Understanding which of those standards are used where, and which standards are being

adopted or phased out, can make or break your strategy. This is particularly true when it is time to automate the sharing of content with other departments or agencies, or sending content to outside organizations such as news agencies or community calendars. Technical standards also make content accessible to people with disabilities, as described in Chapter 12, Ensuring Accessibility for People with Disabilities, or when filtering content — for example, showing a subset of content based on a narrower topic.

- *Accessibility standards*. Government sites must pay particular attention to ensuring that content can be consumed by those who use adaptive technologies to "read" copy on the Web. This includes people who are colorblind or have other visual disabilities, who use screen readers, and people with mobility issues, who cannot use a mouse and/or keyboard. A content strategist ensures that incoming copy conforms to structures and standards that meet accessibility standards, such as W3C or the American Section 508 standards.
- *Search*. Ensuring content findability is not a luxury, but a necessity; searching accounts for a significant percentage of the ways people look for content. The major search engines have hundreds of factors in their search-ranking algorithms, which affects search engine results (Singhal, 2011). Optimizing on-site search has a different set of factors. It may be tempting to "just use a better search engine" but if the content does not measure up to the standards used by the search engine, the results will still be inaccurate. For these reasons, it is critical to include search as part of the content strategy (Mathewson, Donatone, & Fishel, 2010). Managing search engine result pages (SERPs) is a specialized strategy that overlaps with metadata and linking strategies. Understanding the most important factors that search engines use to identify what they consider to be the best links involves a diverse and complex array of factors — far too many to discuss here — from metadata text, to the construction of headings, to how page content is written, to the number of sites that link to the page, to how old the page link is, and so on. These factors change on a daily basis, as the major search engines adjust their algorithms to prevent people from gaming the system for their own benefit.
- *Metadata*. This data *about* data is the equivalent to an index for web sites. It organizes content, helps with browsing, and helps people search using common terms (when content does not use them). Without a robust taxonomy, other aspects of your content strategy will fail.
- *Links*. A sophisticated linking strategy ensures that new content appears higher in search results than similar, but old, content. Linking has become a sophisticated and complicated science, and needs to be tackled as part of a content strategy, particularly in the context of making site search work. Major search engines use a host of factors, plus searches by millions of other users, to decide which links are most relevant, while a search tool on a site has a limited number of searches and amount of related data to make search decisions. Search engines give high ratings to machine-understandable links, links with longevity, links that are not buried too deeply below the top level of navigation, and so on. The more pages a site has, the more important a link strategy is for content findability.
- *Mobile*. There has recently been a phenomenal increase in mobile use as the sale of smartphones continue to dominate the market (Gartner, Inc., 2010). Having content optimized for mobile consumption has become a necessity for organizations that want to meet the needs of their content consumers, who are increasingly accessing information from small-screen devices such as touch-screen tablets and smartphones (Kuang, 2011). Consumers increasingly expect content to be optimized for mobile devices; they expect to download mobile applications for specific interactions, such as entering an address and being shown a map with directions. (See Chapter 13, Mobile Access, for more information on mobile devices.)

- *Pass-through content.* Content consumers bring their expectations of being able to subscribe to content feeds, share content with friends and followers, and learn about items of importance in your organization through social networks. The tie-in between social media, social content, and other engagement channels needs core business content to succeed.

The role of governance

Informational interviews with over a dozen content strategy professionals in a range of jurisdictions across the United States, Canada, Britain, and Southeast Asia — from municipal to state or provincial and federal governments, federal agencies, and quasi-governmental organizations — revealed a consensus that implementing an appropriate governance model is the single-most common stumbling block when it comes to achieving project success. *Governance* is about getting everyone on the same page, from the creation processes to approval processes, from brand and relevance to site mandate. The strategists who were interviewed revealed the commonality of concerns about governance, in several different areas:

- In theory, sponsors — executives, management, or sponsoring stakeholders — want to support the adoption of governance but find it difficult to overcome the organizational obstacles related to implementing a governance model.
- Project teams tend to collaborate well at the level of the subject matter experts, but tensions among upper levels of management (Welchman, 2011) over control of features, quality, and resources cannot be resolved until issues around unarticulated de facto standards are uncovered and dealt with. This requires an informed authority at a higher level, such as a director or general manager, to make governance decisions by which the organization must abide.
- As a side effect of the governance gap, the project team is left vulnerable in its ability to move forward in time-critical ways. Without the authority to implement standards — and sometimes without governance guidelines to enforce — the project team cannot prevent content owners from digging in their heels about their own content on the site, or refusing to engage in any exercise to cull content or bring added value.
- Executives who have little technical knowledge unwittingly make decisions that result in serious technical implications and have a huge impact on the design, user experience, and larger content strategy. The problem is compounded because the project team generally has insufficient time to respond to directional changes; often they have little or no access to the executive level in order to explain the consequences of straying from tested best practices.
- Inevitably, there will be change-resistant bureaucrats who fail to understand the multitude of ways that publishing has changed over the years, and who insist on staying within their comfort zone. Their contribution to derailing the project is holding up content publication with unduly long approval processes. Some organizations have reported, in conversation, that content takes weeks or even months to get publishing approval, which is far too long for content such as responses to social media posts.

CONTENT STRATEGY DONE RIGHT

The City of Vancouver, in British Columbia, Canada, began a Web redevelopment project in 2009, culminating in a new site (launch: May 2012). This was at least the fourth attempt to introduce a comprehensive approach to web asset management, and was by far the most successful one. The reason?

The corporate management team recognized that the web site problem they wanted to fix was neither a communications nor a technology problem (though the lack of a content management system was certainly a significant problem for efficient publishing) but, rather, a business problem.

The site is content driven, as are most government sites, and the content was organized around departmental silos instead of around the mental models of typical site users. As a result, the site had become bloated to over 60,000 pages with a mix of useful and irrelevant content, much of it having fallen into time-lapsed inaccuracy with no centralized governance to provide a mandate for managing the site as part of a larger digital strategy.

The project, headed by the former Director of Communications, followed a user-centered design process: initial user research yielded an understanding of how residents thought about the activity of finding city information, and drove how the site architecture was developed, as shown in Figure 10.4. The result, viewable at www.vancouver.ca, is a drastic departure from the department-based information silos.

FIGURE 10.4 Mock-up of redesigned City of Vancouver home page

(For the color version of this figure, see the Web version of this chapter.)

For example, all information about a resident's property was grouped together in one menu area, no matter what the task: paying property taxes, applying for a permit to remove a tree, ordering a new recycling bin, renewing a dog license, or learning about home safety and fire prevention.

Personas resulting from the user research were used to understand the main audiences for the city web site. In this case, over 5000 surveys and interviews revealed seven personas who were the main site users. The personas made it possible to devise typical scenarios for each one from the frustrated user who simply wanted to complete an online transaction and get out, to the contented citizen who wanted the story behind the sound bite on the news; from the citizen who wanted to get, and stay, involved, to the business professional whose wasted time meant lost profits, and so wanted to ensure his interactions with the CITY were efficient and productive.

The personas and scenarios provided a framework in which to develop content. A team of highly skilled content strategists and content developers was brought on board and charged with reworking the content, starting with the 15% of pages that received the most visits during the past couple of years. They had a mandate to do two things: reduce the page counts, and rewrite the content. The final content had to meet plain language, accessibility, and technical standards, all of which were needed to increase content comprehension, technical flexibility, and findability through search.

Reworking the content for the large government site looked, from the outside, to be a daunting task, but by adhering to some core principles, the team managed to stay focused and productive.

The content strategists met with each business unit within the city, and learned about the needs of each unit. From the unit's business objectives, the strategists teased out the tactical activities that were web-worthy, keeping in mind the three cornerstones of intention — *provide information, allow transactions, facilitate engagement* — and then pulled out the content that would support those activities (See Figure 10.5). That became the basis for the content for the new site launch. The business units were assured that their content would be dispersed to the appropriate menus, in the logical places that users would look for the content — and those menu structures underwent usability testing to confirm any assumptions.

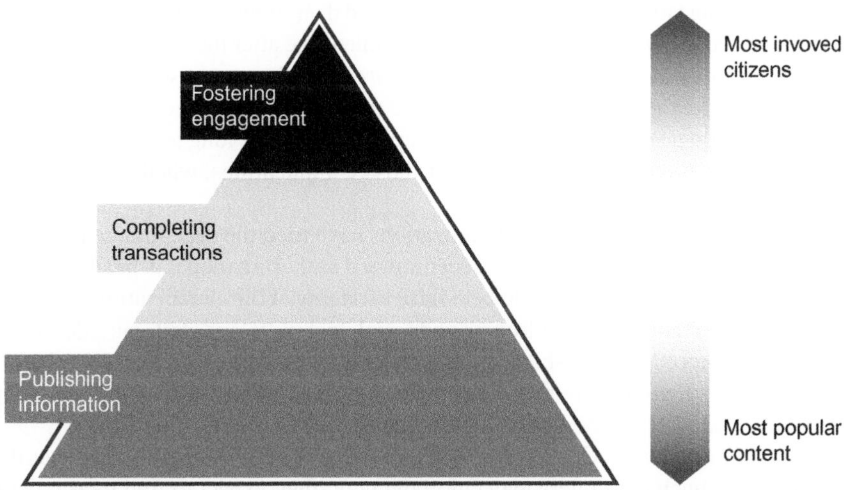

FIGURE 10.5 The demand hierarchy: Information, transactions, engagement

Throughout all of this, the project director gently pushed the governance discussion — many times, in fact — until the project sponsors were ready to hear the message about the need for governance and the recommendations for a model that made sense for the city. For the duration of the project the director received interim authority to make project-level decisions, which allowed the project to move forward, unimpeded by the types of issues reported by professionals on other projects. Some of the governance questions worked themselves out via technical requirements — for example, needing to program workflow into the content management system. Other questions became resolved as project roadblocks needed to be removed: who gets to decide about Level 1 issues, what is the approval process for mobile applications, and so on. Without these conversations, and without interim authority, the project could not have moved forward to completion.

SUCCESS FACTORS

The content strategists and other communications professionals who shared their experiences as part of the research for this chapter had a common goal in mind: to pave the way for the success of future projects by identifying the issues encountered in the course of their work, and to identify the factors that could be put into place to achieve success. Here are some of their success factors:

- *Recognize the Web as a business tool.* Unlike the print side of publishing, which is by and large under control, most government sites continue to be treated as an online presence secondary to their bricks-and-mortar and print presences. The public use of the Internet and mobile devices to access information and resources has grown by leaps and bounds. Developing a common vision for how business will be done online, and then creating the infrastructure to do so, is the foundation for all the other factors that follow.
- *Adopt Web Operations Management guidelines.* A fundamental aspect of moving Web operations up the Information Process Maturity Model. (Hackos, 2004) is to acknowledge Web Operations Management as an extension of governance (Welchman, 2009). This provides a common framework by which an organization can measure its success, and then continuously improve to keep pace with demand — a necessary component of content maintenance after the initial site launch.
- *Invest strategically in a technology infrastructure.* Use the expertise of the vendors, but own the process. Resist the temptation to outsource the entire project because it feels complicated. Your organization needs to manage those complications in the long term, so use vendors to *help* the organization to understand and conquer those complications, whether they be governance, technology, or user research.
- *Invest in specialized content skills.* Organizations have tried the decentralized authoring model, and it has not worked. The allure of a decentralized authoring model is head count and budget, which has proven again and again to be a false economy. Your organization probably lacks the skills required to manage content from the editorial, technical, and strategic sides of content, and the need for advanced content skills will not disappear after the project is "complete." Investing in content strategy will ensure that the content does not devolve after the initial launch, and it reduces the need later on for a costly rectification project.
- *Have form follow function.* Consider the design as a treasure hunt and the content as the treasure. No matter how much consumers may enjoy the hunt, they expect to find treasure at the end of the hunt. The design and architecture should support, not shape, the content (Jones, 2011).

- *Set priorities and boundaries.* Trying to "boil the ocean" may jeopardize project success. Prioritize the content to be reworked according to the severity of the problems, or spread the depth of content over multiple publishing phases. It is best to start with less, and carefully to add more quality content during subsequent phases. On the City of Vancouver project, the realization that processing over 60,000 pages was neither useful nor possible provided the impetus to distinguish between "must-have" and "nice-to-have" information, and to rework the most critical content first.
- *Keep the content aligned with business objectives.* Users must be able to do business with your organization online as smoothly as in person. You can make that happen by ensuring that content rolls up to the tasks that people want to accomplish online or the information they need to find, in the context of the organization's business goals. This alignment cuts out the ambiguities that lead to content clutter.

SUMMARY

A content strategy can succeed only within a larger framework that supports the project as a whole. As best practices for developing and maintaining web sites continue to progress, the focus has moved from being technology driven to operations driven. As government bodies make the shift to online information and services, the web site as a business tool is being considered as part of their larger digital strategies. Content is one of the pillars needed to support a successful project, and depends on the other pillars equally to build a good user experience. When organizations recognize that their online operations are rapidly becoming a primary way of doing business, they value and tend the infrastructure that allows it to operate and thrive. Content strategy is quickly becoming a recognized part of that infrastructure.

For content to be the effective agent to facilitate the provision of information, completion of transactions, and engagement of citizens, content needs to be managed reliably and effectively, throughout its entire lifecycle. Paying attention to the content lifecycle ensures that the increasing complexity of delivering content to multiple audiences is handled in ways that keep content at the center of an organization's digital strategy.

References

Bailie, R. A. (2010). *Content strategy. Content strategy: A community exploration of an emerging field of practice.* Retrieved 6 November 2011 from http://www.backbonemag.com/files/PDF/Speakers/2011-10-understanding-the-content-strategy-landscape.pdf

Campbell, A. (2008, September) *Government website trends.* Retrieved 6 November 2011 from http://www.theappgap.com/government-website-trends.html

Gartner, Inc. (2010, August). *Gartner says worldwide mobile device sales grew 13.8 percent in second quarter of 2010, but competition drove prices down.* Retrieved 6 November 2011 from http://www.gartner.com/it/page.jsp?id=1421013

Hackos, J. (2004). *The Information Process Maturity Model: A 2004 update.* Retrieved 6 November 2011 from http://www.infomanagementcenter.com/pdfs/Hackos_IPMM_04_update.pdf

Jones, C. (2011). *Clout: The art and science of influential web content.* Berkeley, CA: New Riders.

Kuang, C. (2011, June). *Infographic of the day: 15 facts about the internet in 2015*. Retrieved 6 November 2011 from http://www.fastcodesign.com/1663953/infographic-of-the-day-15-facts-about-the-internet-in-2015

Mathewson, J., Donatone, F., & Fishel, C. (2010). *Audience, relevance, and search: Targeting web audiences with relevant content*. Stoughton, MA: IBM Press.

Rutter, K. (2008, February 6). *Indi Young tells Kate about mental models & her new book*. Adaptive Path. Retrieved 6 November 2011 from http://adaptivepath.com/ideas/e000865

Singhal, A. (2011, May 6). *More guidance on building high-quality sites. Google webmaster central blog*. Retrieved 6 November 2011 from http://googlewebmastercentral.blogspot.com/2011/05/more-guidance-on-building-high-quality.html

Welchman, L. (2009, May). *Web Operations Management Primer*. Welchman*Pierpoint*. Retrieved 6 November 2011 from http://www.welchmanpierpoint.com/article/web-operations-management-primer

Welchman, L. (2011). *Empires, confederations & federations: Three web governance models that work*. Welchman*Pierpoint*. Retrieved 6 November 2011 from http://www.slideshare.net/welchmanpierpoint/three-web-governance-models-that-work

Further reading

Mulder, S., & Yaar, Z. (2007). *The user is always right: A practical guide to creating and using personas for the web*. Berkeley, CA: New Riders.

CHAPTER

Plain Language in Government

11

Janice (Ginny) Redish*, Susan Kleimann†

Bethesda, MD, USA Rockville, MD, USA†*

"Plain language is about creating documents for real life and for real people. . . . We take into account that our readers may not be experts in reading, or in [the language in which we are writing], or in the topic, and that they are probably very busy. . . . So we strive to make texts that will give them what they need, when and how they need it, in a way that's as quick, simple, easy, and effective as can be."

— D. Joseph (2011)

INTRODUCTION

Government agencies want citizens, immigrants, and visitors to comply voluntarily with the country's laws and regulations, to fill out forms correctly, to have the benefits to which they are entitled, and so on. All these interactions depend on communication — by phone, by email, by written document or web page, or through social media. Successful user experiences require successful communication, and successful communication requires plain language.

In the United States, it's the law!

The *Plain Writing Act of 2010* requires US federal agencies to write all new material for the public in a "clear, concise, well-organized" manner that follows the best practices of plain language writing. The law applies to web sites, forms, notices, and all other communications (except regulations) (US Congress, 2010).

To include regulations in the plain language requirement, President Obama issued an executive order in January 2011 requiring that regulations be "accessible, consistent, written in plain language, and easy to understand" (White House, 2011).

Some states also have plain language requirements

At the state level in the United States, we also see movement toward plain language. Oregon law requires all state agencies to prepare public communications in language that is as clear and simple as possible (Oregon.gov, 2011). The state of Washington requires plain language in all public documents, including regulations (Washington State, Office of the Governor, 2011). Washington calls its program Plain Talk; and, in the exuberant spirit of the ever-changing English language, Washington writers have made the adjective and noun into a verb. You will hear Washington teams saying, "We need to plain talk that letter/form/document/web content."

Other countries also use plain language

Michelle Asprey, a plain language expert in Australia, provides a comprehensive summary of laws, regulations, and activities related to plain language for 24 countries and the European Union in the fourth edition of her book, *Plain Language for Lawyers* (Asprey, 2010).

Some countries work hard to have legislation in plain language because so many other government documents stem from laws. In Sweden, for example, since 1976, every piece of proposed legislation must go through review by language experts and lawyers in the Ministry of Justice's Division for Legal and Linguistic Draft Revision. The language experts' job is to ensure that acts and ordinances "are as easy as possible to read and understand" (Ehrenberg-Sundin, 2004).

DEFINITION

Plain language means creating communications that work for both writer and reader.

The Norwegian government works with a simple, broad definition: plain language means a document is clear, correct, and user-centered (Kvarenes, Reksten, Stranger-Thorsen, & Aarønæs, 2010, translated by S. Motzfeldt, October 25, 2011).

In the United States, the official guidance for complying with the *Plain Writing Act of 2010* is at the web site of the Plain Language Action and Information Network (PLAIN). PLAIN says that the guidance is meant to achieve the following:

improve your writing — and your agency's writing — so your users can

- *find what they need,*
- *understand what they find, and*
- *use what they find to meet their needs.* (PLAIN, 2011a)

The US nonprofit organization, the Center for Plain Language, also uses this definition based on users' behavior (Center for Plain Language, 2011a). The International Plain Language Working Group has proposed a similar definition (Cheek, 2010).

Notice how compatible our definition is with what you are reading about successful user experiences (UX) in other chapters of this book. Plain language is a critical component of successful UX and both focus on the three key measures: *find, understand, use.*

Our broad definition has at least these important implications:

- Plain language applies to all types of information.
- Plain language means focusing on your readers.
- Plain language is more than words and sentences.

Plain language applies to all types of information

Plain language is critical in every type of communication:

- web content
- Social media messages

- Emails
- Forms
- Surveys
- Documents
- The words and images in applications (from menu items to help text to messages)

For plain language as it specifically applies to forms and transactions on the Web, see Chapter 4 of this book, UX of Transactions, and Jarrett and Gaffney (2009).

Plain language is necessary to successfully carry out a content strategy. (For more on content strategy, see Chapter 10 of this book, Content Strategy, and Halvorson, 2012.)

Plain language means focusing on your readers

Plain language is sometimes called reader-focused writing. If we look again at the definition of plain language — with italics for emphasis this time, we can see that plain language is not a "one size fits all" proposition:

... writing — so *your users* can

- find what *they* need,
- understand what *they* find, and
- use what *they* find to meet *their* needs.

What is plain language for one set of readers may not be so for another. For example, the US National Cancer Institute (NCI) has two sets of information on each type of cancer — one directed at patients and their families, the other directed at health-care professionals. Both should be in plain language — with clear headings, logical organization, short paragraphs, straightforward sentences, and common words for most of the writing. But what is covered might differ between the two because what new cancer patients need and want to know is different from what health-care professionals need and want to know. Also, we would expect medical terms in the information for patients to come with explanations (in words and perhaps also in pictures). In the information for health-care professionals, the same medical terms might not need explanations.

Know your readers

The people who use what you write decide how much time and effort to spend trying to find, understand, and use. Therefore, to communicate successfully, you have to find out who your readers are, what they already know about your topic, and what words they use to talk about the topic. You also have to understand the situations in which they will get, open, look at, scan, read, and use what you write for them. (UX specialists call this the "context of use")

One way to keep your readers in mind as you write is to create *personas* (Adlin & Pruitt, 2010; US Department of Health & Human Services, 2011a). A persona is an exemplar for a group of people — a fictional person who realistically represents one of your major audiences/sets of readers or site visitors. Each persona has a name, a picture, demographic characteristics, and often a quote that the persona wants you to keep in mind when writing to the people the persona represents.

Shift your goals to focus on what readers should do

The first key to successful communication is knowing your readers. The second is understanding your purposes (what you want to achieve through this communication).

All communications in the workplace are functional — meant to achieve something. When planning any communication, focus those goals not on what you have to say but on what you want to achieve — on what you want or need your readers to do. Here is an example of the difference:

- Writer-focused goal:
  We must publish the guidelines for submitting proposals.
- Reader-focused goal:
  We want people to submit proposals on time, to the right place, and with the right information.

The reader-focused goals keep you thinking about how you can help readers accomplish that. You will find yourself saying, "To get to that goal, we have to select and arrange the information and write it so people who should submit proposals can easily find, understand, and use the information."

If you combine personas with reader-focused goals, you will write as if you were having a conversation with your readers. Redish (2007) shows you how to use both of these UX techniques to communicate successfully, thinking of content as conversation. And thinking of content as conversation will lead you to plain language.

Plain language is more than words and sentences

Plain language = successful communication. Therefore, plain language includes four essential components:

- What you say (selecting the content)
- The order in which you say it (organizing the content)
- The way you say it (choosing your words and arranging them into sentences, lists, or fragments)
- How you present it (selecting the font, layout, and design)

Although some plain language specialists want to separate language from design, most (including us) consider both language and design critically important to any plain language project.

Thus, plain language requires that you consider features such as these:

- Overall page or screen layout (what elements go where)
- Alignment (margins, indents, justified or ragged right)
- Headings — both how they look and what they say
- Labels in forms and applications — again both where they come and what they say
- Presentation of the information (when to use paragraphs, lists, tables, images, video, or other media)
- Space (where on the page or screen to include space and how much)
- Typography (fonts, font size, line length, spacing between lines)

All these features on a page or screen can help or hinder people in both finding what they need and being willing and able to work with what they find.

To summarize this section on defining plain language: you meet your goals best by focusing on your readers (users/site visitors) and thinking about what they want to know and need to do, their situations, how they will use what you write (or the multimedia you produce), the words they know and do not know, and what makes information easy or hard for them to find, understand, and use.

TWO CASE STUDIES

Does plain language work? Does it help people? Can we make the business case for revising material to be in plain language? The answer to all these questions is yes. In this section of the chapter, we give you two case studies that show the value of plain language.

Saving money through plain language

In 2010, the Swedish Agency for Higher Education Services saved 25% of the cost of its contact center by revising web text, forms, and emails into plain language. Figure 11.1 shows one example of what they did in the original Swedish. Figure 11.2 is the English translation.

Karin Hansson, a plain language expert at the agency, shared the story with us for this chapter (Hansson, personal communication, September 20, 2011). Here is Karin's story in her words:

The context

The main task of the agency is to process applications for Sweden's universities and colleges. We also run online application services — one for Swedish speakers and one for English speakers. We serve almost 40 universities and colleges that offer 15,000 courses and programs. We serve about 800,000 applicants.

The team

In 2009, we formed a team to work toward clear language in a planned and structured way. We chose the eight people on the team because they work closely with call center staff and admissions officers who reply to emails from applicants and talk to applicants on the phone every day. The idea was to gather as much knowledge about user needs as possible.

Before

Om du redan har ett konto med ditt personnummer ska du **inte** skapa ett till här. Ta kontakt med Antagningen om du vill ha hjälp med ditt konto.
Du kommer att kunna anmälan dig till högskolan, följa din anmälan, ändra dina adressuppgifter samt svara på antagningsbeskedet här på studera.nu.
Däremot får du **inte tillgång till de registrerade uppgifter** som finns om dig (till exempel meriter). För detta krävs att du loggar in med svenskt personnummer.
Du som har sekretessmarkerade personuppgifter ska skicka din anmälan per post direkt till VHS, Box 24 070, 104 50 Stockholm och skriv "sekretessmarkerade uppgifter" på blanketten. Anmäler du dig via internet blir samtliga uppgifter offentliga.

After

Har du sekretessmarkerade personuppgifter?
För att samtliga uppgifter i din anmälan inte ska bli offentliga ska du anmäla dig med pappersblankett och skicka den direkt till VHS, Box 24 070, 104 50 Stockholm. Skriv "sekretessmarkerade uppgifter" på blanketten. Läs mer om sekretessmarkerade personuppgifter.

Har du redan ett konto med svenskt personnummer?
Då ska du använda det och **inte** skapa ett konto till.

Har du frågor?
Använd kontaktformuläret för att ställa en fråga till Antagningen.

FIGURE 11.1 The original message in Swedish (left) and the revised message (right)

Before

If you already have a user account with your Swedish civic registration number, do not create a new account. Please contact University Studies in Sweden if you need assistance. You will be able to submit an application, follow your application, change your address and reply to the notification of selection results here at studera.nu. However, you cannot access your qualifications. This requires that you create an account with a Swedish civic registration number. If you have non-disclosable personal details you must apply by mail directly to VHS, PO Box 24070, 104 50 Stockholm, and write "non-disclosable personal details" on the application form. If you apply via the internet, all the information in your application will be available to the public.

After

Do you have personal details you do not want to disclose?
To avoid making the personal details in your application available to everyone, you must apply by submitting an application form directly to VHS, PO Box 24070, 104 50 Stockholm. Write "non-disclosable personal details" on the application form. Read more about non-disclosable personal details.

Already have an account with a Swedish civic registration number?
Then you must use it and not create a new account.

Any questions?
Use the contact form to ask a question to University Studies in Sweden.

FIGURE 11.2 English translations of the original message (left) and of the revised message (right)

None of the people on the team had any training in clear writing before this project. My role as plain language expert was to guide the group to reader-centered writing.

The task

The task was to revise 200 pieces of content for our online application service and about 30 prewritten emails that the online service sends automatically. Team members gave about 5% of their work time to the project, about 2 hours per person per week.

The process

We used various plain language techniques, always starting with these questions:

- What is the purpose of this text? What do we want to achieve?
- Where in the application process are the readers? What do they need to know at this stage in the process? What do they want to know? What do they already know?

Furthermore, we looked at the whole process. We always considered what we were revising in context — all the material relating to one part of the application process, such as searching for courses and applying, or logging on to read the selection results and replying to offers. This was a critical aspect of the project, one that had not been considered before.

The changes

Here is how we improved the web pages and emails:

- Added headings
- Moved the most important information to the beginning
- Added information on how to ask questions and what to do if something is wrong
- Removed information that is not relevant to the applicant at that stage of the process
- Put instructions into numbered lists

The result

After a few months, we started noticing the effects of our work: many fewer calls and emails. By the end of 2010, we concluded that the cost of our contact center that year had been almost *25% less* than we had expected.

Plain language makes a difference! And the Swedish Agency for Higher Education Services won the Swedish plain language prize, the Plain Language Crystal, for 2011.

Karin's story ends here. It gives us some key takeaways:

- Take on plain language as a project.
- Put together a team with relevant skills — subject matter knowledge, plain language knowledge, contact with and knowledge of the readers.
- Focus on purpose (what you want to achieve) and readers (including their context of use).
- Select something doable and work over time. Make it a sustained effort — not a one-off push.
- Iterate — each version gets better as you get feedback.

Next, we go from what a single agency can do to how a group of agencies can cooperate to create plain language documents.

Achieving plain language through iterative usability testing

Government agencies are often concerned not only with their own communications but also with how the businesses they regulate communicate with consumers. Our second case study shows how a group of government agencies working together with plain-language specialists were able to develop a model document and get many businesses to communicate in plain language. It also demonstrates the power of another UX technique: testing with users — having representative users try out your communication before you send it to hundreds or thousands or millions of people.

The official guidance for complying with *The Plain Writing Act of 2010* says this:

> *Testing your documents should be an integral part of your plain-language planning and writing process, not something you do after the fact to see if your document (or your website) is a success. . . . we recommend testing websites, documents, brochures, applications, mobile websites, videos, social media, and public affairs messages.* (PLAIN, 2011b)

Susan Kleimann, the second author of this chapter, and her team collaborated on this project with eight government agencies. This is Susan's story:

The context

Privacy is a huge concern in many aspects of our lives today. In the United States, the law says that financial institutions (such as banks or credit unions) must send customers a *financial privacy disclosure*[1] every year. The notice must explain

- How the institution collects and uses the customer's personal information
- Whether and how the customer can opt out of some ways that the institution shares that personal information

[1]The notice is required by the Financial Modernization Act of 1999, known as the Gramm-Leach-Bliley Act (GLBA). Financial institutions do not have to use the official model, but if they do they can satisfy the GLBA requirement and have a "legal safe harbor" about the elements required by law to be disclosed. The safe harbor does not apply to the nature of the individual institution's practices.

Today, financial institutions can comply with disclosure aspects of the law by using the official government model — and many do. The model is a research-based plain language document.

The problem

In the early years of the law, typical financial privacy notices were long, dense, full of legalese, and often in tiny type. People got them, but most did not read or understand them. Figure 11.3 shows one example. Although some disclosures used "we" and "you," the length and density often meant that people did not read or understand them.

The solution

Figure 11.4 shows the plain language notice we developed with our client team (Kleimann Communication Group, 2006). You can see how to customize the model notice to fit a specific institution's practice at the web site of the Federal Trade Commission (Federal Trade Commission, 2011). This example comes from the final round of usability testing. Neptune is not an actual bank. The final model disclosure is a template that financial institutions use, and we thought it would be better to show a filled-in example. This is very close to the final model.

What is the difference?

Comparing Figures 11.3 and 11.4, you can see at a glance that the plain language notice is visually more appealing and easier to use. If you delve into the organization and language, you also see that the plain language version has at least three other major differences:

- It starts with "Facts: What does [name of bank] do with your personal information?" That is longer than "Privacy Notice" which many old notices had as the title, but it is much clearer. Usability testing showed that consumers thought that there was no action to take with a "Privacy Notice" and, thus, no reason to read it. The new name engages customers. They now read what follows.
- It answers customers' questions right at the top: Why? What? How? Most people do not even know that banks share their personal information. Usability testing showed that people need this contextual information, and the use of familiar questions (like a newspaper story) further encourages customers to read.
- It uses a table to show the key facts about what the bank does. Usability testing showed that people can and do use the table both to understand what this bank does and to compare their options from different banks.

In Figure 11.4, you see only the first page of the plain language notice. After that comes a page with answers to typical customers' questions, definitions, and some other legally required information — all in plain language.

How did we get there?

This project shows how a user-centered design approach with lots of usability testing can bring about a plain language model even when eight different regulatory agencies are involved, the document is a legal notice, and industry representatives are skeptical.[2]

[2]The agencies included Board of Governors of the Federal Reserve System, Commodity Futures Trading Commission, Federal Deposit Insurance Corporation, Federal Trade Commission, National Credit Union Administration, Office of the Comptroller of the Currency, Office of Thrift Supervision, and Securities and Exchange Commission.

We value your privacy.

Inside you will learn about:

1. SAFEGUARDING YOUR INFORMATION
2. KEEPING YOUR INFORMATION ACCURATE
3. COLLECTING YOUR INFORMATION
4. PROTECTING INFORMATION ABOUT YOU FROM OUTSIDE MARKETERS
5. SHARING YOUR INFORMATION
6. CHOICES YOU CAN MAKE
7. ACTIONS YOU CAN TAKE
8. JUPITER BANK COMPANIES

This policy covers the information we collect about you, or "your personal information" as we refer to it in this notice, which means personally identifiable information about a consumer or a consumer's current or former relationship with Jupiter Bank. This policy applies to all Jupiter Bank companies and is provided to you as required by federal financial privacy laws.

1. SAFEGUARDING YOUR INFORMATION

We maintain physical, electronic and procedural safeguards to protect your personal information. Employees are authorized to access your personal information only when they need it to provide you with products and services or to maintain your accounts. Our code of ethics requires our employees to provide confidential treatment for your personal information and they are subject to disciplinary action if they fail to follow this code.

2. KEEPING YOUR INFORMATION ACCURATE

Keeping your account information accurate and up-to-date is very important. You have access to your account information through various means, such as through your account statements, and using our online banking services, and in response to your requests. If your account information is incomplete, inaccurate, or not current, please call or write to us at the telephone number or address listed on your account statement, bank records, or other documentation. We will promptly update or correct any errors. You can also write to us at:

Jupiter Bank
2004 Main Street
Plano, TX 75432

Please contact us if you have questions.

3. COLLECTING YOUR INFORMATION

We collect and use various types of information to service your accounts and make your dealings with us as easy as possible.

We keep the following types of customer information:

Application Information—information that you provide to us, such as on your applications and your account information, for example, your assets, income, and debt.

Transaction and Experience Information—information about your transactions and account experience, as well as information about our communications with you. Examples include your account balances, payment history, parties to transactions, credit card usage, requests for copies of checks, and preapproved credit offers.

Consumer Report Information—information from a consumer report, for example, your credit-worthiness and credit history.

Other Information—information from outside sources regarding your employment, credit and other relationships, as well as public records. Examples include your employment history, loan balances, credit card balances, property insurance coverage, and other information.

4. PROTECTING INFORMATION ABOUT YOU FROM OUTSIDE MARKETERS

Jupiter Bank does not sell or share any of your personal information with outside marketers who may want to offer you their own products and services. <u>You don't need to take any action to stop this type of sharing.</u>

5. SHARING YOUR INFORMATION

We manage the way in which information is shared among Jupiter Bank companies, with companies that work for us, and with other parties.

Sharing information among Jupiter Bank companies

Jupiter Bank is a group of financial companies, such as our mortgage company and credit card company, and nonfinancial companies such as our operations and servicing subsidiaries. Please review the section on *Jupiter Bank Companies* for a current list of our companies, all of which comply with this privacy policy.

Jupiter Bank may share any of your personal information among our companies:

To protect you. The information we maintain about your customer relationship helps us identify you and helps prevent unauthorized persons from accessing your information, or your accounts and services. For example, we may use information about your ATM and credit card transactions to identify unusual activity, and then contact you to learn if your card has been lost or stolen.

For your convenience. If you have an account with one of our companies and would like to open an account with another of our companies, we may share information you have previously provided to us. By sharing this information, you may not need to furnish the same information to any of our companies twice.

To provide quality service. Your customer information allows us to respond quickly to your needs—from obtaining cash through ATMs, to speedy approval of your mortgage loan application.

To tell you about new or improved financial services. By understanding your relationship, we can better meet your needs and determine whether other Jupiter services could be of value to you. We offer our customers a wide range of financial products—banking services, investment and brokerage services, mortgage services, and insurance products—and we can tailor our products and services to fit your personal needs.

To improve our products and services. Our products and services reflect the ways our customers actually use their accounts. We collect and analyze information about customer activity and history, so that we can design new types of loans, checking, and other accounts—all to meet your personal needs.

Sharing information with companies that work for us

We may share your personal information with companies that work for us. All the companies that act on our behalf to provide various services for you are contractually obligated to keep the information we provide to them confidential and to use the personal information we share only to provide the services we ask them to perform. Such companies may include companies that assist us in processing your transactions, printing your checks, mailing statements, and responding to your requests.

In addition, we may share any of your personal information with companies that work for us to provide marketing support services.

Some of our own companies may provide any of these services for us.

Other Sharing

We also may disclose any of your personal information to credit bureaus and similar organizations and when required or permitted by law. For example, your personal information may be disclosed in response to a subpoena or other legal process, a fraud investigation, and where required in public records, such as recording a deed of trust. Your personal information may be disclosed to companies that process your requests for products or services, or in the event your loan account is sold to another financial institution. We may also share your personal information outside of Jupiter Bank companies if we have your consent.

6. CHOICES YOU CAN MAKE

You can choose not to disclose some of your personal information to Jupiter Bank companies and to limit direct marketing solicitations by Jupiter Bank companies to you.

Sharing among Jupiter Bank companies

You may request that certain of your personal information, such as your application information and consumer report information, not be shared among Jupiter Bank companies. During the normal course of doing business, we will continue to share your transaction and experience information among our companies in order to service your accounts.

Direct marketing

You can choose not to receive marketing offers from us by direct mail, telephone, and/or e-mail. This preference applies to offers from us about our products and services, and about other products that we think may be of interest to you.

If you choose not to receive information about our products and services by direct mail, telephone or e-mail, you will continue to:

- Be contacted as necessary to service your account
- Receive marketing information included with your regular account mailings and statements, and when you visit us online or at an ATM

To help you understand how we record your preferences, you should know that:

- Your preferences will be honored among all Jupiter Bank companies
- Since some marketing programs may already be in progress, it may take up to 45 days for your preferences to be fully effective

7. ACTIONS YOU CAN TAKE

Remember that Jupiter Bank goes beyond the law and does not sell or share any of your personal information with outside marketers.

<u>No action is required for you to receive this benefit.</u>

FIGURE 11.3 A typical financial privacy disclosure from the early days of the law that requires them

FACTS	WHAT DOES NEPTUNE BANK DO WITH YOUR PERSONAL INFORMATION?
Why?	Financial companies choose how they share your personal information. Federal law gives consumers the right to limit some but not all sharing. Federal law also requires us to tell you how we collect, share, and protect your personal information. Please read this notice carefully to understand what we do.
What?	The types of personal information we collect and share depend on the product or service you have with us. This information can include: ▪ social security number and income ▪ account balances and payment history ▪ credit history and credit scores When you close your account, we continue to share information about you according to our policies.
How?	All financial companies need to share customers' personal information to run their everyday business—to process transactions, maintain customer accounts, and report to credit bureaus. In the section below, we list the reasons financial companies can share their customers' personal information; the reasons Neptune Bank chooses to share; and whether you can limit this sharing.

Reasons we can share your personal information	Does Neptune Bank share?	Can you limit this sharing?
For our everyday business purposes— to process your transactions, maintain your account, and report to credit bureaus	Yes	No
For our marketing purposes— to offer our products and services to you	Yes	No
For joint marketing with other financial companies	Yes	No
For our affiliates' everyday business purposes— information about your transactions and experiences	Yes	No
For our affiliates' everyday business purposes— information about your creditworthiness	Yes	Yes *(Check your choices, p.3)*
For our affiliates to market to you	Yes	Yes *(Check your choices, p.3)*
For nonaffiliates to market to you	Yes	Yes *(Check your choices, p.3)*

Contact Us	Call 1-800-898-9698 or go to www.neptunebank.com/privacy

FIGURE 11.4 An example of the new financial privacy disclosure with plain language and clear information design

The team used these UX methods:

- Reviewed many notices and the literature about notices to understand the problem and the context
- Held early focus groups to learn more about consumers and their use of the notices
- Put design and language together, creating drafts for testing with best practices in both information design and writing
- Iterated — went through several rounds of iterative design and usability testing

- Dealt with feedback from many interested reviewers — regulators in the partner federal agencies, industry representatives, and consumer groups
- Did usability testing with more than 60 consumers across eight cities

What did we learn?

Plain language and UX practitioners can take away these six key practices from our research (Kleimann, 2011):

1. *Keep it simple — but include what people need.* Consumers are overwhelmed by too many words, complex information, and vague sentences. If they think the information is complex, they often will not try to read it. We stripped away redundancies, cut out words, used simpler words, and put key information up front to set the context. But we did not oversimplify. The challenge in plain language is to find the balance between writing as few words as possible and giving people relevant and sufficient information.
2. *Use good design.* Good design delivers information in a format that reinforces the content. An easy-to-read design makes consumers more willing to use the document and better able to understand it. Headings, white space, bold text where appropriate, bulleted lists, the table, larger font size, and even putting the notice on regular, full-size paper all helped. Consumers recognized that the model disclosure looked different from typical legal disclosures. They said it looked more inviting and it created the impression that the financial institution wanted them to read and understand the notice.
3. *Be accurate, truthful, and objective.* In developing the plain language model disclosure, we had to be very careful not to introduce any bias for or against opting out of sharing because some consumers want the sharing. Also, the reality of many government documents is that they must satisfy the needs of different groups. In this case, to have consumers benefit from the model document, financial institutions must be willing to use the model. And financial institutions do not want the document to bias consumers against sharing. To assure that the model disclosure is accurate, truthful, and objective, in each round of usability testing, we listened carefully for comments, reactions, and perceptions from consumers that might indicate bias in any direction. Iterative testing let us choose design and wording that is clear and neutral. Careful design decisions ensure neutrality.
4. *Put context up front and explain when people need it.* Our research shows that people need context before details, and they need reasons to help them decide what to do. Most consumers have not understood that financial institutions share information, whom they share with, and what they and these other groups do with the information. In our plain language model, the top explains enough about financial sharing laws and personal information — in language that makes sense to consumers — so they can then use the table. In the table, we show — again in plain language — the reasons financial institutions can share information. Without this context, consumers are lost; they understand almost nothing of the notice.
5. *Standardize to help people find, understand, and use.* Creating a model that many institutions use helps consumers. In our research, standardizing the form and content helped consumers recognize the notice and the information in it. They learned where to look for differences between financial institutions' sharing practices. Standardization reduces cognitive burden because consumers recognize the information without having to read each notice word for word.

6. *Use tables to help people understand and compare*. The table is the heart of the plain language model notice. Simple, concise, and visual, the table simplifies highly complex, required information into a design that works—almost at a glance. In our research, consumers were able to understand and use the information in the table with greater ease than when that information was in paragraphs. They were more accurate at comparing practices across financial institutions. And they preferred the tables.

Where are we now?

This government project was a success. Consumers are benefiting because many industry leaders are voluntarily using the model privacy notices, including Bank of America, BB&T, CapitalOne, Chase Bank, and the Treasury Federal Credit Union.

The Federal Trade Commission and the other agencies won a ClearMark Award from the Center for Plain Language for "Best Original Public Document" for the model notice (Center for Plain Language, 2011b). Judges said the notice "reflects the balance of required regulation and industry comments in an easy-to-understand and well-organized design" (Judges' review forms, shared with competition entrant, 2010).

Plain language is possible! You can do it — even for legal documents, even with many stakeholders, even in government documents and documents that government develops for others to use.

ENCOURAGEMENT AND SUPPORT

As with so many aspects of UX, plain language does not magically happen even when law and executive order require it. In most government agencies, plain language practitioners must be advocates, champions, and evangelists. They must convince lawyers, managers, and other subject matter experts to change old habits, old models, and old philosophies.

We can encourage and support plain language in government in at least these four ways:

- Research
- Awards
- Training
- Usability testing

Research

As our first case study shows, we can sometimes get quantitative measures of how plain language helps — by saving money, reducing errors, reducing the need for secondary documents, and so on. Kimble (2012) gives many examples. We need even more.

Other types of research can also help, including basic research, research related to literacy levels, and research with specific audiences, such as judges.

Basic research

Guidelines that plain language practitioners follow have research behind them. That research comes from many academic fields, including cognitive psychology, linguistics, and research on reading and writing. It also comes from studies of entire documents, primarily through usability testing.

Tasks completed successfully	% of tasks Before	After	Improvement
Low-literacy web users	46%	82%	+77%
High-literacy web users	68%	93%	+37%
All users	59%	89%	+52%

Time spent on tasks	Time (min) Before	After	Improvement
Low-literacy web users	22:16	9:30	+134%
High-literacy web users	14:19	5:05	+182%
All users	17:50	6:45	+164%

FIGURE 11.5 Results from usability testing of an information-rich site

(For color version of this figure, see the web version of this chapter.)

For an early compilation of guidelines with their research base, see Felker, Pickering, Charrow, Holland, & Redish (1981). For a more recent compilation related to web sites, see US Department of Health & Human Services (2006).

Helping low-literacy people helps high-literacy people even more

Kathryn Summers and her team tested a web site with both low-literacy and high-literacy Web users. They then revised the site to resolve the problems the low-literacy Web users had. And they tested the new site with both low-literacy and high-literacy Web users (Summers & Summers, 2005).

The changes they made include many of the guidelines for plain language: starting with key messages; organizing in a logical, linear fashion; making the organization and hierarchy of the information obvious; using meaningful headings; keeping paragraphs very short; using lists; keeping sentences short and straightforward; using the simplest word that has the right meaning.

As you can see in Figure 11.5, the changes helped low-literacy site visitors get what they needed faster and more accurately. And those same changes helped high-literacy site visitors even more!

High-literacy readers are likely to be the busiest and least patient of your site visitors. When we use plain language, we are not "dumbing down" what we write. We are respecting our busy readers' time!

Judges find plain language more persuasive

In several studies over the past 25 years, legal researchers have shown that judges want plain language in the documents they must deal with. In the most recent study, more than half of the 292 judges reviewing a typical legal document and a plain language revision said the plain language version was more persuasive (Flammer, 2011). Flammer reports (p. 51), "More specifically, the rates for federal trial, federal appellate, state trial, and state appellate judges were 52%, 73%, 72%, and 65%" finding the plain language version more persuasive. Past studies with other documents have found judges preferring the plain language version by even higher percentages (Kimble, 1987, 1990).

Awards

Everyone values recognition for their work. Many groups encourage plain language through award programs.

Norway and Sweden both have an awards program for government agencies (Norway, 2011; Sweden, 2011). The US National Institutes of Health (NIH) has had a plain language awards program for many years (US National Institutes of Health, 2011). The Center for Plain Language began an annual awards program in 2010 with both ClearMark awards (for the best plain language) and WonderMark awards (for the worst, as in "we wonder what they were thinking when they wrote this"). In the second year, the Center introduced the TurnAround award for groups that had "won" a WonderMark award, taken it seriously, and done a good job of revising the communication. The Center's awards are judged in separate categories for entries from government agencies, not-for-profit organizations, and commercial companies (Center for Plain Language, 2011c).

Professional societies, including the Society for Technical Communication (STC), have national and international awards programs that receive many entries from government writers (STC, 2011). Commercial companies in several countries also have awards programs.

Training

Writing is both an art and a skill. We *can* teach the skills of writing clearly. And we need to do that because most people in government specialize in fields other than writing.

If your academic degree is in political science, policy, law, economics, chemistry, biology, meteorology, and so on, you may never have had a course in clear writing for the workplace. You may not have realized how much of your work time would be spent writing. You may be a technical professional who writes, not a professional writer or editor.

Even if you took composition classes in school or university, what you learned may have been how to write an academic paper—not at all the type of writing that you do for your work. As you will see in the final section of this chapter, writing in the workplace requires different guidelines from the ones that are typically rewarded in school.

Training is, therefore, an important part of getting people both to appreciate the need for plain language and to be able to communicate in plain language. Plain language consultants in many countries offer training courses.

In the United States, some government agencies, such as the Internal Revenue Service (IRS) and the Veterans Administration (VA), have developed plain language courses to train their employees. Also, any US government agency can request free training through the PLAIN web site (PLAIN, 2011c).

Usability testing

One of the best ways to make plain language (or any other aspect of UX) happen is to show its value through usability testing. In a usability test, you find out how well a document or web site works for the people who have to use it by having some of those people try it (US Department of Health & Human Services, 2011b; Chapter 20 of this book, Evaluation in Government Environments; Barnum, 2011; Dumas & Redish, 1999; Krug, 2010; Rubin & Chisnell, 2008).

Even a little usability testing helps

As our second case study shows, the best documents emerge from rounds of drafting, usability testing, drafting again based on what you learned in the usability test, testing again, and so on. Although that project went through several rounds over several years, most projects are only able to do much less. And yet they learn a great deal even in a short time and a few rounds.

Usability testing does not have to be formal, lengthy, or expensive. In the United States, the NCI has been conducting usability tests for more than a decade. The General Services Administration (GSA) helps agencies usability test their materials following Steve Krug's very quick method in which you focus on very specific issues with a promise to fix what you found within the next month (GSA, 2011).

Other US agencies, such as the Federal Reserve Board, the newly-created Consumer Financial Protection Bureau, and the Department of Health and Human Services, frequently use usability testing for major consumer documents.

Usability testing should cover "understand" and "use" as well as "find"

Remember our definition of usability: *find, understand, use*. Too many usability tests stop at "find." They do not learn whether people "understand" or how they would "use" the information.

Test content, not just navigation and search. People do not come to web sites for the joy of navigating or searching. They want the answer to a question. They want to do a task.

In a usability test, have people get information or do a task. Have real content in the material you test, not fake words (often shown as *Lorem ipsum*). Watch and listen to find out whether the content does the following:

- Gives people the information they need; answers their questions
- Follows an order that makes sense to them
- Includes headings that help them
- Uses words they know
- Puts the information in sentences, paragraphs, lists, or tables that they are willing and able to read and understand

Do not assume that if people looked at the information, they understood it. Ask them to explain what they found. Ask further questions to see if they can use the information.

Even in early testing with only some of the pages of the document or web site, you can have real information in at least part of the document or web site. Test that part. Test with real text and images.

Usability testing works for paper documents, too

With forms, you can watch and listen as people fill out the form. With notices and letters, you can ask people questions that show whether they understand what the notice is telling them and what they should now do. You can give them situations (scenarios) just as you do in testing web sites. For example, if you were testing a mortgage form, you might ask your usability test participants, "What amount would you write on your check to the lender for your first loan payment?"

Do not just ask people for their reaction (whether they like the document or not). Learn whether they understand and can use the document.

GUIDELINES FOR PLAIN LANGUAGE

The list you just read of what to look for when testing content (in a web site or a paper document) reflects some of the guidelines for plain language. We cover those and a few more in this last section of the chapter.

As part of the work for the International Plain Language Working Group, Harris, Kleimann, and Mowatt (2010) developed a list of seven key characteristics of communicating in plain language.

In Table 11.1, we adapt and add to these, making them a brief set of guidelines to help you communicate in plain language both online and on paper.

Table 11.1 Guidelines for Plain Language

Category	Guidance for Writers
1. Purpose, audience, and approach	Answer these questions before you write: • What do you want to achieve by writing this? • Who will use it? (create personas) • Why will they use it? • What tasks will they do with it?
2. Design	Use design and layout to make it easy for your readers/site visitors to see, understand, and use the information: • Separate sections, paragraphs, and lists with enough space to make the information manageable. • Use a grid so elements of the page line up neatly. • Show the hierarchy of the information in your design. For example, make first level headings bigger than lower-level headings. Perhaps put a key message in bold at the top of the page. • Set all text flush left and ragged right. Do not center text. • Group information visually. For example, put more space above each heading than between the heading and the text that follows it. If you use lines with the headings, put them over the heading not under it. • Use a legible font in a size large enough for easy reading. • Do not use all capitals.
3. Structure/ organization/ navigation	Keep the structure and navigation obvious and well-marked so the audience can find the information they need: • Organize logically for the reader. Follow the flow of a conversation with your reader. • Use headings to divide information. • Write meaningful headings using words your readers know. Meaningful headings can be questions, statements of key messages, or calls to action with verbs. Nouns work well only to name categories. They don't work as well for headings within documents. • Make the headings stand out visually, using bold or color or other design elements.
4. Hierarchy	Create a hierarchy that helps your readers distinguish between critical and less important information: • Put the key message first. • Give an overview to show the parts and how they fit together to make the whole. • Use design elements, such as size or graphics, to show the levels of information.
5. Language	Use words and sentences that work for all the people who must deal with what you produce: • Write short, straightforward sentences. • Keep each sentence to one or two tightly-connected thoughts. • Put extra material in another sentence (or fragment). • Use words your readers know. • Use the simplest, shortest word that has the right meaning.

Continued

Table 11.1 Guidelines for Plain Language—cont'd

Category	Guidance for Writers
	• Write to your readers. Use pronouns, "you" and "we." • Write with strong verbs, not nouns made from verbs. For example: In the sentence "Retention of a copy for your files is mandatory," the grammatical verb is "is"; and the noun "retention" hides the real action, "retain." Instead write, "You must keep a copy for your files." or "Keep a copy for your files." • Prefer the active voice.
6. Tone	Watch the tone so that you as the writer and your organization come across as reliable and trustworthy • Consider how people are going to "hear" what you are saying. When confronted with a document that has 100-word sentences and archaic legalisms, such as "heretofore" and the "said" program, people may just hear, "you aren't going to understand this." And they may think you are not dealing with them in good faith. • Although we encourage you to use "you" and "we," consider the situation. Be careful not to use "you" in an accusatory way or "we" in an arrogant way. Tone is always about balance.
7. Testing	Test your web site or document using a method that is appropriate for the purpose, importance, and type and number of people who will use what you are writing and designing. Test with early prototypes or drafts so that you have time to revise based on what you learn in the tests.

SUMMARY

Plain language is writing that helps readers find what they need, understand what they find, and use what they find to meet their needs. In the United States and elsewhere, laws and regulations require government writers to communicate in plain language.

The main keys to plain language are to focus on your readers and to remember that plain language is more than words and sentences:

- Selecting the content that your readers need
- Organizing logically for your readers
- Breaking up the information into manageable pieces with clear headings
- Using language your readers know
- Writing in short, straightforward sentences with lists, tables, and graphics where appropriate
- Designing the communication so that alignment, space, fonts, and so on help your readers

Our two case studies show the value of plain language. The Swedish Agency for Higher Education Services saved 25% of the cost of its contact center through plain language. A consortium of eight US federal agencies developed a model plain language notice that most major US financial institutions have adopted. The case studies give government writers several specific take-aways for developing plain language.

In this chapter, we have also identified four ways to encourage and further plain language in government: showing research results, providing awards programs, offering training, and helping with usability testing. A table in the last part of the chapter gives government writers specific guidelines for plain language.

References

Adlin, T., & Pruitt, J. (2010). *The essential persona lifecycle: Your guide to building and using*. Burlington, MA: Morgan Kaufmann.

Asprey, M. (2010). *Plain language for lawyers* (4th ed.). Annandale, NSW, Australia: Federation Press.

Barnum, C. (2011). *Usability testing essentials—Ready, set ... test!*. Burlington, MA: Morgan Kaufmann.

Center for Plain Language. (2011a). *What is plain language?* Retrieved 23 October 2011 from http://centerforplainlanguage.org/about-plain-language/

Center for Plain Language. (2011b). *2010 Clearmark award winners*. Retrieved 23 October 2011 from http://centerforplainlanguage.org/awards/past-years/clearmark2010/

Center for Plain Language. (2011c). *Awards*. Retrieved 23 October 2011 from http://centerforplainlanguage.org/awards/

Cheek, A. (2010). Defining plain language. *Clarity*, *64*, 5–15.

Dumas, J. S., & Redish, J. C. (1999). *A practical guide to usability testing* (Revised edition). Exeter, England: Intellect.

Ehrenberg-Sundin, B. (2004). *Plain language in Sweden, the results after 30 years*. Retrieved 23 October 2011 from http://www.plainlanguage.gov/usingPL/world/world-sweden.cfm

Federal Trade Commission. (2011). *Interagency notice research project and model form rule*. Retrieved 23 October 2011 from http://business.ftc.gov/documents/financial-privacy-rule-interagency-notice-research-project

Felker, D. B., Pickering, F., Charrow, V. R., Holland, V. M., & Redish, J. C. (1981). *Guidelines for document designers*. Washington, DC: American Institutes for Research.

Flammer, S. (2011, September). Writing to persuade judges. *Michigan Bar Journal*, *90*(9), 50–51. Retrieved 23 October 2011 from http://www.michbar.org/journal/pdf/pdf4article1900.pdf

Halvorson, K. (2012). *Content strategy for the web* (2nd edition). Berkeley, CA: New Riders.

Harris, L., Kleimann, S., & Mowatt, C. (2010). Setting plain language standards. *Clarity*, *64*, 16–25.

Jarrett, C., & Gaffney, G. (2009). *Forms that work—Designing web forms for usability*. Burlington, MA: Morgan-Kaufmann.

Joseph, D. (2011, September 6). Excerpted with permission from message posted to http://groups.yahoo.com/group/plainlanguage/

Kimble, J. (1987). Survey: Plain English wins every which way. *Michigan Bar Journal*, *1024*.

Kimble, J. (1990). Strike three for legalese. *Michigan Bar Journal*, *418*.

Kimble, J. (2012). *Writing for dollars; Writing to please*. Durham, NC: Carolina Academic Press.

Kleimann, K. (2011, February 8). *Leading practices for developing clear, concise financial privacy notices*. Retrieved 23 October 2011 from http://kleimann.com/wordpress/?page_id=41

Kleimann Communication Group. (2006). *Evolution of a prototype financial privacy notice*. Retrieved 23 October 2011 from http://www.ftc.gov/privacy/privacyinitiatives/ftcfinalreport060228.pdf

Krug, S. (2010). *Rocket surgery made easy*. Berkeley, CA: New Riders.

Kvarenes, M., Reksten, T., Stranger-Thorsen, I., & Aarønæs, L. (2010). *Klar, men aldri ferdig*. Oslo: Language Council of Norway and the Agency for Public Management and e-Government (Difi). Available from http://www.sprakrad.no/nb-NO/Klarsprak/Sprakhjelp/Klarsprak/

Norway. (2011). *Plain language in Norway's civil service*. Retrieved 23 October 2011 from http://www.sprakrad.no/nb-NO/Klarsprak/Fakta/Klarsprak/

Oregon.gov. (2011). *Plain language*. Retrieved 23 October 2011 from http://plainlanguage.oregon.gov/

PLAIN. (2011a). *Federal plain language guidelines—Introduction*. Retrieved 23 October 2011 from http://www.plainlanguage.gov

PLAIN. (2011b). *Federal plain language guidelines—Testing*. Retrieved 23 October 2011 from http://www.plainlanguage.gov

PLAIN. (2011c). *Free plain language training.* Retrieved 23 October 2011 from http://www.plainlanguage.gov/resources/take_training/freetraining.cfm

Redish. (2007). *Letting go of the words—Writing web content that works.* San Francisco, CA: Morgan Kaufmann.

Rubin, J., & Chisnell, D. (2008). *Handbook of usability testing* (2nd edition). Indianapolis, IN: Wiley.

Society for Technical Communication. (2011). *International summit awards.* Retrieved 23 October 2011 from http://stc .org/membership/recognition/competitions

Summers, K., & Summers, M. (2005). *Reading and navigational strategies of web users with lower literacy skills. Proceedings from ASIS&T 2005.* Retrieved 23 October 2011 from http//iat.ubalt.edu/summers/papers/Summers _ASIST2005.pdf

Sweden. (2011). *Plain Swedish language.* Retrieved 23 October 2011 from http://www.sprakradet.se/plain_language

US Congress. (2010). *The plain writing act of 2010.* Retrieved 23 October 2011 from http://www.fdic.gov/plainlanguage/plainwritingact.pdf

US Department of Health & Human Services. (2006). *Research-based web design & usability guidelines.* Washington, DC: US Government Printing Office. http://www.usability.gov/guidelines/index.html

US Department of Health & Human Services. (2011a). *Develop personas.* Retrieved 23 October 2011 from http://www.usability.gov/methods/analyze_current/personas.html

US Department of Health & Human Services. (2011b). *Usability testing.* Retrieved 23 October 2011 from http://www.usability.gov/methods/test_refine/learnusa/index.html

US General Services Administration. (2011). *First Friday's product testing program.* Retrieved 23 October 2011 from http://www.howto.gov/web-content/usability/first-fridays

US National Institutes of Health. *Plain language,* Retrieved 23 October 2011 from http://www.nih.gov/clearcommunication/plainlanguage.htm

Washington State, Office of the Governor. (2011). *Plain talk.* Retrieved 23 October 2011 from http://www .governor.wa.gov/priorities/plaintalk/

White House. (2011, January 18). *Improving regulation and regulatory review—Executive order.* Retrieved 23 October 2011 from http://www.whitehouse.gov/the-press-office/2011/01/18/improving-regulation-and -regulatory-review-executive-order

Further reading

Center for Plain Language. www.centerforplainlanguage.org

Clarity (an international organization focusing on clear legal documents). www.clarity-international.net

European Commission. (2011). *How to write clearly.* (Available as a free PDF in 23 languages). Retrieved 23 October 2011 from http://bookshop.europa.eu/is-bin/INTERSHOP.enfinity/WFS/EU-Bookshop-Site/en _GB/-/EUR/ViewPublication-Start?PublicationKey=HC3010536

Plain Language Association International. www.plainlanguagenetwork.org

Plain Language Action and Information Network (PLAIN). www.plainlanguage.gov

Stephens, C. (Ed.), (2010). *Plain language in Plain English.* Vancouver, BC: PlainLanguageWizardry.com

US Department of Health & Human Services. (2011). *Writing for the web.* Retrieved 23 October 2011 from http://www.usability.gov/methods/design_site/writing4web.html

US Federal Register. (2011). *Plain language tools.* Retrieved 23 October 2011 from http://www.archives.gov/federal-register/write/plain-language/

US Securities and Exchange Commission. (2011). *A plain English handbook.* Retrieved 23 October 2011 from http://www.sec.gov/pdf/handbook.pdf

CHAPTER

Ensuring Accessibility for People with Disabilities 12

Jonathan Lazar*, Brian Wentz†
Towson, MD, USA Frostburg, MD, USA†*

"Blind Americans are outraged that the government is failing to comply with its own guidelines to make government information and services available to citizens with disabilities . . . given that use of the Internet is critical to education, employment, access to government benefits and services, and all other aspects of modern life, there is no excuse for [government] failure to follow and rigorously enforce these guidelines."
— Dr. Marc Maurer, President, National Federation of the Blind

INTRODUCTION

Accessible interfaces are computer interfaces that can be successfully used by people with various disabilities. Historically, governments have focused both on employment of people with disabilities and on providing public information in multiple formats to ensure the widest distribution of information to the public. The focus on people with disabilities typically occurs in the government sector before the private sector gives similar attention to them. The same pattern holds true for the accessibility of information technology. Governments, through policies and laws, make technology accessibility a priority or a requirement, spurring interest and actions (such as technology development) within the private sector. Often, when laws exist for the government sector, they are later broadened to cover the private sector.

Information technology accessibility in the government typically has multiple goals and aspects, including technology access for employees with disabilities to do their daily work, making sure that citizens with disabilities can access government information, bringing attention to the topic of people with disabilities, and building partnerships to help spur private sector efforts in accessibility. Government policies related to accessibility do have an impact outside of the government. For instance, governments are large purchasers of information technology. When requests for proposals (RFPs) for government procurements specify technical requirements that include accessibility features, only companies whose products include accessibility features can respond to them, and that may spur other companies to add accessibility features so that their products could potentially be sold to the government. And although it is theoretically possible for a company to have two different versions of a product (an accessible version and an inaccessible one), the overhead and the logistics required often mean that only one version of a product is developed — and that version is accessible.

Information technology accessibility within the government is a years-long process involving many different steps: publicly stating accessibility as a priority, developing laws, creating technical standards (which are periodically updated) that specify how to meet the laws, and managing the iterative cycle of compliance and enforcement. The mechanisms for compliance and enforcement are different depending on the technologies involved: accessibility enforcement primarily occurs using the procurement process for acquiring hardware, software, and telecommunications devices. Accessibility enforcement occurs using regular usability evaluation (usability testing, expert reviews, or automated tests) for web sites (public or internal). And it is important to note that while government IT accessibility is typically viewed as something that only covers core government agencies, various government IT accessibility laws usually also cover public institutions such as public universities, public libraries, and government-funded museums.

WHAT IT ACCESSIBILITY MEANS

Before we discuss specific laws, it is important to discuss what accessibility means. From a practical point of view, IT accessibility means that someone with a perceptual or motor impairment can effectively use an interface, web site, or device. For web sites, blind people need web pages that work properly with screen reader software or refreshable Braille displays, so that they can access web page text and markup, such as links, tables, labels, and graphics. Blind people also are likely to be unable to use a pointing device (such as a mouse). Figure 12.1 shows a PAC Mate Braille display from Freedom Scientific.

People with motor impairment need to be able to interact with a web page without using a pointing device, and typically using an alternative input device (such as a modified keyboard, speech recognition, or eye tracking) to enter data. People who are deaf or hard of hearing need to have full transcripts for audio and captioning for video. For operating systems and application interfaces, these same types of flexibility hold true. For physical devices, there must be equivalents for people with perceptual and motor impairments, so that, for instance, a copier or mobile touch screen provides methods for blind people to interact — either tactile cues or speech output so that blind people can interact with the device without seeing the display. For people who are deaf or hard of hearing, equivalents might include captioning for any output that exists via audio or vibration, rather than an alarm sounding. For people with motor impairments, voice input or larger tactile input might be appropriate.

Rather than add one feature for blind people, one feature for deaf people, etc., designers follow a set of design guidelines, so that their designs cover the widest range of potential users. The technical standards themselves (discussed later in this chapter) address primarily people with perceptual and motor impairment, but typically do not address many types of cognitive impairment. There are multiple reasons for this: whereas the human-computer interaction community has a track record of more than 30 years of

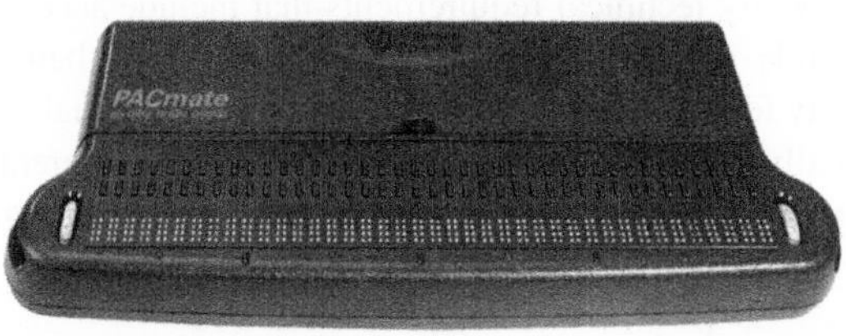

FIGURE 12.1 Assistive technology: PAC Mate Braille display

designing interfaces for perceptual and motor impairment, there is a very limited track record (8-10 years only) of research on cognitive impairment. Furthermore, there are no clear design recommendations on how to design interfaces for people with all types of cognitive impairment — although some design guidelines, such as providing the ability to ask for more time to complete a task, could be interpreted as such.

LAWS AND TECHNICAL STANDARDS

The laws and standards that mandate government accessibility often vary dramatically throughout the world. Since 1998 in the United States, Section 508 of the Rehabilitation Act of 1973 ("Section 508"), which essentially dealt with employment, has served as a primary guideline for government accessibility. Section 508 has been enforceable since 2001. Several other mandates also apply, including Section 504 of the Rehabilitation Act of 1973 and the E-Government Act (Jaeger, 2004). Section 504 provides equal access to a public education for individuals with disabilities, and the E-government Act encouraged accessibility and usability of government information. Section 508 specifies the accessibility standards for government web sites and technology. The Americans with Disabilities Act of 1990 (ADA) began requiring employers to provide "reasonable accommodation" to employees with disabilities—this includes access to computer systems and other technology (Gunderson, 1994). In 2010 the US Department of Justice began a process to develop technical standards for web sites of private companies that are considered "public accommodations" under the ADA and therefore must be accessible to people with disabilities.

The Twenty-First Century Communications and Video Accessibility Act legislation, signed into law in the United States in late 2010 (US Department of Justice, 2010), attempts to ensure access to Internet communication devices and video for those with disabilities (Committee on Energy and Commerce, 2010). Section 508 has, since 2008, been undergoing a revision to address changes recommended by the Telecommunications and Electronic and Information Technology Advisory Committee. Under the version of Section 508 currently in effect, web sites must conform to the paragraphs that are somewhat based on the Web Content Accessibility Guidelines (WCAG) 1.0, which the World Wide Web Consortium (W3C) published as part of its Web Accessibility Initiative (W3C, 2011). The current version of WCAG is 2.0, and as of this writing, Section 508 is being updated simply to use WCAG 2.0 (US Access Board, 2008).

In the United States, many accessibility measures have been related more to the procurement of accessible technology instead of the more difficult ongoing monitoring and maintenance. Because many web sites are developed "in house," and the content changes frequently, this often provides an accessibility "loophole" for web sites, where there is no oversight of accessibility. US accessibility laws also apply to both internal and public-facing systems, unlike in many other countries, where such laws often only apply to public-facing systems. Software applications used by federal employees (such as enterprise-wide database programs) as well as personal office automation applications (such as word processing and spreadsheeting), and data analysis software (such as statistical and scientific software) are generally purchased with multiple levels of financial approvals. These approval steps can provide an opportunity to evaluate software for accessibility, and reject procurements of software that do not meet legal accessibility requirements.

Under disability laws (in the United States, for example), governmental entities can claim that an accessibility accommodation is not financially or practically reasonable (an "undue burden" under the law). By current law, if the accommodation is an undue burden, then the entity does not need to provide the accessibility accommodation. This is also true in an instance where the requirements of a particular job require a certain physical ability (such as eyesight). The undue burden clause has been somewhat overused, since the court systems seem to accept most claims related to this clause (Lazar & Jaeger, 2011).

In the United Kingdom, the Disability Discrimination Act specifies accessibility standards for web sites and other technology that might cause discrimination by a lack of accessibility, but its focus has been on government web sites (Office of Public Sector Information, 2005). It has been updated by the Equality Act 2010, which attempts to strengthen the impact of the previous legislation, including pre-employment disability-related inquiries (Government Equalities Office, 2010). The new law is now proactive, in that organizations can no longer wait until a person with a disability attempts to use a service to comply with the law, but must be proactive in determining in advance, and on a regular basis, what should be done to provide accessibility (RNIB, 2011). This law applies to both the public and private sector. For web sites, the current law allows conformance to either WCAG 1.0 or WCAG 2.0.

Across the European Union (EU), eEurope 2002 mandated WCAG 1.0 conformance for all EU Commission web sites (Europe's Information Society, 2010). This initiative attempts to broaden e-inclusion and accessibility throughout Europe. Individual member states also have specific legislation related to accessibility. In France, the Government Circular of 1999 encouraged web sites to provide accessibility, and the more recent Law No 2005-102 of 2005 required all government web sites to conform to WCAG 2.0 by May 2011 (European Union, 2010a). Germany's 2002 Federal Ordinance on Barrier-Free Information Technology mandated compliance to WCAG 1.0, but an update begun in 2006 now mandates compliance to WCAG 2.0 (Federal Ministry of the Interior, 2002). Italy's Law No. 4/2004 requires that information technologies support access for those with disabilities (European Union, 2010b). For all government web sites in Italy, WCAG 1.0 is required. In Spain, Law 56/2007 established an obligation for general accessibility; however, the law provides exceptions for functions or services that do not allow for accessibility (Inter-Parliamentary Union, 2007). Spain is an active participant in the EU Mandate 376, which details the accessibility requirements for ICT procurement in the European Union (Joint Working Grouping Group for M376, 2011).

Other countries such as Hong Kong, New Zealand, and Australia also have similar laws or regulations in place. In Hong Kong, all government web sites must conform to WCAG 1.0 level AA, and there has been a focus on web site accessibility since late 1999 (Home Affairs Bureau, 2001). E-Government Web Standards in New Zealand, as required by the Human Rights Amendment of 2001, require adherence to WCAG 2.0 level AA (Office of the GCIO, 2009). In Australia, the Disability Discrimination Act specifies that all government and non-government web sites should comply with WCAG 2.0 level AA by 2013 (Minister for Finance and Deregulation, 2010). In Thailand, the TH-WCAG (similar to WCAG 2.0 level A) is used to promote the accessibility of e-government (e-Gov) (Mitsamarn, Gestubtim, & Junnatas, 2007).

It is important to note that while discussions about government IT systems accessibility typically occur at the national or federal level, local governments also have technology and web sites which must be accessible for people with disabilities. While local and regional governments typically are considered to have less experience in IT usability and accessibility than federal/national governments, two recent studies found that state governments in the United States may outperform the federal government when it comes to Web accessibility. Yu and Parmento (2011) found that US state government web sites, on average, were more accessible than US federal government web sites. Olalere and Lazar (2011) found that stronger accessibility policy statements on federal web sites did not result in more accessible web sites, which is a different result from the Rubaii-Barrett and Wise (2008) finding that stronger accessibility policy statements on US state web sites did mean that the web sites were actually more accessible.

Table 12.1 provides a summary of IT accessibility laws from various national governments.

Table 12.1 Sample of Accessibility Laws and Enforcement Around the World

Country	Related Laws	Link to Legislation	Enforcement
Australia	Disability Discrimination Act	http://www.comlaw.gov.au/Series/C2004A04426	Human Rights Commission
Canada	Human Rights Act of 1977, Common Look and Feel for the Internet	http://www.tbs-sct.gc.ca/pol/doc-eng.aspx?section=text&id=23601	Treasury Board of Canada
France	Law No 2005-102	http://www.legifrance.gouv.fr/affichTexte.do?cidTexte=JORFTEXT000000809647	Unknown
Germany	Federal Ordinance on Barrier-Free Information Technology	http://www.einfach-fuer-alle.de/artikel/bitv_english/	Federal Ministry of the Interior
Hong Kong	Digital 21 Strategy (not legislation)	http://www.digital21.gov.hk/	Home Affairs Bureau
Italy	Stanca Act, 2004 Provisions to Support the Access to Information Technologies for the Disabled	http://www.pubbliaccesso.gov.it/normative/law_20040109_n4.htm	Unknown
New Zealand	Human Rights Amendment of 2001	http://www.legislation.govt.nz/act/public/2001/0096/latest/DLM121285.html	State Services Commission
Spain	Act 11/2007, Electronic Access of Citizens to Public Services, 2007 Act on Public Sector Contracts	http://fundacionorange.es/fundacionorange/analisis/eespana/e_espana10.html	Ministry of Labour and Social Affairs
Sweden	EU Mandate 376 (also applies to all EU countries)	http://www.mandate376.eu/	Legal, Financial, and Administrative Services Agency
United Kingdom	Equality Act	http://www.legislation.gov.uk/ukpga/2010/15/contents	Equality and Human Rights Commission
United States	Americans with Disabilities Act, Section 508, Section 504, E-Government Act, 21st Century Communications and Video Accessibility Act	http://www.ada.gov/pubs/ada.htm, http://www.section508.gov	US Department of Justice

IT ACCESSIBILITY MONITORING AND ENFORCEMENT

One of the core challenges with IT accessibility in government is that even when laws exist requiring accessible IT in government, often they are not enforced. Governments often purchase inaccessible IT, and develop and maintain inaccessible web sites. Often, there is no one supervising the implementation of accessibility laws. Furthermore, many times, there is no clear guidance on *how* to implement them. A common problem is that government agencies often refuse to share their data on IT accessibility with the public, or even with other government agencies within the same country. While this may in some cases be a violation of public records laws (in countries where they exist), it does occur.

Enforcing IT accessibility in procurement of hardware and software, in our opinion, is an easier task than enforcing IT accessibility in web sites because government agencies typically have well-established procurement processes in place. (For more information on government procurement, see Chapter 16, Getting UX into the Contract.) Oftentimes, web sites are developed in house, without any procurement approval processes. Furthermore, even if a web site is developed by an outside company and goes through a procurement process, web sites (both public and internal) tend to change on a daily basis, and very rarely are there compliance monitoring processes in place. If copier machines are being purchased, if an enterprise-wide database application is being procured, if a kiosk for travelers entering the United States is being procured, if software for online training for federal employees (such as software to deliver webinars) is being procured — all of these types of IT must be accessible and typically would go through a procurement process. Purchasing inaccessible IT for use by government employees in their work automatically puts government employees with disabilities at a competitive disadvantage.

Procuring IT requires the approval of monetary expenditures at multiple levels, and these serve as natural checkpoints for ensuring accessibility. If inaccessible IT is going to be procured (because there are no viable options that are accessible), then paperwork must be filled out to justify the inaccessible purchase and document the departure from the normal procurement process. Because web sites change daily, without any monetary expenditure, there often are no approval or maintenance processes in place, and so, unfortunately, it is much easier for government to avoid the issue of Web accessibility. Web sites (both public sites as well as intranets for employees) are often not procured but developed in house, and procurement is where the most effective controls for accessibility often take place. Even if a web site is developed outside of the government and goes through a procurement process, often there are no compliance checks once the site is launched.

Another challenge is that, unfortunately, government does not widely employ the user-centered design processes that are necessary for monitoring web site accessibility compliance on an ongoing basis. There is hesitation to do user-centered design — or sometimes, there is outright hostility toward it. As one US government official (who shall remain nameless) told us, "User studies consistently undermine accessibility efforts" because "users themselves are notoriously bad at use of computing technologies." So there may be resistance to doing user-based testing.

In the United Kingdom, the Equality Act of 2010 mandates accessibility and attempts to strengthen previous requirements of the Disability Discrimination Act. Section 29(1) of the Act states: "A person . . . concerned with the provision of a service to the public or a section of the public (for payment or not) must not discriminate against a person requiring the service by not providing the person with the service" (Government Equalities Office, 2010). The British Standards Institute (BSI) launched a new Web accessibility code of practice to address the challenge of Web accessibility (BSI, 2011). A study conducted in 2009 noted that 97% of official web sites in the United Kingdom had accessibility violations (Kuzma, 2010). Because the Act went into effect only recently, it remains to be seen whether its implementation and enforcement will have a stronger impact than prior legislation. With the new legislation enacted, one area of significant interest to web site operators (and Web hosts) is that the Act allows Web hosting providers actually to shut down inaccessible web sites. Schedule 25 states that hosting providers will be exempt from liability under the Act in relation to inaccessible content they host if they did not have knowledge of it, and if they "expeditiously remove" it once they are aware that it is inaccessible (discriminatory) in nature (Government Equalities Office, 2010).

There is no single standard or accepted practice for how to monitor government web sites on an ongoing basis. The key approaches for accessibility evaluations, which are rooted in user-centered design processes described as, could be described as (1) usability testing involving people with disabilities, (2) expert reviews, and (3) automated accessibility testing by software applications. Although automated testing is generally not considered to be as effective as usability testing or expert reviews, the large-scale need for evaluation (millions of web sites) makes automated accessibility likely to be a component of any government web site accessibility plan. The Swedish government uses an interesting approach where they perform automated accessibility evaluations and publicly post the results, which encourages ongoing compliance (Gulliksen, Von Axelson, Persson, & Goransson, 2010). Mirri, Muratori, and Salomoni (2011) recently developed an application called the "Accessibility Monitoring Application", which can be used to evaluate certain aspects of Web accessibility on a geopolitical level. This tool is currently being used by the Emilia-Romagna region of Italy to conduct regular monitoring of more than 370 regional, provincial, and municipality web sites for compliance with the WCAG and the Stanca Act (Italian law related to accessibility). Rui, Gomes, and Carrico (2010) describe how Web archives (in their example, the Portuguese Web Archive), which store copies of millions of web pages, could potentially be utilized to evaluate accessibility on a large scale. This study evaluated the accessibility of over 25 million web pages that were in the Portuguese Web archive. While these large-scale overviews may be useful to get a snapshot of accessibility and determine if, overall, the situation is getting worse or better, the feedback provided about improving specific web sites is limited.

The Treasury Board of Canada Secretariat (TBCS) posts the "Common Look and Feel for the Internet" guide to maintain consistent Web accessibility (TBCS, 2010). This is based on the responsibilities in the Canadian Human Rights Act of 1977. The current version of the guidelines is based on WCAG 2.0. The Common Look and Feel for the Internet Guide has been in effect since 2001. In August of 2011, an updated "Standard on Web Accessibility" took effect. The law notes that deputy heads of government agencies will be responsible for monitoring and reporting requirements as well as taking corrective measures. On a government-wide basis, the TBCS is responsible for monitoring compliance (TBCS, 2011). Despite having these measures in place, accessibility remains a problem for government systems throughout Canada. Because of this, in late 2010, a Canadian federal court judge ordered that all government web sites needed to be made accessible within 15 months (Lancaster House, 2011). The action of citizens, rather than government enforcement, has encouraged accessibility in Canada. In 2010, Australia released the Web Accessibility National Transition Strategy to describe the implementation of WCAG 2.0. The plan requires all web sites of federal agencies to conform to level A by December 2012 and to level AA by December 2014. The Australian Human Rights Commission enforces and monitors government accessibility in Australia (Conway, 2011).

In 2009, Sweden ratified the UN Convention on the Rights of Persons with Disabilities. As this law was ratified, it became the basis for disability policies in Sweden. Sweden has implemented a set of guidelines for interface accessibility that is intended to support the procurement, development, and maintenance of public administration web sites so that they are accessible. The current guidelines are based on a version of WCAG 2.0. Gulliksen et al. (2010) report that automated tools are used to regularly evaluate the accessibility of public administration web sites and that as of 2007, 90% of the web site administrators were familiar with the guidelines. Unfortunately, Verva (the agency which supervised the accessibility efforts in Sweden) was shut down in late 2008, but a new delegation for e-Gov is being established to improve and carry on the efforts. The EU Mandate 376 details how accessible procurement should be conducted, and the Legal, Financial, and Administrative Services Agency in Sweden is responsible for such procurement (ICT Standards Board, 2011). As such, this agency will be involved in implementing the EU Mandate. As of 2007, across EU member states, the government and parliament web sites in Sweden ranked first in accessibility compliance.

Another example is that of Portugal, which was an early leader in web accessibility legislation — but within ten years of its supporting early legislation, evaluations revealed low compliance by government web sites. It is probable that the lack of clear goals and implementation guidance, combined with a lack of enforcement or penalties, was primarily to blame. A new government directive from the prime minister resulted in 95% compliance within three years, and a UN report then ranked the Portuguese government at second place in terms of web site accessibility (Goodwin, Susar, Nietzio, Snaprud, & Jensen, 2011).

ACHIEVING COMPLIANCE AND ACCESSIBILITY

Governments may not have ongoing "checkpoints" where compliance is monitored in computer interfaces, except when a monetary expense is involved. For most hardware devices, operating systems, and software applications, there is indeed a point of purchase, a monetary expenditure, and a process to be followed. Generally, governments have been more successful with procurement as far as compliance to accessibility is concerned. For example, the US federal government provides a wizard to help determine accessibility requirements and obtain standard accessible IT wording for use in RFPs (see www.buyaccessible.gov). The federal government in partnership with industry developed the Voluntary Product Accessibility Template (VPAT), which many companies offer to provide details about the IT accessibility compliance of their product. For instance, Even Grounds (an accessibility consulting company) offers a VPAT directory (http://www.evengrounds.com/resources/vpat-directory) containing a list of major IT companies that offer VPATs, with links to those specific sites. Figure 12.2 shows the "BuyAccessible" wizard provided by the General Services Administration for US federal agencies.

A few US federal agencies and federal projects have been open and transparent in describing how they strive to meet legal requirements for Web accessibility. It seems as though federal agencies that employ full-time Section 508 coordinators often may do a more thorough job with implementation and enforcement than do those agencies that assign it to an individual as a collateral job duty. Some agencies and federal projects that have been open about describing their 508 compliance processes include the US Census Bureau, the US Food and Drug Administration (FDA), and the web site of the American Recovery and Reinvestment Act (Recovery.gov) (Lazar & Olalere, 2011). Documenting best practices is especially important since recent studies have listed inaccessible web sites across the federal government and in state governments (Lazar et al., 2010; Olalere & Lazar, 2011; Yu & Parmento, 2011), and this problem has been identified for a number of years (Jaeger, 2006).

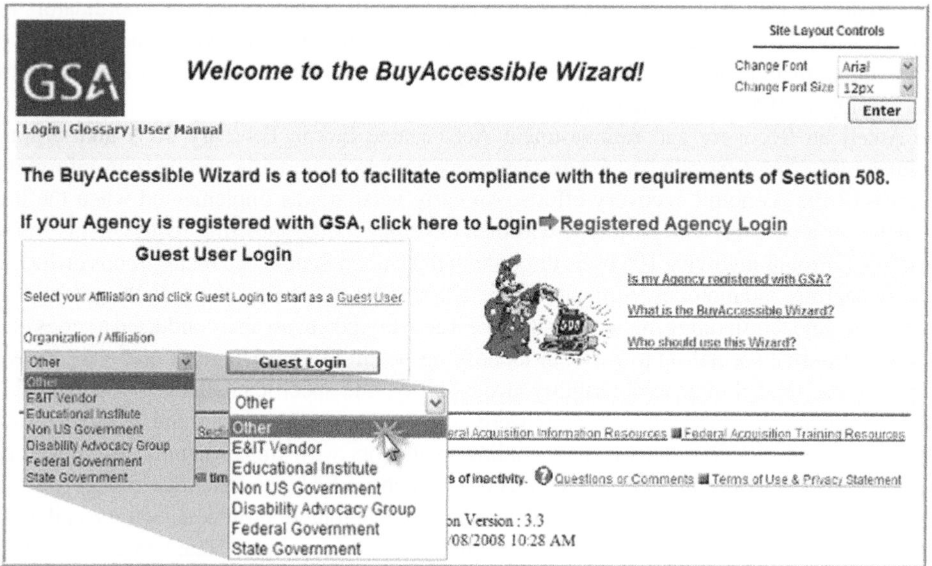

FIGURE 12.2 The BuyAccessible Wizard of the US General Services Administration

(from http://www.buyaccessible.gov/ on October 18, 2011). (For the color version of this figure, see the Web version of this chapter.)

The US Census Bureau operates under the Department of Commerce to collect census and other data about the population of the United States. These data are used by government, business, and individuals for decision making (US Census Bureau, 2010). The Census Bureau employs a full-time Section 508 coordinator for ensuring compliance with Section 508. To increase the accessibility of Web-based information, the Bureau uses web page templates and a number of automated tools to analyze compliance. The automated software tools evaluate 90% of Census Bureau web sites for accessibility on a monthly basis, and the reports are sent to the individuals responsible for maintaining that content. In addition, blind individuals regularly participate in usability tests with JAWS a type of (screen reader software) to ensure usability. Contractors interacting with the Census Bureau are also required to comply with Section 508 and are provided with suggestions for improvement when they produce content that does not comply. To further encourage a culture of accessibility compliance, a monthly technology newsletter includes Section 508 news and tips, and the Census Bureau posts its accessibility statement on its public web site (Lazar & Olalere, 2011).

The FDA is the part of the US Department of Health and Human Services (HHS) that protects public health in the United States by assuring the safety, efficacy, and security of human and veterinary drugs, biological products, medical devices, the food supply, cosmetics, and products that emit radiation (FDA, 2011). To implement accessibility, the FDA uses a content management system (CMS). (For more information about the use of CMSs, see Chapter 10, Content Strategy.) Because the FDA has more than 800 contributors to the content of their web site, they created a Section 508 compliance group to maintain and promote compliance throughout the agency. The group relies on a panel of users with disabilities to conduct usability testing to inform 508 compliance activities. Before creating a CMS account for a content contributor, the FDA requires a signed contract stating that only Section 508-compliant materials will be posted and that the content contributor understands that repeated offenses could result in losing account privileges. The FDA holds monthly meetings with all their Section 508 coordinators as well as training sessions on compliance, which are also available to all FDA employees. The compliance team is also seeking to include Section 508 in the new employee orientation as mandatory annual training for all HHS employees (Lazar & Olalere, 2011).

The American Recovery and Reinvestment Act became law in February 2009 and required the establishment of a "user-friendly" web site (Recovery.gov) to provide the public with information on the progress of the economic recovery efforts. An early version was implemented when the law was signed, however a new web site prototype was then developed after gathering requirements from users during 10 focus groups involving 105 users throughout the United States. The focus groups included users with vision, hearing, and motor impairments and results were used to help determine the potential layout, design, content, and terminology of the web site. The Recovery.gov team also conducted a series of expert reviews with external specialists to assist in identifying potential improvements and challenges in the prototypes. These related to general usability, accessibility, and specific challenges of geospatial maps and data visualizations. After initial designs were complete, usability testing and a formal evaluation for compliance with Section 508 (again including evaluators with impairments). The developers of Recovery.gov also evaluated the web site with JAWS, Watchfire XM (automated accessibility evaluation tool), and a head-pointing device (Lazar & Olalere, 2011). All content providers, editors, and approvers for Recovery.gov receive accessibility training, and all new content or features are evaluated for compliance with Section 508 before being posted.

The EU Commission on Employment, Social Affairs and Inclusion is a major driver behind the monitoring and encouragement of IT accessibility throughout the EU (European Commission on Employment, Social Affairs and Inclusion, 2011). The support of this Commission has prompted further legislation and methods of compliance throughout the EU. One such example is Spain, where the 2007 Act, "Electronic Access of Citizens to Public Services," has resulted in a strong push for greater electronic accessibility and universal access in public sector technology, in public procurement, in research and development, in education, and even in private industry (Soto, 2009). The Spanish National Council of Representatives of Persons with Disabilities has partnered with the Spanish government to achieve accessibility. The European Internet Accessibility Observatory has been involved in assessing the results of European efforts for accessible web sites since 2004 (Manchester Metropolitan University, 2005). European Design for All e-Accessibility Network (EDeAN) has been an outgrowth of these EU directives. The purpose of this network of organizations in EU member states is to be a forum for universal design issues, to support the EU e-inclusion initiatives, to raise awareness in both the public and private sectors, and to provide an online resource on the topic of universal design (EDeAN, 2007). EDeAN serves as a repository for case studies and best practices on training for and benchmarking accessibility (drawing much information from relevant international conferences).

It is important to note that there is often a difference between mere legal compliance and true accessibility. Laws often specify the basic minimum of accessibility features, not full accessibility. Some advocate basic compliance through the use of only means automated tools without involving actual human users. True accessibility implies going beyond mere compliance toward a goal of universal access. Achieving true accessibility requires conformance to national and international guidelines but also conducting regular user evaluations of technology products (including web sites). User evaluations often yield surprising results that would not have been discovered through strict accessibility evaluations using automated tools. Accomplishing universal access in government requires collaboration between governments, advocacy groups, academia, and private industry.

SUCCESS FACTORS

To increase the probability of achieving successful IT accessibility in government, we suggest the following:

- *Use training sessions and public awareness strategies to encourage IT accessibility.* This can be useful in both the public and private sectors to ensure that individuals understand both the need for accessibility and how IT can be accessible.
- *Highlight visible examples of best practices.* This enables government agencies to see what ongoing monitoring activities and practices in IT accessibility are exemplary.
- *Enforce IT accessibility, for software, web sites, and the IT procurement process.* Simply passing regulations to require accessibility is a far cry from enforcing accessibility in government.
- *Maintain openness and transparency.* This ensures that compliance to accessibility can be verified and monitored.
- *Address the emergence and popularity of mobile applications.* Often, areas of emerging technologies (such as mobile devices and electronic health records) are not covered by current regulations or actively monitored for accessibility by government agencies.
- *Work to harmonize IT accessibility regulations.* This is essential across international, federal, state (or province), and local government levels. The more changes that are made to guidelines which move them further away from the international standards, the less likely that existing software tools will be able to test for those guidelines.

These strategies start with simple steps that governments can take to address the need for accessibility and build to the more challenging steps that are needed to ensure long-term accessibility. Achieving government accessibility must be a planned, structured endeavor, rather than merely scattered attempts with the hope of somehow reaching that goal.

SUMMARY

Accessible information technology refers specifically to the ability of individuals with disabilities to be able to access and use information technology. Because of the services it provides and its responsibility to act as a positive exemplar of universal access, it is crucial that governments exhibit a high level of technology accessibility, both internally and externally. Government regulations and case examples also often form the foundation for accessibility compliance in the private sector.

There is a wide range of regulation — and compliance to that regulation — by governments around the world. Some countries have very clear regulations on accessibility, while others have few or no guidelines. It varies from country to country: some countries have transparency and enforcement mechanisms, even without strong laws, and other countries have laws but no enforcement or discussion of the laws. Monitoring and enforcing accessibility is an ongoing challenge, and it is clear that successful government accessibility will be achieved only by combining the use of training, best practices, credible enforcement, transparency, and regulation harmonization.

If government leads the way in IT accessibility, universal access will ultimately reach beyond government to all areas of life.

References

British Standards Institute. New web accessibility standard launched. (2011). Retrieved 13 July 2011 from http://www.bsigroup.com/en/Standards-and-Publications/Newsletters–press/Latest-news/Technical-design-and-innovation-news-homepage/New-web-accessibility-standard-launched/

Committee on Energy and Commerce. The Library of Congress. (2010). Retrieved 23 August 2011 from http://thomas.loc.gov/cgi-bin/query/z?c111:S.3304

Conway, V. (2011). Website accessibility in Australia and the Australian government's national transition strategy. In *Proceedings of the international cross-disciplinary conference on web accessibility (W4a '11).* New York: Association for Computing Machinery, Article 15.

EDeAN. European design for all e-accessibility network. (2007). Retrieved 24 August 2011 from http://www.edean.org

Europe's Information Society. eEurope 2002 action plan. (2010). Retrieved 25 August 2011 from http://ec.europa.eu/information_society/eeurope/2002/index_en.htm

European Commission on Employment, Social Affairs and Inclusion. What we do. (2011). Retrieved 24 August 2011 from http://ec.europa.eu/social/main.jsp?langId=en&catId=1

European Union. eInclusion factsheet—France—Legal framework. (2010a). Retrieved 25 August 2011 from http://www.epractice.eu/en/document/365309

European Union. eInclusion factsheet—Italy—Legal framework. (2010b). Retrieved 25 August 2011 from http://www.epractice.eu/en/document/329684

Federal Ministry of the Interior. Federal ordinance on barrier-free information technology. (2002). Retrieved 23 August 2011 from http://www.einfach-fuer-alle.de/artikel/bitv_english/

Goodwin, M., Susar, D., Nietzio, A., Snaprud, M., & Jensen, C. (2011). Global web accessibility analysis of national government portals and ministry web sites. *Journal of Information Technology & Politics*, *8*, 41–67.

Government Equalities Office. Equality act 2010. (2010). Retrieved 23 August 2011 from http://www.equalities.gov.uk/equality_act_2010.aspx

Gulliksen, J., Von Axelson, H., Persson, H., & Goransson, B. (2010, May). Accessibility and public policy in Sweden. *Interactions*, *17*(3), 26–29.

Gunderson, Jon R. (1994). American with Disabilities Act (ADA): Human computer interaction for persons with disabilities. In *Conference companion on human factors in computing systems (CHI '94),* Catherine Plaisant (Ed.), (pp. 381–382). New York, NY, USA: ACM.

Home Affairs Bureau. Legislative council panel on information technology and broadcasting: Web access by people with disabilities. (2001). Retrieved 23 August 2011 from http://www.legco.gov.hk/yr00-01/english/panels/itb/papers/a774-02e.pdf

ICT Standards Board. European accessibility requirements for public procurement of products and services in the ICT domain. (2011). Retrieved 24 August 2011 from http://www.mandate376.eu/m376.htm

Inter-Parliamentary Union. Law 56/2007 on measures to promote information society. (2007). Retrieved 24 August 2011 from http://www.ictparliament.org/node/1782

Jaeger, P. T. (2004). Beyond section 508: The spectrum of legal requirements for accessible e-government web sites in the United States. *Journal of Government Information*, *30*(4), 518–533.

Jaeger, P. (2006). Assessing section 508 compliance on federal e-government websites: A multi-method, user-centered evaluation of accessibility for persons with disabilities. *Government Information Quarterly*, *23*(2), 169–190.

Joint Working Group for M376. European accessibility requirements for public procurement of products and services in the ICT domain. (2011). Retrieved 29 February 2012 from http://www.mandate376.eu

Kuzma, J. M. (2010). Accessibility design issues with UK e-government sites. *Government Information Quarterly*, *27*(2), 141–146.

Lancaster House. Judge orders federal government to make its websites accessible to the blind but Ottawa digs in. (2011). Retrieved 25 August 2011 from http://www.lancasterhouse.com/about/headlines_jan20.asp

Lazar, J., Beavan, P., Brown, J., Coffey, D., Nolf, B., Poole, R., et al. (2010). Investigating the accessibility of state government websites in Maryland. In P. Langdon, P. Clarkson & P. Robinson (Eds.), *Designing inclusive interactions—Proceedings of the 2010 Cambridge workshop on universal access and assistive technology*, (pp. 69–78). London: Springer-Verlag.

Lazar, J., & Jaeger, P. T. (2011). Reducing barriers to online access for people with disabilities. *Issues in Science and Technology*, *17*(2), 68–82.

Lazar, J., & Olalere, A. (2011). Investigation of best practices for maintaining section 508 compliance in U.S. federal web sites. In *Proceedings of the human computer interaction international conference 2011* (pp. 498–506), Berlin: Springer-Verlag.

Manchester Metropolitan University. European internet accessibility observatory (EIAO). (2005). Retrieved 20 August 2011 from http://www.cerlim.ac.uk/projects/eiao/

Minister for Finance and Deregulation. Government releases website accessibility national transition strategy. (2010). Retrieved 20 August 2011 from http://www.financeminister.gov.au/archive/media/2010/mr_372010_joint.html

Mirri, S., Muratori, L., & Salomoni, P. (2011). Monitoring accessibility: large scale evaluations at a Geo political level. In *The proceedings of the 13th International ACM SIGACCESS Conference on Computers and Accessibility (ASSETS '11)*, New York, NY, USA: ACM, 163–170.

Mitsamarn, N., Gestubtim, W., & Junnatas, S. (2007). Web accessibility: A government's effort to promote e-accessibility in Thailand. In *Proceedings of the 1st international convention on rehabilitation engineering & assistive technology: in conjunction with 1st Tan Tock Seng hospital neurorehabilitation meeting (i-CREATe '07)*, 23–27. New York: ACM.

Office of Public Sector Information. The disability discrimination act 2005. (2005). Retrieved 23 August 2011 from http://www.opsi.gov.uk/acts/acts2005/ukpga_20050013_en_1

Office of the GCIO. New Zealand government web standards. (2009). Retrieved 25 August 2011 from http://webstandards.govt.nz/meeting-the-standards/

Olalere, A., & Lazar, J. (2011). Accessibility of U.S. federal government home pages: Section 508 compliance and site accessibility statements. *Government Information Quarterly*, *28*(3), 303–309.

RNIB. UK law for websites. (2011). Retrieved 25 August 2011 from http://www.rnib.org.uk/professionals/webaccessibility/lawsandstandards/Pages/uk_law.aspx

Rubaii-Barrett, N., & Wise, L. (2008). Disability access and e-government: An empirical analysis of state practices. *Journal of Disability Policy Studies*, *19*(1), 52–64.

Rui, L., Gomes, D., & Carrico, L. (2010). Web not for all: A large scale study of web accessibility. In *Proceedings of the 2010 international cross-disciplinary conference on web accessibility*, Berlin: Springer-Verlag.

Soto, I. (2009). *11/2007 Law guide.* Retrieved 20 August 2011 from http://www.ogov.eu/guia-de-la-ley-112007/

Treasury Board of Canada Secretariat. Common look and feel for the internet 2.0. (2010). Retrieved 20 August 2011 from http://www.tbs-sct.gc.ca/clf2-nsi2/index-eng.asp

Treasury Board of Canada Secretariat. Standard on web accessibility. (2011). Retrieved 25 August 2011 from http://www.tbs-sct.gc.ca/pol/doc-eng.aspx?section=text&id=23601

US Access Board. Report to the Access Board: Refreshed Accessibility Standards and Guidelines in Telecommunications and Electronic and Information Technology. (2008). Retrieved 25 August 2011 from http://www .access-board.gov/sec508/refresh/report/

US Census Bureau. About us. (2010). Retrieved 21 August 2011 from http://www.census.gov/aboutus/

US Department of Justice. Advance notice of proposed rulemaking on accessibility of web information and services provided by entities covered by the ADA. (2010). Retrieved 20 August 2011 from http://www.ada.gov/anprm2010/factsht_web_anprm_2010.pdf

US Food and Drug Administration. FDA fundamentals. (2011). Retrieved 20 August 2011 from http://www.fda.gov/AboutFDA/Transparency/Basics/ucm192695.htm

W3C. WCAG overview. (2011). Retrieved 20 August 2011 from http://www.w3.org/WAI/intro/wcag

Yu, D., & Parmento, B. (2011). US state government websites demonstrate better in terms of accessibility compared to federal government and commercial websites. *Government Information Quarterly*, *28*(4), 484–490.

Further reading

Microsoft Government Accessibility Guide: www.microsoft.com/industry/government/guides/accessibility

United States Access Board: www.access-board.gov

WebAIM: webaim.org

CHAPTER

Mobile Access

13

George Buchanan
School of Informatics, City University London, London, UK

"It isn't just about making the Web you know today work on mobile phones.... The innovations which will really count are the things which I can't imagine now."
— Sir Tim Berners-Lee

INTRODUCTION

Effective interaction design for mobile services needs to consider, as with any information technology (IT) system, the likely users of the system. Government — local, regional, and national — has some services (e.g., garbage, or rubbish, collection) used by almost everyone in the community, and others (e.g., care services) used mainly by very specific sectors of the public. These two situations can interact in both particular and unpredictable ways. While pavements[1] are used by everyone, a certain section of pavement may be used particularly often by the elderly when it provides access to a care center. For those familiar with that specific location, it may seem "obvious" that older people often use it: it is not so straightforward to systematically identify all such locations or circumstances within a locality.

In the case of mobile services, problems of particular knowledge and particular profiles of use recur. Anticipating accurately the "right" cross-section of users is far from simple. This challenge is even sharper for government bodies; they are more vulnerable to criticism that suggests noncompliance with statutory obligations such as the UK Disability Discrimination Act, or the US Americans with Disabilities Act. The wise, or at least cautious, approach is to ensure that a wide variety of users are included in requirements gathering and the design phase of any mobile service, with others included during user testing of prototypes and developed systems. Some government services will particularly focus upon users with disabilities and impairments. When this is the case, particular attention needs to be paid to inclusive design, as detailed in Chapter 12, Ensuring Accessibility for People with Disabilities.

Added to this complexity is that individual mobile users are prone to behaving differently when they use a service in varied locations, times, or circumstances (Church et al, 2007). This makes developing usable mobile services more difficult than for Web-based systems targeted at static desktop users (Jones & Marsden, 2005).

[1]"Sidewalks" in the United States.

Examples of the significant problems the impact of varying mobile context has on actual usability are not hard to imagine: a young mother may experience no difficulty in using her mobile phone to pay for a parking ticket when on her own, but with a toddler, baby carriage, and baggage, using the same phone one-handed, while distracted by her children, may prove much more problematic. Reproducing such situations in a "classic" laboratory-based user test is inherently difficult. Similarly, capturing the full range of similar differences through traditional requirements gathering processes is harder when context is so variable in practice. Users of IT systems are not analytically studying when or why they experience systems as being difficult to use. Personnel with strong usability and implementation skills are needed to ensure that a good quantity of this information is gathered during early parts of any development project (see Chapter 18, User-Centered Requirements Definition, for further information).

Problems of the variability of users' context are not unique to government services, but they typically apply with greater frequency than would be the case for, say, a general retail web site. Providing a service for all users may be seen as — at best — desirable by a commercial organization; any political or statutory body will typically face less flexible expectations — as is discussed in Chapter 23, Service Design and Channel Shifting.

Before even starting to examine the more technical issues surrounding mobile user experience, we need to pay some attention to ensuring that the overall software development process (as described in Section IV, and in particular in Chapters 18, User-Centered Requirements Definition, and 19, Models as Abstract Representations for Supporting the Development of e-Procedures) has frequent points where feedback on real users' needs will inform the design and implementation of the final system.

USER-CENTERED DESIGN

IT experts repeatedly report that usability testing is a critical part of the early development of interactive systems, but the predominant culture is to approach usability experts to validate or endorse a particular design much too late in the development process. If errors cause problems with desktop systems, they are almost always fatal to mobile services, thus ensuring that traditional methods have to be maintained and expected savings are not realized. Chapters 17, ISO Standards for User-Centered Design and the Specification of Usability, and 19, Models as Abstract Representations for Supporting the Development of e-Procedures, give some valuable insights into software development, user-centered design, and the main relevant standards that ought to be taken into account.

Applying the user-centered design approach to mobile interaction naturally requires particular attention to the contexts in which mobiles are used. We will look at three key concerns: choosing representative users, identifying contextual scenarios, and scoping the design.

Choosing users

Choosing appropriate representative users and studying their needs in a realistic setting is a major barrier. If this is not successfully resolved, it is likely that any implemented system will prove to be ineffective in use.

Our experience of testing real government services, both using mobile devices and desktop computers, in the City Interaction Laboratory,[2] has underlined these general points with real cases.[3]

[2]http://hcid.soi.city.ac.uk/cityinteractionlab/.

[3]We are unable, for reasons of commercial confidentiality, to provide case study details.

We have encountered situations where target users of a new system lacked both access to the needed computer technology, and the IT skills to use it. Even well-designed interfaces cannot realistically hope to overcome such significant barriers to use. Similarly, apparently "generic" services, which one might reasonably expect to be used by "everyone," quite often are used with particular frequency by the elderly or disabled. While this knowledge was typically transparent to those in the "front line," project specifications had failed to identify and record this, and major problems emerged late in the development cycle, with the consequently high cost associated with remedial action.

Using front-line staff as a source of knowledge about users is a simple and effective method. Identifying a few representative users — demonstrating the anticipated "normal" profile — is a good start, but also needed is an understanding of user groups on the margins, who might have particular problems. The vital information is what mobile devices people are actually using. Current best-selling phone lists may seem persuasive, but, in reality, many people retain and use older phones, and carry and use a phone in very different ways.

Getting real information on real users and their behavior can be done through simple, semiformal interviews. For mobile devices the normal caution on avoiding questionnaires and surveys to gain information about real use applies with double force. Even knowledge from the previous year may be inaccurate or redundant — and the opinion of the phone enthusiast in the development team is clearly not impartial. Approaching even a few likely users informally will provide more information than will a standardized form. Ethnographic style methods can be particularly helpful, as they emphasize understanding people's lives and activities from their own point of view (Jones & Marsden, 2005).

Our knowledge of the use of mobile phones from primary research is surprisingly limited; there are still few concrete, proven guidelines of "typical" use that can actually inform generic design of mobile interfaces. This means we must all do our own research on what our users do. In identifying our users, we can identify the mobile devices they have access to and some general mobile usage patterns. We now need to be more specific, and to focus on where, when, and how they will be using a mobile service.

Understanding the context of use

As well as identifying an individual user's immediate personal needs and their devices, it is vital to understand where and when they would use a mobile service. Many investigative methods are available but the popular use of questionnaires is a poor choice. Most especially when using mobile devices, where use is interrupted, often opportunistic, and regularly unplanned, users have a poor recollection of when they use a mobile service. A questionnaire or survey is a very limited tool; if the wrong questions are asked, vital details will not be revealed, and a misleading picture can be formed that will lead to a poor-quality design. Many people are misled by the apparently simple expertise required to perform surveys — while it is easy to create a questionnaire, it is, in fact, torturously difficult to design a truly effective one (Ozok, 2009).

Problems in obtaining large-scale information on such contexts of use through surveys have privileged the major service providers. Yahoo or Google can access large-scale logs that unveil deep insights into user behavior but such resources are not publicly available due to their commercial value; few governmental bodies will be so fortunate as to have such data to draw upon.

Diary studies (e.g., Grawemeyer & Johnson, 2011) are prone to incomplete participation (users drop out of the study or provide only partial data) but can provide valuable clues at little cost. A participant completes an entry for each day, or when a specific type of event occurs, and provides some details about use of the system. When accompanied by interviews, this method can provide a good insight with even modest numbers of participants. A diary study can be followed up by a questionnaire informed by real behavior, and will be more likely to deliver good data for design work. If appropriate users have been identified, then diary studies or contextual interviews (Beyer & Holtzblatt, 1997) can really help to obtain a good picture of the environments in which people may use a service.

The more distracting and busy the situation is, the simpler the system must be. It is a common error to design as many of the full-service features into a mobile interface as is possible. If the system is really used at home, in a quiet place without interruption, by someone familiar with IT, it may well be usable. For a parent on a downtown street with three children to keep an eye on, the same interface will most likely fail catastrophically.

Understanding the physical context will also help identify the services really likely to be useful. To take two obvious cases, a retired person going shopping may need to pay for parking but is unlikely, at that moment, to want to check the environmental policies of the city council. Conversely, when at home, she may want to check on the recycling collection schedule, but will not want to buy another parking ticket. Such needs are — bizarrely — often given equal importance on government web sites. Some services are a natural fit for the mobile context; others really are more at home on the desktop Web.

Given enough primary data, you can draw a truly useful picture of your user's real-world requirements. Once a list is created, you can group similar and related requirements. Requirements can be prioritized by the proportion of users who share the requirement and its importance for those users. Practical considerations such as development time can also be used in prioritization. Given the limited scope of most mobile systems, this need not require specialist tools or methods.

Too many organizations structure their online presence around their internal structures. The negative consequences of such navel-gazing apply with particular force to mobile interaction. Stripping away unnecessary content may rankle internally, but overburdening services with too many options causes many more external problems. Many useful services have limited relevance to mobile users. The actual requirements of the real-world behavior can help reduce your services to the right ones. Given small screens and time-consuming input methods, limiting any software to a few well-implemented features will produce a more usable mobile service.

Scoping the design

One vital element of any interactive system is working out what functionality is required. Given the context of use, one can construct a set of requirements, with associated constraints and issues.

One simple guideline is to focus ruthlessly on a limited, specific feature of high importance first, and expand from there. The ideal feature is a "low-hanging fruit" that requires limited development effort, but can produce short-term successes. The first goal must be clearly set in a broader strategy, with a staged plan that will roll out functionality to other areas. If not, a fragmented and inconsistent potpourri of features will emerge.

For example, if a parking scheme is to use mobile phones for payment, simply providing a fixed-term ticket for a fixed fee, timed from the moment that the user buys the ticket, reduces both interaction design and interface development costs. The initial system may only use a simple Web-based interface, before progressing to provide more complex interfaces.

An SMS interface might be developed for simpler phones, but this requires a more specific infrastructure. Designing good text-messaging services is surprisingly difficult — errors can produce repeated texts, texting produces no immediate feedback — which can make using the service a daunting experience. SMS services, however, have the advantage that they do not require private information to be divulged. An initial service can be tried out with a few selected users, to provide vital further information on other users' actual needs and requirements.

Clearly segmenting features into consistent and coherent sets rolled out in iterative phases will allow for focused design work at each stage, minimize the risk of design error, and increase the chances of good take-up. Making early releases of a service comply with local regulations and standards and careful staging ensures that any statutory compliance requirements are fulfilled in a stepwise process alongside the interface design.

A cautious approach will avoid over-elaboration of services. Minimizing complexity is a vital goal and all parties should repeatedly reconsider what is really required. Representatives of the user community can verify the importance of unresolved issues — some needs appear less important once a basic service exists, while others, which appeared to be superficial, become more useful.

Users who self-identify as being technologically aware will often demand complex service functionality. Increased elaboration of features demonstrates their self-ascribed technological mastery. Pressure from such users for more complex features needs to be tempered against a wider range of users and abilities. Good-quality default options in a simplified interface will reduce the interaction demands for casual and occasional users.

Lowering the cost of usability

While many experienced analysts can recall project failures caused by poor user-based research, many development team leaders lack user research skills, and are unsure in distinguishing between market research and studies that assist the design of interfaces and software. Time and financial constraints can also prohibit original user research. Where there is a willingness to learn about usability methods, the time required to acquire new skills is hard to judge, and, typically, when faced with uncertain costs for uncertain benefits, people will do nothing.

In mobile services, two projects may develop very different pieces of software, but many user contexts may be shared between them. Just as software engineering benefits from reusing existing software, knowledge of users' needs can be transferred between projects. This can be done both internally and externally to other parts of government and, even, industry. Taking our example of a mother facing difficulties when using her mobile phone, if one lesson drawn was that an interface should be useable single-handed (which is almost always a good guideline for a mobile system), then it seems likely to be a relevant usage scenario for other services.

INTERNAL SYSTEMS

When developing internal government IT systems, the principles for public-facing systems still apply. It is easier to get participants for gathering user needs and for evaluation. Just as understanding what the public does is difficult, managers will seldom appreciate every detail of their employees' work. The real needs of staff, from the front line to strategic management, may prove more limited and focused than speculation suggests. The BlackBerry's success may now be fading, but its superiority for simple messaging tasks — the commonplace of management work — demonstrates the importance of a small range of work for even the President of the United States (Barack Obama being a flagship BlackBerry user).

The pressure of workplace politics needs to be understood with care. Managers often wish for designs that will unintentionally impede front-line work, and will try to ensure that developers only receive information that complies with their expectations. Interviewing internal users away from management oversight is vital, as many internal IT projects have failed when this was not done.

Nonetheless, well-designed mobile IT projects have proved particularly successful. The Nomad Project on UK local government use of mobile devices has resulted in some spectacular successes — the London Borough of Sutton obtained a 30% leap in productivity for their financial assessors. An external audit (Audit Commission, 2007) reported that running an extensive pilot scheme that maximized the influence of front-line staff in designing the project was a major factor in the project's success. This project demonstrates many other points of best practice, as highlighted in Chapter 23, Service Design and Channel Shifting.

When working with professional staff, drawing on the ideas of participatory design — where future users become design advisors who contributed directly to the design of systems that they will later use — is particularly powerful. Typically, such staff have a useful grasp of the potential of IT systems, and can enhance the quality of ideas generated during the design phase of the project.

INTERNATIONAL PERSPECTIVES

In Western Europe and North America, mobile phones are complementary devices that are used alongside desktop computers, laptops, etc. This has led to an emphasis on transferring PC-based knowledge, and interface metaphors, to mobile applications. It is worthwhile looking from a wider, global perspective as has been done also in Chapter 21, Adapting e-Gov Usability Evaluation to Cultural Contexts, Chapter 22, Design for Policymaking, and Chapter 24, UX and e-Democracy in Asia.

In many emerging markets, the mobile phone is not only the most commonplace, but in many cases the only computational device that people have (Jones & Marsden, 2005). Furthermore, many of the phones in these countries are "second market" phones that have been refurbished or newly manufactured at lower cost. Consequently, the level of technological sophistication of the device, and also the mental model of the device held by users, are radically different from the proliferation of touchscreen phones and PC metaphors that hold sway in a large metropolis.

Devices are only part of the picture: many countries are likely to skip directly to a predominantly wireless infrastructure. Cabled networks require a large investment, and where users are sparse, this is not economically viable. These practical constraints affect remote areas in developed countries as well as sparsely populated areas of developing nations. While such similarities do exist, the urban realities for, say, Delhi versus Toronto (or India versus Denmark, as discussed in Chapter 21, Adapting e-Gov Usability Evaluation to Cultural Contexts) are very different.

One major consequence for service usability is that simply transferring desktop-based metaphors will doubly fail in emerging and developing economies. Even basic considerations such as literacy may be a problem, and infrastructure may not be consistently reliable. The plague of variable coverage may be an irritation in Berlin, but it is likely to be much worse in Hanoi. The economics of services also differ — many users of mobile phones in Africa predominantly use SMS rather than voice calls — particularly for advanced services such as broadband wireless.

To avoid using the wrong metaphor, there must be an emphasis on the early stages of user-centered design — identifying what designs have any chance of success early, at limited cost. Paper prototyping is ideal, and can be done with many people with simple materials. The issue of limited wireless broadband means that services may have to use SMS and design stand-alone applications that require only periodic data connections. Successful designs embrace these limitations, and use limited communications within a simple interaction.

STANDARDS AND GUIDELINES

ISO 20282 (International Organization for Standardization, 2006a, 2006b), is an ISO standard that provides ease-of-use standards for everyday products. Many phone manufacturers use this standard, and it both specifies the design process used to create products and proposes a set of evaluation processes for different types of products. ISO 20282 can help design a thorough usability process. However, the test processes are specified as having 50 participants. This is certainly state-of-the art, but the costs involved are significant. (Other usability-related ISO standards can be found in Chapter 17, ISO Standards for User-Centered Design and the Specification of Usability.) The general usability issues addressed by those standards apply with equal force to mobile services and systems.

The general World Wide Web Consortium (W3C) Web Content Accessibility Guidelines (WCAG) (W3C, 2008a) are a second commonplace standard, and the importance of the issue of accessibility has been noted earlier in this chapter and also in Chapter 2, Usability of Public Web Sites, Chapter 4, UX of Transactions, and Chapter 12, Ensuring Accessibility for People with Disabilities. For mobiles, W3C produces a guide for Mobile Web Best Practices (W3C, 2008b). This is not aimed specifically at accessibility but the approach has a close relationship with the different elements of the WCAG. The W3C notes similarities between mobile users and disabled users of web sites, and its Web Accessibility Initiative discusses the cost and process advantages of taking this approach. It is wise to remember, however, that mobile users and users with disabilities are not the same group, and following this similarity too closely is unwise.

Earlier standards still persist in some areas — as was noted in the International Perspectives section above, technology deployments vary from country to country, and earlier standards like the Wireless Application Protocol (WAP) still persist. While redundant in most of "the West," low-bandwidth, conservative technology persists elsewhere as an affordable alternative to more developed forms of mobile Web access. The practices of local service providers and national radiofrequency communication laws also lead to varying usability practices. The different histories of technology deployments and current standards lead to significantly different user expectations of technology.

NTT Docomo in Japan was an early innovator in mobile interactive services, but led with both interaction designs and advanced services, not simply providing of wireless Internet. Even now, the Japanese mobile phone market is distinguished from others by the commonplace use of "wallet" payment technology, integrated train ticket support, etc. through to the support of long text messages. Some issues are due to Japan's cultural expectations of public behavior while others have been driven by the early deployment of Japan's mobile Internet service.

When transferring systems from one country to another, both the direct and lingering effects of differing technologies need to be identified if local standards are to be meaningfully complied with.

A SHIFTING TECHNOLOGY BASE

Mobile technologies are continually changing, shaped by a mixture of global innovation and the transfer of technology between countries. This creates real challenges for longer-term usability. Japan's i-Mode mobile Internet technology was adopted by many countries, but several have now ceased using the standard when complete third-generation (3G) broadband services rendered it redundant. Similarly, wireless application protocol (WAP) services of the early 2000s quickly became archaic due to changes in communication technology.

An awareness of the current constraints of public networks in a country can inform current design, but it is wise to consider foreseeable future changes. If a system will rapidly become redundant, its short lifespan will limit its viability. From a usability point of view, some future-proofing (identifying how a technology can be incorporated into a system at a future date) can allow for better planning. For example, in Europe, the use of radiofrequency identification technology (RFID) seems likely to increase, particularly as a means of payment. Considering how, conceptually, this technology could be included in a current or future system should not be a costly exercise. Avoiding the need to make radical changes to the interface will save development costs, but will also ensure that users experience a smooth progression from one technology to the next — with the interface changing in an apparently minimal manner.

Digital democracy

One element of governance that has attracted considerable discussion is the use of mobile devices to facilitate voting — either within the context of elections or the simple canvassing of opinion. Mobile devices can have positive attributes in remote areas or widely dispersed populations but potential malpractice is a very real concern. Someone other than its owner may misappropriate a phone, or anonymous phones may be used to overrepresent particular points of view. There is a complex, and sometimes contentious, tension between openness and the traditional checks of representative government.

The complex issues surrounding user experience and e-Democracy are addressed in Chapter 24, UX and e-Democracy in Asia, and apply to both mobile systems and desktop applications. Concerns of privacy and security (see Chapter 5, Privacy and the Citizen, and Chapter 14, User Issues in Security) similarly have a direct impact on the usability and design of mobile services. The main concern in the mobile-specific issue is user location data. Mobile phone manufacturers often have specific limitations that they apply to their devices, and applying the usual methods for ensuring that log data are securely kept on your servers usually suffices.

PRACTICAL MOBILE USABILITY

What about the pragmatic realities of developing usable mobile systems? This section discusses some of the common interaction design pitfalls that can be readily addressed, regardless of the specific services being developed or the differing technologies being used.

Text size

The first major limitation of mobile usability is the small display size. While some technologies improve the readability of small text, the readability of content remains a significant practical problem. For older or partially sighted users, technology can only mitigate the problems of small text. Reducing the volume of text to be read on any display is a much better approach than squeezing more content onto a small screen.

Touchscreen phones are a particular problem, as "clicking" depends on both seeing a small piece of content and pressing accurately the on-screen target. My own recent research has shown that even on an iPad, many web pages become difficult for users to navigate, particularly when links are close together. Increased white space between links has surprisingly little effect. If text becomes smaller than 10 "real" points (approx. 1/7th of an inch or approx. 3.5 mm) on the display, selection performance drops rapidly. Large web pages will often result in most text being smaller than this on typical touch-screen mobiles. Even this limited size would be practically difficult for many users, so increasing the size to 1/6th inch (4 mm) or more will usually prove necessary.

Scrolling

Increases in text size lead to a greater demand on scrolling. Mobile research has demonstrated that vertical scrolling is much easier for users than horizontal scrolling, and mobile phone manufacturers take pains to avoid horizontal scrolling in their interfaces. This is a simple lesson that should be adhered to scrupulously: horizontal scrolling is to be avoided.

Some content providers try to avoid this problem by using tabs to flip between different parts of a larger page (also a common pattern in general Web design these days), but this results in problems when the content is closely connected and the reader has to remember the content of one tab as it becomes immediately invisible when switching to another.

Text entry

Even with touchscreen phones or the full keyboards found on devices from Research in Motion (such as the BlackBerry), typing on a mobile phone is demanding. Error correction takes longer than on a traditional computer, and moving position is slower than with a mouse. It is therefore imperative to minimize the amount of typing needed on any service interface. Some values are also very difficult to type in when a user is using predictive text on a keypad phone — try typing a number "1" or "0" on most Nokia phones without switching off predictive text.

Some strategies can avoid input problems. Drop-down boxes and the like, despite their limitations (particularly when lists are long), are often quicker than typing. Some simple approaches can help data entry further — e.g., if entering a time, does the user need to specify to the minute? Using 5-min blocks makes a drop-down list a mere 12 items. If words are difficult to type, or numbers tricky to input, you could just have saved the user significant amounts of time, even if the method is not quite as smooth on first appearance as what one would design for a web page on a desktop!

Moving between pages on a web site is also slow — and all too often desktop interactions make users move between pages to correct errors or work around unexpected problems (e.g., when a desired time is unavailable to book an appointment). Web connections on phones are much slower than desktop computers, and the phone lacks processing power. Whenever possible, allow corrections without moving between pages — for example, suggesting three alternative times when a wanted one is booked already, or making unavailable times visible before times are requested. These points may seem simplistic, but an interaction that appears convincing when tested on a mobile phone on a developer's laptop can appear to be unworkable when tried on the real thing. Getting the design right early will save many problems later!

INCLUSIVE DESIGN

Individual variations between people can be particularly pronounced in the case of mobile devices. Inclusive design emphasizes the importance of addressing a wide variety of users and factors (such as cultural and ethnic background, age, education, and gender) within the design process. A retired metalworker may be physically able, yet face difficulties in using a mobile service because of strong cultural expectations of a mobile as a phone, and limited exposure to office computers. Similarly, particular metaphors rely on cultural expectations that may be commonplace in one community, but prove totally opaque to another group. In the limited display space of the mobile phone, these differences are less readily fixed by additional help text than on a desktop computer.

A systematic investigation of who the users of a service are will help in recruiting representative individuals but some communities may be wary of outsiders, and such individuals may have to act as intermediaries between the group and the development team. Participatory design methods — including recruiting potential users as design partners, not simply as usability test participants and sources of requirements information — are often effective when minority groups form a significant portion of the final user group.

SUCCESS FACTORS

Achieving success with mobile applications requires five key measures:

- *Get clear user data.* Identify actual user needs and prioritize ruthlessly on the major features that will be needed. Focusing on the wrong services will lead to failure. Ensure you encompass the right variety of users and stakeholders.
- *Identify organizational and local factors.* Respond to local expectations of technology from your user data, and tailor approaches that have worked in different contexts accordingly.
- *Limit the scope.* Keep services to the key essentials, and plan a staged roll-out for more advanced features when initial user feedback and data suggest they are required.
- *Minimize content.* Reduce content to avoid scrolling (particularly horizontal scrolling) and ensure that all content is actually needed.
- *Review and revise.* Repeat the design process in steps; do not try to develop the perfect service in one step.

Jones and Marsden (2005) provide a detailed expansion on these key points.

SUMMARY

Creating usable mobile services for government is difficult. Local, national, and cultural contexts all play a part in shaping the expectations and skills of users. Mobile services provide an opportunity to leap the digital divide where many citizens lack access to traditional PC technology and many services fit naturally into a mobile context. The novelty and rapidly changing nature of mobile technology means, however, that development and implementation costs can be high.

Government bodies not only need to ensure that they scope down the complexity of their mobile services to attain long-term sustainability, but also that they are genuinely usable for the communities they serve.

References

Audit Commission. Seeing the light: Innovation in local public services, case study 7, London Borough of Sutton: Using tablet PCs in financial assessments. (2007). Retrieved 6 December, 2011, from http://www.audit-commission.gov.uk/localgov/goodpractice/partnership/Pages/suttonpcs.aspx

Beyer, H., & Holtzblatt, K. (1997). *Contextual Design: Defining customer-centered systems.* New York: Morgan Kaufmann.

Church, K., Smyth, B., Cotter, P., & Bradley, K. (2007). Mobile information access: A study of emerging search behavior on the mobile internet. *Transactions on the Web, 1*(1), 1–38.

Grawemeyer, B., & Johnson, H. (2011). Using and managing multiple passwords: A week to a view. *Interacting with Computers, 23*(3), 256–267.

International Organization for Standardization. (2006a). Ease of operation of everyday products — Part 1: Design requirements for context of use and user characteristics, ISO 20282-1.

International Organization for Standardization. (2006b). Ease of operation of everyday products — Part 2: Test method for walk-up-and-use products, ISO 20282-2.

Jones, M., & Marsden, G. (2005). *Mobile interaction Design.* London: Wiley.

Ozok, A. A. (2009). Survey design and implementation in HCI. In A. Sears & J. A. Jacko (Eds.), *Human computer interaction: Development process* (pp. 254–271). London: CRC Press.

W3C. Web content accessibility guidelines (WCAG) 2.0. (2008a). Retrieved 6 December, 2011, from http://www.w3.org/TR/2008/REC-WCAG20-20081211/

W3C. Mobile web best practices 1.0. (2008b). Retrieved 6 December, 2011, from http://www.w3.org/TR/mobile-bp/

Further reading

Buchanan, G., Jones, M., Thimbleby, H., Farrant, S., & Pazzani, M. (2001). Improving mobile internet usability. In *Proceedings WWW 2001.* Hong Kong/New York: ACM Press, pp. 673–680.

Oulasvirta, A., Tamminen, S., Roto, V., & Kuorelahti, J. (2005). Interaction in 4-second bursts: The fragmented nature of attentional resources in mobile HCI. In *Proceedings of the SIGCHI conference on human factors in computing systems, Portland, Oregon, United States.* New York: ACM Press, pp. 919–928.

Preece, J., Rogers, Y., & Sharp, J. (2011). *Interaction design: Beyond human-computer interaction* (3rd ed.). London: Wiley.

Roberts, D. (2010). *Usability and mobile devices.* Retrieved 6 December, 2011, from http://www.usability.gov/articles/newsletter/pubs/052010news.html

Teevan, J., Karlson, A., Amini, S., Bernheim Brush, A. J., & Krumm, J. (2011). Understanding the importance of location, time, and people in mobile local search behavior. In *Proceedings of the 13th conference on human computer interaction with mobile devices and services (mobile HCI).* Stockholm/New York: ACM Press, pp. 77–80.

CHAPTER

User Issues in Security

14

Karen Renaud
University of Glasgow UK

"Security is, I would say, our top priority because for all the exciting things you will be able to do with computers — organizing your lives, staying in touch with people, being creative — if we don't solve these security problems, then people will hold back."
— Bill Gates

INTRODUCTION

Governments have trailed behind industry in moving online but are losing no time catching up now that industry has demonstrated the benefits and viability of this modern communication and interaction mechanism. Driving this activity is the clear benefit of a self-service approach rather than the traditional and time-consuming approach that relies on letters and telephones answered by people. Hence the era of e-Government (e-gov) has changed the way government interacts with citizens. This is clearly more economical and efficient, and the benefits of a personalized online service are rather compelling drivers (Hyden, Court, & Mease, 2004). (For a more detailed discussion of this aspect, see Chapter 23, Service Design and Channel Shifting.)

E-gov systems offer services and information to users. The information supporting this provision comes out of databases owned and maintained by the government itself. The security of the information in the databases — i.e., the *integrity, confidentiality*, and *availability* thereof — must be guaranteed. Another essential aspect is that of *nonrepudiation*, which basically means that any change to data must be traceable to the person who made the change and the person cannot repudiate that change (i.e., cannot deny having made it). Ensuring that these aspects are guaranteed is essential if government is to maintain the necessary level of trust from citizens.

E-gov tends to evolve in a predictable and staged fashion (Layne & Lee, 2001), as illustrated in Figure 14.1. The first stage is information provision, giving information to the general population in a broadcast fashion. The second stage starts engaging with the citizens, allowing transactions to be carried out. Whereas the previous stage, being a broadcast mechanism, did not need the user to identify him- or herself, this stage and successive stages do indeed require users to prove their identity and participate in a security-related activity.

The next two stages happen behind the scenes and involve various government services collaborating in a variety of ways in order to share information, and linking to each other. The challenge here is managerial as well as technological. In terms of user experience, this is mostly positive as citizens

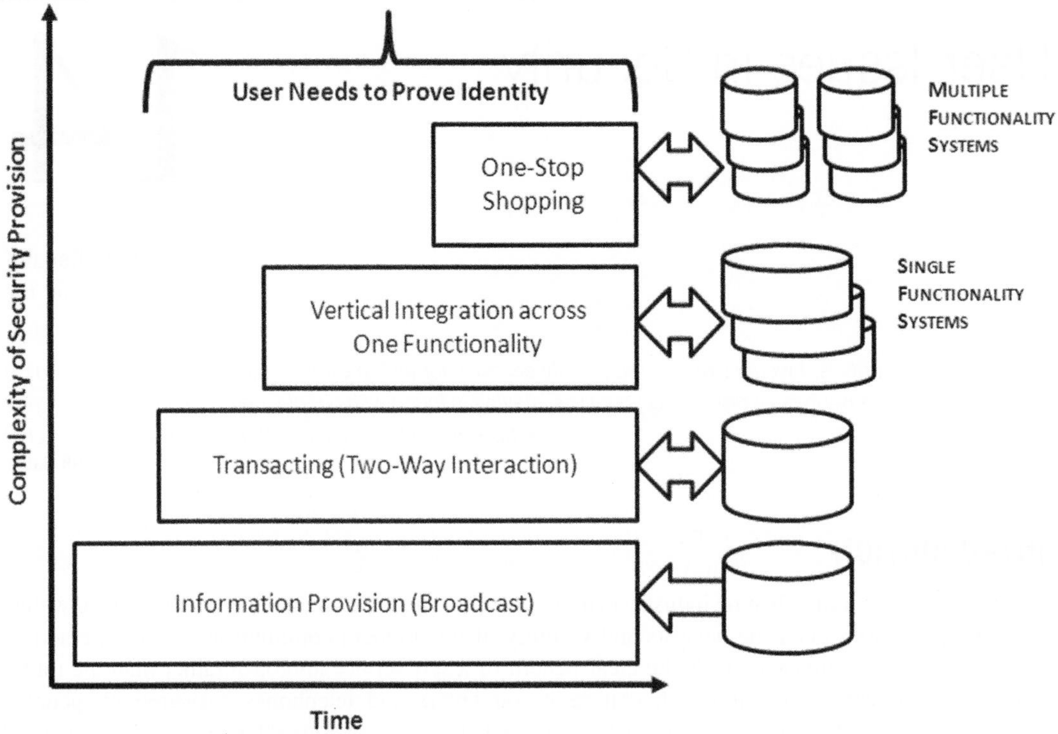

FIGURE 14.1 Escalating complexity of security provision

can apply for a particular service, or provide information, once, and the request is propagated to all relevant departments without requiring the citizen to make the same request to all departments involved in the service. The proviso is that the communications between functionally independent units do not result in data leakage and that data are secured properly.

Unfortunately, as pointed out by Johnson and Raue (2010), such integration efforts are rarely conducted with the required level of assurance in terms of data integrity and confidentiality. They point out that a focus on costs will often lead to essential controls not being implemented, which will ensure that information is shared properly, with due consideration of the security thereof.

If this sharing is done correctly, the citizens' direct experience with the security of e-gov systems will usually begin and end with establishing their identity so that the provider can ensure that the citizen is entitled to the services he/she is applying for. This need is widely accepted and understood, but achieving it in a digital era is not as simple as it seems.

Establishing an identity

To establish an identity online, a citizen starts off by proffering a unique identity string. Some countries — Australia and Sweden, for example — issue citizens with identity numbers, and this is then the unique identifier of choice. Countries without these, such as the United Kingdom, need to improvise in this respect. In these countries, each system often maintains its own identifiers or makes use of an identifier which most citizens have, usually one which was originally intended for another purpose. Many UK government web sites make use of the National Insurance number, something everyone has to have in order to be employed.

Having claimed an identity, the citizen has to prove that he or she is indeed the person associated with that identity in the e-gov system's databases. This step is called *authentication*, and can theoretically be achieved in one of three ways: by means of something the citizen *knows*, such as a password, by means of something they *hold*, such as a card, or by means of something they *are*, such as a fingerprint. (See Chapter 21, Adapting e-Gov Usability Evaluation to Cultural Contexts, for a case study of a usability test of such a system.) If the system is being used online, the first mechanism — the password, is used almost ubiquitously. If the system is being used in a government building, with the citizen present, then biometrics can be used. Countries using fingerprint biometrics to identify their citizens include Hong Kong and South Africa. Some countries use biometrics to identify visitors to their shores. A well-known example of this is the US-VISIT program, which takes the thumbprint of every non-US citizen as they enter the country. (For a detailed discussion of the usability of biometric systems, see Chapter 15, Usability of Biometric Systems.)

In an ideal world, citizens would simply say who they are and there would be no need to authenticate — but we live in a far from ideal world. There will always be those who wish to use another's identity to carry out a variety of illegal activities. The first recorded case goes back to Biblical times — when Jacob pretended to be Esau — so identity theft is hardly a modern crime. E-gov systems hold a veritable gold mine of information that an identity thief will find invaluable in masquerading as another. E-gov systems have to be designed to withstand such attacks, even more so than commercial sites since they are the sole issuer of identity documents. This is especially true because people have no choice in the matter: they *have* to supply personal information and entrust it to government systems. It ill behooves a government to lose the trust of its citizens (Van de Wallea & Bouckaerta, 2003), since that could make them vote for the opposition at the next opportunity. Governments therefore need to give priority to ensuring the security of any information they hold. Carter and Belanger (2005) noted that the more citizens trust the e-gov provision, the more they will use the services provided by e-gov systems.

Trust is not the only factor influencing the success of e-gov systems. The traditional approach in designing the interface to systems is to ensure that the system is as *usable* as possible. Usability is traditionally measured in terms of effectiveness, efficiency, and satisfaction — in other words, to what extent can someone carry out their intended tasks, how quickly can they complete the tasks, and how satisfied are they with the system as a whole (once again, judged in terms of the tasks). In terms of usability, the designer and the end user are both striving toward the same objective: both are happy if the system is as usable as it can be. In the last few years, there has been a move toward designing with the *user experience* in mind. This is more dynamic, subjective, and context-dependent than pure usability, and depends on the user's accumulated experiences of the system over a longer time period than a single usability evaluation.

Designing for user experience

What does "designing for user experience" mean in terms of security? For the average computer user, "security" is not something they anticipate with pleasure. No one looks forward to coming up with yet another password, or to encrypting their memory stick. Users are primarily focused on convenience,

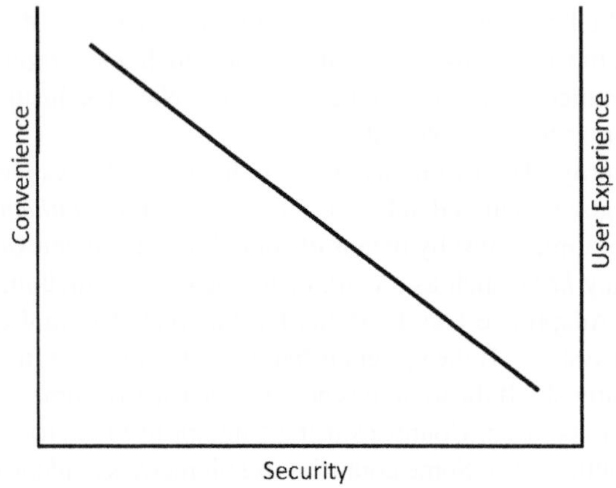

FIGURE 14.2 Relationship between security, convenience, and usability

and any effort spent on extraneous activities — e.g., security-related activities — will be resented if there is a perception that it is too time consuming or inconveniences them too much. The traditional view can be depicted as shown in Figure 14.2: the more secure the system, the more effort it is going to demand from users, and the poorer and less convenient the user experience will be. On the other hand, the user's experience is bound to be negatively affected if their account is breached by an intruder. The focus on user experience is therefore likely to be particularly challenging for those professionals designing interfaces to secure systems.

The end user's perspective, thus, is often "how much does 'security' get in the way of carrying out my primary task?" Most users consider security a necessary evil, much in the same vein as death and taxes; something that interferes with the execution of their day-to-day tasks. If the security-related and required activities become too arduous, their user experience is poor and a negative attitude is likely to be the result.

In this chapter, we are interested in the experiences of the end user using e-gov systems. This chapter seeks to inform design decisions made by security professionals and interaction designers of these systems.

KEY CONSIDERATIONS

One cannot consider "security" as some attainable state of a system since no system is ever 100% secure. Security is very much a tradeoff between the value of what is being secured and the cost of the applied mechanisms used to secure the system. Here we consider cost in both monetary and human terms. To introduce rigor into the process, we secure according to perceived threats, and we are constrained by budgetary and human limitations.

One very popular threat-classification technique is identified by the mnemonic STRIDE (Swiderski & Snyder, 2004), taken from the first letter of threats in each of the following categories (illustrated in

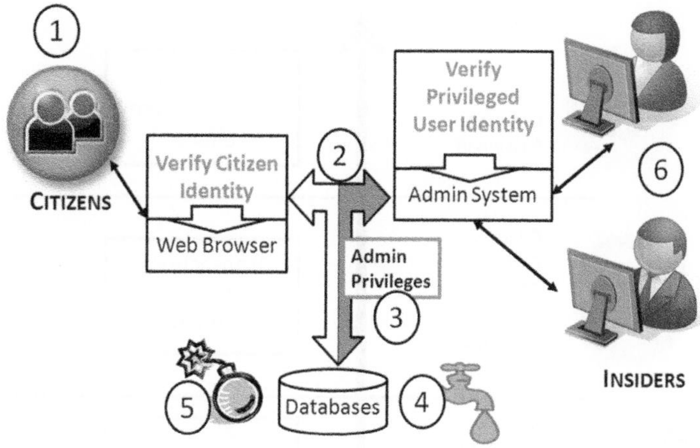

FIGURE 14.3 Applying STRIDE to e-gov systems

(For color version of this figure, see the Web version of this chapter.)

Figure 14.3, with the circled numbers in the figure referring to the numbers below and showing what is being attacked):

- *Spoofing* — can someone masquerade as another citizen?
- *Tampering* — is it possible to change data in transit between systems involved in a transaction?
- *Repudiation* — can we ensure that illicit actions can be traced back to the responsible person?
- *Information disclosure* — can data be obtained by unauthorized parties?
- *Denial of service* — can the system's legitimate operation be interfered with?
- *Elevation of privilege* — can a person using the system gain extra privileges to carry out unauthorized actions?

Spoofing, tampering, information disclosure, and elevation of privilege potentially impact the confidentiality and integrity of the information held by the government's databases. Denial of service impacts availability and nonrepudiation ensures that those who have exploited vulnerabilities in the system can be identified. An example of this appears in the Case Studies section.

Mitigation of threats

Once the threats have been identified, the next step is to decide how, or whether, these threats can be mitigated. For example, most systems will use an authentication mechanism to mitigate the threat of spoofing. The strength of the chosen authentication mechanism should be directly related to the value of the information and functionality being protected. An example of this is given in Figure 14.4, where the initial authentication step is augmented by a more stringent authentication for transactions with side effects. Other threats are easily prevented by means of modern encryption techniques, and the end user remains oblivious to these efforts if they work properly. Hence "security" for the citizen equates to authentication, usually in the form of a user name and password. This works moderately

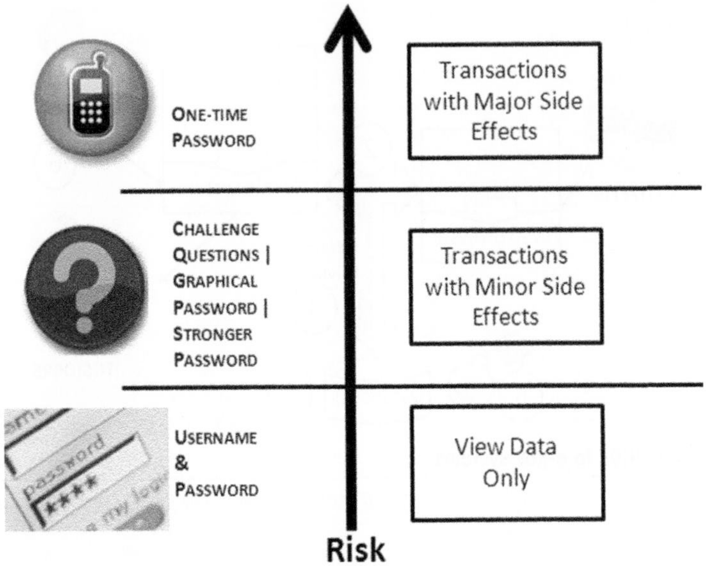

FIGURE 14.4 Matching authentication requirements to risk

(For color version of this figure, see the Web version of this chapter.)

well for outsiders (citizens), but the techniques required to mitigate these threats for insiders (employees) are far more challenging. To achieve nonrepudiation, all activities need to be logged and regularly audited, and the system administration needs to be tailored so that insiders cannot easily elevate their privileges.

Designing for the user

How do we design for an optimal user experience? Having decided on the required level of security, we need to ensure that the mechanism used to establish the citizen's identity matches the requirements. This usually translates to the choice of authentication mechanism. For example, if the decision is made to use a password, then decisions need to be made about the implementation: Will the password be issued or chosen by the user, what will the required "strength" of the password be, and how will passwords be replaced if they are forgotten? If systems issue passwords, users are more likely to forget them — so the majority of systems will allow users to choose their own passwords. As far as password strength is concerned, there is a widely accepted myth that the longer and stronger the password, the more secure the system will be. The reality is exactly the opposite.

A blog entry (Anonymous, 2008) titled "Annoying password criteria" demonstrates this very aptly. The writer says:

> *The criteria for the DVLA password is:*
>
> - *be between 8 and 12 characters*
> - *contain a combination of letters and numbers*

- *contain two or more numbers which are separated by one or more letters*
- *not contain spaces or the word "password"*
- *not contain three adjacent letters or numbers the same (e.g., "aaa" or "999")*

So what is the first thing you do after creating such a secure password? Write it down, thus defeating the whole point in the strict security.

The UK Driver and Vehicle Licensing Agency (DVLA) designers thought that by applying stringent password criteria they were strengthening the security of the site, but as this blog post shows, they are actually having the opposite effect. It would be far better to provide registering users with some password generation tips than applying fairly stringent password strength criteria, which results in a weakening of the security of the system — exactly the opposite of what the designers thought they were achieving. It would be better to let users provide a long password in the form of a sentence (passphrase) than requiring them essentially to define a password that is impossible to remember (Inglesant & Sasse, 2010).

Authenticator replacement

Authenticator replacement is not a simple matter. Since most systems use passwords, they often simply email the forgotten password to the user. This is very convenient, but equally insecure since someone who breaks into the user's email account can then access their e-gov account very easily, clearly an undesirable outcome. At the other end of the spectrum, the system can require users to phone in, to request a password reset. This is more secure but also very inconvenient and potentially expensive. This will have a negative effect on the user's experience. Some systems use a relatively low-cost option of deploying a secondary authentication mechanism such as challenge questions. So, for example, when the person first registers, he or she answers some questions such as "what is your mother's maiden name?" or "what is the name of your primary school?" The massive uptake of social networking sites makes these questions a severe vulnerability (Rabkin, 2008) and probably unsuitable for e-gov systems.

Cost, benefit, and user experience

In making these choices, the designers have to balance cost and benefit, and one of the costs is related to the effort required of citizens (Whitley & Hosein, 2010). The only way to achieve this balance is to ensure that the applied security matches the risk associated with a particular action. So a low-risk transaction must not require the user to provide the same credentials as a high-risk transaction. Furthermore, the chosen mechanism has to engender trust and confidence in the general populace. Security is as much about perceptions as it is about reality, and great care needs to be taken to build up levels of trust.

Passwords initially appear a cheap and easy option, but there are many hidden costs associated with replacing passwords and fielding service-desk calls related to passwords. The other cost, which is much harder to quantify, is related to the impact on the citizen's experience of the system when password requirements are too stringent, when passwords are forgotten, and when password replacement is overly arduous.

A common mistake is to consider authentication as a binary issue — the person is either authenticated or rejected. A far better solution is to have a system where citizens are given graduated access to system functionality, and are authenticated with increasing vigor when they want to carry out transactions with increasingly significant side effects, as shown in Figure 14.4. Registration of a birth or death has major implications and should therefore be a maximum risk transaction. Confirmation of voting credentials could be a medium risk transaction but the changing of these credentials should require an extra authentication step. For example, a citizen could be required to provide a simple password to view basic details such as their address. To make a change to the address, they need to provide additional proof that they are who they say they are. In this case, the system should also incorporate an extra verification step such as asking the user to respond to an email to confirm the change.

There is a lack of innovation in this area as far as e-gov is concerned, given the wealth of research into alternative authentication techniques over the last decade. Most systems impose a password requirement when it is clearly the wrong technique. Others fail to implement the controls which will ensure the integrity of information. Examples of these are detailed in the next section.

CASE STUDIES

Here two cases act as examples of where the citizen's experience of the security of e-gov systems has been suboptimal.

Insider violation of information security

In 2004, a newspaper article appeared in South Africa's newspapers that urged South African women to visit the home affairs web site to check their marital status. One online newspaper (Brits, 2004) stated the following:

> *Home Affairs Minister Nosiviwe Mapisa-Nqakula launched a special "Check Your Status" campaign in KwaMhlanga, Mpumalanga, partly in a bid to curb the problem of women being married to foreigners without their knowledge. Some of this was probably the work of the department's own officials, and efforts were being intensified to bring these to book, the minister said in a prepared speech.*

The fraudulent changes to these marital records provide a clear example of the integrity of the data being compromised by insiders: officials within the department of home affairs were bribed to register "fake" marriages between South African citizens and foreign nationals who wished to remain in the country. It is interesting that an e-gov web site was made available to allow citizens to check on their own marital status. This demonstrates the government's commitment to e-gov. Unfortunately, with a broadband penetration rate of only 7% (as of December 2010) (Vermeulen, 2010), it is likely that many of the (un)married women will be unable to use this service and these scam "marriages" will go undetected. On a more positive note, a mechanism for implementing an audit trail (keeping a log of all actions carried out on the data held by a system), and achieving nonrepudiation, is now being used. The system requires officials to provide a fingerprint biometric whenever they enter data into any internal database. While they may not be able to prevent these kinds of scams, they will be able to identify the miscreant immediately should irregularities be uncovered.

This is not an isolated event; such crimes appear in the news worldwide. For example, in Scotland a tax worker invented and added four children to the births database so that she could claim benefits for them (BBC, 2011). In the United States, an employee of Veterans Affairs was prosecuted for identity theft (*Fayetteville Observer*, 2011). Government workers, with elevated privileges, are in a particularly strong position to do major damage because of the value of the information recorded in government databases, and the variety of services which rely on the integrity of this data.

Citizen experience of information security

The awards agency used by students of a particular country has a web site that citizens use to apply for student loans. In principle this is a good idea, since the majority of students have access to information technology via their universities or schools. The agency requires their users to remember two pieces of information, a user name and a password. It also facilitate the provision of a hint which will be displayed to prompt them should they forget their passwords. If the user has forgotten the password, he/she is directed to a screen asking for his/her mother's maiden name. If this is entered correctly the hint is shown. If the hints fail to jog their memory they can request an emailed reminder. This mechanism does not always work, which then necessitates a telephone call to request a password reset. If the email does arrive, the users have to define a new password when they log in using the reset password.

It is instructional to consider the threat model. Different categories of people could try to hack into a student's account, ranging from a complete unknown to a very close friend or family member. The aforementioned technique will probably prevent a complete unknown from spoofing the account since the user name does not necessarily link directly to the account holder and therefore does not provide an easy link to the requested mother's maiden name. A brute-force attack is resisted by the web site. However, consider an ex-partner, probably the greatest threat. He/she might easily guess the user name, and know the person's mother's maiden name (easily determined from social networking sites). Depending on how well he/she knows the target and the obscurity of the password hint, it might be relatively easy to gain access to the account.

Furthermore, the agency fails to satisfy their customers as far as information security is concerned. There is a Facebook page titled "We hate ***" (the name of the awards agency). The top entry is particularly revealing, where the user complains: "I love *** money, only annoyance for me is trying to reset the bloody password! Grrr" (Facebook, 2011). Students forget their passwords. This forgetting is not only predictable but inevitable, since they use the passwords only once a year. They either have to request a password reminder by email, if they can remember their user name, or use a pay-by-minute phone number to do so, and the calls are not answered quickly. A quick Twitter search comes up with a number of tweets complaining about the frustration being experienced by the users of this system. One tweet says: "*** I hate you." Another says "*** I hate you. That's more than a week now I haven't even been able to get on the waiting line." Many are related to the difficulty of contacting the agency to query things, and of course password resets suffer from the same problem. The Facebook page also demonstrates a clear issue with the integrity of the data in the system — a student complains about having been incorrectly marked as "withdrawn." A blog entry provides anecdotal evidence of the level of frustration being experienced by some users of this e-gov system:[1]

> *I did get the privilege of speaking to 3 different people today, including a case manager! Person no 1: We have not received the information you have now sent us on 6 occasions.*
>
> *Person no 2: We have received it but it's not the information we need even though it's what we told you we need.*
>
> *Person no 3 (case manager!): we have now lost the information that we found 2 minutes ago but if we do find it again, we will not need anything else other than a letter stating why you cannot provide details of your*

[1]This blog will remain anonymous because providing a reference would identify the funding body.

partner's income.... Yes I know there is a letter somewhere confirming your separation but that does not explain why you cannot provide the details.

Hmmm... THINK IT THROUGH

I think I was well within my rights to scream at them! You couldn't make it up. I am actually considering going down to the offices but I'd probably end up being charged with assault.

Sorry this has turned into quite a rant!

The system fails to implement the proper controls to secure and maintain their data, and the resulting user experience leaves much to be desired.

There are many problems with this system, and here the word "system" refers to the software as well as the accompanying infrastructure and help desk staff. If we focus on the security aspects only, it is clear that the agency's use of an authentication mechanism (the password), which fails predictably because of its relatively infrequent use, does not help. Furthermore, their password replacement procedure is insecure and inconvenient, to say the least. Students react to the predictable forgetting in two ways. Some record their passwords in some way, either by writing them down or (24%) by storing them on their mobile phones (Credant, 2010). Many phones are lost or stolen. Accounts are easily compromised by anyone who finds these records. Those who do not record their passwords are very likely to forget them, request a reset, get frustrated, and generally have a poor user experience — directly as a consequence of the poor design of the identity management system.

ESTABLISHING AN IDENTITY

Much security can be hidden from users. For example, users probably assume that communications are encrypted, that passwords are encrypted in the database, that employee actions are audited, and that the servers are carefully configured to make them as resistant as possible to the efforts of external hackers. If their assumption is wrong, and information is leaked, their user experience is negatively affected — and severely so.

The one area where the users have to be involved is in establishing their identity. The mechanism of choice for 99% of systems is the password. Unfortunately, the widespread misuse of the password mechanism has been its undoing, and its usage often has more to do with ease of implementation for developers than efficacy in achieving its purpose. There is no widely established and accepted standard for matching the strength of the password to the requirements of the system. Much password practice is steeped in beliefs of the 1970s. End users are commonly told to include a special character, an upper case letter, and a number in their password. This is poor advice, since the latest technology makes breaking this kind of password child's play (Mah, 2007), and the inevitable difficulty of remembering the password makes this advice particularly bad. The kind of brute-force attack this complex password defends against is easily prevented by the system locking the attacker out after three incorrect attempts.

Choosing an authenticator

What is needed is a completely new approach to authentication. The first step is to acknowledge that authentication needs to be implemented with some deliberation, with due consideration of the end user. If the system is going to be used infrequently, passwords are particularly problematic. In these cases, it would be preferable not to rely on imperfect human memory. Other techniques should be used such as, for example, sending the person a one-time password to their registered mobile phone number, or posting a number to their registered address when they need to return to the system. Some systems, such as the awards agency mentioned above, have entirely predictable usage patterns: students use the system once a year only, and usually during a particular 3-month period. This use can therefore be anticipated and the means for accessing the system provided. This might well be in the form of a letter containing a one-time password sent to the students, or a one-time password sent to their mobile device, or even the use of an authenticator which does not put as much strain on frail human memory. One good example is the Passface system (Brostoff & Sasse, 2000) which relies on human memory for faces, something humans do almost effortlessly. When people enroll, they are given four faces to remember. When they return to the system, it will display successive screens displaying nine faces, one of which is one of their "secret" faces. The users click on their face in each set and if they have identified all of them correctly they are authenticated.

If the system is going to be used often enough to make remembering a password a reasonable expectation, one should be sensible about (1) password requirements and (2) the password replacement mechanism. Strength requirements that make the password hard to remember are self-defeating. Passwords made up of sentences are equally strong, but also easier to remember. Hence, when the user defines the password, the wise system administrator will provide advice such as "make up a memorable sentence and type the whole sentence in as your password" right next to the password entry field in the interface.

Authenticator replacement

If the authenticator can be lost or stolen, a replacement mechanism needs to be incorporated into the system. Such a replacement mechanism should not require human intervention, since this adds an intolerable delay to the process and is expensive in monetary terms as well. The chosen mechanism should match the security of the system. So, for example, systems that affect people's privacy or financial details will require a more stringent mechanism than a system that is less risky. In many countries, the mobile phone market penetration is over 100%.[2] This, together with the fact that phones are very much a personal device, means that users should be able to get password reminders sent to their phones. This is very convenient and also far more secure than sending details to email accounts, which can often be breached from anywhere in the world. One proviso is that the owner of the mobile phone should secure the device with a good password so that such texted password reminders cannot be accessed should the phone be mislaid or stolen.

Less risky systems could also deploy carefully designed challenge questions. Challenge questions should avoid asking about details that can be obtained via Social Networking sites and also not use questions already used by other sites. For example, Renaud and Just (2010) proposed a system where people chose a picture, and said whom they associated with the picture. Their research showed that this was far harder to guess than asking someone for their mother's maiden name.

Another option is to use one of the alternative authentication techniques as a fallback mechanism (Renaud & De Angeli, 2009). Since these mechanisms are not widely deployed, and the secrets are less widely disseminated, it makes it harder for an attacker to guess the person's secret.

[2]http://mobithinking.com/mobile-marketing-tools/latest-mobile-stats. Retrieved 13 November 2011.

Another option is to provide a cue. Some sites ask users to provide a cue to jolt their memory, should they need it. This is done at enrollment when they provide the password. This is rather risky because some users simply type their password into the reminder field, and others provide cues that are far too helpful to attackers. Some authors have proposed using cueing mechanisms. For example, Renaud, McBryan, and Siebert (2008) proposed using Inkblot-like images to cue passwords. Since people see different things in inkblots, the cue is much stronger than a textual cue.

A range of alternative authentication techniques have been proposed by a host of researchers over the last decade. These are simply waiting for the perceptive developer to deploy them. The user experience will be much improved as a result.

SUCCESS FACTORS

When designing security mechanisms for e-gov systems, keep the following in mind:

- *Match the risk.* Choose the authentication mechanism that matches the risk associated with the use of the system. Figure 14.4 provides some guidance in this respect.
- *For infrequently used systems, use a mechanism that does not rely on memory.* A knowledge-based mechanism will almost inevitably fail for infrequently used systems.
- *For low-risk systems, consider using an alternative authentication mechanism that relies on a stronger memory than alphanumeric strings.* This could also be used as an additional mechanism to authorize higher risk actions on the person's account.
- *Provide a convenient authentication replacement mechanism that does not require human intervention.* In the modern age, with individually owned and almost ubiquitous mobile phones, this is probably the best channel for delivering replacement authenticators.

In conclusion, five abiding principles should guide security professionals in securing e-gov systems:

- *Carry out a formal threat analysis for the protected assets.* Decide on the techniques to mitigate these threats so that the imposed security is necessary and sufficient to secure the system.
- *Put as small a burden as possible on the citizen.* If the citizen has to be involved, minimize their effort. If this is not possible, ease the process so that the user is inconvenienced as little as possible.
- *Respect the citizen's desire for privacy and confidentiality of their data.*
- *Ensure that all employee actions are logged to facilitate an effective audit trail.*
- *Secure background systems to the highest possible level.* Put mechanisms in place to guarantee the integrity and confidentiality of citizen data.

These guidelines are so simple that they may well appear to be "common sense." Stephen Covey puts it aptly (Covey, 2005, p. 325):

> *Common Sense is seldom Common Practice.*

It is therefore worth enumerating these, so that they can be used to guide good practice and inform responsible developers.

SUMMARY

The user experience of the security of e-gov sites is probably going to be based largely on how it handles the identity verification process. Such verification is achieved by means of authentication. A measure of the citizen's perception will also depend on how well back-end systems are secured, but since the user is not inconvenienced by these measures they are unlikely to form the basis of their user experience unless they fail.

Identity verification has two stages: identify and authenticate. Authentication has four components: registration, subsequent authentication, authenticator replacement, and account closure. Many systems reach for the ubiquitous password without putting sufficient thought into the registration or replacement processes and very few are concerned with account closure. These failures lead to frustration and poor user experiences.

All that is required is for some rigor to be interjected into the process, so that the burden being imposed on the user is considered, and reduced as much as is possible, while security is maintained.

References

Anonymous. Annoying password criteria. (2008). Retrieved 13 November 2011 from www.haywoodsbrain.co.uk/2008/11/30/annoying-password-criteria

BBC. (2011, July 26). Woman invented four kids for £90 000 tax claim. *BBC News*, Retrieved 5 November 2011 from www.bbc.co.uk/news/uk-scotland-tayside-central-14289785

Brits, E. (2004, July 28). Unwitting (un)wedded bliss. *News 24*, Retrieved 5 November 2011 from www.news24.com/SouthAfrica/Politics/Unwitting-unwedded-bliss-20040727

Brostoff, A., & Sasse, M. A. (2000). Are Passfaces more usable than passwords? A field trial investigation. In S. McDonald, Y. Waern, & G. Cockton (Eds.), *People and computers XIV — Usability or else!: Proceedings of HCI 2000* (pp. 405–424). London, UK: Springer.

Carter, L., & Belanger, F. (2005). The utilization of e-government services: Citizen trust, innovation and acceptance factors. *Information Systems Journal, 15*, 5–25.

Covey, S. R. (2005). *The 7 habits of highly effective people*. London, UK: Simon & Schuster.

Credant Technologies. (2010, March 18). UK businesses left vulnerable by naïve mobile phone users. *Credant*, Retrieved 5 November 2011 from www.credant.com/news-a-events/press-releases/208-uk-businesses-left-vulnerable-by-naive-mobile-phone-users.html

Facebook. (2011). We hate ****. Retrieved 5 November 2011 [Link removed to preserve anonymity].

Fayetteville Observer. (2011, August). Ex-VA employee gets prison in identity theft case. Military.com syndicated article from *Fayetteville Observer*, Retrieved 15 September 2011 from www.military.com/news/article/ex-va-employee-gets-prison-in-identity-theft-case.html

Hyden, G., Court, J., & Mease, K. (2004). *Making sense of governance: Empirical evidence from sixteen developing countries.* Boulder, CO: Rienner Publishers.

Inglesant, P. G., & Sasse, M. A. (2010). The true cost of unusable password policies: Password use in the wild. In *Proceedings of the 28th international conference on human factors in computing systems (CHI '10)*, (pp. 383–392). New York: ACM.

Johnson, C. W., & Raue, S. (2010). On the safety implications of e-governance: Assessing the hazards of enterprise information architectures in safety-critical systems. In E. Schoitsch (Ed.), *Proceedings of SAFECOMP 2010,*

29th international conference on computer safety, reliability and security, LNCS 6351, (pp. 402–417). Vienna, Austria: Springer.

Layne, K., & Lee, J. (2001). Developing fully functional E-government: A four stage model. *Government Information Quarterly*, *18*, 122–136.

Mah, P. (2007). Graphics card cracks passwords 25 times faster. *TechRepublic*, Retrieved 23 October 2011 from www.techrepublic.com/blog/tech-news/graphics-card-cracks-passwords-25-times-faster/1433

Rabkin, A. (2008). Personal knowledge questions for fallback authentication: Security questions in the era of Facebook. In *Proceedings of the 4th symposium on usable privacy and security*, (pp. 23–25). Pittsburgh, PA: ACM.

Renaud, K., & De Angeli, A. (2009, December). Visual passwords: Cure-all or snake-oil? *Communications of the ACM*, *52*(12).

Renaud, K., & Just, M. (2010). Examining user responses to association-based authentication. In *Proceedings HCI 2010*, University of Abertay, Dundee. To appear.

Renaud, K., McBryan, A., & Siebert, P. (2008). Password cueing with cue(ink)blots. In *IADIS computer graphics and visualization 2008 (CGV 2008) conference*, (pp. 74–81). Amsterdam, The Netherlands: Inderscience.

Swiderski, F., & Snyder, W. (2004). *Threat modeling*. Redmond, WA: Microsoft Press.

Van de Wallea, S., & Bouckaerta, G. (2003). Public service performance and trust in government: The problem of causality. *International Journal of Public Administration*, *26*(8-9), 891–913.

Vermeulen, J. (2010, December 6). Broadband penetration: It's not looking good for South Africa. *mybroadband*, Retrieved 13 November 2010 from mybroadband.co.za/news/broadband/17085-broadband-penetration-it-s-not-looking-good-for-south-africa.html

Whitley, E. A., & Hosein, G. (2010). *Global challenges for identity policies*. Houndmills, UK: Palgrave Macmillan.

Further reading

Cohen, S., Ben-Asher, No., & Meyer, J. (2011). Towards information technology security for universal access. In *Proceedings universal access in HCI. Lecture notes in computer science 6765*, (pp. 443–435). Vienna, Austria: Springer.

Hassenzahl, M. (2011). User experience and experience design. User experience (UX): Towards an experiential perspective on product quality. In *Proceedings IHM 2008 conference*, (pp. 11–15). New York: ACM.

Horsburgh, S., Goldfinch, S., & Gauld, R. (2011). Is public trust in government associated with trust in e-government? *Social Science Computer Review*, *29*(2), 232–241.

Law, E. L., Roto, V., Hassenzahl, M., Vermeeren, A. P. O. S., & Kort, J. (2009). Understanding, scoping and defining user experience: A survey approach. In *Proceedings of CHI*, (pp. 719–728). New York: ACM.

Silcock, R. (2001). What is e-government. *Parliamentary Affairs*, *54*(1), 88–101.

Tolbert, C., & Mossberger, K. (2006). The effects of e-government on trust and confidence in government. *Public Administration Review*, *66*, 354–369.

Welch, E., Hinnant, C., & Jae Moon, M. (2004). Linking citizen satisfaction with e-government and trust in government. *Journal of Public Administration Research and Theory*, *15*, 371–391.

CHAPTER 15

Usability of Biometric Systems

Mary Frances Theofanos, Brian Stanton
National Institute of Standards and Technology, Gaithersburg, MD, USA

"Trust in biometrics technology will be earned by virtue of system performance meeting user expectations."
— National Subcommittee on Biometrics and Identity Management, Executive Office of the President

WHAT ARE BIOMETRICS?

Biometrics are measurable anatomical, physiological, or behavioral attributes that can be used for automated recognition (a fingerprint, a photo of a face, a person's gait — the manner in which they walk — etc.). Biometrics can also be a process of automated methods of recognizing an individual based on anatomical, physiological, or behavioral characteristics (see www.biometrics.gov). Clearly the use of fingerprints and photographs has a long history of use in law enforcement. The New York State Prisons began using fingerprints for the identification of criminals in 1903. During the twentieth century, more and more local police identification bureaus established fingerprint systems. This increased use of fingerprints led to the establishment of the Identification Division of the Federal Bureau of Investigation.

In addition to using biometrics operationally, the US federal government has also invested in the research, development, testing, evaluation, and standardization of biometric systems and technologies since the mid-1960s. From automating fingerprint identification processing to face recognition and iris and speech technologies, the US government has led research in new biometric technologies and systems, and the federal policies required to implement and develop them. The terrorist attacks of September 11, 2001 ("9/11") accelerated the deployment of biometric systems, including the use of biometric applications to aid in promoting national security and in identifying and managing vast numbers of individuals at US borders. Biometric applications for physical and data access control, employee security management, and personnel verification application were also deployed quickly. These applications were no longer used solely by law enforcement but were used by the general public. Yet in the rush to deploy, the biometrics community forgot about this new user.

Many countries and governments have deployed biometric systems in use, including the United Kingdom, France, Australia, Japan, and Singapore. Many more countries participate in international standardization efforts for biometric systems, in the International Organization for Standardization (ISO) Subcommittee 37 and Working Group Six, which focus on usability and societal implications where usability awareness, results, and lessons learned are shared. This chapter, however, will focus on biometric usability studies and lessons learned in the United States because of the access and availability of data and reports.

What about the user?

On January 4, 2004, the US Department of Homeland Security's (DHS's) US Visitor and Immigrant Status Indicator Technology (US-VISIT) program began collecting right and left index fingerprints, two thumbprints, and a digital photograph of all foreign travelers entering the United States. Unfortunately, little attention was given to the human-computer interaction (HCI) of the devices or to the system and process, which resulted in long lines, confusion for international travelers, and overall distrust of the system (National Science and Technology Council, 2008). Although HCI and usability guidelines were well established for desktop systems and applications, and for Web applications (see www.usability.gov), which allowed developers to design systems according to HCI principles and established baselines, no such guidelines existed for biometric systems. In 2004, the National Institute of Standards and Technology's (NIST's) Visualization and Usability Group recognized this need and worked with the DHS Science and Technology Directorate to establish a program to develop HCI guidelines and standards for biometric systems.

Unfortunately, the biometrics community viewed the user as a passive source of the biometric sample rather than as an interactive part of the system. The community had never watched "real" users actually use the system. They never considered that users would be totally unfamiliar with the technology — and a little scared by it. Therefore when DHS determined the system throughput, they thought it was simply a matter of multiplying the capture time of the biometric device by the number of prints to be captured. Using this logic, if it takes 3 s to capture a print, it would take 9 s (3 s each for a right index, a left index, and the simultaneous thumbs) to process a person through US-VISIT. As US-VISIT discovered, this is not true. This view does not take into account any of the user's interactions or behaviors. Our goal was to understand how users' behavior, cognition, perception, and anthropometric qualities impact system performance metrics (both throughput and quality), in order to convince the biometrics community of the value of HCI and usability, and persuade them to incorporate usability standards and guidelines into their development and implementation processes. The ultimate goal is the development and testing of usability guidelines for biometric systems that enhance performance (throughput and biometric sample quality), improve user satisfaction and acceptance, and provide consistency across biometric system user interfaces.

Incremental steps

As a standards organization, we began with the ISO definition of usability: "extent to which a product can be used by specified users to achieve specified goals with effectiveness, efficiency and satisfaction in a specified context of use" (ISO 9241-11:1998, p. 2). This definition makes clear that usability can be measured, but more importantly we were hoping to connect with the measurement side of the biometrics community. From that perspective it was necessary to speak their language. The biometrics community was focused on system performance — primarily throughput, image quality, and errors. Thus it was necessary to measure biometric usability in terms of such measures, and to show the impact of usability and the user on biometric performance. From our perspective, we needed to identify and understand three factors:

1. *The users* — Who are the users of the biometrics systems? What characteristics of the user affect performance? We needed to consider age, gender, physiology, experience, and ability among other factors, and to show their impact on throughput and quality.

2. *The context of use* — How does the environment influence performance? What about instructions, anthropometrics, affordance, and accessibility — and how do they contribute to system performance?
3. *What to measure*:
   - Effectiveness: a measure of accuracy and completeness; in this case, we measured the quality of the captured images and number of errors the user made in attempting to use the biometric device.
   - Efficiency: a measure of resources expended (task time); in this case, we measured the user's total interaction time with the biometric device instead of just the time required for the device to capture and process an image.
   - User satisfaction: the degree to which the product meets the user's expectations, or the level of comfort the user experiences — a subjective response.

We began our work by visiting airports and spending hours observing US-VISIT in action. We documented how the US Customs and Border Protection officers interacted with travelers and how travelers interacted with the devices. We also looked at exactly what the environment was: we measured the counter heights, the widths of the lanes, how the instructions were provided, etc. We timed the process from the point where the traveler was asked to leave a fingerprint to the point where they had left all three images correctly . . . and the list goes on. This list became the material from which we designed our controlled experiments where we accurately measured time on task and quality of the biometric images with respect to the variables we were testing.

At the airports, we made the following general observations that we believed required further investigation:

- The fingerprint capture process started with the left index finger, yet travelers seemed to want to start the process with their right hand.
- The counter heights varied in the airports, but most counter heights were quite high.
- The fingerprint instructions seemed confusing to many of the travelers.
- Many travelers entered the country frequently such as airline personnel and used the fingerprint scanners often. We wondered if throughput and quality changed with repeated use.
- We observed a wide range of ages. US-VISIT collects prints from travelers from 17 to 79 years old. We wondered about the influence of age and gender.

From our visits to the airports and our list of observations, we began our research studies and the identification of those human factors that influence biometric system performance.

Most importantly, our research has led to a holistic system view. Previously the biometrics community held a system-centric view, which is illustrated by the right side of the arrow in Figure 15.1.

Up to now the user had been left out of the system. But the user is the key to the process. The user initiates the process, and the user's sample determines the success of the process. As our studies have demonstrated and Figure 15.1 illustrates, the user has inherent characteristics that affect the quality of the biometric sample and the time required to acquire the sample. We have shown that these characteristics include age, gender, height, experience, perception, and ability. These inherent characteristics require that the biometric system addresses anthropometrics, accessibility, the environment, instructions, and affordances.

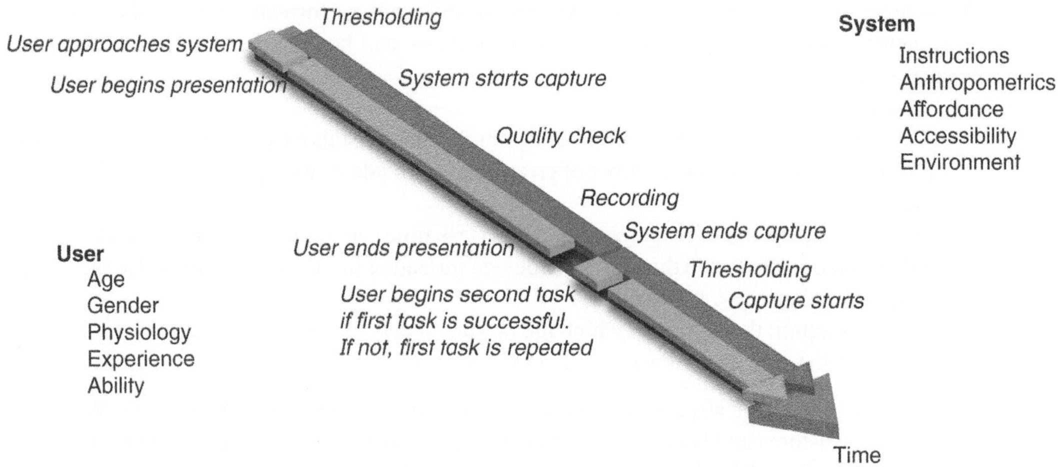

FIGURE 15.1 Holistic view of biometric systems

(For color version of this figure, see the web version of this chapter.)

CASE STUDIES: REDUCING LONG LINES, CONFUSION, AND DISTRUST THROUGH USABILITY TESTING

As described earlier, little attention was given to the HCI of the devices, the system, or the process when DHS implemented the US-VISIT program resulting in long lines, confusion for the international travelers, and overall distrust of the system. The initial system was implemented at border points of entry, such as airports and seaports, where visitors are fingerprinted and photographed to help ascertain and verify the identities of travelers entering the United States. When the program began, US-VISIT required visitors to have their two index fingers electronically printed and a face photograph. Over time, they have migrated to a process that collects all 10 fingerprints and a face photograph.

The NIST usability team, primed with the observations from the airport and a list of questions regarding the system and the travelers' behaviors, began a series of usability tests.[1] In the first test, we examined habituation, or acclimatization: Do user behavior and interaction with the device over time improve or degrade user performance? The second study focused on anthropometrics and the height of the work surface and scanner placement. Is there a relationship between the scanner's height and the quality of captured images? Our third test studied the use of instructional materials. Do people perform better with oral, video, or poster instructions?

[1]These tests were supported by the US DHS. Specific hardware and software products identified in this report were used to perform the evaluations described. In no case does such identification imply recommendation or endorsement by the NIST, nor does it imply that the products and equipment identified are necessarily the best available for the purpose.

Habituation and feedback

The habituation and feedback study (Theofanos, Micheals, Scholtz, Morse, & May, 2006) was designed to determine if a user's behavior could potentially change as a result of habituation. Does habituation, the process of becoming accustomed to the device, affect the user's performance and the acquisition of quality images? Fingerprint image quality might improve as one learns how to use the system, or might decrease in quality since comfort with the system could translate into carelessness. Additionally, how does feedback affect habituation and image quality? There are many types of feedback to consider. For most biometric systems, the granularity of feedback presented to the user is typically quite coarse. For example, a fingerprint-based access control system might include only feedback indicating when a person should start and stop pressing a finger on the scanner or might indicate whether a claim of identity was accepted or rejected (e.g., the door opens or remains closed). What information helps the user improve fingerprint image quality?

This study identified a number of external factors that affected the image quality and usability of index fingerprints collected by an electronic reader. These factors include age and gender but also the absence or presence of immediate feedback.

We collected the data in two phases (for details on the experiment see Theofanos et al., 2006). In each phase, we collected two impressions of left and right index fingers for 30 participants, over a period of 15 days. In phase one, the operator indicated when a participant should place and remove his/her finger. The operator manually triggered image capture and the participants received no information about image quality.

In this phase, we found the following:

- Younger participants submit higher quality images than older participants.
- Women's images, on average, are of poorer quality than men's.
- Habituation has no effect on image quality without feedback.

In phase two, participants decided in which order to scan their fingers, saw a dynamic scale bar of image quality, received encouragement to collect as many samples as needed to achieve desired quality, and decided when to submit the image to the database.

In phase two, we found the following:

- When feedback was introduced, older participants tried more times.
- Feedback allowed older participants to produce images that were of higher quality over time.
- Younger subjects still submitted higher quality images.

Anthropometrics

In a second study, we examined the influence of the height of the sensor on the quality and time required to collect fingerprints (Theofanos, Orandi, Micheals, Stanton, & Zhang, 2006). Most entry-point counters were fairly high and we had observed shorter travelers struggling to leave fingerprints, yet there were no data that compared the work surface heights. This study compared work surface heights of 26 inches (660 mm), 32 inches (813 mm), 36 inches (914 mm), and 42 inches (1067 mm) not including the height of the scanner. We used a scanner that was 6 inches high, resulting in a scanner platen height that was 6 inches above the work surface. For each scanner height, the participants were asked to leave a left "slap" (the left hand without the thumb), a right slap (right hand without the thumb), each individual thumbprint, and both thumbprints together. The study included 75 participants, and we collected timing data in addition to the fingerprint images.

The analysis of sensor height and fingerprint image quality was based on image quality as formally defined by the NIST Fingerprint Image Quality (NFIQ) metric (Tabassi, Wilson, & Watson, 2004). Our study examined the distribution of the frequency of NFIQ scores for each finger and found that image quality is affected by scanner height. In particular, we identified the following factors affecting image quality:

- The right index finger was not sensitive to height. The right index finger is the only finger where no reliable difference was found.
- The thumbs are more sensitive to height than the slaps.
- The left slap is more sensitive than the right slap.
- The data indicate a dramatic drop in quality from individual thumbprints to simultaneous thumbs. This observation suggests that individual thumbs give higher quality images across all heights.

We identified the following conditions for optimal scanner placement with respect to counter height:

- *For the simultaneous thumbprint*: The work surface height that yielded the poorest image quality was 42 inches. Participants were consistently able to provide higher quality thumbprints at work surface heights lower than 42 inches. The work surface height yielding the highest image quality is at 26 or 32 inches.
- *For the left slap*: The work surface height yielding the poorest image quality was 42 inches. Participants were consistently able to provide higher quality prints at work surface heights lower than 42 inches. The work surface height yielding the highest image quality is at 26 inches.
- There were no clear trends for the right slap or for the individual thumbs with respect to optimal scanner height.

We also found that a counter height of 36 inches (914 mm) gives the fastest performance. Finally, starting a capture sequence with the right slap was most efficient.

Instructional materials

A third study examined the effect of instructional modes on user performance. Users who are accustomed to leaving two index fingerprints at US-VISIT will not be familiar with the 10-fingerprint capture process. Therefore this study measured not only the time necessary to acquire a 10-print image, but also evaluated how to present instructional information to the users. The study was designed to answer three questions:

- How does the instructional mode (poster, video, or verbal) affect user performance?
- How long does it take to capture a 10-print image?
- What is the nature of the errors that occur in this process?

This study also identified a number of external factors that affected the user performance and image quality of the collected prints including the instructional mode.

For this experiment, each of the 300 participants received instructions on how to complete the 10-print collection process in one of the three formats: a 76 × 115-cm poster (no text), verbal instructions spoken by the test conductor, or a 50-s soundless video. The instructional materials portrayed three steps: participants were asked to present a left slap, a right slap, and both thumbprints simultaneously. After completing a user satisfaction survey, participants were asked to repeat the fingerprint collection task leaving reference prints. The second set of images is important for performing matches of images. This fingerprint task was assisted by the operator as necessary.

This experiment showed that instructional mode and operator interaction are significant factors in user performance and even in image quality. We reported five findings:

- Those who received instructions via the poster had the most difficulty performing the fingerprinting task. Statistical analysis shows that participants who received the poster instructions took significantly longer to complete the 10-print collection process than did participants in the video or verbal instructional groups. Fewer participants in the poster condition were able to complete the task and made significantly more errors than either the video or verbal conditions. Only 56% of these participants were able to complete the fingerprinting process successfully.
- Operators are critical to the acquisition process. From the reference prints, it appears that operators are able to assist individuals to overcome the deficits of the instructional materials. With operator assistance, 98% of the participants were able to complete the fingerprint process successfully.
- On average, the time required to capture a 10-print sequence (a right slap, a left slap, and simultaneous thumbs) without operator assistance ranges from 48 to 64 s and the medians ranged from 45 to 59 s, and with operator assistance from 50 to 54 s (the medians ranged from 45 to 46 s) for our biometric system configuration The minimum time to complete a capture sequence of the three images successfully in our configuration is approximately 30 s. This includes approximately 21 s for image capture and 9 s of overhead for initialization and other operational chores.
- Participants who received the verbal and video instructions performed equally well on the first collection. Verbal instructions were rated highest in preference by participants followed by video, and poster was rated the lowest of the three instructional modes. Verbal instructions may be difficult in an operational setting. Video instructions may be presented to many people waiting in line simultaneously providing an effective instructional delivery method by adding no additional time for the operator during the collection process and still providing optimum capture times and low-error incidence.
- Participants who received instructions via the poster left the poorest quality images using NFIQ. Statistical analysis shows that the image quality of prints from participants who received the poster was significantly lower than the quality of the images collected from participants who received either the verbal or the video instructions.

Each of these studies has resulted in a set of guidelines for use by DHS, as well as operational changes in the field that have increased efficiency and effectiveness. What does this mean? The lines are shorter, the processing time is faster, and travelers are more satisfied with the overall process.

One of the most far-reaching findings of these studies is that the accuracy of biometric systems can be radically enhanced by improving the usability of the systems. This is a paradigm-shifting result, as previous attempts at improving accuracy focused mainly on developing better biometric technologies. Now US-VISIT seeks input and requests studies from the NIST usability team.

Angling fingerprint scanners

When DHS was moving from the two-print process to the collection of all 10 fingerprints, they were faced with the challenge of how to perform the collection without adversely affecting throughput while collecting good quality prints. DHS was worried that the quality and throughput could be adversely affected by the height of the fingerprint scanner. As we described earlier, the entry point counters were fairly high for safety reasons. Lowering all the counters at every entry point was considered too costly. DHS wanted an alternative solution. A possible solution was angling the fingerprint scanner so that the platen of the scanner was tilted toward the visitor. DHS asked us to investigate what would be the best angle for a fingerprint scanner given the current counter heights.

We ran a usability study that tested the most common height of 39″, the tallest height of 49″, and the practical midpoint of 45″ (there were no 44″ tall counters in use). Using computer-aided design software we arrived at four probable angles: 0°, 10°, 20°, and 30°. We designed an adjustable platform with pegs to angle the scanners, as illustrated in Figure 15.2.

Each of the 126 participants completed five tasks. Participants were asked to present a left slap followed by a left thumb, or a right slap followed by a right thumb (known as a 4-1-4-1 slap). Once both hands and single thumbs had been collected, we prompted them for both thumbs simultaneously. Fingerprint images were collected from each participant at the four different angles for one counter height. The order of the angles was counterbalanced, meaning all possible combinations of angles were accounted for, and whether the participant started with the right or left hand was randomly selected.

The order of presentation of the slaps was provided to the participants as verbal instructions generated by the software.

We found that angling the fingerprint scanners had no impact on quantitative performance. There was no significant difference in time to complete the tasks; the angles had no effect. Nor did the angles affect the quality of the captured images. But with respect to user satisfaction for both scanners, the angled scanners proved to be much more comfortable to use at the taller counter heights. The least comfortable angle appears more dependent on the participant's height (see Figures 15.3 and 15.4). Finally, as the height of the counter increased, more people preferred single thumb prints to positioning both thumbs together. This preference was further elaborated in the participants' comments. In responses to the question of whether they had difficulty positioning themselves for any of the trials, most of the comments concerned positioning of the thumbs. They also indicated that it was uncomfortable to place both thumbs simultaneously on the platen of the fingerprint scanner. Comments included "this is awkward" and "kind of hard."

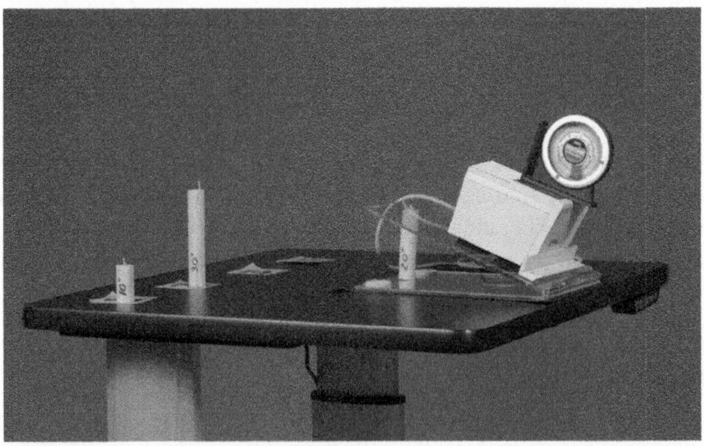

FIGURE 15.2 Angled scanner with pegs

(For color version of this figure, see the Web version of this chapter.)

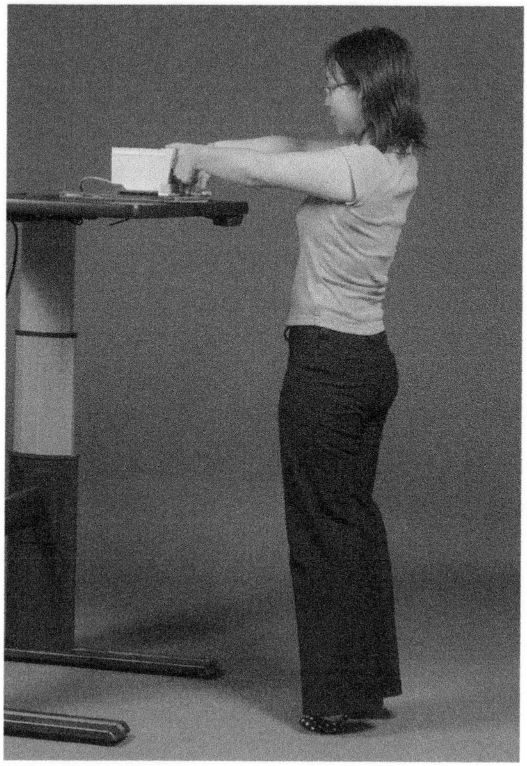

FIGURE 15.3 Shorter participant with flat scanner

(For color version of this figure, see the Web version of this chapter.)

In 2008, when US-VISIT fully implemented 10-print fingerprint capture, they angled the scanners at 20° at all the airports, as illustrated in Figure 15.5. They also eliminated the capture of simultaneous thumbs.

Take-aways

The NIST biometrics team has identified a number of user characteristics that affect fingerprint performance:

- Inherent characteristics of a person such as age, gender, height (anthropometrics)
- Experience — familiarity with the device or the technology
- Ability — physical limitations
- Perception — level of comfort or acceptance of the device or process. Two percent of the population has expressed concerns about the possibility of germs on the scanner. The tactile feedback from the smooth glass and metal surface is perceived to be sticky. Automated Teller Machines are usually made of hard matte-textured plastic surfaces to minimize this impression.

FIGURE 15.4 Taller participant with 30° scanner

(For color version of this figure, see the Web version of this chapter.)

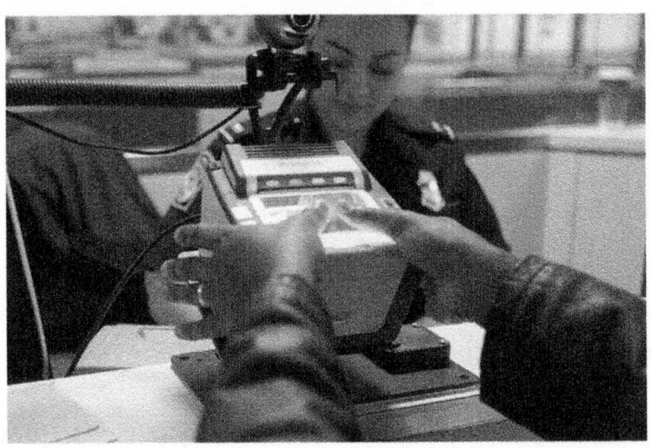

FIGURE 15.5 Angled scanner at border entry point

(For color version of this figure, see the Web version of this chapter.)

These user characteristics require that we examine certain biometric system factors:

- *Physical characteristics of the device* — How high is it? How should the device be positioned? What color should the fingerprint platen be? Should it feel warm or cold?
- *Affordance* — The inherent ability of the device to relay its use: Consider a door. Is it a push or pull door? It should be obvious from the knob or the push bar. It should not require a sign that says push or pull. In this case, the shape and configuration of the scanner should convey where to place your fingers and give feedback that the prints have been captured.
- *Instructions and learning materials* — Not everyone speaks English. What form should the instructions take?
- *Accessibility* — What about Section 508 of the Rehabilitation Act? How should the technology adapt for people with disabilities? (See Chapter 12, Ensuring Accessibility for People with Disabilities, for more information on accessibility for people with disabilities.)

SUCCESS FACTORS

The studies we completed and the two perspectives of biometric systems previously discussed have taught us that there are four key factors to consider when designing biometric systems or integrating biometric devices into systems:

- context
- users
- system characteristics
- usability testing

Context

Successful implementation of biometric systems is highly dependent on their environment. Environmental factors are critical to the capture of good quality images, especially five major ones:

- *Climate* — temperature, humidity, very wet, or very dry conditions. Many biometric devices, especially fingerprint devices, are sensitive to temperature and humidity. Fingerprint capture using today's digital scanners may be very difficult in extreme conditions. Consider, for example, the dry conditions at a border crossing in the southwest, the extremely wet conditions on a Coast Guard cutter, or the extreme cold in the winter at the Canadian border; all of these are current fingerprint scenarios for DHS within the United States.
- *Illumination* — lighting and type of lighting. Capturing good facial images requires appropriate lighting. Overhead lighting, especially fluorescent lighting, tends to cast shadows across the image. Collection of iris images is also affected by lighting. There have been examples of facilities placing an iris scanner in front of a window, which negatively affected the quality of the images.
- *Position* — placement of biometric devices must be carefully designed. Many factors influence performance. As discussed in the case study above: the counter height affected fingerprint capture performance. The height and angle of the iris scanner and the camera will also affect

the quality of the iris and facial images and the throughput of the overall biometric system. The placement of the biometric system must take into account pedestrian traffic flow and provide for the queue.

- *Hygiene* — biometric devices may need cleaning. It may be necessary to include cleaning of the biometric device into the standing operating procedures in order to capture good quality images. In many environments, after repeated use the fingerprint platen may become sticky and covered with latent fingerprints, which can significantly affect image capture.
- *Location* — indoors or outdoors. Many times biometric devices are used for access control for entry, and as such are placed outdoors. In this case, the devices and system must be "hardened" for outdoor use. This may also impact the type of biometric device that may be appropriate and its throughput that can be achieved. Finally, consideration must be given to the safety of the user if the user is queued up outside for any length of time.

Users

For biometric applications, it is important to know users' physical characteristics; after all, biometrics are physical characteristics. Gather as much information as possible about your user population.

The following three factors have been shown to have a specific influence on biometric systems:

- *Demographics* such as age, gender, and ethnicity have a direct effect on image quality. Large biometric data collections have shown that as we age, our ridges are less pronounced and our fingers are drier. Similarly, these collections have shown that women are harder to fingerprint, generally because their fingertips are drier. User perception is an important factor to consider and is often related to ethnicity. Different cultures view biometrics differently and users may be apprehensive or sensitive to having their biometrics collected. Currently, collecting iris images is not well accepted because of a science fiction movie in which a more advanced version of the technology was misused. Collecting a good facial image requires an individual to remove any headgear, eyeglasses, or anything else obstructing his/her face; many cultures are uncomfortable with this requirement.
- *Professions* have also been shown to have a direct effect on image quality. Consider, for example, anyone who works with his/her hands — construction workers, hairdressers, and day laborers all are traditionally more difficult to fingerprint because of their jobs and the materials with which they work.
- *Anthropometrics* — the study of the measurement of humans — and the *ergonomics* of the biometric device environment affect the performance of the overall system. As described in the case study above, the relationship of a biometric device and a person's height is an important feature for all three major biometric devices — fingerprint, face, and iris. It is not just a matter of placing a scanner on a convenient surface; each decision must be designed and carefully assessed. Other factors such as those addressed by the Section 508 law must also be considered.

System characteristics

The design and characteristics of the overall system also affect the system's performance, especially the throughput. The research has shown that the following three factors are of key consideration:

- Design-in affordance — as much as possible the biometric device should encourage its use and convey its intended function. Many people are not familiar with biometric devices; their only exposure is what they have seen on TV. Unfortunately, this does not give them an accurate picture of biometrics. Biometric devices must have good affordance to help overcome these misperceptions.
- Avoid negative affordance — an affordance that is not in congruence with the actual use. Many times it is in violation of a population stereotype. Consider, for example, a fingerprint platen that is glowing red. This glow may be perceived as *hot* or *stop, don't touch*. Other biometric devices may require a user to insert his/her arm in an enclosure — again, this is perceived as a risk to his/her well-being.
- Provide instructional materials — if the system does not have good affordance, instructional materials are necessary. These materials require careful development, taking into account cultural differences, languages, and method of presentation.

Usability testing

As our studies showed, usability testing can predict the efficiency (throughput) and effectiveness (quality) of biometric systems. Therefore it is important to test your biometric system with representative users in a representative environment, so that you can truly understand the performance of the overall system.

Resources

As we completed each study, we prepared a NIST Internal Report (NISTIR) that completely documented the experiment and the results. Many times we also submitted a paper to a journal or conference. Through these studies we have discovered several factors that affect biometric system performance:

- Counter height (Theofanos, Orandi, et al., 2006)
- Repeated use — but only if feedback is provided (Theofanos, Micheals, et al., 2006)
- Gender and age (Theofanos, Micheals, et al., 2006)
- The method of conveying information and instructions (Theofanos, Stanton, Orandi, Micheals, & Zhang, 2007)

Our studies have also uncovered some optimal methods and parameter values:

- Fingerprint sequence (Theofanos, Orandi, et al., 2006)
- Expected time to capture all 10 fingerprints (Theofanos, Stanton, et al., 2007)
- Expected number of recaptures (Theofanos, Stanton, et al., 2007)
- The best way to improve face acquisition (Theofanos et al., 2008a)
- The preferred vendor system (Theofanos et al., 2008b)

All of these documents are available on our web site (zing.ncsl.nist.gov/biousa).

In 2008, as the biometrics community began to incorporate usability principles, we developed a usability and Biometrics handbook (National Institute of Standards and Technology, 2008) for designers and developers of biometrics devices. The handbook introduced designers to the concept of usability and the user-centered design (UCD) process and showcased the ways in which a properly implemented UCD process can improve a system's efficiency, effectiveness, and user satisfaction. This handbook was distributed at the International Workshop on Usability of Biometrics and at the NIST booth at BCC in September of 2008. The handbook was so popular that we printed CDs, "Usability and Biometrics 101," for distribution at the BCC booth in September of 2009. The handbook is also available on our web site.

SUMMARY

In 2004, when biometric systems were first widely introduced to the public, the user was not considered an integral part of the system. Today we have evidence to show that the user is critical to the success of the biometric system. Designing with the user in mind can significantly improve the performance of the overall system — both the system throughput and the quality of the captured images. We have shown that the findings of the NIST experiments and usability tests do translate directly into the field. This is a paradigm shift for the biometric industry, as previous attempts at improving accuracy and performance focused mainly on developing better biometric technologies. As a result, we have been able to identify four key factors that must be addressed to implement successful biometric systems that integrate the user.

References

International Organization for Standards. (1998). ISO 9241-11 Ergonomic requirements for office work with visual display terminals (VDTs) — Part 11: Guidance on usability. Geneva, Switzerland: Author.

National Institute of Standards and Technology. (2008). *Usability & biometrics: Ensuring successful biometrics systems.* Gaithersburg, MD: Author.

National Science and Technology Council. Biometrics in government post-9/11. (2008). Retrieved on 14 August 2011 from http://www.biometrics .gov/nstc/publications.aspx

Tabassi, E., Wilson, C., & Watson, C. (2004). *Fingerprint image quality (NISTIR 7151).* Gaithersburg, MD: National Institute of Standards and Technology.

Theofanos, M., Micheals, R., Scholtz, J., Morse, E., & May, P. (2006). Does habituation affect fingerprint quality? In *Proceedings of CHI 2006.*

Theofanos, M., Orandi, S., Micheals, R., Stanton, B., & Zhang, N. (2006). *Effects of scanner height on fingerprint capture (NISTIR 7382).* Gaithersburg, MD: National Institute of Standards and Technology.

Theofanos, M., Stanton, B., Orandi, S., Micheals, R., & Zhang, N. (2007). *Usability testing of ten-print fingerprint capture (NISTIR 7403).* Gaithersburg, MD: National Institute of Standards and Technology.

Theofanos, M., Stanton, B., Sheppard, C., Micheals, R., Libert, J., & Orandi, S. (2008). *Assessing face acquisition (NISTIR 7540).* Gaithersburg, MD: National Institute of Standards and Technology.

Theofanos, M., Stanton, B., Sheppard, C., Micheals, R., Zhang, N., Wydler, J., et al. (2008). *Usability testing of height and angles of ten-print fingerprint capture (NISTIR 7504).* Gaithersburg, MD: National Institute of Standards and Technology.

Further reading

Choong, Y., Stanton, B., & Theofanos, M. (2010). Biometric symbol design for the public — Case studies in the United States and four Asian countries. In *3rd International conference on applied human factors and ergonomics (AHFE), Miami, Florida, USA.*

Guan, H., Theofanos, M. F., Choong, Y. Y., & Stanton, B. (2011), Real-time feedback for fingerprint systems. 2011 International joint conference on biometrics (IJCB).

Sasse, M. A. (2007). Red-eye blink, bendy shuffle, and the yuck factor: A user experience of biometric airport systems. *IEEE Security & Privacy*, 1540-79937, 78–81.

Theofanos, M. F., Micheals, R., Scholtz, J., Morse, E., & May, P. (2006). Does habituation affect fingerprint quality? In *Proceedings of CHI 2006.*

Theofanos, M. F., Micheals, R., & Stanton, B. (2009). Biometrics systems include users. *IEEE Systems Journal*, *3*(4), 461–468.

Theofanos, M. F., Orandi, S., Micheals, R., Stanton, B., & Zhang, N. (2008). How the subject can improve fingerprint image quality, *Journal of Electronic Imaging*, *17*(1), 011007-1–011007-10.

Theofanos, M. F., & Stanton, B. (2007). Making biometric systems usable: Let's not forget the user!. *Defense Standardization Journal*, 77–81.

Theofanos, M. F., Stanton, B., Orandi, S., & Micheals, R. (2007a). Effects of scanner height on fingerprint capture. In *Proceedings of human factors and ergonomics society annual conference.*

Theofanos, M. F., Stanton, B., Orandi, S., & Micheals, R. (2007b). Biometric systematic uncertainty and the user. In *IEEE conference on biometrics Theory, application and systems.*

Theofanos, M. F., Stanton, B., Orandi, S., Micheals, R., & Zhang, N. F. (2007). Usability testing of ten-print fingerprint capture. In *Proceedings of human factors and ergonomics society annual conference.*

Theofanos, M. F., Stanton, B., Sheppard, C., & Micheals, R. (2008). Usability testing of face image capture for US ports of entry. In *Proceedings of the IEEE conference on biometrics Theory, application and systems.*

Theofanos, M. F., Stanton, B., Sheppard, C., Micheals, R., Zhang, N., & Wydler, J. (2008). Does the angle of a fingerprint scanner affect user performance? In *Proceedings of human factors and ergonomics society annual conference.*

SECTION

Procurement and Development IV

"All truths are easy to understand once they are discovered; the point is to discover them."
— Galileo Galilei

This section maps usability and user experience processes to government systems development processes, from initiation through to evaluation. The section comprises six chapters:

- *Chapter 16*, Getting UX into the Contract
- *Chapter 17*, ISO Standards for User-Centered Design and the Specification of Usability
- *Chapter 18*, User-Centered Requirements Definition
- *Chapter 19*, Models as Representations for Supporting the Development of e-Procedures
- *Chapter 20*, Evaluation in Government Environments
- *Chapter 21*, Adapting e-Gov Usability Evaluation to Cultural Contexts

These chapters discuss the conduct of UX processes under the requirements and constraints that governments worldwide impose on how they procure electronic and information technology and related services — constraints that are aimed at obtaining the best value for the taxpayers' money, promoting competition among vendors and contractors, and ensuring the transparency of the process. The key factors in government procurements are that they must be open, competitive, cost-effective, and free of fraud, waste, and abuse. For readers who are already familiar with government procurement, the chapters in this section provide insights into how those processes can incorporate UX. For readers who are familiar with UX, they provide insights into government procurement environments and how UX processes can be adapted to fit into them.

- In Chapter 16, **Timo Jokela** (Finland) and **Elizabeth Buie** (USA) discuss how governments invite prospective contractors to bid on projects and how usability and UX have been and should be incorporated into that process. Government systems continue to demonstrate poor usability for two main reasons: agencies fail to specify usability in a way that ensures the production of adequately usable systems, and they are not prepared to ensure usability and good UX for themselves. Jokela and Buie look at various ways in which governments initiate system development projects and contracts, and explore how they prepare requests for proposals. They discuss the difference between the question of who conducts the UX activities and who takes responsibility for usability, and propose some approaches that both purchasers and contractors can take. To illustrate these concepts, the authors draw on their experience in government contracting in Finland and in the United States. Constraints arising from lack of time, money, expertise, or organizational support, Jokela and Buie tell us, "can make it impossible for purchasers and bidders to give usability its proper place in the RFP and the proposal, respectively. Nonetheless, usability and UX are gaining recognition in the government systems environment, and the situation is improving. . . . The purchasers are in the key position; if UX is truly required, the contractors will follow."

- In Chapter 17, **Jonathan Earthy** (UK), **Nigel Bevan** (UK), and **Brian Sherwood Jones** (UK) describe the processes by which systems are made usable and how ISO standards that define how to perform these processes can facilitate making government systems usable. International standards for usability and human-centered design (HCD) are flexible enough to support appropriate user-centered design and measurable enough to allow conformance. The authors introduce international standards for usability, detail the requirements for ergonomics and HCD, and describe the ISO process models, HCD processes, and design guidance. They describe the application of the ISO HCD process to government systems from the perspectives of risk reduction, process improvement, product specification, and validation. They also discuss the effect of project scale and provide the details of relevant standards. "Conformance to these standards," they emphasize, "gives usability and user-centered design status in systems development. These international standards can be used in contracts (both for specification and monitoring), and for the management of development and testing."

- In Chapter 18, **Alistair Sutcliffe** (UK) and **Jan Gulliksen** (Sweden) review requirements analysis and definition methods and techniques that can help improve government system usability, and illustrate the process with case studies of e-government requirements analysis. Requirements play an essential role in all types of system development, and the authors stress the special importance of requirements for government systems. They point out, however, that new development approaches and technologies, combined with changes in legislation, are moving requirements analysis to become more user-centered and more central to the communication between developers and users. Sutcliffe and Gulliksen illustrate their points with examples from their own experience in defining requirements for public-sector projects in the United Kingdom and in Sweden. "These techniques," they assert, "contribute to a further development of requirements engineering to manage the evolving demands of current systems development practice."

- In Chapter 19, **Philippe Palanque** (France) and **Marco Winckler** (France) describe a modeling approach to the development of systems that support electronic procedures, explaining how model-based approaches can help in developing complex e-procedures and conveying design options to a multidisciplinary team. Their approach develops a task model for the user activities and a system model for the implementation, and matches the two to ensure that the developed system will support the user tasks appropriately. The authors illustrate their approach with an example of designing a system to support student financial aid applications, which involve both members of the public (students and their parents) and government employees (high-school principals[1] and administrative staff). They show how such models can provide useful information for understanding and matching user tasks and needs with system behavior along the different steps in the workflow. "Without appropriate support from models," contend Palanque and Winckler, "the development team will get lost and the chance of unexpected and undesired behaviors will increase. These models provide different points of view on the same sociotechnical system, so that when working in multidisciplinary teams all stakeholders can use the most suitable model to make their concerns and requirements explicit, to be embedded in the final application."

- In Chapter 20, **Whitney Quesenbery** (USA) describes usability evaluation and its critical role in system development and explains the unique challenges and constraints of evaluating usability in a government environment. She begins with an overview of usability evaluation in general — when, why, and how to conduct evaluation effectively — and discusses the difference between qualitative and quantitative analysis of results. She then describes in detail the specific requirements of usability evaluation in a government context. Touching on legal and ethical issues such as privacy and informed consent, she describes test participant recruitment for government projects (especially public-facing systems), and explores the challenges that confront usability evaluation in government projects, especially that of following good research practice while still providing the transparency needed for public projects. "Within a user-centered process," she stresses "it is important to check the work in progress as well as the final result and make sure that all the elements of the system have come together to meet the usability requirements."

- In Chapter 21, **Torkil Clemmensen** (Denmark) and **Dinesh Katre** (India) discuss "cultural usability" — the effect of cultural factors on usability — and explain how to adapt usability evaluation to different cultures. They argue that e-government usability evaluations must draw on studies from the geographical region and the culture in which the government

[1]"Head teacher" in the UK.

operates, to provide an understanding of the issues that are important to the populations in question. The authors illustrate their points with two usability evaluations of public-facing government systems: an expert review of 28 state government portals in India, and a usability test of a Danish e-gov authentication system. The Indian study found that visual design and other nontraditional factors impacting on usability (e.g., ownership and branding) were important to varying degrees; the Danish study found that user acceptance of a single-sign-on system to online government services was fairly high despite severe usability problems, because users developed workarounds and because they recognized its usefulness despite the problems. Clemmensen and Katre offer some advice for how to take a "broad and context-oriented approach" to evaluating e-gov systems in different cultural environments. "In general, usability professionals working with adapting e-gov usability to cultural contexts should pay particular attention to the culturally specific relationships between the human work, the design artifacts, and the interaction design. The combination of the analysis of human work in e-gov systems with the interaction design of e-gov systems should identify 'cultural models of use' — in the form of existing systems, as well as sketches and prototypes of future systems — of a given technology (e.g., a web site) for each user group and geographical region."

These chapters appear, roughly, in chronological order according to the sequence of the activity in the procurement process.

CHAPTER

Getting UX Into the Contract

16

Timo Jokela*, Elizabeth Buie†
Joticom Oy, Helsinki, Finland Luminanze Consulting, Silver Spring, MD, USA†*

"It's a very sobering feeling to be up in space and realize that one's safety factor was determined by the lowest bidder on a government contract."
— Alan Shepard, first American in space

INTRODUCTION

Government agencies no longer select contractors solely on price, for the most part. However, as previous chapters have shown, government systems continue to suffer widely from poor usability and give citizens and public servants a less-than-pleasant user experience (UX).

Why does poor usability persist in government systems? In our view, the main reason is that government agencies fail to specify usability in a way that ensures the production of adequately usable systems, or are not prepared to ensure usability by themselves. In this chapter, we look at how governments initiate system development projects, and we propose some approaches to solving the problem.

Getting UX into a government project depends on defining requirements, activities, and selection criteria up front, so that the agency can evaluate proposals, select a contractor, and verify that the contractor has delivered what was agreed. *Usability* is defined in terms of effectiveness, efficiency, and satisfaction (International Organization for Standardization [ISO], 1998) — which can be *specified and measured* as attributes of a system. *User experience*, in contrast, is the user's subjective experience of the system. UX as a field is not yet mature enough to have developed generally accepted ways of specifying or measuring the desired system features or UX parameters so that a system can be validated against them. However, although UX itself does not encompass usability, usability is required for a good UX, and UX work addresses usability.

A final note about scope: governments worldwide vary widely in their approaches to system development. In writing this chapter together, we have learned something about this variety, just by discovering some of the differences between a member country of the European Union (Finland) and the United States. We cannot begin to cover all the possibilities here — we are, after all, drawing on our own experiences and resources in our own countries — but we hope that our discussion and examples provide enough variety that all of our readers will find something useful in them.

Project structures

Government system development can occur within a variety of project structures. Figures 16.1 through 16.4 depict four common types:[1]

1. *In-house development* (Figure 16.1): The agency assigns a project to its own staff, who design, develop, and maintain the system. Numerous government web sites fall into this category.
2. *Project contract* (Figure 16.2): The agency issues a contract for a single project to a single contractor.[2] The contract has the same scope as the project, and is competitive.
3. *"Umbrella"*[3] *contract with a single contractor* (Figure 16.3): The agency issues a contract to a single contractor for an unspecified amount of a certain type of service. The agency assigns projects to that contractor as needed, and may add work to existing projects. This "umbrella-single" contract is awarded on a competitive basis, but individual projects within it are not.

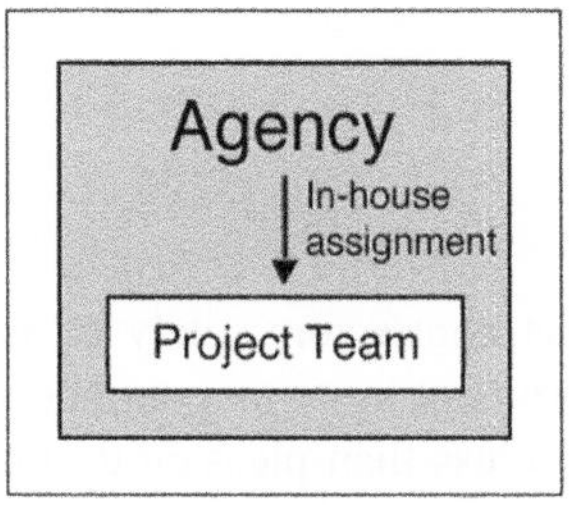

FIGURE 16.1 In-house project structure

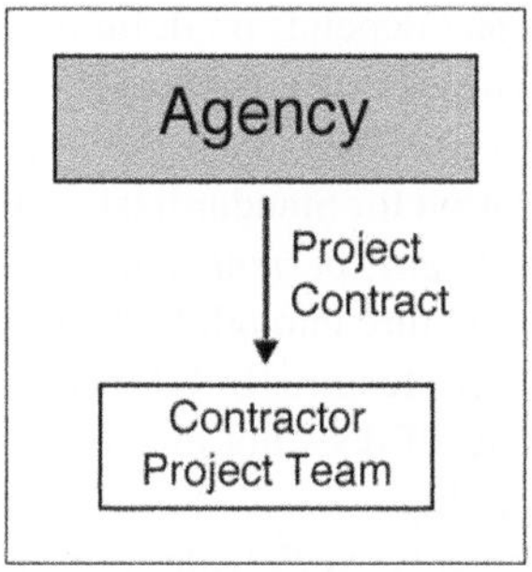

FIGURE 16.2 Project contract structure

[1]The actual structures are more numerous and may be more complex than what we have described, but these four illustrate the issues that are important to the analysis of getting UX into government projects.

[2]When we talk about "a single contractor" we mean a contractor team led by one prime contractor. The team may or may not include subcontractors, but that makes no difference, and we treat the team as a single contractor entity.

[3]"Umbrella" is the general term we use in this chapter to indicate that the contract may cover more than one project. We use "umbrella-single" for an umbrella contract with one contractor and "umbrella-multiple" for one with more than one contractor. Although the concept comes from the United States' "IDIQ" contract structure (as explained below), we have devised this term to describe the salient features without using the terminology of any particular country.

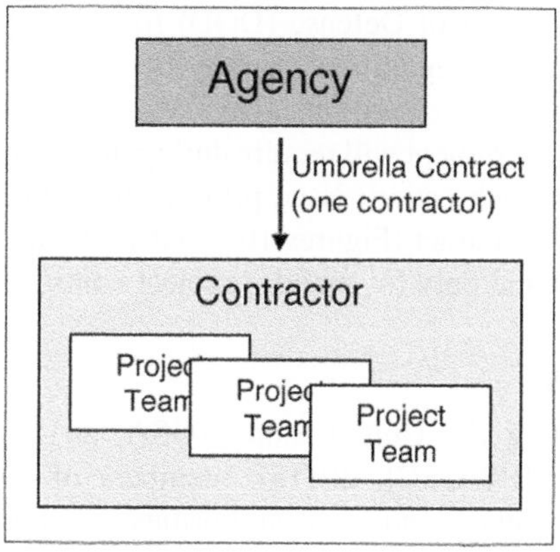

FIGURE 16.3 **"Umbrella-single" contract structure**

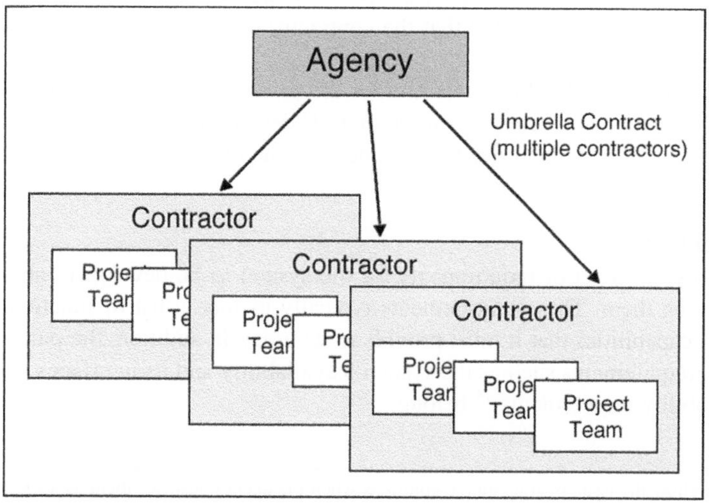

FIGURE 16.4 **"Umbrella-multiple" contract structure**

4. *"Umbrella" contract with multiple contractors* (Figure 16.4): The agency issues a contract to multiple contractors for an unspecified amount of the same type of services. Essentially, the contractors have "prequalified" to bid on projects for this type of work. The agency defines new projects as needed, and the prequalified contractors compete for each one. Both the "umbrella-multiple" contract itself and all of its projects are competitive.

An example of an umbrella contract is the United States' "indefinite delivery, indefinite quantity" (IDIQ) contract structure, which can be issued by the General Services Administration (GSA) for civilian work and by the Department of Defense (DOD) for military work. According to the GSA (2011a), IDIQ contracts "procure an indefinite quantity of services during a fixed period of time. They are used when the GSA can't predetermine, above a specified minimum, the precise quantities of supplies or services that the government will require during the contract period." IDIQ contracts may even cover multiple agencies, which can all issue project orders under that contract. In the United States, both types of "umbrella" contract (Figures 16.3 and 16.4) fall into this group.

A number of governments issue only (or mainly) project contracts.

Government procurements

Many governments — including the United States (GSA, 2011b), Canada (Public Works and Government Services Canada [PWGSC], 2011a), members of the European Union, and their various component states, provinces, and local authorities — operate under a legal requirement to use open competition in selecting contractors for government projects. For most procurements in these jurisdictions, the government authority — the "purchaser" — must issue a public, competitive[4] request for proposals (RFP).[5]

To initiate a project under an umbrella contract, an agency issues what we will call a "project order" to define the project and its requirements. Under an umbrella-multiple contract, the project order is usually competitive among the contractors; under an umbrella-single contract, it is not competitive but is given to that contractor provided that the contractor commits to satisfying its requirements in terms of scope and price.

Three components of an RFP or project order are critical for selecting the contractor and also relevant to UX: system requirements, contractor task descriptions (CTDs), and selection criteria. The role of UX in the procurement depends on the contents of these components and their presence in the RFP.

System requirements

The purchaser provides a set of requirements for the system to be developed, and all bidders must commit to satisfying them. These requirements typically include a list of functions that the system must possess and capabilities that it must provide to its users. In addition, the purchaser may impose "nonfunctional"[6] requirements such as the system's availability and its interfaces with other systems; here is where usability requirements[7,8] belong.

---

[4]Some governments allow the issue of sole-source contracts when the agency justifies them as such, and some allow their agencies to issue contracts noncompetitively for any procurement below a certain price.

[5]The RFP may also be called by other names, such as call for tenders, invitation to tender, or invitation to bid. This chapter uses "RFP" to refer to all such calls.

[6]"Nonfunctional" seems to be the term of art (see, for example, Eide, 2005; and a Google search for "non-functional" on ieee.org yielded approximately 3750 results on November 1, 2011), but it seems odd because it implies that these other requirements do not work. However, that is what the industry calls these requirements, and it is what we will call them as well.

[7]These requirements may address the system at a higher level than those covered in Chapter 18, User-Centered Requirements Definition.

[8]This chapter does not address issues of accessibility, such as those covered by the US law known as Section 508, although accessibility requirements, too, belong in the nonfunctional requirements. For information on accessibility, see Chapter 12, Ensuring Accessibility for People with Disabilities.

Contractor task descriptions

The purchaser describes, usually at a high level, the work to be performed by the contractor. In many cases, RFPs define contractor tasks in the form of a statement of work (SOW) that prescribes the activities in some detail. An[9] SOW defines these tasks as "structured in logical phases separated by major decision points called milestones" (DOD, 1996, p. 20), or it is "a narrative description of the work required and stipulates the deliverables or services required to fulfill the contract" (PWGSC, 2011b). The SOW generally specifies what must be accomplished but leaves much of the "how" up to the bidders. In other cases, the RFP includes, instead of an SOW, a performance work statement (PWS), which is intended to focus on contractor performance criteria as a measure of project success rather than defining the activities. Nominally, the PWS places less emphasis on the "how" than an SOW does. However, in practice the SOW and the PWS are often used interchangeably (D. Lang, personal communication, October 29, 2011), although they are by definition different approaches.

In some cases, instead of constituting a separate part of the RFP (e.g., SOW or PWS), the CTD comprises "process" requirements in the System Requirements section.

Regardless of whether the CTD appears in a separate part or within the requirements, it is a good place for requiring UX activities as part of the project. Requiring such activities does not *per se* guarantee usability or a good UX. It can, however, go a long way toward achieving good UX, especially if agency constraints do not allow for specifying usability requirements in the RFP.

Selection criteria

The purchaser describes the criteria by which it will evaluate the proposals or quotes and by which it will select the contractor(s). These criteria always include price. In addition, they may include characteristics of the proposals, of the bidders (particularly their past performance on similar contracts), and of any prototypes or demonstrations that accompany the proposals. The bidders, whose proposals respond to the requirements and/or the CTD, as appropriate, receive scores based on the selection criteria. Generally, the purchaser must select the bidder (or bidders, for an umbrella-multiple contract) whose proposal receives the highest score. Here is where a bidder's past performance in UX may play a role in the selection of the contractor.

Different procurements may use different methods of evaluating proposals. The US government, for example, provides for a "best value" continuum with two endpoints: Tradeoff and Lowest Price Technically Acceptable (LPTA) (Defense Acquisition University, 2010; GSA, 2011c). If using the Tradeoff method, the purchaser may weigh quality against cost and choose the proposal that provides best value. According to GSA (2011c), this method "allows the Government to accept other than the lowest priced proposal. The perceived benefits of the higher priced proposal shall merit the additional cost, and the rationale for tradeoffs must be documented" according to the Federal Acquisition Regulation. If using LPTA, however, the purchaser must identify the proposals that meet or exceed the technical criteria and must select from those the one that offers the lowest price, and proposals "are not ranked using the non-cost/price factors" (GSA, 2011c). Some in the government procurement community have expressed concern that the LPTA method is finding its way into procurements where it might actually be counterproductive. According to Alan Chvotkin, writing in the *Washington Business*

[9] We write "an SOW" because the term "SOW" is most often pronounced by its three letters, not as the word "sow" (which means "female pig") and because the pronunciation of the name of the letter "s" (usually written "ess") begins with a vowel sound. So "an SOW" is pronounced "an s-o-w."

Journal (Chvotkin, 2011), LPTA "is undergoing a troubling expansion by being inappropriately applied to procurements for high-skilled, complex services and solutions." Chvotkin continues:

> *This trend is so concerning that a senior government official addressing the Professional Services Council's Annual Conference said he questions buying services with LPTA evaluation techniques, because government is generally not able to write requirements with the specificity needed to effectively use price as the sole or primary discriminator for purchases other than for commodities or routine services.*

In Finland, a representative member of the European Union, the overall basis for selecting a proposal is "most economically advantageous." The purchasing agency needs to turn this into concrete criteria: a combination of price, quality factors, product options, etc. The concrete criteria and their relative weights depend on the judgment of the agency, so they vary greatly between RFPs, even for similar kinds of systems.

The role of UX in the procurement

UX may take varying roles in RFPs, according to the type of contract. For a project contract — the most common type in many countries — the RFP can specify both the usability of the system and the selection criteria for the contractor. However, as case study 1 (below) shows, this is not easy. For either type of umbrella contract, however, the RFP cannot specify usability for a system because the system has not yet been identified, let alone defined. However, even in an umbrella contract, usability requirements can still appear in the agency's orders for individual projects. In fact, project orders can also include contractor tasks, and the competitive ones can even include selection criteria.

For the purposes of this chapter, a competitive project order is analogous to an RFP, and except as indicated otherwise, from here on out we will use "RFP" to refer to both documents.

Implications for usability and UX

In responding to an RFP, bidders naturally prepare their proposals to be as competitive as possible. In Europe, and under LPTA in the United States, contractor selection must be based on the predefined criteria. In the United States, under the Tradeoff method, the bidder may show how its proposal adds important value and better enables the proposed approach to satisfy the requirements.

Generally, bidders propose UX only to the extent that it has significance in the selection process:

- Usability requirements appear among the system requirements
- UX activities appear in the CTD
- UX factors appear in the selection criteria

If UX *does not* appear, bidders may well omit such considerations from their proposals — and understandably so. If the purchaser does not require usability, proposing usability activities could lead to a more expensive proposal and thereby make the bid less cost competitive.

If usability appears in the *requirements*, ideally the purchaser has written usability requirements so that their satisfaction means a truly usable system. Each one should be verifiable, valid, and comprehensive:

- *Verifiable*: A means exists for determining objectively whether the requirement is satisfied or not (so that there is no room for disagreement between purchaser and contractor).

- *Valid*: The content of the requirement is correct, so that its satisfaction has a positive effect on the usability of the system.
- *Comprehensive*: The requirement covers the system substantially enough.

If UX appears in the *CTDs*, the activities should be valid — well-established, user-centered methods and techniques that are known to aid in producing good UX. (Chapter 17, ISO Standards for User-Centered Design and the Specification of Usability, describes ISO standards for human-centered design [HCD] activities, an excellent basis for CTDs.)

Note, however, that relying on UX methods and techniques carries some risk: the use of design methods and evaluation techniques does not guarantee quality of the outcome, in the absence of defining the requirements for usability. The results of the Comparative Usability Evaluation (CUE) study (Molich & Dumas, 2008) show that even usability testing is not an adequately robust method, but its results depend on who conducts the test. Usability testing — even with multiple tests — does not by itself ensure good usability.

In addition, if UX appears in the *selection criteria*, those criteria should also be valid, so that more points mean the contractor is likely to deliver a better UX. Especially important is the past performance of a bidder in achieving good UX.

How purchasers approach usability today

The topic of usability in RFPs has not been much studied, and we would like to see more research undertaken. One of the few examples is a study of usability in 38 public software system RFPs that were issued in 2009 by government authorities in Finland (Lehtonen, Kumpulainen, Jokela, & Liukkonen, 2010) for project contracts (see Figure 16.1, above). Nine of the 38 RFPs made no attempt to include usability in the requirements in any way. In the 29 that did, the statements regarding usability fell into four main categories:

1. *Vague "requirements"*: Typical usability requirements or selection criteria were very vague, such as "The system shall be easy to use"; "The user's memory load shall be minimized"; "The software shall have a modern and user-friendly interface."
2. *Design requirements*: Some requirements addressed precise design features, such as "every screen shall have an exit."
3. *Process requirements*:[10] Another type of requirement covered some aspect of the development process — e.g., "The software must be usability tested. A certificate of the test shall be provided."
4. *Users' subjective assessment of demonstrations*: A typical scheme for including usability in selection criteria was that the representatives of the purchaser (who often included potential users) gave a subjective rating to the demonstrations presented by the prospective contractors.

None of these is a true usability requirement — verifiable, valid, and comprehensive:

1. Vague usability requirements are not objectively verifiable. How can anyone determine whether an implemented system avoids error situations or minimizes the user's memory load? Not real requirements, these statements can be regarded as wish lists, which contractors need

[10]In countries where RFPs include an SOW or a PWS, these activities would appear there. Finland generally does not place the CTD in a separate component of the RFP, and these statements appear as requirements for process.

not fulfill — because they *cannot*. However, they do indicate something that the purchaser wants, and bidders would be wise to take them under consideration. In a competitive setting, however, these "wants" are easily ignored because it is more important for the bidder to focus on the real requirements of the RFP.

2. The more precise design requirements are verifiable, but their coverage is very limited. Such general requirements cover usability only marginally: satisfying them does not ensure that the system will support users' tasks.
3. Process requirements of the sort "usability testing shall be conducted and a certificate [or report] provided" are verifiable: the existence of "a certificate" or "a report" can be established. Validity is the issue here: the contractor may satisfy these requirements without providing appropriate usability. As discussed earlier, the results of the CUE study show that the quality of results of methods and techniques — even a basic method such as usability testing — depends heavily on who performs the activity.
4. Having users give subjective ratings of demonstrations, especially without using the products demonstrated, also has a validity problem: this is not a recognized usability evaluation method, and user approval of a demonstration does not guarantee adequate usability of the delivered system. It may address some aspects of UX outside of usability, but it cannot assure usability.

In all, *none* of the RFPs analyzed in the Finnish study included usability requirements or selection criteria that were verifiable, valid, and comprehensive.

KEY CONSIDERATIONS

Getting usability into a project requires answering two main questions:

- *Who will carry the responsibility for achieving good UX?* Who will bear the cost of making changes (or the consequences of not making them) if the delivered system does not provide the desired UX?
- *Who will perform the UX activities?* Will the activities be allocated to the purchaser, to the contractor, or to a collaboration between the two?

These are two different questions, although they are somewhat related. We will look at each in turn.

Responsibility for achieving good UX

The purchaser has two options regarding the responsibility for achieving usability or UX in the system:

- Assign the responsibility for usability to the contractor
- Assume the responsibility for UX as the purchaser

To assign responsibility to the development contractor, the purchaser needs to take the necessary steps to ensure that the contractor will deliver adequate usability. The RFP or project order must include actual usability requirements, the satisfaction of which is verified through a summative usability test (see Chapter 17, ISO Standards for User-Centered Design and the Specification of Usability, and Chapter 20, Evaluation in Government Environments), to assess whether or not the system meets the usability requirements and the contractor has fulfilled its usability obligation to the project. To make the summative test rigorous, one can follow the guidelines of the "CIF" — the Common Industry Format for Usability Test Reports (ISO/IEC, 2006). The purchaser could include UX in the selection criteria for contractor past performance and use reputation databases in evaluating bidders.

If the purchaser assumes responsibility, the usability requirements can evolve as the design progresses — as more detail is known and interim evaluations are made (see Chapter 18, User-Centered Requirements Definition) — and "big UX" (the part above and beyond usability) can be more easily included. However, the purchaser needs to have (or hire) UX capabilities that are independent of the development contractor.

Sometimes the purchaser has insufficient up-front resources (time, budget, expertise) to define usability requirements as we have described. In this case, it is necessary for the purchaser to assume the responsibility for usability and UX, and to make ongoing tradeoffs to determine when they are "good enough."

Let us look at these two options in more detail.

Assign the responsibility for usability to the development contractor

Many attempts to define usability requirements in RFPs indicate that purchasers hope to place the responsibility for usability on the contractor. One would expect that purchasers might find this an attractive option, as it means that they would not need to bother with usability themselves, just turn it over to the contractor. If the system were to have usability problems, the obligation and costs of fixing the design would fall to the contractor. However, as mentioned above, this may occur very rarely if at all: the study in Finland found no RFP where usability would truly be the responsibility of the contractor.

Furthermore, this approach offers two main challenges. First, writing usability requirements so that the responsibility lies with the contractor is not easy: the usability requirements need to be verifiable, valid, and comprehensive. Defining these kinds of requirements is possible (see the first case study, below), but it is quite difficult, and more research is needed into tools and techniques to make it easier.

The second challenge — a cultural one — may be more profound. This approach would mean a different development culture from what seems to prevail today. Today, development contractors have their design solutions approved by the purchasers. This means, in practice, that at the moment when the purchaser approves the design solution, the responsibility for the solution — and its usability — is transferred to the purchaser.

Placing usability entirely into the hands of the development contractor, then, logically means that purchasers would approve, not designs, but systems that satisfy the usability requirements (whatever the design solution might be). Naturally, the contractor has to follow the standards, style guides, and other such items that the purchaser may have defined in the RFP. It may also be challenging to prepare a fixed-price proposal.

In summary, it is probably not a realistic approach to assign the responsibility for usability to the contractor. The reasons are threefold: there are methodological challenges to defining verifiable, valid, and comprehensive usability requirements; it is very much contrary to what seems to be the current development culture; and it may be difficult for bidders on competitive projects to estimate the required usability efforts in their proposals. And as we have noted, "big UX" can be very difficult to specify in a way that will allow objective verification.

Assume the responsibility for usability as the purchaser

This is the *de facto* setting of today in Finland. However, the many attempts to require usability in RFPs, as found by the aforementioned study (Lehtonen et al., 2010), indicate that many purchasers probably do not realize this.

If purchasers take the responsibility for UX, naturally they will need to carry out appropriate activities and have appropriate resources and skills (or hire another contractor to do it for them). In particular, purchasers need to conduct user needs analysis (including context of use definition), usability requirements definition, and usability evaluation.

Under this model, the design of the user interface would be the task of the development contractor because they would know the technical capabilities and limitations. The purchaser's task would be to guide the design work because they, in the end, have the responsibility for the quality of the design.

What does this approach mean for RFPs? Even if the responsibility for UX is on the purchaser, the designers should have good knowledge of usability and UX. Therefore, usability expertise of the interaction designers or past performance in achieving good UX is among the requirements that purchasers should consider specifying. One criterion that appeared in some RFPs in the Finnish study was project experience, but this does not necessarily relate to skills.

Allocation of UX activities

From a high-level project standpoint, UX activities fall into three main categories:

- *Define usability requirements and, if appropriate, UX goals.* Three scenarios are possible here:
  1. The purchaser defines usability requirements and UX goals without contractor input.
  2. The contractor recommends a set of requirements for the purchaser's consideration.
  3. The purchaser and the contractor collaborate on defining usability requirements and UX goals during the project.

  Ultimately, however, all usability requirements that drive the project must receive approval from the purchaser.
- *Design and develop system.* The contractor always does the development and usually does most if not all of the design. The level of independence at which the contractor proceeds with this work varies from project to project; oftentimes the purchaser guides design and/or approves design decisions.
- *Test system against usability requirements.* During design and development, the contractor should conduct interim tests or other usability evaluations to make sure the design is proceeding in the right direction. But the responsibility for the final testing can fall on either side: the contractor tests the system and delivers a report to the purchaser, or the contractor delivers the system and the purchaser conducts the usability test (or hires a different contractor to do it). This is a kind of acceptance testing.

These activities must occur regardless of who bears the responsibility for usability.

CASE STUDIES

Space and time make it impossible for us to include case studies for each of the possibilities. We provide two case studies to illustrate our experiences with different approaches. Both involved project contracts.

Case study 1: purchaser-defined usability requirements and assigned responsibility for usability to the development contractor

This case study (Jokela, 2010) had the goal of defining usability requirements to be included in the RFP for a health-care system. We took the following approach:

- *Verifiable requirements*: Define measures, measuring instruments, and target values.
- *Valid requirements*: Base usability requirements on user task performance.
- *Comprehensive requirements*: Identify user tasks systematically and define task objectives.

We found all of these to be challenging exercises.

Defining measures

We chose Nielsen's (2001) task success rate ("the percentage of tasks that users complete correctly") as the basis of our measure and modified it in two ways. First, we changed the measure itself to *task completion success rate*: "the percentage of users who complete [task] correctly." This change would enable the purchaser to identify specific tasks with which users have problems in using the system.

Second, we modified the "percentage." It is not possible to verify "90% of users must complete [task] correctly" — unless one tests with the entire user population, which is virtually never feasible. Testing with a sample population yields only a certain level of confidence regarding the minimum and maximum percentage of users who can complete a task correctly. So we redefined this measure to take a statistical form: *95% confidence that at least 75% of the target population will complete [task] correctly*. (For a good explanation of this topic, see Sauro, 2004.)

Measuring instrument: usability testing

The usability test approach defined items such as the selection criteria for test participants, the tasks that the participants were to do, and the criteria for task completion. It allowed the purchaser to choose "any set of user tasks, presuming that they represent the natural order of work flow of the test participant" (Jokela, 2010). It provided the development contractor the opportunity to comment on the test tasks, before the tests were carried out.

A task was defined as complete when both of the following conditions held:

- The user believes that he/she has achieved the correct outcome.
- The outcome of the task is actually correct.

Otherwise, the task was defined as not complete.

User tasks and target-completion levels

For comprehensive requirements, we needed to define "completion" for each task. This took 70 pages. We assigned each task a name, user group, and task objective. Using the target level as described above, if we tested with 10 users, all had to be successful.

Case study 2: the government specifies a usability process in the RFP and monitors the contractor's activities

One of us (Buie) has been a contractor on several US government projects whose CTD specified usability activities. This case study regards a project in which an agency issued an RFP for usability services to redesign an intranet web site. The SOW began:

[Client] requires contractor services to provide usability testing, standards development, information architecture and navigation design, and page wireframe (content placement) support for [Client] information on the Intranet.

[Client] wish[es] [the contractor] to employ methods that may include, but are not limited to, eye-tracking, card sorting, and focus groups for the design, development, and implementation of a standard information architecture frameworks and usability testing to improve the usefulness and organization of [Client]'s information on internal and external websites as they move from an organizational based content structure to a topical-based content structure.

The SOW went on to define a fairly detailed work breakdown structure beginning with kickoff and planning, proceeding to usability analysis, information architecture, navigation, and page template design, and ending with usability test of IA/navigation/template design. Our team's proposal followed the client's basic outline and also recommended some modifications to the proposed sequence of activities, based on the prime contractor's established process and noting that the RFP left some details of the activities open to the bidder to suggest. The proposal explained how our team's approach would best meet the client's needs.

The client's budget was not large enough to support defining usability requirements or conducting a summative test; their goal was to obtain substantially better usability and UX than their existing intranet gave them, and they had confidence that a well-established UX design consultancy who tailored its process to their project's needs would help them achieve that. The client also had enough understanding of UX to know that they needed to hire a specialist rather than attempting to do it in-house.

Our team met with the client numerous times during the months-long project. We collected information about their needs and their users, and we reviewed and discussed with them our plans for user-based activities (interviews, card sorting, and formative[11] usability testing), the results of our activities, and our interim designs for the information architecture and the page templates. At each step, we explained how our designs were based on the data we had collected, and we incorporated their feedback so that the new design would meet the needs of both the organization and the users.

In this project, the purchaser took responsibility for both usability and "big UX," and we worked together to understand their goals. Although our team would not develop the new intranet, the design was ours and so, effectively, was the UX. Iterative usability testing, conducted by an individual who had not created the design, gave the client confidence that our design was an improvement over their existing intranet.

SUCCESS FACTORS

Both purchasers and contractors have many opportunities to incorporate usability and good UX into their projects.

Purchaser success factors

If you are a purchaser of contractor services, you have many ways to bring UX into your projects:

- *Decide whether to assume the responsibility for usability or assign it to the contractor.* Even if the latter choice may seem attractive, be aware that it requires specifying verifiable, valid, comprehensive usability requirements and instituting project practices very different from

[11] A formative usability test aims to find usability problems during the design and development process, so that they can be fixed. For more information see Chapter 20, Evaluation in Government Environments.

the current development culture. Do not expect contractors to take responsibility for usability in fixed-priced projects unless you can do those things.

- *Be prepared to take the responsibility for usability.* This may mean hiring an outside usability consultant to help you prepare the RFP, guide the design, and monitor your development contractor's deliverables.
- *Give weight to contractors' UX expertise.* Define your selection criteria to include, if possible, UX successes among the contractor's past performance, and require capabilities such as usability engineering and interaction design among the skills and experience of the contractor's personnel.
- *Build your own UX competencies.* Prepare yourself to integrate UX into your RFPs and to work with your contractors to achieve good usability. Before preparing the RFP, conduct the necessary background work to understand and define the users' needs and goals. Allocate adequate resources to these activities.
- *Specify usability tasks in the project.* If your RFP or project order will include CTDs, integrate usability into them. Draw on ISO 9241-210:2010 (ISO, 2010) for HCD activities. Although HCD activities are not *sufficient* — they do not guarantee good usability without a specification of what that means for the system — they are *necessary*, in that usability cannot realistically be achieved without them.

Overall, consider including UX in the requirements, rather than in the selection criteria. A weak proposal in terms of UX selection criteria may win if it is strong in other selection criteria.

Contractor success factors

When the RFP specifically identifies UX as a factor in the procurement, it makes your job easier. What you must do is this:

- *Examine the usability content of the RFP.* If the RFP includes usability in the system requirements, the CTD, or the selection criteria, consider carefully what is required by the purchaser and what the selection criteria are. Allocate appropriate specialists and draw on established processes, such as those described in ISO 9241-210:2010 (ISO, 2010), to ensure that your proposal responds to the usability content in a way that has been shown to produce results.

Even when an RFP does not explicitly mention usability or UX, depending on your country you may have several ways of including it in your proposal:

- *Highlight previous successes.* In describing your company's related experience, describe the ways in which your previous UX activities enhanced the satisfaction of requirements on your projects. You will probably need to focus on nonfunctional requirements in this part.
- *Emphasize return on investment (ROI).* Also in the related experience section, emphasize ways in which your previous UX activities saved your government clients' money. Explain, for example, how they helped achieve operational efficiencies among staff, enabled and encouraged citizens to use online services more easily and thus decreased in-person visits to government offices, or reduced calls to the help desk for technical support. Bias and Mayhew (2005) give many examples of ROI for usability activities.
- *Include personnel with UX expertise.* If your proposal mentions specific personnel, include at least one person with UX expertise and list that among his or her capabilities. It is not necessary to present UX as that person's main focus on the project.

- *Take advantage of any flexibility.* To the extent that the RFP allows flexibility in defining your activities, seek to identify and apply ways in which UX can play a role in your proposal. If the RFP includes vague statements about "ease of use" or "user friendliness," describe how your technical approach will derive true usability requirements for those qualities.

In some countries, you may not be permitted to include UX in a proposal if the RFP does not mention it explicitly; or the page count allowed for your technical approach may not allow for describing additional activities beyond what are specified in the RFP. However, you may still find opportunities to include it in the project if you win:

- *Do as much UX during design and implementation as your resources allow.* Even if your client does not formally require usability, do as much as you can during the project. At least you will gain a better reputation, and you can cite these successes in future proposals.

In any case, you should be prepared for purchasers to issue RFPs that give you the responsibility for usability. This implies that you will need to commit to producing a system that is approved on the basis of how well it supports users' performance (as opposed to the purchaser approving your designs), and you will be required to modify the designs at your expense if they do not meet the criteria.

SUMMARY

Government systems continue to demonstrate poor usability and to provide the public and their own employees with a less-than-satisfying UX. This situation persists mainly because government agencies fail to specify usability in a way that ensures the production of adequately usable systems, or are not prepared to ensure usability and good UX by themselves. We have looked at how governments initiate system development projects and contracts, explored how they prepare RFPs, and proposed some approaches to solving the problem. To illustrate these concepts, we drew on our experience in Finland (as an example of a European country) and in the United States.

Constraints often preclude the purchaser from writing usability into the RFP in an ideal way, via usability requirements, CTDs, and selection criteria. These constraints may arise from lack of time, money, expertise, or organizational support. They can make it impossible for purchasers and bidders to give usability its proper place in the RFP and the proposal, respectively. Nonetheless, usability and UX are gaining recognition in the government systems environment, and the situation is improving. We encourage you to foster the trend. The purchasers are in the key position — if UX is truly required, the contractors will follow.

References

Bias, R., & Mayhew, D. (Eds.). (2005). *Cost-justifying usability: An update for the internet age.* (2nd ed.). Boston, MA: Morgan Kaufmann.

Chvotkin, A. (2011, November 2). When "low price technically acceptable" is unacceptable. *Washington Business Journal.* Retrieved 14 November 2011 from http://www.bizjournals.com/washington/blog/fedbiz_daily/2011/11/when-low-price-technically-acceptable-is.html

Defense Acquisition University. Proposal evaluation. (2010). Retrieved 4 March 2012 from https://acc.dau.mil/CommunityBrowser.aspx?id=341735

Eide, P. L. H. (2005). *Quantification and traceability of requirements.* Norwegian Institute of Science and Technology. Retrieved 29 October 2011 from http://www.idi.ntnu.no/grupper/su/fordypningsprosjekt-2005/eide-fordyp05.pdf

General Services Administration. Subpart 15.2 — Solicitation and receipt of proposals and information. (2011a). Retrieved 29 October 2011 from https://www.acquisition.gov/far/html/Subpart%2015_2.html

General Services Administration. Indefinite delivery, indefinite quantity (IDIQ) contracts. (2011b). Retrieved 30 October 2011 from http://www.gsa.gov/portal/content/103926

General Services Administration. Best Value Continnum. (2011c). Retrieved 4 March 2012 from https://www.acquisition.gov/far/current/html/Subpart%2015_1.html#wp1095853

ISO. (1998). *9241-210:2010 Ergonomics of human-system interaction — Part 11: Guidance on usability.*

ISO. (2010). *9241-210:2010 Ergonomics of human-system interaction — Part 210: Human-centred design for interactive systems.*

ISO/IEC. (2006). *25062:2006 Common industry format (CIF) for usability test reports.*

Jokela, T. (2010). Determining usability requirements into a call-for-tenders: A case study on the development of a healthcare system. In *Paper presented at the NordiCHI 2010 conference, Reykjavik.*

Lehtonen, T., Kumpulainen, J., Jokela, T., & Liukkonen, T. (2010). How much usability truly matters? A study on usability requirements in call-for-tenders of software systems, issued by public authorities. In *Paper presented at the NordiCHI 2010 conference, Reykjavik.*

Molich, R., & Dumas, J. (2008). Comparative usability evaluation (CUE-4). *Behaviour and Information Technology*, *27*(3), 263–281.

Nielsen, J. (2001). *Success rate: The simplest usability metric.* Retrieved 17 November 2011 from http://www.useit.com/alertbox/20010218.html

Public Works and Government Services Canada. Supply manual. (2011a). Retrieved 29 October 2011 from http://www.tpsgc-pwgsc.gc.ca/app-acq/ga-sm/index-eng.html

Public Works and Government Services Canada. Statement of work. (2011b). Retrieved 1 November 2011 from https://buyandsell.gc.ca/for -government/define-the-requirements/statement-of-work

Sauro, J. (2004). *Calculating sample size for task completion (discrete-binary method).* Retrieved 1 November 2011 from http://www.measuringusability.com/comp_sample.php

US Department of Defense. MIL-HDBK-245D: Handbook for preparation of statement of work. (1996). Retrieved 11 November 2011 from https://www.acquisition.gov/comp/seven_steps/library/DODhandbook.pdf

CHAPTER

ISO Standards for User-Centered Design and the Specification of Usability

17

Jonathan Earthy*, Brian Sherwood Jones†, Nigel Bevan‡

Lloyd's Register Group, London, UK. Process Contracting Ltd., Coylton, Scotland, UK.†, London, UK.‡*

"I'm not sure why standards get such short shrift. After all, they are a distillation of the best practice prepared by the peers of those who should be glad of their support."

— Danny Dresner (UK National Computing Centre)

INTRODUCTION

This chapter is about the standards for usable systems from the International Organization for Standardization (ISO). It explains how to conform to the ISO standards for user-centered design and the specification of usability. To emphasize the impact on stakeholders who might not typically be considered as users, ISO uses the term "human-centered" rather than "user-centered." To avoid misunderstanding when referring to or describing the content of the ISO standards, this chapter uses the term "human-centered design" (HCD).

If your job is related to the acquisition of systems, these standards are a convenient way to specify the way that you want suppliers to develop and test a usable system, and your own organization to support it. (See Chapter 16, Getting UX into the Contract, for more information on getting UX into the project.) If you are supplying a system, the standards can be used to justify the work you need to do to incorporate user-centered design, and to define and demonstrate the usability of the system. They also describe how to develop a usable system.

The chapter introduces the main standards related to the ISO-HCD process, then describes the application of this family of standards through examples of the application of ISO usability standards to government systems, and concludes with success factors for applying these standards.

INTERNATIONAL STANDARDS FOR USABILITY

International standards represent the agreement of the world's experts on a topic. Stewart (1991) explains that standards play an important role in improving the usability of systems:

- They offer the possibility of consistency, even at the international level.
- They provide a disciplined framework for human factors recommendations and make them accessible to nonspecialists.
- They represent consensus about good practice.

He goes on to explain that ISO has four aims for standards: mutual understanding; health, safety, and the protection of the environment; facilitating compatibility; and fitness for purpose. All of these contribute to usability. Standards allow acquirers to set appropriate procurement requirements and provide a basis for evaluation of suppliers' offerings. They allow suppliers to check their products during design and manufacture and provide a basis for making claims about the quality of products. They allow regulators to assess quality and provide a basis for testing of products.

The early standards for information technology (IT) ergonomics specified design features (such as character height on a display). Although this encourages consistency and achievement of basic ergonomic properties, it does not take account of the interactions that occur in use. The next generation of standards defined measures based on use, initially for physical devices (such as displays) and eventually for system usability — measured as a user's effectiveness, efficiency, and satisfaction in the performance of a task. The latest standards set requirements for the management, performance, and documentation of HCD.

For a subject that is relatively new — and that has a background of diverse, individual practice and several definitions for its core concepts — international standards represent a significant maturing of the discipline. They give a defensible framework for addressing usability in a project or contract (Earthy, Sherwood Jones, & Bevan, 2001). Used together, the standards related to usability provide a framework that can be used for developing (by good practice), specifying (by mandates), and ensuring (by conformance) usability in government system acquisition.

ISO 9241-11:1998 introduced a broad definition of usability, closely aligned with business objectives. The most recent definition of usability, in ISO 9241-210:2010, is "the extent to which a system, product, or service can be used by specified users to achieve specified goals with effectiveness, efficiency, and satisfaction in a specified context of use." The software quality model ISO/IEC 25010:2011 describes this as "quality in use," to distinguish it from narrower interpretations of usability as just the ease of use of an interface. The broader interpretation (sometimes referred to as "big usability") is the user's experience of the quality of the product, system, or service and thus a critical goal for systems design — i.e., the extent to which users can successfully achieve their goals in an acceptable amount of time, and are satisfied with the experience.

ISO requirements for ergonomics and user-centered design

ISO has recently published standards for ergonomics principles and HCD activities. These place requirements on the practice and process of user-centered design. They provide a context for the detailed recommendations and guidance in standards that address the application of ergonomics. This application framework and the setting of requirements are useful in the promotion of usability in the government sector.

ISO 26800:2011 brings together in one document the basic principles and concepts of ergonomics. ISO 9241-210 provides requirements and recommendations for HCD principles and activities throughout the lifecycle of interactive systems; it is for use by those responsible for planning and managing projects that develop interactive systems. It addresses technical human factors and ergonomics issues to the extent necessary to enable understanding of their relevance and importance in the design process as a whole.

The following lists (derived from Earthy & Sherwood Jones, 2010) summarize the collated requirements of these two standards. They characterize HCD and how it is achieved as a series of objectives. As you can see, these requirements do not constrain the methods used or the solutions provided: they delineate what HCD is and how to recognize that it is being done.

Fundamental principles of ergonomics and HCD:

- Ensure the project understands what the users want or need to achieve and the environment in which they work or live.
- Ensure the designers know who the users are and how the system should fit into their lives or their work.
- Make the demonstration of usability (in the broad sense of quality in use) the objective of the design team.
- Have a flexible team that can understand and address all aspects of the users' experience with the system.

Required project activities:

- Facilitate a focus on usability from the very beginning of the project.
- Help the users to develop a clear understanding of their actual requirements.
- Set targets for user interaction and performance with the system.
- Ensure that the team takes account of relevant ergonomics knowledge and the users' requirements.
- Ensure that quality in use is an early and continued target for the designers.
- Select and provide methods and tools suitable for doing HCD work on the project.
- Make sure HCD work is done and that the results are used.
- Make sure the findings from HCD work, and their impact, are communicated to all the right people.

Required organizational management activities:

- Include and integrate HCD into the overall project plan and all phases of the product lifecycle.
- Integrate milestones for human-centered activities into the overall design and development process.
- Allocate time for iteration and the incorporation of user feedback, and for evaluating whether the design solution satisfies the users' requirements.
- Involve workers or users (or potential workers or users) in the process.
- Identify the range of skills and viewpoints required in the team in addition to the staff, public, and other users.
- Define the responsibility for achieving each of the above objectives and allocate sufficient authority to fulfill these responsibilities.

The traditional (slow and expensive) defense system acquisition process produced a number of standards for Human Engineering Program Plans (HEPPs), which have also been used for non-defense government acquisition. These standards fall short of the above objectives for HCD and do not satisfy fully the needs of modern defense acquisition. With support from the US Army, the US National Academy of Sciences (NAS) has supported the development of the Incremental Risk Model (Pew & Mavor, 2007), which is of potentially wider application.

ISO process models

Early attempts to manage IT resulted in the definition of detailed and prescriptive development methodologies. These were found to be too constraining, and the Software Engineering Institute (SEI) at Carnegie-Mellon University applied the concepts of maturity and business process reengineering to the problem of identifying a lead indicator of IT project success (Paulk, Weber, Curtis, & Chrissis,

1993). This resulted in the Software Capability Maturity Model (CMM) and then the superseding Capability Maturity Model Integration (CMMI). Equivalent standards have been produced by ISO/IEC JTC1/SC7, including ISO/IEC 15504, which provides a framework for assessing an organization's capability in performing processes.

Processes are related collections of responsibilities described in terms of ongoing sets of activities, characterized by an outcome and an owner (James Moore, personal communication, June 26, 2003). A process has a purpose and fulfills a business requirement. Activities often include the creation of a work product.

Process models are structured collections of processes that describe an aspect of business from a defined perspective. A disciplined evaluation of an organization's processes against a model is called process assessment. Process assessment seeks to establish first whether or not processes are performed successfully and then the degree to which processes are under control.

Process modeling and assessment provide the following three benefits:

- A means to analyze the ability of an organization to implement good practice
- A description of the factors that hinder this ability
- The means of addressing such shortcomings and mitigating risk

The activities described in ISO 9241-210 have been formalized in two ISO-HCD process models: ISO TR 18529:2000 and, for larger or more complex projects, ISO TS 18152:2010. These are the repository of industry, academic, and government knowledge on how to achieve usability. As such, these process models provide a valuable means of achieving usable systems for government applications. These standards are cited as a means of assuring usability in the ISO/IEC 15288:2008 process model for systems, and the ISO/IEC 12207:2008 process model for software.

The processes to address HCD within a project or organization, and to fulfill the objectives listed above, fall into four categories:

- *Focusing the enterprise on usability*: Establishes and maintains awareness and sensitivity for risks arising from stakeholder and user needs across the organization, and keeps usability and user experience an inherent element in an organization's business strategy.
- *Enabling HCD across and within projects*: Ensures that HCD activities are resourced, conducted, and matched to the whole system lifecycle process and the enterprise.
- *Executing HCD within a project*: Carries out HCD activities as appropriate, to ensure that the system is safe, accessible, and usable.
- *Introducing and operating a system*: Identifies unsatisfied needs and unsatisfactory system attributes during introduction, support, and maintenance of the system, to meet stakeholder and user requirements continuously.

As shown in Table 17.1, the performance of these categories of process is the responsibility of particular organizational roles. Each category addresses certain types of risk and facilitates particular types of decision. International standards that are relevant to each category are listed. These standards are described at the end of this chapter.

User-centered design process issues for government projects

Figure 17.1 shows the simple process model in ISO 18529. This sets out seven HCD processes (referenced as HCD 1-7) for focusing, enabling, executing, and introducing and operating systems and services. (Large, complex projects require the use of the more sophisticated ISO TS 18152 model.)

Table 17.1 Responsibilities for Categories of HCD Process and the Relevant Standards

Process Category	Responsible	Type of Risks Addressed	Type of Decisions Made	Relevant Standards
Focusing the enterprise on usability	C-level executives Usability Management in terms of "facilitating usability across the organization"	Image/society Business survival Human-system issues in governance Human-system issues in services	Approach to policy Investment Strategy/ic Development	38500, 18152
Enabling HCD across and within projects	"The group that makes things happen (or not)" Program managers Project managers Product manager Usability managers Process owners Technical specialists with cross-project/ organizational responsibilities	Resource Functional Human-system issues in program Human-system issues in project Quality of product	Governance Program Lifecycle Standards Project Process improvement	15288, 20000, 25000, 9241-210, 18529, 18152, 25060, 25062, 26800, 9241-11, 9241-110
Executing HCD within a project	Usability professionals Practitioners	Technical Human-system issues in products	Technique and design Process implementation	26800, 9241-210, 18529, 62508, 9241-110, 9241-100 series
Introducing and operating the system	Service managers Support managers Usability professionals Practitioners	Operational Human-system issues in services Quality of service	Support Contextual Investment	20000, 6385, 18529, 18152

This section highlights the systems lifecycle issues for government projects for these processes, followed by illustrations from the introduction of e-government (e-Gov) in the United Kingdom, which remain equally relevant to current e-gov systems.

HCD 1 is a focusing process, whose purpose is to establish and maintain a focus on stakeholder and user issues in each part of the organization that deals with system markets, concept, development, and support. Citizen-centered Electronic Service Delivery (ESD) has been seen as essential to modernizing government. To make this effective, policy has to reflect the centrality of users and a user-centered approach:

> *The delivery of public services that are focused on the needs of customers and citizens is one of the central aims of the Scottish Executive's strategic vision for the modernization of government. Developing a customer/citizen focused approach to the delivery of public services is an integral element of key cross cutting initiatives such as Best Value, Community Planning, and 21st Century Government. It is also a central feature of a range of other initiatives in key policy areas such as health, education, housing, planning, and social justice.*
>
> **— Stevenson and Gibson (2002, p. 3).**

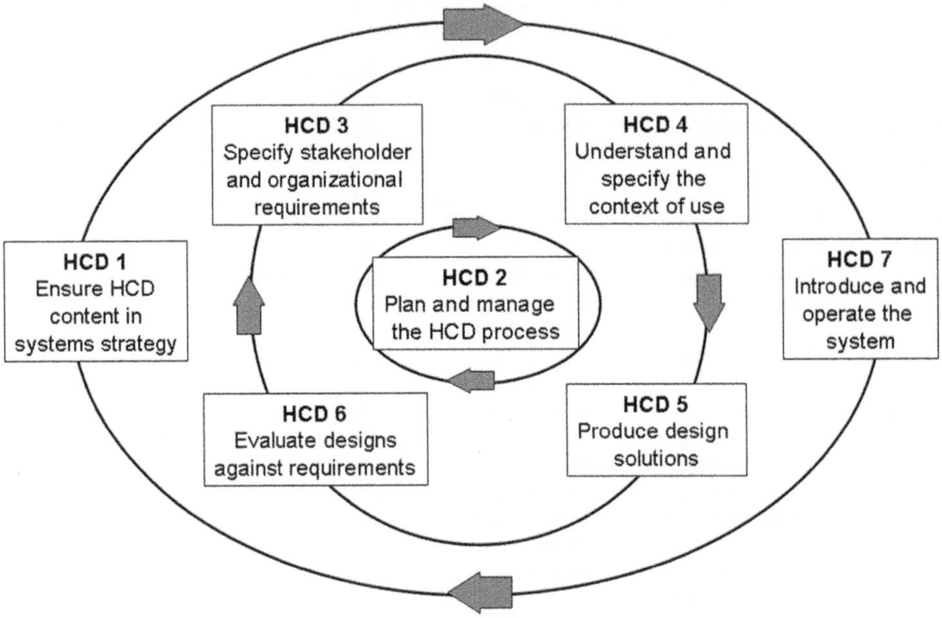

FIGURE 17.1 HCD processes in ISO 18529 and their linking

HCD 2 is the key enabling process, whose purpose is to specify how the human-centered activities fit into the whole system lifecycle process and the enterprise. In the context of citizen-facing government systems, planning the HCD process may be a demanding activity in itself. Maintaining the focus on the user through the development and implementation process can also be a demanding management task:

> *. . . initiatives that span multiple agencies require a disproportionate amount of political backing and funding. The result is that over 60% of e-government projects are doomed to failure.*
>
> **— Gartner Inc. (2002).**

HCD 3 is an executing process, whose purpose is to establish the requirements of the organization and other interested parties for the system. This process takes full account of the needs, competencies, and working environment of each relevant stakeholder in the system. User requirements form a vital link between policy aspiration and technical implementation. Usability metrics based on achieving requirements can form a central role in assessing the value of the system. Failure to establish user requirements can lead to the failure of systems to deliver usability:

> *". . . the public may see no advantage in accessing services electronically and take-up may be low. To overcome this departments need to set take-up targets and provide incentives such as cost savings to users" (UK National Audit Office, 2002, p. 4). Individual members of the public interact with and have an interest in the work of public service providers in a number of different capacities*

> *and "wearing a number of different hats" —as customers, citizens, and members of communities of place and interest. This is an important factor that needs to be taken into account in developing effective mechanisms for seeking feedback from and consulting with members of the public*
>
> **— Stevenson and Gibson (2002, p. 1).**

HCD 4 is an execution process, whose purpose is to identify, clarify, and record the context of use: the characteristics of the stakeholders, their tasks, and the organizational and physical environment in which the system will be used. This process complements a transactional view of the system functionality:

> *People have different needs. Departments, therefore, need to have a good understanding of the needs and preferences of the users of their services. The elderly for example, have a range of requirements depending on their income, health, general well-being, and where they live. Other groups such as students, children, parents, the unemployed, and businesses will have different requirements. There is, however, considerable variation in the quality of information which departments have on their key users and client groups for example on the frequency and ways in which citizens access government services.*
>
> **— UK National Audit Office (2002, p. 4).**

HCD 5 is an execution process, whose purpose is to create potential design solutions by drawing on established state-of-the-art practice, the experience and knowledge of the participants, and the results of the context-of-use analysis. The development of multiple design prototypes is a change from traditional requirements-driven procurement. The timing and management of this process is critical in relation to software development commitments:

> *This document therefore seeks to provide Government web managers with specific guidance around usability issues relevant to public sector websites and in particular awareness of issues that need to be addressed under the relevant human centered design standards*
>
> **— HMRC, UK Cabinet Office (2003, p. 2).**

HCD 6 is an execution process, whose purpose is to collect feedback on the developing design. This feedback will be collected from end users and other evaluation activities.

Evaluation may need to inform both design and policy. Metrics need to be at a task level, rather than a transaction level. Design reviews need to be against use scenarios rather than reviews of screens. The selection of users to target for surveys, etc., needs to reflect the system personas and their usage patterns.

> *Public sector organizations are less likely to analyze feedback from customers to monitor trends or identify potential service improvements than to respond to individual cases.*
>
> **— Stevenson and Gibson (2002, p. 1).**

HCD 7 is an introducing and operating process, whose purpose is to establish the human-system aspects of the support and implementation of the system. The rollout and deployment of a new government service may require new partnerships to work, the readiness of permanent and temporary support facilities, awareness material, in-service monitoring, and feedback resources, etc.

> *Perhaps the greatest challenge the government faces in delivering services electronically is in developing the organizational capability to do so.*
>
> **— Performance and Innovation Unit (2000, p. 69).**

Design guidance

The defense sector has developed a number of standards for product characteristics, such as MIL-STD-1472F (US Department of Defense, 1999). Since these are aimed at a military population, they are not appropriate for the design of public-facing government systems, but of course are required for defense systems.

There have been a number of attempts at writing guidelines for government web sites. An example of this is the US Department of Health and Human Services' (HHS's) "Research-Based Web Design and Usability Guidelines" (www.usability.gov) (HHS, 2011), which has a number of sections of design guidance

Such guidance has the challenge of being maintained in the face of rapid technological change, including the use of mobile technology and tablets. The guidance available is best seen as a resource for the development of project style guides. At the time of writing, sources of government guidelines for web sites are available from HHS (2011), Central Office of Information (2011), and Kranz (2011).

ISO 9241 provides extensive design support in the 9241-100 series of standards, including 9241-171:2008, guidance on software accessibility, and ISO 9241-151:2008 on web design. The design standards in the ISO 9241 series provide recommendations for ergonomic systems that can be customized to a particular context. The result of this customization is a binding and verifiable style guide for developers.

The scale of the challenge in maintaining any attempt at comprehensive guidance is evident. As a consequence of these difficulties, ISO has increased its emphasis on process, including the definition of an appropriate baseline for a project.

APPLICATION OF ISO USABILITY STANDARDS TO GOVERNMENT SYSTEMS

Applying ISO standards provides a credible, industrial-strength, internationally recognizable way of ensuring that usability is addressed in government projects. The easiest way to ensure that a standard is used is to have the contract require conformance to that standard. Each international standard contains a section that describes how conformance is to be demonstrated. The rest of this chapter explains how the ISO standards introduced above can be applied to government projects and what conformance to these standards gives you in terms of control over the usability of a system. The order of the sections is broadly the order in which decisions are made about how to address issues related to achieving a usable system.

HCD as a means of reducing risk in contracts

The contractual and commercial constraints on government systems are different from those in the private sector, and are subject to political influences. It is not appropriate for a government department to specify or adopt a proprietary method that is subject to intellectual property rights restrictions. An international standard provides a defensible framework for a project or contract. Insofar as "big" usability is indisputable as an objective for government public-facing systems, standards for HCD are default requirements for the development process.

Government IT failures are well publicized (e.g., the UK Rural Payments Agency, and National Health Service IT). Lack of user input at an early stage appears frequently. Adopting an HCD process can provide mitigation against major well-known risks.

The practicalities of system acquisition, particularly for large systems, are that contracts (at various levels of the supply chain) may be placed with less than total assurance of receiving a usable system. This may be because the user requirements have not been fully defined (or cascaded), or may be recognized as subject to change. The nature of the design solution(s) may still be unclear, either in the delivery medium (cellphone texts vs. computer web browser vs. call center, etc.) or in the arrangements for back-office functions. In such situations, assessing the HCD capability of candidate suppliers before contracts are placed is the most promising resource available to the customer organization.

Government systems have attempted to transfer risk to other parties, not always successfully. Risks to the usability of a service (possibly aggregated from different systems) are likely to remain with the government department. Subsidiary to this may be the risks associated with the usability of an online system that meets part of the government service obligation, perhaps held by an agency. A lower-level risk, such as ease of interaction on a display, may be held by a supplier. Clear assignment of risk ownership and hence conformance is necessary in all contractual arrangements. This means that, in addition to clear ownership of risk, arrangements for risk identification and mitigation across boundaries need to be in place. For example, usability trials should be holistic and their scope not be constrained by contractual boundaries.

Adoption of ISO 9241-210 as a standard for projects introduces a set of requirements to deliver usable systems through HCD. Inclusion and enforcement of a clause such as the following in contracts would require a supplier to produce evidence that projects' user-centered design needs are assessed, and internal and external project activity monitored against good practice benchmarks.

> *The contractor shall adopt iterative human-centered design in accordance with* ISO 9241-210:2010 Human-centred design for interactive systems. *The conformance procedure described in Clause 8 and Annex B of ISO 9241-210 standard shall be applied. The client reserves the right to conduct an assessment of the usability of the developing or finished service or system. The client reserves the right to conduct an assessment of potential contractors' capability to conduct user centered design.*
>
> *For the purposes of this contract,* ISO 9241-210 Clause 5, Planning human-centred design, *extends to an iterative program of evaluation and improvement for the human-centered design process. Process improvement shall be based on a validated assessment scheme such as that described in* ISO/IEC 15504-2:2003 Process assessment, ISO 9004:2009 Managing for the sustained success of an organization, *or the SEI CMM and may be integrated with process improvement based on models that conform with these schemes. Process assessment shall be based on* ISO TR 18529:2000 Human-centred lifecycle process descriptions. *The improvement program and its findings shall be reported to the client.*

Process improvement using capability assessment is described in the next section.

Conformance to the requirements and recommendation of 9241-210 is managed conveniently using Annex B of ISO 9241-210. Editable versions of the checklist are provided on the ISO TC Internet site

(ISO, 2010). This annex contains a checklist of all requirements and recommendations from the standard. This checklist is used to present three pieces of information:

- Evidence of which recommendation is applicable
- How compliance with requirements and applicable recommendations is going to be demonstrated
- Whether or not this has been achieved

The checklist is used to manage agreements on exactly how HCD is to be done on a project, with the understanding that you are following (or agreeing to not follow) the international standard approach to HCD. Alternatively, a supplier can unilaterally use a completed table as evidence that they have followed the internationally agreed approach to HCD.

Usability may be a key discriminator in international acquisition. Systems from suppliers in other nations may have been developed to meet similar legislation, provide similar software functions, and operate in a similar technical environment, but the context of use and user requirements may be very different. It may be possible to use usability test results to evaluate proposals for products or systems based on commercial, off-the-shelf (COTS) packages, but it may also be necessary to draw on resources such as early user-centered design activity by the acquiring department, or to assess the candidate suppliers. Where organizations from other nations are bidding to develop government systems, pre-contract award capability evaluation becomes a powerful form of risk mitigation. The existence of international standards enables such evaluation to be justified in a government system context. (For further details on usability evaluation in different countries, see Chapter 21, Adapting e-Gov Usability Evaluation to Cultural Contexts.)

Improving user-centered design processes

Many organizations lack the skills and processes needed to implement even the simplest user-centered design activities. Despite good intentions, the organization may be unable to produce products with acceptable usability. A traditional approach to improving usability has been to start by introducing usability testing at the end of the development process to highlight shortcomings in usability, in the hope that this will motivate the more important activities that are needed earlier in the lifecycle. However, this has the disadvantage that it is often too late to make any significant improvements, and these types of bottom-up initiatives are often conducted at the whim of the individual project manager. They are therefore not adequate as a basis for award of contract.

Lasting improvements can come only from a top-down policy for improvement of usability. ISO TR 18529 and ISO TS 18152 are comprehensive models of good practice in HCD. These provide the basis for the pre-contract assessment of the usability maturity/capability of an organization. Process assessment is essentially a series of guided, in-depth, structured interviews with relevant project stakeholders in an organization and a selection of representative projects. The results provide a profile of technical and managerial capability. This profile is analyzed to identify strengths and weaknesses. Demonstration of timely improvement in the areas of weakness is included in the conditions of contract. If necessary, regular third part audits can also be stipulated.

The cultural milieu for the development and operation of government systems differs from that around commercial systems. Pre-contract award capability evaluation can be used to counter political pressure to award contracts to suppliers without user-centered design capability. The issue of government department or agency capability is more sensitive but can be addressed using capability assessment.

The ISO standards for HCD are "quality manager friendly" and acknowledged best practice. Process improvement using standards derived from ISO/IEC 15504 is likely to be accepted in government system acquisition, and is compatible with overarching frameworks such as Control Objectives for Information and Related Technologies (COBIT) V (Information Systems Audit and Control Association, 2011). Less formal assessments may be of benefit to both government departments and their supply chain. Bevan, Bogomolni, & Ryan (2001) describe the use of process improvement internal to a government organization.

Because risks associated with usability are likely to be held by the government department or agency, a process capability evaluation is of value at all stages in the supply chain, not just external suppliers. Capability assessment should therefore include the HCD processes performed by the acquiring department and operating agency.

Managing user-centered design in large-scale systems

The ISO-HCD standards provide the resources necessary to plan and manage usability-related activities for large complex systems. Larger systems are disproportionately more difficult to manage. In terms of contracts, there is the added difficulty of passing usability requirements down supply chains. In terms of the definition of system requirements, problems can arise from conflicting service delivery goals between departments. At a working level, it is no longer possible for a UX team to keep informal track of what implementers are doing. The scale of use cases, user requirements, personas, etc. require formal management. Risk and issue management becomes formalized. Project planning and management reporting become more demanding and more important. The UX team's challenge is to retain the agility and economy of UX methods, while operating in a large project context. HCD process models, particularly the Human-Systems model in ISO TS 18152, have been developed to address these problems. Large system integration, undertaken using the Systems Engineering processes described in ISO/IEC 15288, offers particular benefits because the Human-Systems model has been designed to integrate with this standard.

The increase in management effort for large projects is illustrated by the differences between ISO TR 18529, with its one process for the planning and management of HCD, and the 13 lifecycle and integration processes in ISO TS 18152.

Several types of government systems have consequences of failure that are substantial. For such high integrity systems, the consideration of usability extends the existing approach to mechanical and logical dependability, as described in standards such as IEC 62508:2010. IEC 62508 categorizes the ISO TS 18152 activities by project stages and gives guidance on how they are applied to achieve whole system integrity.

Including usability in product specification

To ensure that a product meets user needs, the requirements specification should include all the aspects of quality that are important for that product to be successful. ISO/IEC 25010 provides a comprehensive checklist of quality characteristics. From a user-centered perspective, the most important characteristics are likely to be functional suitability, usability, and freedom from risk. It is essential that user and other stakeholder needs be identified (ISO/IEC DIS 25064:2011), taking account of the context of use (ISO/IEC DIS 25063:2011). These needs should be translated into a set of functional requirements that support the user needs, and into requirements for usability in terms of *effectiveness*, *efficiency*, and *satisfaction* in typical and critical contexts of use. ISO 9241-11 provides guidance on these measurements. The product should be designed so that it is usable in all the intended *contexts of use*: for all intended types of *users, tasks,* and *physical, technical, and organizational environments.* Those usability requirements that are essential for the success of the product should be given priority if there is any need to trade off these requirements against other requirements.

As mentioned above in the section on Design Guidance, the ISO 9241-100 series provides recommendations on interaction and interface design. Each standard includes an annexed checklist for use in assessing the relevance of each recommendation and demonstration of compliance to that recommendation. This checklist can be made part of a contract and used as the basis of both a style guide and the requirements for the product test program.

Validating usability

The only way to ensure that a product will meet user needs is to carry out usability testing in representative scenarios of use (ISO 9241-11). This type of testing is important to manage the risks to project success that could arise from poor usability. Usability testing should be a routine activity for any major system. Even for a smaller project, where usability testing cannot be justified, it is important to establish the usability requirements, as considering these during development can have a major influence on the design. ISO TR 16982:2002 provides guidance on methods for evaluation of usability. ISO/IEC 25062:2006 provides a means to report usability testing. Further details on validating usability can be found in Chapters 20, Evaluation in Government Environments, and 21, Adapting e-Gov Usability Evaluation to Cultural Contexts.

SUCCESS FACTORS

The ISO standards for HCD offer a range of benefits in the acquisition and supply of government systems. Here are some factors that can help you succeed in achieving these benefits:

- *Use the framework and status that the standards provide.* Proprietary methods are all very well and good, but you cannot stick them into a government contract. ISO provides an integrated set of standards with a common philosophy that avoids the risk of using specifications that are inflexible or incorrectly prescriptive. They provide a means of requiring and assessing conformance, and matching what is done to the capability of the client organization.
- *Integrate conformance to standards with contract and quality.* Conformance makes things happen. Ensuring that processes and products conform to standards may be the first time that usability people are useful to a project manager. Up until now, they have probably been seen as a cost and a risk. However, usability professionals do not normally encounter standards and

should watch and learn from those who do. In particular, understand conformance and how it integrates with contract and quality. For usability people unfamiliar with using standards to advantage, a good primer is Dresner (2003).

- *Use standards to provide a common language and concepts.* Internationally agreed terms, concepts, and principles remove arguments over terminology and the best way to do things. Of course they need to be interpreted for particular situations, but this is a valuable part of the planning process. Having a standard to argue from places user-centered design on a level playing field with other engineering disciplines, and can also be used to counter noncommercial barriers in government acquisition.
- *Use HCD standards to make the user viewpoint harder to ignore in design.* The activities and deliverables of HCD force the user viewpoint to be considered. Many governmental IT standards are compatible with the user viewpoint, but documents specific to usability (e.g., user requirements, style guides, usability evaluations) can be buried in the list of other requirements that receive greater emphasis.
- *Use standards for usability to make the user viewpoint harder to ignore in operation.* Big usability provides a policy-level counter to the point of view adopted by many service providers and adopted in standards such as BS8477 (British Standards Institution, 2007). The viewpoint provided by HCD also provides a counter to the transaction-level view of service delivery and associated metrics (e.g., five days to reply to a letter), giving formal expression to the user task and context of use (e.g., a battered wife and her children taken into a refuge).

SUMMARY

Standards have particular importance in the highly monitored world of government systems development, and there has been significant investment in this area. International standards for usability and HCD exist that are flexible enough to support appropriate user-centered design and measurable enough to allow conformance. Conformance to these standards gives usability and user-centered design status in systems development. These international standards can be used in contracts (both for specification and monitoring) and for the management of development and testing.

References

Bevan, N., Bogomolni, I., & Ryan, N. (2001). Incorporating usability into the development process at the Inland Revenue and Israel Aircraft Industries. In M. Hirose (Ed.), *Human-computer interaction—INTERACT'01* (pp. 862–868). Amsterdam, The Netherlands: IOS Press.

British Standards Institution. BS 8477: Customer satisfaction—Code of practice for customer service. (2007). http://shop.bsigroup.com/ProductDetail/?pid=000000000030137880

Central Office of Information. Web standards and guidelines. (2011). http://coi.gov.uk/guidance.php?page=188

Dresner, D. (2003). *Guidelines for IT managers—Desert island standards.* National Computer Centre Guideline 275, NCC, 2003. Retrieved 27 March 2012 from http://www.ictknowledgebase.org.uk/fileadmin/ICT/pdf/NCC/Desert_Island_Standards.pdf (Also the new version can be retrieved from http://wwwncc.co.uk/publications/management-guidelines/desert-island-standards-ii-pdf)

Earthy, J., & Sherwood Jones, B. (2010). Best practice for addressing human element issues in the shipping industry. In O. Turan, J. Bos, J. Stark & J. L. Colwell (Eds.), *Proceedings of the international conference on human performance at sea (HPAS) 2010 conference*, (pp. 523–534). Glasgow, UK University of Strathclyde.

Earthy, J., Sherwood Jones, B., & Bevan, N. (2001). The improvement of human-centred process—Acing the challenge and reaping the benefit of ISO 13407. *The International Journal of Human-Computer Studies, 55*, 553–585.

Gartner Inc. Majority of e-government initiatives fail or fall short of expectations. (2002). http://www.govtech.com/e-government/Gartner-Majority-of-E-Government-Initiatives-Fail.html

HMRC. Quality framework for the UK government website design. (2003). http://webarchive.nationalarchives.gov.uk/20081105160428/archive.cabinetoffice.gov.uk/e-government/resources/handbook/introduction.asp

Information Systems Audit and Control Association. COBIT 5: Process reference guide exposure draft. (2011). www.isaca.org

ISO. 9241-210:2010 Human-centred design for interactive systems, Annex B, Sample procedure for assessing applicability and conformance. (2010). http://isotc.iso.org/livelink/livelink?func=ll&objId=8265864

Kranz, P. (2011). *Standards schmandards—A practical approach to web accessibility.* http://www.standards-schmandards.com/projects/government-guidelines/

Paulk, M., Weber, C., Curtis, W., & Chrissis, M. (1993). *Capability maturity model for software, version 1.1, (CMU/SEI-93-TR-024 ESC-TR-93-177).* Carnegie Mellon University, Software Engineering Institute.

Performance and Innovation Unit. e.gov, Electronic government services for the 21st century. (2000). London, UK: Institute of Education, University of London. http://dera.ioe.ac.uk/9905/ Cabinet Office Performance and Innovation Unit

Pew, R., & Mavor, A. (Eds.), (2007). *Human-system integration in the system development process: A new look.* Washington, DC: National Academies Press *http://www.nap.edu/catalog/11893.html*

Stevenson, R., & Gibson, P. (2002). *Customer and citizen focused public service provision.* Edinburgh: The Stationery Office Scottish Executive Central Research Unit.

Stewart, T. (1991). *Directory of HCI standards, usability now!.* London, UK: British Library Document Supply Centre UK Department of Trade and Industry (DSC:4515.48026).

HHS. US Department of Health and Human Services. Research-based web design and usability guidelines. (2011). http://www.usability.gov/guidelines/

UK National Audit Office. (2002). *Better public services through e-government.* London: The Stationary Office Report by the Comptroller and Auditor General. HC 704-I, Session 2001-2002: 4 April 2002.

US Department of Defense. (1999). *Design criteria standard: Human engineering (MIL-STD-1472F).* Available from http://www.public.navy.mil/navsafecen/Documents/acquisition/MILSTD1472F.pdf

Further reading

The recommended further reading is ISO 9241-210:2010 *Human-centred design for interactive systems.*

Details of Standards

Tables 17.2–17.4 list the international ISO standards related to human-centered design. Table 17.5 describes the types of standard listed in the other three. ISO standards are available from your national standards body or directly from ISO at www.iso.org.

Table 17.2 Standards That Define HCD

Title	Type of Standard	Description
ISO 9241-210:2010 *Human-centred design for interactive systems*	Fundamental & Management system	Guidance and requirements for management of HCD projects. Requirements and recommendations for HCD activities. It is a revision of ISO 13407:1999, ISO's initial definition of HCD.
ISO TR 18529:2000 *Human-centred lifecycle process descriptions*	Assessment model	15504-compliant set of processes for HCD of interactive systems. Processes for enabling, executing, and assessing HCD within organizations. This model will be developed as ISO 9241-220 *Processes for enabling, executing, and assessing HCD within organizations*.
ISO TS 18152:2010 *A specification for the process assessment of human-system issues*	Assessment model	A set of 15504-compliant processes that address issues associated with humans throughout the lifecycle. This specification provides a bridge between standardization in the area of Ergonomics (by ISO TC159) and the lifecycle standardization being carried out by ISO/IEC JTC1/SC7 *Systems and software engineering*.
ISO/IEC 25060:2010 *General framework for usability-related information*, ISO/IEC 25062:2006 *Common Industry Format (CIF) for usability reports*, ISO/IEC DIS 25063:2011 *Common Industry Format (CIF) for usability: Context of use description*, ISO/IEC DIS 25064:2011 *Common Industry Format (CIF) for usability: User needs report*	Information/ work product	A developing family of information product descriptions related to HCD processes. These standards describe how to define and report information related to usability.

Table 17.3 Standards Related to the Design of Usable Systems

Title	Type of Standard	Description
ISO 26800:2011 *General approach, principles, and concepts*	Fundamental	Description of the ergonomics viewpoint and specific perspectives within ergonomics. Requirements for ergonomics design process.
IEC 62508:2010 *Guidance on human aspects of dependability*	Detailed/view	Elaboration of HCD for safety-related systems.

Continued

Table 17.3 Standards Related to the Design of Usable Systems—cont'd

Title	Type of Standard	Description
ISO 9241-11:1998 *Guidance on usability*	Guide	Guidance on defining and measuring usability and defining context of use.
ISO 9241-110:2006 *Dialogue principles*	Design standard	Principles for the design of user interfaces.
ISO 9241-100 *Software ergonomics* (series)	Design standard	Recommendations for the design of software user interfaces.
ISO 16982:2002 *Usability methods supporting human-centred design*	Guide	An overview of existing usability methods that can be used on their own or in combination to support design and evaluation.

Table 17.4 IT Process Standards That Set a Framework for HCD and Usability

Title	Type of Standard	Description
ISO/IEC 38500:2008 *Corporate governance of information technology*	Fundamental	Principles for executive/top management-level staff on the effective, efficient, and acceptable use of IT within their organizations.
ISO/IEC 15288:2008 *System lifecycle processes*	Process model	Defines a set of processes and associated terminology for the full lifecycle, including conception, development, production, utilization, support, and retirement. This standard also supports the definition, control, assessment, and improvement of these processes.
ISO/IEC 25000 *Software product Quality Requirements and Evaluation* (SQuaRE series)	Fundamental & management system	A family of standards defining aspects of quality and measurement for software intensive systems.
ISO/IEC 15504 *Process assessment* (series)	Guide/ assessment model	A family of standards that describe how to perform process assessments, set requirements for conformance assessment and provide exemplar assessment models derived from ISO/IEC process reference models, including 15288.

Table 17.5 Types of Standards

Type	Instructions
Fundamentals	Set requirements on or recommendations for the scope, definition, and implementation of processes. This includes principles, approaches, frameworks, vocabulary, conformance, formats, etc. Concepts and terminology are often included.
Information/work products	Specify the outputs from a process both in terms of a generic classification scheme products and a catalog of descriptions of the content of particular instances of products.
(Process) assessment models	Elaborate process reference models for the purpose of assessing process capability. The elaborations usually consist of capability levels (steps toward a particular aspect of organizational achievement) and assessment indicators (work products, practices/tasks).
Detailed process descriptions	Elaborate one or more processes for the purpose of implementation. This typically includes setting in a range of contexts, further description of the outcomes, responsibilities, methods, and techniques for implementing tasks, content, and format of documents produced.
Guides	Provide advice on application, implementation, improvement, etc.
Management systems	Define a context and business purpose for process implementation and/or assessment and specific requirements on a range of procedure, lifecycle, competence, policy, method, and documentation matters for the implementation of activities or tasks. They usually set the requirements for a certification scheme.
Process views	Present lifecycle activities from a particular stakeholder perspective. This usually entails defining attribute or profession-specific purposes and outcomes and comments contextualizing the intent of activities and tasks.
Design standards	Contain sets of recommendations on some aspect of the properties, performance, or features of an artifact or interface. As well as providing the basis for a design, they often specify how tests are to be carried out.

CHAPTER

User-Centered Requirements Definition

18

Alistair Sutcliffe*, Jan Gulliksen†

Manchester, UK. KTH – Royal Institute of Technology, Stockholm, Sweden.†*

"Every truth passes through three stages before it is recognized. In the first, it is ridiculed, in the second it is opposed, in the third it is regarded as self-evident."

— Arthur Schopenhauer

INTRODUCTION

The process of requirements analysis and specification is one of the most critical parts of any system development. Getting requirements wrong leads to cost overruns and, in the worst cases, abandoned systems and wasted public funds. For many workers in public authorities, abandoning the system is not an option, so the consequences can be frustration, stress, and eventually work environment problems. Unfortunately, government systems have experienced many failures that can be traced to poor requirements analysis; for example, the London Ambulance Service system has become the canonical case study of how not to do requirements analysis. Similarly, in Sweden, the development of a software support system for national patient records for the healthcare sector has an equally bad reputation. There are many other examples from all over the world of government systems that do not meet their expectations or fulfill the goals of their users, with causes that in many cases can be attributed to a poorly functioning requirements specification process.

Although poor methods and practice can carry the blame for many failures, the public sector is not alone in experiencing system disasters, as the financial sector discovered when implementing a new trading system in the London Stock Exchange. So why do government systems experience such problems? Complexity is one factor that makes requirements analysis difficult. Many government systems exist to implement legislation and manage transactions with the public, such as payment of taxes, provision of social benefits, registration for driving licenses, passport applications, and so on. In spite of politicians' endeavors to create simple rules, during the lifetime of most government systems more and more exceptions and special cases arise, and new rules are devised to deal with them. Engineering and control applications, common in the defense sector, are naturally complex, given their increasing scale of automation, integration, and capability. Complexity inevitably increases as users' ambitions drive product capability and system sophistication.

As governments attempt to reduce the costs of public administration, developers of public-facing, government-to-people (G2P) systems have to deal with further problems. The system is complex, yet the users' capacity to deal with all the details of government legislation is limited; hence the requirements analyst has to simplify the complexity by filtering essential requirements to make the system digestible by the general public. Further demands arise from the need to make user interfaces not only easy to operate but also interesting and attractive. Unless public systems engage users, take-up will be limited, and this becomes critical in public-facing systems where use is discretionary, such as e-health campaigns to raise awareness of lifestyle issues, obesity, smoking, and alcohol abuse.

One problem that many e-government (e-Gov) projects face is an inadequate understanding by users and managers of the time and resources required to build well-functioning computerized systems to support their work. Governments often introduce new legislation and want rapid development of new procedures to support change, without taking into consideration the time needed to build effective computer support. At the same time, the organization that commissions the computer system development will have received competitive bids for the work, and needs to cut costs and development times in the contract negotiations. As a result, development projects are often over-optimistic and important requirements may be neglected in favor of a financially appealing project.

This chapter reviews requirements analysis and definition methods and techniques that can be applied to improve the usability, engagement, and acceptability of government systems, and illustrates the process with case studies of requirements analysis in e-Gov practice.

KEY CONSIDERATIONS

This section introduces requirements definition (also called "Requirements Engineering" in the literature) and explains the key activities.

Requirements Engineering activities and process

Requirements engineering (RE) is, as its name suggests, the engineering discipline of establishing user requirements and specifying software systems. There are many definitions of the term; however, they all share the idea that requirements definition involves finding out what people want from a computer system and understanding what their needs mean in terms of design. It is closely related to software engineering (SE), which focuses more on the process of designing and developing the system that users want. Perhaps the most concise summary comes from Boehm (1981), who believes that requirements are designing the right thing, as opposed to SE's designing the thing right. Nuseibeh and Easterbrook (2000) give a more comprehensive definition of software systems RE as the process of discovering the purpose, by identifying stakeholders and their needs and documenting these in a form amenable to analysis, communication, and implementation.

RE is closely related to user-centered design (UCD), where user requirements are seen as part of the process of a design exploration, prototyping, and evaluation with the user, rather than as the more linear "specify-design-implement" process favored in the SE community, although these differences have become less marked with the growth in Agile development methods (Beck, 1999) that advocate involving users with an approach based on scenarios (as stories).

Process map of requirements engineering

RE follows different routes and mixes of activities, depending on the needs of the project. For instance, requirements might start as problems with a current system, or as examples of products that users want. RE to select commercial off-the-shelf (COTS) products will be dealt with only briefly (see Maiden & Ncube, 1998, for COTS-based RE), and we will focus on the most common, goal-oriented pathway. Requirements are initiated by senior managers and company executives as policies, aims, objectives, and other high-level statements of intent. This route, illustrated in Figure 18.1, necessitates considerable scoping activity, as requirements start with vaguely expressed intentions and users' wish lists. The process borrows from business analysis, such as *Set policy objectives* (1) and *Analyze and model business* (2). Policy can be analyzed within the business context by means of enterprise models. Requirements analysis may use techniques from business modeling, such as value-chain analysis (Porter, 1980), concept maps (Eden, 1988), and critical success factors (Rockart & Short, 1991).

Top-down decomposition is the normal approach whereby policy-level intentions are successively decomposed into goals. The requirements team combines objectives from management with facts, information, and goals from users gathered in the *Elicit requirements* step (3) via interviews, focus groups, workshops, etc. These form the inputs for *Analyze requirements* (4), in which preliminary information, usually in the form of lists and notes, is organized as connections between facts. For example, relationships are added progressively as objectives are understood, in terms of what has to be done to achieve them (goals) and the implications for people (actors) and their organizations (organization unit, objects, etc.). Analyze requirements is interleaved with *Model requirements and domain* (5) as analysis produces models that document facts and their associations. For example, modeling goals in the context of their impact on tasks and the organization is vital not only to the elaboration of the meaning of informal statements of intent but also to assessment of the impact of change. Modeling is

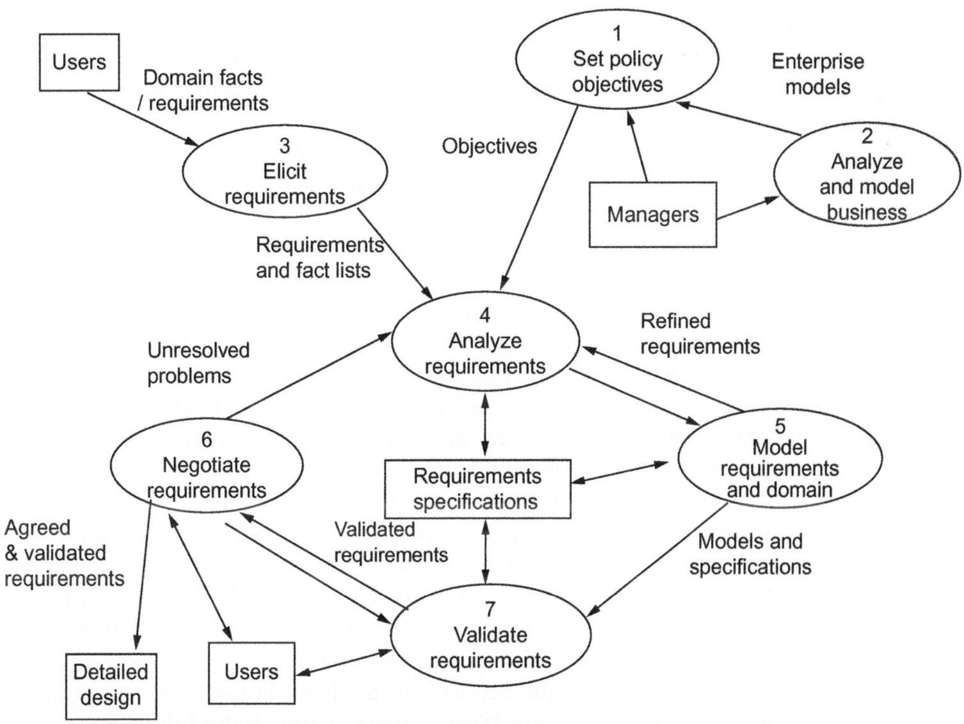

FIGURE 18.1 Process pathway map for requirements analysis

an essential precursor for the *Validate requirements stage* (6), as goals cannot be easily understood without contextual detail about how they may be achieved and their relationship to people and processes. (For more information on the use of modeling, see Chapter 19, Models as Representations for Supporting the Development of e-Procedures.) This stage is usually interleaved with *Negotiate requirements* (7), as discussion among stakeholders and designers leads to requirements being agreed on or rejected, and conflicts between stakeholders resolved. Stages 4-7 in the process form an iterative loop, as requirements are rarely specified correctly the first time; instead, requirements emerge through iterations of analysis, modeling, validation, and negotiation. Once goals have been decomposed to the stage where the desired state of the system can be described, at least informally, the first-cut decisions on the use of technology can be made (see Chapter 19, Models as Representations for Supporting the Development of e-Procedures). Some goals become functional requirements, while others have implications for management alone (e.g., decisions about resources, organization, and human activity). Each stage is explained in more depth in the following sections.

Scoping

Requirements frequently start with a vague statement of intent. The first problem is to establish the boundary of investigation and, inter alia, the scope of the intended system. Unfortunately, this is rarely an easy process, as clients are often uncertain of exactly what they want, and knowledge about the intended system is vague. This stage may be initiated by a *Terms of Reference* document (or a *Request for Proposals*) for externally sourced projects (see Chapter 16, Getting UX into the Contract) — a written document describing the background and aims of the system. Terms of reference, however, are frequently imprecise, and the first part of the investigation is to define the scope of the intended system. *Scoping* tends to be an iterative activity; boundaries become clearer as the understanding of the domain becomes increasingly shared by all the stakeholders. Workshops in the KJ brainstorming method (named after its inventor, Jiro Kawakita) and in Rapid Application Development (DSDM Consortium, 1995) advocate the use of lists and informal maps of the problem space. Writing down the scope tends to focus users' attention on where the boundaries of the system investigation should lie, and helps to identify at least an initial scope for the system.

Take, for example, a system to help epidemiologists with their research, which was the brief for the ADVISES project (Sutcliffe, Thew, & Jarvis, 2011; Thew et al., 2009). The range of possible decision-support tools could include data collection, data preparation, statistical analysis, visualizations, graphs, and maps, as well as group-working support for collaborative discussion of results. The system's owner and scope were not clear since the project was initiated as part of the UK government-supported e-Science research program, with users who were academic researchers in epidemiology and who also collaborated with public-health analysts from local hospitals. Scoping proved to be a long-term process, as collecting all the stakeholders in one workshop and then getting them to come to agreement required time to develop a common understanding. The process was helped by creating informal maps of the systems and interested parties, as illustrated in Figure 18.2.

The organizations involved appear in rectangles as secondary stakeholders — people who have an interest in the system output but are not the primary hands-on users (who are shown in circles). Primary stakeholders — the end users — were public-health analysts in Primary Care Trusts (PCTs are local units of organization in the UK National Health Service) and academic health informatics researchers, who collectively formed the NIHBI unit (North-West Institute of Bio-Health Informatics).

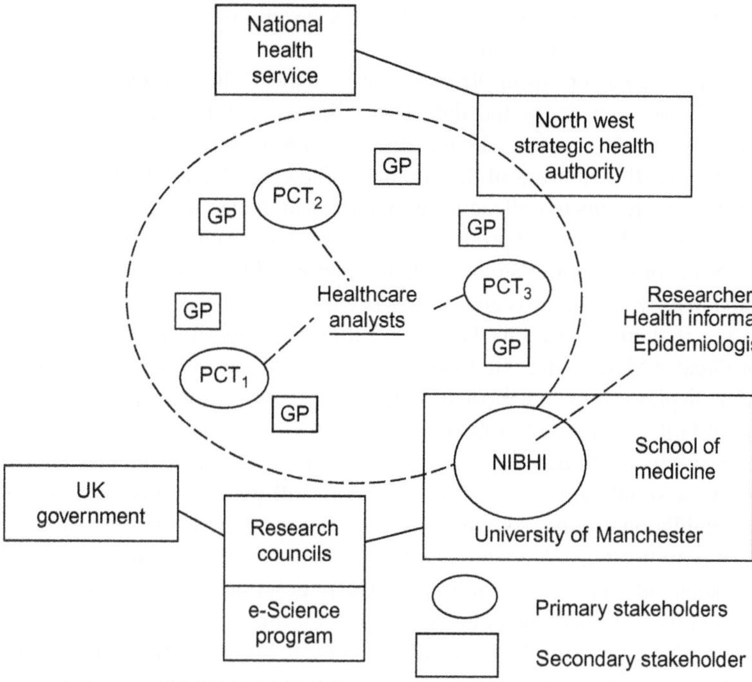

FIGURE 18.2 Informal map of the ADVISES project

Analysis and modeling

Analysis and modeling generally follow top-down approaches, concentrating on goal decomposition. *Analysis* is often driven by five "W" questions: What is the system's purpose (goals)? What objects are involved? Where is the system located? When should things happen? and Why is the system necessary (goals or problems it intends to solve)? One approach to goal analysis uses scenarios to discover obstacles or potential problems, with questions: "What might prevent this goal from being achieved?" or "What could go wrong in this situation/scenario?" These obstacles enable the elaboration of goals for maintaining, avoiding, and repairing situations.

Modeling consumes the output from analysis, structures the facts, and represents them with lists and diagrams, usually borrowed from structured system development methods such as Unified Modeling Language (UML) and the Rational Unified Process (RUP): use cases, data-flow diagrams, and entity-relationship or class diagrams. Analysis and modeling are frequently interleaved to elaborate the requirements as the understanding of the problem domain increases through the act of representation.

Scenarios have several roles in analysis and modeling, from a "cognitive prosthesis" stimulating the designer's imagination to narratives of system use and problems from which requirements emerge. Scenarios can be related to *personas* that amplify narrative experiences by illustrating typical users. Personas complement scenarios by providing a "character sketch" of one or more typical users, describing their background, personality, lifestyle aims, interests, etc., to the extent that those attributes are relevant to their use of the system.

To illustrate with some examples from the ADVISES system, the initial *vision scenario* describes how medical researchers might work in the future:

Epidemiologists view data sets from different parts of the United Kingdom, displayed on maps and different charts. They can query the data using limited natural language commands and by manipulating simple controls such as sliders, and can immediately see the results of different analyses on their data in different areas of the country. When they have found interesting results they can add notes and send the results to colleagues in other research teams. Vision scenarios set the scene for the development project before any prototype exists, so that they focus on the intended outcomes.

Usage scenarios, in contrast, paint a more detailed picture of how the system will operate, and are frequently accompanied by storyboards and prototypes to illustrate the design:

Iain wants to see if there is any link between asthma and obesity in young school children in different areas of Greater Manchester. He loads data sets for the incidence of asthma and obesity in different areas. Map displays show that most areas have little association, apart from two local districts where high levels of both obesity and asthma are shown by color coding in the map. He checks that this is an accurate result by applying an area density correction statistic and then running a correlation analysis. This shows a significant result. However, diet and poor exercise are known to be more common causes of childhood obesity, so Iain loads the location of sports facilities on the map and finds that both asthma-obesity hotspots also have few sports facilities. His investigation continues.

Later in the development cycle, *context and use scenarios* describe system use but with expectations of how the system output may be used, including test probes for use in validation and evaluation sessions:

Jane is a public-health analyst for the Greater Heaton PCT. She is interested in looking at obesity in primary school year 6 (equivalent to US 6th grade) children (age 11) in her area. She makes a new map based on the Middle Layer Super Output Areas, and using a first data set. She loads the younger children data sets and inspects the map display, using sliders to change the view of results by age, gender, and other variables provided. She identifies any general patterns from the maps for males only, females only, and both together.

Scenarios are used in conjunction with models to specify the system goals and agents, leading to more detailed understanding about how the system should operate. See Figure 18.3 and Table 18.1.

Validation

Validation involves getting users to understand the implications of a requirements specification and then agree — i.e., validate — that it accurately reflects their wishes. Walkthrough techniques are a useful approach in which specifications such as data-flow diagrams are critiqued in a workshop of designers and users. The designers explain how the system should operate by describing the process shown on a data-flow diagram. Walkthroughs using diagram specifications are quick and cheap; unfortunately, people often fail to understand even simple diagrams. In contrast, realistic representations such as mock-ups or prototypes are more powerful since users react more strongly to detail and a partially working system. Scenario-based representations using videos, storyboard sketches of screen sequences, or animated simulations also help users see the implications of system behavior and thereby improve validation.

In ADVISES, requirements validation was an iterative process of showing users different designs, initially as storyboards, and later as mock-ups and prototypes,[1] as illustrated in Figure 18.4. This

[1]A video demonstration of the prototype can be found at http://www.youtube.com/watch?v=8EfSM9KG3Dg

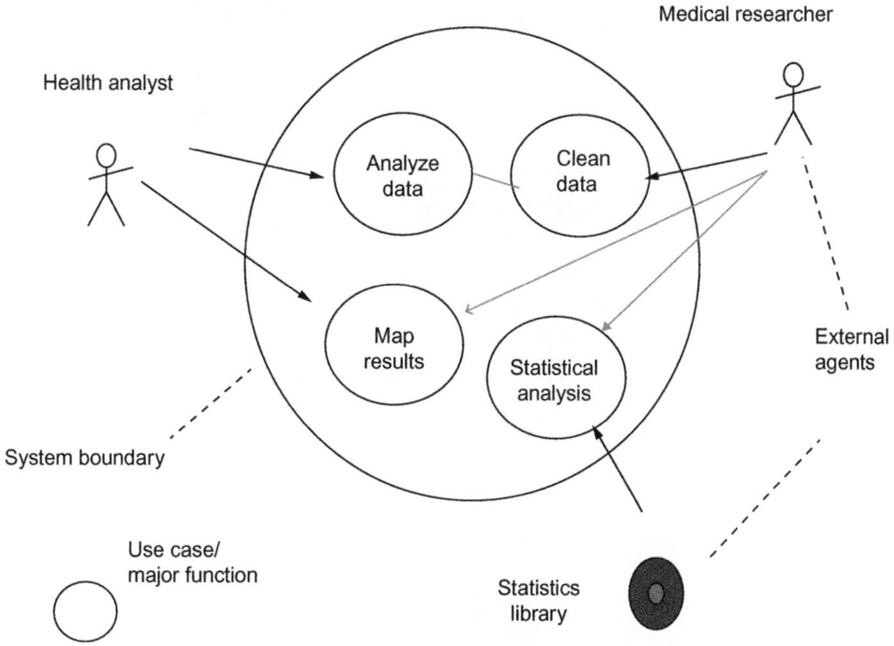

FIGURE 18.3 Use-case context diagram

(For color version of this figure, see the Web version of this chapter.)

Table 18.1 Lower-Level Use Case Specified in an Action Sequence Template

Use-Case Number	EM3
Name	Viewing the name of a map region
Description	Basic theme map has been created
Primary actor	Epidemiologist
Pre-condition	User has successfully created a theme map, divided into geographic regions
Trigger	Map has been created, user is ready to explore map
Basic flow	Selection of a region, viewing of name
Alternate flows	Error handling — name cannot be displayed for the selected region

facilitated discussion with users about exactly what they wanted, and also helped the requirements team learn more about the users' work. Presenting people with designs rarely fails to elicit useful feedback, and this approach is central to user-centered design.

Figure 18.4 shows two configurations of the ADVISES paper prototype designed to support exploration of epidemiological data. The upper one shows a map of a fictitious city, split up according to organizational boundaries. The lower one shows the same map, but now split into smaller sub-areas accompanied by a histogram-like plot for those areas. Acetate transparencies were used as overlays

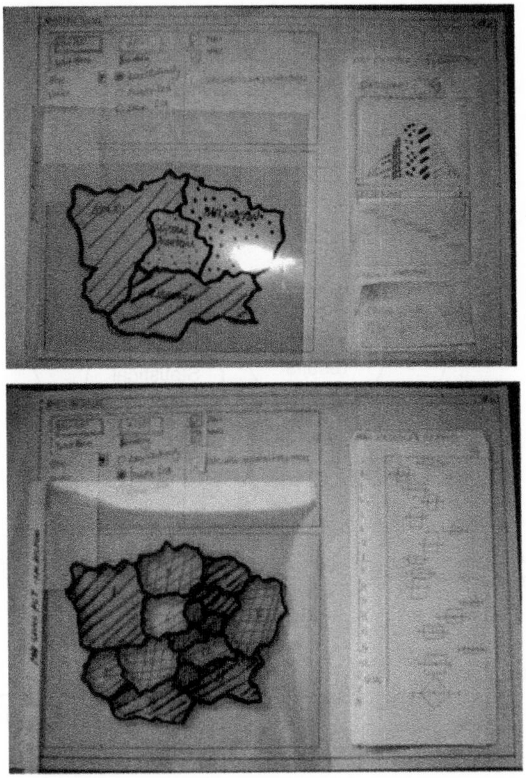

FIGURE 18.4 Illustration of the ADVISES storyboards used in validation sessions with users

(For color version of this figure, see the Web version of this chapter.)

so different options could be presented in an interactive sequence, while Post-it® notes were used to record ideas and feedback suggestions during validation sessions. Users were encouraged to draw on the paper prototypes to illustrate their own design ideas. Design exploration using these techniques helps the requirements process in three ways:

- Designs can show users different possible solutions, which then clarify the requirements in users' minds: the "I'll know what I want when I get it" approach.
- Design exploration engages users in a dialog as they participate in the process of specifying requirements and designs.
- Engaging in the process encourages a sense of ownership of the requirements, as users are more committed to solutions they have chosen.

In complex government systems, such as air-traffic control, integrated battlefield systems in defense, or tax collection and administration, both approaches — requirements specification that concentrates on modeling and documentation, and design exploration using scenarios and prototypes — have their merits. Requirements specification will be necessary to handle the complexity in large-scale systems, while UCD is more suited to elaborating requirements where user needs are unclear.

Negotiation and tradeoff analysis

Requirements are often held by different stakeholders, who may have conflicting views; hence, *tradeoff analysis* is an essential activity for comparing, prioritizing, and deciding among different requirements or design options. Ranked lists or matrix-based techniques using decision tables can help in this type of analysis. Table 18.2 shows an example of tradeoff analysis in ADVISES. Two sets of requirements were gathered, one from the academic researchers, and the other from the public-health analysts. The table shows the relationship between the requirements and different quality criteria, such as accuracy, privacy, and usability.

A check mark ("✓") shows the prioritization of the goals for each group of stakeholders, a minus sign ("−") shows a neutral view, and a double minus sign ("−−") shows disapproval or a goal conflict. A plus sign ("+") implies positive associations between goals and quality criteria with more plus signs indicating a stronger association; no entry shows the default "no association."

Decision tables, decision trees, and flowcharts are other representations that can facilitate negotiation and tradeoff analysis by making the space of options clear, and help stakeholders to see their priorities from the perspective of others.

The negotiation issues in ADVISES are illustrated in Table 18.2. Clearly the two groups of stakeholders have different priorities, with only a few goals in common such as (data errors, maps, and simple statistics). If stakeholder goals do not conflict, then all goals might be included in the design, although this can increase complexity. However, when goals conflict, as was the case in the "prevent analysis errors" goal, negotiation has to reconcile the conflicting views. Health analysts perceived this goal as a slight to their professional integrity; however, when the positive effects of this requirement on improving the accuracy of results were explained, they accepted it.

Representing alternative ideas for negotiation can be helped by Design Rationale diagrams that present alternative design solutions for discussion. In requirements analysis, the gIBIS (Conklin & Begeman, 1988) notation has been adopted to represent user goals as issues, mapped to design alternatives (requirements) with arguments; see Figure 18.5.

Table 18.2 The Dependencies Between Requirements Goals and Quality Criteria for Two Stakeholder Views in ADVISES

	Stakeholder Prioritization		Quality Criteria Association		
Goals	**Medical Researchers**	**Health Analysts**	**Accuracy**	**Security**	**Usability**
Plot data on maps	✓	✓✓			++
Show hotspots on maps	−	✓✓✓			++
Provide simple statistics	✓	✓✓			+
Annotate maps	−	✓✓✓			+
Check data errors	✓✓	✓	++	+	
Provide advanced statistics	✓✓✓	−	++		
Prevent analysis errors	✓✓✓	−−	++		
Encrypt data	✓✓	−		++	
Integrate maps and charts	✓✓	−	+		+

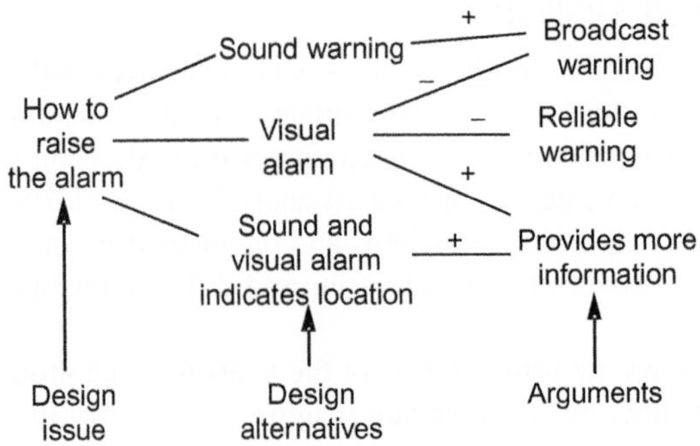

FIGURE 18.5 Design Rationale diagram showing the gIBIS-requirements engineering variant

The design issues illustrated in Figure 18.5 come from a case study of requirements analysis for a safety-critical fire-management system on container ships. Heat sensors detected fire, and then the issue was how to notify the crew. The diagram shows three design alternatives, linked to tradeoff criteria. The top option proposes an audio alarm broadcast throughout the ship, but it does not give vital information on the location of the fire. The middle option of a visual alarm on a panel display is reliable but more localized, while the third option of using visual diagrams of the ship and highlighting the location of the fire provides better information. Design Rationale diagrams allow users to see the tradeoffs between different requirements as design options.

CASE STUDY: THE SWEDISH NATIONAL TAX BOARD (1994-2004)

We have had extensive cooperation with public authorities to improve their computerized work environment and development processes to better fit with the need for change in society and technology. In a 10-year cooperation project, the Uppsala University (Sweden) helped a public authority to change their development processes toward a more user-centered one for ongoing large-scale projects. That project yielded a number of lessons learned about the requirements elicitation process (Gulliksen et al., 2003):

- Unsurprisingly, specifying requirements as use cases or using UML made them difficult to understand for the user organization, which was asked to confirm these requirements before development (Gulliksen, Göransson, & Lif, 2001).
- Prototypes served as excellent tools to help clarify the understanding of the requirements for both the development organization and for the user representatives.
- Usability designers played an important role as "go-betweens" between the user and the developer organization, to explain difficult terminology and to focus specifically on quality aspects from the user perspective.
- The RE process was cumbersome and lasted for a very long time (up to one a year for a larger project was not uncommon). Therefore the need to change or add new requirements late in the process was considered a major problem that risked even further delays, and was therefore forbidden in the requirements revision process, although everybody acknowledged the need for modification.

- Very large and long development projects that lacked the ability to adapt to changing requirements demonstrated a need to leave the requirements focus behind during the later phases of the project and to focus instead on the product at hand.

One of the things we noticed was the lack of interest in understanding and capturing all aspects of the work environment during the process of software development. Much attention was given to the development of the public face of these systems, and to the increased opportunity for citizens to interact directly with the government information that they needed. The changing role of the work conducted by the public authorities received less attention than the user-facing aspects, not only during development but also in requirements elicitation. One of the reasons may be that the public face of the systems receives much media attention, the effects that these systems could have on the staff working with them receive inadequate attention or understanding. In the planning of the public-facing projects, the initial expectation was that it would not necessarily result in a change of system for the staff. We noticed that, in one particular case, the developers logged into the public-facing systems, as the information provided by those systems differed from what was available in the internal case-handling systems.

One important aspect was the necessity to understand and work with the actual competencies and procedures that were already well established. See, for example, Figure 18.6; note the number of documents and "stickies" pasted around the display and on the bookshelves.

Traditionally, requirements communicated the needs determined for the computerized system without considering the full breadth of the work environment that provided the context for such requirements. From looking at the work environment, it was obvious that the established work routines, the organization of the work, and the skills available also provided important information for requirements definition. We needed to understand and evaluate the context of use, so that we could engineer it to meet any new requirements that might be imposed (e.g., from legislative changes, new technology, or organizational development and improvement goals.)

To enable us to understand the complexity of the context of use, we conducted a series of observation-interviews (see Figure 18.7), with the aim of gaining a better understanding of which aspects of the context of use should be maintained and which should be elaborated in greater detail in the development

FIGURE 18.6 A typical work environment from a Swedish public authority (not the Tax Board)

(For color version of this figure, see the Web version of this chapter.)

FIGURE 18.7 Contextual interviews or field studies to gather requirements

(For color version of this figure, see the Web version of this chapter.)

work. The results of the contextual interviews were analyzed and turned into new requirements in that process. A large amount of the knowledge gathered in such field studies, however, does not end up as new requirements; instead, it is maintained as a common repository of knowledge to be shared among those involved in the development work. Contextual knowledge helps developers interpret requirements and refine designs to suit users' needs; not all aspects of users' needs and goals can be captured as formal requirements.

The users themselves are always the people most familiar with, and the most knowledgeable about, the actual procedures in their work; but often they have little or no knowledge about the process of formulating requirements. Many user representatives have participated in requirements gathering work, but they often report a lack of influence, both in terms of what impact their participation actually had on the resulting system and on the contribution they could make because of the methods and tools used.

We used a collaborative prototyping activity to elicit the user requirements. We worked with low-fidelity tools and techniques, with which the users themselves drew sketches and diagrams. Then the users acted out operational sequences in their future system in cooperation with usability designers and system developers. In this way knowledge and understanding of the needs and requirements of the future computerized work situations were increased (see Figure 18.8). Both the users and the developers were very happy with the outcome, in that it clearly communicated the requirements in such a way that the users could understand and relate to them, and the developers could clearly see what the system should look like. The low-fidelity prototypes (see Figure 18.9), the scenarios, and the user profiles then became a part of the formal requirements in a way that felt rewarding for all involved. It also clearly gave more control to the business and user side of the organization in comparison to previous methodologies, in which the users felt like hostages under the control of the software developers. Users, usability designers, and developers participated on an equal footing to design and develop their future vision of the system.

Working with low-fidelity prototypes to elicit requirements provided a mutual language that evened out the power relations between the development team and users; furthermore, it made the team focus

FIGURE 18.8 Collaborative prototyping at the Swedish National Tax Board

(For color version of this figure, see the Web version of this chapter.)

FIGURE 18.9 Low-fidelity prototypes illustrating screen designs and operational sequences

(For color version of this figure, see the Web version of this chapter.)

on developing future work tasks, rather than getting stuck in terminological or detailed graphical design issues that higher-level prototypes can engender.

In our engender evaluation, it turned out that the prototype-based requirements documents gave the developers, for the first time, a clear understanding and overview of the work to be done and a general feel for the requirements. It also worked well as a tool to provide the users with real power in the development phase, and as a result the subsequent system fulfilled its purpose in a much better way than had systems produced by previous development projects.

A prototype-driven development process where prototypes play an important role as a replacement or complement to the standard requirements specifications is more effective in meeting development goals; it decreases the risk of project failure or abandonment and increases quality and a sense of participation among the users.

SUCCESS FACTORS

This section summarizes the key message in terms of tips on how development should be conducted to better deliver requirements that will contribute to increased usability and more effective work projects.

- *Conduct field studies and contextual interviews.* These serve the purpose of increasing the understanding of the work tasks, the users, and the context of use. Field studies can identify goals, wishes, and demands from the users. Interpret all of this information into requirements that can aid the development process. A collaborative process of distinguishing these requirements and also spotting tacit knowledge — knowledge of which the users may not be aware — is very important for subsequent development.
- *Involve users in requirements elicitation and further development.* User involvement is the key to success, and more active involvement will result in a better fit between the system's functionality and the users' goals and expectations. Conducting the development process in an open fashion with user participation throughout the process will avoid many risks. Bringing users in at an earlier stage, where their input can be more effective, can prevent many burdensome and expensive late changes.
- *Use prototypes to illustrate the key ideas.* The role of prototypes in the requirements process has risen in importance as systems become more complex. In particular, low-fidelity prototypes increase the opportunities for effective user participation, increase the developers' understanding of the actual requirements, and support creativity in designing work tasks. The process of design should go hand-in-hand with requirements, without the engineering process dominating the decisions.
- *Iterate the requirements.* Iterations are essential for meeting users' expectations, since their understanding of what is possible will unfold only gradually as successive visions of the new system are presented. Iterative design and revising the requirements as the team's knowledge increases are necessary for successful development and for delivering the values that the users expect, need, and deserve. Despite this, many fear iterative design, viewing it as leading to lack of control and oversight (due to the risks of delays and to not meeting initial requirements) and subsequent inefficient development. Recent developments in SE and Agile development methodologies (Beck, 1999) could mitigate such fears. Through iterative development and design, the delivery of usable systems can be more effectively and efficiently realized: additional prototyping cycles save effort later on in system maintenance as change requests arrive from dissatisfied users.
- *Accommodate Agile approaches.* A user-centered requirements definition process needs to accommodate Agile approaches. Agile development is becoming increasingly important, posing new challenges when it comes to requirements definition and use. Agile methodologies, with their heritage from lean manufacturing, aim to make decisions as late as possible; hence, the initial requirements specification contains less detail and moves many additional requirements to the end of the project. Agile approaches have downgraded the importance of requirements and left the requirements generation process for other methods (Larusdottir, Cajander & Gulliksen, in press). When using the Scrum methodology, for example, express changed requirements as new user stories and ensure that these stories communicate well, both to the developers and to the users.

- *Consider the means of procurement.* In many public sector systems, ready-made software will be purchased either as a customizable Enterprise Resource Plan (ERP) or as COTS packages. In these situations, the product's functions are predetermined, so the requirements process becomes a "goodness-of-fit" matching process. Tradeoff matrices (see the Negotiation and Tradeoff Analysis section of this chapter; Hauser & Clausing, 1988) are useful tools for comparing the fit between requirements and the product features from different suppliers. Remember to add in the cost of support (training, customization, and maintenance) and supplier factors (reliability). To arrive at a decision, use weighted decision tables to prioritize the relative importance of cost, requirements fit, and supplier/support factors.

Offshoring development increases the need for requirements, as direct contacts between developers and user/procurer are difficult. Today, system development projects, particularly those that are fairly standardized, may be sent for offshore development in less expensive developing countries. There are several examples of such projects from less business-critical systems and Web services, particularly from smaller public authorities that do not have their own development organizations in house. Several factors make it increasingly necessary to specify clearly in advance what is to be done. These include different time zones, cultures, and language barriers, as well as different attitudes to the development of software versus the need to deal with a different organization or business. Our experience of development in offshoring contexts has shown a return to more traditional requirements-based development deliveries that conflicts with an iterative, user-centered process. There is a need to introduce more user-centered features into the requirements in such situations, to replace the need for direct contact between developers and users.

SUMMARY

In this chapter, we have reviewed methods and techniques for user-centered requirements analysis and definition in government projects. We have illustrated based on case studies from the public sector, the techniques that can improve the usability, engagement, and acceptability of government systems. These techniques contribute to a further development of requirements engineering to manage the evolving demands of current systems development practice.

References

Beck, K. (1999). *Extreme programming explained: Embracing change.* New York: Addison-Wesley.

Boehm, B. (1981). *Software engineering economics.* Englewood Cliffs, NJ: Prentice Hall.

Conklin, J., & Begeman, M. L. (1988). gIBIS: A hypertext tool for exploratory policy discussion. *ACM Transactions on Office Information Systems, 6*(4), 303–331.

DSDM Consortium. (1995). *Dynamic systems development method.* Farnham, Surrey: Tesseract.

Eden, C. (1988). Cognitive mapping. *European Journal of Operational Research, 36*, 1–13.

Gulliksen, J., Göransson, B., Boivie, I., Blomkvist, S., Persson, J., & Cajander, Å. (2003). Key principles for user-centred system design. *Behaviour & Information Technology, 22*(6), 397–409.

Gulliksen, J., Göransson, B., & Lif, M. (2001). A user-centred approach to object-oriented user interface design. In M. van Harmelen (Ed.), *Object modeling and user interface design: Designing interactive systems* (pp. 283–312). New York: Addison-Wesley.

Hauser, J., & Clausing, D. (1988). The house of quality. *Harvard Business Review*, *5*, 63–73.

Larusdottir, M., Cajander, Å., & Gulliksen, J. (in press). User-centred evaluation in Scrum projects in practice. *Interacting with Computers*.

Maiden, N. A. M., & Ncube, C. (1998). Acquiring requirements for Commercial Off-The-Shelf package selection. *IEEE Software*, *15*(2), 46–56.

Nuseibeh, B., & Easterbrook, S. (2000). Requirements engineering: A roadmap. In *Proceedings: International Conference on Software Engineering (ICSE-2000), Limerick 4-11 June*, New York: ACM Press.

Porter, M. E. (1980). *Competitive strategy*. New York: Free Press.

Rockart, J. F., & Short, J. E. (1991). The networked organisation and the management of interdependence. In M. Scott-Morton (Ed.), *The corporation in the 1990s: Information technology and organisational transformation*. New York: Oxford University Press.

Sutcliffe, A. G., Thew, S., & Jarvis, P. (2011). Experience with user-centred requirements engineering. *Requirements Engineering*, *16*(4), 267–280.

Thew, S., Sutcliffe, A. G., Procter, R., De Bruijn, O., McNaught, J., Venters, C., et al. (2009). Requirements engineering for e-science: Experiences in epidemiology. *IEEE Software*, *26*(1), 80–87.

Further reading

Conferences

ACM conferences include DIS (Designing Interactive Systems), NordiCHI, and CHI, which all cover user-centered design and the HCI angle on requirements definition.

IEEE hosts the annual International Conference on Requirements Engineering, covering both academic and industry-oriented topics; and Requirements Engineering for Software Quality (RESQ).

Journals

Requirements Engineering, published by Springer. Like the IEEE conference, it tends to have an SE perspective.

RESG: Requirements Engineering Special Interest Group, a SIG of the British Computer Society, publishes a *Newsletter* with topical articles on requirements issues for practitioners as well as academics. The web site has links to many other sources of information on requirements definition: www.resg.org.uk. [Accessed 26 October 2011].

Textbooks

Robertson, J., & Robertson, S. (1999). *Mastering the requirements process*. Harlow: Addison Wesley. Probably the best practical requirements analysis book, written by expert RE consultants from the Atlantic Systems Guild.

Sutcliffe, A. G. (2002). *User-centred requirements engineering*. London: Springer Covers. HCI and SE perspectives.

Van Lamsweerde, A. (2009). *Requirements engineering: From system goals to UML models to software specifications*. Chichester: Wiley. The most comprehensive textbook on requirements definition and processes. Everything you could possibly want to know, but written from an SE background.

CHAPTER

Models as Representations for Supporting the Development of e-Procedures

19

Marco Winckler*, Philippe Palanque†

ICS-IRIT, University Paul Sabatier, France LIIHS-IRIT, University Paul Sabatier, France*†

"Everything should be made as simple as possible, but no simpler."

— Albert Einstein

INTRODUCTION

Government agencies are increasingly moving toward providing Web support for their administrative procedures. Such Web applications must do five important things:

1. Ensure the security of information exchange (authentication of users, date, and time, secure transfer of data, etc., as discussed in Chapter 14, User Issues in Security).
2. Provide an efficient notification system that helps all users (citizens and organizations) to monitor the progress of the process.
3. Provide flexible support to complex business rules (which might change according to new regulations and laws).
4. Support data exchange among several databases and legacy systems.
5. Be accessible and usable for a large and diverse group of users.

The development of successful electronic procedures is a complex activity that requires diverse expertise in administrative processes and software development. Such expertise can be acquired only by a multidisciplinary team, which should be able to harmoniously combine technical issues and expectations of all users, including citizens and administrative clerks (which we call, respectively, external and internal users). Despite the fact that e-procedure applications often focus on citizens as target users, we should not forget the important role played by stakeholders. By "stakeholder" we mean the internal users, administrative clerks, and agents in charge of receiving citizens' applications, analyzing the data provided, and deciding the outcomes. These stakeholders work on the back end of the e-procedure application, and as a consequence they have a different view of e-procedures. (See Chapter 18, User-Centered Requirements Definition, for a detailed discussion of the underlying complexity of eliciting and defining stakeholders' requirements for e-government applications.) Indeed, some complex administrative procedures will ultimately require the processing of pieces of information by many stakeholders, who work for different agencies and departments; quite often, only a few stakeholders have the entire view of the underlying workflow. In this context, it seems extremely important to provide each participant involved in the development process with multiple views for e-procedures:

- An overall view of the different steps in the underlying workflow process
- A detailed view of tasks that users should perform at every step of the procedure
- A detailed view of how the system supports user tasks in the execution of a procedure

This chapter shows how to employ abstract representations (called models) to support these three views of e-procedure applications. Such models can be used to communicate design options and design decisions to all participants of the development process, including the stakeholders. Beyond that, models are the ideal means of stimulating information exchanges, for sharing them, and for recording them. The approach presented in this chapter combines several notations for representing models that can additionally be used for engineering interactive systems. Our main goal is twofold:

- Define in an unambiguous way the behavior of several components (mainly user tasks and e-procedure application behavior).
- Provide a means to ensure the cross-consistency between these two complementary views of the same sociotechnical system.

For this very purpose, we use two different notations for describing two types of models: task models that represent the actions users should perform at every step of an administrative procedure, and system models that describe how design options can be implemented by the system to support user tasks. The word "system" is used here to refer to the interactive and functional part of the e-procedure application. It does not encompass the hardware and network parts, though they could be modeled with adequate notations. We illustrate user task modeling by using a hierarchical notation called HAMSTERS (which stands for Human-centered Assessment and Modeling to Support Task Engineering for Resilient Systems). The system's behavior is described by the means of the StateWebCharts (SWC) notation dedicated to the modeling of Web-based applications (Winckler, Barboni, Farenc, & Palanque, 2004). The use of these notations is illustrated in a real case study extracted from the French Regional Administration (Région Midi-Pyrénées). When used in an integrated and complementary way, these models can provide the various stakeholders with detailed and structured information to understand the interrelations between individual user's tasks and the system's behavior.

DEVELOPMENT PROCESS FOR e-PROCEDURE APPLICATIONS

Models are valuable tools for reducing ambiguities of specifications, making large and complex projects more manageable, documenting the design, and supporting the communication among developers and stakeholders. Models can be useful at a specific phase of development as well as throughout the application lifecycle. The main goal of this chapter is to show how model-based approaches can contribute to the development process of e-procedure applications. To help in understanding this, Figure 19.1 depicts a lifecycle that illustrates the use of models throughout the development process of Web applications as proposed by Scapin et al. (2000). Currently, there is no consensus on which phases of development are required or which lifecycle better describes the development process of e-procedure applications. Nonetheless, the lifecycle for Web development can be helpful in understanding how e-procedure applications are developed to be deployed on the Web platform. As we shall see, the lifecycle presented in Figure 19.1 is an iterative process made up of six steps:

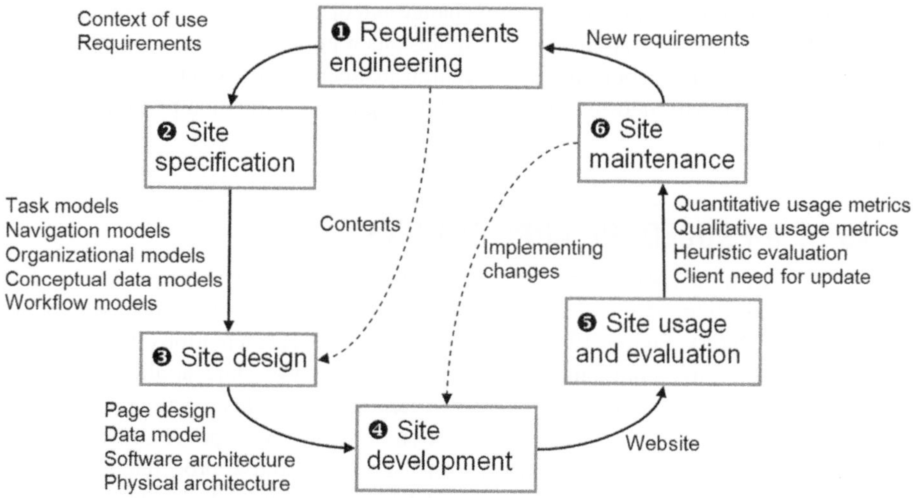

FIGURE 19.1 Lifecycle of Web application development

1. *Requirements engineering*: Identify the context of use, the requirements, and the main goals of stakeholders (see Chapter 18, User-Centered Requirements Definition).
2. *Specification*: Produce models for describing the context of use and requirements gathered in the previous phase. Detailed models formalize requirements including user tasks and e-procedure application behavior, for instance.
3. *Design*: Refine the specifications according to their content. At the end of this phase, a navigation map and page templates are prepared. This phase produces detailed specification to guide the implementation of the Web application.
4. *Development*: Construct the Web application, produce the Web pages, and integrate tools for visualizing media (e.g., sound, video). At the end of this phase, all the pages have content, links, and graphic elements incorporated: the application is delivered.
5. *Site usage and evaluation*: Evaluate advanced prototypes with end users. The product of previous phases is checked with respect to the requirements and the context identified in the first phase. For further information about usability evaluation throughout the development process the interested reader should refer to Chapter 17, ISO Standards for User-Centered Design and the Specification of Usability.
6. *Maintenance*: Gather new information, and plan modifications that have been requested from the use and evaluation phase.

The process in Figure 19.1 is cyclical, going sequentially through the six phases presented above. However, it is widely known that interactive applications development requires faster and sometimes incomplete iterations, especially when prototyping activities have to be performed. Fast iterations are represented in the model by the two arrows (in dotted lines) in the middle of the loop. In Figure 19.1, the arrow on the left-hand side indicates possible shortcuts of the specification phase. Indeed, at the beginning of design, the information architects and Web designers may immediately start to design the site, to have precise information to exchange and discuss with the stakeholders. The arrow on the right-hand side (implementation changes) represents a possible shortcut for increasing development speed and taking into account in a more central manner the usage and the evaluations.

In the next section, we will focus on models used during the specification phase of administrative e-procedures.

MODELING OF e-PROCEDURE APPLICATIONS

An e-procedure application should coordinate seamlessly the relationships between information concerning the organization, the underlying workflow process, and the database (see Pontico, Farenc, & Winckler, 2006). Figure 19.2 presents a graphical representation of such information exchange between these three components in the case of an e-procedure application dealing with the submission and evaluation of students' requests for scholarships. This example is similar to many currently available e-procedures in terms of coordination of activities, responsibilities, and resources. This example does not exhibit the critical aspects of the administrative procedures and of the data handled in such contexts, but it has the advantage of both simplicity and of conveying most of the concepts we want to address in this chapter.

As we can see in Figure 19.2, a user can evaluate a submission only if the corresponding document is available in the database and if the organization grants him or her the rights associated to the role of reviewer. Notice that the task "Evaluate a submission" is represented only through the relationships between actors. This way of representing user tasks can be easily justified from an information systems point of view, but it raises a big problem for understanding user activity on the system, especially when

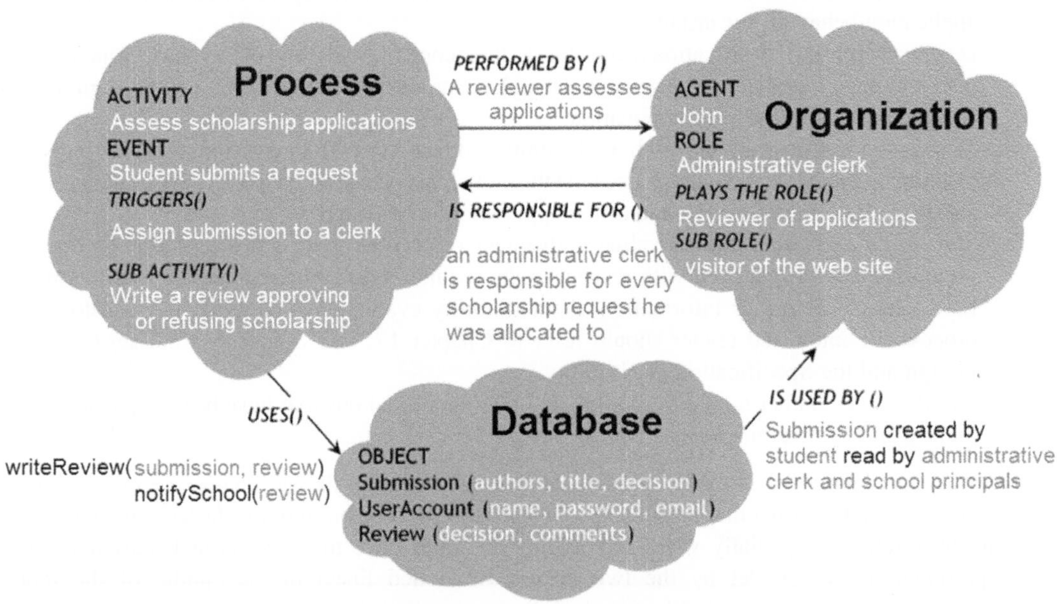

FIGURE 19.2 Information flow between the organization, the process, and the database

actors must cooperate to perform a single activity (e.g., support the discussion of a student application between administrative clerk and possibly a school principal). Such graphical representation is usually perceived by the developers of data-intensive Web applications as sufficient (Ceri et al., 2003) as it supports quite efficiently the identification of information that has to be stored in the database. However, when it comes to the design of the interactive part of the e-procedure application, there is a need to provide a more accurate behavioral description. In order to do so, two complementary perspectives have to be described: all the tasks a user can perform with the system (this representation is called tasks model), and a specification of all function- and scheduling-centered behaviors that should be embedded into administrative e-procedure applications (this description is called the system model). These two models, including the information they embed and how they are built, are described in the following sections.

Modeling user tasks

Task modeling has been proposed as a means of recording information gathered in the task analysis phase and is widely recognized as one fundamental way to focus on the specific user needs and improve the general understanding of how users may interact with a system via a user interface (UI) to accomplish a given interactive goal (Diaper & Stanton, 2004). Task models do not imply any specific implementation, so that one can focus on dependencies between activities, availability of resources required to perform tasks, and steps that users should follow to achieve a task.

Most notations for describing tasks feature a hierarchical organization of goals that are connected by logical and temporal operators for expressing dependencies between them. A task model should describe what users must do to accomplish a given goal without including how the system processes information even though this might determine the outcomes of a task execution. This is usually represented by alternative paths in the task model making explicit the possible outcomes. For this reason, many scenarios (which describe a unique sequence of task execution) can be produced from a single task model. As we shall see in the case study below, one of the advantages of modeling user tasks and scenarios is they help to analyze conflicts between users and administrative goals long before system constraints are considered.

Modeling the system

Several UI description languages (UIDLs) exist for describing the UI and the expected system behavior (see Shaer, Jacob, Green, & Luyten, 2009). A UIDL might cover one or more of three different aspects of the UI: the static structure of the UIs (including the description of UI elements — i.e., widgets — and their composition), the dynamic behavior (the dialog part, describing the dynamic relationships between components, including event, actions, and behavioral constraints), and the presentation attributes. For the sake of simplicity, we will focus only on the behavioral aspects of the systems and, in particular, how we can represent all the user navigation available on a Web portal featuring e-procedure applications. This exhaustive set of navigations is called the system model and should provide a clear description of system behavior, including how the system processes user inputs and generates appropriate output. This system model must then be exploited for prototyping the UI and in the implementation phases of the development process.

CASE STUDY: MODELING e-PROCEDURE APPLICATIONS

To illustrate the complementary use of task and system models, this section presents a case study[1] of an e-procedure application provided by the Regional French Administration Midi-Pyrénées (RMP, www.midipyrenees.fr). We introduce all actors involved and their interactions along the administrative procedures; however, due to space constraints the models only embed citizens' interactions.

Informal description of the case study

Our case study concerns an e-procedure developed as part of the BRPE program (the French acronym for "Regional Scholarship for First Equipment") whose aim is to provide students with scholarships for buying the required equipment (e.g., for hospitality students the purchase of knives, aprons, and suits) for attending classes in vocational high schools. Like many other governmental programs, BRPE is a complex program that integrates actors with diverse juridical status such as citizens (students/parents), units of the regional governmental (RMP) state governmental units (the accounting department), and educational units (high schools). Educational units are controlled by Education Offices, which negotiate once a year BRPE scholarships' entire budget with RMP. For the sake of simplicity, Education Offices, accounting departments, and national banks will be considered as "state units."

A student can apply for a BRPE scholarship only once, and only while attending a specific technical program in a vocational high school. High-school principals are in charge of advising students about the calendar and procedures and helping them prepare applications. BRPE applicants obtain forms from high-school principals. For students under the age of majority, their parents or legal guardian must sign the form. They send the forms and required documents (e.g., a bank account statement) to the high-school principals, who verify the completeness of the forms and send the completed ones to RMP. On receipt, RMP agents analyze BRPE applications. If the application is accepted by RMP, the accounting department (a state institution distinct from RMP) pays the BRPE scholarship through bank transfer to the account of the student (or his or her parents). Figure 19.3 shows the general procedure and depicts how the BRPE processes (gray boxes) are connected to outside processes (black boxes).

From an administrative point of view, the procedure starts with the annual definition of the amount of money allocated per scholarship which varies according to the technical program (Figure 19.3, step 1). Scholarships are subject to annual budget approval from the RMP's council (step 2), which determines the number of scholarships that can be founded. Students do not send applications directly to RMP: the process is mediated by the principals, who notify students (step 4) and explain how they should fill in the form (step 5). Principals are also responsible for checking that all required documents are present and that students regularly attend a vocational high school (step 6). RMP receives student applications and verifies again their correctness and eligibility (step 8). Problems (e.g., fraud, missing information) are reported to the principals (step 7), who can also monitor (step 6) the status of applications of students attending a program at their schools. Eligible applications are duly recorded, and letters of credit are sent to recipients (step 9). Finally, RMP addresses a payment request (step 10) to

[1]This case study omits some internal aspects of the application.

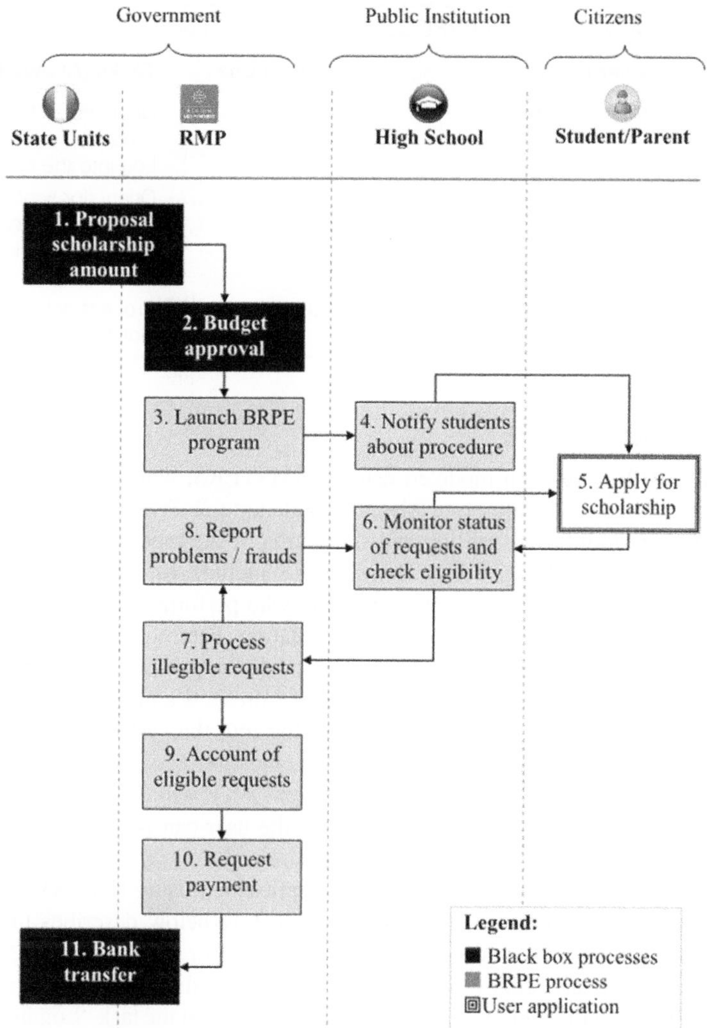

FIGURE 19.3 Overview of the BRPE process

(For color version of this figure, see the Web version of this chapter.)

the accounting department (step 11). Table 19.1 shows the roles that have been identified for the application — "student" and "administrative clerks" — and their corresponding (allowed) tasks. The role "student" includes profiles "students without login" and "registered students." The task "Query (for scholarships)" is available to everyone, but a user can apply for a scholarship only if s/he is logged in the system. The user role "Administrative clerks" refers to someone who is responsible for supervising the submissions.

Table 19.1 Tasks Associated with BRPE Scholarship Applications

Role	User Profile	Preconditions	Tasks (Allowed)
Student	Student without login	None	Query (for scholarships) Create an account Log into the system
	Registered students	Logged in	Query (for scholarship) Update user account Apply for scholarships Monitor status of requests
Administrative clerks	Full control over scholarship applications	Logged in	Process scholarship request Notify students

Modeling user tasks for BRPE

User tasks for the BRPE have been modeled using HAMSTERS, which is a graphical notation for describing task models hierarchically (see Martinie, Palanque & Winckler, 2011). The notation is supported by a software tool for the editing and simulation of the models and is publicly available.[2] The elements of task models described by HAMSTERS include various task types (e.g., abstract, system, user, and interactive tasks) aimed at expressing who performs the task. Similar to other task model notations such as the Concur Task Tree (CTT) notation (Paternò, Mancini, & Meniconi, 1997), temporal and logical operators (e.g., "[]" for choice, ">>" for sequence, "|||" order independency) are used to define the relationships between tasks. Figure 19.4 presents a task model describing the set of actions and their temporal ordering to allow a user to log into the system (user goal represented at the top level of the task model). To reach this goal, the user has to perform the abstract task "Provide identification," which, in sequence (operator >>) will be processed by the system "Validate user ID." To perform the identification task, the user can perform in any order (operator |||) the "provide email" and "provide password" tasks.

Figure 19.5 shows the task model of the students represented using HAMSTERS notation corresponding to the goal "Submit BRPE." The level immediately below describes the tasks that users can perform without having a user account, such as "Query (for scholarships)," "Create account," and "Select scholarship" in any order (operator |||). Connected to that operator, the sequence operator ">>" indicates the fact that the user must perform, in sequence, first the task "Log into the system" and then the task "Manage account." The decision to start this sequence is performed in any order with the tasks of the same level. The task "Select scholarship" is a cognitive task which refers to user's inner decision process. The process of refinement of tasks proceeds until all the details for understanding the user goals and activities have been reached. For example, the task "Query (for scholarships)" is decomposed into "provide keyword" and "show results" (which have to be performed in sequence (">>")), representing respectively the expected user input and the outcome provided by the system.

The task "Apply for scholarship" encompasses a set of subtasks that are required to accomplish the procedure that follows Figure 19.5 (administrative constraints cause the administration to request paper-based certificates, so the subtask "provide certificates" is not supported by the system).

[2] http://www.irit.fr/ICS/hamsters

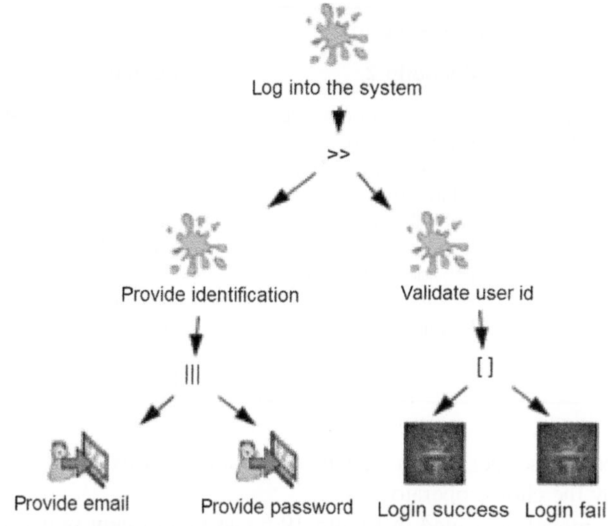

FIGURE 19.4 Task model in HAMSTERS, describing a simple user login

(For color version of this figure, see the Web version of this chapter.)

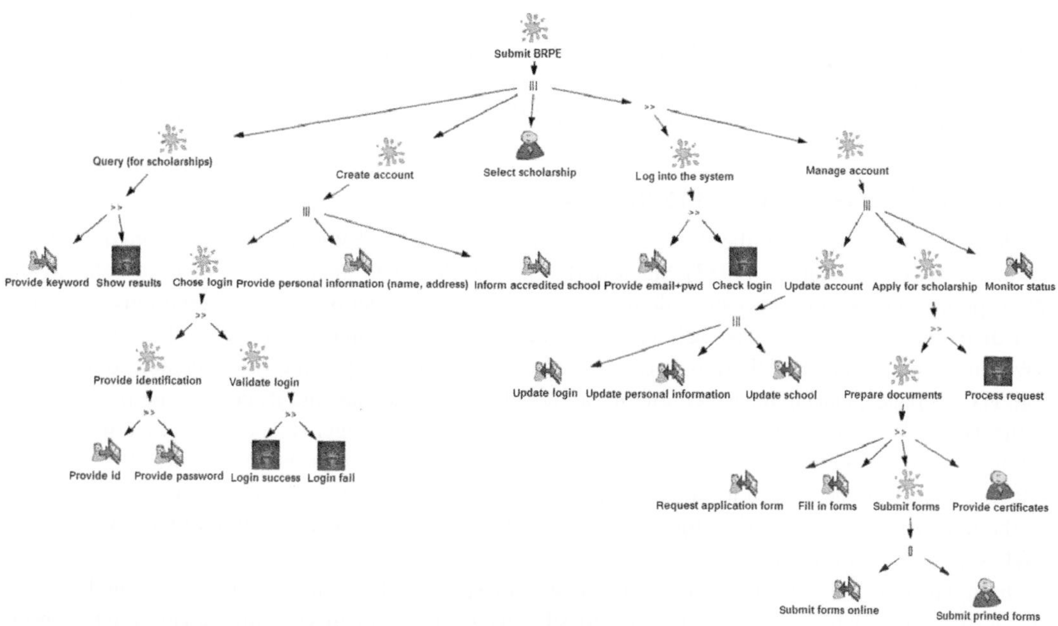

FIGURE 19.5 HAMSTERS task model for the application for BRPE

(For color version of this figure, see the Web version of this chapter.)

Table 19.2 Three Scenarios Related to the "Manage Account" Subtask

Scenario 1	Scenario 2	Scenario 3
Apply for scholarship	Apply for scholarship	Apply for scholarship
Prepare documents	Prepare documents	Prepare documents
Request application form	Request application form	Request application form
Fill in forms	Fill in forms	Fill in forms
Submit forms	Submit forms	Submit forms
Submit forms online	Submit printed forms	Submit forms online
Provide certificates	Provide certificates	Provide certificates
Process request	Process request	Process request
Monitor status	Monitor status	Update account
		Update school
		Monitor status

Similarly, the task model describes how a student can "submit forms" either online or on its printed version (represented by the choice operator "[]").

Exploiting the task model presented in Figure 19.5 can yield many scenarios. Table 19.2 shows three possible scenarios for the task "Apply for scholarship." Scenario 1 considers the situation of a student that connects to the system and ultimately submits forms online. In scenario 2, the user also connects to the system but finally decides to submit printed forms. Scenario 3 describes the situation where a user updates account information after the application is submitted. This might violate the constraint of applying for a scholarship only while attending a specific technical program in a vocational high school. Notice that these scenarios do not impose any particular implementation; user tasks can be better understood without having information about how the system will support them. This kind of analysis is possible because it considers user tasks from the perspective of the users' needs from the application, rather than how to represent the user activity using a particular system.

Modeling the navigation in the BRPE systems

To describe the navigation of the BPRE application, we employ the SWC notation, a formal description technique based on Harel's (1987) StateCharts and developed to specify the dynamic behavior of Web applications. StateCharts can be defined as a set of states, transitions, events, conditions, variables, and their interrelationships. The behavior described in SWC is directly related to the UI. States in SWC are depicted on the UI by means of containers for objects (graphic or executable objects) — e.g., HTML pages. During the execution of the model the current state and its content are made visible to the users. SWC transitions explicitly represent how user events trigger state changes in a model: user actions appear as continuous arrows. Autonomous behaviors appear as dashed arrows. When a user selects a transition the system leaves the current state, which becomes inactive, letting the target state be the next active state in the configuration. Figure 19.6 presents an excerpt of a system model using SWC supporting user login.

In Figure 19.6, the state "login" contains three static states: "fill in email and pwd," "logged in," and "error: try again," which describe the three possible pages the user can see while navigating the application. The state "check password" is a transient state that represents the information processing performed at the server side without any visual representation to the user. The round shape represents

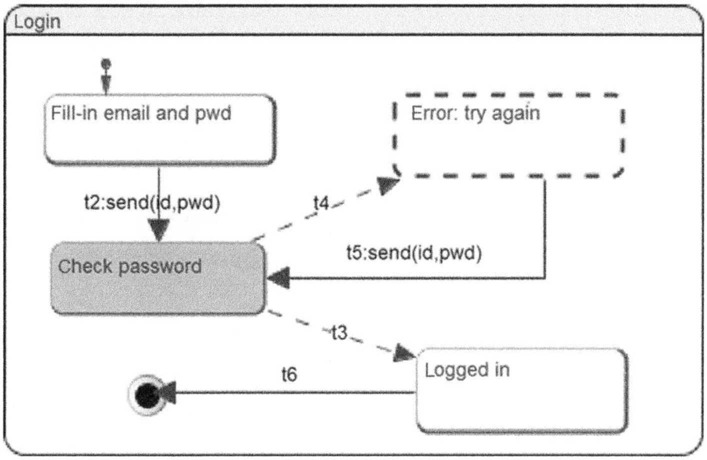

FIGURE 19.6 Simple login described using SWC

(For color version of this figure, see the Web version of this chapter.)

an "end state," used to describe the end of the execution of the application. The SWC model presented in Figure 19.5 is just one of many alternatives for defining the system behavior for performing the task login depicted in Figure 19.4; nonetheless, it describes one agreed-upon design for the navigation of the login part of the BRPE application.

Figure 19.7 shows the complete navigation model for BRPE system, including the support for the tasks "Log into the system" and "Query (for scholarships)." In addition to the functions required to support the tasks represented in the task model, it features some transitions supporting content-based navigation such as "home" and "connected." Simply by connecting states by means of transitions, we can create all of the navigation required by the users, whether it concerns content-based navigation or is navigation required to follow a specific procedure.

Prototyping e-procedure applications from specifications

SWC notation is supported by a computer tool suite that makes it possible to edit and execute models. This specificity supports iterative prototyping as described in the development process of Figure 19.1. After we have created and verified that the navigation model incorporates our requirements, we can create the Web pages for the e-procedure application that corresponds to the SWC model. When the navigation is described, the graphical part of the UI can be connected to the states of the model while user events can be connected to transitions. Executing the models thus allow for simulation of the UI according to the high-fidelity prototyping philosophy. The SWCEditor supports the simultaneous simulation of SWC models and the execution of the corresponding Web pages. Figure 19.8 provides a view-at-a-glance of this process. The navigation modeling for the digital library of BRPE is presented on the left-hand side of Figure 19.8, highlighting the current state in the simulation (the state "home"). Its right-hand side presents the corresponding implementation of the home page. We also can observe in the center of Figure 19.8 a dialog window showing a list of transitions going out from the current state "home." This list represents the set of links currently available for the user navigation.

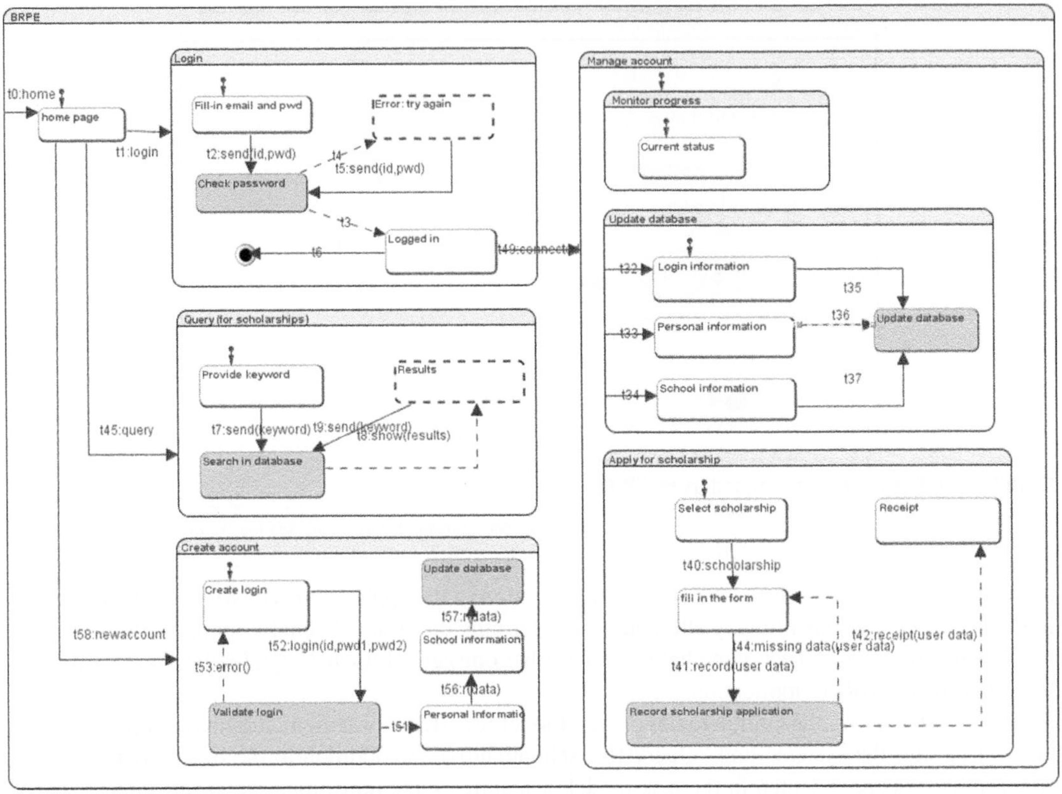

FIGURE 19.7 SWC modeling for BRPE e-procedure application

(For color version of this figure, see the Web version of this chapter.)

ADVANTAGES AND DRAWBACKS OF MODEL-BASED APPROACHES

Most of the existing development methods for Web applications base their conceptual modeling on their objects (or data) and their related methods, functions, or services; and they derive tasks from the traditional CRUD (Create, Read, Update, Delete) pattern: tasks are limited to basic operations on objects and their relationships (Ceri et al., 2003). CRUD patterns can be effective from a developer's point of view of the system but they constrain graphical and interaction designers' creativity around UI presentation and navigation.

The use of task models reinforces the focus on users during the development process of application. Indeed, to help users navigate the application effectively and efficiently, we must pay attention to the users' tasks. Several other approaches for designing e-procedures exist, many of which do not include explicit representation of user tasks. Task modeling is widely considered as a helpful design approach that lets design analyze the user activity without the influence of technological constraints, the actual use of task models for the design of e-procedure applications. However, task modeling is often misunderstood, mainly because current approaches for the design do not provide any guidance on

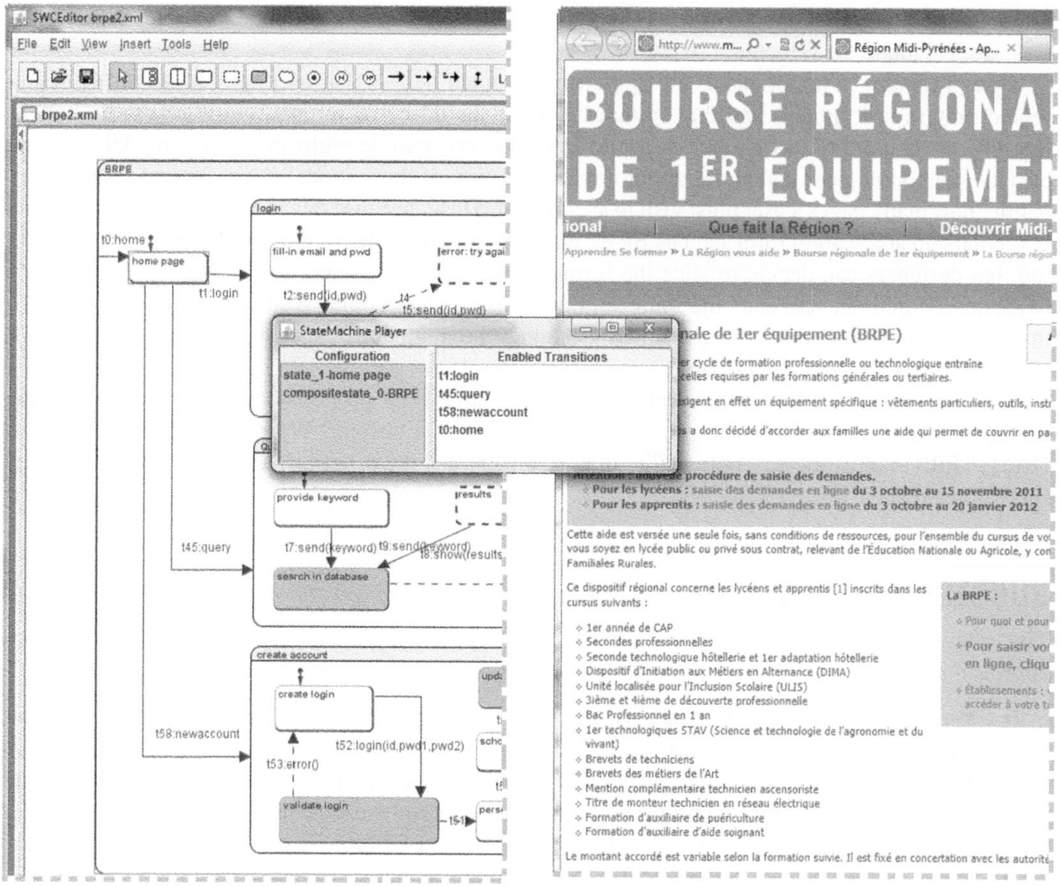

FIGURE 19.8 Prototyping BRPE using SWC models connected to a Web page

(For color version of this figure, see the Web version of this chapter.)

how to integrate task models into the design process. This chapter focused on tasks models and system models rather than on the underlying workflow process of e-procedure applications. Nonetheless, the workflow can be derived from the co-execution of task models and navigation models.

One of the key contributions of the models presented in this chapter is that task models (HAMSTERS) and system models (SWC) can be integrated and their compatibility assessed prior to implementation. For instance, if the task model features four interactive tasks, the system model should embed the same set of transitions between states. Beyond that lexical compatibility, syntactic compatibility has to be insured as well. For instance, if a sequence of actions in the task model describes a constraint in user activity (which can be administrative, physical, or cognitive), the system model must also reflect this constraint. This is precisely where the power of models can be better appreciated. Although checking-by-testing such compatibility is impossible because of the potentially very large number of states and state changes, model bisimulation and model-checking techniques can provide efficient solutions. Bisimulation of task models and system models is detailed by Barboni, Ladry, Navarre, Palanque, & Winckler (2010).

One of the key assumptions of the approach presented here is that user activity should be represented only in task models and that system behavior should be represented only in system models. Keeping the content of task models separate from (but compatible with) the system models helps to provide methodological guidelines about the construction of these models. A task model should not feature how many pages a user must visit to accomplish a task, because this is often a system constraint. A scholarship application form such as BRPE might feature a single page in a Web browser on a desktop, but designers can decide to slice the form in several pages according to groups of information requested. Moreover, accessing the same application through a mobile Web browser will require that the form be sliced into many pages. Notwithstanding the number of pages used to present the BRPE form, the user task remains the same.

It is important to note that several other models have been proposed over the last decade that might fit with the objectives and processes presented in this chapter. We presented only SWC and HAMSTERS to illustrate the applicability of the concepts and the benefits that can be gained following such an approach.

SUCCESS FACTORS

The following checklist is designed to help the reader with key information while using a model-based approach and a model-based development process as presented in this chapter.

- *Keep the task and system models separate.* Ensure that the two models contain different information — user behavior in task models and system behavior in system models.
- *Make sure the system model supports indefinite sequences of a single behavior.* This is an important requirement for supporting the same tasks to be executed by several users one after the other. The execution of one task should not affect its future execution.
- *Verify that the task model terminates.* An iterative task model would specify infinite sequences of action that are required for reaching a goal.
- *Look for appropriate tool support before starting to edit your models.* If you start editing before making sure your tools will support everything you need to do, you will have to start over with tools that will.
- *Use a simulation engine.* The effective use of a model depends on being able to "see" how the model behaves.
- *Make sure to reflect in the models all the changes that are made on the application.* If models are not updated accordingly, they will lose their interest as a tool for analysis and information sharing.
- *Make sure that your models are readable and understandable by the various stakeholders.* This will enable multidisciplinary teams to validate and modify them. Reading a model requires different skills from building one — i.e., do not expect stakeholders with nontechnical backgrounds to build system models.
- *Ensure cross-models compatibility.* If you use a multiple models approach, make sure that there is a support to assess cross-models compatibility, as performing it by hand is usually unmanageable.
- *Do not try to use models everywhere.* Keep models for the complex part of the system and for the complex user tasks. The rest of the system can be built using prototyping approaches.

SUMMARY

The development of successful electronic procedures is a complex activity that requires diverse expertise in administrative processes and software development. Such expertise requires a multidisciplinary team that should combine technical issues and expectations of all users, including citizens and administrative clerks. This chapter has illustrated the use of task models and system models for dealing with the development of e-procedure applications. The case study presented might look small, but it illustrates the huge importance that models will play in the development of even more complex applications. Without appropriate support from models, the development team will get lost and the chance of unexpected and undesired behaviors will increase. These models provide different points of view on the same sociotechnical system, so that when working in multidisciplinary teams all stakeholders can use the most suitable model to make their concerns and requirements explicit, to be embedded in the final application.

References

Barboni, E., Ladry, J.-F., Navarre, D., Palanque, P., & Winckler, M. (2010). Beyond modelling: An integrated environment supporting co-execution of tasks and systems models. In *Proceedings of ACM symposium on Engineering Interactive Systems (EICS' 2010)*, New York: Sheridan.

Ceri, S., Fraternali, P., Bongio, A., Brambilla, M., Comai, S., & Matera, M. (2003). *Designing data-intensive Web applications*. San Franscico: Morgan-Kaufmann Publishers.

Diaper, D., & Stanton, N. A. (2004). *The handbook of task analysis for human-computer interaction*. Mahwah, New Jersey: Lawrence Erlbaum Associates.

Harel, D. (1987). StateCharts: A visual formalism for complex systems. *Science of Computer Programming*, *8*(3), 231–274.

Martinie, C., Palanque, P., & Winckler, M. (2011). Structuring and composition mechanism to address scalability issues in task models. In *Proceedings of IFIP TC13 conference on human-computer interaction (INTERACT 2011)*, Berlin: Springer, 593–611 LNCS 6949.

Paternò, F., Mancini, C., & Meniconi, S. (1997). ConcurTaskTrees: A diagrammatic notation for specifying task models. In *Proceedings of the IFIP TC13 conference on human-computer interaction (INTERACT'97)*, London: Chapman & Hall, 362–369.

Pontico, F., Farenc, C., & Winckler, M. (2006). Model-based support for specifying eService eGovernment applications. In *Proceedings of the 5th international workshop on TAsk MOdels and DIAgrams (TAMODIA'2006)*, Berlin: Springer, 54–67 LNCS 4385.

Scapin, D., Vanderdonckt, J., Farenc, C., Bastide, R., Bastien, C., Leulier, C., et al. (2000). Transferring knowledge of user interfaces guidelines to the Web. In *Proceedings of TWWG 2000: International conference on tools for working with guidelines*, London: Springer, 293–304.

Shaer, O., Jacob, R. J. K., Green, M., & Luyten, K. (2009). User interface description languages for next generation user interfaces. *Special Issue of ACM Transactions on Computer-Human Interaction (ACM TOCHI)*, *16*(4), 1–4.

Winckler, M., Barboni, E., Farenc, C., & Palanque, P. (2004). SWCEditor: A model-based tool for interactive modelling of Web navigation. In *Proceedings of international conference on computer-aided design of user interface (CADUI'2004)*, Funchal, Portugal: Kluwer Academic Publisher, 55–66.

CHAPTER 20

Evaluation in Government Environments

Whitney Quesenbery*

*WQusability, High Bridge NJ, USA**

"Everything gets tested for usability in the end. The only question is whether we are there to observe or whether we wait to learn from the real experience of real users."

— Anonymous

INTRODUCTION

One premise of this book is that it is important for government systems to be easy to use, whether the users are members of the general public, people within the government, or specialists in the system's domain. Earlier chapters have looked at different aspects of a user-centered design process and ways to approach the design to reach that goal.

Now we turn to evaluation. This chapter looks at the best way to check and measure progress toward the goal of usable products with a good user experience: usability evaluation. We will talk about two types of evaluation: usability testing (evaluation with users) and evaluation without users.

- A usability test, at its simplest, consists of a single facilitator working with a user — usually one on one — watching as they work with a system, printed material, web site . . . or anything else.
- Evaluation without users includes techniques for experts to review a system against a checklist of good practices or model the interaction with the system to assess its usability.

Usability evaluation can be both *quantitative* and *qualitative*. That is, it can produce both measurable, statistically valid results and insights based on patterns of behavior or attitudes.

One reason to conduct usability evaluations instead of just asking users or stakeholders for their opinion is that people often have difficulty reporting on their own actions and motivations. They can accurately report why they came to your web site today and they may be able to report whether they consider the visit a success. People, however, are unreliable when asked to explain their route through the web site or analyze why they made specific choices.

How is usability defined?

Usability is defined by the users of a system in terms of their own experience. A widely cited international standard (ISO, 1998, 2010) as discussed in Chapter 17, ISO Standards for User-Centered Design and the Specification of Usability, defines usability as follows:

> *The extent to which a system, product or service can be used by specified users to achieve specified goals with effectiveness, efficiency, and satisfaction in a specified context of use.*
>
> — **ISO 9241-210:2009**

This ISO standard mentions three core qualities (effectiveness, efficiency, satisfaction), but many sources expand this list to include the time it takes to learn a system, how easy a system is to remember, how many errors users make, and how easily a user can recover from errors (Nielsen, 1993; Quesenbery, 2003; Shneiderman, 1980, 1998):

- *Effective* — How accurately and completely users can use the system to meet their own goals
- *Efficient* — The resources, including time, it takes to meet those goals
- *Engaging* — The degree to which using the system is appealing or creates a satisfying emotional experience
- *Error Tolerant* — How well the product allows users to recover gracefully from errors
- *Easy to Learn* — How easily users can learn both basic and advanced functions as they use the product.

These definitions are as useful for evaluating systems used in government as they are for evaluating those used in any other context. The nature of the relationship between users and government is an additional consideration for government systems. In their description of the layers of a form, Caroline Jarrett and Gerry Gaffney (Jarrett & Gaffney, 2008) point out that users may approach a form (or any interaction) in an emotional state based on their relationship with the organization, and Kate Walser describes the role of relationship in citizen engagement in Chapter 3, Usability and Government 2.0.

Interacting with government can be stressful. As more government services are offered only online, more people will find that they are required to use a software program, web site, or other system for activities such as these:

- Complying with a law or regulation
- Exercising their rights as citizens
- Receiving government benefits or services
- Interacting with government agencies or officials.

All of this adds up to the need to ensure a high standard of usability for government systems.

What is the focus of usability evaluation?

Usability evaluation focuses on understanding how well a system supports users in meeting their goals. One type of evaluation, usability testing, evaluates a system by observing behavior. In a usability test, participants are asked to complete tasks or interact with a system based on a scenario, to see what they do and how successful they are in this interaction. This may take place in a usability lab, (or laboratory) as shown in Figure 20.1, where a notetaker observes the participant and moderator through a one-way window; or it may occur in a more informal setting.

A usability test may focus on measurement — for example, using *quantitative* metrics such as success rates or time spent on a task — or may be entirely *qualitative*, aimed at identifying patterns of behavior and insights into problems with the usability of the system.

Other ways of collecting input and feedback from users can be used alongside usability testing:

- *Focus groups* — group discussion sessions to gather opinions and attitudes about features of a system

FIGURE 20.1 A usability test session in a usability lab. Photo courtesy of UserWorks, Inc. (www.userworks.com)

(For color version of this figure, see the Web version of this chapter.)

- *Surveys* — instruments that gather information about facts and opinions, often from large samples of people
- *Search and server log analytics* — records of search terms, paths through a site, and other records from the use of the system
- *Checklists* — a set of guidelines or regulatory requirements against which the system can be checked

Each of these techniques provides valuable information about aspects of the user experience, although they are not replacements for usability testing. All of them can be combined with usability testing to create a strong program for evaluating the usability of a system.

What are the goals of usability evaluation?

During a project, you may have many different questions, and you can conduct a usability evaluation to answer them. Each of these questions is a variation on the overall goal of learning how well the system supports users in doing their work or completing their own tasks in their own way.

Type of evaluation	Questions answered
Benchmarking	Can we measure the usability of the current system, so that we will know if the new system or redesign is an improvement?
Comparison	How do two systems used for similar tasks or functions compare?
User research	How do people interact with the current system? What can we learn about their goals, behavior, or preferences that will help us design a new system or improve the current one? (See Chapter 18, User-Centered Requirements Definition, for more information about ways to gather requirements.)
Diagnostic, or formative	How well does a system in development work for users? What usability problems can we find early and fix before the design is complete? What is working well and should be kept as part of the design?
Measurement, or summative	Can we measure the overall usability of a system? A summative test at the end of a project can be used as the benchmark for a future redesign.
Compliance	Does this system meet the requirements of a standard or a regulation?

INCLUDING USABILITY EVALUATION IN A PROJECT

Usability evaluation must be included in the project plan. The ISO standard for user-centered design ISO, 2009) defines five key activities in the project, as Figure 20.2 shows, starting with the requirement to plan for user-centered design and usability, and then proceeding through an iterative cycle of activities including evaluation (ISO, 2010).

Two points of advice emerge from the writing on usability evaluation. First, evaluation must be integrated into the overall process. Whether the evaluations are conducted by members of staff or an outside company, the results are used better when the designers and developers are able to observe and contribute to the work.

Second, evaluation should occur early and often, during the active design and development process. Smaller evaluations including both checklist reviews and usability tests are easier and less expensive to run. The knowledge and insights from evaluation are also cumulative, with each one building on the last. With less time between evaluations, each one is less critical, and recommendations can be used with more confidence (Krug, 2010; Tognazzini, 1998).

Because evaluation can have many different goals, they can be used in many different places in a system's lifecycle. As a general guideline, the more quantitative evaluation techniques are used early and late in a project, in combination with activities aimed at understanding user requirements. During the design and development process, qualitative techniques are most often used to check the progress of the system, ensuring that it is on track to meet those requirements.

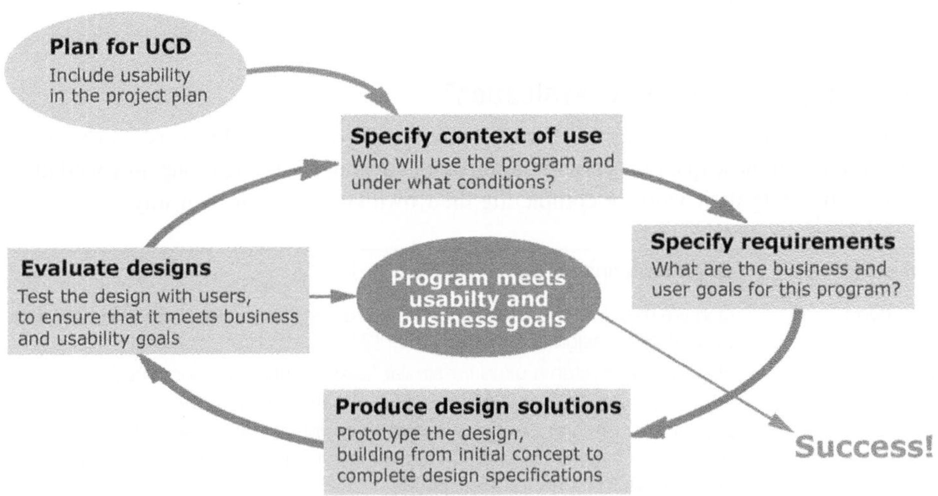

FIGURE 20.2 The user-centered design cycle in ISO 9241-210

(For color version of this figure, see the Web version of this chapter.)

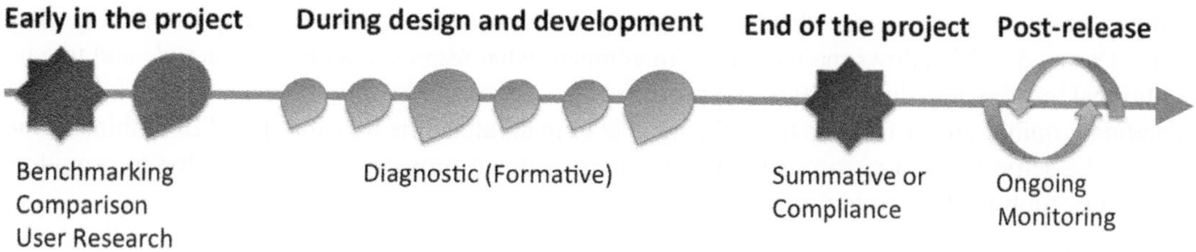

FIGURE 20.3 Types of evaluation at different stages of a project

(For color version of this figure, see the Web version of this chapter.)

One way to think about how to include usability evaluation in the process of a system design and development project is in several stages (see Figure 20.3):

- *Early in the project*, evaluations to benchmark the usability of the current system or to compare it to other systems provide input to the requirements. (User research aimed at understanding user needs and context is also done early in the project.)
- *During the project*, iterative diagnostic tests evaluate the work in progress. These evaluations might be scheduled to coordinate with Agile sprints[1], or other units of work. Larger tests can be scheduled at periodic milestones, to ensure that as the pieces of the project come together, the system has good overall usability.
- *At the end of the project*, a final summative test evaluates whether the system is ready to release because it meets the requirements or shows improvement over the benchmarks.
- *After release*, ongoing monitoring includes reviewing technical support logs or analytics, but might also include a periodic usability evaluation to be sure the system continues to meet its goals.

CONDUCTING USABILITY TESTING

The procedure for conducting a usability test is well established. Typically, a moderator works with one participant (or sometimes a small group), observing their interaction with the systems being tested (Barnum, 2010; Dumas & Redish, 1999; Rubin & Chisnell, 2008). The moderator suggests goals or tasks to the participant, or works with the participant to define a goal that is relevant to the individual (Quesenbery, 2009). As the participant works, the moderator takes notes of any problems, successes, or failures.

In addition to observing behavior, the goals for usability evaluation often include understanding *why* a particular problem occurs. In some usability test methods, participants are asked to "think aloud" (Lewis & Rieman, 1993), narrating their actions and sharing their thoughts as they work. "Ask them to

[1]Software Engineering rapid development project management methodologies are termed "agile". The more generally-used term is an "iteration", a "sprint" is the term used in the Scrum methodology.

tell you what they are thinking: what they are trying to do, questions that arise as they work, things they read" (Sec. 5.5). This allows the moderator to compare what users *say* with what they *do* and to gain additional insights into the specifics of a problem. Is it, for example, a problem caused by not understanding terminology, or is it due to not being able to manipulate the user interface? Both think-aloud during the activity and a retrospective review afterward can provide the clues needed to provide a strong direction for how to improve the system.

Testing for measurement

The idea of a single quantitative metric for usability is attractive. Unfortunately, it is not possible to measure "usability" directly, in the same way that you measure number of visits or speed of download. Instead, quantitative evaluation collects data on metrics that are considered to be indicators of good usability. For example, to determine whether a redesign has improved the usability of a system, a useful measure is the degree to which users succeed in completing the same tasks, or give higher scores on a satisfaction survey. In one approach to quantitative scoring, SUM (Sauro & Kindlund, 2005) creates a single usability metric by combining data from several different measurable aspects of a system.

In general, usability tests that are intended to collect measurement data are conducted with a high degree of procedural rigor. For example, the interaction with the moderator is often controlled to reduce any variation between participants in the instructions given to them or in any prompts or hints offered.

One of the values of conducting summative usability testing is that it makes it easier to compare two versions of one system, or different systems. A project led by the US National Institute of Standards and Technology (NIST undated) led to a standard format for usability reports — the "Common Industry Format" (CIF) — for reporting on summative tests (ISO/IEC 25062:2006). A goal of this standard is to make it possible to compare reports of different products, or conducted by different companies.

Testing for design insights

In contrast to testing for measurement, a qualitative test focuses on the insights that can be gained by discovering patterns of interaction and understanding the system from the user's perspective. For example, usability testing of a system for searching for cancer clinical trials focused on how users searched, what criteria they used to identify a list of trials appropriate for a patient, and what information in the search results was most helpful in making decisions. The insights from this testing was used to improve the clinical trial search form.

Although the basic methodology for all usability tests is similar, with a focus on observing participants as they interact with a system, tests for design insights can be conducted with a less formal protocol, fewer users, and less focus on producing measurable events. Originally called "discount usability," a term popularized by Jakob Nielsen (1989, 2009), it was contrasted with the more formal summative measurement. This style of evaluation is now common, the norm for most testing. This approach is characterized by three factors:

- testing more often, in smaller tests aimed at steering the design
- testing with fewer users in each round of testing
- testing with prototypes, sometimes as simple as mockups on paper, rather than waiting for a fully interactive program.

These usability tests may be conducted in a formal setting, with observation rooms and other technical support, but they can be just as effective when run in any convenient location, such as the meeting room setting shown in Figure 20.4. In Washington State, staff from the Department of Elections tested new

FIGURE 20.4 In this usability test, a participant works with a paper prototype while an observer watches and takes notes

(For color version of this figure, see the Web version of this chapter.)

voter registration forms outdoors at a farmer's market, making it easy to recruit participants from people at the busy market.

In practice, a single usability test can provide both quantitative and qualitative results, as long as it is set up with these dual goals in mind. For example, usability evaluations can also collect subjective preference or opinion data through satisfaction assessment questionnaires such as SUS (Brooke, 1996), SUMI (Kirakowski & Corbett, 1993), and PSSUQ (Lewis, 1992).

Two examples of usability testing programs in the United States that focus on evaluation for design insights have expanded the number of projects and systems that receive usability evaluation by streamlining the process.

- "First Fridays" takes a rapid evaluation approach, with the goal of identifying a short list of problems to be fixed equally rapidly.
- "Open Call" is an omnibus evaluation series, in which several different projects are tested together.

"First Fridays"

"First Fridays" is a usability testing program of the US General Services Administration (GSA, 2011a) based on concepts in Steve Krug's *Rocket Surgery Made Easy* (2010) — conducting a small number of test sessions aimed at producing a list of changes to make within the next month. The program is structured to make it easy for busy teams to participate. The entire test happens on a single day, including three test sessions and a meeting to identify the top usability problems found. The program requires that the team commit to making changes to the system based on the results (GSA, 2011b). The GSA also uses First Fridays to train agencies to conduct their own usability testing and invites anyone from the federal government to observe as a way to learn about usability testing.

"Open Call"

A program of the US National Cancer Institute (NCI), called "Open Call," provides an opportunity to test small projects and online content that might otherwise not be tested at all. It is run by US National Cancer Institute's (NCI's) Office of Communication and Education, which manages the flagship web site, cancer.gov, along with cancer publications such as the PDQ® Cancer Treatment Summaries.

Open Call tests, scheduled every other month, group several different projects into a single session. This allows NCI teams to evaluate projects as diverse as new content portal pages, early concepts for a mobile site, or print brochures. As in the First Fridays program, members of the project team are required to observe the sessions and be part of the feedback sessions.

In addition to the obvious value of making more frequent usability testing available, Open Call has a secondary value in building the level of usability knowledge among the communications staff and cross-pollination among projects. For example, the web portal managers might test a new idea on one portal, but then use what they learn in many different parts of the site.

Evaluation without users

Testing with users — whatever technique is used — is the "gold standard" for usability evaluation. It is especially important in government systems, where the differences in understanding, perception of value, and relationship to the program can be very different for government insiders and the citizens the systems serves. However, there are some usability evaluation methods that do not include direct work with typical users.

Persona-led reviews

One approach to evaluating a system without users is a technique called a persona-led review. Instead of basing the review solely on expert opinion or heuristics, this style of review builds on user research by enacting the interaction through the lens of a persona. In their work to understand how older adults use the Web, Dana Chisnell and Ginny Redish (Chisnell & Redish, 2004) selected two personas and performed the tasks that were realistic for each one. They recorded their observations while performing the task, as though observing a real user.

The advantage of this technique is that it can be done at low cost and with minimal preparation. Chisnell & Redish reported, "In the guise of our personas, we made observations that were much like the 'think aloud' verbal commentary that we typically get from participants in a usability test" (p. 6). This technique assumes that there is already a good understanding of user requirements and a solid set of personas.

In another technique for bringing user perspectives into a review, Jarrett & Quesenbery (2006) used a simplified version of this approach in an evaluation in which experts compare a system to best practices. The persona led review can also be adapted for a project team, to extend the users' perspective into informal discussions and help make design brainstorming user-centered.

Testing for conformance

All of the ways of conducting a usability evaluation that have been discussed so far are intended to determine how the usability of a system compares either to similar systems or to its own requirements. Although there are some standard design requirements aimed at supporting good usability, few broad standards exist that can be used as a benchmark against which to measure a system.

The US Election Assistance Commission (EAC) develops standards for voting systems. If the Voting Performance Protocol is approved, it will be the first standard requiring a human performance test with pass-fail benchmarks for conformance. (EAC, 2007, Section 3.2.1; User-Centered Design, Inc. & NIST (2006)). The current draft standard includes a requirement that to be certified for conformance a voting system must pass a test in which participants achieve predefined levels of accuracy in completing a set of standardized voting tasks.

Remote or in person

Remote usability testing, with the participant and moderator in different locations, has become popular as new tools make it easier to share screens and even use two-way video to communicate over distance. It is not always practical either to bring participants to the evaluation location or to have those conducting the testing travel. Working with participants in other time zones can allow for test sessions to be conducted at a time that is convenient for participants (such as evening), but within working hours for the project team.

Another general advantage is that participants are using their own equipment, so the evaluation includes a more accurate view of the range of computers, operating systems, connection bandwidth, browsers, and other personalization.

Remote testing has some specific advantages for evaluating government systems:

- Government agencies are often concentrated in capital cities, where even people who do not work directly for the government are often more aware of it than are people in other parts of the country.
- Agencies often operate under political requirements to ensure that systems work with a diverse audience or to be sure that they are accounting for regional variations among users.
- Some government systems are intended for a specialized audience. A site that, for example, provides agricultural information must be tested with people who work in this field.

Remote testing can also be more comfortable for participants. It can be intimidating for a person to come to a government or corporate office, especially if the work of the agency has emotional overtones, such as a tax authority. Even if the relationship between the participants and the agency is a positive one, it can affect the evaluation. Cancer advocates may feel honored to be asked to test a new system that is part of the fight against cancer, for example. One solution is to rent neutral facilities, or to conduct tests in an office not identified as an official government building.

Usability evaluation and accessibility

Many countries now have national laws requiring accessibility (see Chapter 12, Ensuring Accessibility for People with Disabilities). These regulations often focus on easily testable requirements — for example, that alternatives are provided for visual or auditory information. These requirements ensure that basic access is possible, and they are a critical first step.

Unfortunately, they do not ensure that the systems are usable by people with disabilities or using different types of assistive technology. For that, usability testing, as described in this chapter, is needed. Advocates for accessibility urge the inclusion of people with disabilities in usability testing and consideration of their issues in all usability evaluation (Henry, 2007).

- Testing in person with participants with disabilities builds richer insights into how they interact with the system, as well as deeper understanding of their physical requirements.
- Unmoderated remote testing, using a service such as the "Usability Exchange" in the United Kingdom (http://www.usabilityexchange.com) or "Knowbility Access Works" in the United States (http://www.knowbility.org), allows participants to conduct the test activities in their own physical and computer environment, and pause to rest as needed.

MANAGING EVALUATION IN A GOVERNMENT CONTEXT

In most ways, usability evaluation in a government context is no different from anywhere else. However, government systems have a few aspects that must be taken into account, especially in the relationship with usability test participants.

How many participants?

Ever since Jakob Nielsen (1989) suggested that five users are enough for "discount usability engineering," there has been debate over how many users are needed. Early work focused on how many people needed to discover a problem. This issue is important in government systems for several reasons:

- Government systems serve a public function and are often required for use.
- They often have very large audiences, so it is important to be sure that design decisions are not based on limited user perspectives or outliers.
- The audience is diverse. Government agencies have to consider the full range of users, including possible differences based on geography, race/ethnicity, income/education, language preferences, literacy, and the need for assistive technology.

Despite the need to cover a broad audience, it is still possible to conduct effective usability tests with a small number of participants. Jeff Sauro (2004) suggests focusing on tasks rather than users. His approach suggests that "12 users completing 10 tasks would be representative enough to draw many conclusions." Steve Krug (2010) suggests that you "recruit loosely and grade on a curve" — that is, worry less about finding participants who are an exact demographic representation of the audience in favor of more frequent tests.

In a project for the UK Small Business Service, the agency originally planned for 15 sessions, each lasting 1-2 hours. However, after the first five sessions were completed, the project partners of agency staff and usability experts agreed (against agency expectations) "that there would be limited returns to adding further participants unless changes had been made to the site" (Elliott & Jarrett, 2001, p. 668).

Ethical treatment of participants

You may have noticed that this chapter has referred to "participants" in a usability test, rather than calling these people "subjects," as one might when talking about a psychological or medical experiment. The reason is simple: the system is the "subject" of the evaluation, not the people.

It is important that anyone conducting a usability evaluation ensure that the test participants are treated with care. In an evaluation of a government system, there is an extra need to pay attention to ethical practices because of the imbalance of power between a government agency and a citizen.

In medical and social research, institutional review boards (IRBs) oversee the work to ensure that participants are treated ethically. Some government agencies maintain their own IRB and require that plans for any research be reviewed. Usability evaluations are often given an exemption from a full IRB review because they offer little chance of harm to the participants. As usability evaluation has become more common in the government, some agencies are updating their rules. The US Department of Health and Human Services, for example, proposed updates to its rules for human-subject research (HHS, 2011) to update the way risk to participants — especially medical patients — is assessed.

Informed consent

Many moderators start a usability evaluation with an introduction that reassures participants that they are not being judged. This introduction is often similar to this excerpt from the Usability.gov "Test Facilitator's Guide" (HHS, undated).

> *Thank you for agreeing to participate in this web site evaluation. Today we are asking you to serve as an evaluator of this web site and to complete a set of scenarios. Our goal is to see how easy or difficult you find the site to use. We will record your reactions and opinions; so, we may ask you to clarify statements that you make from time to time. . . .*
>
> *Here are some things that you should know about your participation:*
>
> - *This is not a test of you; you're testing the site. So don't worry about making mistakes.*
> - *There is no right or wrong answer. We really just want to know if we designed the site well for you.*

In addition to this verbal information, participants are often asked to sign an informed consent form, especially if they will be recorded during the session. For a meaningful consent, it is important that the form be written in plain language, explaining what will happen, without using any jargon.

At the NCI Office of Communications and Education usability lab, the consent process is divided into two parts for any sessions where the recording includes images of the participant:

- Before the session begins, the participant reviews and signs an informed consent and gives permission for the recording to be started.
- After the session, when the participant knows what is on the recording, the participant is asked to sign a release form for use of the recording within NCI. If the participant does not agree, the recording is erased while they watch.

This may seem excessive for a simple usability test, but participants in NCI's tests often use their own medical history to help complete activities, and may reveal more personal information than they feel comfortable preserving on video. In one case, a participant whose emotions overwhelmed her as she recalled her own cancer treatment asked for the recording to be erased, saying that she was embarrassed that she had broken down.

Privacy and identification

A part of good research ethics, most informed consent forms for usability testing say that the information from each participant will be aggregated so that no individual can be identified. Concerns about privacy are especially serious in a government context where these data could be made public either in the normal course of government transparency or though a legal request for government information. A usability test that includes sensitive information such as medical or financial details carries an even greater need to handle test data carefully.

- Challenges for working with the general public include the risk of accidentally revealing private personal details. In some health contexts, for example, it is common to avoid making recordings that include the participant's face.
- When the participants are experts or work in advocacy organizations, there is a risk that the statements and activities of the individual could be associated with their organization. In small communities, government staff often knows many of the people in their field, adding to this risk.
- For participants from government staff, there is a risk that personal details may be made known to their colleagues.

Data handling

All of the risk to the privacy and anonymity of participants requires careful handling of any data related to usability tests. Good practices include these:

- Identifying participant data through an anonymous code or number, kept separate from personally identifiable information (PII)
- Ensuring training in research ethics for all testing staff and observers
- Establishing policies to control access to test data, including dates for the destruction of notes, raw data files, and recordings

Establishing good practices for planning, running, and following up ensures that a team can conduct usability tests with confidence that they will be able to gain all the benefits of insights into the usability of a government system, while minimizing the risk to the privacy of any participants.

SUCCESS FACTORS

To conduct usability evaluations successfully in a government context, incorporate the following practices:

- *Plan for evaluation from the beginning of a project.* It is more difficult to add a new step to a project than it is to complete one that is part of the project plan. Evaluation is one part of a strong user-centered design process.
- *Test early and often.* Do not wait until a system is almost complete to conduct usability evaluations. Usability testing and other evaluation techniques are most useful when they can be used to find and fix problems early.
- *Be clear about your goals.* Evaluation is a way of answering both broad questions like, "Can people use this system effectively, efficiently, and with satisfaction?" and targeted questions about design details. Use the right usability method at the right time and to answer the right questions.
- *Collect both quantitative and qualitative usability data.* Quantitative data can help identify problematic aspects of a system; qualitative data look more deeply at why the problem exists and how it can be corrected.
- *Consider both remote and in-person testing.* Conducting usability tests in person gives you rich data, but can limit the range of participants, especially for specialized audiences. Remote testing allows a broader geographical reach, and allows you to schedule tests at times convenient for both the team and the participants.
- *Work with a diverse set of participants.* Be sure that the demographics and other characteristics of usability participants are as broad as the actual audience. Include people with disabilities, especially those who use a good range of assistive technologies.
- *Treat participants ethically.* Remember that you are working with *people*, not "subjects" or "guinea pigs." Follow good ethical and privacy practices. This is especially important in the government contexts, where there are often guidelines for handling data that can be matched to a specific person.

SUMMARY

Evaluation, especially usability testing, is a critical part of developing usable government systems. Within a user-centered process, it is important to check the work in progress as well as the final result and make sure that all the elements of the system have come together to meet the usability requirements. The primary form of evaluation is usability testing, which may be conducted in both formal labs and informal settings and with a relatively small number of participants. Usability testing can provide both quantitative analysis and qualitative insights into usability problems.

References

Barnum, C. (2010). *Usability testing essentials: Ready, set... test!*. Burlington, MA: Morgan Kaufmann.

Brooke, J. (1996). SUS: A "quick and dirty" usability scale. In P. Jordan, B. Thomas & B. Weerdmeester (Eds.), *Usability evaluation in industry* (pp. 189–194). London: Taylor & Francis. See also http://www.cee.hw.ac.uk/~ph/sus.html

Chisnell, D., & Redish, J. C. (2004). *Designing web sites for older adults: Expert review of usability for older adults at 50 web sites.* Retrieved 20 November 2011 from http://redish.net/images/stories/PDF/AARP-50Sites.pdf

Dumas, J. S., & Redish, J. C. (1999). *A practical guide to usability testing* (Revised edition). Exeter, England: Intellect.

Elliott, C., & Jarrett, C. (2001). Assessing the customer experience: Lessons from the early evaluation of the SBS website. In *24th ISBA national small firms policy and research conference,* 14-16 Nov 2001, Leicester, UK. pp. 663–676.

Henry, S. L. (2007). *Just ask: Integrating accessibility throughout design.* Madison, WI: ET\Lawton. Also available from http://www.uiAccess.com/JustAsk

International Organization for Standardization. (1998). ISO 9241-11:1998, Ergonomic requirements for office work with visual display terminals (VDTs) — Part 11: Guidance on usability.

International Organization for Standardization. (2006). ISO/IEC 25062:2006, Software engineering — Software product Quality Requirements and Evaluation (SQuaRE) — Common industry format (CIF) for usability test reports.

International Organization for Standardization. (2010). ISO 9241-210:2009, Human-centered design for interactive systems (formerly ISO 13407:1999).

Jarrett, C., & Gaffney, G. (2008). *Forms that work: Designing web forms for usability.* Burlington, MA: Morgan Kaufmann.

Jarrett, C., & Quesenbery, W. (2006). *How to look at a form — In a hurry.* Retrieved 20 November 2011 from http://www.formsthatwork.com/files/Articles/how-to-look-at-a-form.pdf

Kirakowski, J., & Corbett, M. (1993). SUMI: The software usability measurement inventory. *British Journal of Educational Technology, 24,* 210–212. See also http://sumi.ucc.ie

Krug, S. (2010). *Rocket surgery made easy.* Berkeley, CA: New Riders.

Lewis, C., & Rieman, J. (1993). *Task-centered user interface design: A practical introduction.* Retrieved 20 November 2011 from http://hcibib.org/tcuid

Lewis, J. R. (1992). Psychometric evaluation of the post-study system usability questionnaire: The PSSUQ. In *Proceedings of the human factors society 36th annual meeting,* (pp. 1259–1263). Atlanta, GA: Human Factors Society.

Nielsen, J. (1989). "Usability engineering at a discount." In G. Salvendy & M. J. Smith (Eds.), *Using human-computer interfaces and knowledge-based systems* (pp. 394–401). Amsterdam: Elsevier.

Nielsen, J. (1993). *Usability engineering.* London: Academic Press.

Nielsen, J. (2009). *Discount usability: 20 years.* UseIt.com Alerbox, September 14, 2009. Retrieved 26 November 2011 from http://www.useit.com/alertbox/discount-usability.html

Quesenbery, W. (2003). Dimensions of usability. In M. Albers & B. Mazur (Eds.), *Content and complexity: Information design in technical communication.* Mahwah, NJ, USA: Erlbaum.

Quesenbery, W. (2009). *Letting participants choose their own tasks.* Retrieved 20 November 2011 from http://www.wqusability.com/handouts/participant%20tasks.pdf

Rubin, J., & Chisnell, D. (2008). *Handbook of usability testing: How to plan, design, and conduct effective tests* (2nd ed.). New York: Wiley.

Sauro, J. (2004). *Calculating sample size for task completion (discrete-binary method).* Retrieved 20 November 2011 from http://www.measuringusability.com/sample.htm

Sauro, J., & Kindlund, B. (2005). A method to standardize usability metrics into a single score. In *CHI 2005, April 2-7, 2005, Portland, Oregon, USA.* See also http://www.measuringusability.com/SUM/index.htm

Shneiderman, B. (1980). *Software psychology: Human factors in computer and information systems.* Waltham, MA, USA: Little, Brown and Co.

Shneiderman, B. (1998). *Designing the user interface.* Boston, MA, USA: Addison-Wesley Publishing Company.

Tognazzini, B. (1998). *$1.98, Close-coupled usability testing.* AskTog, June 15, 1998. Retrieved 26 November 2011 from http://www.asktog.com/columns/001closecoupledtesting.html

User-Centered Design, Inc. and NIST. Preliminary report on the development of a user-based conformance test for the usability of voting equipment. (2006). Retrieved 20 November 2011 from http://www.nist.gov/itl/vote/publications.cfm

US Election Assistance Commission (EAC). Voluntary voting system guidelines, VVSG 1.1 (drafts). (2007). Retrieved 20 November 2011 from http://www.eac.gov/testing_and_certification/voluntary_voting_system_guidelines.aspx

US General Services Administration (GSA). First Friday's product testing program. (2011a). Retrieved 11 November 2011 from http://www.howto.gov/web-content/usability/first-fridays

US General Services Administration (GSA). Letter of intent template. (2011b). Retrieved 11 November 2011 from http://www.howto.gov/sites/default/files/first-fridays-letter-of-intent-final-template.pdf

US Department of Health and Human Services (HHS). (undated). Test facilitator's guide. Usability.gov. Retrieved 20 November 2011 from http://www.usability.gov/methods/test_refine/learnusa/preparation.html

US Department of Health and Human Services (HHS). Information related to advanced notice of proposed rule-making (ANPRM) for revisions to the common rule. (2011). Retrieved 22 November 2011 from http://www.hhs.gov/ohrp/humansubjects/anprm2011page.html

US National Institute of Standards and Technology (NIST). (undated). Industry usability reporting (IUSR). Retrieved 11 November 2011 from http://zing.ncsl.nist.gov/iusr

US National Institute of Standards and Technology (NIST). (undated). NIST and the Help America Vote Act (HAVA). Retrieved 11 November 2011 from http://www.nist.gov/itl/vote

Further reading

Albert, W., Tullis, T., & Tedesco, D. (2010). *Beyond the usability lab: Conducting large-scale online user experience studies.* Burlington, MA: Morgan Kaufmann.

Bold, N., & Tulathimutte, T. (2010). *Remote research: Real users, real time, real research.* New York: Rosenfeld Media.

Dumas, J. S., & Loring, B. A. (2008). *Moderating usability tests: Principles and practice for interacting.* Burlington, MA: Morgan Kaufmann.

Tullis, T., & Albert, W. (2008). *Measuring the user experience.* Burlington, MA: Morgan Kaufmann.

US Department of Health and Human Services. Research-based web design & usability guidelines. (2006). Washington, DC: US Government Printing Office. Also available from http://www.usability.gov/guidelines/index.html

CHAPTER

Adapting e-gov Usability Evaluation to Cultural Contexts

21

Torkil Clemmensen*, Dinesh Katre†

*Copenhagen Business School, Denmark**

Centre for Development of Advanced Computing, Pune Area, India†

"I hate this, I HATE this . . . so wildly that I will go back to saving coins in my mattress . . ."

— Anders Matthesen, Danish stand-up comedian and user of e-gov solution

INTRODUCTION

In the global world of today, e-government (e-gov) usability has to be defined and evaluated in an increasing number of different cultural contexts. The complex interplay and information exchanges between the models of government-to-government (G2G), government-to-business (G2B), and government-to-citizen (G2C) in different countries and cultural contexts pose different kinds of challenges for designing e-gov systems. The analysis of human work is critical in public information systems (IS) design because the procedures, working styles, and organizational contexts differ among public-sector organizations. In parallel with analyzing human work issues, the interaction design of the e-gov system and public IS must address the user experience (UX) needs of diverse users such as people from varied educational and professional backgrounds, senior citizens, people with physical disabilities, and people with low or no literacy, different languages, and cultural preferences. The combination of human work analysis and interaction design for e-gov systems must adapt itself to diverse delivery media such as Web, desktop, touch-screen kiosks, control centers, and mobile devices.

Globally, local governments and organizations such as the World Bank and United Nations Educational, Scientific and Cultural Organization (UNESCO) are promoting the computerization of governmental processes and services to benefit citizens and uplift the socioeconomic situation. In many e-gov projects, operational systems fail to win acceptance from stakeholders because of major usability problems. Heeks (2003) estimates the success rate of e-gov projects in developing countries as follows: approximately 50% of e-government projects are failures, 35% are partially successful, and only 15% can be seen as full successes. Both the World Bank and UNESCO have emphasized the need for enhancing the usability of e-gov systems in developing countries for reaching out to ordinary people (UNESCO, 2005). A large proportion of e-gov portals, web sites, and software systems are apparently difficult for citizens to use due to complicated systems and unusable interfaces.

In the global context, new definitions of usability, and adaptation of existing usability methods to local cultural contexts, are necessary to disseminate usability across e-gov initiatives.

KEY CONSIDERATIONS

Studies of cultural aspects of usability — here defined as "cultural usability" — have applied different definitions of "culture." Two of these are particularly important.

Usability defined as cultural values

The background for many studies of cultural usability has been Hofstede's (1980) framework of national cultural dimensions: power distance, individualism-collectivism, masculinity-femininity, and avoidance of uncertainty (Clemmensen & Roese, 2010). When we use this framework, usability — at least in the West — can be defined as an issue of equality (universal access) for individual users. There is a tendency to favor "masculine" values of effectiveness and efficiency rather than emotional and social aspects, and to focus on safe and secure use of IT. In the research fields of information systems (IS) and human-computer interaction (HCI), nationally shared cultural value dimensions have been the dominant concepts of cultures. This is clear from three review studies conducted within the last 10 years. Ford, Connelly, & Meisterr (2003) found that 22% of global IS research papers cited Hofstede's framework; Leidner & Kayworth (2006) defined and developed a value-based approach to the study of information technology (IT) and culture; and Kappos & Rivard (2008) applied a definition of culture as patterns of meaning, which link visible artifacts and practices to the beliefs, assumptions, and values of everyday life. However, the preference for focusing on values as central to cultural usability is not limited to IS research. Most culture and design theorists, many professional designers across all disciplines, and even some users believe that national cultural value dimensions pervade every human activity and every artifact, including user interfaces (Marcus, 2002).

Usability defined as cultural representations in situations

Those who oppose the cultural value approach to usability argue that it is not appropriate to rely on overly simple guidelines about how to address differences in cultural values. It is difficult to identify who the users are, based only on national cultural values. A value-based design process tends to build stereotypes — which may later become design rules! Merely identifying different cultures as groups or geographical regions that share one specific set of values does not really take into account cultural heterogeneity. Instead of using this overly simple cultural value approach, usability professionals should consider that the meanings of icons, symbols, and text in user interfaces lie in the cultural contexts. They should think of culturally determined usability problems in interfaces as resulting from users' (mis)understandings of the symbols, icons, and texts used in the design (Bourges-Waldegg & Scrivener, 1998). Culturally specific usability problems occur because the symbols, icons, texts, and other representations used are too foreign, are not available in the local culture, or are simply not appropriate in social situations in the local culture.

Cultural usability

The culture-specific approach to usability in e-gov and public IS that this chapter suggests and illustrates with case studies assumes that usability is something different for different cultural groups and geographical regions of the world. We believe that it is worthwhile to consider and study the usability problems in e-gov that are emerging in diverse regions and countries around the world. Furthermore, this must be done by drawing on studies that are indigenous to the region/country in question; no one from the outside can appreciate what are the critical problems in a local design solution (Clemmensen, 2011).

CASE STUDIES: USABILITY IN e-GOV IN DIFFERENT COUNTRIES

To illustrate what is meant by usability in cultural contexts and to demonstrate how to adapt usability testing of e-gov to new cultural contexts, we present two case studies: one on 28 state Web portals in India and one on a government single-sign-on system in Denmark.

India

One of us (Katre) participated in a project that conducted expert usability reviews of the 28 Indian state government Web portals, each created by a state for the citizens of that state. The review was conducted by a usability expert from the Human-Centered Design and Computing Group at the Centre for Development of Advanced Computing (C-DAC), a scientific society of the Ministry of Communications and Information Technology, Government of India. This study aimed to identify the scope for usability improvements of these portals.

The Indian government, through its National e-Governance Action Plan, plans to invest approximately $10 billion on creating 100,000 Citizen Service Centres and 27 mission-mode e-gov projects at the national, state, and district levels. Clearly, these massive investments will benefit the citizens only if the systems are sufficiently well designed and usable. Therefore, considering the lack of awareness about usability, particularly in the Indian government sector, we decided to conduct an expert usability review of these portals.

To identify the criteria for the reviews, we undertook a literature survey of e-governance usability evaluation methods applied by researchers from Asian countries. Latif & Masrek (2010) carried out an accessibility evaluation on specific Malaysian e-gov web sites which were based on the World Wide Web Consortium's (W3C's) Priority 1 accessibility checkpoints. Sidi and Junaini (2007) reviewed the credibility of 13 Malaysian state e-gov web sites. Dominic, Jati, Sellappan, & Nee (2011) used diagnostic tools to evaluate Asian e-gov web sites in terms of technical aspects such as loading time, page rank, frequency of update, traffic, mark-up validation, and accessibility errors. Wangpipatwong, Chutimaskul, & Papasratorn (2005) evaluated the quality of information on Thai e-gov web sites, using criteria such as accuracy, relevance, and timeliness. Liu, Chen, & Wang (2010) evaluated Chinese government portals on the basis of content functional and construction indexes.

We wanted to include findings from a few studies in Europe and the US. Atagloglou & Economides (2009) evaluated European ministries' web sites based on 100 criteria, grouped under 13 main dimensions. This study included abstract evaluation parameters such as comprehensiveness, esthetics, simplicity, and appropriate mix of media. Baker (2009) provided measurable criteria for content analysis of e-gov web sites in the United States, addressed as enhanced usability benchmarks. Stowers (2003) evaluated US federal web sites based on the availability of desired features relating to legitimacy, services, navigation aids, information architecture, user help, etc.

Our literature survey indicates that people from different countries and regions of the world appreciate different aspects of usability (for further evidence on this issue, see Frandsen-Thorlacius, Hornbæk, Hertzum, & Clemmensen, 2009; Hertzum & Clemmensen, 2012; Hertzum et al., 2011). In our opinion, the choice of criteria for usability evaluation in these studies reflects the technical, social, cultural, and political context in the respective countries.

India-specific usability parameters

What makes for good web site usability in the Indian context? This has not yet been clearly defined. The published guidelines for Indian government web sites (Verma & Joshi, 2009) do not provide any coverage of usability and human work analysis for interaction design. The use of regional languages in state Web portals is important in the Indian context, as India has 22 officially recognized regional languages. Surprisingly, although every state in India insists on using its regional language for official communications, regional language does not often appear in the state Web portals: 20 of them provide information in English only. Therefore, provision of the Web content in Indian languages and application of Unicode[1] fonts were selected as the usability parameters as part of accessibility. We also reviewed the links related to the Right to Information (RTI) Act, which is an important concern for Indian citizens, who expect their state governments to demonstrate a visible commitment to transparent governance.

Furthermore, while selecting various parameters, we decided that the broad categories for our usability evaluation of these portals should include ownership and branding. Some portals seemed at first glance to demonstrate greater ownership and responsibility by providing the contact details of ministers, officers, and service-based or needs-based officials to help the citizens. For example, the Gujarat state Web portal provides for contacting the Chief Minister, but other portals did not publish contact details. We surmised that some states were taking the opportunity to engage in "branding," building an image of the state and trying to sell it to investors, tourists, and their own citizens. The design of these portals reflected their proactive and marketing approach. Therefore, we decided to compare all states on the branding parameter as well. This differs from what we found in the literature review about usability evaluation of e-gov in other national cases in Asia, so our study also emphasized evaluation of information content.

The method that we used to carry out the expert usability review was formed by our view that India is less developed in the e-gov area. Instead of focusing only on one particular aspect such as accessibility, credibility, content, or services, in India we must take a holistic approach that takes into account all of the most relevant aspects of e-gov portals. To develop the set of parameters, we used a qualitative, iterative approach of switching between looking at Web portals and reflecting on our set of parameters. Using this approach, we identified seven different aspects of web site usability that we believed were important across all of the Web portals: accessibility, navigation, visual design, information content, interactivity, ownership, and branding. These seven aspects were based on 79 different usability parameters, found in the iterative, qualitative review of the 28 Indian state Web portals (Figure 21.1).

During the review, we ensured that the selected parameters were not abstract but were tangible in terms of observable factors and indicators in the web site — for example, whether or not the portal displayed the state's logo. We avoided subjective parameters such as esthetics or comprehensibility of information.

Review method

During the usability review, we checked the presence or absence of the each particular parameter or its applicability, and coded this as present or absent. For example, the presence of Cascading Style Sheets (CSS) as a parameter of clean visual design was recorded as (1) while its absence (an indicator of poor

[1]Unicode is a computing industry standard that provides a unique number for every character, no matter the platform, no matter the program, no matter the language.

Accessibility
Site map
Information in English
Keyword search
Use of alternative text for images
Font size adjustment for readability
Web content in local languages
Application of Unicode fonts
Appropriate page titles
Declaration of recommended browser and display resolution
Screen reader support
Page alignment in browser
Scalable or fixed layout
Management of linked URLs
Visible link to return on home page
Indicate Doc, PDF, Images as downloads
Use of bookmarks for long text
Rich Site Summary (RSS) feeds
Meta tags

Interactivity
Online services
Online QA for citizens, discussion forums
Polls, participatory features
Online tracking of proposals, applications
Application of Web 2.0

Navigation
Dropdown menus / tabs
Use of breadcrumb trails
Indication of internal and external links
Logical structuring of information
Highlight hyperlinks on mouse over
Prioritization based on importance to users
Task / Goal orientation

Information content
Government's agenda and priorities
Persuasive information
Schemes and services
Guidance on disasters / state calamities
State news
Announcements, decisions, orders, policy
Daily state weather info.
Media information
Tenders
Right To Informaction (RTI) Act
State statistics
Latest and upcoming events
Awards and achievements
Declaration of assets by council ministers
Profile of Chief Minister
List of departments
Rule & regulations
Forms and other information
Grievance
FAQs
Maps
Market rates

Visual design and layout
Color scheme / thematic colors
Simple layout
Grid based structural design
Highlighted categories
Use of Cascading Style Sheets (CSS)
Quality / size of images / graphics
Logical arrangement of contents
Effective use of font styles and text size
Color code for text / labels in image
Proper use of scrolling text
Proper use of bullets
Effective use of animation
Consistency of presentation

Ownership
Write to Chief Minister
Web directories
Contacts of ministers, key position holders
Contacts of secretaries, district officials
Departmental feedback
Emergency contacts
Security / quality certification
Contact Webmaster
Web site designed by

Branding
State / Web site logo
Projection of state vision, slogan, mission
Projection of local culture
Photo gallery
State newsletter

FIGURE 21.1 The parameters of e-gov usability in the Indian context

design) was recorded as (0). We clicked every link on the home page of all 28 portals. We did not review the functionality of online services, as it required a login name and password for registered citizens belonging to the particular state. However, our objective was to review comprehensively the overall usefulness and usability of the state government Web portals. Another limitation of our approach was the that it concerned only the state Web portals during the year 2010-2011, and obviously the observations and ratings might change if the state Web portals are modified or enhanced in the future. Table 21.1 summarizes the findings of the usability review of the 28 Indian state Web portals.

Analysis of the usability review

A holistic picture of usability of e-gov in India emerges from the details in Table 21.1. Under each category, the total number of parameters appears; for example, accessibility consists of 18 parameters. Each row presents results from the usability review of a state in India. The last column gives the total results (out of 79 parameters) for every state. The Web portal of the Jammu and the Kashmir state governments started to display the "web site under construction" page after we completed the accessibility review; hence no review of these portals was done.

To keep the analysis simple and clear, we decided to consider the state Web portal to be in compliance with a web site usability aspect when at least half of the parameters for that aspect were present. For example, the accessibility aspect comprised 18 parameters, so a state Web portal would meet the requirements for accessibility if it met nine or more of them.

Table 21.1 Results of Usability Review of India State Web Portals

Names of States (no. of parameters)	Acces-sibility (18)	Navi-gation (7)	Visual Design (13)	Info. Content (22)	Inter-activity (5)	Owner-ship (9)	Branding (5)	Total (79)
Haryana	4	1	1	6	1	4	0	17
Mizoram	5	1	1	6	4	1	1	19
Andhra Pradesh	8	6	12	15	2	8	1	52
Himachal Pradesh	4	4	11	13	3	6	2	43
Nagaland	4	1	2	7	0	4	0	18
Arunachal Pradesh	4	1	1	9	0	4	2	21
Jammu/Kashmir	2	–	–	–	–	–	–	2
Orissa	4	5	12	17	3	7	4	52
Assam	6	2	11	8	0	4	3	34
Jharkhand	7	4	9	9	4	3	2	38
Bihar	6	4	12	9	0	5	2	38
Karnataka	2	3	6	8	2	4	2	27
Punjab	5	3	10	7	0	4	1	30
Kerala	6	3	8	13	2	5	1	38
Rajasthan	5	2	5	12	1	3	2	30
Chhattisgarh	2	1	0	8	2	2	0	15
Sikkim	3	0	1	14	0	3	3	24
Madhya Pradesh	4	2	7	18	2	5	2	40
Tamil Nadu	7	5	11	18	2	6	2	51
Maharashtra	5	2	2	12	1	2	1	25
Tripura	2	1	1	6	0	4	1	15
Manipur	1	2	2	8	0	3	1	17
Uttar Pradesh	1	0	0	8	0	4	1	14
Goa	3	2	6	10	1	4	1	27
Meghalaya	5	3	4	15	1	4	1	33
Uttarakhand	13	4	11	14	2	7	2	53
Gujarat	11	6	12	18	4	6	3	60
West Bengal	8	4	12	18	2	6	3	53

As Table 21.1 shows, only two portals (Uttarakhand and Gujarat) met the accessibility requirements. The other 26 portals were found to be below our criteria of 50% compliance with accessibility parameters. Likewise, few (four) portals met the usability requirements for navigation, as most of the portals suffered from great inconsistencies in the placement of search features, use of local language (often only English was used), and use of "home" links. Visual design parameters, on the other hand, were met by nearly half of the portals, which displayed neatness and appropriate composition of various elements. Like visual design, aspects of usability requirements for the information content (e.g., FAQ for general citizen services, persuasive information about business opportunities, emergency contacts, and guidance for disaster response) were met by half of the portals. For example, the links pertaining to "RTI" in the

Andhra Pradesh state portal were rated highly as it provided contact details of information officers in all government departments, educated the people about their information rights, and offered access to important decisions by the government.

Online services and interactivity are very useful for citizens, but very few portals scored high on this aspect of usability. The Gujarat state portal did offer various participatory features such as interact with the government, participating in contests, making pledges, contributing to Gujaratpedia (encyclopedia of Gujarat), participating in opinion polls, and receiving e-greetings.

Ownership is another usability parameter that is relevant in India, but was not frequently met by state portal designs. For example, a "Write to chief minister" feature appeared on very few portals. Finally, regarding the branding aspect (e.g., displaying government logo), the study found very few state portals (Orissa, Gujarat, and West Bengal) to be effective.

In discussion of the results, we give a sociopolitical interpretation of the usability evaluation results, and of the broad categories of usability that we developed and used for this review (Table 21.2). The aspects best covered by Indian state portals were visual design and information content. We found five state portals to have good visual design, which in the Indian context can be understood as neatness, attractiveness, and caring for people. The other well-covered aspect was information content, which in the Indian context can be understood as communicativeness, effort to inform the citizens, and reaching out.

We can interpret a positive score on accessibility parameters as better transparency and a negative score as poor transparency. Similarly, we can derive other parameters, as the right column of Table 21.2 shows. On the negative side, the condition of most of the Indian state Web portals indicated a lack of synchronization and consistent information flow between the Web teams and various state government departments. The overall web site framework and content structure were generally not designed for scalability and incremental growth of information. This apparently resulted in unstructured layouts, patchy information blocks, flat presentation, and information overloading with too many hyperlinks on the home page itself. The content published on state Web portals may reflect that the state governments seem to lack clarity about what kinds of information will actually help the citizens. (See Chapter 3, "Usability and Government 2.0," Chapter 10, "Content Strategy," and Chapter 22, "Design for Policymaking" for detail on how this may be achieved).

Table 21.2 Interpretation of Broad Aspects of Web Site Usability in the Indian Context

Aspects of Evaluation	Manifestation of Quality of Governance
Accessibility	Transparency, caring for people
Navigation	Organized approach, structured clarity, understanding of the activities and portfolios
Visual design	Neatness, attractiveness, caring for people
Information content	Communicativeness, effort to inform the citizens, reaching out
Online services and interactivity	Effort to serve the citizens, participation
Ownership	Willingness to be accountable to citizens, commitment
Branding	Welcoming, enterprising, marketing approach Seriousness about business and development
Usefulness and usability	Overall citizen-centricity

From this review, we found that visual design in the form of neatness, attractiveness, and caring for people is an important feature of e-gov portals across India, as is information content in the form of communicativeness, effort to inform the citizens, and reaching out.

Denmark

The other author of this chapter (Clemmensen) analyzed the design of the Danish government's single-sign-on authentication system called "NemID." In 2011, the Danish government was behind the creation of a single digital signature for all Danes, with the aim of accelerating the Danish vision of one login for public and private services on the Internet DanID A/S (2012). The idea was that this login could be used in many places — to access online banking services, local public authorities' self-service, insurance companies, government tax authorities, and more. The idea was not new, but having a working, practical solution *was* new. The solution provided cross-platform access via any device connected to the Internet — work computers, home computers, Internet cafes, smartphones, and more. The signature worked by having a user name, a password, and a paper-based code card, which the user carried around, presumably in her/his wallet — i.e., a "something you have" solution (Paul, Morse, Zhang, Choong, & Theofanos, 2011), as shown in Figure 21.2.

As this figure illustrates, the single-sign-on solution has three input text fields. After the user has entered the user name and password, the system generates a four-digit number, which the user then finds on the paper code card; next to that there is a six-digit number that the user has to enter into the card code key field, and — voilà! — the user is signed in. The figure also nicely illustrates one of the problems with this solution: the user in this case did not discover that she was supposed to punch out a part of the card and carry only that around (or she did not take the time to do the punching out), so the card appears large and unwieldy.

History of the design

The history of the NemID design has two high points: in 2007, when the government put the solution out to tender, and in January 2011, when the solution became operational. The previous history included many designs, among them "Den Fælles Pinkode," which was halted in March 2011. All were

FIGURE 21.2 The Danish NemID solution

(For color version of this figure, see the Web version of this chapter.)

part of the Danish government's strategy for digitization Danish e-government strategy 2007–2010, June 2007). By April 2011, more than 3 million Danes (the total population is 5.6 million) had activated their digital signatures, which made it a success.

Usability problems

The usability and user experience problems were, however, plentiful. Despite the long history of development with many previous versions behind the NemID, many Danish users expressed their dissatisfaction with the new solution in blogs, letters to newspapers, interviews in the media, etc. Most famous among the expressions was a YouTube video (www.ANDEN.dk, 2011), in which a Danish stand-up comedian showed the problems that he had; among the biggest was having to carry the paper-based code card, which he saw as a very outdated method in this mobile era. After NemID became operational it was tested by students in an HCI group at the University of Copenhagen (Pedersen, 2011), who wrote a report that was cited in the Danish Parliament by the responsible minister. The report applied a classic approach to usability evaluation: the testers identified several user tasks for usability testing and conducted usability tests with two different user groups. They found 8-10 critical usability problems and many more serious ones. With regard to broader user experience aspects, this evaluation focused on traditional subjective satisfaction. The results indicated that users were medium satisfied ("middelmådige subjective satisfaction"; Pedersen, 2011, p. 113), which the usability evaluators interpreted as a poor result considering the large amount of money used to develop the system. The final conclusion from the evaluation was that up to 300,000 users could experience severe usability problems with NemID.

This dissatisfaction emerged despite the fact that the NemID solution had been tested thoroughly by a usability consultancy company during the development, which was an optimal situation even for the mature Danish market at that time. Although we will not report on the results of this here, we will state some general observations of importance for usability of e-gov in Denmark and probably most of Europe and which address some of the issues raised in Chapter 23, "Service Design and Channel Shifting" (A. Thrane, CEO "Interfazes," personal communication, August 2, 2011):

- Some people (user groups) will never become users of e-gov solutions.
- Marginalized groups will always have problems with self-service. Instead, this user group needs direct face-to-face contact with specialists. This is, however, not easily acknowledged by clients paying for usability evaluations. Certain stereotypes of users that are widespread and quite common in public administration are unrealistic, from a professional point of view; one example is the low-literate, low-income, single parent, who has so many and such specialized interactions with the welfare state that an e-gov solution is inappropriate. The problem here is not the group into which these users fall, but the fact that public administration employees — clients who pay for the usability work — often expect e-gov to be a solution for marginalized groups.
- Perhaps more seriously, people with computer skills — including young people with lots of gaming experience — can experience serious problems with e-gov solutions, because they simply do not understand the concepts for using the system. One example is the (Danish) public library, which has two concepts for ordering a book online — "reservation" and "ordering" — the meaning of which relates to whether the book is already at the local library or needs to be sent from another library. Many users do not understand such terminology (although it is very useful to librarians).

These and other similar observations about the importance of context for e-gov usability suggest possible explanations for the apparent dissatisfaction expressed by users of e-gov systems in Denmark. To remedy such a situation, we should study the context.

Analysis of usability problems

What would a study of the context tell us about the user experience of NemID? Our team did a bottom-up analysis based on a wide variety of materials and data that we could acquire (other people's usability reports, government strategic documents, our own analysis, and more) to find patterns and themes in the NemID case material (see Clemmensen, 2012). We analyzed all relevant documents that we could collect regarding the NemID case. Our analysis included 39 documents, which we segmented into 49 bits of text that we then gave 40 different labels or "codes." We then used the codes to create a network consisting of codes with linked relationships between the codes. We identified a total of 47 relationships that connected the analysis of human work in sign-on situations to the interaction design of the solution. Somewhat surprisingly, we found that the users' emotional relations to the design were related to both their social/organizational world and to their emotional experience of using the design. For example, users' unsafe workarounds (e.g., scanning and saving pictures of the paper card code on their mobile phone) connected what went on in user forums (debates about workarounds and more) with the user experience (anticipated and real perceptions and responses). This can be illustrated by an excerpt from two users' dialog in a social media forum (Wicked & DanielPT, 2011, translated from the Danish):

> *[DanielPT]...Has anybody scanned their NEM-ID or found an app that could put a password on a pdf doc?*
>
> *[Wicked] I have just taken a picture of my NemID card, if that is what you mean ...*
>
> **Wicked & DanielPT (2011)**

When we see this dialog in the context of the results of the post-implementation usability study — "... people do apparently like the NemID less and less as the months pass, and their critique is related to use of an analogue code card in a digitized world..." (Pedersen, 2011) — we see that the definition of good usability may change across temporal contexts, and other kinds of contexts as well. Apparently the users, across time, create workarounds in order to accept the new e-gov solution; a study of temporal context should have shown this. More generally, we suggest that the usability and user experience of e-gov require that theories and studies of user experience take context into account, which most academic studies of user experience do not do today (Bargas-Avila & Hornbæk, 2011), though a great many practitioners already do.

Furthermore, the Danish case indicates that the context of e-gov usability cannot be studied only by means of ethnographic field studies, which after a while may not identify much that is new. Long-term studies with a hundred thousand users would also be important. Finally, the case analysis illustrates that although the usability (and user experience) of the code card continues to be a problem, this is only one small thing in the larger picture of the design of the NemID authentication. Thus, a "medium subjective satisfaction" user experience which might usually be seen as a negative result may actually be an acceptable result for a culturally acceptable design in the long run. Although you are allowed to feel something when you use e-gov solutions, there is no need to get agitated about your use.

SUCCESS FACTORS

We have made a few important assumptions in this chapter. First, all user experience design for e-gov is cultural. We have touched briefly on one aspect of these difficulties — namely, that traditional definitions of usability need to be adapted to new user groups and new geographical regions, and that new usability methods must be developed. Second, it is even more difficult to do cross-cultural usability evaluation and design because of the greater diversity among user groups and geographical regions. Hence we need to take a broad and context-oriented approach to cross-cultural e-gov usability.

Cross-cultural success factors

The two case studies in India and Denmark yield five important success factors for interaction design and usability evaluation in governments that serve multiple cultures:

- *Analyze the human work.* Determine what users want to do with the e-gov system. Do this analysis for each different user group (minorities, majorities, language groups, etc.), and geographical region (states, countries, continents).
- *Identify cultural models of use.* Combine the analysis of human work in e-gov systems and the interaction design of e-gov systems to identify "cultural models of use" — in the form of existing systems, as well as sketches and prototypes of future systems — of a given technology, (e.g., a web site) for each user group and geographical region.
- *Be as broad as possible.* Conduct your analysis in "grounded theory" style — bottom-up analysis based on as many kinds of materials and data that you can get (other people's usability reports, government strategic documents, your own analysis, more), and then seek patterns and themes in the material.
- *Identify relationships.* Pay particular attention to the types of relationships that you see between analysis of human work, the design artifacts, and the interaction design activities. These relations may not be the same, or even very similar, in different regions of the world.
- *Encourage participation.* Encourage participation of all possible stakeholders such as various types of citizens, government officials with different roles and responsibilities, and the user agencies while designing the e-gov systems.

Success factors for India

The case study of expert usability evaluation of 28 state portals in India offers the following guidelines for e-gov usability in that culture:

- Consider the overall national context (technical, social, cultural, economic, and political) while selecting key aspects of e-gov usability for evaluation.
- Define common specifications and user interface patterns to avoid very basic design errors.
- Urge government authorities to introduce third-party usability evaluation as a standard procedure with some level of regularity. The Indian government cannot depend on voluntary initiatives like the expert usability evaluation described above.

Success factors for Europe

The Danish case study gives the following guidelines:

- Do not design e-gov solutions for the marginal user with specialized needs, without making it very clear to clients that these users require additional support from human specialists.
- Be aware that western European users, even when computer literate, do not necessarily understand the idea behind many e-gov and public IS — that is, what to do with these systems.
- Study the context by sampling diverse case material and look for relations between these, with a focus on the connection between human work (how should this system be used) and interaction design (usability and user experience of the e-gov design solution).
- Take into account that user experience of e-gov unfolds in stages, and has a temporality — and, for example, that a possible "medium subjective satisfaction" identified as a negative result in a classic usability study may be an acceptable result for a culturally acceptable design in the long run. It may take a long time (years) for individual users as well as for user populations to learn to use e-gov systems.

In this chapter, we have assumed that the purpose of design is to let the e-gov system support the users' diversity; obviously this is not always the case, as for political purposes government may want to use e-gov to homogenize its people. In addition, certain e-gov solutions may (as may any other software) become more widely popular for different reasons, and the implicit models of use built into such solutions should be studied in detail, for example, what kind of democracy they tend to support.

SUMMARY

In this chapter, we have discussed how to define and evaluate e-gov usability in India and Denmark. From an evaluation of 28 Indian state Web portals, we found that visual design and information content are important aspects of e-gov usability in India, and that other nontraditional aspects of usability (for example branding and ownership) were important to varying degrees. In addition, there were some very basic usability problems in many of the e-gov web sites. The recommendation to people working with e-gov usability in India is to consider the overall national context (technical, social, cultural, economic, and political) while selecting key aspects of e-gov usability for evaluation.

The Danish case of e-gov usability focused on a single-sign-on solution that had severe usability problems and a mediocre user experience, but which in the long run turned out to be accepted by a majority of the Danish population. This was due to the users' development of creative work around the usability problems, and because it was made clear to the intended users how the solution was highly useful for them for many different purposes. The recommendation from the Danish case is to admit that even a good usability of e-gov solutions can never be a quick fix for government's interaction with marginalized user populations, and that, on the other hand, if the purpose of using the e-gov system is made clear, citizens high in computer literacy will eventually use the solution.

In general, usability professionals working with adapting e-gov usability to cultural contexts should pay particular attention to the culturally specific relationships between the human work, the design artifacts, and the interaction design. The combination of the analysis of human work in e-gov systems with the interaction design of e-gov systems should identify "cultural models of use" — in the form of existing systems, as well as sketches and prototypes of future systems — of a given technology (e.g., a web site) for each user group and geographical region.

References

Atagloglou, M. P., & Economides, A. A. (2009). Evaluating European ministries' websites. *International Journal of Public Information Systems*, *3*, 147–177.

Baker, D. L. (2009). Advancing E-Government performance in the United States through enhanced usability benchmarks. *Elsevier's Government Information Quarterly*, *26*(2009), 82–88.

Bargas-Avila, J. A., & Hornbæk, K. (2011). Old wine in new bottles or novel challenges: A critical analysis of empirical studies of user experience. *CHI2011* (pp. 2689–2698). NY: ACM.

Bourges-Waldegg, P., & Scrivener, S. A. R. (1998). Meaning, the central issue in cross-cultural HCI design. *Interacting with Computers*, *9*(3), 287.

Clemmensen, T., & Roese, K. (2010). An overview of a decade of journal publications about culture and Human-Computer Interaction (HCI). In D. S. Katre, R. Orngreen, P. G. Yammiyavar & T. Clemmensen (Eds.), *Human work interaction design: Usability in social, cultural and organizational contexts.* Vol. 316 (pp. 98–112). Hamburg: Springer.

Clemmensen, T. (2011). Designing a Simple Folder Structure for a Complex Domain. *Human Technology: An Interdisciplinary Journal on Humans in ICT*, *7*(3), 216–249.

Clemmensen, T. (2012). Usability problem identification in culturally diverse settings. *Information Systems Journal*, *22*(2), 151–175.

Danish e-government strategy 2007–2010 - Towards better digital service, increased efficiency and stronger collaboration. (2007). Retrieved 8 November 2011 from http://modernisering.dk/fileadmin/user_upload/documents/Projekter/digitaliseringsstrategi/Danish_E-government_strategy_2007-2010.pdf

Dominic, P., Jati, H., Sellappan, P., & Nee, G. K. (2011). A comparison of Asian e-government websites quality: Using a non-parametric test. *International Journal of Business Information Systems*, *7*(2), 220–246.

Ford, D. P., Connelly, C. E., & Meister, D. B. (2003). Information systems research and Hofstede's culture's consequences: An uneasy and incomplete partnership. *IEEE Transactions on Engineering Management*, *50*(1), 8–25.

Frandsen-Thorlacius, O., Hornbæk, K. A. S., Hertzum, M., & Clemmensen, T. (2009). Non-universal usability? In *CHI 2009—Designing for other cultures* (pp. 41–50). New York: ACM.

Heeks, R. (2003). *Success and failure rates of eGovernment in developing/transitional countries: Overview.* Manchester, UK: IDPM, University of Manchester. Retrieved 8 November 2011 from http://www.egov4-dev.org/success/sfrates.shtml

Hertzum, M., & Clemmensen, T. (2012). How do usability professionals construe usability? *International Journal of Human Computer Studies*, *70*(1), 26–42.

Hertzum, M., Clemmensen, T., Hornbæk, K., Kumar, J., Shi, Q., & Yammiyavar, P. G. (2011). Personal usability constructs: How people construe usability across nationalities and stakeholder groups. *International Journal of Human Computer Interaction*, *27*(8), 729–761.

Hofstede, G. (1980). *Culture's consequence: Comparing values, behaviours, institutions and organizations across nations.* Thousand Oaks, CA: Sage Publications Inc.

Kappos, A., & Rivard, S. (2008). A three-perspective model of culture, information systems, and their development and use. *MIS Quarterly*, *32*(3), 601–634.

Latif, M. H. A., & Masrek, M. N. (2010). Accessibility evaluation on Malaysian e-government websites. *Journal of E-Government*, 2010, 1–11.

Leidner, D. E., & Kayworth, T. (2006). Review: A review of culture in information systems research: Toward a theory of information technology culture conflict. *MIS Quarterly*, *30*(2), 357.

Liu, Y., Chen, X., & Wang, X. (2010). Evaluating government portal websites in China. In *PACIS 2010 proceedings.* Paper 88. http://aisel.aisnet.org/pacis2010/88

Marcus, A. (2002). Fast forward: Culture class vs. culture clash. *Interactions*, *9*(3), 25–28.

Paul, C., Morse, E., Zhang, A., Choong, Y. Y., & Theofanos, M. (2011). A field study of user behavior and perceptions in smartcard authentication. In *INTERACT 2011* (pp. 1–17). Lisboa: Springer.

Pedersen, A. B. (2011). *Usability evaluation of NemID (in Danish, usability-evaluering af NemID)*. Unpublished Master's thesis, University of Copenhagen, Copenhagen. Retrieved 8 November 2011 from http://www.andersbp.dk/studier/dat/SPECIALE/speciale.pdf

Sidi, J., & Junaini, S. N. (2007). Credibility review of the Malaysian states e-government web sites. *Public Sector ICT Management Review*, *1*(1), 41–45. Retrieved 8 November 2011 from http://citeseerx.ist.psu.edu/viewdoc/download?doi=10.1.1.137.8229&rep=rep1&type=pdf

Stowers, G. N. L. (2003). The state of federal websites: The pursuit of excellence. In M. A. Abramson & T. L. Morin (Eds.), *E-government 2003* (pp. 17–52). Oxford: Rowman and Littlefield Publishers, Inc.

UNESCO. (2005). *E-government toolkit for developing countries*. New Delhi, India: UNESCO Office New Delhi National Informatics Centre (India) (209 pages).

Verma, N., & Joshi, L. (2009). Guidelines for Indian government websites: Standards for enhancing web usability. In *Proceedings of the 3rd international conference on theory and practice of electronic governance*, (281–286). Bogota, Colombia: ACM.

Wangpipatwong, S., Chutimaskul, W., & Papasratorn, B. (2005). Factors influencing the adoption of Thai eGovernment websites: Information quality and system quality approach. In *Proceedings of Fourth International conference on eBusiness*, November 19-20, 2005, Bangkok, Thailand, Special Issue of the International Journal of the Computer, the Internet and Management, Vol. 13 No.SP3, pp. 141-147.

Wicked & DanielPT. Fede Android app.!!!!. Retrieved 28 October 2011 from http://www.mobildebat.dk/archive/index.php?t-152146-p-31

www.ANDEN.dk (Producer). NemID eller?. (2011, November 2). Retrieved 8 November 2011 from http://www.youtube.com/watch?v=qE-bbRoSrR4

SECTION

Wider Considerations

V

"The greater danger for most of us lies not in setting our aim too high and falling short; but in setting our aim too low, and achieving our mark."
— Michelangelo Buonarroti

This section takes a broader view and considers user interactions with government "in the large." The section has three chapters:

- *Chapter 22*, Design for Policymaking
- *Chapter 23*, Service Design and Channel Shifting
- *Chapter 24*, UX and e-Democracy in Asia

The chapters in this section take a step back from users' direct interactions with information and communications technology and thus from usability and UX as the field traditionally considers them. The authors in this section take a larger view of UX in government, addressing the user experience of the government itself and how design can play a role in enhancing that and making it more effective, efficient, and satisfying.

- In Chapter 22, **Jess McMullin** (Canada) discusses the role that design can play in making public policy. Design, he asserts, can facilitate innovation in public policymaking and can contribute beyond improving service delivery — which itself often needs underlying policy changes.

By working at the level of government's "decision DNA," design can make a greater impact and policymakers can find a new set of tools and perspectives to help their efforts succeed. Experienced as they are in improving the ways in which people interact with organizations, he observes, designers are well positioned to bring their skills and their tools to policy as the larger picture of that interaction. This chapter shows the similarities and differences between policy and design, provides an introduction to the policymaking process, and points to useful design activities to complement specific stages of that process. McMullin illustrates his points with two brief case studies of using design approaches for policy and follows them with some useful recommendations for policymakers and designers who seek to collaborate. "Design for policymaking," he says, "is a fundamental long-term shift, not an overnight transformation, and it is worth it. As designers and policymakers work together there are exciting, deeply meaningful opportunities for innovation in the policy process and the programs and services that government delivers." McMullin urges us, "Go out and discover them."

- In Chapter 23, **Neil Sandford** (UK) and **Angus Doulton** (UK) discuss two concepts that are currently attracting high levels of interest in customer-focused "one-stop shop" applications. They discuss the ways in which attention to the quality of service-delivery processes and the use of digital technologies and enhanced or multiple communication channels allow widespread and convenient access to services with fast or immediate responses, thus helping to meet government targets for efficiency, transparency, and cost savings. They point out that, although governments have operated for two decades under the assumption that low-cost ubiquitous IT will transform how they do business with their citizens, their piecemeal adoption of technology and lack of organizational commitment have hardly improved the situation for the citizen. They conclude that the key to making a public services more effective and efficient cannot be found in simply moving them to lower cost channels, but in making the services themselves more approachable and more accessible. They cite two case studies: (1) Centrelink, which centralizes access to government services in Australia's Department of Human Services and undergoes continual improvement and (2) the central government in the United Kingdom, whose "archaic processes and incoherent decision making" have impeded service delivery instead of improving it.

- In Chapter 24, **Daniel Szuc** (Hong Kong), **Josephine Wong** (Hong Kong), and **Raven Chai** (Singapore) describe some ways in which UX design practitioners in Asia are helping improve their countries by getting involved in e-government. Dealing with government sometimes feels, they comment, "like jumping into the unknown without a parachute." They argue that one of the most challenging tasks for any government is to support both the individual needs of the citizens and the growth — usually the economic growth — of the nation as a whole. Gross domestic product per capita is often considered an indicator of a country's standard of living, but they wonder if that is the right indicator. Szuc, Wong, and Chai end with an exercise for the reader: "Looking ahead," they ask us, "if we were to transform government to a friendly place where we could get the answers we need, what would that look like, and what would our design goals be for a future government?"

These three chapters all take a larger perspective on UX than the design of web sites and interactive computer-based systems and encourage us to think of other ways in which UX professionals can contribute to improving government's interactions with its citizens.

CHAPTER

Design for Policymaking

22

Jess McMullin
Centre for Citizen Experience, Edmonton, Canada

"No foreign policy, no matter how ingenious, has any chance of success if it is born in the minds of a few and carried in the hearts of none."
— Henry Kissinger

INTRODUCTION

The chapters in this book cover a wide variety of topics on improving the user experience of government web sites, applications, and systems. Some authors have also focused on improving service delivery across channels, including face to face and call centers.

But when we talk about design and government we should not stop with better service delivery alone. Design methods are a largely untapped gold mine to help make better organizational decisions of all kinds. For designers working in the public sector, it means getting involved in the policy process. (For additional perspective on this topic, see Chapters 23, Service Design and Channel Shifting, and 24, UX and e-Democracy in Asia.)

Why policy matters

When the discussion turns to policy, many UX practitioners suddenly remember another pressing engagement. Visions of dusty binders full of obscure rules cannot compete with the thrill of designing for the latest shiny technology. For many, policy is the essence of bureaucracy and comes with all the corresponding baggage and associations with stifled innovation, stodgy organizations, and the arcana of government machinery. The very word "policy" evokes images of paperwork in triplicate, endless lines at the Department of Motor Vehicles (DMV), or constant shuttling between reps in government call centers punctuated only by hold music procured from the lowest bidder.

It is true — those are real problems with policy.

And that is precisely why policy design matters so much.

If you want to simplify paperwork, or streamline the DMV, or get a citizen's issue settled in as few calls as possible, you cannot just come up with a new design. You need to deal with the policy behind those things.

Policy is the decision DNA within organizations: just as its genetic code determines a living organism's features, so policy is the code that determines an organization's functionality. It sets the internal patterns, priorities, and constraints that emerge in the world as visible services, touchpoints, and interactions.

Of course, good genes have to have the right environment to thrive, and even great policy cannot guarantee good practices without other success factors. Organizational culture, constraints, and the constant gravitational pull of the status quo can mire even the best policies and limit their benefit. But good policy can enable amazing things. Policy is a key foundation for making fundamental shifts in improving the citizen experience, especially by lowering barriers to rethinking and refining programs and services. The benefits of designing for policy do not stop there, though.

Daily policy decisions have a tremendous impact on how well government works across the board, not just in service delivery. Designers have an opportunity to contribute to the general policy process as well. This contribution comes largely through facilitation of that process, including design research insights, exploring and imagining futures, helping frame the conversation, and communicating options and outcomes both for the policy team and for other stakeholders.

Despite this broad potential, design is not a panacea that promises a flawless policy process or perfect policies. Instead, it is a new set of tools to add to the toolkit for public servants and policymakers of all kinds, and some new perspectives to guide the use of those tools. Together, a design toolset and design logic can make policymaking better.

For organizations, the benefit of this design toolkit is in saving money and time while lowering risk, accelerating the policy process without compromise, producing policy that more accurately reflects the needs of citizens and other stakeholders, and increasing the success rate of achieving the desired outcomes.

For designers, the benefit is the opportunity to move upstream and increase their impact. The design community has an ongoing conversation about how to "get a seat at the table". That seat is here, working on policy design, right next to the binder full of regulations in triplicate.

For both designers and organizations, the question comes down to *how*: How can we use design to improve policy?

The rest of this chapter will start to answer that question and provide pointers to more resources to help you develop your own practice of designing for policy, whether you are a policymaker or a designer.

KEY CONSIDERATIONS

The following sections highlight similarities and differences between policy and design, touch on the policy process, and show why, and how, design can contribute. These considerations are aimed at providing designers with some useful background and perspective as they look for policy opportunities. Policymakers will also find these points useful in finding common ground as they look to work with designers.

What is policy?

Before we can design for something, we have to know what it is. *Policy* is a complex topic with many valid definitions and perspectives — not unlike design itself. However, for our purposes here, policy is simply a decision about how government will act to achieve its goals. Policy both guides and constrains further decisions and actions taken by government, outlining what is and is not allowable in a given situation. Policy is both permission and purpose for action.

Policymaking as design

Nobel laureate Herbert Simon (1996) declared, "Everyone designs who devises a course of action aimed at changing existing situations into preferred ones" (p. 111). In this broad sense, policymaking is a design practice in its own right. As such, policy is also a design medium, an "intervening substance . . . through which a force acts or an effect is produced" (Dictionary.com, 2011). This recognition draws out further similarities to more common design practices, and the possibility that these design practices are a useful addition to policymaking.

The most significant similarity is that design and policy both deal with "wicked" problems. Wicked problems are large-scale, intractable challenges without simple solutions or routine methods for addressing them. Designers began to adopt the idea of wicked problems in earnest in the early 1990s (Buchanan, 1992), and wicked problems are now a staple principle used to characterize design as a practice. However, designers may not realize that wicked problems were first defined to describe policy challenges in the late 1960s (Rittel & Webber, 1973).

This common concern for wicked problems points to specific parallels between design and policy. The following four parallels are not an exhaustive list, but they form a core of commonality rising from their "wicked" nature:

1. *Policy and design anticipate the future.* Through their action, they try to not only anticipate but also actually create specific desirable futures. However, as future-facing practices, both confront the limits of foresight and prediction — policy and design solutions operate in an ambiguous environment of imperfect information.
2. *Policy and design act within and upon complex systems.* Success in both disciplines relies on insight into the connections, relationships, forces, and influence throughout that system. However, these elements are difficult to map or model; developing a complete picture of a complex system is possible only through approximation. Within these models, both design and policy look for leverage points — opportunities to intervene to create a desired outcome. Both practices have their own prevailing stock of accepted interventions as they seek to influence systems. Policy and design often achieve their goals through modifying people's behavior, whether it is reducing smoking or making an ATM transaction easier for new users.
3. *Policy and design have no single answers.* Because of the complexity of systems and the wide divergence of stakeholder values — including contradictory values — it is impossible to formulate a definitive goal for intervention. Further, no single definitive goal means that no one single solution exists for addressing a wicked problem. New solutions emerge over time, through iteration and observing the outcomes of earlier solutions. There is no correct answer, only a range of possibilities — what is right for one person in one situation may actually prove wrong for someone else.
4. *Policy and design solutions may both generate unintended consequences.* Because of the complexity of the system and uncertainty of the future, we cannot predict all the outcomes of a policy or design intervention. Operating within a complex system introduces new variables that alter the system itself, in both expected and unexpected ways. Some of those ways may shift the system enough that the model of the original system is no longer valid, jeopardizing solutions based on that now-faulty model. For example, improving roadways to relieve traffic congestion may encourage increased driving and result in a return to gridlock.

As well as a shared connection to wicked problems, policymaking and design are both decision-making processes. Torjman (2005) characterizes policy as "... a deliberate and (usually) careful decision that provides guidance for addressing selected public concerns" (p. 4). These decisions are then expressed as the priorities and activities that shape the organization and its offerings. For design, decisions involve the strategy, scope, and form of a product or service.

We can see additional similarities of decision processes in design and policymaking:

1. *Design and policy deal with groups making decisions.* Few design or policy decisions are made alone. As the scale of the decision grows, so does the scale of the groups involved. With increasing diversity comes increasing complexity, with competing interests working to turn the decision process toward an outcome that benefits them. Most federal legislation in the United States has fallen victim to this complexity, with provisions and amendments inserted by various lobbyists, think tanks, elected officials, and other people jockeying for advantage.
2. *Both design and policymaking occur within a specific context.* This context is the largest factor that determines the types of solutions considered, proposed, and supported (Schneider & Ingram, 1997). As an Internet company Google focuses its products on the browser as a delivery platform, even when other dedicated applications often provide a better experience.
3. *Context determines how decisions, problems, and opportunities are represented.* The framing of the design or policy process encourages certain directions while actively inhibiting others. The range of options generated is determined by the context and framing accepted by decision makers. Sometimes a group cannot even express or acknowledge an option if it does not fit their context. Different framing is a large reason why Democrats and Republicans in the US find it difficult to work together — their competing viewpoints have become so polarized that it is difficult to even consider the other's alternatives.
4. *Design and policy decisions have to work in the real world.* While both can work to pilot, prototype, simulate, or test a decision, the real outcomes are visible and understandable only once the course of action takes place in the world. For example, US President George W. Bush administration's simulation of the Iraq war showed victory in a very short time period, but did not anticipate the strength of the ongoing insurgent resistance until troops were on the ground facing guerilla warfare.

These important factors are common between design and policymaking practice. But there are important differences as well.

Differences between policymaking and design

Policymaking is not simply design in a different medium. It is the force that operates to shape government and its role in society. In turn, it is responsible for the citizen experience — the collective interactions, perceptions, and relationships between citizens and government. Together, those experiences are a reflection of a nation and determine much of its character, culture, and attitudes.

Because of this scope, policy and design often differ in scale; that is the most significant difference between them. Design commonly focuses on a product, service, or interaction. Policy may have similar outputs at times, but it also operates on a far larger scale, from fiscal and monetary policy to social programs to national defense. Design must recalibrate itself to support operations at scale:

1. *With a larger scale comes a longer cycle time.* For a designer used to working with the Web where new changes can be rolled out literally overnight, the speed of policy design, implementation, and feedback can seem glacial. Design must prepare for a longer horizon to effectively contribute to policy. At the same time, policy may find opportunities to reduce cycle time through design insights.

2. *Policy affects everyone*. Many policies are aimed at the public at large, consciously rejecting the insight and differentiation that comes from focusing on specific users in the name of equitable treatment for all. Alternatively, policy may aim at certain target *populations* with a focus on aggregate group behaviors, in contrast with design's focus on specific *user groups* where design goals concentrate on individual behavior. Again, this difference in scale provides opportunities for both designers and policymakers to learn from each other.
3. *Policy is often abstract, while design is often concrete*. Policy is put into place through policy instruments — the actions, decisions, standards, or regulations aimed at achieving certain outcomes. Often these are indirect instruments, such as changing interest rates to moderate inflation and manage economic growth. In contrast, design is much more direct, aiming to produce a certain result through a product or service.
4. *Policy is often driven by ideology, while the market often drives design*. Many policy decisions are directed and shaped by political ideology or expediency. Political leaders set policy direction based on their platforms, and often ignore contradictory evidence or research (or forbid such potential research from even being conducted). Political leaders will also promote policy that responds to current sentiment — whether ignited through media coverage or through loud and large civic action such as the 2011 Tea Party or Occupy protest movements in the US — and later worldwide.
5. *Policy is often put in place by a government monopoly without competitors*. In a monopoly, attitudes can sometimes be that a policy is good enough or that people can "take it or leave it". This is compounded by the lack of a profit motive — governments are often more concerned with political capital than with financial solvency. For years, shuffling through the gauntlet of the DMV characterized this inefficiency and lack of empathy. There is nowhere else you can get a driver's license, so citizens had no alternative and the DMV seemed to have little motivation to improve. Thankfully, over the past decade, DMVs in most states have simplified and streamlined their processes.
6. *Policy is biased toward quantitative methods and measures*. This is true even when policymakers are able to take a research-based approach. They often question the validity of qualitative approaches because of both abstraction and scale. Quantitative measures also bring a sense of security and confidence when they support a position and allow policymakers to invoke the mantra of data when confronted about their decisions.
7. *Qualitative policy research is often limited to citizen engagement activities*. These activities often reflect traditional market research tools and include open houses, town halls, focus groups, surveys, and, more recently, social media outreach. Often these activities are about gauging response to a preferred or determined direction, or are simply a risk management tool so policymakers can say that they have consulted their constituencies. Policymakers use these efforts to claim they are citizen-centric even when they are only paying lip service to a citizen focus. In these cases, citizen engagement is about public relations rather than public consultation.

For designers to recalibrate their practice to contribute to policymaking, they need to build on similarities, respect and learn from differences, and find opportunities to integrate with the policymaking process.

Policymaking 101

The policymaking process comes in a wide variety of styles, approaches, and steps, depending on who makes the policy. This snapshot of the policy process will describe two useful models.

The strategic triangle

The first model comes from Mark Moore's 1995 book *Creating Public Value: Strategic Management in Government*. Moore's model of strategy (and the policy to direct and realize that strategy) includes three elements that form a strategic triangle (p. 71):

1. *Public value*: The policy must create something of real, substantial value to a given population.
2. *Legitimacy*: The policy must have political legitimacy, supported by elected officials and their constituents. This legitimacy is necessary to authorize, implement, and maintain a policy initiative, including the financial capital required.
3. *Feasibility*: The organization must have both the will and the capability to design and implement the policy. This includes appropriate skills, expertise, information, and insight. It also includes the commitment and capacity to apply those resources to this specific policy effort.

Policymaking strives to align these three elements, and it fails if any of these pieces is missing. Failures of public value, political legitimacy, or organizational capability may not keep a policy from implementation, but they will prevent meaningful policy outcomes even if the typical policy process is followed.

A typical policy process

Harold Lasswell (1951) articulated the first serious consideration of policy process and his model influences many of the variations that followed.

This process follows six stages:

1. *Problem identification*: Observation, public demand, or political ideology serves to identify issues or problems.
2. *Agenda setting*: Those with authority for addressing these issues decide which problems are prioritized and addressed through policy development.
3. *Policy formulation and selection*: For a given issue or problem, the organization considers policy options and decides which policies to advance.
4. *Adoption*: Selecting a specific course of action is insufficient; both the organization and their stakeholders must endorse and accept a policy for it to be legitimate and move ahead successfully.
5. *Implementation*: The organization works to realize policy goals by using the policy instruments available and authorized to address the issue.
6. *Evaluation*: Organizations evaluate policy outcomes and policy implementation.

Evaluating policy provides input into problem and issue identification, and the cycle is repeated. By understanding the policy cycle and the underlying strategic triangle that guides it, designers can find opportunities to contribute.

The power that design brings to policy

When I have asked designers what benefits they see design contributing to policy, the answers are often about innovation and improved programs or services. Those are important, but in my experience the most important power that design brings to policy is *making the right decisions, faster*.

A simple model of decision making can help us understand how design can accelerate policy decisions. Individuals make judgments by comparing a given option to their internal model of the world, a model determined by context. They use this comparison to predict how well that choice will work in the future (Klein, 1999). How accurate these predictions prove depends on how well that internal model actually approximates to the world.

Groups decide this way too, except that they need to agree on a shared model to evaluate possibilities efficiently. Having this common ground or shared frame of reference speeds up group decisions because participants can focus on how well an option will work. Without this common ground, groups spend their time negotiating about that shared understanding and advocating their own individual points of view to be adopted as part of the overall criteria.

Design helps people decide faster because it can inform and represent both *context* (to help shape that shared model of the world) and *options* (to facilitate easy mental simulation, comparing options to the model to predict outcomes). Together, these two contributions make policy that better reflects the needs of citizens and that lowers risk, improves outcomes, and brings clarity to the decision process.

This clarity is especially valuable when compared with the typical reliance on verbal thinking that dominates most business and policy decisions. As policymakers strive to reach common ground and then generate and select options, they spend most of their time talking or writing (and writing . . . and talking). Working in this verbal mode opens the door to ambiguity — language is flexible, sometimes too flexible. When we rely mostly on words, it takes more effort to understand one another and to be confident in making a decision together.

Fortunately, design complements verbal thinking and goes beyond the typical assumptions expected in policymaking to shorten the time needed to create a good decision environment. This ability of design to help make the right policy decisions faster is grounded in the commonalities and differences that were explored earlier in this chapter. Design offers new ways for policy to confront wicked problems, improve as a decision process, and operate at scale.

Design tools for policymaking

Design helps policy across the entire lifecycle, from initial ideas to final implementation and evaluation. Specific design approaches help in each stage of the policy process. While detailed method descriptions are beyond the scope of this chapter, these tools fall into five broad activities.

- *Real-world observation*: Designers develop insights by going out into the world and watching and talking with people in their natural settings, whether that is at work, home, or play. That fieldwork includes activities such as ethnographic studies and contextual inquiry, which observe and interview people where and when they go about their lives; diary studies, where people record their experiences and interactions in a given context over several weeks; and digital fieldwork, where this same kind of observation and conversation is brought to social media and online communities (e.g., learning about tourism in Canada's Northwest Territories by reading blogs about people's holidays there, instead of the expense of a far north field study).
- *Co-design*: As well as going out into the world, designers bring people into the studio for participatory design sessions. Giving people simple tools to design together with designers and with each other provides a new level of insight. Some of the models, representations, or sketches made may actually be built. More importantly, making tangible objects taps into a new way of articulating and expressing needs. These artifacts provide a new lens for conversations with people about their values, priorities, hopes, and dreams — and that points to new opportunities for innovation and optimization.

- *Analysis, insight, and framing*: Analyzing the collected data of real-world observation and co-design produces insights that allow designers to better understand and represent problems, systems, and contexts. This framing activity helps individuals and groups make sense of the complex situations they face and develop a common reference for generating and judging alternatives. Some related tools include affinity diagramming (an activity using sticky notes where similar concepts are clustered together), concept models (graphical models of the system, its nodes, and relationships), personas (richly descriptive user profiles), journey maps (graphical representation of someone's experience over time), task analysis, and mental model diagrams (which align granular activities with features, functions, or content of a given program or service).
- *Visual and tangible thinking and making*: One of the key tools of design to make sense of things, to frame a certain context, or to represent a problem or solution is visual and tangible thinking. This includes tools such as sketching, prototyping, storytelling, infographics, concept videos, and other tools to make the abstract concrete. Realism ranges from napkin sketches to prototype concept cars. Teams can generate and evaluate more options by working with rough sketches, while more polished versions are useful for communicating ideas broadly for buy-in and understanding.
- *Value-centered evaluation*: Too often, organizations set objectives in their own terms — meeting certain benchmarks or targets in staff efficiency, cost reductions, or similar factors. Design defines success as a shared value, both for the organization and for the people it serves. This value-centered approach demands that evaluation consider how well something works for people as well as how well it works for the organization. This limits unintended consequences, such as call-center reps hanging up on calls to reduce average call times. Tools may include analytics (based on tracking usage data), usability testing (having real people use a prototype, a production system, or a process to accomplish certain tasks), or key performance indicators grounded in the goals and outcomes that people find valuable (as discovered through real-world observation and co-design).

Designers apply these approaches and related tools using design logic. Design logic is the logic of possibility, of asking "what if?" and of generating new alternatives instead of working from what we already know (Simon, 1996, p. 121). Design logic operates with a deep empathy for human needs and works to generate and iterate options by managing the appropriate level of fidelity in its discovery, analysis, and visualization work (Conley, 2004).

Comparing these methods to the steps in the policy process helps find places to contribute (see Table 22.1).

EXAMPLES OF DESIGNING FOR POLICY

The following examples illustrate some of these design contributions to the policy process in action.

British Columbia Public Service Dragon's Den

In 2011, the Government of British Columbia (BC) began holding week-long design intensives for teams to address challenging issues in their ministries. The week takes its cue from the British and Canadian reality show *Dragon's Den*, where entrepreneurs pitch their ideas to a panel of investors for on-the-air investment or rejection (B. Moran, personal communication, September 22, 2011).

Table 22.1 Contributions of Design to the Policy Process

Policy Process	Design Helps ...
Problem identification	Discover and model the system using real-world observation, co-design, and analysis, insight, and framing
Agenda setting	Set priorities and find common ground by framing and using visual and tangible thinking to provide a concrete touchstone for groups to agree on criteria
Policy formulation and selection	Generate, represent, and evaluate options using visual and tangible thinking to explore options, insight, and framing to represent how those options fit in a specific context, and value-centered evaluation to select which options to pursue
Adoption	Communicate options, rationale, direction, and vision so that the organization buys in to a chosen direction using analysis, insight, and visual and tangible thinking. Frame the option so that it fits with the prevailing context in the organization. Help explain abstract concepts in concrete terms
Implementation	Explore, define, and specify solutions. This is the traditional domain of design, and all the practices mentioned are brought into play to create new programs and services, innovate in service delivery, and improve outcomes. The practice of service design (see Chapter 23, Service Design and Channel Shifting) is particularly relevant in the public sector
Evaluation	Compare, measure, judge, and select options or areas for improvement. The value-centered perspective of design evaluation is invaluable for effective policy assessment

Hosted by the Citizen Engagement team within the Ministry of Labour, Citizens' Services and Open Government, each week-long session involves four or five teams. As of this writing, two cohorts have participated, with a third scheduled. Teams apply to participate, and outline a significant challenge that the Ministry faces. These challenges have typically been identified by the Ministry for several years but are not yet resolved. Each team works on its own live challenge over the course of the week.

The week starts off with an orientation and an introduction to different kinds of tools for deep, meaningful citizen engagement, including social media. Then, facilitators from the government's central user experience group work with each team to identify a persona (a profile of an archetypal user focused on needs, motivations, and goals instead of simple demographic segmentation). The teams use these personas to map characteristic journeys, the chain of touchpoints, interactions, and experiences that define the particular scenarios (such as getting audited) that are related to the overall challenge they wanted to address.

These journey maps provide a common way to look for breakdowns in the citizen experience and to find places to make a difference. Teams sketch and brainstorm possible solutions across the range of interactions identified, from small adjustments to wholesale reinvention. Choosing from the ideas generated, the teams refine them into a specific proposal for a pilot (either completely new or modifying an existing program or service). Teams present their proposals on Friday to a panel of senior government executives, who offer feedback and can make an on-the-spot decision to fund a pilot.

For the first two rounds of policy design intensives, six out of nine proposals were approved and are now moving forward. Just as importantly, demand for participation in the program is skyrocketing, and BC public servants are learning to use design in their decision making.

Building the future brick by brick

Edmonton (Alberta, Canada) city councilor Don Iveson ran for reelection in October 2010. He wanted to explain his vision for a more livable city, so he made a video — using Lego®! This video followed up on earlier writing and speeches where Councilor Iveson used Lego models to explain urban policy. He narrated the video showing the kinds of transportation, planning, and economic policies he advocates. This introduced his ideas to a broad audience and contributed to a larger conversation during the campaign about the kind of city Edmonton should become (D. Iveson, personal communication, October 11, 2011).

The city's planning department extended that conversation. Encouraged by Iveson's earlier work, they planned their own conversation. In November 2010, the city launched its *The Way We Move* challenge. City planners built a model neighborhood of a future Edmonton with Lego® and displayed it at the Space and Science Centre. Then the city invited the public to come and build their own additions over 2 days. The city supplied the bricks, and citizens contributed their vision. In 48 hours, everyday people's dreams and needs came to life with small plastic blocks.

Those entries were judged by Councilors Iveson, Henderson, and Leibovici, and the winning entries were added to the larger model. This model remained at the museum for another 6 weeks, and now sits in city hall, where it is used to promote conversations about the city's future. Parts of the model now make school visits, and the city plans that it will become a pattern for even larger efforts to involve the citizens of Edmonton in shaping policy, using similar tools to make that conversation concrete, accessible, and participatory (Figure 22.1).

SUCCESS FACTORS

Designers cannot simply decide to design for policy — they must have the right opportunity to contribute. The following factors help find that opportunity so that designers and policymakers can be more successful together.

FIGURE 22.1 Edmonton City Councilor Don Iveson with *The Way We Move* model

(For color version of this figure, see the Web version of this chapter.)

- *Find the opportunity next door.* First, look for adjacent opportunities. Where is policy that is connected to your current work decided? How could your work inform those decisions? This is especially easy with design research projects — ask early in the scoping for such projects about opportunities to share results beyond the project team, especially with policymakers. The less you have to stretch from your current work, the easier it will be to have a successful start. Government 2.0 efforts (see Chapter 3, Usability and Government 2.0), citizen engagement, and policy for service delivery are all natural extensions of design work. Similarly, local and state or provincial issues are often easier than federal or international ones, simply because of having a more manageable scale.
- *Avoid ideology.* Exercise caution when dealing with ideological policymaking. Evidence-based policy efforts are often a better fit for design contributions. A policy process driven by ideology will not welcome a "better" context or evidence — ideology *is* framing and context, and attempts to reframe or introduce contradictory evidence jeopardizes the group's sense of meaning and purpose. This threatens the group's core identity and places the designer in a weak adversarial position, hardly the place to make a difference. Even when you personally agree with the ideology in question, opportunities to contribute are limited more to working within the ideological framework rather than exploring a full range of possibilities, and that limits innovation and opportunity.
- *Be humble.* Recognize that you have only part of the puzzle. Design offers a useful toolkit, but it is not the only toolkit. Arrogance in assuming that "design thinking" offers superior methods, or designers dismissing existing work, only limits success. Designers work best in policy by *complementing* existing efforts, such as the verbal talking and writing that permeates policymaking. Those words are important — and design can make them work even better. Humility is especially important because designers often lack the deep domain expertise of policy experts. Respect that expertise, and work as a partner and facilitator to smooth the way and unlock its full potential.
- *Rise to design's potential.* Counterintuitively, as you work to unlock others' potential you will realize your own. Design can do more, and *should* do more to improve our public sector. The citizen experience desperately needs the help, and governments all over the world are in a crisis state that demands innovation and bold maneuvers. Working with policy has the potential to profoundly change the world and make a difference in the daily lives of citizens, and that has the potential to elevate design. Pairing design for policy with design for service delivery is a compelling combination.

In all these efforts, look for the right partners. Having smart, passionate collaborators from policymaking, design, and other disciplines is the greatest success factor of all as you tackle new challenges.

SUMMARY

Great public sector design fosters a great citizen experience. To reach that full potential we need to include design for both service delivery and policymaking. By working at the level of government's decision DNA, design can make a greater impact and policymakers can find a new set of tools and perspectives to help their efforts succeed (Table 22.2).

Table 22.2 New Tools and Perspectives for Policy and Design

Policy Expects	Design Offers
Abstraction	Concreteness
Problem set by political agenda	Alternative representations and reframing
Preference-driven market research	Behavior-led design research
Verbal thinking	Visual and tangible thinking
Policymaking as exercising expertise	Policymaking as participatory codesign

Design for policymaking is a fundamental long-term shift, not an overnight transformation, and it is worth it. As designers and policymakers work together they can find exciting, deeply meaningful opportunities for innovation in the policy process and the programs and services that government delivers. Go out and discover them.

References

Buchanan, R. (1992). Wicked problems in design thinking. *Design Issues*, *8*, 5–21.

Conley, C. (2004). Leveraging design's core competencies. *Design Management Review*, *15*(3), 45–51.

Klein, G. A. (1999). *Sources of power: How people make decisions*. Cambridge, MA: The MIT Press.

Lasswell, H. D. (1951). The policy orientation. In D. Lerner & H. D. Lasswell (Eds.), *The Policy Sciences*. Palo Alto, CA: Stanford University Press.

medium. (n.d.). *Dictionary.com unabridged*. Retrieved 5 November 2011 Dictionary.com web site: http://dictionary.reference.com/browse/medium

Moore, M. H. (1995). *Creating public value: Strategic management in government*. Cambridge, MA: Harvard University Press.

Rittel, H. W. J., & Webber, M. M. (1973). Dilemmas in a general theory of planning. *Policy Sciences*, *4*(2), 155–169.

Schneider, A., & Ingram, H. (1997). *Policy design for democracy*. Lawrence, KS: University Press of Kansas is in Lawrence, KS.

Simon, H. A. (1996). *The sciences of the artificial* (3rd ed.). Cambridge, MA: The MIT Press.

Torjman, S. (2005). *What is policy?* Ottawa, ON: Caledon Institute of Social Policy.

CHAPTER

23

Service Design and Channel Shifting

Neil Sandford*, Angus Doulton†

Putting People Before Computers, Teddington, UK CDW & Associates, Bletchingdon, UK†*

"I didn't say there is a problem. There isn't a problem. The system is fine. The [Pay As You Earn] people put the extra digits in when they entered your reference code."

— A hard-pressed Revenue Service call center agent

INTRODUCTION

Interaction with government systems cannot be considered in isolation without also understanding the profound effect of the underlying, often convoluted or archaic, government policies and procedures. Improving the user experience (UX) of government services requires commitment to end-to-end transformation of the way those services are delivered.

We base our argument on case studies of two very different approaches. The first describes an attempt to encourage changes in customer[1] behavior to move demand away from expensive face-to-face interfaces toward less expensive Information and Communications Technology (ICT)–enabled self-service channels (known as channel shifting) without considering the sometimes vital role of a human intermediary. Often, one of the first things that a front-line service agent has to learn is how to "beat the system" to achieve the best result for the customer.

The second case study is about rethinking the delivery of government services end to end, from governance issues to the types of questions asked during the initial diagnosis of customer need. Service design (or redesign) of that kind goes beyond conventional business process reengineering or conventional user-centered design approaches.

The public and voluntary sectors are responsible for a vast range of services for citizens and businesses. The actual mechanisms for delivering those services will vary from country to country but we can make some general statements about the differences between service design for the public sector and for the private sector.

[1]*Customer or client?* Everybody is a citizen and every citizen is a potential customer for its government's services. No other service provider has a broader potential customer base. Local government is responsible for services that people need (such as education), those they want (such as leisure services), and those they may not want but have to have (such as local taxes).

For most citizens, for most of their lives, the relationship will be a straightforward one. However, some citizens will, at some point, experience a crisis that turns them from an everyday customer into what a social services worker might prefer to call a "client," someone who needs professional help and may need an advocate.

SERVICE DESIGN

In the private sector, most products and services are designed to be as attractive as possible to as many people as possible and the interactions between customer and supplier are as straightforward and as robust as possible. If a particular market segment is "too difficult" the supplier has the option of not entering that market. Brand and UX are at the core of the offering.

The only aspect that the public sector worker would recognize from this picture is that most — but not all — public sector transactions are (theoretically, at least) very straightforward. The exception arises when the problem requires urgent attention from one or more service organizations because the person in need is coping with a crisis and is probably under duress.

Dealing with government is a complex business, even if it all seems routine to the agent dealing with the case — because the procedures have been designed to suit the provider of the service, not to suit the recipient. The citizens may, for example, be unaware of the need to bring with them identification and verification of their circumstances.

Because the procedures, terminology, and culture of the public sector are unfamiliar, the citizen may need to be represented by an advocate — typically a member of the family, the community, or the voluntary sector. If no advocate is available, the service agent needs to be able to take on that role.

The concept of "User Experience" has entered the lexicon of public-sector service design only within the last few years, but with the advent of modern technologies, it provides the opportunity to challenge the way a service process has run, usually without change, perhaps for decades. In the public sector, the tendency is to evaluate only the new. Ruth Flood of the UK Design Council found that, out of a sample of 44 public authorities, 66% "always" or "regularly" involve users in the design of a (new) service but only 32% would observe users while they actually use a service (Flood, 2008). Put another way, service designers in two-thirds of the authorities start without knowing how *approachable* and *accessible* the current service is.

Discussions about service design often tend to focus on the most "expensive" channels (one-to-one discussion with an intermediary) and ways of deflecting demand toward cheaper solutions that are often based on self-service (automated telephony, web site). Assessment of the true cost of the replacement channel has to include the relative *effectiveness* of the interaction and the *efficiency* of its response to and meeting user needs without fail.

KEY CONSIDERATIONS

Good design starts with commitment to resolving customer needs. As we move toward more sophisticated channels capable of integrating support from several agencies, underlying processes have to be seen as parts of an overall system. The focus, end to end, has to be on services that comply with the demands of the customer rather than the other way around. Stripping out anything that does not contribute to that commitment results in four desirable outcomes:

- *Approachable* services with an identifiable and fully functional multichannel one-stop entry point
- *Accessible* services with resilient front-end processes that address customer needs, regardless of circumstances
- *Effective* services that resolve queries, reliably, at the initial point of contact
- *Efficient* services with determination to get it right first time, every time — not as a target, but as a principle

The benefit of this customer-focused approach can be measured in the contribution that outcomes (not outputs) make to delivery of policy goals such as enhanced social capital or community well-being. The effectiveness of an antipoverty initiative, for example, can be determined by the increase in wealth circulating in the target community, leading to less reliance on welfare benefits. From a "public purse" perspective, every family taken off benefits represents a major saving.

THE RELATIONSHIP BETWEEN COST SAVING AND SERVICE QUALITY

Our first case study is about "modernization" of local government service delivery in the United Kingdom, where cost was the main driver and best practices in service delivery have emerged "bottom-up" or "from the front in" via the development of customer focus through front-line staff and customers. Adherence to principles of customer focus in the development of a new service-delivery agency in our second case study, from Australia, exemplifies the benefit of a top-down approach. Our conclusion is straightforward: *You can reduce cost by improving the quality of your service-delivery processes, but you cannot improve service delivery by cutting costs.*

Failure demand and other forms of wasted work

The consequence of waste on the cost-effectiveness of production has been a mainstay of theories about quality since the period between the two world wars, and was subsequently revitalized by W. Edwards Deming and his champions. Four types of waste are most relevant to the provider of public services:

- *Duplicated work* — such as insisting that each part of each government department (each hospital, health center, and doctor's surgery[2] in the case of the UK National Health Service) maintains its own records.
- *Unnecessary work* — such as demonstrating compliance with statistical performance targets or processing customer feedback without learning how to improve.
- *Reworking* — correcting mistakes — often the result of the culture of setting targets that add nothing to the value of work and say nothing about the impact of that work on individual customers or on whole communities.
- *Failure demand* — avoidable contact resulting from failure to adopt the ethos of "get it right first time, every time" and failing to provide feedback at regular intervals if a request for service is delayed. This is difficult to verify and implies that every contact has four follow-up contacts.

CUSTOMER FOCUS AND TRANSFORMATION

In theory, using digital technologies and channels to enable and enhance communication channels provides "access to services with quicker — sometimes immediate — responses, which are available in more convenient places and at more convenient times" (CITU, 1996). According to a UK Government Green Paper (HM Treasury, 2003), four steps lead to achieving the desired outcomes of better and more efficient services, greater efficiency and openness, and substantial cost savings for the taxpayer:

[2]"Surgery" is the British term for what in the United States is called the doctor's office.

- Deploying an electronic customer interface, leaving internal processes and operations essentially unchanged
- Automating, but not fundamentally changing, internal processes
- Transforming internal processes
- Effecting end-to-end transformation, combining internal transformation with e-enabled interaction, with three purposes:
  - Reduce effort: removing duplicate steps and steps that do not add value
  - Save time: combining steps or conducting them in parallel rather than in series
  - Consolidate operations: reducing the number of offices, call centers, and data centers

The Green Paper explicitly recognized that services "will also appear quite different from the arrangements we are all used to. They will only work if a substantial proportion of the public (both businesses and citizens) find the new forms of service delivery attractive." What it failed to recognize was that the most significant resistance to change would come from within government itself and that the problems would be organizational, not technological. The main barriers are as follows:

- *Failure to address customer quality at a strategic level*: Departmentalizing the various service providers (education, social care, housing, etc.) resulted in silo-based service delivery with no organization-wide strategy and no senior manager empowered to ensure customer-centered design of all services.
- *Communication barriers between departmental "silos"*: Silos frequently lead to maverick behavior. One senior management team agreed to a customer-centered system design strategy, which the Head of Housing refused to support. More recently, an authority tried to "integrate" the various members of the service team by relocating them all in the same building — but placed council employees on the ground floor and their private-sector service partners (i.e., contractors) upstairs.
- *Lack of incentive for change*: The discipline of service design evolved from the emergence of "awareness of the lack of an organic and autonomous design culture" to balance the financial drivers for service delivery (Mager, Maffei, & Sangiorgi, 2005). Innovation in service design is a response to the needs of service managers and those developing new delivery mechanisms. Vision is a prerequisite for change, and the voice of the customer often went unheard.
- *Lack of vision of the enabling role of ICT*: In a market driven by specialized application vendors and customers with legacy systems, innovative integrative developments were few and far between and their potential value misunderstood. Customer Relationship Management (CRM), for example, was often seen as middleware for integration of legacy systems rather than anything to do with customer relationships.
- *Indifference toward wasted work*: Grossly inefficient processes, often built around collecting, updating, and retrieving paper records, were endemic, causing errors and delays for the customer in requesting and receiving service. Payment of benefits, for example, could be wildly inaccurate (in overpayment or underpayment) as long as the average led to consumption of the available budget. Equally inefficient were the "foolproof" processes designed to protect the department or an individual officer against the consequences of mistakes. These could be disastrous, both for the customer and the officer and the result in one District Council was typical: a nine-step process to find out whether planning permission was required.

CASE STUDY: e-GOVERNMENT IN THE UNITED KINGDOM

This case study charts the progress in England up HM Treasury's ladder toward electronic enablement of services, as described in the Green Paper previously discussed. Starting in 2001, local government was required to "enable interactions between the citizen and the council to be undertaken by electronic means as far as legally permissible within five years" (House of Commons, ODPM, 2005).

The scope was defined as follows and corresponds to the first rung on the ladder:

> *Any contact between the citizen and the council including: providing information; collecting revenue; providing benefits and grants; consultation; regulation (such as issuing licenses); applications for services; booking venues, resources and courses; paying for goods and services; providing access to community, professional or business networks; and procurement.*

This exposed a significant knowledge gap in terms of how existing channels were being used, which services customers actually needed, and how front- and back-office processes really worked.

The "proof" that people would migrate to a less-expensive channel, given the choice, came from a 1999 study from the United Kingdom's Henley Management College (unavailable), which reported very high (94%) acceptance of the telephone as a local government channel, almost the same as acceptance of the face-to-face channel. Given no other significant variable, the implication was that very few people would object to moving from face-to-face to telephone contact. Of course, the conclusion ignored the whole question of fitness-for-purpose of the channel.

"Proof" that migration produced savings was published in the widely read *Municipal Journal* in 2000 (unavailable). It claimed that a telephone "transaction" at £1.37 (US $2.20) was five times less expensive than a letter (£7 or $11.20), while a face-to-face interview cost £77 (US $123.20), eleven times as much. These figures went into popular mythology when they were quoted by the Improvement and Development Agency (IDeA, 2001) and were frequently cited by authorities in Best Value Reviews, Implementing Electronic Government (IEG) statements, and Cabinet papers.

It is unclear where these numbers originated, especially since the call-center industry practice is to express costs in terms of cost per call-minute (typically in the range £0.40-0.60, or $0.65-0.97) rather than per transaction. In 2002, a UK National Audit Office survey of 133 government call centers found 24 that could not disaggregate call-center costs at all and a further 36 that did not record call duration. Forty percent of the remainder had a cost-per-minute rate of more than double the industry average. The most expensive were Equality Direct at £27.50 ($44) per call-minute and the Electronic Integrated Arable Compensation Scheme Help Desk (£23.00 or $36.80) (House of Commons, PASC, 2003).

In 2002, one authority attempted to quantify potential savings by adding estimated volumes to the IDeA figures. Their 2.8 million face-to-face visits notionally cost £215 million ($344 million). Add 1.6 million postal items (£11 million or $17.60 million) and 3 million telephone calls £4 million, or $6.4 million. That means, if the figures are to be believed, that over 60% of the organization's total £370 million ($592 million) annual budget was spent on communication!

Nowhere have we found an authority that distinguishes between fixed and variable costs to separate the "cost of doing nothing" from demand-related costs. Nowhere in this contradictory picture was there any attempt to define the scope of a "transaction," whether the cost included fulfillment, what quality of service could be expected, or even what range of services were included in the estimate.

In short, no one in the local government seems to have heeded HM Treasury's (2003) advice about how to write an e-gov business case.

This did not detract from the focus on the IIEG program. By 2002, the role of the central government had been defined in a Public Service Agreement as "assisting local government to achieve 100% capability in electronic delivery of priority services by 2005, in ways that customers will use" (House of Commons, ODPM, 2003). By the middle of the decade, pressure to reduce the cost of public services was increasing and three deep-rooted structural problems were acknowledged — lack of customer focus, large-scale duplication of activity, and shortage of relevant ICT skills in both the public and private sectors. One response was a portfolio of collaborative "national projects" focused on enabling technologies — CRM, workflow, and smart cards, for example — and applications addressing 14 national priority areas such as education, democratic renewal, transport, and support for vulnerable people. They met with varied success. Some of the applications were widely implemented, taking local government to the second rung of the ladder: internal automation. However, it was not until the publication of *Transformational Government* (Cabinet Office, 2005) that the UK government began to rise to the challenge of *Transformation, not Automation* set by Daniel Steadman-Jones (2001).

David Varney (2006) echoed a point made by Steadman-Jones — viewing government service users as customers resulted in undue emphasis on the transaction, leaving citizens to navigate a route through "service islands" and join up those services themselves. This was particularly important for those most likely to need multiple services — the most vulnerable.

At the same time, leading local authorities were hungry to utilize their customer contact channels more widely by moving from simple automation to service transformation. However, Varney firmly told us in a private meeting in 2005 (D. Varney, personal communication, 2005) that restructuring the relationship between local and central government was out of scope.

Varney's report signaled the end of extra funding for e-gov in the *Invest to Save* tradition,[3] arguing that future investment in transformation would come from rationalization of front- and back-office processes:

> *Service transformation is not about further increases in public spending or investing in new technology. Building on the work done in the 2004 Spending Review on efficiency, there is an opportunity to coordinate services more directly around the needs of citizens and businesses and to deal with more problems at the first point of contact.*
>
> *... this approach could drive out efficiencies by improved performance and coordination of front-line e-services, contact centers and local offices and reducing duplication of business processes through shared use of an identity management system. Over the longer term further efficiencies and service enhancements could be made by reducing the back office functions that would no longer be required.*

While *Transformational Government* looked primarily at gaining efficiencies within central government departments, Michael Lyons (2007) raised a fresh line of thinking about the role of local government and its relationship with other local agencies, which he termed "place-shaping". Lyons' thinking had

[3]A UK government-wide funding program for welfare benefits payments based on an innovative financing agreement between the Department of Work and Pensions and HM Treasury.

been influenced by his close understanding of developing approaches to service delivery among leading local government organizations and based on his experiences as Chief Executive.

Case study conclusions

The *Transformational Government* strategy had proposed that "government should steer citizens and businesses to the lowest cost channels consistent with meeting policy objectives and customer acceptability. At an appropriate time, legacy channels should be closed . . . unless there are compelling policy reasons that cannot be achieved by other means" (Lyons, 2007). The business case for e-gov was assumed proven but a service provider would have to justify continuation of existing services and ways of working; central government did not share Lyons' deeply rooted background in local services and failed to recognize that the customer's needs are the starting point, not an adjunct, to the discussion.

The customer sees "government" as a haphazard and illogical network of services, the route to which is full of unnecessary or repeated tasks. She would not be wrong. What the customer needs most of all when she approaches a public-service provider for help is a "one-stop shop" empowered to mediate on her behalf.

WHAT THE CUSTOMER WANTS

Most citizens do not deal with government until they have to do so. They tend to be very unfamiliar with its rules, regulations, processes, and — most especially — language. They need support from people who are experts in government and who can mediate between them and service providers.

In England, a death can involve the next of kin or another relative in up to 86 possible interactions involving two doctors (plus a medical referee if the person died in hospital), a coroner, a pathologist, the Registrar of Births, Marriages, and Deaths, three local authority teams (Bereavement Services, Housing Benefits, and Social Services), and central government in the form of the Benefits Agency, a Probate Office, the Treasury Solicitor, and two separate departments of HM Revenues & Customs (HMRC) — as well as funeral directors, a housing agency, the deceased's employer, bank, insurers, pension providers, and others. Nearly all of these interactions require the original paper Death Certificate to be taken in, copied, and returned.

The Wolverhampton Bereavement Centre in the UK initiated a project in 2001 to address this wasteful and stress-inducing situation. As project reviewers, we watched them steadily develop a one-stop solution to giving all bereaved people a single place to go a Contact Centre.

Customer focus as a service design principle

Except in the very simplest cases, no two individuals' circumstances will be identical. The agent navigating the maze of regulations that affect eligibility needs precise case detail, including as much of the back history as possible, and must ensure that appropriate and up-to-date regulations are being applied. The agent must also be empowered to involve multiple service providers.

A one-stop shop "provides the public with a 'single face of government'" (Doulton & Wilson, 1999). Opening a new one-stop reveals a staggering amount of previously unmet demand among customer groups who had failed to engage with their Local Council. (See case studies in the Exchanging Information with the Public report series, e.g., Doulton, Sandford, and Wilson (1995).)

Customers want resolution and should never face any of these discoveries:

- They have started in the wrong place, or they have to take the results of this first step to another location.
- They have come without the right documents.
- They cannot understand the form they have to fill in — especially since they are well aware that a mistake could remain with them for years.
- Something has gone wrong within the "system" and they will have to start again.

All these result in avoidable contact caused by badly designed processes. None of them are the customer's fault. Getting it right first time, every time, is the way to avoid escalating costs associated with reworking, as well as giving resolution to people in an unfamiliar and often stressful situation.

A one-stop shop provides a relatively local place where the agent behind the desk will be able to cope with procedures in place across the whole of the government sector. People do not mind being told that they do not qualify for benefits of various kinds, so long as the reasons for the decision are clearly and openly given. Nor do they mind being told that a process will take a certain number of days and that they will hear again at a specified time, as long as that promise is not broken.

Basic design principles recur each time there is an opportunity to incorporate new ways of working and new technologies. Lessons learned from successful one-stop shops informed the design of multi-channel Contact Centres. As service organizations depend more and more on Internet channels it is vital that the lessons are not forgotten.

Customer-focused service providers have long recognized that situations such as the bereavement scenario identified above are damaging both to the citizen and to the provider. Adoption of a "Tell Us Once"[4] approach allows all service providers to share information such as a change of address or a death. Restrictions on communication between the UK government databases sometimes limit Tell Us Once participants to rekeying data that have been circulated by email. Where digital data sharing is permitted, the added benefit is a reduction in variations and errors in that data.

Opportunities to remove barriers to one-stop services must also be taken. The critical success factor for a one-stop operation is the ability of the organization to break down the silos and overcome inertia in order to integrate all aspects of service delivery into one seamless end-to-end system. We recently undertook a single-client study of the way one-stop shops have evolved, and found two major types of changes:

- The most obvious change is improvement of in-house ICT skills and more imaginative applications. Integrating information management, geo-demographic applications, and customer-tracking facilities within service delivery systems, for example, allows prediction of customer demand leading to more effective deployment of scarce resources
- Organizations with robust infrastructure and IT-enabled processes have more easily exploited new technology-enabled channels such as the Web, call centers, SMS, automated voice systems, and direct-debit funds transfers. These developments have generally produced significant improvement in the quality of service available and a reduction in wasted work.

[4]The Tell Us Once notification service aims to reduce the number of local and central government departments that UK residents have to notify when they have had a baby or suffer a bereavement.

We also asked one-stop shop managers who were still in the post from the early days what, with 10 years of hindsight, they would do differently. They were unanimous: *Make sure all other front doors were closed on day one.*

Allowing different service providers, even within the same organization, to maintain their own reception desks operating their own standalone processes simply cannot be justified if you subscribe to the business benefits of customer focus. In particular:

- The efficiency and effectiveness gains delivered by a customer-focused approach require commitment to transformation throughout the organization.
- The vision to be delivered by transformation has to be justified by a robust business case.
- The business case will necessarily include evidence of the improvement in performance arising from avoidance of waste.
- Identifying and then eliminating waste are essential for both customer and organization.
- There needs to be one overarching approach to service delivery that is managed centrally, agreed on, and implemented across the organization.
- Face-to-face channels (fixed one-stop and roaming), contact centers (including email and letter), automated telephony, web sites, and links into the web sites of local partner organizations must all be "owned" by the customer-service function.

Organizations must apply appropriate measures to monitor and learn from the changes they have made: "Measures to analyze the quality of local authority services are deficient if they concentrate solely upon technical quality and need to be supplemented by non-technical measures in which perceptions and reactions of consumers are systematically captured" (Hart & Byrne, 2005, p. 10).

However, conventional surveys are subjective and may be inadequate: "People bring different expectations — often shaped by their own circumstances and backgrounds — to service experiences; all [that] satisfaction measures is the extent of the gap between those expectations and perceptions" (Parker & Heapy, 2006, pp. 68–69).

CHANNEL STRATEGIES

If there were such a thing as a perfect channel, it would always be "on," nearby, free, and instantaneous. The "channel of choice" is — or should be — an individual's choice, not the provider's, and can be selected for particular purposes on a case-by-case basis. Channel strategies based solely on benefit to the organization are doomed to failure. As of this writing, the most recent Cabinet Office advice on channel strategy (Fogden, 2009) makes explicit reference to the tension between the organization's need to reduce cost and the customer's need for confidence, or reassurance, in the channel in use.

Customers will choose the channel that offers the most effective solution and greatest ease of use for each specific task. In the UK, Surrey County Council's Channel Strategy (Surrey County Council, 2010) gives the example of the choices available to the recipient of a bailiff's notice about recovery of an already-settled debt. The optimal solution, from the Council's perspective, would be for the person to locate appropriate advice in the web site FAQs, but the customer would undoubtedly prefer to call the Contact Centre for reassurance and would probably ask for a letter confirming that no further action was required. All of these channels must be open.

Four considerations are paramount for channel strategies that assume channel shifting:

- Predictions of the effect of channel shifting must include the impact on third-party services (e.g., the voluntary sector) whose own channels and services may be seen as alternatives to the "official" channels.
- Plans must include mechanisms for accessing services, appropriate for those unable or unwilling to use digital technologies, such as 70% of the UK families in social housing — as identified by the National Housing Federation (NHF, 2009).
- Accessibility solutions must be determined for disabled users, such as the 10 million or 18% of UK citizens protected by equality legislation (EFD, 2009).
- Interoperability or full functionality across all channels must be specified.

A channel strategy should include at least the following activities:

- Provide appropriate channels for the hard-to-reach, such as mobile telephony, SMS messaging, and low-call-cost phone numbers for pay-as-you-go users.
- Enhance channels that can be used by the disabled with, for example, text-to-voice.
- Evaluate existing provision, in recognition that channels evolve, emerging opportunities such as Voice over Internet Protocol (VoIP) phone services and social media.
- Treat the Council web site as a baseline for channel functionality, so that a service designed for delivery on the Web will not fail on other channels.

New handheld mobile devices enable entirely new channels, transforming the original concept of face-to-face services. Customers no longer have to travel to often inconvenient offices because Councils can operate, literally, at the front line. They bring the functionality of the office to people's homes. In the UK Gloucestershire County Council deployed "Village Agents" to visit elderly people at home. One agent could work with several service providers (such as housing, health, fire, and police) to ensure that such people had all the services for which they qualified and that they needed.

In this scenario, the cost of the primary channel is almost irrelevant compared to the scale of benefit that the organization can achieve. Each person who could stay in her own home because of the availability of high-quality support, rather than entering a care home, saves the council many thousands of pounds.

Seeing the full picture

Channel shift is not simply about switching one channel on and another off. Self-service on petrol station forecourts[5] worked because the technology was available and the process was easily modified. The benefit for the customer was reduced queuing times in exchange for having to do the work. When the technology and/or process design is inadequate, as in many UK supermarkets, it causes longer queues than simply letting a skilled intermediary (the cashier) do the work for the customers.

When instigated by the customer, channel shift is both natural and beneficial to all parties. When it is the result of enforced behavioral change motivated by cost-cutting, the potential saving can be vastly outweighed by the consequences of disenfranchisement.

[5]"Gas station" in the United States.

Customers will *not* necessarily benefit from self-service, as they run the risk of losing access to well-trained intermediaries and advocates. They will *not* necessarily accept poor service simply because there is no alternative. If they encounter difficulty in trying to use an unfamiliar interface, people may simply drop out without taking up services to which they are entitled. This, inevitably, compounds the problem they originally tried to address. It becomes extremely expensive to solve, often requiring concerted efforts from several different agencies over a lengthy period of time. Getting it right first time is the least expensive thing to do.

Switching off conventional channels — as has already been done for specific interactions with HM Customs and Excise, Department of Work and Pensions (DWP), and elsewhere in UK government — leaves the service user with three choices:

- Accept the intended replacement channel.
- Fail to reach service at all.
- Find an alternative route to service.

As has been pointed out, people tend not to differentiate between different parts of government. Faced with rationalization (i.e., closure) of local facilities, many will find their way to another department or agency, or the voluntary sector. Unfortunately, the budget for providing the support they need rarely follows them. Closing one central government office simply transfers demand to other service providers — including the voluntary service.

In 2010, the UK government's "Digital Champion," Martha Lane Fox, endorsed two key recommendations from the *Transformational Government* agenda (Fox, 2010), albeit in more strident terms ("*Revolution, not Evolution*"):

- Make "DirectGov" more than simply a portal giving access to government services, by giving its developers "*absolute control*" over its contents.
- Turn everything else off.

Tom Loosemore led the customer insight research into a prototype of the portal (alpha.gov.uk) and blogged (Loosemore, 2011) feedback on the trials:

Amongst much else, the research stresses the importance of:
- *browse/category/related links, as much for orientation as navigation*
- *clearer design differentiation between audience types, again to help orientation*
- *ensuring we do not edit down the content *too* much (some felt it was too basic to be 'the government')*
- *internal search not being noticed, with people invariably returning to the search engine from which they came*
- *more thinking needed to understand how to make location work well for everyone*

Orientation is clearly critical, especially when users are arriving deep in a very large site. Do the users think they are in the 'right' place? What clues can we offer to help them? How can we help them understand when they are in the wrong place, as well as the right one?

"Orientation" clearly is critical, and if everything else has been turned off, where do the disoriented go? Savings will be made at the heart of government and the impact felt elsewhere.

In a survey of government web sites, the now defunct business2www said in 2003, "Government, political and public services web sites are relatively large, approximately equal in size with the average

UK FTSE 100 corporate web site. The average UK corporate web site when tested by B2W had 85 errors; the government average was 600 — nearly 7 times as many." The new Direct.Gov.uk will incorporate the content from perhaps 900 of the government web sites identified as part of the *Transformation Government* work; we leave readers to draw their own conclusions.

CASE STUDY, CENTRELINK, AUSTRALIA

The Australian Centrelink initiative was influenced by the separation of policy making from service delivery in New Zealand during the radical reforms of 1984 (Boston, Martin, Pallot, & Walsh, 1996). The new Commonwealth Service Delivery Agency integrated largely parallel delivery networks from the departments of Social Security and Education, Employment, Training and Youth Affairs. Instead of sitting within one government department, the agency has supplier/purchaser relationships with its client departments and is accountable to the federal government and the political agenda of the day. The third key stakeholder group is, of course, the customer and the need for customer focus was explicitly recognized from the outset.

Centrelink opened in 1997, with an inherited customer base of 8 million social welfare recipients and responsibility for handling nearly one-third of government expenditure. It was mandated to compete to deliver services on behalf of other departments. By 2002, it was operating about 1000 delivery points with 23,000 staff, including mobile agents in sparsely populated areas. These are genuine one-stop shops, delivering services on behalf of a wide range of government departments, not just multiple services from one authority.

A UK Education and Employment Select Committee delegation studied Centrelink in 1998 and their Report to Parliament (House of Commons, EESC, 1998) highlights the differences between the two countries:

> *One can envisage a time when the full range of government services are provided in a client-friendly, attractive environment. We can see that a similar model could provide real opportunities in the UK for the unified delivery of central and local government services. Of particular interest are the implications of a single IT platform with its capacity to reduce the amount of duplication that exists in the collection of information from clients.*
>
> *Another exciting feature is the possibility of de-stigmatizing the use of welfare offices, by expanding the range of clients and the reasons for their attendance. We believe that the scope here is almost limitless. The incorporation of tax services, for example, would mean that payments to, as well as payments by, the government could be dealt with on the same site. There is scope to achieve more than simply a cosmetic change. We sense that this represents a real opportunity to overcome the tendency for unemployed people to experience social exclusion.*

Halligan and Wills (2008) document the evolution of Centrelink and the difficulties it faced in maintaining its unique position as an autonomous multifunctional agency. As the service matured and evolved, a key aspect of the relationship between the agency and its users emerged. Having multiple client departments had led naturally to the one-stop-shop delivery model, making the service approachable. The customer no longer had to find out which door to walk through. But they still had to access the solution to their needs once they arrived.

Recognizing that the response to a request had to be formulated by the front line led to a service architecture based on *life events*. That was a natural model to follow because it helped to bring order to the very large number of possible queries: "The range and complexity of the services provided by Centrelink and its predecessors had confused customers about the system and the support they were entitled to." Customers would no longer "have to spend their time trying to locate the part of Centrelink that deals with their particular situation. However they choose to approach us the response they receive will be guided by the 'life event,' which has prompted their contact with us" (Vardon, 2000, as reported in Halligan & Wills, 2008).

> *The life-events model identified the key times of change or crisis in people's lives and designed services around them. To make it easier for customers, they would be asked to identify only their problems; Centrelink staff would then take responsibility for recognizing what services would best meet their customer's needs. The onus would be shifted from the customer to Centrelink staff, supported by their IT system, to ask questions of the customer that would enable a complete and accurate matching of needs with available products and services, including internal and external referrals.*

Figure 23.1 is a simplified model of the situations that the "front line"[6] can identify and address. These will be familiar to anybody working in local government customer services. What will be different in most cases is that Centrelink has responsibility for services from up to 18 government departments and the ability to join up David Varney's service islands on behalf of the customer.

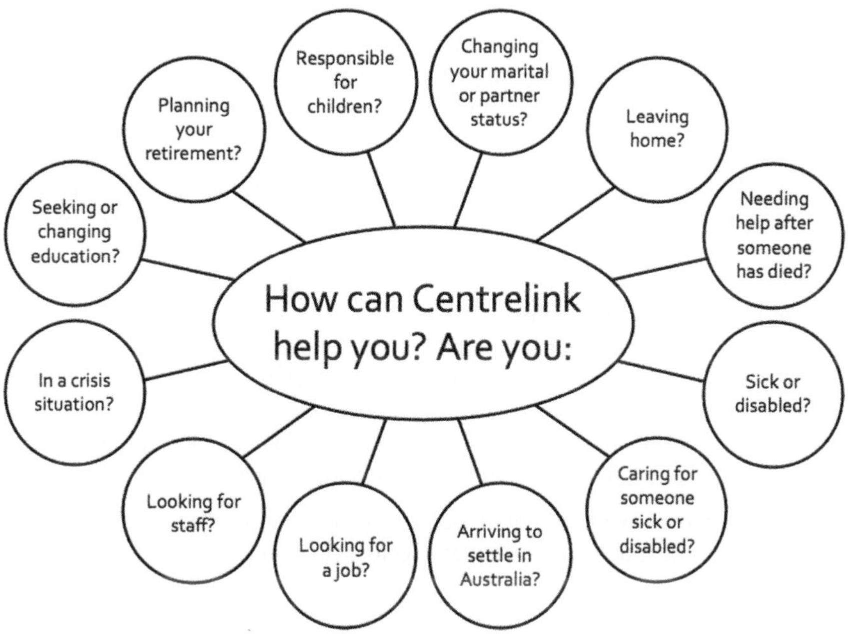

FIGURE 23.1 Expressions of need, courtesy of John Halligan

[6]In the late 1990s, the front line would have been a person speaking face-to-face and one-to-one with the customer. Today there could be a number of electronic interfaces offering the same capability.

Case study conclusions

The Centrelink "experiment" has been exposed to some extraordinary challenges that are beyond the scope of this chapter. However, some generic issues must not be overlooked.

The ability of the organization to respond to customer needs depends on its governance structure and its mandate. Centrelink was set up as a one-stop shop, not answerable to a single government department and not constrained to deliver one specific type of service. Its design started with a "clean sheet of paper".

The value of adopting a life-events model as a way of integrating several different types of service offering cannot be overestimated. This was not part of the initial Centrelink design concept but arose out of a need to guide the customer toward the most appropriate service responses. Customers who pursue the wrong area of service, or find they are ineligible, as well as would-be customers who find the right service too late, if at all, are major sources of wasted work and associated expense.

SUCCESS FACTORS

The UK Select Committee Report on Centrelink (House of Commons, EESC, 1998) identified the significant impact of having a single, integrated IT platform capable of supporting a range of channels, especially the face-to-face channel, which is crucial in controlling exclusion. The issue of harmonizing access channels is normally addressed within an access to services strategy. From our studies of these strategy documents, we have observed the following to have the greatest impact on the success of service delivery — from the customer's perspective as well as the organizational view:

- Ensure that the service users can be confident that they will receive the necessary support in accessing service, regardless of which channel is used and which service providers are ultimately responsible for those services.
- Resolve the vast majority of requests for information, advice, help, support, or intervention in (or as a result of) one transaction.
- Empower the service agent to work effectively with "back offices" (the service professionals such as planners, school managers, care providers) through internal interfaces and processes that have been designed as one seamless end-to-end operation.
- Take a "whole person" approach that identifies service needs more promptly and results in reduced failure demand and other forms of avoidable contact.

We have encapsulated our findings within our Customer Focus Framework for service design professionals working in the public and voluntary sectors (Doulton, 2007).

SUMMARY

From reading the account of Halligan and Wills (2008) in detail, it should be clear that reduction of costs was one of the key justifications for setting up the Centrelink agency in the first place, and that has been delivered through a focus on cost-effectiveness and continual improvement so that the benefits are felt by the whole of society, not just taxpayers.

The very different approach taken by central government in the UK has led to the failure to protect the most vulnerable members of society. Service users in general, who should have benefited from joined-up government, still suffer from archaic processes and incoherent decision making. The system is overweight and being starved in the name of austerity. Had the vision of end-to-end transformation been pursued instead of the development of more and more processes for reporting "progress" toward parochial forms of e-gov, the system would now be leaner and better placed to deliver much-needed societal outcomes.

References

Boston, J., Martin, J., Pallot, J., & Walsh, P. (1996). *Public management: The New Zealand model.* Auckland: Oxford University Press.

Cabinet Office. Transformational government enabled by technology. (2005). London: HMSO. Retrieved 12 November 2011 from webarchive.nationalarchives.gov.uk/+/www.cabinetoffice.gov.uk/media/141734/transgov-strategy.pdf

CITU (Central IT Unit). Government direct green paper. (1996). Available from Centre for Technology Policy Research London: HMSO. Retrieved 26 July 2011 from http://ctpr.org/wp-content/uploads/2011/03/Government-Direct.pdf

Doulton, A. (2007). *The EIP customer focus framework.* Bletchingdon, Oxon: CDW & Associates.

Doulton, A., Sandford, N., & Wilson, R. (1995). *Local government decentralisation and community information systems.* United Kingdom: Dragonflair Publishing, Church Stretton, UK.

Doulton, A., & Wilson, R. (1999). *Single access points for public service.* United Kingdom: Dragonflair Publishing, Church Stretton, UK.

Employers' Forum on Disability (EFD). Disability in the UK. (2009). United Kingdom: London. Retrieved 12 November 2011 from http://www.efd.org.uk/media-centre/facts-and-figures/disability-in-uk

Flood, R. (2008). What can design add to the sector? In E. Thomas (Ed.), *Innovation by design in public services* (pp. 44–47). United Kingdom: SOLACE Foundation Imprint.

Fogden, S. (2009). *Channel strategy guidance.* London: HMSO, Cabinet Office. Retrieved 12 November 2011 from http://www.cabinetoffice.gov.uk/media/261368/channel_strategy_modules.pdf

Fox, M. L. (2010). *Direct.Gov 2010 and beyond — Revolution not evolution.* London: HMSO, Cabinet Office. Retrieved 12 November 2011 from http://www.cabinetoffice.gov.uk/resource-library/directgov-2010-and-beyond-revolution-not-evolution

Halligan, J., & Wills, J. (2008). *The centrelink experiment — Innovation in service delivery.* Canberra, Australia: ANU-E Press. Retrieved 26 July 2011 from epress.anu.edu.au/anzsog/centrelink/html/frames.php

Hart, M., & Byrne, P. (2005). *Using e-government to improve the quality of local authority services.* Retrieved 4 August 2011 from mikehart-papers.co.uk/tutorials/lit_rev/egovqu_2.doc

HM Treasury. Measuring the expected benefits of e-government. (2003). Retrieved 12 November 2011 from ctpr.org/wp-content/uploads/2011/03/HMTGuidelinesVersion1_4.pdf

House of Commons, Office of the Deputy Prime Minister. IEG4: Delivering e-government benefits. (2005). London: HMSO. Retrieved 4 August 2011 from www.egovmonitor.com/reports/rep12027.pdf

House of Commons, Office of the Deputy Prime Minister: Housing, Planning, Local Government and the Regions Committee. Annual report. (2003). London: HMSO. Retrieved 12 November 2011 from www.publications.parliament.uk/pa/cm200304/cmselect/cmodpm/102/102.pdf

House of Commons, Select Committee on Public Accounts. Twentieth report. (2003). London: HMSO. Retrieved 12 November 2011 from www.publications.parliament.uk/pa/cm200203/cmselect/cmpubacc/373/37305.htm

House of Commons, Select Committee on Education and Employment (EESC). (1998). *First Report.* London: HMSO, Retrieved 4 August 2011 from http://www.publications.parliament.uk/pa/cm199899/cmselect/cmeduemp/163/16305.htm

Improvement and Development Agency (IDeA). Call and contact centres in local government—Getting it right!. (2001). United Kingdom: IDeA/Employers Association for Local Government. Retrieved 4 August 2011 from www.idea.gov.uk/idk/aio/68969

Loosemore, T. (2011). *Alpha.gov.uk wrap-up.* Government Digital Service. Retrieved 4 August 2011 from digital.cabinetoffice.gov.uk/2011/07/29/alpha-gov-uk-wrap-up/

Lyons, M. (2007). *Place-shaping: A shared ambition for the future of local government, Lyons' enquiry into local government.* London: HMSO. Retrieved 12 November 2011 from www.lyonsinquiry.org.uk/

Mager, B., Maffei, S., & Sangiorgi, D. (2005). Innovation through service design. From research and theory to a network of practice: A user driven perspective. In *Joining forces: International conference on design research, Helsinki, Finland.* Retrieved 12 November 2011 from www.service-design-network.org/system/files/10_Mager_Innovation_0.pdf

National Housing Federation (NHF). Digital exclusion and social housing. (2009). United Kingdom: National Housing Federation. Retrieved 12 November 2011 from raceonline2012.org/sites/default/files/resources/digitalexclusionandsocialhousing2009.pdf

Parker, S., & Heapy, J. (2006). *The journey to the interface—How public service design can connect users to reform.* London: Demos. Retrieved 4 August 2011 from www.demos.co.uk/publications/thejourneytotheinterface

Steadman-Jones, D. (2001). *Transformation not automation, the e-government challenge.* London. Retrieved 12 November 2011 from www.demos.co.uk/files/Transformationnotautomation.pdf

Surrey County Council. Channel strategy. (2010). Retrieved 2 August 2011 from www.surreycc.gov.uk/

Vardon, S. (2000). *We're from the government and we're here to help—Centrelink's story. Australian Journal of Public Administration,* 59, 3–10.

Varney, D. (2006). *Service transformation: A better service for citizens and businesses, a better deal for the taxpayer.* London: HMSO. Retrieved 12 November 2011 from www.official-documents.gov.uk/document/other/011840489X/011840489X.pdf

CHAPTER

UX and e-Democracy in Asia

24

Daniel Szuc*, Josephine Wong*, Raven Chai†
Apogee Usability Asia Ltd., Hong Kong UX Consulting Pte Ltd., Singapore†*

"Let go of the need to be an 'expert,' work alongside the people who live the situation every day and let the new thing be born through that collaboration."
— Marc Rettig

DON'T MAKE ME DEAL WITH GOVERNMENT!

Dealing with the government and government departments feels, at times, like jumping into the unknown without a parachute. Sometimes it feels as if we, the citizens, want to have as little interaction with the government as possible, expecting nothing more than poor experiences, frustration, waiting for answers in places where we do not know how to get answers, with the aim of making better lives for ourselves (see Figure 24.1). When citizens are forced into situations where they have to deal with the government, it feels as though they are being pushed to work with something big, unknown, scary, and unwieldy — a large machine with a heavy user manual that has been lost between some filing cabinets in a basement office that the government has forgotten about.

People often do not know where to start with the government, whom to approach when visiting government buildings and departments that force a person into a bureaucracy, with drab appearances and poor signage, filled with unhappy people who unfortunately are not always rewarded for good service. It seems the less we have to deal with the government the better.

Slow and frustrating

Governments can be slow to react to people, who are becoming better connected and knowledgeable via social networks, which in turn makes it much easier for them to bypass the need to deal with the government for answers. Government web sites also provide little help, with content organized by government departments, copy transferred directly from documents that use technical and policy language, contact phone numbers that are impossible to find, and an inaccurate search — which all add up to an overall frustrating experience, when citizens are already expecting this to begin with.

Transforming government experience

This raises the question: Looking ahead, if we were to transform government to a friendly place where we could get the answers we need, what would that look like, and what would our design goals be?

FIGURE 24.1 We do not always get the service we expect when we need it most

(For color version of this figure, see the Web version of this chapter.)

Would a future government do these things?

- Be open and transparent
- Serve the people, but not by drafting policies to serve the administration of government with the primary aim of reelection
- Treat citizens not as numbers but as real people, with lives, problems, aspirations, and dreams
- Be forward thinking about future benefit for all and not just short-term benefit for government
- Work as a team toward these future benefits, and not as siloed departments, each focused only on its own concerns
- Share resources and knowledge intelligently

What would it take to improve the experience we have with governments as they reposition themselves in the new connected global economy?

- How do we want citizens to feel when they walk into a government building with the goal of getting answers they need?
- What feelings would citizens want to have when they visit a government office for inquiries?
- How would this extend to the "look and feel" of government web sites, signage, and documents?
- How does a government overhaul its communications strategy to find better ways to communicate with its citizens?
- How do we empower people within government, giving them the flexibility to make faster decisions for the citizens and avoid trapping them in consultation loops?
- How does a government transform its model of governance toward understanding better what it takes, not just to serve its citizens but to delight them?

Designing for change

People usually want to change when they are unhappy with the current situation and either recognize a *better future state* or are introduced to one. We also find that people are losing patience with large entities (see Figure 24.2) that are or appear to be self-serving and not listening or empathizing with the needs of their citizens. People do not always know what the future state will look like, how to

FIGURE 24.2 How do we move away from silos, departments, and divisions toward a more connected and organic way of working together for greater good?

(For color version of this figure, see the Web version of this chapter.)

articulate it, or know how to get there. They may also think they have no great motivation to change, as it is just too difficult to do. Change usually signifies movement or something different to people, as they look to others to show them the necessary and relevant elements to make change happen.

USER EXPERIENCE DESIGNERS AS LEADERS FOR POLITICAL CHANGE

User experience (UX) design leaders, both regionally in Asia and globally, are starting to ask themselves what role they can play in making large organizational systems change politically and economically toward helping society. They accept that the role of UX designers may be in helping organizations achieve that aim, and in designing tactics that will change organizational thinking. UX designers can help and mentor people in experimenting with change, and can nudge such change along where they themselves work. This new voice and growing confidence in Asia is influencing how we view our political leaders and what people expect of leaders and institutions today.

Skills and attitude

We must recognize, however, that to help create change in government and the government projects on which we work, UX designers will need special skills and attitudes:

- *Planning and facilitation*: We need to have the confidence to stand in front of groups of people, to provide activities that work on both tactical and strategic issues. We need to be comfortable in helping government leaders outline strategies and roadmaps.

- *Communications style*: How do we want people to feel after they have worked with us? How do we want our positive energy to transfer to their colleagues and people outside their team? How can our style teach people how to create change in their work?
- *Solutions, not problems*: We should listen carefully to existing problems as part of learning about how we can help. But we also need to be good at presenting possible solutions to help people shift their thinking and ultimately to help the government achieve its goals.
- *Shifting and challenging the status quo*: It is our role to teach people in government to question and discuss alternative ways of doing things, not for the sake of keeping things as the status quo, but as moving toward something better for all.
- *Empathy*: We work in a human field, so we should embed the elements of empathy in every way in which we work with people (see Figure 24.3).

Asia perspectives

Many countries — Burma, China, North Korea, Indonesia, Japan, the Philippines and Taiwan, for example — have suffered terribly from corruption, scandals, leadership changes, and a genuine lack of citizen trust in the government. The same is happening to varying degrees in other parts of the world, as evidenced by recent protests in the Middle East and even in the United States. The occurrence of these events demonstrates a lack of government transparency, and has not increased citizens' trust in their government or given them any confidence that designing a new way of governance can be undertaken.

Younger generations in Asia have a better education, more access to knowledge, and more money than did the generations before them. They see much more of the world through travels and the Internet, are more globally aware and connected with independent thinking, and expect more from their governments in terms of creating a better life. Unfortunately, in many respects government is still running the same way as it did for generations — which frustrates younger people who see other parts of the world changing more quickly, and for the better.

Government needs to redesign itself from the inside out and look at how it operates internally, to change its face to the people who interact with it locally, regionally, and globally. Perhaps governments

FIGURE 24.3 Spaces can invite people to work together more effectively

(For color version of this figure, see the Web version of this chapter.)

spend too much time and money maintaining their grip on political power when they could be opening Government itself up and improving consultation paths for its citizens.

One of the most challenging tasks for any government is to balance the needs and happiness of its citizens without sacrificing the nation's growth. In virtually all cases "growth" means economic growth via increasing the country's Gross Domestic Product (GDP) per capita. While GDP per capita is often considered an indicator of a country's standard of living — and it is absolutely without doubt that most of us want to improve our standard of living — we (including the government) should start asking ourselves these key questions:

Are we using the right indicators to measure our standard of living?

What do we, as citizens, perceive as the values in life, and how do we hope the government resonates with us through decisions and policies?

Use of media

The use of traditional media to communicate and interact with citizens is undergoing a change. With the dominant use of mainstream media such as television, radio, newspapers, and other print publications, governments can design "communication packages" to portray their positive sides. With the emergence of social media, almost everyone can post videos of "evidence" where policymakers communicated poorly with the public. They can write articles and publish them in Facebook, or write personal blogs to express grievances and voice alternative views from that of the government. This emergence of social media has taken the government by surprise as it struggles to "design" its "communication packages" consistently in both mainstream and new media channels. Government officials have pledged to listen to all different views from all media channels. They now need to harness stronger communication and interpersonal skills, as they have to be seen as articulating their own thoughts and views directly through social media channels, without the protection of censorship.

Ministers, politicians, and government officials are now facing a situation where they need to answer citizens' questions directly and face their scrutiny. Their personal values will be evaluated, their decision-making processes will be watched and debated intensely by citizens, and their voices and thoughts will be communicated directly via new media. The whole approach and concept of governance may require drastic "redesign" for them to govern and lead in a more effective manner.

DESIGN OPPORTUNITIES

Based on the above issues, we can explore a couple of design goals and opportunities:

What if we could help redesign the government to better understand and meet citizen needs and values (Figure 24.4)? The underlying question is an opportunity for citizens and government (both politicians and administrators) to sit down together to agree on the *kind of societal values that are right for our culture*, and to start using these "agreed values" as the guiding principles for designing future policies.

Consider the following four examples of such values:

- Satisfaction level when using public transport system
- Eco-friendliness and sustainability level of infrastructure design
- Percentage of personal time versus working hours
- Gross National Happiness

FIGURE 24.4 Designing for the future state

(For color version of this figure, see the Web version of this chapter.)

We can use collaborative design activities when drafting policies (see Chapter 22, Design for Policymaking, for in-depth analysis and case studies). During the initial stage of drafting policies, government policymakers should hold a series of brainstorming and fact-finding sessions with citizens who will be affected by the policies. Domain experts on the subject matter should also be involved in these sessions, to help create real-life, practical constraints to shape the design activities. In such a scenario, citizens will have a chance to co-create the policies that are meant for them, while policymakers can truly address the citizens' concerns in closer proximity and domain experts can provide advice in a practical context. All concerned stakeholders will be present for the same design activities.

The main challenge is who this type of person should be and what kind of soft skills he/she must have, to facilitate such collaborative design activities. We recommend choosing someone who has strong communication skills and is highly respected by citizens, policymakers, and domain experts — and more importantly, is a person of high integrity, who views matters with the national interest at heart.

GOVERNMENT 2.0 (GOV 2.0) IN ASIA

So what does this mean for the future of governments in Asia and their service offerings to citizens? The key word here is *collaboration* — only through collaborative design activities with all the concerned stakeholders can all voices be duly heard and a more balanced decision be made when drafting policies. (See Chapter 3, Usability and Government 2.0, for a more in-depth discussion of Gov 2.0.)

In a future government, politicians will still hold the executive powers (rightly so, since they are elected by the people to do just that), but they would (we hope) take a more consultative approach where users (citizens) would have more opportunities to shape the policies through collaborative design activities. Government services are intended for citizens, so it is only logical that citizens should be involved in creating the services for themselves. It also makes sense that citizens would be rewarded for their efforts. If the method of collaborative design yields a higher success rate in drafting sound policies, we see a chance that we might eliminate extreme elitism, with its current mindset that only highly educated individuals are capable of governing the country. Since all stakeholders would now share the effort and ownership of policies, we citizens could then focus more on electing politicians with high integrity and social values rather than just competence and intelligence.

Is not that the essence of the democratic process? As citizens we aim to elect people who represent the people and resonate with our values, and we communicate our views to them so that, maybe by adopting a collaborative design approach as part of the policymaking process, we can have at least a slim chance of fulfilling the ideal concept of future government.

Designing for future generations

UX designers are also looking past current leadership models, toward simpler and more open ways of communicating between the government and its citizens:

What experiences do citizens want to have with Gov 2.0, and are we capable of designing this for our future generations? Here are some potential design opportunities for governments in Asia:

- *One view*: Create a one-to-one relationship with government, with one login and one place to manage all the activities, including taxation, driver's license, utility usage, voting, and rewards (e.g., citizens who reduce their use of electricity or water would receive a reward).
- *Accessibility*: Place a priority on accessibility — to ensure that people with special needs can easily access government web sites for the information and services they need. (Chapter 12, Ensuring Accessibility for People with Disabilities, covers this topic in depth.)
- *Plain language*: Encourage and educate politicians and government workers to avoid "political speak" but instead be able to translate not only the needs of people into government action, but also policy into a language people can understand. (Chapter 11, Plain Language in Government, covers that topic; and Chapter 9, Legislative Drafting Systems, discusses the language of legal policymaking.)
- *Openness*: Provide publicly available information to help citizens understand *how and why* government decisions were and are made.
- *Integration rather than silos*: Ensure that when citizens have a question or a problem, they do not have to know or find out which government department can address it. (See Chapter 23, Service Design and Channel Shifting, for a more in-depth discussion of this topic.)
- *Friendliness*: Hire and train people to provide open, happy, clear help to citizens ("service with a smile," for example), and reward them for doing so.
- *Spaces*: Design public offices so that they offer places to sit, relax, and connect while we wait to be served by the government.

AN EXERCISE FOR YOU: DESIGN OF GOVERNMENT SERVICES

The key theme of this chapter is one of improving ways for citizens (ourselves) to connect with our governments and to better understand how decisions are made. If you could design a dashboard — such as the one you see in your car to indicate speed, gas, temperature, etc. — to show your relationship with government services and the community in which you live, what would that look like?

Draw it!

SUMMARY

With recent citizen discontent about Government, social uprisings, and breakdowns in financial and economic models that produce global "occupy" movements, people are beginning to question today's political leadership and looking for a helping hand to point them to alternative solutions. People are also questioning the notion of "economic growth" and asking if this is in fact a truly scalable indicator to measure a "quality" standard of living. We are also seeing the rise of social networks where people no longer have to rely on large entities to provide answers. Finally, as Asia gains more global economic power, UX design leaders in Asia are also asking themselves what role they can play in helping larger entities embrace change toward a better understanding of their new role towards helping society locally and globally. We hope this chapter has helped answer these questions and has generated discussion of what our future governments should look like.

Further reading

Quesenbery, W., & Szuc, D. (2011). *Global UX: Design and research in a connected world.* Waltham, MA: Morgan Kaufmann.

Szuc, D. (2011). *UX trends.* Retrieved 1 October 2011 from http://www.uxmatters.com/mt/archives/2011/03/ux-trends.php

Szuc, D., & Wong, J. (2011a). *Designing for change: "Be water my friend"* Retrieved 1 October 2011 from http://johnnyholland.org/2011/09/12/designing-for-change-be-water-my-friend/

Szuc, D., & Wong, J. (2011b). *User experience design in Asia.* Retrieved 1 October 2011 from http://www.uxmatters.com/mt/archives/2011/01/user-experience-design-in-asia.php

Closing Thoughts

Although nature commences with reason and ends in experience it is necessary for us to do the opposite, that is to commence with experience and from this to proceed to investigate the reason.

Leonardo da Vinci

This book has addressed a wide range of topics relevant to usability and user experience in government systems, from history to principles, from design features to process. We have explored these in diverse types of systems, from public web sites to military command-and-control systems, from the anthropometrics of fingerprint scanners to the highest level systems of public policy. The authors of these chapters have illustrated the ways in which these issues affect the lives of citizens and the quality of their government and have shown us many steps we can take and techniques we can use to enhance and improve the usability of government systems and the user experience of the people who use them.

This book also touches on several emerging topics that bear watching:

- **Social media**. Although social media have been around for a long time — since the first computer bulletin boards in the 1970s (Bennett, 2011) — as of this writing, many governments are still working to understand and define where it fits into their public outreach program.
- **Voting systems**. Recent years have seen a great deal of attention paid to voting systems in the United States — ballot design has been determined to have influenced the outcome of elections (Wolf, 2008), and voting machine usability is an important enough issue that the US's 2002 Help America Vote Act gave the National Institute of Standards and Technology (NIST) a key role in helping to achieve improvements in voting systems and listed human factors among its research activities (NIST, 2009).
- **Service design**. In particular, new work is emerging in multi- and cross-channel considerations (e.g., Gagnon, Posada, Bourgault, & Naud, 2010) linked to mobile growth, telecommunications infrastructure, accessibility, and the digital economy.
- **User experience.** As mentioned in Chapter 16, Getting UX into the Contract, the field of user experience is not yet mature enough to have developed generally accepted means of specifying and measuring user experience as the user's subjective experience separates from usability. We look forward to seeing that grow.

We also point out some current issues that will grow in importance (and which we have not covered in detail in this book): Multicultural populations, personalization and customization, health systems, crisis response, e-democracy and e-governance, e-health and health records, and behavior change.

CLOSING WORDS

There is so much more to say. Unfortunately, time and space prevent us from saying any more in this book right now. Except this:

> *I have been impressed with the urgency of doing. Knowing is not enough; we must apply. Being willing is not enough; we must do.*
>
> **Leonardo da Vinci**

We hope that this book has inspired you to go out and *do*.

References

Bennett, S. (2011). *A short history of social media (1978–2011).* Retrieved 22 November 2011 from http://www.mediabistro.com/alltwitter/history-social-media_b12770

Gagnon, Y., Posada, E., Bourgault, M., & Naud, A. (2010). Multichannel delivery of public services: A new and complex management challenge. *International Journal of Public Administration 33*(5), 213–222.

NIST (2009). *NIST and the Help America Vote Act (HAVA).* Retrieved 22 November 2011 from http://www.nist.gov/itl/vote

Wolf, R. (2008). *Study: Poor ballot designs still affect U.S. elections.* Retrieved 22 November 2011 from http://www.usatoday.com/news/politics/election2008/2008-07-20-ballots_N.htm

Acronyms and Abbreviations

ACM	Association for Computing Machinery
ACTD	Advanced Concept Technology Demonstration
AI	Artificial Intelligence
AJAX	Asynchronous JavaScript and XML
AmbI/AmI	Ambient Intelligence
ANSI	American National Standards Institute (US)
ATM (i)	Air Traffic Management
ATM (ii)	Automatic Teller Machine
BCC	Biometric Consortium Conference
BCS	British Computer Society (UK)
BLS	Bureau of Labor Statistics (US)
BSI	British Standards Institute (UK)
CBC	Canadian Broadcasting Corporation (Canada)
CBP	Customs and Border Protection (US)
CBRNE	Chemical, Biological, Radiological, Nuclear. Explosives events
CCTT	Close Combat Tactical Trainer
CFP	Call for Proposals
CFT	Call for Tenders
CHI	Computer–Human Interaction
CIF	Common Industry Format for Usability Test Reports
CLG	Department of Communities and Local Government (UK)
CMM	Capability Maturity Model
CMS	Content Management System
CNIs	Critical National Infrastructures
CONOPS	Concept of Operations
COTS	Commercial, off-the-Shelf
CRM	Customer Relationship Management
CTD	Contractor Task Descriptions
CUE	Comparative Usability Evaluation
DARPA	Defense Advanced Research Projects Agency (US)
DAU	Defense Acquisition University (US)
DHS	Department of Homeland Security (US)
DIN	Deutsches Institut für Normung eV (Germany)
DMV	Department of Motor Vehicles (Canada, US)
DOD	Department of Defense (US)
DRDC	Defence Research & Development Canada (Canada)
DTD	Document Type Definition
DVLA	Driver and Vehicle Licensing Agency (UK)
DWP	Department of Work and Pensions (UK)
EIP	Exchanging Information with the Public
EMS	Emergency Medical Services

EPCIP	European Programme for Critical Infrastructure Protection (EU)
ESL	English as a Second Language
ESPRIT	European Strategic Programme for Research in Information Technology (EU)
FAA	Federal Aviation Administration (US)
FAR	Federal Acquisition Regulation (US)
FBI	Federal Bureau of Investigation (US)
FDA	Food and Drug Administration (US)
FEMA	Federal Emergency Management Agency (US)
FERC	Federal Energy Regulatory Commission (US)
FIS	Forensic Identification Specialist
fMRI	Functional Magnetic Resonance Imaging
fNIR	Functional Near-Infrared System
GDP	Gross Domestic Product
GIS	Geographic Information Systems
GNC	Guidance, Navigation, and Control
GPS	Global Positioning System
GSA	General Services Administration (US)
GUI	Graphical User Interface
Hazmat	Hazardous material (Canada, US)
HCD	Human-Centered Design
HCI	Human-Computer Interaction
HF&E	Human Factors and Ergonomics
HFI	Human Factors Integration
HHS	Department of Health and Human Services (US)
HMRC	Her Majesty's Revenues and Customs (UK)
HMT	Her Majesty's Treasury (UK)
HSI	Human-Systems Integration
HTML	HyperText Markup Language
HTTP	HyperText Transfer Protocol
HTTP-S	Secure HyperText Transfer Protocol
IA	Information Architecture
ICS	Incident Command System
ICT	Information and Communications Technology
ICU	Intensive Care Unit
ID	Interaction Design (UK), Industrial Design (US)
Ident	Forensic Identification Specialist
IDIQ	Indefinite Delivery, Indefinite Quantity
IEC	International Electrotechnical Commission
IEG	Implementing Electronic Government
IHM	Interaction Humaine-Machine (France)
IRB	Institutional Review Board
IS	Information Systems
ISO	International Organization for Standardization
IT	Information Technology

ITB	Invitation to Bid
ITT	Invitation to Tender
IxD	Interaction Design
JMET	Joint Military Essential Tasks
LPTA	Lowest Price Technically Acceptable (US)
LTPA	Lightweight Third-Party Authentication
LRE	Launch and Recovery Element
MAC	Multi-Aircraft Control
MANPRINT	Manpower and Personnel Integration (US)
MedPost	Medical & Casualty Command Post (Canada)
MEDS	Multifunction Electronic Display System
MEG	Magnetoencephalography
MEMA	Mississippi Emergency Management Agency (US)
MMS	Multimedia Message Service
MWBP	Mobile Web Best Practices
NASA	National Aeronautics and Space Administration (US)
NCARAI	Navy Center for Applied Research in Artificial Intelligence (US)
NCI	National Cancer Institute (US)
NFIQ	NIST Fingerprint Image Quality (US)
NHS	National Health Service (UK)
NIH	National Institutes of Health (US)
NIMS	National Incident Management System (US)
NIST	National Institute of Standards and Technology (US)
NIST IR	NIST Internal Report (US)
NSTC	National Science and Technology Council (US)
NTIA	National Telecommunications and Information Administration (US)
OCS	Operator Control Station
OMB	Office of Management and Budget (US)
ONP	Open Network Provision
OODA	Observe, Orient, Decide, and Act
OSD	Office of the Secretary of Defense (US)
PDF	Portable Document Format
PDF/A	Portable Document Format - ISO standard 10-1
PLAIN	Plain Language Action and Information Network (US)
PP	Partido Popular (Spain)
PPE	Personal Protective Equipment
PURPA	Public Utility Regulatory Policy Act (US)
PWGSC	Public Works and Government Services Canada (Canada)
PWS	Performance Work Statement
QR	Quick Response
REMIS	Reliability and Maintainability Information System
RFID	Radio Frequency Identification
RFP	Request for Proposals
RNIB	Royal National Institute for the Blind (UK)

ROI	Return on Investment
RPA	Remotely Piloted Aircraft
RSS	Real Simple Syndication
RTI	Right to Information Act (India)
RTMW	Rapid Triage Management Workbench
SAA	Sense and Avoid
SAGE	Strategic Air-Ground Environment
SARS	Severe Acute Respiratory Syndrome
SE	Software Engineering
SERP	Search Engine Results Page
SETA	Systems Engineering and Technical Assistance
SIGCHI	Special Interest Group on Computer and Human Interaction (ACM)
SMS	Short Message Service
SOW	Statement of Work
SSA	Social Security Administration (US)
STC	Society for Technical Communication
STRIDE	Spoofing, Tampering, Repudiation, Information Disclosure, Denial of Service, Elevation of Privilege
TIGERS	Tactical Information GUI Engineering & Requirements Specification
TTPs	Tactics, Techniques, and Procedures
UbiComp	Ubiquitous Computing
UCD	User-Centered Design
UI	User Interface
UPA	Usability Professionals Association
UPS	Uninterruptible Power Supply
US-VISIT	United States Visitor and Immigrant Status Indicator Technology (US)
USA PATRIOT Act	Uniting and Strengthening America by Providing Appropriate Tools Required to Intercept and Obstruct Terrorism Act (US)
USDA	US Department of Agriculture
UX	User Experience
VoIP	Voice over Internet Protocol
VUG	NIST Visualization and Usability Group (US)
W3C	World Wide Web Consortium
WAI	Web Accessibility Initiative (W3C)
WBS	Work Breakdown Structure
WCAG	Web Content Accessibility Guidelines (W3C)
WHO	World Health Organization
xGEA	Government Enterprise Information Architecture (UK)
XIT	Commercial eXplosives Identification Tool
XML	Extensible Markup Language

Glossary of Terms

Access to Services Strategy: A CRM approach for local government information services that separates customer contact management from the delivery of complex services.

Accessibility: The usability of a product, service, environment, or facility by people with the widest range of capabilities (ISO 9241-20). Also, the provision of equal access to all individuals, particularly users with disabilities, to interact with technology, regardless of the method of access (e.g., mobile device or assistive technology).

Agile processes: Software engineering methodology based on iterative and incremental development, where requirements and solutions evolve through collaboration between self-organizing, cross-functional teams. The term stems from the 2001 "Agile Manifesto."

Air traffic management: The direction of aircraft by ground-based controllers to ensure collision avoidance (via separation assurance and "see and avoid"), air traffic flow, airspace efficiency, and flight safety.

Anthropometrics: The study of human body measurements.

Assistive technologies: Products, devices, or equipment, whether acquired commercially, modified, or customized, used to maintain, increase, or improve the functional capabilities of individuals with disabilities. Such technologies are increasingly "smart," digital, unobtrusive, and home-based.

Authentication: Any process by which a system verifies the identity of a user who wishes to access it; essential to effective security.

Autonomy: The automation of tasks by machine to increase speed, safety, repeatability/predictability, sustainability, effectiveness, and/or efficiency (freeing up humans to do higher level tasks). The "degree" of autonomy — the degree of machine independence from human control — can range from none (manual control) to partial automation (often with the human "in the loop" manually performing some of the tasks), to supervisory control (human "on the loop," overseeing and often guiding tasks or selecting among possible alternative actions), to full autonomy (no human intervention other than to start or cancel an operation).

Benefits Agency: An executive agency of the UK's DWP between 1991 and 2001.

Best Value Review: The statutory basis (Local Government Act, 1999) on which UK local councils plan, review, and manage their performance. The resource provides guidance and advice on managing performance indicators, developing performance plans, conducting reviews and procuring the right solution, and ensuring integration with other local and national initiatives and strategies.

Biometrics: A measurable biological (anatomical and physiological) or behavioral characteristic that can be used for automated recognition.

Bisimulation: A binary relation between state transition systems, associating systems which behave in the same way in the sense that one system simulates the other and vice versa.

Card sorting: A UCD method for increasing the findability of information. Participants sort a set of items of content (information or functionality) into groups that make sense to them, and the analyst aggregates the results for all participants to get the "best fit" solution for the user population.

Channel: The means of communication; in the service context this would typically include face-to-face contact over a counter, a call center for telephone callers, a contact center (a call center with added capacity for outbound calls, email, and letters), kiosk, or Internet.

Citizen engagement: Interactions and discussions, between a government agency and citizens, in which citizens provide ideas, suggestions, and recommendations related to the agency's current and future plans and activities.

Codesign: A process in which users and designers work together to conceive and develop new concepts and products in a more collaborative and interactive manner.

Cognitive overload: a.k.a. *information overload.* A term used in psychology to describe the condition in which a person receives more information at one time than he or she can take in or process.

Consolidation of legislation: The generation of the correct wording of a legislative act taking into account a modification act that contains only editing instructions such as "delete this structure" and "add these words."

Context of use: Users, tasks, equipment (hardware, software, and materials), and the physical and social environments in which a product is used.

Crowdsourcing: Asking the public to contribute information and ideas. In the case of Gov 2.0, agencies ask citizens to contribute ideas and review information.

Cultural usability: The study and consideration of differences in usability for different cultural groups and geographic regions of the world.

Culture: The characteristic features of everyday existence (as diversions or a way of life) shared by people in a place or time. Here, it is the situation-specific meanings of representations (icons, symbols, and texts) in user interfaces used by different groups and geographical regions.

Customer focus: The principle that service delivery should meet the needs of the customer, not the convenience of the provider.

Customer relationship management: A widely implemented strategy for managing a company's interactions with customers, clients, and sales prospects.

Digital democracy: a.k.a. *e-democracy*. The use of information and communication technologies in political and governance processes, aimed at broader and more active citizen participation.

District Council: UK local government body at the town rather than city level.

e-Government (e-Gov): The conduct of government business and the provision of government services electronically, usually via the Internet.

e-Procedures: Software allowing users to manage administrative procedures electronically, usually through the Internet.

Effectiveness: The accuracy and completeness with which users achieve their specified goals.

Efficiency: The resources expended (e.g., time) with respect to effectiveness.

Emergency response: An effort to mitigate the effect of an incident that threatens public health and safety.

Ethnography: A qualitative field-based method for gathering empirical data on human societies and activities, stemming from anthropology and sociology. Data collection occurs through participant observation, interviews, and questionnaires. UCD projects can be informed by ethnographic studies of the environments in which users will be interacting with the proposed system.

Ex-ante legislative phases: All the workflow steps a legislative bill undergoes before official endorsement by the empowered authority.

Ex-post legislative phases: All the workflow steps a legislative bill undergoes after official deliberation (e.g., publication in an official medium).

External house processes: All activities regarding a legislative bill between houses and other institutions of the state, including the government, the head of state, etc.

Failure demand: The interaction resulting from (typically) a mistake or delay in service provision.

Formative usability test: A test that aims to find usability problems during the design and development process, so that they can be fixed.

Freedom of Information laws: Laws that guarantee access to data held by the state. They establish a "right-to-know" legal process by which requests may be made for government-held information, to be received freely or at minimal cost, barring standard exceptions.

Functionality weakness: A usability problem in a tool where the user expects the tool to help him/ or her in performing a specific task, when in fact it does not.

Government 2.0: A more active and open form of government that involves government collaborating with citizens, often using social media and Web 2.0 tools.

Heuristic: A high-level design principle that is used (in conjunction with others) by experts to assess a product's ease of use. A heuristic evaluation can be part of a usability assessment; it is less expensive than testing with product users. Studies have shown that heuristic evaluation and usability testing find different problems, so they are not interchangeable.

Human factors integration: A set of management and technical processes that provide assurance that the system will be operable and supported by the proposed target audience description in defined operability scenarios.

Human-centered design: Approach to system design and development that aims to make interactive systems more usable by focusing on the use of the system; applying human factors, ergonomics, and usability knowledge and techniques. The term "human-centered design" is used rather than "user-centered design" in order to emphasize that this standard also addresses impacts on a number of stakeholders, not just those typically considered as users — in practice, these terms are often used synonymously. Usable systems can provide a number of benefits, including improved productivity, enhanced user well-being, avoidance of stress, increased accessibility, and reduced risk of harm.

Infographics: (Information Graphics) Illustrations and charts that convey information that would be difficult or impossible to convey with only text.

Information architecture: The structural design of shared information environments; the art and science of organizing and labeling web sites, intranets, online communities, and software to support usability and findability; and an emerging community of practice focused on bringing principles of design and architecture to the digital landscape. From the IA Institute: http://iainstitute.org/en/learn/resources/what_is_ia.php

Internal house processes: All activities regarding a legislative bill within a specific house, including the activities of individual commissions within it.

Legislative drafting: Activities in support of the choice of the actual wording of the content of a legislative bill, often performed by specialized personnel.

Life cycle: Evolution of a system, product, service, project, or other human-made entity from conception through retirement. Usability requires an iterative approach to design and the use of prototyping at multiple design levels. A number of strategies are available for interfacing this iteration with overall system engineering life cycles.

Low literacy: A low level of the knowledge and skills required to understand and use information from text or textual documents.

Lowest price technically acceptable: A method of proposal evaluation conducted by the US Government, in which the proposals that meet or exceed the technical criteria are identified and the lowest-priced one among them is selected. Not used for cost-type contracts.

Mashup: An application or presentation that combines multiple data sources, services, or applications (e.g., mapping) to present information or services in a novel way.

Nonfunctional requirements: Requirements other than functional requirements (e.g., design, process, standards).

Nonrepudiation: A characteristic of a system such that any change to data must be traceable to the person who made the change and the person cannot repudiate that change (i.e., cannot deny having made it).

Offshoring: Outsourcing to an organization in a different country, usually to save money by taking advantage of the lower cost of labor in that country.

Outsourcing: The contracting out of a function or service, possibly one that could be performed in house. Services are outsourced for a variety of reasons, from taking advantage of a contractor's specialized capabilities to avoiding the burden of hiring and managing staff with the capability to do the required work.

Persona: An imaginary person — a fictional representative member of a user group — that can help designers focus on users as people and can guide design decisions. A profile of an archetypal user focused on needs, motivations, and goals instead of simple demographic segmentation.

Platen: A flat plate, as in the flat plate of glass on some fingerprint scanners.

Point-in-time legislation: The availability of the correct wording of an act at any moment in time, especially if affected in time by a large sequence of modification acts.

Process: A set of interrelated activities that transform inputs into outputs. A process is what is done to develop and operate a system. Processes are performed through methods, techniques, work instructions, etc. A process has a purpose and fulfills a business requirement. There are likely to be several enactments of model processes in different business processes within any one enterprise. For example, different partners in a project will do HFI in different ways and will use human-centered processes differently at different stages in the development of a system.

Process capability: The ability of a process to achieve a required goal. Capability is how well processes are done. The process capability of an organization provides one means of predicting the most likely outcomes to be expected from the next project the organization undertakes. A capability level is a set of attribute(s) that work together to provide a major enhancement in the capability to perform a process. Each level provides a major enhancement of capability in the performance of a process. The levels constitute a rational way of progressing through improvement of the capability of any process. A capability level can be defined as a point on an ordinal scale (of process capability) that represents the increasing capability of the performed process. Each level builds on the capability of the level below (typically five or six levels).

Process improvement: Action taken to change an organization's processes so that they meet the organization's business needs and achieve its business goals more effectively.

Quick response code: A barcode that can store data such as a web site address and be scanned by a mobile device.

Radio frequency identification: A technology that incorporates the use of electromagnetic or electrostatic coupling in the radio frequency (RF) portion of the electromagnetic spectrum to uniquely identify an object, animal, or person. It is coming into increasing use in industry as an alternative to the bar code. The advantage is that it does not require direct contact or line-of-sight scanning.

Recommender system or technology: A systems that automates user choices (about what to buy, how to spend leisure time, etc.) based on algorithmic approaches for generating personalized buying proposals (such as collaborative and content-based filtering), user logging, and knowledge-based approaches. Recommender systems increasingly contribute to consumer buying behavior theory for the social web.

Remotely piloted aircraft: A flying machine that is controlled from a distance by an operator using line of site and/or satellite communications.

Requirements analysis: Process of eliciting users' needs and goals for a new computer system and refining those needs into a specification and a design.

Screen reader: Assistive technology software that interprets the operating system, software, web site, or application for the user, presenting the information and interaction options audibly.

Selection criteria: The criteria by which a government agency selects a contractor (or contractors) from among the bidders.

Service agent: Person working face to face with the user/customer for a service.

Service design: Design of the interface to, and functionality of a service.

Single sign-on: An authentication process in which the user can enter one username and password and have access to a number of resources within an organization.

Situation awareness: a.k.a. *situational awareness*. Being aware of what is happening around you and understanding what the information means to you now and in the future.

Social Web: a.k.a. *Web 2.0*. The second generation of the World Wide Web, which focuses heavily on user-generated content, communities, networking, and social interaction.

Summative usability test: A test that establishes how well the system meets the requirements for effectiveness, efficiency, and satisfaction.

Surveillance: The observation or "watching over" of people, things, and events, typically from a distance, often employed for the purpose of detecting and tracking threats.

Synopsis table: A comparative view of a returning bill (i.e., a bill first approved by one house, then approved by the other with modifications, and then returning to the first house for the final approval in the modified wording) in which every difference between the old and the new version is emphasized appropriately by typographical choices.

System: Combination of interacting elements organized to achieve one or more stated purposes. A system may be considered as a product or as the services it provides. In practice, the interpretation of its meaning is frequently clarified by the use of an associative noun, e.g. aircraft system. Alternatively, the word "system" may be substituted simply by a context-dependent synonym, e.g., aircraft, although this may then obscure a system principles perspective.

System models: System models describe important aspects of the user interface such as the set of states the system can be in, the set of actions the system is able to perform, the set of events the system is able to react to, and the state changes that occur when such events or actions are performed. System models help designers build the application (by describing its behavior in the details) before it is implemented.

Task models: Logical descriptions of the activities to be performed to achieve a goal. Task models are intended to improve the understanding of how users may interact with a given user interface when carrying out a particular interactive task.

Technology enablers: Web sites, social media, smartphones, and other technological tools that facilitate different methods of collaboration.

Trade-off method: A method of proposal evaluation conducted by the US Government, in which price can be balanced against quality factors, so that the proposal that is judged to provide best value for money is selected.

Transformation: In service design, the replacement of top-down, silo-based service delivery with a better integrated and more customer-focused approach.

Transparency: The open conduct of government and of public business, to promote accountability and provide citizens with information about what government is doing.

Unicode: A computing industry standard that provides a unique number for every character, no matter the platform, no matter the program, and no matter the language.

Universal access: Access to information and communications technology by everyone in a population.

Usability: The quality of a product reflected in how well users can use it to achieve their goals. Also, the methods employed for making designs easy to use.

Usability definition, ISO: The extent to which a system, product, or service can be used by specified users to achieve specified goals with effectiveness, efficiency, and satisfaction in a specified context of use (based on ISO 9241-11: 1998).

Usability weakness: A usability problem in a tool where the tool does provides the necessary function, but the user could not use it, or could hardly use it, or found it unhelpful or less than satisfactory.

User experience: A person's perceptions and responses that result from the use and/or anticipated use of a product, system, or service, including all the users' emotions, beliefs, preferences, perceptions, physical and psychological responses, behaviors, and accomplishments that occur before, during, and after use. UX is a consequence of brand image, presentation, functionality, system performance, interactive behavior, and assistive capabilities of the interactive system; the user's internal and physical state resulting from prior experiences, attitudes, skills, and personality; and the context of use. Usability, when interpreted from the perspective of the users' personal goals, can include the kind of perceptual and emotional aspects typically associated with user experience. Usability criteria can be used to assess aspects of user experience.

User-centered design: An iterative approach to design that focuses on the people who will use a product with the goal of creating an easy-to-use and useful product. From ISO 13407, "Human-centered design is characterized by: the active involvement of users and a clear understanding of user and task requirements; an appropriate allocation of function between users and technology; the iteration of design solutions; multi-disciplinary design."

Web 2.0: Second generation of the World Wide Web that uses open standards, JavaScript, and programming languages to provide dynamic, often interactive web pages. Its dynamic nature enabled many social media tools such as blogs, Facebook, Google+, and Twitter.

Web portal: A web site that functions as a point of access to information in the World Wide Web.

Index

Note: Page numbers followed by *b* indicate boxes, *f* indicate figures, *t* indicate tables, and *ge* indicate glossary terms.

D

E

Q

R

S

W

X

Related Titles from Morgan Kaufmann

Information Visualization, 3rd edition
Perception for Design
Colin Ware
ISBN: 9780123814647

Sketching User Experiences: The Workbook
Saul Greenberg, Sheelagh Carpendale, Nicolai Marquardt, Bill Buxton
ISBN: 9780123819598

The UX Book
Process and Guidelines for Ensuring Quality User Experience
Rex Hartson and Pardha Pyla
ISBN: 9780123852410

Quantifying the User Experience
Practical Statistics for User Research
Jeff Sauro and James R. Lewis
ISBN: 9780123849687

Grounded Innovation
Strategies for Creating Digital Products
Lars Erik Holmquist
ISBN: 9780123859464

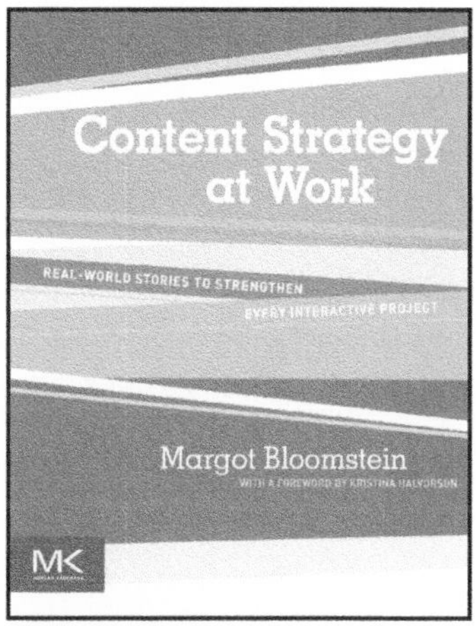

Content Strategy at Work
Real-world Stories to Strengthen Every Interactive Project
Margot Bloomstein
ISBN: 9780123919229

MK
MORGAN KAUFMANN

mkp.com

Printed and bound by CPI Group (UK) Ltd, Croydon, CR0 4YY
03/10/2024
01040310-0005